POPULATION AND SOCIETY

An Introduction to Demography

This comprehensive yet accessible textbook is an ideal resource for undergraduate and graduate students taking their first course in demography. Clearly explaining technical demographic issues without using extensive mathematics, *Population and Society* is sociologically oriented, but incorporates a variety of social sciences in its approach, including economics, political science, geography, and history. It highlights the significant impact of decision-making at the individual level – especially regarding fertility, but also mortality and migration – on population change. The text engages students by providing numerous examples of demography's practical applications in their lives, and demonstrates the extent of its relevance by examining a wide selection of data from the United States, Africa, Asia, and Europe. This thoroughly revised edition includes four new chapters, covering topics such as race and sexuality, and encourages students to consider the broad implications of population growth and change for global challenges such as environmental degradation.

Dudley L. Poston, Jr., is Professor of Sociology and the George T. and Gladys H. Abell Endowed Professor of Liberal Arts at Texas A&M University. He holds adjunct professorships at Renmin (People's) University, Beijing, China; Fuzhou University, China; and Nanjing Normal University, China. He previously served on the rural sociology and sociology faculties, respectively, of Cornell University and the University of Texas at Austin. Professor Poston has coauthored or edited eighteen books and has authored or coauthored more than 300 journal articles and book chapters on various sociological and demographic topics.

Leon F. Bouvier, at the time of his death in 2011, was Professor of Sociology at Old Dominion University. He was also Adjunct Professor at the Payson Center for International Development at Tulane University. He previously served as Vice President of the Population Reference Bureau, Washington, DC; as a demographic consultant to two congressional committees; and as a consultant to the United States Agency for International Development. He coauthored or edited fifteen books and numerous articles and book reviews.

POPULATION AND SOCIETY

An Introduction to Demography

Dudley L. Poston, Jr.
Texas A&M University

Leon F. Bouvier[†]
Old Dominion University

CAMBRIDGE
UNIVERSITY PRESS

CAMBRIDGE
UNIVERSITY PRESS

University Printing House, Cambridge CB2 8BS, United Kingdom

One Liberty Plaza, 20th Floor, New York, NY 10006, USA

477 Williamstown Road, Port Melbourne, VIC 3207, Australia

314–321, 3rd Floor, Plot 3, Splendor Forum, Jasola District Centre, New Delhi – 110025, India

79 Anson Road, #06–04/06, Singapore 079906

Cambridge University Press is part of the University of Cambridge.

It furthers the University's mission by disseminating knowledge in the pursuit of
education, learning, and research at the highest international levels of excellence.

www.cambridge.org
Information on this title: www.cambridge.org/9781107042674
DOI: 10.1017/9781107337237

First published 2017
Reprinted 2019

Printed in the United Kingdom by TJ International Ltd. Padstow Cornwall

A catalogue record for this publication is available from the British Library.

Library of Congress Cataloging in Publication Data
Names: Poston, Dudley L., 1940– author. | Bouvier, Leon F., author.
Title: Population and society : an introduction to demography / Dudley L. Poston, Jr,
  Leon F. Bouvier.
Description: Second edition. | New York : Cambridge University Press, 2017. | Revised edition of
  the authors
Identifiers: LCCN 2016035986 | ISBN 9781107042674 (hardback)
Subjects: LCSH: Population. | BISAC: SOCIAL SCIENCE / Demography.
Classification: LCC HB849.4 .P678 2016 | DDC 304.6 – dc23
LC record available at https://lccn.loc.gov/2016035986

ISBN 978-1-107-04267-4 Hardback
ISBN 978-1-107-64593-6 Paperback

Contents

Detailed Contents

Preface

The first edition of this book had its genesis when I met Leon F. Bouvier for the first time in April 1974 at the annual meeting of the Population Association of America, held that year in New York City. When two demographers meet for the first time, they usually want to tell each other about the demographic research they are conducting, along with the interesting and important facts and findings they are producing. Strangely, this was not the case when I first met Leon. We found ourselves talking not about our research, but, instead, about what was then, and for me still is today, our first love: the teaching of demography.

Beginning in 1974 until he died in 2011, Leon and I became very good and dear friends, as did our families. We saw each other once or twice a year and communicated frequently by email. We coauthored a book about the population of Texas and wrote several research articles that dealt with immigration, congressional apportionment, and the relationship between the two. But, over the years, whenever we were together, our conversations would always seem to lead to our talking about teaching demography. For the first three decades of our friendship, we always seemed to be talking about the topics we were covering in our classes, the teaching tools and techniques we were using, the books and readings we were assigning, and the importance and relevance of demography to society and the world. Every now and again in the 1990s, I would say to Leon, or he would say to me, "Some day we need to write our own demography text." But we never did, at least not for the first thirty years of our friendship. Finally, in the early 2000s, I said one day to Leon, "If we are ever going to write our demography book, we had better do it pretty soon." Thus, in late 2005, Leon and I prepared a book prospectus and chapter outline for an introductory demography text. In early 2006, we shared it with Ed Parsons of Cambridge University Press, who a few months later gave us a contract to write *Population and Society: An Introduction to Demography*. The first edition of *Population and Society* was published in late spring 2010.

A lot of people helped us write that first edition. We will forever be indebted to all of them. Each is mentioned by name in the Preface of the first edition.

On January 26, 2011, just nine months after our book was published, Leon Bouvier died of heart failure in Norfolk, Virginia. He was 88 years old. Leon was very proud of our book. He very much enjoyed writing it with me. It took us more than two years to write it. So during that time Leon and I were in constant communication revising and rewriting one chapter after another. Indeed, Sidney Goldstein of Brown University, who was Leon's mentor when he was a graduate student in the 1960s at Brown University, wrote to me a few weeks after Leon's death that the joy that Leon received in writing that demography book likely kept him alive that last year or so.

In early 2014, Robert Dreesen of Cambridge University Press asked me to consider writing a second edition of *Population and Society*. I knew well that our book needed an updating. But I wondered how I could write a new edition without Leon. I thought about Robert's request for several months and finally decided to take on the task of writing the new edition, realizing full well that it would be a different experience without Leon as my co-author. Robert gave me a contract in 2014. I spent the next several months preparing a new outline, dropping some chapters and outlining new ones (the second edition has sixteen chapters, two more than the first edition), and gathering new data and materials. I did the bulk of the writing in the spring, summer and fall of 2015. I delivered preliminary drafts of the sixteen chapters to Robert in late August and December 2015, and then a final draft of the book in April 2016.

I learned a great deal writing this edition. It is a second edition, but it is really pretty much a brand new book. I certainly missed having Leon help me with the writing. There is a little bit of him still in a couple of the chapters. But the bulk of the book, around 95 percent or so, is mine. Nevertheless, I decided to keep Leon listed as my coauthor. He and I began this project several decades ago. I want him on as a coauthor.

The writing of the second edition of *Population and Society* would not have been possible without the help and patience of many people. First, I thank my editor at Cambridge University Press, Robert Dreesen, for his many suggestions and encouragement and patience.

I asked many of my former and current graduate students, and several of my undergraduate students, to read, edit, and critique chapters, to check references, and to help me assemble tables. Also, work I published with some of these students has been adapted and referenced in various chapters of the book. I thank all these conscientious and helpful and ever so faithful students, listed here alphabetically: Taylor Bates,

Amanda Baumle, Yuting Chang, Christopher Cherry, D'Lane Compton, Eugenia Conde, Rachel Traut Cortes, Cristina Cruz, Mary Ann Davis, Danielle Xiaodan Deng, Bethany DeSalvo, Haijun Dong, Ceylan Engin, Nicole Farris, Layton Field, Ginny Garcia, Nayoung Heo, Lindsay Howden, Heather Kincannon, Hannah Elisabeth Klein, Michael Koets, Sherri Lander, Danny Malone, Guadalupe Marquez-Velarde, Angelica Menchaca, Misael Obregon, Jeffrey Passel, Brittany Rico, Richard Rogers, Cheryl Rollman-Tinajero, Fabian Romero, Chris Russell, Juyin Helen Wong, Qian Kate Xiong, Dan Yin, and Huanjun June Zhang.

I also thank friends and colleagues who read one or more chapters and provided feedback, suggested improvements, and alerted me to the work of others. Some answered questions I raised about chapter topics, geography, and page referencing. Others listened and sometimes reacted to my discussions about one or more of the chapters and themes. Some listened to a lot of my discussions and comments, possibly more than they wanted to. These friends and colleagues, listed alphabetically, are Eduardo Bonilla-Silva, John Boies, David Carlson, Elwood Carlson, Stephanie Coontz, Alex Dessler, Joe Feagin, Nadia Flores, Mark Fossett, William Frey, Geoffrey Gilbert, Melanie Hawthorne, Daniel Lichter, John Macionis, Keith Maggert, Kyriakos Markides, Ramiro Martinez, Peter Morrison, Nancy Riley, Rogelio Saenz, Sophie H. Savage, Jane Sell, Nancy Zaro Shaw, Jackson Shultz, Diego von Vacano, and James Weatherby.

My long and time-consuming efforts in writing this edition were assisted by the support, understanding, patience, and love of my family. I thank my children, Nancy and Dudley III, and my son-in-law, Rick Espey, and my grandchildren, David, Kara, and Daniel Espey (David and Kara deserve special praise; each of them read all sixteen chapters and sent their grandfather over the course of several months the comments and reactions of a recent college graduate and a current college sophomore, neither of whom had completed an undergraduate demography course).

Last, but certainly not least, I thank my wife and best friend, Patricia, my marriage partner of fifty-three years, who also has never completed a demography course, but knows more about demography and demographers than do most people. She has lived with a demographer for more than half a century, and she deserves five Purple Hearts for doing so. I dedicate this edition of *Population and Society* to Pat.

Dudley L. Poston, Jr.

Introduction

The media these days are rediscovering population dynamics and the subject of demography. The first real heyday for demography was probably in the 1960s and 1970s with the "discovery" of the global population problem. In recent decades, demographic behavior and demographic characteristics have received increased attention in the popular media. And the term *demographics* has seeped into our vocabulary. This is an encouraging sign. Forty-five years ago when I first began studying and teaching demography, the subject was nowhere near as recognized and discussed as it is today. Now, the importance of population change, in terms of size, composition, and distribution, has become increasingly relevant in policymaking at the local, state, national, and international levels. There is an increasing awareness not only of population growth and decline, but also of compositional change in age, sex, and racial identity.

Care must be taken, however, to evaluate the works of journalists and others who use, or fail to use, demographic data, and nevertheless comment about demography and its dynamics. It is very easy to make errors when reporting on and interpreting population behavior. Hopefully, readers of this book will become attuned to these types of errors, which seem to appear every so often in the popular media.

Population and Society: An Introduction to Demography is intended for undergraduate students, as well as graduate students, taking their first course in demography. It is sociologically oriented, although economics, political science, geography, history, and the other social sciences are also used to inform some of the materials I cover and discuss. While the emphasis is on demography, I well recognize that at the individual level, population change is related to private decisions, especially in relation to fertility but also to migration and even to mortality. I thus consider in some detail, early in the book, the role of individuals in population decision-making. At the level of countries, and even the world, changes in population size have an important effect on environmental and related challenges facing all the world's inhabitants. I often wonder why the media, when discussing issues such as global warming or immigration, tend sometimes to minimize the role of demography and demographic data and patterns.

A significant and very necessary component of demography is its techniques. The study of demography involves much more than theories, concepts, and data. Demography, more so than any of the other social sciences, has a body of methods and approaches uniquely suited for the analysis of its concepts and events. In this book, I present some of the basic techniques that are needed to better understand demographic behavior. But the methodological discussions in the chapters per se are introductory. Students interested in pursuing the techniques in more detail will need to take a course or two dealing with demographic methods and/or consult any of a number of excellent texts focusing on demographic methods (e.g., Hinde, 1998; Pollard, Yusuf, and Pollard, 1990; Preston, Heuveline, and Guillot, 2001; Rowland, 2003; Siegel and Swanson, 2004; Smith, 1992; Yusuf, Martins, and Swanson, 2014).

I also hold that students of demography should be conversant with the basic sources of demographic data. Thus, on the Cambridge University Press web page that is maintained for this book, I have placed detailed instructions on how to locate population data through the Internet and other sources. I am hopeful that in addition to learning about the relevance and importance of demography and its concepts, theories, and methods, students will also gain some knowledge about the richness of data available from a wide variety of governmental sources. This knowledge should come in handy in many future endeavors.

In sum, I have tried in this book to provide students and others interested in this exciting and relevant field with as much information as possible in a readable manner mostly absent of professional jargon.

1 An Introduction to Demography

WHAT IS DEMOGRAPHY?

This book is an introduction to **demography**. A short definition of demography is the systematic and scientific study of human populations. The word *demography* comes from the Greek words δημος (*demos*) for "population" and γραφια (*graphia*) for "description" or "writing," thus the phrase, "writings about population." The term *demography* was first used in 1855 by the Belgian statistician Achille Guillard in his book *Elements of Human Statistics or Comparative Demography* (Borrie, 1973: 75; Rowland, 2003: 16). Most demographers (Hauser and Duncan, 1959; McFalls, 2007; Micklin and Poston, 2005) agree about the objectives and definition of demography.

Demography is the social science that studies: (1) the size, composition, and distribution of the human population of a given area at a specific point in time; (2) the changes in population size and composition; (3) the components of these changes (**fertility, mortality**, and **migration**); (4) the factors that affect these components; and (5) the consequences of changes in population size, composition, and distribution, or in the components themselves. Hence, demography may be more broadly defined as the scientific study of the size, composition, and distribution of human populations and their changes resulting from fertility, mortality, and migration. Demography is concerned with how large (or how small) are the populations; how the populations are composed according to age, sex, race, marital status, and other characteristics; and how the populations are distributed in physical space (e.g., how urban and rural they are) (Bogue, 1969). Demography is also interested in the changes over time in the size, composition, and distribution of human populations, and how these result from the processes of fertility, mortality, and migration. The chapters of this book discuss these topics in much more depth and detail and will provide you with a thorough introduction to demography.

I will start this first chapter with the following point: every one of us, you and I, whether we are aware of it or not, have already contributed, and will continue to contribute throughout our lives, to the subject matter of demography. I will next elaborate on the definition of demography introduced above. I will then consider the so-called demographic equation. Two of the most important variables used by demographers are age and sex; hence, I will then give some examples of the relevance of age and sex to demography and to society. I will next discuss the issue of population distribution and review briefly some of the major sources of demographic data. Finally, I will conclude this first chapter by discussing the phrase "Demography is destiny."

WE ARE ALL POPULATION ACTORS

We are all population actors. This is a major theme of this book. Think about it: your parents performed a demographic act when you were conceived. You, in turn, perform similar demographic acts when you decide to have, or not to have, children. Sometime during your lifetime you will move – once or perhaps numerous times. These, too, are demographic acts. Finally, you will die.

Now, you may think that your dying is not the same kind of demographic act as the decision-making of your parents when you were conceived because you yourself do not really decide how long you will live and when you will die. However, we do indeed have a lot to say about how old we will be when we die. That is, we have many options that may, or may not, extend our lives. These include such behaviors as stopping or never beginning smoking, limiting alcohol intake, eating a healthy diet, and exercising. Another very important behavior that will extend our lives is education, specifically obtaining a college degree.

Let me compare women and men at age 25 with and without a college degree. On average, women with a college degree will live sixty-two additional years (beyond age 25) compared with those with just a high school degree, who will live around fifty-six more years, a difference of six years. At age 25, men with a college degree are expected to live another fifty-seven years compared with another fifty-one years for men who have only completed high school, again a difference of six years (Hummer and Hernandez, 2013; Rostron, Boies, and Arias, 2010).

So, one of the first pieces of important and relevant information for your life and livelihood that you have learned by just reading the first pages of this book is the following: stay in school, graduate from college, and you will add more than just a few years to your life. In summary, we are all population actors. We are very much involved in demography in our day-to-day lives, even though we may not always realize it.

Demography is the study of some of the most important events in our lives, and we are very much involved in them. Ask yourself: what are the only two times in your life when you will have a very good chance of being identified by name and listed in your local newspapers? When you are born and when you die. These are two of the events that demographers study. Other very important events in the lives of many of us include getting married and, also for some of us, getting divorced. These are two more behaviors studied by demographers. Another really important event that almost every one of us will do at least once, if not many times, in our lives is moving from one residence to another. Demographers also study residential changes. So, as I often tell my students who are enrolled in my "Population and Society" undergraduate course, it is not at all an overstatement to say that demographers study the beginning and the end of our lives, as well as many, if not most, of the really important events that occur in between. Or as the eminent demographer Samuel Preston (1987: 620–621) once stated: "The study of population offers something for everyone: the daily dramas of sex and death, politics and war; the interlacing of individuals in all their ... (groups); and the confrontations of nature and civilization." In the next chapter, I begin elaborating on these and related points.

DEFINITION OF DEMOGRAPHY

I have already defined demography at the start of this chapter as the systematic and scientific study of human populations. I return now to a fuller consideration. Demography is the study of three basic processes: fertility, migration, and mortality. These are referred to as the **demographic processes**. In an important sense, that is really all there is to demography. When populations change in size, composition, or distribution, the changes depend solely on one or more of these three demographic processes. Hence, a discussion of the three demographic processes will comprise a major portion of this text.

THE DEMOGRAPHIC EQUATION

It should be clear to you that the size of a population can change only through the processes of fertility, mortality, and migration. There are only two ways of entering a population – being born, or moving into it. There are also two, and only two, ways of leaving a population – dying, or moving out of it. One of the fundamental facts about population change, therefore, is that populations can only change by way of a limited, countable number of events.

For example, consider the population size of a country. Suppose that this country at time t contains P_t persons, and that one year later it contains P_{t+1} persons. We may write this as the following equation:

$$P_{t+1} = P_t + B_{t\,to\,t+1} - D_{t\,to\,t+1} + I_{t\,to\,t+1} - E_{t\,to\,t+1} \qquad (1.1)$$

where $B_{t\ to\ t+1}$ and $D_{t\ to\ t+1}$ are, respectively, the number of births and deaths occurring in the population between times t and $t+1$; and $I_{t\,to\,t+1}$ and $E_{t\,to\,t+1}$ are, respectively, the number of immigrants (or in-migrants) to and emigrants (or out-migrants) from the population between times t and $t+1$. Equation (1.1) is known as the basic **demographic equation**, or sometimes as the demographic balancing or accounting equation. It states that the size of an area's population can change because of only three types of event: births, deaths, and migrations. These three events are known as the components of demographic change and also as the three demographic processes.

The quantity $(B_{t\ to\ t+1} - D_{t\ to\ t+1})$ is the difference between the number of births and the number of deaths that occurred during the time period $t\ to\ t+1$ and is known as **natural increase**; if $B_{t\ to\ t+1} < D_{t\ to\ t+1}$, then the number of deaths exceeds the number of births during the interval $t\ to\ t+1$, meaning negative natural increase, that is, **natural decrease**. The quantity $(I_{t\ to\ t+1} - E_{t\ to\ t+1})$ refers to the difference between the number of immigrants (persons who enter a country) and the number of emigrants (persons who leave a country) during the time period, and is known as net international migration (or, in the case of **in-migration** minus **out-migration**, net internal migration). If $I_{t\ to\ t+1} < E_{t\ to\ t+1}$, then more persons leave (emigrate from) the area than enter (immigrate into) the area, and the quantity is known as negative net international migration. Finally, if the quantity $I_{t\ to\ t+1} > E_{t\ to\ t+1}$, then we have positive net international migration.

In the United States, we almost always have positive net international migration because it is the situation in the United States and in most developed countries that $I_{t\ to\ t+1} > E_{t\ to\ t+1}$. The United States is, thus, a receiving country when it comes to international migration. In many developing countries, there is very frequently negative net international migration because $I_{t\ to\ t+1} < E_{t\ to\ t+1}$. Countries such as Mexico, China, India, and the Philippines are referred to as sending countries; they have more people leave their countries than enter and are hence characterized by negative net international migration. The Philippines sends around 1.5 million persons abroad every year, including 300,000 who work on ships around the world. Around 10 percent of the country's population lives abroad (Martin, 2013).

Within countries, however, there is usually a lot of significant variation in the demographic equation. Large older cities often have net out-migration. If the extent of natural increase does not surpass the level of out-migration, then the city loses population. The Detroit–Dearborn–Levonia, Michigan metropolitan area is an example with such a demographic pattern. Between 2010 and 2012, its total population fell by 29,045 inhabitants. Yet it had a natural increase of 12,980 persons (52,969 births minus 39,989 deaths). However, 42,025 more people moved out of the Detroit metropolitan area than moved into it. Hence, this net out-migration of 42,025 more than offset the natural increase of 12,980.

Some places have natural decrease because its elderly population comprises a large share of the population. A metropolitan area in Florida, The Villages (located in central Florida midway between the Gulf and Atlantic coasts, about an hour north of Orlando), had a total population in 2013 of over 107,000 persons. Between 2012 and 2013 it was the fastest growing metropolitan area in the entire United States (it was also the fastest growing metro area between 2013 and 2014). In the year between 2012 and 2013, The Villages grew by 3,470 persons. But there were 1,215 deaths in the year and only 442 births, resulting in 773 more deaths than births. To offset that loss, net migration amounted to 4,243. Why the high number of deaths? The in-migration to The Villages primarily consisted of retirees, resulting in a very large elderly population. The Villages is said to be the largest gated retirement community in the United States (Cohen, 2009). There are many of these so-called retirement areas in Arizona, California, Florida, North Carolina, and Texas.

Some populations have both natural decrease and negative net migration. For example, in the Charleston, West Virginia metropolitan area, between 2010 and 2012, there were 5,943 births and 6,456 deaths, and there were 592 more people moving out of the metropolitan area than moving in; so more people died than were born in Charleston, and more people left than entered Charleston. The area's high number of deaths reflects, in part, an older population. However, in The Villages metropolitan area, as I just mentioned above, their natural decrease was offset by a very high net in-migration.

This phenomenon of natural decrease is of increasing importance and relevance in the United States and especially in Europe. To illustrate, in 2008, more than half of all the counties in Europe had more deaths than births. These include almost all the counties of Germany, Hungary, Croatia, Romania and Bulgaria, the Baltic states, Greece, and Italy. "A long-term continuation of natural decrease will result in the continual diminution of the population, and eventually lead to its disappearance, unless the excess of deaths over births is offset by population increase due to net migration" (Field and Poston, 2013: 2; Johnson, Field, and Poston, 2015).

From these examples, we can see that all three of the demographic processes play important roles in determining not only the size, but also the composition of any population. Changes in the variables themselves are the result of our behavior as population actors. This is the heart of demography: understanding how the many factors that cause changes in demographic behavior and that are the consequences of this behavior are all interrelated.

AGE AND SEX

Changes in any one of the demographic processes yield equally important information about how populations are composed, that is, their structure. The most important characteristics that tell us about population structure are age and sex. These two characteristics are so important to the study of demography and the demographic processes that they are referred to as **the** demographic characteristics.

Let me show you how closely age and sex are tied in with the three demographic processes. With regard to fertility, defined by demographers as the actual production of children, more males are born than females, usually around 105 males for every 100 females. **Fecundity**, that is, the ability to produce children, varies by sex; specifically, the childbearing years of females are, for the most part, between the ages of 15 and 49, and for males they are generally between the ages of around 15 and 79 (Poston, 2005; Zhang, Poston, and Chang, 2014).

Regarding mortality, that is, the frequency with which death occurs in a population, females have lower death rates than males at every age of life. Death rates are high in the first year of life and then drop to very low levels. In modern populations, the death rates do not again reach the level of the first year of life for another five to six decades. Also, cause-specific mortality is often age related. For instance, causes of "mortality such as infanticide, parricide and suicide are ... age (and sex) related" (Goldscheider 1971: 227; MacKellar, 2003). Two renowned demographers, Jacob Siegel and Henry Shryock, have written that "in view of the very close relation between age and the risk of death, age may be considered the most important demographic variable in the analysis of mortality" (Shryock, Siegel, and Associates, 1976: 224; McGehee, 2004).

Migration also differs by age and sex. Traditionally, males and females have not migrated to the same places in equal numbers. Long-distance migration has tended to favor males, and short-distance migration, females, and this has been especially the case in developing countries. However, with increases in the degree of gender equity in societies, the migration of females now tends to approximate that of males. In fact, almost half of the international migrants worldwide are now women, and more than half of the legal immigrants to the United States are women (PRB, 2007: 9). Internal migration is also age selective, with the largest numbers of migrants found among young adults (Bernard, Bell, and Charles-Edwards, 2014).

Age and sex are not the only important compositional variables in demography. Other variables are also related to the three demographic processes. Knowing something about marital status, for example, is important when studying fertility. Race is strongly associated with socioeconomic status. On average, blacks, whites, Asians, and Hispanics all have somewhat different lifestyles, and these are related to the basic demographic processes. Education is an especially important variable to consider. In general, the higher the education attained, the lower the fertility and the lower the mortality.

These are just hints of the many compositional variables that demographers consider. The number is large, giving demographers a wide field to study. They are interested in most everything that is related to demographic behavior.

Finally, compositional variables are both the cause and the effect of population change. In turn, demographic changes can affect the compositional variables. I will have much more to say about this issue later.

AGE COMPOSITION: AN EXAMPLE

I now consider an example that illustrates well the central importance in demography of **age composition**. It is an example that will be mentioned and discussed later in our book. It is the famous **baby boom**, which began in the United States and in some other Western countries around 1946 at the conclusion of the Second World War and lasted until about 1964. Right after the end of the Second World War, the young adults of that period decided to have more children than those in previous generations. This resulted in a "bulge" in the age composition – a bulge, as I will note later, that resulted in numerous challenges for every institution in US society. The bulge is easy to see in Figure 1.1, which is an age and sex population pyramid for the United States in 2010. A **population pyramid** is a graph showing the numbers of males and females according to their ages. I will cover these in greater detail in Chapter 10.

Have a look at the pyramid in Figure 1.1. The baby boom bulge is most evident in the 45–54-year age groups; and many of the babies of the baby boom babies, that is, the children of the baby boomers, are evident in the 15–24-year age groups. In future decades, the baby boom bulge will be

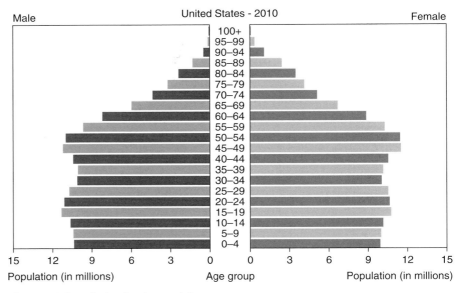

Figure 1.1 Population by Age and Sex
Source: US Census Bureau, International Data Base, available at: www.census.gov/
population/international/data/idb/region.php?N=%20Results%20&T=12&A=separate
&RT=0&Y=2010&R=-1&C=US, last accessed April 29, 2016.

visible higher and higher up in the country's pyramid. McFalls, Gallagher, and Jones (1986) have noted that we can think, figuratively, of the people born during the baby boom period as a group, that is, a **cohort** that passes through the population from the youngest ages to the oldest ages, as a pig that has been swallowed by a python.

Those people born from the mid-1940s to the mid-1960s are known as baby boom babies, or baby boomers, because there were so many of them compared with the numbers of babies born before them and after them. The baby boomers have experienced problems throughout their lives. Their attendance at elementary and secondary school and at college was often marked by overcrowded classrooms and a shortage of teachers. When they entered the labor market, many of them discovered that there were not enough jobs to go around. Housing for many of them has been scarce. The older members, most of whom have now reached retirement age, are finding that their demands on the US social security system are producing and will continue to produce strains between the financial demands of their large cohort and the smaller number of younger workers who must finance the system. These are examples of some of the problems that are likely to occur when one age group is considerably larger than groups before it or after it (Carlson, 2008).

In contrast, the babies born after the baby boomers, say, those born in the 1970s, have had a much easier time during their lives. In the 1970s, there were 33 million babies born in the United States, a figure 10 million fewer than the number born in the ten years between 1955 and 1964, the latter part of the period when most of the baby boom babies were born. The babies born after the baby boom, starting in the mid-1960s through the early 1980s, are referred to as the **baby bust** cohort, and also as the "Generation X" cohort (Carlson, 2008). They followed the enormously large group of baby boomers and have been in a much more favored position during their lives. Education facilities have been more than adequate for them, and many more jobs have been available for them than for the baby boomers who preceded them. But the Generation X babies will have a big responsibility financing the retirement of the baby boomers.

I was born in 1940, before the start of the baby boom. My cohort, often referred to as the Lucky Few cohort, extends from around 1929 through 1945. There were many fewer of us compared with the large number of baby boomers, around 41 million "Lucky Few" versus 78 million baby boomers (Carlson, 2008). We enjoyed higher employment rates and a greater variety of social opportunities than Americans in the preceding or in the following generations; and much of this was due to our small population size.

Clearly, being a member of the Lucky Few, or the baby boom, or Generation X, can have a significant impact on one's chances of success in life. I am not suggesting a form of demographic determinism. Indeed, individuals can and do succeed on their own. But it goes without saying that being born as a member of a large or a small cohort does in fact alter one's odds for later success in life (Carlson, 2008). Our generational location has a big influence on our life and our life chances. I will discuss this issue in greater detail in Chapter 10.

I have noted here the importance of age and age composition in demography and also some of the ways in which the size of one's age cohort can influence many aspects of one's life and livelihood. I turn now to a consideration of sex and **sex composition**.

SEX COMPOSITION: AN EXAMPLE

I mentioned earlier that most societies in the world have **sex ratios at birth** (SRBs) of around 105, that is, 105 boys are born for every 100 girls. (And around 110 or so males are conceived for every 100 females.) The so-called biologically normal SRB level of about 105 is likely an evolutionary adaptation to the fact that females have higher survival probabilities at every age than do males. Since at every year of life more males die than females, around 105 or so males are required at birth per every 100 females for there to be approximately equal numbers of males and females when the two groups reach the marriageable ages (although there are often slightly more males than females at the beginning of the marriageable ages).

Later in this book, I will discuss in more detail the sex ratio at birth. But I note here that since the mid-1980s and the 1990s, several countries, for example, China, South Korea, Taiwan, India, and a few others have been having SRBs (i.e., the number of male births per 100 female births) that are much higher than the biological average of around 105 (Hudson and den Boer, 2002, 2004; Jha et al., 2006; Poston and Glover, 2005; Poston and Morrison, 2005; Poston, Conde, and DeSalvo, 2011). Indeed, in 2012, China had an SRB of 119; this means that in 2012 in China, there were 119 baby boys born for every 100 baby girls. The SRBs in China between 2005 and 2011 have hovered around 120.

My students, Eugenia Conde and Bethany DeSalvo, and I, have estimated that there have likely been born in China more than 41 million Chinese boys who, when they reach their mid-twenties and are looking for brides, will not be able to find Chinese girls to marry. Our numbers do not take into account the likelihood of some daughters at birth being underreported (Goodkind, 2011), so the figure of over 40 million may be a little high. Nevertheless, there will be many millions of extra boys in the country. What might be some of the outcomes?

The Chinese government could well turn to a more authoritarian form of government so as to be better able to control these millions of excess bachelors. Sociological research has shown that when large numbers of men do not marry, they are often more prone to crime than if they were married (Laub and Sampson, 2006; Sampson and Laub, 1990). Banditry, violence, and revolutions could occur in areas with large numbers of excess males (Hudson and den Boer, 2002).

Another implication of this unbalanced sex ratio at birth is the potential for an HIV/AIDS epidemic of a scale previously unimagined. This will occur if many of the excess Chinese bachelors move to the big cities in China, and if China's commercial sex markets in the cities expand to accommodate the many millions of surplus males (Parish et al., 2003; Tucker et al., 2005). The numbers of HIV cases in China in the next decade and later, owing to the bachelors and other factors (e.g., China's extremely large floating population – a topic I will cover in Chapter 8) could well rival the HIV numbers in sub-Saharan Africa. In 2013, in sub-Saharan Africa, there were 24.7 million adults infected with HIV, which is almost 71 percent of the

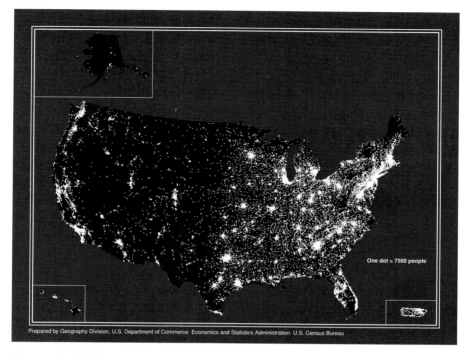

Figure 1.2 2010 Population Distribution in the United States and Puerto Rico

total number of adult infections worldwide (UNAIDS, 2014). China could well equal, if not exceed, these numbers by 2020–2030 (Tucker et al., 2009). These are the kind of societal impacts that could occur when the sex ratio becomes significantly unbalanced.

POPULATION DISTRIBUTION

I edited the final draft of this chapter in late October 2015. The "World Population Clock" at the US Bureau of the Census (US Bureau of the Census, 2015b) estimated that the size of the population of the world in October 2015 was nearly 7.3 billion people. But these billions of inhabitants are not equally distributed across the planet. Some areas are densely populated; others are not. Some areas are deserts; others are mountains. Consider, for instance, the population distribution of the United States. Figure 1.2 is a map of the United States produced by the US Bureau of the Census showing the distribution of the population using data from the 2010 census. Land area is shown in black and population locations are shown with white dots. Each white dot represents around 7,500 people.

Look at the map and you will notice that the northeastern region of the country has the highest population density of population per square mile, but the southern region has the most people.

Population distribution reflects levels of fertility, mortality, and migration. Earlier in this chapter, I noted that the Detroit metropolitan area was losing population mainly through out-migration. The same is true of many older large cities in the United States. Other, often newer, cities tend to grow quite rapidly. I mentioned Florida's The Villages metropolitan area, whose growth is due solely to in-migration, even though the area has many more deaths than births. I commented on other places where deaths outnumbered births and where the number of out-migrants exceeded the number of in-migrants.

Humans are constantly moving from place to place. We are indeed peripatetic. We always have been and always will be. The interesting point for demographers is that all three demographic processes are involved in this ongoing shift by the residents of our planet.

DEMOGRAPHIC DATA

I need to address another topic in this introductory chapter: the data that are used to study demography. Where do we find these data? We demographers are more fortunate than many of our social science colleagues who oftentimes must gather and develop their own data. Generally speaking, most of the data that demographers use have already been gathered for us. I will cover this topic in more detail in Chapter 3.

The US Census Bureau is an incredible source of demographic data. The data that the Census Bureau makes available and easily accessible to everyone on its web page pertain not only to the United States. The international database of the US Census Bureau is especially thorough and of great relevance.

Another important source of data is the US National Center for Health Statistics (NCHS), particularly data dealing with fertility, **morbidity** (the prevalence of sickness in a population), causes of death, and mortality. The US Citizenship and Immigration Services (USCIS), a branch of the Department of Homeland Security, makes available extensive data on immigration. In addition, most of the US states have their own demographic data centers, and much information can be gleaned there (see, e.g., the web page of the Texas State Data Center at: http://txsdc.utsa.edu).

The United Nations (UN) Population Division also publishes extensive demographic information for every country in the world, as does the US Central Intelligence Agency. The Population Reference Bureau (PRB) is a private nonprofit organization in Washington, DC that focuses on population, health, and the environment. The PRB provides a great amount of demographic information on its web page, much of which I will use in this book.

At one time, finding and gathering data from these monumental sources were torturous. When I was an undergraduate student studying for my BA degree in sociology at the University of San Francisco in the late 1950s and early 1960s, we had to go to a library and find the different locations of all the various government publications; then we had to find the actual books and census volumes; and then we had to code the data by hand. But today, almost all these sources are available on the Internet. On the Cambridge University Press web page that is maintained for our *Population and Society* book, I have placed specific sources for the various kinds of demographic data discussed in the chapters, with detailed directions about accessing them.

DEMOGRAPHY IS DESTINY

We often hear the expression, "Demography is destiny." Indeed, the founding father of sociology, Auguste Comte, is believed to be the first person to have made such a statement (Thompson, 1975: 156–157). Today, commentators and news analysts often use the phrase as an explanation of how things are, and how they got that way, and how they will be. Some demographers, however, tend to shy away from the expression. While there is some validity to the phrase, there are far too many other variables that intervene in determining where an individual or a society stands at any given point in time. Nevertheless, there are instances in the study of demography, particularly with respect to population behavior occurring in relatively short periods of time, when it can indeed be argued that demography is destiny.

For instance, and again citing the baby boom example I introduced earlier, we have known for many years that by the year 2020, a very large population increase in the numbers of elderly people in the United States and in most countries of the developed world will have occurred. Why? Because we know how many people were born during the baby boom period and we can be fairly accurate as to how many have already entered and will be entering the elderly years of life. A similar statement can be made with regard to the many, many millions of baby boys already born in China, Taiwan, South Korea, and India who, when it is time for them to marry, will not be able to find Chinese, or Taiwanese, or South Korean, or Indian brides. These boys have already been born, and we know that they far outnumber the women who will be there for them to marry.

Thus, one could very well argue that demography is destiny. But we should not carry the analogy too far. Nevertheless, I hold that an educated person should have at least a basic knowledge of demography and how it affects almost every aspect of our lives and our institutions. I hope that the following chapters in our book will convince you of this argument.

2 Theories of Demography

Demographers have developed several theories or explanations about why and how populations change their size. Many have written about world population growth and decline. In this chapter I consider first the general meaning of the term "population." Then, I review the works of some of the early writers who discussed population and population change. Since Malthus is perhaps the most well known of the early scholars, I discuss him and his writings in some detail. I follow my discussion of Malthus with a somewhat shorter discussion of Karl Marx. I then turn to a detailed discussion of **demographic transition theory** (DTT) and its major extensions. Finally, I discuss some of the principal theories and perspectives that demographers have developed that focus specifically and separately on fertility, mortality and migration.

WHAT IS A POPULATION?

Demography is the study of human populations. The word *population* is from the Latin *populare*, to populate, and the Latin noun, *populatio*. McNicoll has written that in ancient times, the verb *populare* "commonly meant to lay waste, plunder, or ravage," and the noun *populatio* "was a plundering or despoliation" (2003: 730). These usages became obsolete by the eighteenth century. According to Landry (1945), the modern use of the word *population* first appeared in 1597 in an essay by Francis Bacon (McNicoll, 2003).

Strictly speaking, a population is a group or collection of items. To a demographer, a population is a group or collection of people. Preston, Heuveline, and Guillot (2001: 1) have distinguished between a specific population or group of actual people alive at a given period of time (e.g., the population of China as of November 1, 2010) and the population that persists over time even though its actual members may change (e.g., the population of China during the past 4,000 years). But as McNicoll has noted, the more common use of the term *population* by demographers and in modern English usage is with regard to a "well-defined set, with clear-cut membership criteria" (2003: 731), such as the population of the People's Republic of China as identified and enumerated in its 2010 census on November 1, 2010.

In a similar vein, Ryder (1964: 448) considered a population to be an aggregate of individuals defined in spatial and temporal terms. It is not necessarily a group, which in sociological terms requires some form of interpersonal interaction and the development of a sense of community. The analysis of human populations is inherently dynamic because attention is focused on changes in the population over time.

Ryder also stated that the population model is both microdynamic and macrodynamic. This means that processes of change in fertility, mortality, and migration can be identified at both the individual (micro) and the aggregate (macro) levels. This distinction lies at the very heart of the population model because it introduces Lotka's ([1934] 1998) important distinction between the persistence of the individual and the persistence of the aggregate. All human beings are born, live for some period of time, and then die. But a population aggregate is not temporally limited, provided that enough individuals continue to enter the population, usually through births, to replace those exiting. The population aggregate in this sense is immortal.

Population aggregates, both in terms of the changes in numbers and the characteristics of those entering and exiting, can experience changes not reducible to individuals who constitute the population. For instance, when individuals enter a population through birth or through in-migration, they will "age" by becoming older. But the population aggregate cannot only become older; it can also become younger, provided that births exceed deaths and that the in-migrants are younger than the out-migrants. Indeed, all human institutions and organizations may be thought of in these terms. Indeed, one way that social change may be studied is by the monitoring of compositional change caused by entrances and exits (Ryder, 1964).

EARLY WRITINGS ABOUT POPULATION

Interest and concern about population change have not been limited to demographers. In 1848, the great English philosopher John Stuart Mill wrote the following: "If the earth must lose that great portion of its pleasantness which it owes to things that the unlimited growth of wealth and population would extirpate from it, for the mere purpose of enabling it to support a larger, but not a happier or a better population, I sincerely hope, for the sake of posterity, that they will be content to be stationary, long before necessity compels them to it" ([1848] 1965, Book 4: 756–757).

Actually, concerns about population per se go back to Genesis 1:28, where humans were encouraged to "be fruitful and multiply and fill the earth."

Plato had his own ideas about population size. He believed that a community should not be larger than 5,040 citizens; otherwise, too many people would lead to anonymity. The farsightedness of Plato and some of the other Greek philosophers of that time remains amazing to me today. A major concern of sociologists in the twenty-first century is the lack of face-to-face communication because of the Internet, iPods, iPhones, smart watches, and other new inventions. I can only speculate as to how Plato would react to these decreasing levels of face-to-face communication were he alive today!

Plato's ideas resonate well with the writings of the nineteenth-century sociologist, Émile Durkheim, who visualized two types of societies: mechanical and organic. The former was small, with a simple **division of labor**, whereas the latter was considerably larger, with an extensive division of labor as well as increasing anonymity (Durkheim, [1893] 1984).

The fourteenth-century Arab philosopher Ibn Khaldun was also concerned with population growth. He posited that societies pass through stages of population growth as they mature – much like individuals do: "The inhabitants of a more populous city are more prosperous than their counterparts in a less populous one . . . The fundamental cause of this is the difference in the nature of the occupations carried on in different places" (Issawi, 1987: 93).

MALTHUS

The most well-known early scholar who wrote about population growth is Thomas Robert Malthus. He was born in England in 1766. He did not use the name "Thomas," but instead either "T. R. Malthus" or "T. Robt. Malthus." He was educated at Jesus College Cambridge. At the age of 22 he became a curate near his family home in Surrey and later in Lincolnshire. In 1805, he was appointed a professor of history and political economy at East India College, Haileybury, a position he occupied until his death in 1834. It his early years at age 32 when he was a rural clergyman, he published anonymously the first edition of his famous work, *An Essay on the Principle of Population as it Affects the Future Improvement of Society, with Remarks on the Speculations of Mr. Goodwin, M. Condorcet, and Other Writers.* According to Petersen, this publication immediately made Malthus a very controversial figure. This first edition was mainly a "deductive book" of around 55,000 words, whereas the second edition (see below) expanded the theory and provided a great deal of illustrative data, resulting in around 200,000 words (Petersen, 1979: 52–53). Subsequent editions, ending in the seventh edition published posthumously in 1872, included relatively minor changes. The best edition is the second, with revisions, contained in two volumes and edited by Patricia James (Malthus, [1803] 1989).

Malthus' main argument was that the growth of a population is fueled by a natural urge to reproduce. He claimed that material resources such as food and shelter can grow only at an arithmetic rate, while populations grow at a geometric rate. The rate of increase for population, in each generation, is 1–2–4–8–16–32–64, while that for subsistence, in each generation, is 1–2–3–4–5–6–7. If unchecked, population levels would double in size about every twenty-five years. Because productive capacity can never maintain this rate of growth for long, the growth in population must be continually checked. Subsistence, however, does not necessarily grow exponentially. In 225 years, the population would be at 512 billion – 511 billion more than at time 1. Yet in that same time period, the means of subsistence would only have increased by 10. In 2,000 years, the difference between population and production would be incalculable.

Malthus argued that population growth was held in check in two ways, by **preventive checks** and by **positive checks**. The major preventive check was "moral restraint," or the postponement of marriage (see below). The positive checks included wars, famine, pestilence, and other forms of misery. If population was left unchecked, it would grow much faster than material resources and lead to human misery, ultimately resulting in poverty.

Malthus' second edition of his essay was written as a result of his travels in search of ethnographic and statistical evidence to support the principle of population. In this edition, he focused more on moral restraint as a means to limit the number of births. It referred to the postponement of marriage until an individual had prospects for supporting a family. In addition to the theory of progress, his second essay was also concerned with questions of practice. Under the assumption that the "principle of population" was thought to be a natural law, Malthus wanted to see if human action could remove or limit the evil effects of this law.

Malthus' essay needs to be placed and considered in historical context. It opposed two very influential schools of thought, **mercantilism** and **utopianism**, and cast doubt on the hope of human perfectibility. Winch has written that "Malthus showed that any attempt to create an ideal society in which altruism and common property rights prevailed would be undermined by its inability to cope with the resulting population pressure" (2003: 169).

Eversley (1959) has noted that Malthus is sometimes misunderstood by people who have never read him or is misquoted by those who claim to have read him. He observed that Malthus was a good sociologist and his population theory important, although unsystematic and poorly written, but it is impossible to ignore the "Malthusian problem."

Glass (1953) has observed that when Malthus wrote his first essay, it was to attack the belief in the ideals of William Godwin and the Marquis de Condorcet regarding the perfectibility of man and society; indeed, the names of Godwin and Condorcet are in the book's subtitle. Glass has contrasted Malthusian theory with historical problems. He noted that Malthus' precepts of conduct are no longer relevant for preventing conflict between population and subsistence. Malthus was a poor prophet because the only nation that followed the Malthusian way was Ireland. Glass urged readers to respect Malthus as an important economist, but to be wary of many of his ideas.

Malthus' essays have sparked much debate from the time the first edition was published. However, it is likely that many more people talk about Malthus' views than truly understand them. Today, scholars are still debating Malthus' ideas regarding population. Many nonbelievers note that Malthus' arithmetic analysis has faults, an argument with which Malthus may not have disagreed. According to Thompson and Lewis, Malthus actually noted that he used the geometrical ratio for population and an arithmetical ratio for subsistence mostly to illustrate his point (Thompson and Lewis, 1965). However, Malthus always held that population growth was faster than subsistence. Some of the other arguments attributed to Malthus are that he ignored the impact of contraception on controlling population growth; however, as a clergyman he was not able to recognize birth control within marriage as a check. Winch wrote that Malthus was "opposed to birth control on the grounds that such 'unnatural' experiments ran contrary to God's design in placing humankind under the right degree of pressure to ensure its development" (Winch, 2003: 620). Thompson and Lewis also stated that Malthus never clearly defined subsistence as either food or means of subsistence, which is synonymous with standard of life (Thompson and Lewis, 1965).

Bogue (1969) may have written one of the better appraisals of Malthus. He believed that Malthus' contribution to the development of demography was, at best, modest. He stated that Malthus' defenders often find solace in stating that those who do not accept him have not read him; however, Bogue disagrees. He wrote a detailed examination of Malthus' work, pointing out that he was not methodologically or substantively original. He observed that Malthusian principles were not valid for Europe or for North America because the industrial revolution has shown that increases in subsistence have far exceeded the human tendency to reproduce (Poston, 2006b).

The writings of Malthus are said to have influenced the work of Charles Darwin, Herbert Spencer, David Ricardo, John Maynard Keynes, and many others. For instance, Darwin wrote in his *Autobiography* ([1887]

1958: 42–43) that: "fifteen months after I had begun my systematic enquiry, I happened to read for amusement Malthus on population, and being well prepared to appreciate the struggle for existence which everywhere goes on from long-continued observation of the habits of animals and plants, it at once struck me that under these circumstances favourable variations would tend to be preserved and unfavourable ones be destroyed. The result of this would be a new species. Here, then, I had at last got a theory by which to work."

MARX

Karl Marx, the economist and philosopher, disagreed with Malthus about the universal nature of the problem of overpopulation. Marx was writing at a time when the Industrial Revolution was reaching its apex. He argued that there were two classes of people, namely, the bourgeoisie (capitalists) and the proletariat (the workers) (Marx and Engels, [1848] 1935: 32). It was to the advantage of the bourgeoisie to encourage high fertility because this would result in a surplus of workers. Such a surplus would lead to more profits, the goal of the capitalists. According to Malthus, population was an **independent variable** and was the cause of much distress, such as poverty. In contrast, Marx argued that population was the **dependent variable**: "Whenever the reserve army of labor is relatively depleted and the level of wages tends to rise reducing the rate of surplus value, the capitalist class will adopt measures (i.e., technological improvements, foreign investments, and so forth) which, while increasing the productivity of labor and the rate of profit, will render obsolete the number of jobs" (Gimenez, 1971: 4). In other words, Marx believed that capitalism was the culprit that ended up causing poverty, whereas Malthus believed that population growth per se was the main cause of poverty.

Marx was aware that population growth could be a problem. Indeed, Friedrich Engels, his long-time friend and collaborator, wrote that "there is, of course, the abstract possibility that the number of people will become so great that limits will have to be set to their increase. But if at some time communist society finds itself obligated to regulate the production of human beings, just as it has already come to regulate the production of things, it will be precisely this society and this society alone which will carry this out without difficulty" (cited in Gimenez, 1971: 4).

DEMOGRAPHIC TRANSITION THEORY

The most prominent explanation for the growth of human populations is demographic transition theory (DTT). Changes in the size of the world's

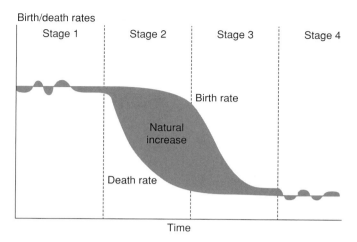

Figure 2.1 The Classic Stages of Demographic Transitions
Source: McFalls, 2007: 27 (reprinted with permission of the PRB).

population over a certain period of time are due entirely to changes during the same time period in fertility and mortality (migration, obviously, does not figure into the equation when the focus is on the world). The world population changes its size over a given time interval by adding persons born during the period and subtracting persons dying.

Demographic transition theory was first developed by Warren S. Thompson (1929) and Frank W. Notestein (1945), and extended by Kingsley Davis (1963). The theory proposes that four stages of mortality and fertility change occur in the process of societal modernization (see Figure 2.1). Stage 1 is the pretransitional or preindustrialization stage. It lasted for thousands and thousands of years when the world was characterized by high birth and death rates and stable population growth. It shows high rates of fluctuating mortality and high fertility. The relative instability of the mortality rates means that during this stage, there were some periods of natural increase and some of natural decrease, but that over the longer period, there was very little change in population size.

The pretransitional stage was followed by a transition to the second stage. For numerous reasons, mortality began to decline in many countries of the world (I discuss these reasons in more detail in Chapter 12). With the onset of industrialization and modernization, many societies transitioned to lower death rates, especially lower infant and maternal mortality rates, but maintained high birth rates; rapid population growth was the result. It would take another generation or so before fertility would begin to fall. Thus, during Stage 2, population growth was intense.

The next stage (Stage 3) was characterized by decreasing population growth due to lower birth and death rates. It was during this period that fertility began to decline. In the final stage (Stage 4), called incipient decline, both fertility and mortality are very low. In Stage 4, populations grow only when there are increases in fertility, such as in the baby boom in the United States after the Second World War. During this stage, however, there are slight fluctuations in fertility. Thus, both natural increase and natural decrease will occur owing to these fluctuations. The term incipient is used because it is not really possible to determine how low fertility will go. In recent years, fertility has fallen so low in many European countries and in Japan that the number of deaths exceeds the number of births (Poston, Johnson, and Field, 2015).

The theory of demographic transition is the most popular of the demographic theories of population change (Browning and Poston, 1980). There are numerous applications of the theory in European and other populations (Coale and Watkins, 1986), and they show that it does not work the same way in every population (Hirschman, 1994; Knodel and van de Walle, 1979; K. Mason, 1997; Poston, 2000). Its major contribution is its utility less as a predictor than as a general description of population change (Poston, Zhang, and Terrell, 2008).

The demographic transition in most less developed countries (LDCs) is not as yet complete. Many African countries are early in Stage 3 of the transition, with falling death rates and high, though falling, birth rates, and others are late in Stage 2. This is also the case in much of the Middle East. Some countries in Latin America are moving toward the stage of incipient decline, but are not there yet. This is also true of the United States.

These variations in demographic transition between the more developed and the LDCs are resulting in some interesting changes in population distribution. One in particular is that most of the population increase in the world between now and 2050 will be mainly among the developing countries and not among the developed countries. In 2014, over 83 percent of the world's population (almost 6 billion people) lived in the LDCs and just under 17 percent (just over 1.2 billion) in the more developed countries. Just a century ago, the pattern was reversed, with a majority of the Earth's population residing in the more developed countries. "The conclusion is obvious: not only has population growth been enormous in the 20th century, it has also led to a complete reversal of population distribution with the poorer regions gaining and surpassing the richer sections in the process" (Bouvier and Bertrand, 1999: 10). The share of population living in the LDCs will increase even further during the twenty-first century given the very low fertility rates in the developed nations.

I mentioned above that Stage 4 of the demographic transition is referred to as that of incipient decline because fertility and mortality are both low. However, major changes throughout society have occurred, along with the very low fertility and mortality. Dirk van de Kaa (1987) and Ron Lesthaeghe (1995, 2010; Lesthaeghe and Neidert, 2006, 2009) have discussed these further fertility declines, along with accompanying demographic behaviors, such as increasing age at first marriage, increases in cohabitation, increases in divorce, the emergence of same-sex partnerships and marriages, increasing rates of nonmarital childbearing, and voluntary childlessness. These have been subsumed under the heading of an extension of DTT that is popularly known as the **second demographic transition** (SDT). I show later in Chapters 4 and 5 that all the above changes are now occurring in the United States and in most of the European countries.

Demographic transition theory has been further revised with the recognition by Coleman (2006) of the increasing tendency, if not requirement, of low fertility countries to rely on immigration to maintain their populations. This means that "the ancestry of some national populations is being radically and permanently altered by high levels of immigration of persons from remote geographic origins," and in some countries is accompanied by "accelerated levels of emigration of the domestic population" (Coleman, 2006: 401). These further changes are popularly referred to as the **third demographic transition** (TDT).

A particularly instructive application of this perspective is Lichter's (2013: 364) observation that the "new immigration has altered America's fundamental character. Immigration has become a national political issue and not just a state or local one." Changes in the racial mix of the United States are first seen among the children and young people of the society (Johnson and Lichter, 2008, 2010), and many of these children are the children of immigrants. Lichter makes the point that these children are in "the vanguard of the Third Demographic Transition that will remake America" (Lichter, 2013: 364).

In summary, then, classic demographic transition now referred to as the first demographic transition, involved the transition or movement of societies from high levels of fertility and mortality to low levels of fertility and mortality. This transition began in 1700 and later in Europe and is still ongoing in many Latin American and Asian countries and in virtually all of sub-Saharan Africa. I mentioned above the major changes that have occurred in demographic behavior in most European countries and other countries experiencing very low levels of fertility. These changes have led to what is now popularly known as the second demographic transition, which is an attempt by demographers to explain "the revolution in living arrangements and sexual behavior, and in the setting for childbearing, now transforming the lives of many inhabitants of Western societies and, it is argued, eventually in developed societies elsewhere" (Coleman, 2006: 402).

But given the very low levels of fertility, so low that in some societies more deaths than births are occurring, there has been a tendency, if not a requirement, to rely on international migration to maintain their populations. Neither the first nor the second demographic transitions explicitly took into account the role of international migration. This lack of attention to the crucial role assumed by international migration has resulted in what has become known as the third demographic transition. This involves bringing increasing numbers of immigrants into the low fertility countries, and in so doing, resulting in significant changes in the "composition of national populations and thereby (their) culture, physical appearance, social experiences, and self-perceived identity (Coleman, 2006: 402). I turn next to various theories that refer specifically to each of the three demographic processes of fertility, mortality, and migration.

FERTILITY THEORIES

Demographers have developed several theories of fertility. Prominent explanations are **wealth flows theory, human ecological theory**, and **political economic theory**. I now give each of these some attention.

Caldwell (1976) revised certain features of the classic DTT (just reviewed) with his fertility theory of wealth flows. It is based on the notion that the "emotional" nucleation of the family is crucial for lower fertility. This occurs when parents become less concerned with ancestors and extended family relatives than they are with their children, their children's future, and even the future of their children's children (1976: 322). He noted that this depends largely on the direction of the intergenerational flows of wealth and services. If the flows run from children to their parents, parents will want to have large families. In modern societies where the flows are from parents to children, they will want small families or maybe even no children (Poston and Terrell, 2006; Poston, Zhang, and Terrell, 2008).

Two other prominent theories of fertility change are based on human ecology and political economy. Both are extensions of DTT but in different ways. Human ecological theory is a macro-level explanation, that is, it focuses on societies and not on individuals. It argues that the level of sustenance organization complexity of a society is negatively related with fertility growth and decline (Poston and Frisbie, 2005). In the first place, high fertility patterns are dysfunctional for an increasingly complex sustenance organization because so much of the sustenance produced must be consumed directly by the population. High fertility will reduce the absolute amount of uncommitted sustenance resources, thereby limiting the population's flexibility in adapting to environmental, technological, and other kinds of societal change and fluctuation. Low fertility is more consonant with the needs and requirements of an expansive sustenance organization. More sustenance would be available for investment back into the system in a low growth and low fertility population than in a population with high fertility. Hence, large quantities of sustenance normally consumed by the familial and educational institutions in a high fertility population would be available as mobile or fluid resources in a low fertility population. Sustenance organization in this latter instance would thus have the investment resources available for increasing complexity, given requisite changes in the environment and technology. This leads to the hypothesis of a negative relation between organizational complexity and fertility and population change (Kasarda, 1971; London, 1987; London and Hadden, 1989; Poston and Frisbie, 2005).

The political economic approach is another way to analyze fertility. Diverse fields of knowledge are integrated into the political economy approach so that research reflecting this perspective is "multileveled," combining both macro- and micro-level explanations. Its complexity requires a methodology that embraces both quantitative and qualitative approaches (Greenhalgh, 1990b, 2008; Poston and Terrell, 2006).

The political economy of fertility is not really a theory of fertility per se, but an investigative framework, or "analytic perspective," for the study of fertility (Greenhalgh, 1990b: 87). A good example of a political economy approach to fertility is Kertzer and Hogan's study of Casalecchio, Italy. The authors tracked one small, rural Italian community during a few change-laden decades of the nineteenth and twentieth centuries, using individual-level data and directed by a life-course perspective. They touched on historical events, such as labor and marriage patterns, often ignored by other studies of demographic change. They showed that fertility rates and fertility reduction vary depending on the class or occupation of the family, thus demonstrating that macro-level socioeconomic factors have idiosyncratic effects on different classes of people (Kertzer and Hogan, 1989).

A THEORY OF MORTALITY

An important theory that demographers use to help them better understand societal changes in mortality and the changing structure of causes of death is **epidemiological transition theory** (ETT). Epidemiological transition theory focuses on the society-wide decline of infectious disease and the rise of chronic degenerative causes of death. According to ETT, as postulated by Omran (1971), there are three stages. The first stage is the age of pestilence and famine, in which the primary causes of mortality were influenza, pneumonia, smallpox, tuberculosis, and other related diseases, with high infant and childhood mortality, and a life expectancy averaging between twenty and forty years. In developed countries, this first stage lasted until around 1875.

The second ETT stage is the age of receding pandemics, in which there was a decline in mortality due to improved sanitation and increases in standards of living and public health, resulting in a steady increase in life expectancy to between thirty and fifty years. According to Rogers and Hackenberg (1987), the stage of receding pandemics occurred around the period between 1875 and 1930. The third ETT stage is known as the era of degenerative and manmade diseases (heart disease, cancer, and stroke), in which mortality declines are due to medical advances in the prevention and treatment of infectious diseases. Life expectancy at birth rises rapidly, so that fertility becomes the primary factor in population growth as life expectancy exceeds seventy years (Omran, 1971). About three-fourths of the deaths in this stage are the result of degenerative diseases in the advanced years (Olshansky and Ault, 1986).

Rogers and Hackenberg have noted a fourth ETT state that they have identified as an "hybristic stage," where mortality is heavily influenced by individual behavior and lifestyle choices. Deaths in this stage are due to social pathologies, such as accidents, alcoholism, suicide, and homicide, as well as to lifestyle issues, such as smoking and diet (Fingerhut, 2003; Poston, Davis, and Lewinski, 2006; Robine, 2003; Rogers and Hackenberg, 1987).

THEORIES OF INTERNAL MIGRATION

I now discuss some of the main theories developed by demographers to account for migration. In this section I focus on internal migration, or the changes in residence that occur within a country. In the next section I focus on international migration, or the changes in residence that occur between countries.

With respect to internal migration, why do people move or not move, and why do some geographic areas grow through internal migration and others do not? I will note in later chapters that fertility and mortality occur in response to both biological/genetic and social factors. For example, the likelihood that a woman will have a child is due in part to her fecundity (biological) and in part to her education (social). The likelihood that a person will die or not die is also due in part to biological and social factors. Migration, however, has no such biological or genetic component. There is no genetic propensity in humans favoring or not favoring residential change. The likelihood that a person will or will not move is due entirely to factors in the physical and social environment at the areas of origin and destination, as well as to personal factors.

The eminent demographer Donald Bogue once wrote that the "human organism tends to remain at rest [that is, in the same residential location] until impelled to action by some unsatisfied need or by the threat of discomfort…Migration [theories thus begin] with the premise that every departure for a new community, i.e., migratory movement, is either a response to some impelling need that the person believes cannot be satisfied in his/her present residence, or is a flight from a situation that for some reason has become undesirable, unpleasant, or intolerable" (1969: 753).

The question of who migrates depends in large part on what demographers refer to as the **push and pull factors of migration**. In every consideration of migration, there is usually some combination of factors pushing or not pushing the person from the area of origin and pulling or not pulling the person to the area of destination. Migration push factors include such considerations as loss of a job; discrimination; low availability of social and life partners; and community catastrophes such as floods, epidemics, or hurricanes. Migration pull factors include better chances for employment, education, or income; gentler environment in terms of climate and living conditions, and in terms of race and sexual orientation; and the lure of new or different types of activity (Bogue, 1969; Lee, 1966).

Demographers have shown that people who migrate, that is, change their residences, in response mainly to "pull" factors at the place of destination tend to be "positively" selected. They generally have more education than those who remain behind (Bouvier, Macisco, and Zarate, 1976). Hence, their departure lowers the overall level of educational attainment in the area of origin and often deprives the area of persons with skills that might be useful. These migrants tend to be more innovative and are often better planners. Indeed, that is one reason why they chose to move in the first place. To the extent that this selectivity is present, the area of origin will likely lose a valuable segment of its population (Macisco, Bouvier, and Weller, 1970).

In contrast, migrants responding mainly to "push" factors in the area of origin tend to be "negatively" selected. They are the people who cannot seem to succeed, either because of poor education or lack of needed talents. They are, in a sense, almost forced to leave in order to better their lot in life. They tend to have fewer of the positive characteristics that are valued in the society. Other things being equal, the area of origin is changed positively by the out-migration of such people (Bouvier, Macisco, and Zarate, 1976).

Lee (1966) noted, however, that there is more to migration than a person calculating the advantages and disadvantages, the positives and the negatives, at both the areas of origin and destination. There are also intervening obstacles that must be considered. Between every two possible areas of origin and destination there are various obstacles that may or may not intervene and have an impact on whether the migration will or will not occur. One is distance. Other things being equal, the greater the distance between two areas, the less likely the migration. Physical barriers and migration laws may also reduce the likelihood of migration.

Thus, at both the origin and the destination, there are positive and negative factors that the person typically considers when deciding whether or not to migrate. Between the origin and destination are obstacles that may or may not influence the migration decision. The pushes and pulls thus are evaluated in light of the costs of overcoming the intervening obstacles.

Many of the specific theories of internal migration developed by demographers to better understand the dynamics of migration begin with this framework. Each theory tends to focus more on certain pushes, pulls, or obstacles than on others. The main theoretical models seek to explain internal migration in terms of (1) the effects of distance, (2) income, (3) the physical costs of migration, (4) information, (5) personal characteristics, (6) individual expectations, and (7) community and kinship ties (Poston, Luo, and Zhang, 2006).

As already mentioned, the distance model states that long distance discourages migration (Lee, 1966) because the costs involved in migration are substantial and are closely related to distance. The income model argues that income and job opportunities provide a better explanation of in-migration than they do for out-migration (Perloff et al., 1960); destination characteristics also help to determine the location to which the migrant will move (Poston and Frisbie, 2005). The physical costs model suggests that physical costs influence resource allocation and migration by influencing the private costs of migration (Greenwood, 1975). The information model emphasizes that "the availability of information concerning alternative localities plays a prominent role in the potential migrant's decision regarding a destination" (Greenwood, 1975: 405). The personal characteristics model argues that personal demographic characteristics (e.g., age, sex, education, number of dependants, networks, and race) exert important influences on the individual's decision or propensity to migrate (Grieco and Boyd, 1998; Nam, Serow, and Sly, 1990). The individual expectations model assumes that the dynamics of migration decision-making are based on individual expectations about the advantages and disadvantages of the home community versus possible alternative destination communities (Fischer, Martin, and Straubhaar, 1997). The community and kinship ties model points out that "the presence of relatives and friends is a valued aspect of life [that] . . . encourages migration by increasing the individual's potential for adjustment through the availability of aid in location at an alternative area of residence" (Ritchey, 1976: 389).

The above theories of internal migration focus mainly on individuals and why they move or do not move. Demographers have developed other kinds of theories that are known as aggregate theories. They focus less on individuals per se and more on populations and their geographic areas. Rather than asking why individuals move, the aggregate theories ask why some areas increase in population size through migration, why others decrease through migration, and why still others are not influenced one way or the other via migration.

Sociological human ecology is an aggregate theory that provides a perspective for considering the effects of migration on populations and geographic areas. From the perspective of human ecology, migration is the major mechanism of social change and adaptability for human populations. Knowledge of migration patterns tells us about how "populations … maintain themselves in particular areas" (Hawley, 1950: 149). The ecological approach asserts that human populations redistribute themselves via net migration in order to attain an equilibrium between their overall size and the life chances available to them (Poston and Frisbie, 1998: 30, 2005; Poston, 2015).

The theoretical foundation of human ecology is based on the interdependence of the four conceptual rubrics of population, organization, environment, and technology. The interrelationships among and between these dimensions inform our understanding of migration patterns. All populations adapt to their environments. These adaptations vary among populations according to their social and sustenance organization, their technology, and the size, composition, and distribution of the population. The environment is comprised of both social and physical factors, and it sets constraints on the population and the form and characteristics of its organization. The technology at the population's disposal sets the boundaries for the form and kind of environmental adaptation that the population assumes. Human ecology posits that of the three demographic processes, migration is the most efficient agent for returning the human ecosystem to a state of equilibrium, or balance, between its size and organization (Poston and Frisbie, 1998, 2005; Poston, 2015).

A hypothesis typically investigated in ecological studies of internal migration (e.g., Poston and Frisbie, 1998; Saenz and Colberg, 1988) is that variability among human groups in their patterns of migration is a function of differences in their patterns of sustenance organization, technology, environment, and population. The **ecological theory of migration** thus focuses on characteristics of the population group to predict the level of migration. Individual attitudes and propensities do not play a role.

Finally, most theories of internal migration, both individual-level theories and aggregate theories, have been influenced in one way or another by the very early work of E. G. Ravenstein, who endeavored in two seminal articles written in 1885 and 1889 to identify the so-called laws of migration. Ravenstein set forth many laws or theorems of migration based largely on his research in England and a few other countries. Included are the following: (1) migration is affected by distance – most migrants move only short distances; (2) migrants often move in stages – as they leave one area, their places are filled by migrants from more distant areas; (3) every migration stream has a compensating counterstream; (4) migrants proceeding long distances often stop, temporarily, at major cities or centers of commerce that are located between the area of origin and the intended final area of destination; and (5) urban residents are less likely to migrate than rural residents.

THEORIES OF INTERNATIONAL MIGRATION

There are several theories of international migration, most of which focus on the determinants of voluntary migration. The **neoclassical economic theory of international migration** is perhaps the oldest and best-known theory of international migration. It focuses specifically on labor migration (Harris and Todaro, 1970; Massey et al., 1993, 1994). According to this model, migration occurs on account of individual cost–benefit decisions to maximize expected incomes through international movement. Workers are attracted from low-wage countries with adequate labor to high-wage countries with limited labor.

The **new economics theory of migration** is an international migration theory developed in recent years to challenge some of the hypotheses and assumptions of neoclassical economics. This theory argues that migration decisions are made not only by isolated individuals, but also by larger units, such as families and households (Massey et al., 1993; Stark, 1984, 1991). Migration occurs not only to increase individual earnings, but also to minimize household risks and to protect the family from market failures.

An approach that differs from both of the preceding is **dual labor market theory**. This theory states that international migration stems from the demands of the economic structure of industrial societies (Massey et al., 1993, 1994; Piore, 1979). International migration is caused not only by the push factors of the origin countries, but also by the pull factors of the destination countries. Inherent tendencies in modern capitalism lead labor markets to separate into two sectors: "the primary sector that produces jobs with secure tenure, high pay, generous benefits, and good working conditions; and the secondary sector typified by instability, low pay, limited benefits, and unpleasant or hazardous working conditions" (Massey et al., 1994: 715). Employers are inclined to turn to migrants to fill the jobs in the secondary sector.

The **world systems theory of migration** argues that international migration is the natural result of the globalization of the market economy

(Massey et al., 1993; Portes and Walton, 1981; Sassen, 1988). In the process of global industrialization, a large number of people are released from traditional industries, such as farming, state-owned industries, and handicrafts, and this creates a mobilized population to move both internally and internationally (Massey, 1988; Massey et al., 1993). The development of the global market economy attracts human capital to a relatively small number of global cities, among them, New York, Los Angeles, and Chicago (Castells, 1989).

Finally, **migration network theory** focuses on networks, that is, the interpersonal ties that connect migrants, former migrants, potential migrants, and nonmigrants in the origin and destination countries. The networks increase the likelihood of international movement by decreasing migrant risks and costs and increasing the net earnings to migration (Massey et al., 1993). Networks make it easier for new migrants to find jobs and gain access to required resources in their destination countries.

These theories and others endeavor to account for the causal process of international migration at different levels of analysis, namely, the individual, the household, the country, and the world. These different perspectives are not necessarily incompatible (Poston, Luo, and Zhang, 2006). Indeed, the key elements of each theory are sometimes all subsumed under the headings of "push" and "pull." There are push and pull conditions facilitating migration in most of the countries of the world. For an individual or group to decide to engage in international migration, there needs to be a push from the origin country and/or a pull to the destination country.

In addition to individual push and pull factors leading to international migration, there are also contextual factors that are operating. For example, after arriving in destination countries, migrants, particularly Asian migrants, sometimes gravitate into what are called ethnic enclaves. An **ethnic enclave** is a community that helps individuals transition into life as immigrants by providing support and environments much like those in their mother countries. The push and pull factors, individual and contextual, can be one or more of any of the characteristics defining the five theories outlined in this section (Cortes and Poston, 2008).

CONCLUSION

I began this chapter by asking about the meaning of "population." I next examined some of the early writings about population. I paid special attention to the work and contributions of Malthus, but also considered other population theorists, for example, Marx. I next covered the major theory of demography, DTT, that was developed by demographers to help our understanding of overall population change that societies experienced as they transitioned from high fertility and mortality rates to low fertility and mortality rates. I then discussed how demographers have revised the theory dealing with this classic, or first, demographic transition into extensions involving the second and third demographic transitions.

I then turned attention to theories focusing specifically on fertility and discussed some of the key perspectives. Next, I reviewed the major features of the main demographic theory of mortality, epidemiological transition theory. I followed this presentation with discussions of theories dealing with internal migration and with international migration. In Chapters 4–14, I will have occasion to refer to many, if not all, of these theories in my reviews of the major substantive issues of demography.

Finally, it is clear from my discussions in this chapter that demography has an abundance of theories. Indeed, the theoretical perspectives of demography rival those of any of the other social sciences. Consider the many different theoretical perspectives I have reviewed in this chapter that focus on fertility and mortality and internal and international migration. Consider also the classic model of demographic transition and its elaborations. Charles Nam argued almost forty years ago that "the issues of demographic journals today are replete with theoretically based articles, in stark contrast to those of the past" (1979: 490; see also Riley and McCarthy, 2003). Occasionally, uninformed social scientists who do not know the demographic literature criticize demography as being atheoretical. They erroneously claim that there is a paucity of theory in demography. The statement that demography is void of theory is clearly incorrect (Burch, 2003). Demography has more formal and substantive theories than almost all the social sciences.

3 The Sources of Demographic Information

I noted toward the end of Chapter 1 that we demographers are more fortunate than many of our social science colleagues who must gather and develop their own data and databases. Generally speaking, most of the data we demographers use have already been gathered for us, although this is not always the situation. Indeed, some demographers do gather their own data, especially those using anthropological perspectives and who engage in ethnographic research (Greenhalgh, 1990b, 1994; Riley, 1998; Riley and McCarthy, 2003). However, most of us use data already gathered and developed by other organizations. In this chapter, I discuss the basic sources of demographic information of which there are three.

The three basic sources of demographic data are national censuses, registers, and surveys. National censuses and registers differ in that the former are conducted on a decennial (or, in some countries, quinquennial) basis, while the latter, theoretically at least, are compiled continuously. Actually, **registration** data of population events are usually compiled and published annually or monthly, but they are gathered continuously. A **census** may be likened to taking a snapshot of a population at one point in time, say, once every ten years or so, and in this snapshot getting a picture of the size of the population, its characteristics, and its spatial distribution. Conversely, a register may be thought of as a continuous compilation of major population events, often births, deaths, marriages, divorces, and sometimes migrations. When a birth or a death occurs, it is registered with the government; the registrations thus occur continuously.

Censuses and registers are intended to cover the entire population. In a national census, it is intended that everyone in the population is enumerated, and all the demographic events (births, deaths, and so forth) that occur in the population are supposed to be registered. Surveys, on the other hand, are, by definition, administered to only a fraction, a sample, of the population. Surveys often contain data items that are also included in censuses and registers, plus additional items of interest that are not included in censuses and surveys. I will now cover in some detail each of these three sources of demographic data.

NATIONAL CENSUSES

A national **census** is "the total process of collecting, compiling, and publishing demographic, economic, and social data pertaining, at a specified time . . . to all persons in a country or delimited territory" (United Nations, 1958: 3). The principal objective of a census is to obtain data about the size, composition, and distribution of the population. A typical census thus includes information about the size of the population and its geographic subpopulations, as well as data on their age and sex composition, and other mainly demographic characteristics. Some censuses also include information about the population's educational composition (levels of literacy and educational attainment, and extent of school attendance), its economically active and inactive populations, the industrial and occupational composition of the working population, as well as economic (salary and income) data. Other population data in a typical census might include information pertaining to country or area of birth, citizenship, language, recent migration experience, religion, and ethnic heritage, which refers to group distinctions based on shared cultural origins (Shryock, Siegel, and Associates, 1976).

The US decennial censuses, since 1940, included most of the above information, and this was the situation up through the census conducted in 2000. There were two census questionnaires known as the short-form or 100% questionnaire, and the long-form or sample questionnaire. Everyone filled out the short-form instrument, and it asked questions about one's sex, age, race, ethnicity, and household relationship. The long-form questionnaire was administered to all persons in about every one of six households, and it asked a host of questions dealing with socioeconomic status, place of birth, citizenship, migration, ancestry, and so forth. Several years ago the Census Bureau redesigned these questionnaires, so that the questionnaire used in the 2010 census included only the questions from the short-form instrument. The more detailed long-form questionnaire is now the major component of an annual survey known as the American Community Survey (I discuss this survey later in the chapter).

The 2010 census questionnaire was one of the shortest questionnaires in US census history. It asked each person to provide only his or her name, sex, age, race, ethnicity, relationship, and whether he or she owned or rented their home. It took the average household about 10 minutes to fill it out.

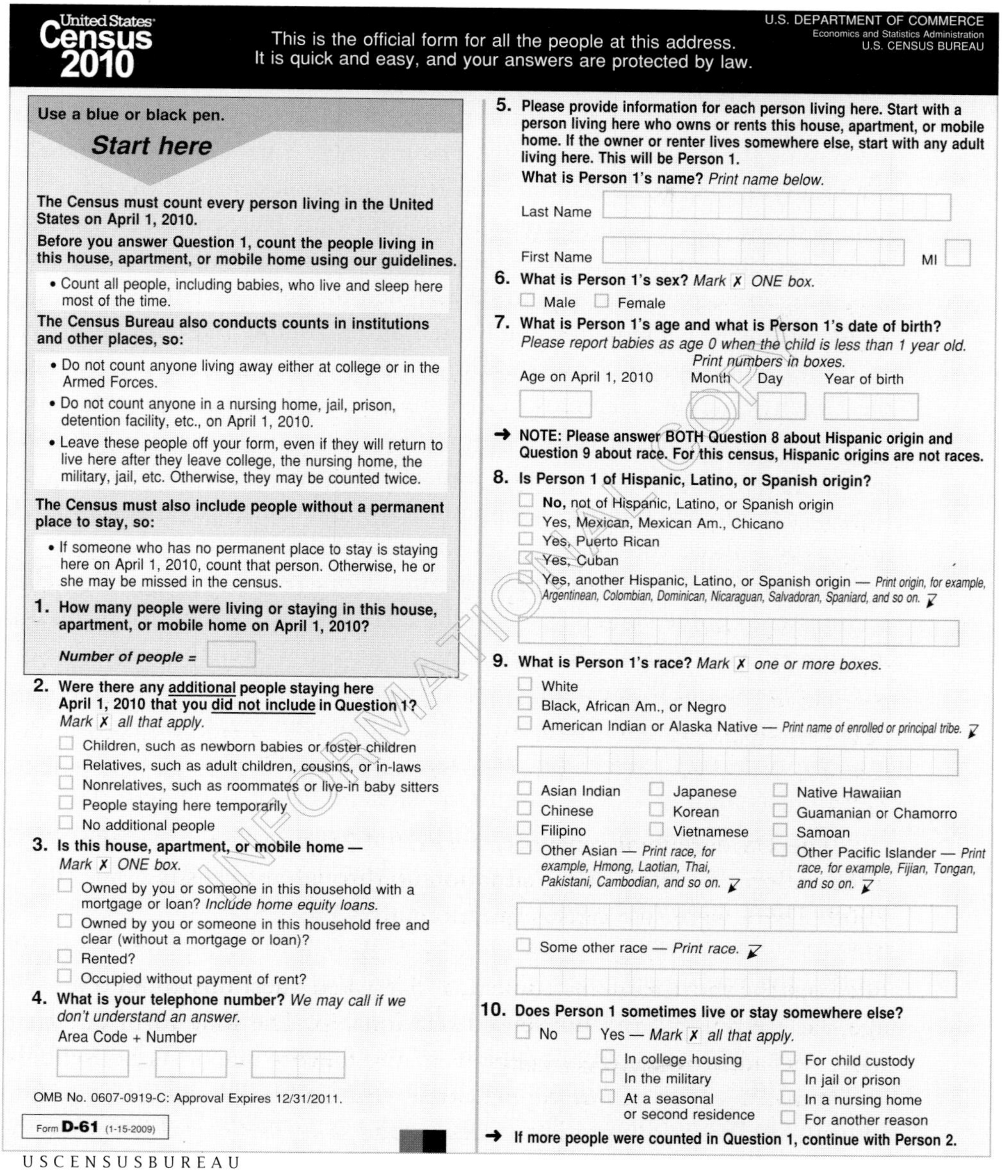

United States Census 2010

This is the official form for all the people at this address.
It is quick and easy, and your answers are protected by law.

U.S. DEPARTMENT OF COMMERCE
Economics and Statistics Administration
U.S. CENSUS BUREAU

Use a blue or black pen.

Start here

The Census must count every person living in the United States on April 1, 2010.

Before you answer Question 1, count the people living in this house, apartment, or mobile home using our guidelines.

- Count all people, including babies, who live and sleep here most of the time.

The Census Bureau also conducts counts in institutions and other places, so:

- Do not count anyone living away either at college or in the Armed Forces.
- Do not count anyone in a nursing home, jail, prison, detention facility, etc., on April 1, 2010.
- Leave these people off your form, even if they will return to live here after they leave college, the nursing home, the military, jail, etc. Otherwise, they may be counted twice.

The Census must also include people without a permanent place to stay, so:

- If someone who has no permanent place to stay is staying here on April 1, 2010, count that person. Otherwise, he or she may be missed in the census.

1. How many people were living or staying in this house, apartment, or mobile home on April 1, 2010?

Number of people = ☐

2. Were there any additional people staying here April 1, 2010 that you did not include in Question 1?
Mark X all that apply.

☐ Children, such as newborn babies or foster children
☐ Relatives, such as adult children, cousins, or in-laws
☐ Nonrelatives, such as roommates or live-in baby sitters
☐ People staying here temporarily
☐ No additional people

3. Is this house, apartment, or mobile home —
Mark X ONE box.

☐ Owned by you or someone in this household with a mortgage or loan? *Include home equity loans.*
☐ Owned by you or someone in this household free and clear (without a mortgage or loan)?
☐ Rented?
☐ Occupied without payment of rent?

4. What is your telephone number? *We may call if we don't understand an answer.*
Area Code + Number

OMB No. 0607-0919-C: Approval Expires 12/31/2011.

Form **D-61** (1-15-2009)

5. Please provide information for each person living here. Start with a person living here who owns or rents this house, apartment, or mobile home. If the owner or renter lives somewhere else, start with any adult living here. This will be Person 1.
What is Person 1's name? *Print name below.*

Last Name

First Name MI

6. What is Person 1's sex? *Mark X ONE box.*
☐ Male ☐ Female

7. What is Person 1's age and what is Person 1's date of birth?
Please report babies as age 0 when the child is less than 1 year old.
Print numbers in boxes.
Age on April 1, 2010 Month Day Year of birth

→ **NOTE: Please answer BOTH Question 8 about Hispanic origin and Question 9 about race. For this census, Hispanic origins are not races.**

8. Is Person 1 of Hispanic, Latino, or Spanish origin?
☐ **No,** not of Hispanic, Latino, or Spanish origin
☐ Yes, Mexican, Mexican Am., Chicano
☐ Yes, Puerto Rican
☐ Yes, Cuban
☐ Yes, another Hispanic, Latino, or Spanish origin — *Print origin, for example, Argentinean, Colombian, Dominican, Nicaraguan, Salvadoran, Spaniard, and so on.*

9. What is Person 1's race? *Mark X one or more boxes.*
☐ White
☐ Black, African Am., or Negro
☐ American Indian or Alaska Native — *Print name of enrolled or principal tribe.*
☐ Asian Indian ☐ Japanese ☐ Native Hawaiian
☐ Chinese ☐ Korean ☐ Guamanian or Chamorro
☐ Filipino ☐ Vietnamese ☐ Samoan
☐ Other Asian — *Print race, for example, Hmong, Laotian, Thai, Pakistani, Cambodian, and so on.*
☐ Other Pacific Islander — *Print race, for example, Fijian, Tongan, and so on.*
☐ Some other race — *Print race.*

10. Does Person 1 sometimes live or stay somewhere else?
☐ No ☐ Yes — *Mark X all that apply.*
☐ In college housing ☐ For child custody
☐ In the military ☐ In jail or prison
☐ At a seasonal or second residence ☐ In a nursing home
☐ For another reason

→ **If more people were counted in Question 1, continue with Person 2.**

INFORMATIONAL COPY

USCENSUSBUREAU

Figure 3.1

(I have provided an Information Copy of the 2010 census questionnaire in Figure 3.1, above.)

In the actual enumeration of the population, there are two ways to count people: by following a ***de jure*** method or by following a ***de facto*** method (Shryock, 1964). In the case of a *de jure* enumeration, the census covers the entire territory of the country and counts persons according to their "usual" or "normal" place of residence in the country. A *de facto* enumeration, on the other hand, also covers the entire territory of the country, but counts each person according to his or her geographical location on the day of the census undertaking. For instance, a person who lives with her family in Dallas, Texas, but who is traveling on census day and is visiting a friend in College Station, Texas, and thus happens to be counted in College Station, would be counted as a resident of Dallas if the census was a *de jure* census, but would be assigned to College Station if it was a *de facto* census. Canada and the United States follow a *de jure* approach, as do most European countries, for example, Austria, Belgium, Croatia, the Czech Republic, Denmark, Germany, the Netherlands, Norway, Sweden, and Switzerland (United Nations, 1998). The censuses of Colombia have been both *de facto* (in 1963 and 1973) and *de jure* (since 1985). Of the more than 230 countries conducting national censuses, however, the *de facto* type is more common than the *de jure* (Wilmoth, 2004: 65).

Shown in Figure 3.1 is an Information Copy of a census questionnaire administered in the United States in the 2010 census. The questions on this instrument were typically answered by one person in every **household** in the United States, and that person typically entered responses to each question for everyone residing in the household. As you can see, there were only a few questions on the 2010 questionnaire.

Census-taking had its origins in ancient Egypt, China, and Rome, among other places, although only a few of these enumerations have survived. There may have been a census conducted in China as early as 3000 BC, but demographic records for China and other countries for the very early periods no longer exist. Several census counts are mentioned in the Bible. One was undertaken at the time of the Exodus in 1491 BC, and another was conducted during King David's era in 1017 BC. Roman censuses were conducted quinquennially for more than 800 years. The Romans extended the census enumeration to the entire Roman Empire in 5 BC, resulting in the popular biblical census story reported in St. Luke's Gospel (Bryan, 2004: 14).

It is difficult to determine with certainty when the first modern census was undertaken. Coverage was highly suspect in the very early censuses, with women and children seldom included. Indeed, the first census conducted in the United States in 1790 was a rather crude undertaking; it only included counts of the number of "free white" males of age 16 and over and those under age 16, the number of "free white" females irrespective of their ages, the number of all other "free" persons irrespective of their sex or age, and the number of slaves irrespective of their sex or age.

Livi-Bacci (2012: 24) has stated that the 1790 US census that counted 3.9 million people, along with the 1787 census of the Kingdom of Spain that counted 10.4 million people, "are the first examples of modern censuses in large countries."

Censuses were often conducted to determine the fiscal and military obligations of the citizens (Bryan, 2004); this is why the 1790 US census differentiated "free white" males by whether they were over or under the age of 16.

Most countries of the world today conduct censuses, although some countries are late to census-taking. For instance, Chad and Oman did not take their first censuses until 1993. Of the more than 230 countries or areas in the world today, the United Nations reports that all but seven (Eritrea, Iraq, Lebanon, Pakistan, Somalia, Uzbekistan, and western Sahara) completed a population census by the end of the 2010 "census round," which covers the time period between 2005 and 2014 (UNSD, 2013). This includes around 96 percent of the world's population. This is a slight improvement from the 95 percent or so of the world's population covered in censuses in the 2000 round, when as many as twenty-six countries did not participate (Johnson, 2000; United Nations, 2007).

Of the seven countries not conducting a census in the 2010 round, Lebanon stands out as the only country never to have conducted an official population census. Most likely owing to the way the country was formed by the French, Lebanon has used national population and household surveys for various enumeration estimates and has avoided, perhaps for political reasons, conducting an actual census (pers. comm., Mary J. Chamie, July 10, 2007).

Population censuses were conducted relatively early in the United States, starting with Virginia in 1624–1625. Various colonial censuses were conducted up to 1767. In the United States, the principal reason and justification for conducting a decennial national census is to provide population counts for the states of the country that are used to apportion the House of Representatives. The requirement for a decennial census was written in 1787 into Article 1, Section 2, of the US Constitution as follows: "Representatives and direct taxes shall be apportioned among the several states which may be included within this Union according to their respective numbers…The actual enumeration shall be made within three years after the first meeting of the Congress of the United States, and within every subsequent term of ten years in such manner as they shall by law direct."

The first national census was conducted in 1790, and one has been conducted in the United States every ten years since. Today, censuses and census data are very important for the functioning of government bodies. As an illustration, I show in Box 3.1 exactly how the most recent apportionment of the US House of Representatives was conducted using data from the 2010 census.

BOX 3.1 USING CENSUS DATA TO APPORTION THE US HOUSE OF REPRESENTATIVES IN 2010

The major objective when apportioning the US House of Representatives is to assign equitably the 435 seats to the fifty states (the District of Columbia is not included in the apportionment; thus, the residents of the District are not represented in the House of Representatives). There are several constraints: (1) the total number of House seats must equal 435; (2) partial representatives cannot be assigned to states, nor can representatives be given fractional votes; (3) representatives may not be shared by two or more states; and (4) every state must be assigned at least one seat in the House.

The first fifty seats are automatically assigned, one per state. The purpose of the apportionment method is to divide up the remaining 385 seats. The apportionment method of "equal proportions" indicates which states should receive second seats, which states should receive third seats, and so forth. However, the US Constitution does not provide instructions on how apportionment should be carried out, only that the underlying assumption must be "one man, one vote." That is, no one person should have more of a voice than another person. As a result, representatives are assigned from states in proportion to their populations. The method of equal proportions was first used to apportion the House in 1940 and has been used ever since. It is a divisor method that first develops a target **ratio** of population to representatives that is based on data for the nation. In 2010, the apportionment population (the population counted by the Census Bureau residing in each state plus certain individuals living overseas who claim the state as their "state of residence," namely, military personnel and US government employees and their dependants) of the United States was 309,183,463. Hence, the target ratio in 2010 was 710,766.6 (or 309,183,463 divided by 435). This ratio, also called a divisor, is then divided into the apportionment populations of each of the states to obtain quotients. The method of equal proportions endeavors to ensure that "the difference between the representation of any two states is the smallest possible when measured both by the relative difference in the average population per district, and also by the relative difference in the individual share in a representative" (Schmeckebier, 1941: 22). The method gives to a state another representative "when its [apportionment] population, divided by the geometric mean of its present assignment of representatives and of its next higher assignment, is greater than the [apportionment] population of any other state divided by the geometric mean of the assignment to such other state and its next higher assignment" (Schmeckebier, 1941: 22).

The first step in using the method of equal proportions is to multiply the apportionment population of each state by the following fraction:

$$\frac{1}{\sqrt{N(N-1)}}$$

where N equals the particular seat being claimed, that is, the second seat, or the third seat, or the fourth seat, and so on. This provides numbers known as priority values. For instance, the proportion used in determining a state's claim to a second seat is:

$$\frac{1}{\sqrt{2(2-1)}} = \frac{1}{\sqrt{2}} = \frac{1}{1.41421356} = 0.70710678$$

The proportion used in determining a state's claim to a third seat is:

$$\frac{1}{\sqrt{3(3-1)}} = \frac{1}{\sqrt{6}} = \frac{1}{2.44948974} = 0.40824829$$

The rounding rule for this method is to round a state's quotient either up or down, "depending on whether or not the quotient exceeds the 'geometric mean' of these two choices" (Balinski and Young, 1982: 62). The geometric mean of two numbers is the square root of their product. Thus, according to the method of equal proportions, if a state had a quotient of 1.39, it would receive one representative because the geometric mean of 1 and 2 is 1.41; however, if a state had a quotient of 1.42, it would receive two representatives.

In the actual apportionment calculations, the rule per se need not be invoked. Instead, one may rely entirely on the proportions developed for the various seats. Thus, once the proportions are developed for determining the priorities for the various seats (I showed above the calculations of the proportions for seats 2 and 3), they are multiplied by the apportionment populations of each of the fifty states. That is, the proportion used for determining the states' priorities for a second seat (0.70710678) is successively multiplied by the apportionment populations of each of the fifty states; this procedure is then repeated using the proportion to determine the states' priorities for a third seat (0.40824829), and so forth.

After all these multiplications have been completed, the resulting priority values are then ranked in order, the largest first and the smallest last. The 385 House seats are assigned to the states with the 385 highest priority values.

In the table below, I report the application of the method of equal proportions in 2010 and identify the states receiving the first six seats and those receiving the last six seats. I also show the states that would have received the three seats beyond the 435th seat if more than 435 seats were available. In the 2010 apportionment, California received the 51st seat. Its priority value for a second seat of 26,404,774 was obtained by multiplying its 2010 apportionment population of 37,341,989 by the "second seat" proportion of 0.70710678. Texas received the 52nd seat with its priority value for a second seat of 17,867,470, which was determined by multiplying its 2010 apportionment population of 25,268,418 by 0.70710678. The 51st and 52nd seats were thus assigned to the two largest states, California and Texas. New York had the third largest population of all the states in 2010, but New York did not receive the 53rd seat because its priority value for a second seat of 13,732,760 was smaller than California's priority value for a third seat of 15,244,803 (the priority value for California's third seat is obtained by multiplying California's apportionment population of 37,341,989 by the "third seat" proportion of 0.40824829). So California received the 53rd seat and New York the 54th seat. Florida received the 55th seat as its second seat, California received the 56th seat as its fourth seat, and Texas received the 57th seat as its third seat.

The table below also shows the states receiving the last six seats in the House, the 430th through the 435th seats. Note, for instance, that Texas' priority value for a 36th seat was slightly larger than California's claim for a 53rd seat, so, therefore, the 433rd seat was assigned to Texas and the 434th to California. Minnesota received the 435th and last House seat; it was allocated as Minnesota's 8th seat. The states of North Carolina, Missouri, and New York were next in line to receive the 436th, 437th, and 438th seats had the House allocated three more seats. For a fuller discussion of apportionment, its history, and calculations see Burnett (2011) for the 2010 apportionment and Baumle and Poston (2004) for the 2000 apportionment.

On this topic of Congressional apportionment, I encourage you also to read Marta Tienda's (2002) very insightful article on "Demography and the Social Contract," which discusses the issues involved in including and excluding immigrants from the apportionment populations of the states. There are some unexpected conclusions.

Numbered seat in House	State	Numbered seat in the State	Priority value
Application in 2010 of the Method of Equal Proportions: Allocating the First Six and Last Few Seats			
First six seats			
51	California	2	26,404,774
52	Texas	2	17,867,470
53	California	3	15,244,803
54	New York	2	13,732,760
55	Florida	2	13,364,865
56	California	4	10,779,704
Last six seats			
430	South Carolina	7	716,890
431	Florida	27	713,364
432	Washington	10	711,868
433	Texas	36	711,857
434	California	53	711,308
435	Minnesota	8	710,231
Three seats beyond the 435th			
436	North Carolina	14	709,063
437	Missouri	9	708,459
438	New York	28	706,337

Censuses are very expensive to conduct. The cost of the 2010 US census was around $13.1 billion, a figure that actually turned out to be 11 percent less than the $14.7 billion that was appropriated for the 2010 count (Roberts, 2010). Census data provide government officials with useful and necessary information about the people in their country. Governments use census data in virtually all features of public policy, for example, how many children the public schools need to serve and where to place new roads. Census results also provide the denominator data for crime rates, death rates, per capita income figures, and other statistics that are needed to administer local and national governments. Private businesses require census data for their market analyses and for advertising activities (Anderson, 2003). Many demographers and other social scientists use census data to test their theories and conduct their analyses.

For instance, one of the questions in the 2010 census asked everyone living in a household with two or more persons about their relationship to the person who is known as "Person 1." This person is often "the member of the household in whose name the home is owned, being bought or rented" (Barrett, 1994: 16). Operationally, it refers to the person taking the major responsibility for filling out the census form. Look at question No. 5 of Figure 3.1 for the actual wording that results in the identification of Person 1. Every person in the household, except Person1, is also asked to respond to a question about his or her relationship to Person 1. (This question about the relationship to Person 1 is not actually shown in Figure 3.1 because the part of the questionnaire that I have included in Figure 3.1 only applies to Person 1.)

The numerous responses that Person 2 and Person 3 and the other persons in the household may use to respond to the "relationship to Person 1" question include the so-called blood or family relationships of husband, wife, son, grandfather, and so forth, and the nonfamily relationships of roomer/boarder, housemate/roommate, unmarried partner, and so forth. The "unmarried partner" response permits researchers to identify a person in the household who is unrelated to Person 1, but who has a "marriage-like" relationship with Person 1. Census procedures allow respondents to check the "unmarried partner" response irrespective of whether the person's sex is the same as that of Person 1. It is thus possible to identify the number of adults in the United States who are unmarried partners with persons of the same sex. Also it is possible, for a few states where in 2010 same-sex marriage was permitted, to count the number of same-sex persons who report that they are the spouse of Person 1. As of the year of 2010, "five states (Connecticut, Iowa, Massachusetts, New Hampshire, and Vermont) and the District of Columbia [were issuing] ... marriage certificates to same-sex couples ... There were also three states that did not perform same-sex marriages but recognized them from other states (Maryland, New York, and Rhode Island)" (O'Connell and Feliz, 2011: 3). As of the end of June 2015, when a near-final version of this chapter was written, the Supreme Court of the United States had ruled that the Constitution guarantees a right to same-sex marriage. By the time this book is published, same-sex marriage will be legal in all fifty states plus the District of Columbia.

It is thus possible to calculate the numbers of same-sex adult males and same-sex adult females who are married or who are not married but living together. Demographers make the assumption that these data on same-sex households (male–male or female–female) represent households inhabited by partnered gay men or partnered lesbians (Baumle, Compton, and Poston, 2009; Black et al., 2000).

My student Yuting Chang and I have used these same-sex data from the 2010 census and calculated gay male partnering rates and lesbian partnering rates for the 366 metropolitan areas of the United States (Poston and Chang, 2013). I cover our research in greater detail later in Chapter 5.

I note first that when analyzing the 2010 same-sex household data Census Bureau researchers "discovered an inconsistency in the responses in the 2010 census summary file statistics that artificially inflated the number of same-sex couples" (Bureau of the Census, 2011). When Dr. Chang and I gathered the same-sex household data for our research, we adapted an adjustment method developed by Gates (2013) in an attempt to address the abovementioned problem (see Poston and Chang [2013] for the details).

We used a gay male/lesbian prevalence index that measures the over- or underrepresentation of "same-sex couples in a geographic area relative to the population" (Gates and Ost, 2004: 24). An index value of 1.0 for a metropolitan area means that "a same-sex couple is just as likely as a randomly picked household to locate" in the metro area (Gates and Ost, 2004: 24). An index value above 1.0 means that a same-sex couple is more likely to live in the metro area than a random household, and a value less than 1.0, less likely.

We showed that the mean index values across the 366 metropolitan areas for gay male households was 0.69 and 0.86 for lesbian households. This means that in the "average" metropolitan area in the United States in 2010, gay male couples were 31 percent less likely to settle there than would be a couple from a randomly selected metropolitan household (i.e., $[0.69 - 1.0] \times 100$); and that a lesbian couple would be 14 percent less likely to settle there than would be a couple from a randomly selected household.

We showed that the San Francisco–Oakland–Fremont, California metropolitan area (hereafter referred to as San Francisco) had the highest gay male couple ratio value, 2.78, and the Ithaca, New York metropolitan area had the highest lesbian couple index ratio, 2.97. The value for the San Francisco area may be interpreted as indicating that a gay male couple is 2.8 times more likely than an "average" US couple to reside in the San Francisco area, or, in other words, 178 percent more likely (i.e., $[2.78 - 1.00] \times 100$). The Ithaca index value indicates that a lesbian couple is almost 200 percent more likely to live in Ithaca than an average US couple is likely to live in Ithaca. San Francisco contains the Castro District, a neighborhood in San Francisco in the Eureka Valley, a well-known gay male enclave, making the high prevalence of partnered gay males in San Francisco unsurprising.

Have you ever wondered why San Francisco's queer communities are so world renowned? Why is San Francisco so welcoming to the gay male and lesbian populations? There are many answers to these questions, beginning with the emergence in the early 1900s of gay bars in San Francisco's tourist districts. See, in particular, Nan Alamilla Boyd's *Wide Open Town* (2003) for its vivid and fascinating chronicling of the history of queer San Francisco.

Regarding the lowest gay male and lesbian ratios of all the metropolitan areas, the Grand Forks, North Dakota–Minnesota metro area has the lowest gay male couple ratio at 0.26, and the Wausau, Wisconsin area has the lowest lesbian couple ratio at 0.32. Gay male couples are about one-quarter as likely (or 74 percent less likely) to live in Grand Forks as a randomly picked US metro household, and lesbian couples are about one-third as likely to live in Wausau as a randomly selected household.

We also found that, for the most part, the gay male indexes tend to vary in the same way as the lesbian indexes. Metropolitan areas with high gay male partnering indexes have high lesbian partnering indexes, and areas with low gay male indexes have low lesbian indexes. But most of the metropolitan areas, 328 of the 366, have higher lesbian index values than gay male index values. From the data it seemed pretty clear to us that partnered gay men have a few favorite destinations in which to reside, including San Francisco, Miami, Seattle, San Diego, Washington, DC, Las Vegas, Los Angeles, Atlanta, Denver, New York, Tampa, Phoenix, Dallas, New Orleans, Honolulu, Chicago, and Houston, where their prevalence scores surpass those of partnered lesbians. Partnered lesbians, conversely, are concentrated more than are partnered gay men in metropolitan areas in general, tending not to prefer particular areas to the degree that gay men prefer them. I will return to some of these issues in more detail in Chapter 5 when I focus on "The Family and Sexuality."

This is but one example of the many and different kind of demographic research questions that may be answered with data from censuses. I turn next to a discussion of the second source of demographic data, **registration systems**.

REGISTRATION SYSTEMS

Whereas censuses provide a **cross-sectional** (one point in time) portrayal of the size, composition, and distribution of the population, registration systems pertain to the population's demographic events (births and deaths and, in some countries, migrations) and measure, that is, register them as they occur. While censuses are static, registers are dynamic and continuous. Registers apply principally to births and deaths, although many countries also maintain registrations of marriages, divorces, and abortions. Some countries maintain a migration registration system.

Strictly speaking, as Ostby (2003: 763) has noted, a **population register** is a list (i.e., a register) of persons that includes the name, address, date of birth, and a personal identification number. Some registers have been maintained for centuries, such as those in church parishes that record the baptisms and the deaths of the parishioners. In Europe, the Nordic countries and the Netherlands maintain population registers, and many developing countries either have them in place or are planning to implement them. In eastern Europe under the Communists, "population registers were used for control (of the people) as well as for administrative purposes, and the successor regimes for the most part have not maintained them" (Ostby, 2003: 763). The United States does not maintain any kind of national population register.

The earliest example on record of a population register of families and related household events is in China during the Han Dynasty (205 BC–AD 220). Indeed, as Taeuber (1959: 261) noted many years ago, a special demographic tradition of China and the East Asian region as a whole was population registration. Its major function, however, "was the control of the population at the local level" (Bryan, 2004: 25) and not necessarily the collection of continuous data on demographic events.

Population registers are of interest to demographers because they contain birth and death records (certificates). But not all birth and death registrations occur in the context of population registers. In fact, since a large number of countries do not maintain them, the registration of many births and deaths occurs outside population registers.

For most countries in the world, the recording of vital events, that is, births and deaths along with marriages, divorces, fetal deaths (stillbirths), and induced termination of pregnancies (abortions), are part of their civil registration systems. But these registration systems need not necessarily be population registers. Indeed, many are not. Although civil registration data are not 100 percent accurate and complete in the countries of the developed world, their quality is far better than that in the poorer nations. Cleland (1996: 435) has observed that although civil registration systems in developing countries are "seriously defective, it would not be correct that the data are of little value to demographers." Demographers have developed special techniques for data adjustment and analysis, yielding a rough notion of trends and differentials in these demographic events (Popoff and Judson, 2004).

Freedman and Weed (2003: 960) have noted that "vital statistics form the basis of fundamental demographic and epidemiologic measures." **Vital statistics** are the data derived from civil registration systems, as well as from the actual records of vital events. The modern origin of vital statistics and their registration may be traced to a 1532 English ordinance requiring that parish clerks in London maintain, on a weekly basis, the registration of deaths and christenings (Bryan, 2004: 25). These reports were begun in response to the plagues of the late sixteenth and early seventeenth centuries and were published in a nearly unbroken series for decades. Merchants used those data as a rough gauge as to the likelihood of their clientele fleeing

---

BOX 3.2   JOHN GRAUNT

John Graunt is deemed by many demographers (Bogue, 1969: 9; Poston, 2006a: 254) to be the founder of demography. He was born in London in 1620, raised as a Puritan, and later in life became a Catholic. He died in London in poverty in 1674. Although lacking any higher education and untrained in the sciences or mathematics, in 1662 he published the first-known quantitative analysis of a human population, *Natural and Political Observations Made Upon the Bills of Mortality*.

The "Bills of Mortality" were weekly accountings and reports of the London parish clerks of all the deaths and christenings. These reports were started in response to the plagues of the late sixteenth and early seventeenth centuries and were published in a nearly unbroken series for decades. Graunt studied this mass of data searching for regularities. He is credited for being the first to recognize that more males are born than females, and that females live longer than males. He also was one of the first to recognize the phenomenon of rural to urban migration. He also developed a crude mortality table that eventually led to the modern life table. (I will show later in Chapter 7 that life tables are the basis for calculating life expectancy.) Graunt also set a precedent for one of demography's oldest traditions, namely, the evaluation of data "to learn the extent, types, and probable causes of errors" (Bogue, 1969: 9). He "carefully evaluated the bills for their numerical consistency and reliability of compilation, and presented his evidence at length so that his readers might judge it independently" (Kraeger, 1988: 129).

When Graunt died in 1674, he was presumably buried beneath the pews of St. Dunston's Church on Fleet Street in London (Aubrey, 1898). With my wife Patricia, I visited this church in London in 2012, but sadly was not able to find any written record there of Graunt or of his burial. The church was rebuilt in 1930, so perhaps this explains why. Although Graunt died in obscurity, his lasting monument is his *Natural and Political Observations*, a very short book that to this day is a joy to read (Poston, 2006a).

---

to the countryside during epidemics (Kraeger, 1988: 129). John Graunt's ([1662] 1939) *Bills of Mortality* is a well-known demographic analysis of these data (see Box 3.2).

With regard to the modern era, Szreter (2007) has written that the registration of one's birth and then death are fundamental human rights. The second clause of Article 24 of the International Covenant on Civil and Political Rights (ICCPR) of the United Nations states that "every child shall be registered immediately after birth and shall have a name" (Szreter, 2007: 67). The ICCPR also states that "for nation states to take appropriate measures to protect and enhance the life expectancy of their populations, they must have at their disposal accurate and detailed information about patterns and trends of mortality" (Szreter, 2007: 68), thus also requiring death registration. (**Life expectancy** is the average number of years yet to be lived by people attaining a given age.)

How complete is the registration of births and deaths in the world today? The United Nations International Children's Emergency Fund (UNICEF) Research Center has estimated that worldwide in the year 2012 there were around 57 million babies born who were not registered; this is roughly four out of every ten babies born in 2012 (UNICEF, 2013). The unregistered children are often found in countries where "there is little awareness of the value of birth registration, where there are no public campaigns, where the registration network is inadequate, or where the costs of registration of children are prohibitive" (UNICEF, 2002: 10). For the most part, the majority of unregistered babies are born in developing nations, largely because these countries are more likely to face political, administrative, and economic barriers to registration. In some countries, gender discrimination and son preference also lead to female babies being excluded from the birth registration (Hudson and den Boer, 2004).

Another measure of the degree of birth registration is "the percentage of children under age five (0 to 59 months) with a birth certificate or whose birth was reported as registered with civil authorities at the time of the survey" (UNICEF, 2013: 11). As of 2012, worldwide, nearly 230 million children under the age of 5 had not been registered. Not being registered, and thus not possessing a birth certificate, have many serious consequences for the child. For instance, the "lack of formal recognition by the State usually means that a child...may be denied health care or education. Later in life, the lack of an official identification document can mean that a child may enter into marriage or the labor market, or be conscripted into the armed forces, before the legal age. If accused of a crime, unregistered children may be prosecuted as adults, due to their inability to prove their age" (UNICEF, 2013: 6). Among the industrialized countries of the world, more than 90 percent of children under the age of 5 are registered. In contrast, less than 20 percent of children under age 5 in many countries in sub-Saharan Africa are registered (UNICEF, 2013).

Not all developing countries have seriously incomplete birth registration. Many countries in the former Soviet Union have virtually universal coverage of births. This is likely to be due to their well-established birth registration systems, good medical facilities, and well-trained medical personnel.

Regarding deaths, we do not know as much about the completeness and coverage of registration around the world. Like the situation with birth registration, incomplete death registration occurs more frequently in developing than in developed nations. The World Health Organization (WHO, 2015a) has estimated that currently only around one-quarter of the population of the world lives in countries with 90 percent or more of their deaths registered, and these countries are almost always high-income countries.

The registration of births, marriages, and deaths in the United States began with registration laws in Virginia in 1632 and later in other colonies. I noted earlier that the US Constitution provides the requirement for a decennial census; but there is no such federal requirement for a national vital registration system. Legal authority for the registration of vital events in the United States lies entirely with the individual states. The first US census was conducted in 1790, but the complete coverage of births and deaths occurred much later.

I have already noted that in seventeenth-century England, the registration and maintenance of baptism, marriage, and burial records were the responsibility of the clergy. This practice was also followed by the English colonies in North America. In 1639, courts in the Massachusetts Bay Colony declared that birth, death, and marriage reporting would be part of their administrative system. Bryan has written that the Massachusetts Bay Colony "may have been the first state in the Western world in which maintaining such records was a function of officers of the civil government" (2004: 26; see also Wolfenden, 1954: 22–23). But even here, registration was voluntary and therefore incomplete. By 1865, however, the reporting of deaths was fairly complete, but this was not the case for births (Bryan, 2004).

Little by little, other US states followed these practices. Since 1919, all the states have had birth and death records on file for their entire areas, even though registration was not complete. Since 1903, Texas has had birth and death records on file for the entire state. For the state of California, the date is 1905.

The US federal government established a Death Registration Area in 1900 and recommended a standard death certificate form. A Birth Registration Area was established in 1915. Ten states and the District of Columbia were members, constituting just over 40 percent of the US population. States were added to the registration areas as they qualified. In theory, writes Bryan, "90 percent of deaths, or births, occurring in the state had to be registered for the state to qualify for admission into the Registration Areas; but ways of measuring performance were very crude" (2004: 27). In 1933, Texas was the last state (of the forty-eight states, at the time) to be admitted to the registration areas.

The US government required that the states in the registration areas transmit copies of their birth and death certificates to Washington every year. Although it is the responsibility of the states to register the births, deaths, and other demographic events, it is the federal government that gathers the materials and publishes them for the country as a whole. Birth and death data are published annually by the NCHS in several series dealing with natality and mortality. These were published in hardcopy volumes into the 1990s, but are now published online.

The registration of marriages and divorces in the United States has lagged behind the registration of births and deaths. The National Registration Areas for Marriages and Divorces were not established until 1957 (marriages) and 1958 (divorces). In the 1990s, the government stopped publishing yearly detailed marriage and divorce data from the states.

Birth certificates typically include the names and ages of the parents, their occupations, and, in some states, their levels of completed education. The mother normally provides the data, but according to Smith, "If she does not know or does not give the infant's father's attributes, they will not appear on the certificate" (1992: 4). Because birth certificate data about the father are sometimes missing or are incomplete, the study of male fertility is much more difficult than the study of female fertility. I discuss some of these issues in Chapter 4.

Birth certificates typically contain a lot of information about the mother and her baby. The birth certificate for Texas, for instance, has sections dealing with pregnancy history, birth weight, obstetric procedures, method of delivery, and congenital anomalies of the child. The states of the United States do not all require exactly the same information on their certificates.

The Texas birth certificate also asks if the mother is married. However, this item and several others are reported as confidential information and are not included on the certified copies of the birth certificate. This practice is followed in most states.

A birth is registered in the following way: the physician, the midwife (or person acting as the midwife), the mother of the child, or the father, is required to file a certificate of birth with the local registrar of the district where the birth occurred within a certain number of days following the birth of the infant. In most states, the birth must be registered within five days.

Death certificates are usually filled out by funeral homes, with personal information about the **decedent** provided by one or more of the surviving family members, as well as by the physician in attendance at the death or by the coroner. In addition to the decedent's age, "which may be misreported by surviving family members, particularly for the elderly, the certificates typically include the decedent's occupation, and place and cause of death information. Space is usually included on the certificate for both immediate and contributing causes of death" (Smith, 1992: 4).

It is likely that at some time in your life, at the death of a parent or close relative, you will serve as the informant to provide personal information to a funeral home official. My parents died in San Francisco in 1977 and 1979. On both occasions my sister Kathleen and I met with the funeral director and provided the personal information about our parents that was entered onto their death certificates.

As an example, the Texas death certificate, and those of most other states, contain basic personal information about the decedent (age, occupation, and so forth), and this is given by one of the surviving members of the decedent's family (the so-called informant) to a staff member of the funeral home, who fills in the certificate. The certificate also includes data on the facts of the death, and these are filled in by the attending physician, or by the medical examiner, or justice of the peace. In most states, the person (undertaker or funeral director) in charge of interment or of the removal of the body from the registration district is responsible for filing a certificate of death with the local registrar. Generally, this registration must occur no later than ten days after the date of the death.

I noted previously that at the federal level, the NCHS gathers the birth and death data from each state and endeavors to make the various birth and death items comparable from state to state. **Nosologists**, that is, persons who study the classification and categorization of diseases and causes of death, then translate the descriptions of the cause of death into cause-of-death codes of the International Classification of Diseases. At the federal level, the United States also maintains a National Death Index (NDI), "which computerizes names and attributes of decedents as well as cause of death information. Among its . . . uses, the NDI allows tracking of individuals lost to medical studies to confirm any deaths that have occurred" (Smith, 1992: 4–5).

One may think that demographic events such as births and deaths are so obvious that they need no definition. Actually, this is not true. I consider now the specific events of births, deaths, and fetal deaths. These are three mutually exclusive categories. A birth must occur before a death. If there is no birth, the **fetus** (the "product of conception") is then classified as a fetal death. I will define these terms very specifically.

First, consider a fetal death, which is defined statistically as follows:

Fetal death: the disappearance of life prior to **live birth**; that is, "the complete expulsion or extraction from its mother of a product of conception, irrespective of the duration of pregnancy. The death is indicated by the fact that after such separation, the fetus does not breathe or show any other evidence of life, such as the beating of the heart, pulsation of the umbilical cord, or definite movement of voluntary muscles" (Shryock, Siegel, and Associates, 1976: 221).

Fetal deaths include miscarriages, abortions, and stillbirths, defined as follows:

Miscarriage: the spontaneous or accidental termination of fetal life that occurs early in pregnancy.

Abortion: the premature expulsion of a fetus, spontaneous or induced, at a time before it is viable of sustaining life. An **induced abortion** is the termination of a pregnancy by human intervention that causes early fetal death.

Stillbirth: a late fetal death of twenty to twenty-eight weeks or more of **gestation.** (Gestation is the carrying of a fetus in the uterus from conception to delivery.)

A death is different from a fetal death. A death must be preceded by a birth; a fetal death, conversely, is not preceded by a birth. A death is defined statistically as follows:

Death: "the permanent disappearance of all evidence of life at any time after a live birth has taken place (postnatal cessation of vital functions without the capability of resuscitation). A death can occur only after a live birth has occurred" (Shryock, Siegel, and Associates, 1976: 221). Deaths, therefore, do not include fetal deaths.

The third demographic event is a birth. Here is its statistical definition:

Birth: "the complete expulsion or extraction from its mother of a product of conception, irrespective of the duration of pregnancy, which, after such separation, breathes or shows any other evidence of life, such as the beating of the heart, pulsation of the umbilical cord, or definite movement of voluntary muscles, whether or not the umbilical cord has been cut or the placenta is attached" (Shryock, Siegel and Associates, 1976: 273).

Strictly speaking, the period of gestation and the state of life or death at the time of registration are not relevant. After being separated from the mother, if the fetus shows any evidence of life (per the above definition), it is a live birth.

In the United States, births and deaths are tabulated on a *de jure* basis. That is, the births and deaths that occur in a state to residents of other states are excluded from the actual tabulations for that state. For example, deaths that occur to Texas residents, regardless of where they die, are included in the Texas death tabulations. A small percentage of births and deaths to residents of a state occurs in other states and places. Knowledge of these events is obtained through an interstate transcript exchange, in cooperation with other states and the NCHS. However, if the death of, say, a Texan, were to occur in California, a California death certificate would be filled out for the decedent. The death information on the California certificate would then be provided to the Texas registration officials to be included in the Texas tabulations, and the death would not be included in the California tabulations.

SURVEYS

Many demographers rely on a third source of demographic data, sample surveys, because censuses and registration systems do not contain the extensive kinds of information needed to address many of the more critical demographic questions. This is particularly true with respect to the analysis of fertility, although it also applies to mortality and migration. Surveys are required for the collection of more detailed information. By administering surveys to carefully selected random samples of the larger populations, demographers are better able to uncover underlying patterns of demographic behavior than is possible with materials only from censuses and registration systems. I will now discuss some of the major surveys that are used by demographers.

World Fertility Surveys

Beginning in the 1970s, coordinated cross-national fertility surveys were introduced in the statistical and demographic communities as an important source of fertility and related demographic information. Between 1974 and 1986, sample surveys to gather data on reproductive behavior and related social and psychological indicators were conducted in sixty-two countries, representing 40 percent of the world's population, under the auspices of the **World Fertility Survey** (WFS) (Cleland and Hobcroft, 1985; Cleland and Scott, 1987).

Demographic and Health Surveys

The WFS was followed by another coordinated international program of research, the **Demographic and Health Survey** (DHS), with more than 260 sample surveys carried out in ninety developing countries since 1984. DHSs are nationally representative household surveys with large sample sizes (usually between 5,000 and 30,000 households). These surveys provide data for many variables in the areas of fertility, population, health, and nutrition. Typically, the surveys are conducted every five years to enable comparisons over time. Interim surveys are conducted between DHS rounds and have shorter questionnaires and smaller samples than the DHS surveys (2,000–3,000 households).

The DHS (as well as the WFS) provides demographic information previously unknown about the countries in which they are implemented. To illustrate, a DHS was recently completed in 2013–2014 in Zambia, a small country of over 14 million people in east Africa. The DHS data for Zambia indicated that if current fertility levels were maintained, a Zambian woman would have, on average, 5.3 children by the time she completed her child-bearing. The DHS data also showed that 45 percent of married women in Zambia used modern methods of contraception, a lower percentage than the 57 percent for married women worldwide, but higher than the 25 percent for married women in Africa as a whole. The 2013–2014 DHS data for Zambia also showed that presently one in every thirteen children in the country do not survive to their fifth birthday. Although this figure is high compared with the much lower level of childhood mortality in the developed world, it is a tremendous improvement compared with its value in 1997 in Zambia when one in every five children did not survive to their fifth birthday (Central Statistical Office, Zambia, and the DHS Program, ICF International, 2014). Important information such as the above would not be available were it not for the DHS.

Other Fertility Surveys

Less ambitious demographic surveys, typically focusing on a single country or community, have been part of the demographer's repertoire for decades. Early endeavors included the Indianapolis study (Kiser, 1953; Kiser and Whelpton, 1953), the Princeton study (Westoff et al., 1961; Westoff, Potter, and Sagi, 1963), and surveys of family and reproductive behavior carried out in Puerto Rico (Hill, Stycos, and Back, 1959; Stycos, 1955).

The number of demographic surveys has grown steadily over the years. There are many surveys conducted in the United States, some of which are conducted by the federal government. Following are two examples of federal surveys.

Current Population Survey

The **Current Population Survey** (CPS) is a monthly nationwide survey sponsored jointly by the US Bureau of the Census and the US Bureau of Labor

Statistics. Its main purpose is to collect **labor force** data about the civilian noninstitutional population. I suppose that many of you have read newspaper stories or watched TV news reports every month or so about the levels of unemployment for the past month in the United States and in its major metropolitan areas. Have you ever wondered where these data come from? These are data that are gathered in the CPS.

CPS interviewers ask questions every month about the labor force participation of each member 14 years of age and older in every sample household. The survey covers around 60,000 occupied households each month and is a nationally representative sample of the US population. A household is in the CPS sample for eight rotations, and the samples are overlapping. Only 25 percent of the households differ between consecutive months. In addition to the basic CPS questions, interviewers also may ask supplementary questions. For instance, the March CPS includes a series of census-type questions (known as the Annual Demographic File) dealing with mobility, marital status, income, poverty, educational status, veteran status, and other census topics.

National Survey of Family Growth

The **National Survey of Family Growth** (NSFG), Cycle 1, was first conducted in 1973 and was followed by five more survey cycles in 1976, 1982, 1988, 1995, and 2002. After 2002, the NSFG has been administered on a continuous basis from 2006 to 2010, then from 2011 to 2015, and continuing beyond 2015.

The NSFG is a nationally representative multistage survey of male and female respondents between the ages of 15 and 44 that collects information on family life, marriage and divorce, pregnancy, infertility, use of contraception, and men's and women's health (NCHS, 2015). The 2002 NSFG was the first to include male respondents. In the first few years of the 2011–2015 period, the NSFG sample consisted of 10,416 men and women; approximately 5,000 more subjects were added in each of the following years of 2014 and 2015. The female questionnaire usually takes, on average, around 85 minutes to complete and the male questionnaire, 60 minutes. Respondent data addressing sensitive topics, such as sexuality, are collected using audio computer-assisted self-interviewing (ACASI) "in which the respondent listens to the questions through headphones, reads them on the (laptop computer) screen, or both, and enters the response directly into the computer" (Mosher, Chandra, and Jones, 2005: 7). Such methods have been shown to "yield more complete reporting of sensitive behaviors, and they also avoid the large amounts of missing data often found on paper and pencil self-administered questionnaires" (Mosher, Chandra, and Jones,

2005: 8). Currently, the surveys have a response rate of 73 percent for women and 72 percent for men.

Another very important source of demographic information about young people is the **National Longitudinal Study of Adolescent to Adult Health** (Add Health), begun by Professor J. Richard Udry in the early 1990s at the Carolina Population Center, University of North Carolina, Chapel Hill. It is a longitudinal study of a nationally representative sample of adolescents in grades 7–12 in the United States in 1994–1995. This adolescent cohort has been followed into young adulthood with four in-home interviews, the last occurring in 2008. Later in Chapter 4 of this book I will discuss important research findings pertaining to adolescent pregnancy and fertility that used data from the Add Health Study.

American Community Survey

In the late 1990s, the US Bureau of the Census began redesigning its decennial long-form questionnaire (see my earlier discussion in this chapter) into an ongoing "continuous measurement" survey, known as the **American Community Survey** (ACS). The ACS became fully operational in 2005. Beginning in 2010, it has taken the place of the decennial long-form census questionnaire. The ACS is now conducted every year in all counties in the United States and Puerto Rico. It provides important economic, social, demographic, and housing data about all the communities in the United States every year, the same type of data that were previously provided only once every ten years. In this sense, the ACS may be thought of as "the decennial 'long form' spread out over 10 years; that is, the data collection occurs throughout the decade rather than just once in ten years" (Taeuber, 2006: 7).

Communities in the United States with 65,000 or more population receive ACS data estimates on all the long-form characteristics on an annual basis and have been receiving these data since 2006. Areas with 20,000–64,999 population receive data each year based on three-year estimates, which began in 2008. Areas with less than 20,000 population receive characteristics data each year based on five-year estimates, which started in 2010. Hence, beginning in 2010, and for every year thereafter, "the nation will have a five-year period estimate available as an alternative to the decennial census long-form sample, a community information resource that shows change over time, even for neighborhoods and rural areas" (US Bureau of the Census, 2006: 2–6). These five-year estimates will be preferred over other ACS estimates because the error will be smaller.

Beginning in 2005, a random sample of households in the United States started to receive the ACS questionnaire each month in the mail. In the 2013 ACS, the sample included approximately 3.54 million housing unit addresses. In earlier years of the ACS, there were fewer sampled households; for instance, between 740,000 and 900,000 households were in the ACS in the years 2000–2004. After the mailing, the selected household receives a telephone follow-up; a face-to-face interview then follows for a subsample of the addresses that do not respond. As noted, the ACS questions are very similar to the decennial census long-form questions.

In closing, I want to emphasize the fact that the ACS is a major change in census operations, indeed, a paradigm shift in census data collection. The ACS was developed so that the US Bureau of the Census would be able to address various problems encountered in recent censuses. These include, but are not limited to, difficulties in recruiting a sufficient number of qualified enumerators, a decline in the mail return of the census questionnaires, and an uncertainty about the completeness of the census address lists and counts, especially in so-called hard-to-enumerate areas. The ACS plan as summarized here (for more detail, see the ACS web site at: www.census.gov/ acs/www) provides an approach for simplifying the enumerators' job by removing the need to learn how to conduct the long-form interview and by identifying hard-to-enumerate areas where special enumeration techniques are needed. The US Bureau of the Census expects that the ACS and its timely data will increase the confidence of users in its results, as well as reduce the number and type of problems encountered during the census operation (for more discussion, see Hillygus et al., 2006).

SUMMARY

In this chapter, I have discussed the three basic sources of demographic data: national censuses, registers, and surveys. Each is an important source of data for demographic study. Some demographers rely more on one or two of these than on the other. But demographic analysis generally requires data from all three sources. In later chapters, I will discuss the three demographic processes of fertility (Chapter 4), mortality (Chapter 7), and migration (Chapters 8 and 9). My discussions in these and other chapters in this book are based on data from all three sources presented and elaborated on in this chapter.

4 Fertility

INTRODUCTION

Fertility refers to the actual production of children, which in the strictest sense is a biological process. A **zygote** is produced when the sperm of a male and the egg of a female are united, and around nine months later a baby is born. Most often in this process, although not always, a man and a woman have sexual intercourse, the woman conceives, and the **conception** results in a live birth. Even though the production of a child is a biological process, the various activities and events that lead to the act of sexual intercourse and, later, to giving birth, are affected by the social, economic, cultural, and psychological characteristics of the woman and the man, as well as by the environment in which they live. The key to this paradox is that engaging in intercourse, conceiving, and giving birth are themselves behaviors that are influenced by other factors, most of them social and cultural. So while we have no influence at all with regard to the family and parents we receive when we are born, we do have a significant influence on our own fertility. We will decide whether or not we produce children, and, if so, the number and timing of the children produced. That is, whether we decide to engage in sexual intercourse, whether this intercourse results in a conception, and whether a live birth is the outcome are all driven largely by social and cultural considerations.

Fertility may be studied in different ways, one of which is cross-sectionally, that is, at one point in time; a cross-sectional perspective is also known as a **period perspective**. Were we to study the fertility behavior of women and men in the year 2015, we would develop cross-sectional fertility measures (also called period measures) that would show the number of births to women and men in the calendar year 2015. Most of the fertility measures I present in this chapter are period measures; they refer to a particular time period. A **period rate** is a rate based on behavior occurring at a particular point or period in time.

Fertility may also be studied over time to give us measures revealing the number and spacing of births to cohorts of women as they pass through the life cycle; this is known as **cohort analysis**. Here, for example, we would take the cohort of women who began their childbearing years at age 15 in, say, the year 1970. We would then follow them each year through to 2005, when they were at the end of age 49 and had completed their childbearing years in order to see how many babies they had produced. Fertility may be measured on a cohort basis, as well as on a period basis.

The demographic study of the fertility of individual women (and men) is known as a **micro analysis** because it is an analysis of the fertility of persons. In contrast, if we were analyzing the fertility rates of the countries of the world we would be engaging in a **macro analysis**.

There are several different ways to study fertility at the micro, that is, individual level: (1) examining the number of births a woman (or man) has produced by a given point in time, such as at the date of a census or survey; (2) examining the number of births a woman (or man) has had by the end of the childbearing years; and (3) focusing on the timing and spacing of births at various stages of the life cycle (say, between the ages of 25 and 29, or between the ages of 45 and 49).

As I noted above, another way to study fertility is to use a macro-level approach, that is, to determine the rate at which births occur in a population or subpopulation during a given period of time. Rather than studying the fertility of persons, macro-fertility analysis studies the fertility of populations (Poston and Frisbie, 2005). One reason demographers measure fertility at the macro-level is to then compare it with mortality, and to compute rates of overall population change. They also compare the fertility levels of different types of subpopulations over time.

In this chapter, I first consider the conceptualization and measurement of fertility. Second, I discuss the so-called **proximate determinants** of fertility. These are the mainly biological factors that lead directly to fertility, and are themselves influenced heavily by social factors. I next consider world fertility patterns and how they have changed over time, and I then focus on fertility trends and differences in the United States. I follow with a discussion of **adolescent fertility**, then **nonmarital fertility**, and then **childlessness**. I conclude the chapter with a discussion of male fertility.

CONCEPTUALIZATION AND MEASUREMENT OF FERTILITY

There are three main fertility concepts. **Fertility** is the actual production of male and female births and refers to real behavior. **Reproduction** is also the actual production of births, but refers to the production of only female births (there is no demographic term to refer to the production of only male births). Fecundity refers to the potential or the biological capability of producing live births.

The **crude birth rate** (CBR) is the first measure of fertility I will consider. It is a cross-sectional (i.e., period) measure and refers to the number of births occurring in a population in a year per 1,000 persons. It is calculated as follows:

$$\text{CBR} = \frac{\text{number of births}}{\text{midyear population}} * 1{,}000 \qquad (4.1)$$

In 2014, the CBR for the world was 20/1,000. This means that in the world in 2014, there were 20 births for every 1,000 members of the world population. Among the continents, the CBR in 2014 ranged from a high of 36 in Africa to a low of 11 in Europe. More than three times as many children per 1,000 population were born in Africa than in Europe in 2014. North America had a CBR of 12 (the CBR of the United States was 13); Latin America and the Caribbean, 18; Asia, 18; and Oceania, 18 (PRB, 2014). The major countries of the world had CBRs in 2014 ranging from lows of 6 in Monaco, and 8 in Japan, Taiwan, Andorra, Bosnia-Herzegovina, and Portugal to highs of 50 in Niger and 48 in Chad. Generally, CBRs above 30 are considered to be high, and those less than 15 to be low.

The CBR is referred to as "crude" because its **denominator**, the midyear population of the area, includes many people who are not at the risk of childbearing, such as young women (under age 15) and postmenopausal women (older than age 49), and men. (An **at-risk population** is the population that is at the risk of the event of interest occurring to them.) Strictly speaking, men do not bear children, so are thus not exposed to the risk of childbearing. However, some demographers do study male fertility, and I consider this topic later in the chapter.

The **general fertility rate** (GFR) is another cross-sectional measure of fertility. It is superior conceptually and statistically to the CBR because it restricts the denominator to women of childbearing ages; its **numerator** is the same as that for the CBR. The GFR is calculated as follows:

$$\text{GFR} = \frac{\text{births}}{\text{midyear population}_{f,15-49}} * 1{,}000 \qquad (4.2)$$

where the numerator is the number of births in the population in the year, and the denominator is the number of females in the midyear population who are in the childbearing ages 15–49.

In the United States in 2013, there were 73,649,960 women of ages 15–49; and 3,932,181 babies were born in 2013 (see Table 4.1). Dividing the latter figure by the former and multiplying the result by 1,000 gives us a GFR value for the United States of 53.4. This means that there were more

Table 4.1 Fertility Data and Rates for the United States, 2013

Age group	Women in age group (midyear population)	Live births to women in age group	Age-specific fertility rates (ASFR) (live births per 1,000 women)	ASFR × 5
Col. 1	Col. 2	Col. 3	Col. 4	Col. 5
15–19*	10,312,774	276,203	26.78	133.9
20–24	11,116,473	896,745	80.67	403.4
25–29	10,620,319	1,120,777	105.53	527.7
30–34	10,582,777	1,036,927	97.98	489.9
35–39	9,818,501	483,873	49.28	246.4
40–44	10,488,928	109,484	10.44	52.2
45–49**	10,710,188	8,172	0.76	3.8
TOTALS	73,649,960	3,932,181		1857.3†

* Birth data are live births to mothers aged 19 and less.
** Birth data are live births to mothers aged 45 and older.
† TFR = Σ(ASFR × 5) = 1,857.3.
Sources: for population data: US Bureau of the Census, at: http://factfinder.census.gov/faces/tableservices/jsf/pages/productview.xhtml?src=bkmk, last accessed June 17, 2015; for birth data, see Martin, Hamilton, and Osterman (2015). Calculations by DLP.

than 53 babies born in the United States in 2013 for every 1,000 women between the ages of 15 and 49.

Sometimes the denominator of the GFR is restricted to women between the ages of 15 and 44. This occurs because, as I show below, not many babies are born to women aged 45–49. For instance, of the 3,932,181 births in the United States in 2013, only 8,172, or 0.21 percent of them, were produced by women over the age of 44 (see Table 4.1).

In Figure 4.1, I show the number of live births and the GFRs for the United States for individual years between 1920 and 2013. The top line in the figure is the number of births and the bottom line is the GFR. Be aware that for the GFRs in Figure 4.1, the denominator is women in the age group 15–44, not 15–49.

In the early 1920s there were around 3 million births each year; the number rose to well over 4 million in the late 1950s and early 1960s, dropped back to almost 3 million in the mid-1970s, and then started increasing to the current levels at about, or slightly less than, 4 million.

The data in Figure 4.1 show that fertility as measured by the GFR (with a denominator of women 15–44) was very low in the 1930s, increased in the 1940s with a big jump in 1946 and 1947 due to the Baby Boom after the end of the Second World War, and then began declining in the 1960s through 1980 to values in the 60s; the fertility rate has remained in the 60s since then.

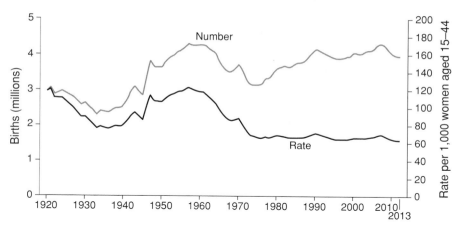

Figure 4.1 Live Births and General Fertility Rates,* 1920–2013
*The denominator of the GFRs is women aged 15–44.
Source: Martin, Hamilton, and Osterman (2015: 3).

In the definition for the GFR, I referred to its denominator as females in the childbearing ages. I consider now what is meant by childbearing ages. In practice, as already noted, few women in a developed country such as the United States give birth before the age of 15 and after age 49, and so demographers usually use the age range 15–49 to mark the limits of the childbearing ages. But, occasionally, births do occur to women before the age of 15 and after the age of 49. In the United States in 2013, there were 3,098 births to women less than 15 years of age, and there were 677 births to women over age 49. But since so few births occur to women younger than 15 or older than 49, the ages 15–49 are used as the childbearing ages.

However, in developed countries, not only are there few births to women over age 49, there are not many births to women over age 44. Hence, as I have already noted, the denominator for the GFR is sometimes restricted to women aged 15–44, as is the case for the GFRs shown in Figure 4.1. So, a good rule of thumb when using the GFR is to use the 15–44 denominator if you are calculating the GFR for women in a developed and modernized country such as the United States.

Who is the oldest woman ever to give birth? I have found evidence of two women in India who gave birth at age 70. In July 2008, the British Broadcasting Corporation (BBC) News agency distributed a story about one of the oldest women ever to give birth. In northern India, in 2008, Omkari Panwar, 70 years old, gave birth to twins. She and her husband, Charam Singh, a farmer in his mid-70s, already had two children, both girls. They badly wanted a son, so they took out a bank loan to pay the costs for *in vitro* **fertility** therapy, the result being a boy and a girl, both weighing around 2 lbs (BBC News, 2008).

Another elderly woman, also from India, reportedly gave birth to a baby when she too was 70 years old. Rajo Devi delivered a baby girl in 2008. Married for many years, she had been trying to give birth until she entered **menopause** when she was 50. She then used a donor's egg that was injected with her 72-year-old husband's sperm, and a baby was born. Rajo Devi stated that "We longed for a child all these years and now we are very happy to have one" (Belkin, 2008).

If you have data available only for the CBR but wish to approximate the value of the GFR, an estimated GFR value (for women 15–44) is given by the following formula:

$$\text{GFR} = \text{CBR} * 4.5 \tag{4.3}$$

To illustrate, CBR values in the United States in 1950 and in 2013 were 24.1 and 13.0, respectively. If we had no other data available and needed GFR values for these two years, we could multiply each CBR by 4.5 and arrive at estimated GFR values of 108.5 for 1950 and 58.5 for 2013. These estimated GFRs (for women 15–44) are not far from the actual GFRs of 106.2 for 1950 and 62.4 for 2013. The constant in this formula and those in other formulas that I show later are based on empirical and analytic relationships between the fertility measures (see Bogue and Palmore [1964] for an example of such an application).

I noted earlier that the GFR addresses the major problem of the CBR by restricting the denominator to women in the childbearing ages. A problem still remains, however, with the GFR. It does not take into account the fact that within the childbearing years of 15–49, there are differences in the extent to which the women produce children. Fertility is low for women 15–19 and is then at its highest for women 20–29; the rates become lower in the 30s and even lower in the 40s. To take into account the fact that fertility varies by age, demographers calculate fertility rates for specific age groups of women.

The **age-specific fertility rate** (ASFR) reflects exactly what its name indicates: it focuses on births to women according to their age. ASFRs are usually calculated for women in each of the seven five-year age groups of 15–19, 20–24, 25–29, 30–34, 35–39, 40–44, and 45–49. The general formula for the ASFR for women in age group x to $x + n$ is as follows:

$$\text{ASFR}_{x \text{ to } x+n} = \frac{\text{births}_{x \text{ to } x+n}}{\text{females}_{x \text{ to } x+n}} * 1{,}000 \tag{4.4}$$

Although most demographic analyses using ASFRs calculate them for these five-year age groups, sometimes thirty-five single-year age groups are used, for example, age group 15, age group 16, age group 17, all the way up to age group 49.

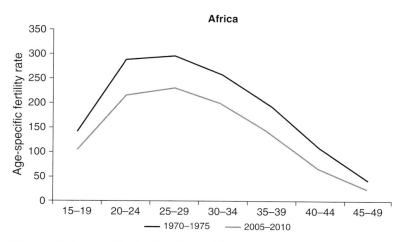

Figure 4.2 Age-specific Fertility Rates, Africa, 1970–1975 and 2005–2010
Source: United Nations (2014a).

Table 4.1 shows the number of women in the United States in 2013 in each of the seven age groups 15–19 to 45–49 (col. 2) and the number of babies born to the women in each of the age groups (col. 3). There were 11,116,473 women in 2013 in the age group 20–24. There were 896,745 babies born in 2013 to women in this age group. Dividing the latter figure by the former and multiplying the result by 1,000 produces an ASFR for women aged 20–24 of 80.67. This means that in the United States in 2013, for every 1,000 women aged 20–24, 81 babies were born to them. All seven ASFRs for US women in 2013 are shown in Table 4.1. The highest ASFR is for women 25–29, the next highest for women 30–34, and the third highest for women 20–24. ASFRs for women in the other four age groups are not as high.

When the seven ASFRs are plotted, they usually form an inverted "U". Such a plot is referred to as the **age curve of fertility**. In Figures 4.2 and 4.3, I show age curve of fertility plots for Africa and Europe, respectively, the two regions with the highest and lowest fertility rates in the world. The curves for the two regions are shown for 1970–1975 and for 2005–2010. Fertility as measured by ASFRs in 1970–1975 and in 2005–2010 is clearly much higher in Africa than in Europe. In Africa in 1970–1975, 20–24-year-old and 25–29-year-old women were having babies each year at a rate of just under 300 per 1,000 women. The African rates dropped to 215/1,000 and 235/1,000 in 2005–2010. Compare these high rates in Africa with the low rates in Europe, where 20–24-year-old and 25–29-year-old women in Europe in 1970–1975 had ASFRs of 150/1,000 and 140/1,000, respectively; the rates in Europe in 1970–1975 were lower than they were in Africa in 2005–2010.

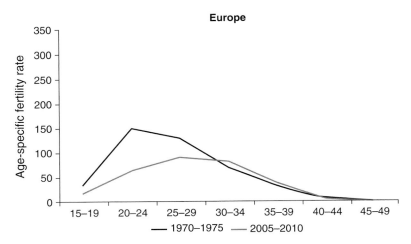

Figure 4.3 Age-specific Fertility Rates, Europe, 1970–1975 and 2005–2010
Source: United Nations (2014a).

The **total fertility rate** (TFR) is the most popular of all fertility rates used by demographers. Like the ASFRs, the TFRs take into account the fact that fertility varies by age. Unlike the ASFRs, which are expressed quantitatively as a series of age-specific rates (usually seven, one for each age group), the TFR provides a single fertility value. The TFR is almost always calculated cross-sectionally, that is, for a specific period of time, although, as I will note later, it may also be calculated for cohorts. A cross-sectional TFR for a particular point in time is an estimate of the number of births that a hypothetical group of 1,000 women would produce during their reproductive lifetime, that is, between the ages of 15 and 49 (or, sometimes, 15 and 44), if their childbearing at each of their reproductive years followed the ASFRs for a given time period. This number of live births that the hypothetical group of 1,000 women would produce is calculated under the assumption that none of the women die during their reproductive years.

The TFR is calculated by summing the ASFRs after multiplying each by the width of the age interval of the ASFRs. If we use ASFRs based on five-year intervals, as is usually the case and as I have done in Table 4.1, we would multiply each ASFR by the value of 5. Here is the formula for calculating the TFR:

$$\text{TFR} = \sum (\text{ASFR}_{x \text{ to } x + n} * i) \tag{4.5}$$

where i = the width in years of the age interval; in most cases, this will be 5.

In Table 4.1, I show the calculation of the TFR for the United States for the year 2013. The ASFRs shown in column 4 are multiplied by the constant of 5 and reported in column 5. These values are then summed, to

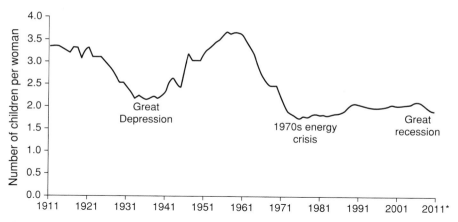

Figure 4.4 Total Fertility Rates, United States, 1911–2011
Source: Mather (2012) (reprinted with permission of the PRB).

yield a TFR of 1,857. This may be interpreted as follows: if 1,000 women went through their reproductive years from when they were age 15 to when they were age 49 and were subjected each year to the ASFRs of the United States for the year of 2013, by the time they reached age 49, they would have produced 1,857 babies, or an average of 1.9 babies each. The TFR refers to the average number of births to 1,000 women, as well as, when divided by 1,000, to the average number of births to a single woman. The TFR is a standardized rate; that is, it is not influenced by the differences in the numbers of women in each age group. Its value is especially useful in interpreting the fertility that is implied by a given set of ASFRs for a particular point in time.

TFRs are shown in Figure 4.4 for the United States for the hundred years from 1911 to 2011. In 1911, the TFR was 3.4, it dropped almost to 2.0 during the years of the **Great Depression** in the 1930s, increased to a high value of 3.7 in 1957 (the peak year of the Baby Boom), dropped to lows of 1.7 and 1.8 during the 1970s energy crisis, and has now stabilized at between 1.9 and 2.1; the TFR for 2013 (see Table 4.1) is just under 1.9.

If one only has CBR data available for an area or country or, alternately, only GFR data, the TFR may be estimated with the following formulas:

$$TFR = CBR * 4.5 * 30 \qquad (4.6)$$

$$TFR = GFR * 30 \qquad (4.7)$$

In 2013, the world TFR was 2.5. It was 2.6 for the **less developed countries** (LDCs) of the world including China, and 3.0 for the LDCs excluding China. The **developed countries** had an average TFR in 2013 of 1.6. TFRs ranged from a high of 7.6 in Niger and 7.0 in South Sudan to a low

Table 4.2 Age-specific Fertility Rates, United States, 1970–1974 to 2010–2014*

	15–19 years	20–24 years	25–29 years	30–34 years	35–39 years	40–44 years	45–49** years	Total fertility rate
1970–1974	62.3	137.1	124.1	62.0	25.5	6.3	0.4	2,088.5
1975–1979	53.0	111.8	109.1	56.1	19.2	4.2	0.2	1,768.0
1980–1984	51.9	110.7	110.5	63.9	21.2	3.9	0.2	1,811.5
1985–1989	52.4	109.5	112.9	72.7	26.5	4.5	0.2	1,893.5
1990–1994	59.8	113.2	115.5	80.0	32.4	5.9	0.3	2,035.5
1995–1999	52.0	107.8	109.4	83.7	35.9	7.1	0.4	1,981.5
2000–2004	43.4	104.4	115.0	93.5	42.2	8.4	0.5	2,037.0
2005–2009	40.1	102.1	115.8	98.6	46.9	9.6	0.6	2,068.5
2010–2014	29.1	83.6	106.6	97.8	48.3	10.4	0.7	1,882.5

* Data for 2014 are preliminary.
** Before 1997, rates are for live births to women aged 45–49 per 1,000 women 45–49; beginning in 1997, rates are for live births to women aged 45–54 per 1,000 45–49.
Table produced by Rachel Traut Cortes and DLP.
Sources: Numerator data from the National Center for Health Statistics; denominator data from the US Bureau of the Census.

of 1.1 in Taiwan and 1.2 in Singapore, Japan, South Korea, Poland, and Portugal (PRB, 2014). If during their childbearing years, 1,000 women followed the ASFRs for Niger in 2013, at the completion of their 49th year, they would have produced 7,600 babies, or an average of 7.6 each. In contrast, if during their reproductive lives, 1,000 women were subjected to the ASFRs of Taiwan for the year 2013, by the time they ended their childbearing years, they would have given birth to 1,100 babies, or about 1.1 each. These are tremendous differences in fertility. I discuss TFR trends and differences among the countries of the world in a later section of this chapter.

I noted earlier that the TFR is most frequently calculated on a cross-sectional basis, that is, for a specific period or year, and is referred to as a period or cross-sectional TFR. Alternately, the TFR may be calculated for cohorts. Rather than subjecting a hypothetical group of 1,000 women to a schedule of ASFRs for a given point in time, that is, as with the cross-sectional TFR, the cohort TFR follows a real group of women through their childbearing years and tabulates their actual fertility as they pass through these years. Table 4.2 presents average annual ASFRs for the years 1970–1974, 1975–1979, and so forth, through 2010–2014. I will now show how to use these data to calculate a period TFR and a cohort TFR.

The cross-sectional TFR may be calculated for any of the years 1970–1974, 1975–1979, up to 2010–2014 by summing the ASFRs across the respective row and multiplying the sum by 5. To illustrate, if we wanted the average annual cross-sectional TFR for the period 1970–1974, we would sum the seven ASFRs for that period, namely, 62.3, 137.1, 124.1, 62.0, 25.5, 6.3, and 0.4, and then multiply the total by 5 to produce an annual period TFR for 1970–1974 of 2,088.5 This value reflects the number of children that a hypothetical group of 1,000 women would produce were they to be subjected to the ASFRs of the United States for the 1970–1974 period. If we wanted the average annual cross-sectional TFR for the period 2010–2014, we would sum the seven ASFRs for that period, namely, 29.1, 83.6, 106.6, 97.8, 48.3, 10.4, and 0.7, and then multiply the total by 5 to produce an annual period TFR for 2010–2014 of 1,882.5 This value reflects the number of children that a hypothetical group of 1,000 women would produce were they to be subjected to the ASFRs of the United States for the 2010–2014 period.

In contrast, if we desired the cohort TFR for those women who started their childbearing years in 1970–1974 (we refer to those women as the 1970–1974 fertility cohort because they initiated their childbearing during those years), we would take the ASFRs on the diagonal line in Table 4.2 for the 1970–1974 fertility cohort of women. When those women were 15–19 in 1970–1974, they had an ASFR of 62.3; when they were 20–24 in 1975–1979, they had an ASFR of 111.8; when they were 25–29 in 1980–1984, they had an ASFR of 110.5; and so forth until they were 45–49 in 2000–2004 and had an ASFR of 0.5. When we sum these ASFRs and multiply the total by 5, we have a cohort TFR of 1,986.5. This is the actual number of children that were produced on average by 1,000 members of the 1970–1974 fertility cohort.

But we had to wait until the women comprising the 1970–74 fertility cohort completed their childbearing years to know what their cohort TFR would be. And by the time they completed their childbearing years, the TFR data for them would be dated and would apply only to an older group of women. Hence, period TFRs are often preferred over cohort TFRs; although period TFRs refer to a hypothetical (sometimes referred to as a synthetic) cohort, they are more timely and current.

A period (i.e., cross-sectional) TFR refers to the fertility of a **hypothetical cohort** (an imaginary set) of 1,000 women, whereas a cohort TFR refers to the actual fertility of a real cohort of 1,000 women. A period TFR for a year, say, the year 2013, refers to the fertility produced by women of all ages in the year 2013, a particular period of time. Alternately, a cohort TFR refers to the fertility of a group of women who have already completed their childbearing years and sometimes may be viewed as out of date. Both period and cohort TFRs are used by demographers, but, as I have mentioned, period TFRs are preferred principally because of their currency.

There are two more fertility measures I will now discuss, although none is as popular as the TFR; these two are based on the concept of **population replacement**. Given a set of fertility rates, what does this mean with regard to replacing the population? Replacement refers to the production of female births, known among demographers as reproduction. In contrast, fertility refers to the production of babies of either sex.

The **gross reproduction rate** (GRR) is a standardized rate similar to the TFR, except that it is based on the sum of age-specific rates that include only female births in the numerators. Sometimes data are not readily available on the number of female live births reported by age of the mothers. Thus, the proportion of all births that are female is usually employed as a constant and is multiplied against the given TFR, as follows:

$$GRR = TFR * \left(\frac{\text{female births}}{\text{births}} \right) \qquad (4.8)$$

The value of the constant multiplier, that is, the proportion of births that are female, varies only slightly from population to population. Most societies, but not all, have about 105 male babies born per 100 female babies. This results in about 51.2 percent of all births each year being male births and 48.8 percent being female births. Hence, we may use the following formula to calculate the GRR:

$$GRR = TFR * 0.488 \qquad (4.9)$$

I noted previously that the TFR in the United States in 2013 was 1857.3 (see Table 4.1). I can thus calculate the GRR for the United States in 2013 as follows:

$$GRR = TFR * 0.488 \qquad (4.10)$$

$$GRR = 1857.3 * 0.488 = 906.4$$

This value of 906.4 may be interpreted as the number of daughters expected to be born alive to a hypothetical cohort of 1,000 women if none of the women died during their childbearing years and if the same schedule of age-specific rates applied throughout their childbearing years.

In Table 4.3, I show the calculation of the GRR for the United States in greater detail than I did above in formula (4.10). In this example, I calculate the GRR for the year of 2005. I begin with a listing of the seven age groups (col. 1) and the midpoint of the age interval for each age group (col. 2). For instance, the midpoint for the age group 15–19 is 17.5. Data on the number of women in each age group in the United States in 2005 appear in column 3. Data on the number of babies born to the women in each age group appear in column 4.

Table 4.3 Calculation of Gross Reproduction Rate (GRR) and Net Reproduction Rate (NRR), United States, 2005

Age group (1)	Midpoint of interval (2)	Number of women in age group (3)	Number of births to women in age group (4)	Number of female births to women in age group (5)	Female births per woman (6)	Female birth rate during 5-year interval (7)	Proportion of female babies surviving to midpoint of age interval (8)	Surviving daughters per woman during 5-year interval (9)
15–19	17.5	10,240,239	414,406	202,230	0.01974	0.09874	0.9889	0.09765
20–24	22.5	10,150,079	1,040,399	507,715	0.05002	0.25010	0.9848	0.24631
25–29	27.5	9,767,524	1,132,293	552,559	0.05657	0.28286	0.9801	0.27723
30–34	32.5	9,906,365	952,013	464,582	0.04690	0.23449	0.9752	0.22868
35–39	37.5	10,427,161	483,401	235,900	0.02262	0.11312	0.9691	0.10962
40–44	42.5	11,475,863	104,644	51,066	0.00445	0.02225	0.9600	0.02136
45–49*	47.5	11,372,141	6,546	3,194	0.00028	0.00140	0.9462	0.00133
						1.00296 = GRR		0.98218 = NRR

* Rates are for live births to mothers aged 45–54 per 1,000 women 45–49.

Sources: Population data: US Bureau of the Census (2008); birth data, Hamilton, Martin, and Ventura (2007); calculations by DLP.

As noted earlier, we sometimes do not have easily accessible data on the sex composition of births by age of mother, so this is often approximated. In the United States, as in most other countries, the **sex ratio at birth** (SRB) is around 105 boys per 100 girls. This means that the proportion of US births that are female is 0.488. I thus multiply the birth data in column 4 by this constant proportion of 0.488, producing in column 5 the data on female births to women in each group. (If the SRB is not around 105, then another constant must be used. For instance, if I was calculating the GRR for China in 2010, I would need to take into account the fact that China's SRB in 2010 was 119. Thus, the proportion of all births in China in 2010 that were female was 0.457. This constant of 0.457 would be the one I would use for calculating the GRR for China in 2010.)

Next, I divide the number of female births at each age (col. 5) by the number of women at each age (col. 3), to produce the age-specific rates of female births (col. 6); these age-specific rates have not yet been multiplied by 1,000.

The age-specific rates of female births in column 6 refer to only a single year, but I will assume that the hypothetical cohort of women will experience these rates during the entire five-year interval. So I now multiply the rates in column 6 by 5 to obtain the female birth rates during the five-year interval; these are shown in column 7.

I then sum the values in column 7 to obtain the GRR. I multiply this sum by 1,000 to get the number of female births born to the hypothetical cohort of 1,000 women. The value of the GRR for the year is 1.00296 (see bottom of column 7 of Table 4.3). I multiply it by 1,000, yielding 1,003. This value of 1,003 may be interpreted as indicating that 1,003 daughters would be produced by a hypothetical cohort of 1,000 women if during their childbearing years they were subjected to the age-specific rates of the United States in 2005. Thus, the 1,000 women would have produced 1,003 daughters, replacing themselves with slightly more (three more) daughters than needed.

I noted above that the GRR makes no allowance for the fact that some of the mothers will die before they complete their childbearing years. Thus, to obtain a more accurate measure of the replacement of daughters by their mothers, demographers have developed another rate, namely, the **net reproduction rate** (NRR).

The NRR is a measure of the number of daughters who will be born to a hypothetical cohort of 1,000 mothers, taking into account the mortality of the mothers from the time of their birth. It may be thought of as the GRR net of mortality. Thus, the NRR subjects the 1,000 mothers not only to a schedule of age-specific reproduction rates, but also to the risk of mortality

attitudes directly concerning fertility as well as attitudes about the proximate determinants themselves are an important feature of any exposition of reproductive change" (Knodel, Chamratrithirong, and Debavalya, 1987: 9).

Bongaarts (1982) has taken the first four of the proximate determinants and quantified them with indexes ranging from 0 to 1, with the lowest value of 0 indicating the greatest possible inhibiting effect on fertility of the proximate determinant and the maximum score of 1 representing no inhibiting effect of the determinant. The marriage-pattern index, Cm, has a value of 1 when all women of reproductive ages are in a marital or consensual union and 0 when none of them is in such a union. The contraception index, Cc, equals 1 if no contraception is used in the population and equals 0 if all fecund women are using completely effective modern methods of contraception. The postpartum-infecundability measure, Ci, is an index that ranges from a value of 1 when no women are experiencing postpartum infecundability to a value of 0 when all women are. The index of abortion, Ca, ranges from a maximum value equaling 1 when there is no induced abortion practiced in the population to 0 if every pregnancy that occurs is aborted.

He then calculated the four indexes for forty-one historical and contemporary (developing and developed) countries and used them to predict the TFRs of these forty-one populations. He showed that 96 percent of the variation in fertility could be explained solely by variation in the four proximate determinants of marriage, contraceptive use, postpartum infecundability, and abortion (see also Bongaarts and Potter [1983]). The other three proximate determinants were less important and did not vary significantly among the populations.

Bongaarts' demonstration is very important because it shows that virtually all of the variation in fertility is due to variation in only the four major proximate determinants. Thus, the effects of any and all of the socioeconomic and attitudinal and other kinds of variable that I mentioned above can have an effect on fertility only if they operate through the proximate determinants.

Stover (1998) has recommended several modifications and extensions to the Bongaarts model to include using sexual activity instead of marriage as the indicator of exposure to pregnancy, extending the sterility index to measure infecundity from all causes, revising the contraception index to take into account the fact that users of sterilization could become infecund before the age of 49, and changing the estimate of total fecundity. These revisions endeavor to take into account the demographic realities of modern societies. For instance, marriage no longer represents one's first exposure to sexual activity. By age 18, more than half of US males and females have engaged in sexual intercourse, and by age 19, over 70 percent (Finer, 2007; Guttmacher Institute, 2014a). The above are important revisions to the Bongaarts model, to be sure. But they should not be seen as reducing or minimizing in any way the contributions of Bongaarts. His path-breaking conceptual and empirical studies, building on the earlier work of Davis and Blake, resulted in a paradigm shift among demographers and their analyses of fertility.

WORLD FERTILITY TRENDS AND PATTERNS

As I noted earlier, in the world in 2013, the TFR was 2.5, but this value hides the tremendous heterogeneity in fertility in the countries around the world. As of 2013, there were 201 countries in the world. As defined by the United Nations (United Nations, 2014a), a country is an internationally recognized country or a territory with a population of 150,000 or more; or, if smaller than 150,000, is a member of the United Nations. Of these 201 countries, there are sixty-six high-fertility countries, that is, countries with TFRs higher than 3.2; and there are seventy low fertility countries, that is, countries with TFRs of 2.0 or less. The remaining sixty-five had TFRs between 2.1 and 3.1. I will focus here on the high fertility countries and the low fertility countries.

High fertility countries are concentrated for the most part in sub-Saharan Africa (forty-five of the sixty). In contrast, while the low fertility countries used to be mainly in Europe, they are now becoming more diverse geographically, with many of them nowadays in Asia and Latin America and the Caribbean (thirty-one of the seventy). Among the high fertility countries, the United Nations expects fertility to decrease in some of them, particularly those in Asia. The fertility declines in others are expected to be much more gradual, especially among those in Africa. The two countries of Mali and Niger (with TFRs in 2013 of 6.1 and 7.6) are not expected to realize marked declines in their TFRs in the next decade or so. Sixteen of the high-fertility countries are projected to reach TFRs of 2.6 or below by 2030. The seventeen countries with projected TFRs of 3.8 or more are all in sub-Saharan Africa.

Most of the low fertility countries are expected to realize modest increases in their TFRs in the next couple of decades. The greatest increases are expected in the countries with the lowest-low fertility rates. For instance, eighteen countries with TFRs currently of less than 1.5 are expected to realize small increases of 0.3 or so in the next two decades. These will be increases to be sure, but their TFRs will still be far below the replacement level of 2.1.

I now consider in more detail the low fertility countries. Let me relax the UN definition and refer to low fertility countries as those with TFRs of 2.1 or less. In 2013, seventy-nine countries had TFRs below 2.1. In contrast, in 1970, there were only ten such countries. They were all in Europe and included Denmark, Finland, Sweden, Hungary, Russia and Greece (PRB, 2014). In these countries, fertility continued to decline and declined so much so that by 2013, they had attained historically and unprecedented low levels of 1.3 children per woman or less (Kohler, Billari, and Ortega, 2002; Morgan, 2003).

Following Billari and Kohler (2004), I will refer to fertility as being "low" when the TFR is between 2.1 and 1.6, as being "very low" when the TFR is between 1.5 and 1.3, and as being "lowest low" when the TFR is under 1.3. Of the seventy-nine countries with TFRs in 2013 of 2.1 or less, forty-three are classified as "low" fertility countries (TFRs between 2.1 and 1.6), twenty-seven as "very low" fertility countries (TFRs between 1.5 and 1.3), and nine as "lowest-low" fertility countries (TFRs under 1.3). The nine lowest-low fertility countries include South Korea, Taiwan, Poland, Portugal, Singapore, Hong Kong, and Macao.

No discussion of world fertility trends would be complete without mentioning **depopulation**, that is, the decline in the size of the population. This is so because depopulation is projected to occur in most countries of the world in the next fifty to one hundred years. Despite the vast amount of attention paid since the late 1960s to the phenomenon of overpopulation (see esp. Ehrlich [1968]; B. Friedman [2005]; Meadows et al. [1974]; Meadows, Randers, and Meadows [2004]), declines in population are expected to occur in around fifty or more countries by the year 2050 and in even more countries thereafter (Howden and Poston, 2008).

Even though the population of the world is projected to continue to grow, reaching around 9.6 billion in 2050, and 10.9 billion in 2100 (United Nations, 2013d) (see my discussion in Chapter 12), a slowing of the rate of population growth is already underway, and a decline in the size of the world population will likely begin around 2100. Europe is experiencing the greatest amount of depopulation, and many of Europe's countries are expected to have smaller populations by 2030.

Actually, in Europe as a whole these days, there is virtually no population growth. In 2014, its crude birth and death rates were both 11/1,000, resulting in a percentage **rate of natural increase** (RNI) of 0.0. (The RNI is the difference between the CBR and the crude death rate, expressed as a percentage.) Only one of Europe's forty-five countries has an RNI of 1.0 or higher, Kosovo (1.1 percent). Seventeen countries have negative rates of natural increase, that is, they had more deaths than births in 2014, the highest being Bulgaria and Serbia at −0.5 percent, and Latvia, Lithuania, Hungary, and Ukraine, all of them with RNIs of −0.4 percent. Three European countries with large populations all have zero or negative RNIs: Russia with a population of 143.7 million has an RNI of 0.0 percent; Germany at 80.9 million has an RNI of −0.2 percent; and Italy at 61.3 million has an RNI or −0.1 percent (Johnson, Field, and Poston, 2015; PRB, 2014).

Indeed, Russia's population is expected to drop from 143.7 million in 2014 to around 134.1 million by 2050. The demographer Nicholas Eberstadt (2009: 51) has written about the severity of this depopulation in Russia as follows: "Russia's human numbers have been progressively dwindling. This slow motion process now taking place in the country carries with it grim and potentially disastrous implications that threaten to recast the contours of life and society in Russia, to diminish the prospects for Russian economic development, and to affect Russia's potential influence on the world stage in the years ahead."

For the majority of countries, including Russia, the reason for depopulation is sustained low fertility. For a population to remain stable, TFRs need to be at or near replacement, that is, around 2.1 children per woman, and the cohorts in the childbearing ages cannot be larger than those in other age groups. If there are large numbers in the population in the parental ages, **replacement-level fertility** alone will not result in depopulation. This is due to what is referred to as negative **population momentum**, that is, the lag between the decline in TFRs and the decline in CBRs that is caused by large numbers of women still in their childbearing years owing to past high fertility. As I have already noted, in 2013 there were seventy-nine countries in the world with fertility at or lower than the replacement level of 2.1.

Many countries with relatively high fertility have started to experience declines in their fertility. This is apparent in Figure 4.2 (presented earlier) showing ASFRs in Africa in 1970–1975 and in 2005–2010. The lower rates of fertility that are occurring these days in the African countries, coupled with lower rates of mortality and immigration, will be responsible for some depopulation even in some of the African countries in the next fifty years or so. For a few countries, population decline is expected to occur even though their fertility is greater than the replacement levels. These countries – namely, Botswana, Lesotho, South Africa, and Swaziland – are being significantly impacted by the HIV/AIDS epidemic, leading to a net loss in population (Howden and Poston, 2008).

The depopulation of most of the countries in the developed world has significant economic impacts and implications. Major effects will likely be felt through the **aging of a population**. As fertility declines, birth cohorts become progressively smaller. These smaller birth cohorts, coupled with increases in life expectancy, lead to an increasingly larger proportion of the population that is older than age 65 and a smaller proportion of the population in the working ages. The United Nations has reported that the period between 2005 and 2050 will see a doubling of the **old-age dependency ratio** (ADR or Aged-DR) (i.e., the ratio of the population aged 65 and older to the population aged 15–64, times 100) in developed countries from 22.6 to 44.4 (United Nations, 2005). For many countries, healthcare and pension programs are not well equipped to handle the large increases in the numbers of elderly, who themselves will live longer than their predecessors (Howden and Poston, 2008).

FERTILITY CHANGE IN THE UNITED STATES

In less than 230 years, the United States has increased tremendously in size from fewer than 4 million people in 1790 to over 317 million in 2014 (see Chapter 13 for more discussion). Earlier in this chapter I showed in Figure 4.4 the TFRs for the United States from 1911 to 2011.

A high fertility rate was an important component of the rapid population increases in the United States in the early years between 1790 and 1860. Indeed, in 1800, the white population had a TFR of 7.0, which was likely the highest fertility rate of any country in the world at the time (Haines and Guest, 2008; Sanderson, 1979). The TFR in 1810 was still around 7.0, but by 1820 had dropped slightly to 6.7. It declined to 5.2 in 1860 and then to just under four births per woman by 1900 (Hamilton, Martin, and Ventura, 2007; Taeuber and Taeuber, 1958; US Bureau of the Census, 1975).

High fertility in the United States resulted from the fact that more than one-half of the population was fecund. The average age of the population was 15.9 in 1790, 17.0 in 1820, and 19.4 in 1860. Another reason for the high fertility was the high levels of rural and agricultural activity. When the first census of the United States was conducted in 1790, 95 percent of the population was rural. The rural portion comprised about 90 percent of the population through 1850 and dropped to only 75 percent by 1900 (Kahn, 1974).

Between 1790 and 1860, when agriculture was dominant, income was directly related to the acreage of cultivated fields. Fields in the west were cheap and easy to obtain, and many people had more children in order to have more laborers. Big families were popular, normative, and economically profitable.

Every modern, economically developed nation has undergone a demographic transition from high to low levels of fertility and mortality. The United States experienced a sustained fertility decline starting in the nineteenth century (Sternlieb and Hughes, 1978). The TFR (for whites) dropped to 4.6 in 1870 and to 3.6 in 1900 (US Bureau of the Census, 1975). By 1920, just after the First World War, the white TFR had dropped to 3.0.

In the decades of the early twentieth century, the United States experienced a rapid transition in its economy, industrialization, and urbanization (Taeuber and Taeuber, 1958). In the late 1950s at the height of the baby boom era, the TFR reached its peak at 3.7. The high (baby boom) fertility following the Second World War was promoted in part by a need to take into account the population losses that occurred during the war.

In the 1960s, the fertility rate started to decline. Many factors influenced this reduction, such as higher living expenses, increases in educational opportunities and expectations, and more women employed in the labor force. Average US family size was reduced. Cheap, easily accessible, and more effective contraceptives, along with abortions (see my discussion in Chapter 6) gave couples greater control over births and, hence, were another factor in the fertility decline. In 1972, the US TFR dropped for the first time below the replacement level of 2.1 (Kahn, 1974; see Figure 4.4); by 1975, it was 1.7. Even during the Great Depression years when fertility was low, it never dropped much below 2.2. Total population increase in 1972 was only 0.7 percent, almost one-half of the average annual increase during the 1960s (Kahn, 1974). Birth rates in the United States kept declining, although not as rapidly as in earlier years. Since 1990, the TFR has remained at just above or below two children per woman (see Figure 4.4).

The US population of 318 million people in 2014 has been growing slowly, with an RNI in 2014 of 0.4 percent. The TFR of 1.9 births in each woman's lifetime is just below the replacement level of 2.1 but, nevertheless, is the highest of any of the developed countries in the world. If these trends continue, the American population is projected to be just over 416 million people in 2060, that is, around 100 million more than in 2014 (see my discussion in Chapter 13). People are living longer, and the US population as a whole is aging.

ADOLESCENT FERTILITY

Adolescent fertility refers to the childbearing of young women. The **adolescent fertility rate** is measured with the ASFR for women aged 15–19. One reason why demographers study adolescent fertility is because "early childbearing is likely to put a young mother on a lifelong path with different choices and opportunities than if she were to postpone her first birth to a later age. She is likely to have more births because of exposure to a longer period of childbearing. Early childbearing may also put a premature end to a young woman's schooling and threaten her economic prospects, earning capacity and overall wellbeing. (And) young mothers may pass on to their children a legacy of poor health, deficient education and meager means of living, creating a hard-to-break cycle of poverty" (United Nations, 2013a: 1).

The adolescent fertility rate for the world for the period 2005–2010 was 48.9 per 1,000. That is, in the 2005–2010 time period, for every 1,000 young girls of the ages 15–19 in the world, there were on average forty-nine babies born to them each year. Among the developed countries, the adolescent fertility rate was 23.6, varying from lows of 4.5 in Switzerland and 4.8 in Slovenia, to highs of 39.7 in the United States and 42.1 in Bulgaria. Except for the United States and Bulgaria, no other developed country in the 2005–2010 time period had an adolescent fertility rate higher than 35/1,000. In the developing countries, the average rate was 52.7, ranging from lows of 0.6 in North Korea and 2.1 in South Korea to highs of 209.6 in Niger, 192.3 in Angola, and 181.9 in Chad. In North Korea and South Korea, for every 1,000 adolescent women, only one or two, respectively, had babies in an average year in the 2005–2010 time period. In contrast, in both Niger and Mali, just under one in five adolescent girls gave birth during this period (United Nations, 2013a: table A1).

The UN data published in 2013 indicate that the adolescent fertility rate is above 100 in thirty-four countries; of these, twenty-nine are in Africa, four in Latin America (Dominican Republic, Nicaragua, Guatemala, and Guyana), and one in Asia (Afghanistan). The rate is 10 or lower in twenty countries, namely, three in Africa (Algeria, Libya, and Tunisia), six in Asia, and eleven in Europe (including Norway, Sweden, Denmark, Finland, and Italy).

I show in Figure 4.5 the adolescent fertility rates in the 2005–2010 time period for the main regions and subregions of the world. It is interesting to observe that the so-called developing countries have both the highest adolescent fertility rates and the lowest adolescent fertility rates in the world. That is, the countries comprising the subregion of Middle Africa have an average adolescent fertility rate of 144 births per 1,000 women in the 15–19 age group, the highest rate of all the subregions in the world; this subregion includes the countries of Angola and Chad with rates of 192.3 and 181.9, respectively. In contrast, the countries comprising the eastern Asia subregion have an average rate of 7.9; included in this subregion are such countries as the two Koreas, with teen fertility rates of 0.6 (North Korea) and 2.1 (South Korea), the lowest rates in the world.

I noted above that in the 2005–10 time period, the United States had the second highest adolescent fertility rate of all the countries of the developed world, namely, 39.7 births per 1,000 adolescents. But according to new data for the year of 2014 that were released in 2015 by the US National Center for Health Statistics (Martin, Hamilton, and Osterman, 2015), the

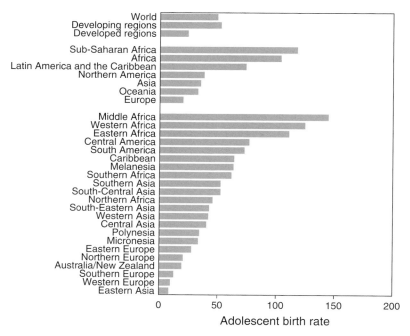

Figure 4.5 Adolescent Birth Rates by Development Groups, Regions and Subregions of the World, 2005–2010
Source: United Nations (2013a: 4).

teen birth rate has fallen markedly in the United States in recent years, reaching a low of 24.2 in 2014 (see Figure 4.6).

Let me first discuss trends in adolescent fertility in the United States since 1940 to present some historical perspective. The US adolescent fertility rates show a long-term downward trend since 1940. The teen birth rate reached its peak in 1957, at 96.3/1,000. In that year, nearly one in ten teenagers gave birth. "The rate dropped almost one-third to 65.5 in 1969," increased slightly in the late 1960s, and then resumed "a decline that continued until 1979–1980 and again until 1986," when the teen rate equaled 50.2. But "from 1986 through 1991, the birth rate rose 23 percent. Since 1991, the rate has fallen 57 percent and the decline has been (pretty much) continuous... The pace of decline accelerated from 2007 forward, with the rate reaching 26.6 in 2013" (Ventura, Hamilton, and Mathews, 2014: 2–3) and 24.2 in 2014. In 1957, nearly one in ten teenage girls and women in the United States had a baby; in 2014, it was one in forty-one teenage girls had a baby.

One interesting change that has occurred among teenage mothers between 1940 and 2014 is the significant increase in the percentage of births to teenagers who are not married. In 1940, only 14 percent of the births to teenagers were to unmarried teenagers. It increased slightly to 15 percent

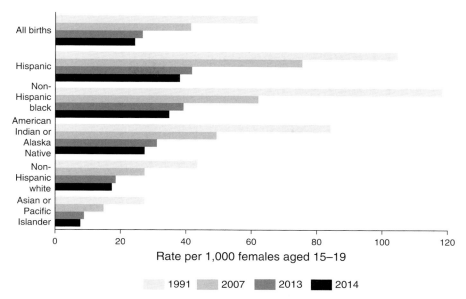

Figure 4.6 Birth Rates for Teenagers (aged 15–19), by Race and Hispanic Origin: United States, 1991, 2007, 2013, 2014
Source: Martin, Hamilton, and Osterman (2015).

in 1960, and then had a very large increase to 48 percent in 1980, and another very large increase to 89 percent in 2013 (Ventura, Hamilton, and Mathews, 2014: 3). Almost half of teenage births in 1980 were to unmarried mothers; almost nine in ten teenage births in 2014 were to unmarried mothers. These days very few teenagers are married, only around 2 percent in 2014.

Another way to examine the fertility of adolescents is to separate them into two groups: younger teenagers (aged 15–17) and older teenagers (aged 18–19). I show in Figure 4.7 the birth rates for these two groups for the years of 1960–2013. (Be aware that the vertical axis in Figure 4.7 is logarithmic.) In 2013, the fertility rate for older teenage women in the United States was 47.3 and for younger teenagers it was 12.3. For every 1,000 older teenagers in 2013, one in around twenty had a baby; for every 1,000 younger teenagers in 2013, one in around eighty had a baby.

The fertility rates of both the younger and the older teenagers have dropped since 1960. Between 1960 and 1975 the rates fell a little more rapidly for the older girls than for the younger girls, falling 50 percent for the former group compared with 18 percent for the latter group. Since the 1990s, the rates have fallen a bit more rapidly for the younger group (Ventura, Hamilton, and Mathews, 2014: 4).

Adolescent fertility for US females varies considerably by race and ethnic group (see Figure 4.6). The lowest adolescent fertility rate for US women

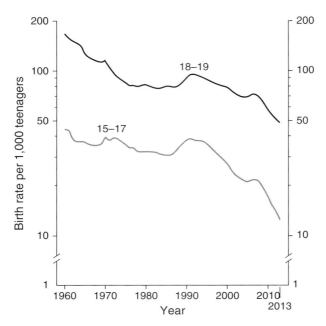

Figure 4.7 Birth rates for Teenagers (aged 15–17 and aged 18–19): United States, 1960–2013
Source: Ventura, Hamilton, and Mathews (2014: 3).

in 2014 was for Asian and Pacific Islander (API) teenagers, 7.7/1,000; a group comprising mainly Asians. Following them with the next highest adolescent fertility rate were non-Hispanic (NH)-white teenagers, then American Indian and Alaskan Native (AIAN) teenagers, then NH-black teenagers, and finally Hispanic teenagers with the highest adolescent fertility rate, 38.0/1,000.

Adolescent fertility rates were much higher in 1991 than in 2014 (Figure 4.6). Indeed, the rates for 2014 are record lows for all the groups. Every race/ethnic group has a lower adolescent fertility rate in 2014 than in 2013, and lower in 2013 than in 2007, and lower in 2007 than in 1991.

Why have these reductions occurred? In terms of the immediate causes, adolescents will have fewer births if they engage in sex less frequently, or if they become more effective users of contraception, or if there is some combination of the two.

There is evidence of a slight reduction in recent years in the percentages of teenagers engaging in sexual intercourse. In 1991, 54 percent of high school students reported that they had ever engaged in sexual intercourse; by 2013, this percentage had declined to 47 percent (Kann et al., 2013). And there is evidence of a significant increase in the percentages of teenagers using contraception. Data for the 2006–2010 time period show that

86 percent of adolescent females and 93 percent of adolescent males stated they had used contraceptives the last time they engaged in sex. These are significant increases from the percentages in 1995, which were 71 percent for females and 82 percent for males (Martinez, Copen, and Abma, 2011).

I stated above that every year Hispanic teenagers have the highest fertility rate of all the race/ethnic groups. But among the Hispanic females, Mexican origin teenagers have the higher rate, followed by Puerto Ricans and then by Cubans. To illustrate, in 2012, Mexican teenagers had a fertility rate of 48/1,000, followed by Puerto Ricans at 43/1,000, followed by Cubans at 16/1,000. My student Eugenia Conde analyzed in her dissertation the race/ethnic patterns and differences in teen fertility. She concluded that one reason why Mexican teenage girls have such high birth rates is the barriers they confront that limit their access to higher education (Conde, 2011).

NONMARITAL FERTILITY

In the preceding section I observed that back in the 1940s very few babies were born to teenage women who were not married. In this section, I focus on the **nonmarital fertility** of all women, not just teenage women. Nonmarital fertility refers to the fertility of women who are not married. An unmarried woman is one who is not married, widowed, or divorced.

When I was born in 1940, less than 4 percent of all births were to unmarried women. At that time, virtually all babies were born to married mothers. So prevalent was this association between the mother's marital status and her having a baby that the term "illegitimate fertility" was used instead of "nonmarital fertility" to refer to births occurring outside marriage. Babies being born to unmarried mothers was so much against the norms of society that these babies were sometimes referred to as "illegitimate."

One reason why demographers study births to unmarried women is because the marital status of the mother is usually an important "marker for the presence or absence of financial, social, and emotional resources. Infants of mothers who are not married have been shown to be at a higher risk for poor outcomes." For example, the mortality rate for infants of unmarried mothers is around 75 percent higher than "the rate for infants of married mothers" (Mathews and MacDorman, 2013: 8).

In 2013, 41 percent of all births were to unmarried women, a dramatic increase from the 4 percent in 1940. But there is considerable variability in the percentage among race/ethnic groups: Asians have the lowest at 17 percent, they are followed by NH-whites at 29 percent, who are followed by Hispanics at 53 percent, following them are American Indians/Alaskan

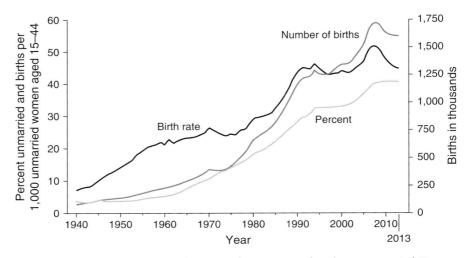

Figure 4.8 Number of Births, Birth Rate, and Percentage of Births to Unmarried Women, United States, 1940–2013
Source: Curtin, Ventura, and Martinez (2014: 1).

Natives at 66 percent, and the group with the highest percentage in 2013 of births to unmarried mothers is blacks at 71 percent.

I show in Figure 4.8 data on the number of nonmarital births, the non-marital birth rate, and the percentage of births to unmarried women for the United States for the years 1940–2013. The number, rate, and percentage were all very low in 1940, then climbed to very high levels in 2008, and since then have been experiencing slight reductions.

The percentage of births to unmarried women was 4 percent in 1940, reached 10 percent in 1970, increased to 18 percent in 1980, then to 28 percent in 1990, to 33 percent in 2000, and to 41 percent in 2010, where it has remained. The nonmarital fertility rate had a low value of 7/1,000 in 1940; for every 1,000 unmarried women aged 15–44 in 1940, only seven of them had babies. The rate increased to 26/1,000 in 1970, to 44/1,000 in 1990, to 52/1,000 in 2008, and then declined slightly to 45/1,000 in 2013. Whereas in 1940, only seven unmarried women per 1,000 had babies, in 2008, fifty-two unmarried women per 1,000 had babies.

It is important to note that nonmarital births "include births to women in cohabiting unions and those to unmarried women not cohabiting" (Curtin, Ventura, and Martinez, 2014: 4). Indeed, these days just under 60 percent of births to unmarried women are to cohabiting women, and about one-half of the births to cohabiting women are intended births, that is, the women planned to have the births when they occurred. Whether or not the mother is cohabiting when she gives birth is sociologically very impor-tant because research has shown that cohabiting parents are more likely to eventually marry than are parents who are not cohabiting; thus, babies of cohabiting parents have a greater likelihood of growing up in a two-parent family (Carlson, McLanahan, and England, 2004). However, in the long run, children of cohabiting parents are more socioeconomically disadvantaged and do not fare as well on a host of behavioral and emotional outcomes when compared with children who were born to a mother and father who are married (Brown, 2004; Child Trends, 2015). I have more discussion of cohabitation and births to unwed mothers in Chapter 5 in the section on the family.

CHILDLESSNESS

Childlessness refers to women having no children voluntarily or involuntarily. Recent years have seen dramatic increases in the percentages of ever-married childless women in the United States. In the 1970s, almost half of white women were childless at age 25. Rindfuss, Morgan, and Swicegood (1988) expected that as many as 20 percent of these white women would still be childless at the end of their childbearing years (see also Morgan and Chen, 1992).

Childlessness is, and has been since the 1970s, much more prevalent than in the 1950s when childlessness was low and little of it, if any, was voluntary (Poston and Kramer, 1983). Indeed, demographers noted that in the 1950s, "voluntary childlessness . . . (was) nearly extinct" (Whelpton, Campbell, and Patterson, 1966: 163). Until the early 1970s, the norms relating to marriage and procreation were pervasive and **pronatalist**, much more so than they are today. The literature written more than forty years ago indicates that childlessness was neither supported nor encouraged by society's normative and value structure (Poston, 1974). The childed state was heavily valued in its own right (Griffith, 1973), and those remaining without children often experienced severe negative sanctions (Blake, 1974; Veevers, 1973).

I have mentioned the very low prevalence of childlessness in the 1950s and 1960s in the United States. However, it would be a mistake to refer to the increases in childlessness since the 1970s as reflecting a so-called secular phenomenon and not as representing the more distant past. For instance, Morgan (1991) has shown that levels of childlessness in the nineteenth century were much higher than those reported for the 1950s and early 1960s. Nonetheless, little attention was given to childless women in the United States prior to the 1970s, and the research that was being conducted at that time focused mostly on involuntary childlessness. These early studies assumed that childlessness was caused primarily by sterility or subfecundity and not by voluntary decisions to stay childless (Poston and Cruz, 2013).

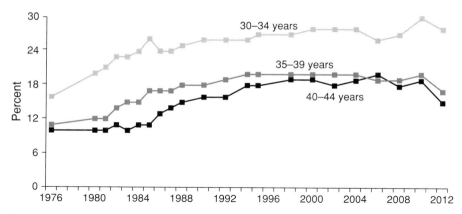

Figure 4.9 Percentage Rates of Childlessness for Women Aged 30–44, United States, 1976–2012
Source: Monte and Ellis (2014: 7).

Interestingly, the percentages of married women aged 15–44 who were childless in the United States have fluctuated over time. In the 1970s when childlessness was increasing, researchers believed that most of the increase was due to women choosing to be childless. More recent studies have supported this idea of increased childlessness especially at the older ages. For instance, Abma and Martinez (2006) focused on childlessness among older women (ages 35–44) and reported that voluntary childlessness rose from 5 percent in 1982 to 8 percent in 1988, and was maintained until 1995 at 9 percent before falling slightly to 7 percent in 2002. They also reported that women who were voluntarily childless tended to have the highest incomes, work experiences, and lowest religiosity (Poston and Cruz, 2013).

Figure 4.9 shows percentage rates of childlessness for US women aged 30–44 for the years 1976–2012. The increases in childlessness over the past several decades are clearly shown in the figure. Thirty percent of women aged 30–34 were childless in 2010, the highest ever for this group. The slight downturns for all three groups of women from 2010 to 2012 are mainly statistical and result from differential sampling weights applied in the surveys (Monte and Ellis, 2014: 7). The increases in childlessness since the 1970s are consistent and remarkable and are due mainly to increases in **voluntary childlessness**, resulting from changes in gender norms, as hypothesized by researchers in the 1960s. Cox and Pendell (2007) discovered that more than 80 percent of respondents in national surveys in the 1980s were neutral or agreed that childless individuals could have fulfilling lives. Their research showed that more positive attitudes toward childlessness were found among females who were college educated and/or childless; the less positive attitudes were found among older, less educated males who were religiously conservative. This suggests that attitudes and norms toward childlessness are becoming more positive overall, which explains in large part the increased levels of childlessness in the United States.

MALE FERTILITY

An important limitation of my discussion in this chapter is that the measures and concepts and research focusing on fertility are all derived from calculations and analyses of females. The fertility of men and the determinants of **male fertility** have rarely been examined and compared with those of females, but they should be. Males are a neglected minority in fertility studies.

Several reasons have been proposed by demographers to justify the exclusion of males from fertility studies. The biological reasons are that the fecundity and the childbearing years of women occur in a more sharply defined and narrower range (15–49) than they do for men (15–79), and that "both the spacing and number of children are less subject to variation among women; a woman can have children only at intervals of 1 or 2 years, whereas a man can (theoretically at least) have hundreds" (Keyfitz, 1977a: 114). There are at least two methodological reasons: one, data on parental age at the birth of a child are more frequently collected on birth registration certificates for the mothers than for the fathers; and, two, when such data are obtained for mothers and fathers, there are more instances of unreported age data for fathers, especially for births occurring outside marriage. A sociological reason is the belief that men are regarded principally as breadwinners and "uninvolved in fertility except to impregnate women and to stand in the way of their contraceptive use" (Greene and Biddlecom, 2000: 83; Poston, Zhang, and Terrell, 2008).

Biological and demographic studies provide us with evidence of the importance of men in fertility and related behaviors. Biologists have found that the male sex in most all species contributes an equivalent amount of genetic information to the next generation as does the female sex. But the variance contributed by the male sex to the next generation is often greater than that of the female sex, especially in species where **polygyny** (a union where a male is simultaneously married to two or more females) is practiced. That is, most females reproduce, some males do not reproduce, and other males have a large number of offspring. This pattern has been found in most mammalian species (Coleman, 2000). In addition, it has been found in many species that there are more childless males than childless females.

Demographically, it has been shown that men have different patterns of fertility and fertility-related behavior. Males' age-specific fertility starts a little later, stops much later, and is typically higher than that of females (Paget and Timaeus, 1994). Also, the TFRs for males and females are not identical. Research has shown that in most industrialized countries, male TFRs are higher than female TFRs (Coleman, 2000). In the 1990s and later, in countries where the male and female TFRs were lower than 2.2, they tended to be more similar than dissimilar; and the opposite was found for countries with male and female TFRs higher than 2.2 (Zhang, 2013). This means that for men and women, if they followed the sex-specific and ASFRs of an area at one point in time, and if they had more than 2.2 children during their childbearing years, these men and women were more likely to have dissimilar than similar fertility rates, and vice versa (also see Myers, 1941; Smith, 1992).

The special importance of male fertility is also seen in the determinants of fertility and fertility-related behaviors, such as cohabitation and marriage. For example, in the United States, men's fertility is more likely to be influenced by their marital and employment status compared with that of women. Being married and employed significantly increases men's number of **children ever born** (CEB), while these factors do not have as strong an impact on women (Zhang, 2013). The relevance of labor-force participation for women's fertility has been emphasized repeatedly. Regarding education, the lower the level of education, the greater the difference between women and men with respect to the number of CEB (Martinez, Daniels, and Chandra, 2012: 5). And with respect to income, research has shown that it has a positive effect on male fertility, but a negative effect on female fertility (Hopcroft, 2015).

In my own research, I have used several independent variables from various fertility paradigms, namely, human ecology, political economy, and wealth flows (see my discussion of these theories in Chapter 2) to predict both male and female TFRs for the counties of Taiwan. The variables are consistently shown to perform better when predicting variation in female TFRs than in male TFRs (Poston, Baumle, and Micklin, 2005; Zhang, Poston, and Chang, 2014).

Men also have different cohabitation and marriage patterns compared with women. In the United States, for birth cohorts born during 1958–1987, living alone, being foreign-born, and living in fragmented families all tended to increase the likelihood of cohabitation for women but not for men. Foreign-born men are more likely to marry than native-born men. But these factors do not seem to have as significant an impact on women's marriage behavior (Zhang, 2013). Researchers have conducted studies examining male and female transitions to adulthood in twenty-four European countries using survey data for the 1980s and 1990s. They found that, in general, the negative effect on fertility of educational attainment is stronger for women than for men. Also, unemployment leads to men's postponement of marriage, whereas it affects women in two distinct ways: it either accelerates or it slows down the timing of marriage for women. The effect of religion is stronger among women than among men. Furthermore, being Catholic and attending church services affect men's and women's parenthood timing in different ways in Catholic-prevalent countries. Other relevant factors such as parental influence seem to have a different impact for males than for females (Corijn and Klijzing, 2001).

Historically, women have been tied to motherhood, and this is deeply rooted in law and policy in the ways that jobs are structured and how family relations are navigated. Studies of fertility and parenthood have been undertaken by demographers in a similar way (Riley, 2005). These, together with the biological and methodological reasons noted previously, have resulted in the decreased attention given to males in fertility research. I mentioned earlier that biological and demographic analyses have shown that fertility and parenting are not simply female issues; they are issues involving both men and women. The study of fertility should not focus only on females. Both Greenhalgh (1990b) and Riley (1998; 2005) have encouraged more discussion of gender issues among demographers, and critical demography has promoted bringing men into population studies (Coleman, 2000; Horton, 1999). It is necessary to incorporate gender studies into studies of demography in order to gain a more balanced picture of demographic issues. Indeed, male fertility is one of the emerging issues of demographic study. Demographers and sociologists need to give more attention to males in their analyses of fertility variation and change. It is essential to take men's roles and commitments into account when considering factors leading to decisions about the bearing and rearing of children.

CONCLUSION

In this chapter, I first considered various measures of fertility and next discussed the so-called proximate determinants of fertility. They are the mainly biological factors that lead directly to fertility and that are influenced heavily by social factors. Indeed, the various social, economic, cultural, environmental, and psychological factors that affect fertility do so only through the "proximate" variables. Both the societal birth rate and the fertility of individual women and men are produced by a combination of those factors. I then considered world fertility patterns and US fertility trends and differences. I next discussed adolescent fertility, nonmarital fertility, childlessness, and male fertility.

I now close this chapter by summarizing some of the major fertility differentials. Fertility rates are much higher in many developing countries, especially those in sub-Saharan Africa, than they are in developed countries. Likewise, different types of people have different patterns of fertility.

Generally, the higher a person's socioeconomic status, the fewer children that person is likely to have. In industrialized societies, women employed in the labor force tend to have fewer children than women who are not so employed. Having a smaller family also increases the woman's availability for employment, and her employment per se encourages a small family. Levels of childbearing also tend to be lower in urban than in rural areas. This is particularly true in more modernized countries, although in the past three or four decades, the difference between rural and urban childbearing rates has diminished. There are few, if any, differences in childbearing between Catholics and non-Catholics in the United States and other more developed countries. The differences are due mainly to differences in socioeconomic status. The fertility of Muslim women, however, is higher than that of Christian and Jewish women, both in developed and developing countries. These differentials notwithstanding, the most important point to remember about fertility is that fertility rates are heavily conditioned by social, economic, psychological, cultural, and environmental factors, all of which eventually affect fertility through the proximate determinants.

5 The Family and Sexuality

INTRODUCTION

In this chapter I discuss two topics of special interest to demography, namely, the family and sexuality. They are important because, as Linda Waite has noted, in most times and places the family is the responsible unit for the production of the next generation, that is, fertility occurs in the family (Waite, 2005: 88). However conceptualized and whatever its structure, fertility, that is, the production of children, operates within the family. Sexuality also has demographic importance because, for one reason, that part or dimension of sexuality dealing with sexual preference often, but not always, leads to the linking or the partnering of two adults within the family setting. And under certain instances, the behavioral dimension of sexuality results in the production of children. I consider later in this chapter in greater detail the three dimensions of sexuality.

I first undertake a historical review of the family, its structure, and form. Today many consider the traditional family to consist of the "male breadwinner working outside the home and the stay-at-home mother taking care of the kids" (Iceland, 2014: 39). This is the kind of idealized family that represented much of America in the 1950s and may be revisited in the reruns of such television programs as "The Adventures of Ozzie and Harriet" and "Leave it to Beaver," shows that I watched almost every week when I was a child. But this family form was not the "traditional" family. As John Iceland reminds us, it differed tremendously from the "traditional families of the colonial era and much of the nineteenth century" (Iceland, 2014: 39). The historian Stephanie Coontz (2000) makes a similar point in her book *The Way We Never Were: American Families and the Nostalgia Trap*. My historical review of the structure and form of the family will show its significant heterogeneity over time.

I follow my historical review with an empirical depiction of the family today. The contemporary family has changed tremendously in the past sixty-five years. For instance, whereas sixty-five years ago 98 percent of children in the United States lived in two-parent "Ozzie and Harriet"-type families, by 2014 it had dropped to 68 percent (Cavanaugh, 2015). Today, as I will show later, people marry later, fewer people marry, premarital cohabitation is normative, and over 40 percent of children are born to unmarried mothers.

The second part of the chapter focuses on sexuality. I first discuss the conceptualization of sexuality and its three principal dimensions. I next show how these dimensions have been researched and operationalized. Then, I use recent data from the NSFG to examine these dimensions of sexuality, principally with respect to heterosexuality and homosexuality.

The last part of the chapter links the two topics of family and sexuality in an empirical examination of **partnering**, that is, two persons living together. I use 2010 US census data to describe the patterns of partnering for the four main configurations: married male and female, cohabiting male and female, married or cohabiting male and male, and married or cohabiting female and female.

THE FAMILY

One would think that defining a "family" should not be a difficult task. After all, the family is so significant to society that it is universal. "The family is one of the most important foundations and agents of socialization; the family is the first place we learn culture, norms, values, and gender roles" (Farris and Poston, 2014: vii). Families exist in all societies, but their constitution varies across cultures and over time. For example, the Western world has traditionally regarded a family as consisting of a husband, wife, and children. But we are seeing these days an increasing number "of one-parent families, gay and lesbian families, blended families and childless families." Moreover, in the United States and in many Western countries, "we use a bilineal system of descent in which we recognize that descent can be traced through both the mother's and the father's side of the family. However in many parts of China, descent is patrilineal" (Farris and Poston, 2014: vii).

Brief Historical Review

Let me start with Thornton and Fricke's very inclusive definition of the family: it is a "social network, not necessarily localized, that is based on culturally recognized biological and marital relationships" (1989: 130). One of the main functions of the family is to produce the next generation. Fertility almost always operates within the family setting. But as Waite (2005: 88) has observed, the "rise of alternative family structures, including gay and lesbian partnerships, and cohabiting couples, sometimes including children, raises the question of whether a family must have a culturally recognized biological or marital relationship." The answer depends on the extent to which the partners are recognized culturally as a family. Marriage clearly converts a cohabiting couple with one or more children into a family. But until recently, gay male and lesbian partners in the United States residing in states where same-sex marriage was illegal and often not recognized (Bryn and Holcomb, 2012) were denied the family legitimizing function of marriage. But this is no longer the situation with the decision of the US Supreme Court on June 26, 2015, legalizing same-sex marriage everywhere in the United States.

I mentioned above the historian Stephanie Coontz, one of the most prolific and articulate writers about marriage and the family. She has another interesting book *Marriage, A History: From Obedience to Intimacy or How Love Conquered Marriage* (2005). I will draw on materials from this book in the next few paragraphs in my historical review of marriage and the family.

Coontz makes several points in her history of marriage that run counter to the idealized perception of the so-called traditional marriage. In the earliest times up to around the seventeenth century, marriages in most societies were not necessarily about love, sex, childrearing, and affection. Although these may have figured into the marriages, the principal objective of marriage was to gain in-laws who would bring legitimacy. Rulers justified their authority on the basis of their ancestry. The best way to bolster one's ancestral legitimacy "was to marry someone who also had an august line of ancestors" (Coontz, 2005: 53). Moreover, marriage was used to establish military and commercial ties. Whereas today rulers and heads of states ratify treaties between countries with their signatures, in the past they would seal "their deals with a marriage ceremony" (Coontz, 2005: 54). And marriages worked in a similar way with similar benefits for the common people. The children who were married off had virtually no say regarding their new partners; their parents and grandparents and the other male relatives made the decisions.

Marrying for the economic and political advantages accruing from such arrangements remained dominant until the eighteenth century. But several hundred years earlier, changes began to occur in western Europe that led the way to the changes in the 1700s. One change was the prohibition around the twelfth century of polygyny. And "by the fifteenth century the children of mistresses had lost the inheritance rights they had had in the early medieval period" (Coontz, 2005: 124). Another change was that increasingly the newly married couple would establish their own household rather than moving in with the parents of the husband. However, despite these changes women still remained subordinate to men. But a wife in these new marital arrangements "could exert more pressure on her husband than in an extended family system, where the husband's authority was reinforced by all his kin" (Coontz, 2005: 130).

By the end of the 1700s, in western Europe a new marriage system had begun to take hold. "For the first time in five thousand years, marriage came to be seen as a private relationship between two individuals rather than one link in a larger system of political and economic alliances" (Coontz, 2005: 145–146). And little by little, the roles of the husband and wife were transformed. The husband assumed the primary role of providing for the family. The wife focused herself morally and emotionally on family life. The "love match" became normative in England in the 1760s, in France in the 1800s, and in other parts of Europe at slightly different times. In America, the norms were also starting to favor the "love match." A few decades after the American Revolution, "New Englanders began to change their description of an ideal mate, adding companionship and cooperation to the traditional expectations of thrift and industriousness" (Coontz, 2005: 147).

During the colonial era in the United States, the traditional family did not have the sharply divided roles and responsibilities we saw in the "Ozzie and Harriet"-type family where the husband was the provider and the wife was the homemaker. The "husband was (still) considered (to be) the head of the family" (Gill, Glazer, and Thernstrom, 1992: 147). But the husband, wife, and children all worked together and contributed economically to the household and household-related tasks. Think of the family farm one hundred or more years ago and the fact that everyone from the grandfather to the youngest baby had a role in its maintenance.

Waite (2005: 88) has described how the societal and structural changes underway in Europe and America worked to influence the change in marriage form. Social changes including industrialization, urbanization, productivity increases, rise of the market economy, and greater individualization gradually shifted control and decision-making away from the family and the extended family to the individuals. With increases in rural to urban migration, more and more adults were working in factories and other non-familial settings. With fewer people employed in family-based activities, for example, the family farm, decision-making became less based on familial issues and connections, resulting in the parents playing reduced roles in mate selection.

Pure demography also played a role in the changes in the importance and form of marriage. I reported in the previous chapter that in the nineteenth century, US white women were having on average seven children each. The TFR started to drop in 1820, but did not reach 4.0 until 1900.

This means that for most of the nineteenth century most women were having their last baby when they were in their 40s. Consider an average woman having her last child (her fifth or sixth, or maybe her seventh) at age 45. She would be 60 years old when her last child was age 15. Female life expectancy at age 60 in 1901 was around fourteen years. So the average white woman in the nineteenth century had fourteen years of life remaining after raising her last-born child to young adulthood. We do not have TFR and life expectancy data for black women and Hispanic women for these periods, but the years of remaining life for black women were surely less than those for whites, and those for Hispanics and whites would have been about the same.

Jump ahead from the nineteenth century to the second decade of the twenty-first century. As I will show below, the average NH-white woman today marries at around age 27. However, 40 percent of babies born today are to unmarried white mothers (the percentages are higher for Hispanic and black mothers). So marriage per se is no longer the precursor to fertility that it used to be. The average mother these days thus has her first baby at age 26. I will assume for the purpose of my illustration that she has her last birth at around age 35 (85 percent of the slightly less than 4 million births in 2012 were to women age 35 or less). By the time the last child of this average mother is age 15, the mother is age 50. Current life tables give this 50-year-old mother another thirty-three years of life. So what does this mean?

The average woman in the nineteenth century had fourteen years of life remaining after she had raised her last child to age 15. Or in other words, by the time her last child was a young adult, the mother had already lived four-fifths of her life and had only one-fifth, or fourteen years left. In contrast, the average woman today has thirty-three years of life remaining by the time she has raised her last child to age 15; so she has used up two-thirds of her life, but has one-third left, or thirty-three more years. The point I am making is that marriage and childbearing are no longer the defining events and activities of our lives. In earlier times they were our identity, and really our only identity. They are much less universal and exclusive than they once were. Or as Coontz (2000: 186) has remarked, "parenthood, like marriage, is a less salient, central, and long-lasting part of life than it used to be."

Marriage and the Family Today

I turn now to a discussion of marriage and the family today, focusing heavily on the situation in the United States. I entertain four main questions:

1. How old are people today when they marry for the first time?
2. How many people get married?

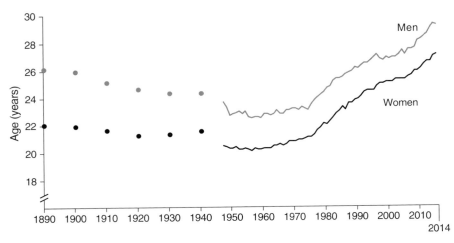

Figure 5.1 Median Age at First Marriage: United States, 1890–2014
Source: US Bureau of the Census, available at: www.census.gov/hhes/families/files/
graphics/MS-2.pdf.

   3. How many people cohabit before marriage?
   4. How many babies are born to unmarried women?

In the "traditional" "Ozzie and Harriet"-type family of the 1950s, males
married at around 22 or 23, and women at around age 20. Almost everyone,
or nearly everyone, married. Very few people cohabited before marriage;
the word "cohabitation" was not even in our vocabulary, even though the
Oxford English Dictionary states that the word "cohabit" meaning "to
live together as a husband and wife: often said distinctively of persons not
legally married" appeared in the English language for the first time as early
as 1530 (Simpson and Weiner, 2000: III: 448). And very few babies were
born to unmarried women; if a woman did have a baby outside marriage,
the baby was usually placed out for adoption. In the next several pages I
will examine the above issues as they exist today and will show how dramatically they have changed. My discussions of them will allow me to paint
a picture of marriage and the family in the contemporary United States and
the changes that have occurred in recent decades.

    I now consider the first question: how old are people these days when
they marry for the first time? Figure 5.1 presents data on the median age at
first marriage for men and women, starting in 1890 and extending to 2014.
Age at first marriage at the end of the nineteenth century was at 26 for men
and almost 22 for women. The trend lines show declines to about the year
1960 to median ages at first marriage of 22.8 years for males and 20.3 years
for females. These data almost perfectly represent me and my wife Patricia.
We married in January 1963. I was just over 22, and Pat was four months

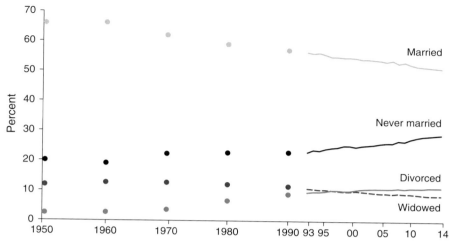

Figure 5.2 Marital Status of Women 15 years of Age and Older: United States, 1950–2014

Source: US Bureau of the Census, available at: www.census.gov/hhes/families/files/graphics/MS-1b.pdf.

shy of 21. And we were not marrying early. We were marrying at about the same time as most of our similarly-aged friends.

Iceland attributes the declines in median age at first marriage from 1890 to the early 1960s to "the growth of well-paid wage labor employment for men that accompanied industrialization...(giving them) a sufficient income to support a family, even at a relatively young age" (Iceland, 2014: 40). And these were also the years of the baby boom, when men and women were marrying earlier and producing more children.

Since the 1960s the trend lines show progressively later ages at first marriage, to 26 years for men and 24 years for women in 1990; to 27 and 25 in 2000; and to over 29 for men and to almost 27 for women in the year of 2014. These days, men and women in the United States are clearly marrying later than they did in earlier times. Indeed, there are no earlier periods in the United States for which marriage data are available showing later average ages at first marriage.

If women and men are marrying later, does this mean that some will never get married? If so, we should see increasing proportions never marrying and decreasing proportions marrying. This is my second question: how many people get married?

Figure 5.2 presents data on the marital status of US women 15 years of age and over, from 1950 to 2014. In 1950, 66 percent of women of age 15+ were married, and 20 percent were never married. I do not show comparative data for men, but they are very similar to those for women, 68 percent married and 28 percent never married. The percent married trend line for women then goes down reaching a low of nearly 50 percent by 2014 (for males it is 52 percent). And the never married trend line for women goes up, reaching a high of 39 percent in 2014 (for males it is 35 percent). So we see a remarkably consistent reduction in the percentages of women and men marrying in the past almost sixty-five years, and a remarkably consistent increase in the percentages never marrying. In the 1950s, more than two-thirds of women and men aged 15 and over were married; in 2014, just over half of women and men were married.

Another way to address the question is to consider data on the percentage in the age group 45–54 who have never married. In 1980, this figure was 5 percent; it was 9 percent in 2000; and it was 14 percent in 2010. Projections developed by demographers at the Pew Research Center place it at 25 percent in the year 2030. In other words, if present trends in the percentages not marrying continue for the next fifteen years, in the year 2030 one-quarter of the population aged 45–54 will have forsaken marriage; this is a fivefold increase from the percentage in this age group not marrying as of 1980 (Wang and Parker, 2014).

More women and men are opting out of marriage or are marrying later. What are they doing? What are their living arrangements? This is my third question: how many people cohabit prior to marriage?

I examine recent data on cohabitation from the 2006–2010 NSFG (see my earlier discussion of the NSFG in Chapter 3). I address two questions pertaining to marriage: does "cohabitation serve primarily as a step toward marriage, much like dating and engagement, or (does it function) as an alternative to marriage?" (Copen, Daniels, and Mosher, 2013:2).

Demographers use the concept **first union** to refer to the first living or partnering arrangement an adult has with another adult that involves commitment, romance, and emotion. The two main first unions are cohabitation and marriage. This is an especially valuable concept because data on first unions at different points in time enable us to determine if there has been an increase or a decrease among heterosexuals in their levels of premarital cohabitation. Figure 5.3 shows data on first unions for women aged 15–44 with data from three NSFGs in 1995, 2002, and 2006–2010.

There has been very little change in the percentages of women aged 15–44 not in a union; they are at about 28 percent. In each of the three time periods, around 28 percent of adult women in the childbearing ages had not yet established a first union. But there have been dramatic changes in the percentages marrying and the percentages cohabiting, and they trend in opposite directions. Women have been increasingly more likely in their first union to cohabit with a partner rather than to marry a partner. In 1995, over one-third of women cohabited as their first union; ten to fifteen years later, almost one-half of the women cohabited as their first union. In

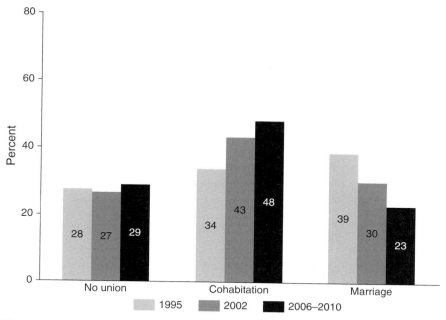

Figure 5.3 Type of First Unions among Women aged 15–44: United States, 1995, 2002 and 2006–2010
Source: Copen, Daniels, and Mosher (2013: 4).

the 2006–2010 period, the percentages for NH-white, black, and Hispanic women cohabiting as their first union were almost the same, 49, 49, and 47, respectively; the percentage for Asian women was much lower at 22 percent. This thus led to lower percentages of women entering into marriage as their first union, dropping from 39 percent in 1995 to 23 percent in 2006–2010.

What happens to the cohabiting women? Do they eventually marry their partners, or do they continue the cohabiting relationship, or do they dissolve it? The median duration of the cohabitations of women in 2006–2010 was two years. But instead of a two-year duration, I will use a three-year duration; this longer interval may indicate greater stability in the relationship.

I ask about the status of the cohabitation three years after it started. Of the nearly one-half of all US women who reported cohabiting as their first union, 40 percent of them had transitioned to marriage after three years had elapsed, a little less than one-third (32 percent) remained in the relationship, and 27 percent dissolved it. More NH-whites transitioned to marriage after three years (44 percent) than either blacks or Hispanics (31 percent). The fact that after three years just under one-third of the cohabitations were still intact indicates that these days it is becoming more and more acceptable, even normative, for women to be in long-term relationships without being married.

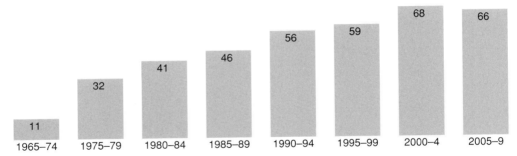

Figure 5.4 Percentages of Women (aged 19–44) Who Cohabited Before their First Marriage, by Marriage Cohort: United States, 1965–1974 to 2005–2009
Source: Manning, (2013:2).

If we examine the data by the age of the women when they first cohabited, we see that by the time the woman are 20 years old, one in four had cohabited; by the time the women are 30 years old, three in four had cohabited. When presented with these data, the demographer Pamela Smock remarked that "the question becomes not who cohabits, but who doesn't" (Aleccia, 2013).

Another demographer, Wendy Manning (2013), asked a similar question about women's cohabiting patterns, but in a slightly different way. Rather than inquiring about women's first unions, she asked women whether they cohabited, or did not cohabit, before their first marriages. Her data pertain to women who were slightly older, 19–44, than the 15–44-year-old women in the NSFG. Manning's data are shown in Figure 5.4.

In 1965–1974, only 11 percent of women reported cohabiting prior to their first marriage; by 1985–1989 it had increased to 46 percent, by 1995–1999 to 59 percent, and by 2005–2009 to 66 percent. Fully two-thirds of women in the 2005–2009 period reported cohabiting before they were married. Today cohabitation is the new normal. It has become increasingly more normative to cohabit, and to cohabit before getting married the first time. Cohabitation over the past several decades has become increasingly a behavior in which most people engage. But it was not normative forty to fifty years ago.

When I was in college and in graduate school (1958–1967), I knew probably no more than five or six male friends who were "living together" with woman friends. We did not use the term "cohabitation"; it was not in our vocabulary. The colloquial term was "shacking up"; the more proper term was "living together." Manning's data (Figure 5.4) indicate that only 11 percent of women in that period cohabited before marriage. The percentage increased sixfold, to 66 percent by 2005–2009.

Women cohabit at different rates depending on their levels of completed education. Figure 5.5 looks at the issue in a slightly different way. It

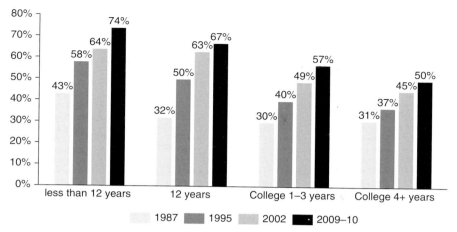

Figure 5.5 Percentages of Women (aged 19–44) Who have Ever Cohabited, by Level of Education Completed: United States, 1987 to 2009–2010
Source: Manning (2013: 3).

presents data on the percentages of women who have "ever cohabited" by years of completed education; the women who have "ever cohabited" may or may not have cohabited before their first marriage. Completed education is viewed in four different categories: completed less than twelve years, completed high school, completed one to three years of college, and completed four+ years of college.

Two points may be gleaned from the data in Figure 5.5. First, irrespective of one's level of education, the percentages who have ever cohabited have increased consistently from 1987 to 2009–2010. More than twice as many high school graduates reported ever cohabiting in 2009–2010 (67 percent) than in 1987 (32 percent). The percentage of women with four or more years college education who ever cohabited increased from 31 percent in 1987 to 50 percent in 2009–2010.

Second, the more education a woman has, the less likely she will have ever cohabited. In the 2009–2010 period, 74 percent of women with less than a high school degree have ever cohabited, 57 percent of women with one to three years of college in 2009–2010 have ever cohabited, and 50 percent of women with four or more years of college have ever cohabited.

I turn now to the last of my four questions: how many babies are born to unmarried mothers? Figure 5.6 shows percentage data on babies born to unmarried women according to their race and Hispanic origin for the years of 1959–2013. In 2013, almost 41 percent of all babies born that year were to unmarried mothers. When I was an undergraduate in college in the late 1950s–early 1960s, few babies were born to unmarried mothers, just over 5 percent of all births.

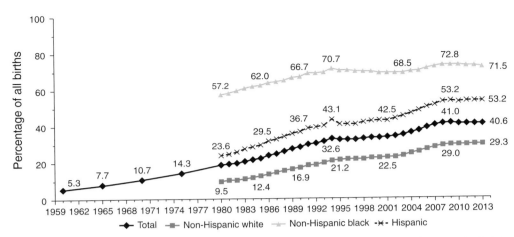

Figure 5.6 Percentages of Births to Unmarried Women, by Race and Hispanic Origin, 1959–2013
Source: Child Trends (2015: 3) (reprinted with permission of Child Trends).

In the 1950s and earlier, if an unmarried woman had a baby, she would most likely not raise the child. Keeping the baby if she was not married could spoil the reputation of her family. And abortion was illegal. So what happened to the young pregnant unmarried woman? She was sent away, often to another city where no one knew her. She would go through her pregnancy there and give birth to the baby. And the baby would then be out-adopted at a very early age, often within the first few months of its birth. How was this done?

In the Parkside neighborhood in San Francisco where I lived for most of the twenty-two years of my life before I married, there was a private facility several blocks from my home that was referred to, in the vernacular of the day, as a "home for unwed mothers." Unwed pregnant women from outside San Francisco, as well as from outside California, lived there until their babies were born. It was located between Vicente and Wawona Streets in a neighborhood in the southwestern section of the city. We all knew what it was, and sometimes we would see young pregnant women walking around the neighborhood; we knew they were from the "home."

My (now deceased) aunt and godmother, Dorothy Kara Zaro, my mother's sister, worked for several decades in the 1960s to the 1980s as an office administrator at another of these "homes for unwed mothers" in San Francisco, known as St. Elizabeth's Infant Home for Unwed Mothers, run by the Daughters of Charity, an order of Catholic nuns. When a pregnant unmarried woman entered St. Elizabeth's, she was given a fictitious name which she used during her tenure there. I can remember my aunt telling me in as early as the 1980s that not as many pregnant unmarried women were boarding at the facility. Fewer unwed pregnant women came to St. Elizabeth's in the 1990s, so they changed their mission. Rather than caring for unmarried women as they progressed through their pregnancies, St. Elizabeth's started to care for married and unmarried mothers with young children. In 1993, St. Elizabeth's was renamed the Epiphany Center for Families in Recovery.

Pregnant unmarried women in the 1960s and earlier were stigmatized and shunned by society. If an unmarried daughter was found to be pregnant, her family would often send her away from her home to a home for unwed mothers in another city or state. She would enter the home – she would be perhaps in her late teen years or early 20s – in the fourth or so month of her pregnancy at about the time she was beginning "to show"; she would remain there until the baby was born. The baby would be taken from her soon after it was born, and it would be out-adopted; the mother would likely never see her baby again. From the start of the twentieth century until around 1970 or so, such establishments were pervasive. Most cities had several of them, and many were owned and operated by religious groups. Most of the young women in a home were from another city or town. The home offered them anonymity and safety. The popular 2013 film *Philomena*, starring Judi Dench and Steve Coogan, is the true story of the experiences of an unwed mother (Philomena Lee, played by Judi Dench) in a home for unwed mothers in Ireland.

The trend data in Figure 5.6 show dramatic increases in the percentages of births to unmarried women, from a low of 5 percent in the late 1950s, to 14 percent by the mid-1970s, to 30 percent by the mid-1980s, to 41 percent by 2013. In the late 1950s, for every 100 babies born, five were to unwed mothers. In 2013, forty-one of every 100 new births were to unmarried mothers. The percentage increased eightfold in nearly sixty-five years.

Homes for unwed mothers still exist, but they are rare today. The reduction in the number of such establishments is due to several factors, such as the legalization of abortion, the widespread availability and enhanced effectiveness of contraception (see my discussion in the next chapter), the increased percentages of single mothers (see Figure 5.6), and the changing societal attitudes regarding single parenthood. The establishments that do exist are no longer called "homes for unwed mothers," but rather, "homes for expectant mothers," or "homes for babies and mothers," or "maternity homes." Often, the names of the establishments do not even contain the words "pregnant" and "unwed." The Edna Gladney Home in Fort Worth, Texas, renamed in 1991 as the Gladney Center for Adoption, was, and is, one of the most prominent institutions in Texas; it has provided services to pregnant single women since the 1930s up to this very day. "Maggie's Place" in Phoenix, Arizona, is another such establishment, as is "Good Counsel Homes" in Hoboken, New Jersey.

The percentage of births to unmarried mothers varies significantly by race and Hispanic origin (Figure 5.6). Race-ethnic-specific data are available starting in 1980. Non-Hispanic-whites have the lowest percentage (bottom trend line in Figure 5.6); it was almost 10 percent in 1980 and was almost 30 percent in 2013; it increased threefold since 1980. Today, almost three of every ten births to NH-white women are to unmarried NH-white women.

NH-black women have the highest percentage. In 1980, 57 percent of black mothers were not married when their babies were born; the rate increased to almost 72 percent by 2013. Today, more than seven of every ten births to black mothers are to unmarried black mothers. The Hispanic percentages are midway between those of the whites and the blacks. In 1980, almost one-quarter of all births to Hispanic women were to unmarried Hispanic women; by 2013, the percentage had more than doubled to over 53 percent. Now, more than half of Hispanic women are unmarried when they have their babies.

Why are the black percentages so much higher than the white percentages? In 2013, almost 72 percent of black births were to unmarried women, compared with around 30 percent of white births. The black rate is almost 2.5 times higher than the white rate. First, the fact that a woman is not married when she has her baby does not mean that the unmarried mothers are raising their babies alone. Of the 72 percent of births to unmarried black women, one-third of the women are cohabiting (Martinez, Daniels, and Chandra, 2012), so there is a father in the household helping to raise the child along with the mother. Another reason is purely demographic, namely, the availability of black men; there are not enough of them. Of the 8 million black men in the United States in the age range 25–54, 1.5 million are not available for the black women. Incarceration and higher mortality are the main factors responsible for taking these 1.5 million men out of the marriage pool. Mass incarceration accounts for 600,000 of them, and higher death rates for much of the balance. "Almost one in 12 black men in this age group are behind bars, compared with one in 60 non-black men" (Blow, 2015: A21).

Since there are many fewer black men available in the marriage market, "some of the men have children by more than one woman, but they can only live in one home at a time" (Blow, 2015: A21). The fact that the father does not live with all his children at the same time, however, does not necessarily mean he is not relating with the children who are not living with him.

The sociologists Kathryn Edin and Maria Kefalas have written a most interesting and provocative ethnography, *Promises I Can Keep: Why Poor Women Put Motherhood before Marriage* (2007). Their book focused on 162 poor mothers living in Philadelphia who were black, Hispanic, or white.

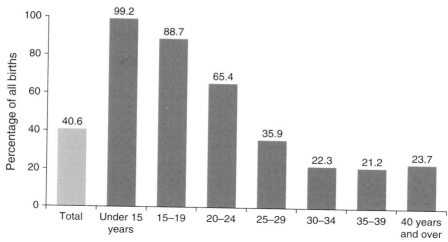

Figure 5.7 Percentage of All Births to Unmarried Women, by Age of Mother: United States, 2013
Source: Child Trends (2015: 4) (reprinted with permission of Child Trends).

Of their many interesting findings, one is of particular relevance for my discussion here: among the poor young women they interviewed, many of them intentionally became pregnant because they wanted to have babies. Having a baby was a legitimation of their personhood. A baby was the woman's identity. Most could not imagine a life without a child, marriage, or no marriage. Not having children was deemed a tragedy. (In my discussion of childlessness in Chapter 4, recall the much lower rates of childlessness among black and Hispanic women than among whites.)

Finally, I ask about the ages of the women who are unmarried when their children are born. How old are they? Figure 5.7 presents data for the year 2013 about the ages of unmarried women giving birth.

Recall that almost 41 percent of all births are to unmarried women. The histogram data in Figure 5.7 indicate that virtually all births in 2013 to women under the age of 15 were to unmarried women; that is no surprise; plus there were very few births to women under age 15, only 3,098 in the United States in 2013 (see Chapter 4). The next age group is 15–19; almost 89 percent of births to women in this group were to unmarried women.

Most of the births occurred to women in their 20s and early 30s (remember the "age curve of fertility" that I discussed in Chapter 4). How many of them are unmarried? Over 65 percent of 20–24-year-old women giving birth are unmarried, almost 36 percent of 25–29 year olds, and over 32 percent of 30–34 year olds. These data mirror very closely the increasing median age at first marriage (Figure 5.1). The older the woman, the more likely it is that she has married and the less likely that she is not married when she gives birth.

I have discussed several dimensions of marriage and the family in the contemporary US society. Men and women are marrying later these days than they ever had previously. Fewer people are marrying than in past decades. More men and women are cohabiting; indeed, cohabitation is now the norm. And, finally, 40 percent of all births are to unmarried women (72 percent for blacks, 53 percent for Hispanics, 29 percent for whites). These four dimensions I chose to examine and discuss are dramatically different quantitatively today compared with the 1950s. In the "Ozzie and Harriet" traditional family, men and women married early, most people married, very few cohabited, and hardly any babies were born to unwed mothers. The "Ozzie and Harriet" days are no longer with us.

SEXUALITY

In this section of the chapter I use sexuality data from the 2006–2008 NSFG to conceptualize and measure the dimensions of sexuality. Much of my discussion here is drawn from some of my previously published research with my student Yuting Chang (Poston and Chang, 2015). I first discuss the two main approaches used by social scientists to conceptualize sexual orientation, namely, essentialism and social constructionism. Next, I review some of the prior empirical literature that has measured sexual orientation. I then specify three different dimensions of sexuality: sexual behavior in one's lifetime; sexual self-identification; and sexual preference. I then use the NSFG data to explore the multiple dimensions of sexuality.

Conceptualizing Sexuality

Most of the social science literature on sexual orientation conceptualizes the phenomenon using two basic perspectives or approaches, or a combination thereof. These two views are known as **essentialism** and **social constructionism** (Baumle, Compton, and Poston, 2009: 19–21; Laumann et al., 1994: 284). Founded in biology, the essentialist view is one of dimorphism; it states that there is an "essential" biological or psychological characteristic or attribute that is common to all persons and that distinguishes them as either of one sexuality or not of that sexuality. This common characteristic, or essence, may be a fundamental drive or trait that establishes a person's inclusion into, or not into, one of the sexual categories of heterosexual or homosexual (Baumle, Compton, and Poston, 2009: 19–20; Laumann et al., 1994: 285).

The social constructionist view, on the other hand, counters and critiques the essentialist perspective. Social constructionism argues against the notion of binary categories, that is, that one either is or is not in a specific sexual category (Baumle, Compton, and Poston, 2009: 20–21; Foucault,

1978). Instead, it argues for a continuum with varying degrees of the categories of sexuality. What in one culture may be defined as "homosexual" may not be so defined in another culture. Or as Blank (2012: xviii) has written, "despite the fact that most of us use the term 'heterosexual' with enormous and cavalier certainty, there seems to be no aspect of 'heterosexual' for which a truly iron-clad definition has been established." And the same may be stated about "homosexual."

Prior to the 1940s and 1950s when Alfred Kinsey and his colleagues (Kinsey, Pomeroy, and Martin, 1948; Kinsey et al., 1953) conducted their sexuality research, most sexuality researchers used an essentialist orientation. It was Kinsey who moved sexuality research away from a position of essentialism.

Perhaps the very best and certainly the most comprehensive analysis of sexuality in the United States is *The Social Organization of Sexuality: Sexual Practices in the United States* by Laumann, Gagnon, Michael, and Michaels, published in 1994. In this book, and indeed in much of the literature on sexuality over the past few decades, a common finding is the fluidity of sexual orientation. Most analyses show that the estimated prevalence rates of homosexuality and heterosexuality and bisexuality and asexuality vary, often considerably, according to the particular dimension of sexuality (behavior, attraction/desire, or self-identification) used. I turn attention now to the dimensions of sexuality. I then apply them to empirical analyses of homosexuality and heterosexuality. In other research (not presented here), I have explored these same issues with regard to bisexuality (Poston and Chang, 2015) and asexuality (Poston and Baumle, 2010) and have shown that bisexuality and asexuality may also be conceptualized with respect to behavior, attraction/desire, and self-identification (see also Compton, Farris, and Chang, 2015).

The Three Dimensions of Sexuality

The three dimensions of sexuality are self-identification, sexual preference, and sexual behavior. Strictly speaking, self-identification is a pretty straightforward issue and should be a simple matter to measure. If persons self-identify as homosexual or as heterosexual, they would be so identified in the data. But this does not necessarily mean that they would respond in a similar manner to questions dealing with other dimensions of sexuality, that is, behavior or desire. That is, a person could self-identify as homosexual, but state that he or she has engaged in sexual activity with both males and females.

Alternately, sexual desire or attraction or preference is a variable that is not as straightforward as personal identification. Desire has to do with individual feelings and wants, regardless of behavior or identification. If a respondent were to declare to desire or prefer sexual relations with someone of the same sex, he or she would be defined as homosexual according to the preference dimension of sexuality.

Behavior is another aspect of a constructed view of sexuality. For instance, a person may engage in same-sex sexual behavior, but not self-identify as homosexual.

The 2006–2008 NSFG includes questions enabling me to directly assess each of the above dimensions of sexuality. I next discuss these issues in more detail.

The NSFG Sexuality Data

The 2006–2008 NSFG questions I used to obtain respondent data on the behavioral dimension of sexuality are two. For females, the two questions are:

> Counting all your male sexual partners, even those you had intercourse with only once, how many men have you had sexual intercourse with in your life?

> Thinking about your entire life, how many female sex partners have you had?

For males, the two questions are:

> How many different females have you ever had intercourse with? This includes any female you had intercourse with, even if it was only once or if you did not know her well.

> Thinking about your entire life, how many male sex partners have you had?

A respondent answering having only opposite-sex partners and no same-sex partners is defined as heterosexual on the behavior dimension of sexuality. A respondent answering having only same-sex partners and no opposite-sex partners is defined as homosexual. It is important to note that this behavioral measurement is limited to assessing behaviors in one's lifetime. Another way to measure behavior is to ask about the past five years, or the past one year. In other studies I have used these alternative questions to measure behavior. The overall patterns of the data are more similar than they are different from data based on the lifetime question.

With respect to the self-identification of sexual orientation, the 2006–2008 NSFG asked each respondent the following question:

> Do you think of yourself as heterosexual or straight; as homosexual, gay or lesbian; as bisexual; or as something else?

Categories	(%)
Behavior	23.19
Desire	22.37
Identity	4.40
Behavior & Desire	0.58
Behavior & Identity	0.63
Desire & Identity	31.21
Behavior, Desire, & Identity	17.62
Sample Size	179
% of total sample (unweighted)	2.43

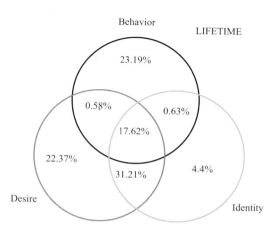

Figure 5.8 Interrelations of Components of Homosexuality, Females, United Sates, 2006–2008
Source: Poston and Chang (2015). Figure prepared by Yuting Chang.

With respect to sexual desire and attraction, the 2006–2008 NSFG asked males the following question, and a similar question was asked of females:

> People are different in their sexual attraction to other people. Which best describes your feelings? Are you ... Only attracted to females; Mostly attracted to females; Equally attracted to females and males; Mostly attracted to males; Only attracted to males; Not sure.

I specified the sexuality of males on the desire dimension as follows. Males who are only attracted to or who are mostly attracted to females are heterosexual; and males who are only attracted to or who are mostly attracted to males are homosexual. I specified the sexuality of females on the desire dimension in a similar way.

Empirical Analyses of Sexuality

I now examine the intersection of the three dimensions of sexuality. I combine the sexuality responses to the above three NSFG questions into seven possible outcomes as follows: the respondent provides a homosexual (or a heterosexual) response (1) only to identification, (2) only to desire, (3) only to behavior, (4) to both identification and desire, (5) to both identification and behavior, (6) to both desire and behavior, and (7) to identification, desire, and behavior. I show the results of my analyses for homosexuality for US females and males aged 15–44 in the Venn diagrams in Figures 5.8 and 5.9.

As Laumann and his colleagues (1994: 298) have written in their discussions of sexuality using similarly prepared Venn diagrams, "these

Categories	(%)
Behavior	12.66
Desire	13.53
Identity	4.27
Behavior & Desire	0.82
Behavior & Identity	0.00
Desire & Identity	40.03
Behavior, Desire, & Identity	28.69
Sample Size	176
% of total sample (unweighted)	2.87

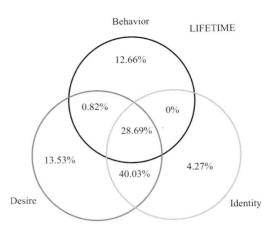

Figure 5.9 Interrelations of Components of Homosexuality, Males, United States, 2006–2008
Source: Poston and Chang (2015). Figure prepared by Yuting Chang.

diagrams make use of overlapping circles to display all the logically possible intersections among different categories (of sexuality)." Whereas the diagrams show all possible combinations, they do not scale the areas of each circle; instead, the percentages attached to each area are shown in the figures. Each circle represents a dimension of sexuality.

Figure 5.8 presents data on the intersection of the sexuality dimensions of homosexuality for females. The Venn diagram shows the degree of overlap among the conceptually distinct dimensions of sexuality applied to female homosexuality. I show in Figure 5.8 exactly how the 179 women who reported any homosexual behavior, desire, or identity are actually distributed across the seven mutually exclusive combinations of the three sexuality dimensions.

The data and diagram in Figure 5.8 indicate that 2.4 percent of all the female respondents in the 2006–2008 NSFG, that is, 179 women of the total NSFG sample of 7,356 women, gave a "homosexual" response to at least one of the three questions pertaining to sexual behavior, self-identification, and desire (see the bottom two rows of data in the table to the left of the Venn diagram). Now look at the Venn diagram in the figure. For purposes of illustration, the part of the "Desire" circle in Figure 5.8 that does not overlap with the "Behavior" or "Identity" circles indicates that over 22 percent of the women giving a homosexual response to any one or more of the three questions reported a desire for persons of the same sex, but did not identify themselves as homosexual and did not report having only homosexual sex in their lifetimes. Only 17.6 percent of the women who gave a homosexual response to at least one of the three questions gave a homosexual response to all three questions (see the overlapping component of all three circles in the center of the Venn diagram). That is, less than one-fifth of the female homosexual sample reported self-identifying as homosexual, *and* having only same-sex sex behavior in their lifetimes, *and* being only or mostly attracted to females. The corresponding percentage for homosexual males is 28.7 percent (Figure 5.9).

The data in Figures 5.8 and 5.9 indicate that very small percentages of females and males gave a homosexual response to at least one of the three sexuality questions dealing with self-identification, behavior, and desire. Just over 2.4 percent of the females and almost 2.9 percent of the males stated that they had only had same-sex sex in their lifetimes, and/or that they desired or were attracted to same-sex persons, and/or that they self-identified as homosexuals.

These percentage calculations assume the truthfulness of persons' responses when answering questions pertaining to nonheterosexual behavior, desire, and self-identification. In an attempt to obtain complete and reliable data on these dimensions of sexuality, the NSFG used an expanded version of ACASI. In ACASI "the respondent listens to the questions through headphones, reads them on the screen, or both, and enters the response directly into the computer. This method avoids asking the respondent to give his or her answers to the interviewer, and it has been found to yield more complete reporting of sensitive behaviors" (Chandra, Mosher, and Copen, 2011: 3). Nevertheless, the stigma in providing truthful responses to questions dealing with nonheterosexual issues may still be present, resulting in lower than the actual percentages of nonheterosexual behavior, desire, and self-identification (Herek, 2007).

However, when I prepared similar Venn diagrams for heterosexuals (the figures are not shown here), I found that an essentialist approach works fairly well for male and female heterosexuals; there is overwhelming support for treating heterosexuals in a binary manner, that is, 75 percent of females and 83 percent of males are heterosexual on all three questions. In other words, 75 percent of females and over 83 percent of males who indicate a heterosexual response to at least one of the three sexuality questions gave a heterosexual response to all three questions. But among homosexuals, there is nowhere near as much agreement. Whereas one could argue that an essentialist approach works fairly satisfactorily for female and male heterosexuality, it does not work well at all for female and male homosexuality. Homosexuality is much more fluid than heterosexuality.

My empirical analyses demonstrate the importance of a social constructionist perspective in developing an understanding of sexuality.

Table 5.1 Percentage Estimates of Female and Male Heterosexuality, United States, 2006–2008

Heterosexuality	Female		Male	
	%	Margin of error	%	Margin of error
Behavior	0.41	+/−0.17	0.11	+/−0.11
Desire	1.38	+/−0.41	0.39	+/−0.18
Identity	0.54	+/−0.25	0.21	+/−0.16
Behavior & Desire	0.48	+/−0.21	0.27	+/−0.15
Behavior & Identity	0.84	+/−0.31	0.22	+/−0.14
Desire & Identity	20.25	+/−2.53	15.47	+/−2.48
Behavior & Desire & Identity	71.54	+/−2.33	79.09	+/−2.45
Sample (*n*)	6,878		5,768	
Total sample (*N*)	7,356		6,139	
Weighted Percentage	*95.43*	*+/−0.83*	*95.77*	*+/−0.88*

Source: Poston and Chang (2015).

Although some individuals provided the same sexual response (e.g., heterosexual or homosexual) on all three dimensions, most of the respondents gave one sexual response (e.g., homosexual) to the NSFG question on one dimension and another sexual response (e.g., bisexual or heterosexual) to the NSFG question on another dimension. Using a social constructionist orientation in an analysis of sexuality provides a much more encompassing understanding of sexuality.

Having examined the interrelations of the dimensions of sexuality for males and females with respect to homosexuality and heterosexuality, I now present prevalence rates by considering the percentages of persons who give one of the two "sexual responses" (heterosexual or homosexual) to one or more of the above three questions. This will allow me to produce percentages of the US population aged 15–44 who are heterosexual and who are homosexual.

I show in Tables 5.1 and 5.2 statistically adjusted percentages for the period of 2006–2008 of the prevalence of female and male heterosexuality (Table 5.1) and homosexuality (Table 5.2).

In the very bottom row of the tables, I show the weighted percentages of persons selecting the respective sexuality response to any one or more of the questions pertaining to identification, behavior, and desire/attraction. For instance, the figure of 95.43 in the female heterosexuality table (Table 5.1) means that in 2006–2008, 95.4 percent of US females aged 15–44 gave a heterosexual answer to at least one of the three questions dealing with sexuality; and 72 percent of US women gave the heterosexual response to all

Table 5.2 Percentage Estimates of Female and Male Homosexuality, United States, 2006–2008

Homosexuality	Female		Male	
	%	Margin of error	%	Margin of error
Behavior	0.43	+/−0.18	0.28	+/−0.20
Desire	0.42	+/−0.19	0.30	+/−0.22
Identity	0.08	+/−0.09	0.10	+/−0.09
Behavior & Desire	0.01	+/−0.02	0.02	+/−0.02
Behavior & Identity	0.01	+/−0.02	0.00	N/A
Desire & Identity	0.58	+/−0.24	0.89	+/−0.29
Behavior & Desire & Identity	0.33	+/−0.16	0.64	+/−0.22
Sample (*n*)	179		176	
Total sample (*N*)	7,356		6,139	
Weighted Percentage	*1.86*	*+/−0.45*	*2.24*	*+/−0.48*

Source: Poston and Chang (2015).

three questions. For males, the corresponding percentages were 96 percent and 79 percent.

So what is the prevalence level of heterosexuality in the United States for females and males in 2006–2008? There is no one answer because it depends on how one defines heterosexuality. To repeat Blank's (2012: xviii) statement that I quoted earlier, "despite the fact that most of us use the term 'heterosexual' with enormous and cavalier certainty, there seems to be no aspect of 'heterosexual' for which a truly iron-clad definition has been established."

So if I define a heterosexual as a person who identifies as a heterosexual, *and* engages in sexual behavior exclusively as a heterosexual, *and* desires or is attracted only to heterosexuals, then the answer for females is around 72 percent and for males 79 percent of the population. But if I invoke a social constructionist approach and define a heterosexual as a person who identifies as a heterosexual, *and/or* engages in sexual behavior exclusively as a heterosexual, *and/or* desires or is attracted to heterosexuals, then the percentages are 95 percent for females and 96 percent for males.

I show in Table 5.2 similar information for female and male homosexuality. What are the percentage levels of homosexuality in the United States in 2006–2008 for females and males? Again, it depends on the definition. If I hold that a homosexual is one who self-identifies as a homosexual, *and* engages in sexual behavior only with persons of the same sex, *and* is attracted to persons of the same sex, then the answer for females is 0.3 percent and for males 0.6 percent of the total US population of males and females aged 15–44. But if I do not insist on such a comprehensive essentialist-type definition, and if I instead define a homosexual in a looser and more fluid manner as one who self-identifies as a homosexual, *and/or* engages in sex only with same-sex persons, *and/or* desires or is attracted to persons of the same sex, that is, if I use a social constructionist approach in my definition of a homosexual, then the percentages are 1.9 percent for females and 2.2 percent for males. A social constructionist interpretation of the data indicates that around 2 percent of the US female population aged 15–44 in the 2006–2008 period was homosexual, and around 2 percent of the male population was homosexual. An essentialist interpretation places the percentage levels of homosexuality much lower.

FAMILY PARTNERING

In the two main sections of this chapter, I focused first on the family and then on sexuality. In this final section I link family and sexuality together in an empirical examination of **family partnering**, that is, two persons living together as a married male and female, or as a cohabiting male and female, or as a married or cohabiting male and male, or as a married or cohabiting female and female. What can we glean from 2010 census data about the patterns of family partnering in the United States?

In Chapter 3, I discussed the 2010 census question that asked everyone living in a household with two or more persons about their relationship with the person who is known as Person 1; this is usually the person taking the major responsibility for filling out the census form. Every person in the household, except Person 1, is then asked to respond to a question about his or her relationship to Person 1. I show in Figure 5.10 a segment of the census questionnaire that is designated for Person 2; look specifically at question No. 2 in the figure.

Observe the numerous responses that Person 2 may use to respond to the "relationship to Person 1" question. They include the so-called blood or family relationships of husband, wife, son, grandfather, and so forth, and the nonfamily relationships of roomer/boarder, housemate/roommate, unmarried partner, and so forth. The "husband/wife" and the "unmarried partner" responses, along with the responses about sex (question No. 3), enable researchers to identify households with two or more adult residents as heterosexual married partnered, heterosexual cohabiting partnered, gay male partnered, and lesbian partnered.

I noted earlier in Chapter 3 that my student Yuting Chang and I (Poston and Chang, 2013) have examined these data on same-sex partners for every one of the 366 metropolitan areas in the United States in 2010 (in Chapter 14, I discuss the concept of the metropolitan area) and developed prevalence

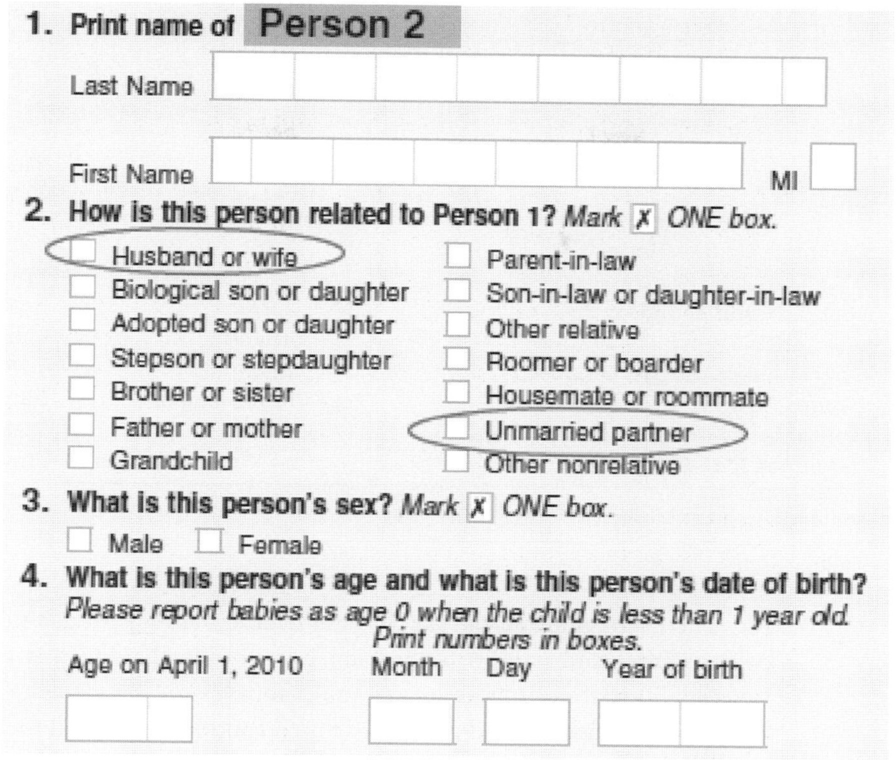

1. **Print name of** **Person 2**

   Last Name [ ][ ][ ][ ][ ][ ][ ]

   First Name [ ][ ][ ][ ][ ][ ]   MI [ ]

2. **How is this person related to Person 1?** *Mark* [X] *ONE box.*
   - ☐ Husband or wife
   - ☐ Biological son or daughter
   - ☐ Adopted son or daughter
   - ☐ Stepson or stepdaughter
   - ☐ Brother or sister
   - ☐ Father or mother
   - ☐ Grandchild
   - ☐ Parent-in-law
   - ☐ Son-in-law or daughter-in-law
   - ☐ Other relative
   - ☐ Roomer or boarder
   - ☐ Housemate or roommate
   - ☐ Unmarried partner
   - ☐ Other nonrelative

3. **What is this person's sex?** *Mark* [X] *ONE box.*
   - ☐ Male ☐ Female

4. **What is this person's age and what is this person's date of birth?**
   Please report babies as age 0 when the child is less than 1 year old.
   Print numbers in boxes.

   Age on April 1, 2010   Month   Day   Year of birth

   [ ]   [ ]   [ ]   [ ]

Figure 5.10 Segment of Questionnaire, 2010 Census of Population, United States

indexes for each of the four types of partnering. I discuss our research here in a little more detail.

The index we used was developed and first employed by Gates and Ost (2004) and then extended by Dr. Chang and myself (Poston and Chang, 2013). When employed to index same-sex partnering, it is a "ratio of the proportion of same-sex couples living in a [metropolitan area] to the proportion of all households that are located in a [metropolitan area]...This ratio...measures the over- or underrepresentation of same-sex couples in a geographic area relative to the population" (Gates and Ost, 2004: 24). An index value of 1.0 for a metropolitan area means that "a same-sex couple is just as likely as a randomly picked household to locate" in the metro area (Gates and Ost, 2004: 24). An index value above 1.0 means that a same-sex couple is more likely to live in the metro area than a random couple household, and a value less than 1.0, less likely.

I show in Table 5.3 descriptive data for the prevalence ratio indexes for gay male partners, lesbian partners, opposite-sex married partners, and opposite-sex cohabiting partners across the 366 metropolitan areas in 2010.

Table 5.3 Means, Standard Deviations (SD), and Maximum and Minimum Values: Ratios of Gay Male Couples, Lesbian Couples, Opposite-sex Married Couples, and Opposite-sex Cohabiting Couples in 366 Metropolitan Areas of the United States, 2010

Rate	Mean	SD	Maximum value	Minimum value
Gay Male Couples Index	0.69	0.31	2.78 San Francisco	0.26 Grand Forks
Lesbian Couples Index	0.86	0.37	2.97 Ithaca	0.32 Wausau
Opposite-sex Married Couples Index	1.02	0.09	1.46 Provo–Orem	0.78 Gainesville
Opposite-sex Cohabiting Couples Index	1.03	1.17	1.63 Lewiston–Auburn	0.34 Provo–Orem

Source: Poston and Chang (2013).

The mean value across the 366 metropolitan areas for gay male households is 0.69 and is 0.86 for lesbian households. This means that in the "average" metropolitan area, gay male couples are 31 percent less likely to settle there than would a couple from a randomly selected metropolitan household (that is, [0.69 − 1.0] × 100); and that a lesbian couple would be 14 percent less likely to settle there than would a couple from a randomly selected household. Opposite-sex married couples are about 2 percent more likely to settle in the average metro area than a randomly selected couple, and an opposite sex cohabiting couple are 3 percent more likely. On average, gay male and lesbian couples are much less likely than a random couple to settle in the average metro area.

Opposite-sex married couples comprise by far the majority of couples in any metropolitan area; they are followed by opposite-sex cohabiting couples, and then by gay male and lesbian couples. Therefore, the statistical odds that opposite-sex couples, especially married couples, would settle in an average metro area are just about even (if the ratio was 1.0, this would mean the odds of settling in the area would be even).

I look next at the maximum and minimum values of the four indexes, as shown in the last two columns of Table 5.3. The highest value for gay males is 2.78; this is for the San Francisco–Oakland–Fremont, California metropolitan area (hereafter referred to as San Francisco). The Ithaca, New York metropolitan area has the highest lesbian ratio at 2.97. The value for San Francisco may be interpreted as indicating that a gay male couple is 2.8 times more likely than an "average" US metro household to reside in the San Francisco area, or, in other words, 180 percent more likely (i.e., [2.78 – 1.00] × 100). The Ithaca index value indicates that a lesbian couple is almost 200 percent more likely to live in Ithaca than an average US metro household is likely to live in Ithaca.

Regarding the minimum values, the Grand Forks, North Dakota–Minnesota metro area has the lowest gay male couple ratio at 0.26, and the Wausau, Wisconsin has the lowest lesbian couple ratio at 0.32. Gay male couples are about one-quarter as likely (or 74 percent less likely) to live in Grand Forks as are a randomly picked US metro household, and lesbian couples are about one-third as likely to live in Wausau as a randomly selected household.

Turning next to the maximum and minimum data for opposite-sex couples, of all the metro areas, the Provo–Orem, Utah area is the most likely to have an opposite-sex married couple located there, with a ratio value of 1.46. And the Lewiston–Auburn, Maine area is the most likely of all the metro areas to have an opposite-sex cohabiting couple residing there. The metro area with the lowest opposite-sex ratio is the Gainesville, Florida metro area with an opposite-sex married couple value of 0.78, and the Provo–Orem, Utah area has the lowest opposite-sex cohabiting couple ratio at 0.34.

These analyses allow me to conclude that the distribution around the United States of four different types of family partnering is very even with respect to opposite-sex partnering, especially married partnering, but very uneven with regard to same-sex partnering. Specifically, gay male households are much more likely to be in some areas than others, and a similar observation may be made for lesbian households. As I already noted in Chapter 3, partnered gay men have a few favorite destinations in which to reside, including San Francisco, Miami, Seattle, San Diego, Washington, DC, Las Vegas, Los Angeles, Atlanta, Denver, New York, Tampa, Phoenix, Dallas, New Orleans, Honolulu, Chicago, and Houston, where their prevalence scores surpass those of partnered lesbians. Partnered lesbians, conversely, are concentrated more than partnered gay men in metropolitan areas in general, tending not to prefer particular areas to the degree that gay men prefer them. Opposite-sex couples, especially married couples, are just about as likely to reside in any of the areas, as is shown by their mean index values of 1.02 and 1.03 (Table 5.3). Yes, there are a few extremes, but these minimum and maximum values are nowhere in the range of the minimum and maximum values for same-sex couples.

CONCLUSION

This chapter had two main sections, one dealing with the family and the other dealing with sexuality. I ended the chapter with a third section bringing the two topics of family and sexuality together in a discussion of family partnering.

In the chapter, I first looked at the family over time, from when they were formed mainly on the basis of economic and related alliances, up to the present time. I showed that today people are marrying later than they ever have, fewer are marrying, most are cohabiting before marriage, and over 40 percent of babies are born to unmarried mothers. The form of the family has not only changed in the past sixty-five years, it has changed in the past 5,000 years.

I then focused on sexuality. I noted that there are two ways to conceptualize sexuality, essentialism and social constructionism. I showed that an answer to the question of how many homosexuals and heterosexuals there are in the United States today depends largely on whether one uses an essentialist or a constructionist point of view. A constructionist approach enabled me to answer that 2 percent of the US female population aged 15–44 is lesbian, and 2 percent of the male population is gay. And a constructionist orientation allowed me to answer that 95 percent of the female population is heterosexual, as is 96 percent of the male population.

In the last part of the chapter, I linked family and sexuality together in an examination of family partnering. I defined family partnering as two opposite-sex or same-sex persons living together in a family or family-type household. I showed that the distribution around the United States in 2010 in four different types of partnering is very even with regard to opposite-sex partnering, especially opposite-sex married partnering, and very uneven with regard to same-sex (lesbian and gay male) partnering.

6 Contraception and Birth Control

INTRODUCTION

Discussions of fertility and the family and sexuality, the topics of Chapters 4 and 5, are not complete without a consideration and review of **contraception** and **birth control**. Most married and unmarried sexually active women and men in the United States and in the countries of the developed world endeavor to limit their family size and/or to control the timing and spacing of their births. In the developing countries of the world, fewer people use birth prevention methods.

There are a variety of methods available to women and men to prevent births. The most popular ones worldwide are contraception, **sterilization**, and abortion. Some methods are more effective than others, and each has its advantages and disadvantages. In this chapter, I first review briefly the history of fertility control. Although fertility control methods have been widely used and publicly accepted in the past five or so decades, attempts to control fertility have characterized human populations for centuries. I follow this review with a description of the general situation worldwide and in the United States regarding the use of contraception, sterilization, and abortion. The main part of the chapter is a description of the major methods of birth prevention, including a discussion of their **effectiveness**.

BRIEF HISTORY OF FERTILITY CONTROL

The idea or notion of preventing births appeared early in human history. Of the many excellent and comprehensive accounts of contraception available today, I call your attention specifically to several. The classic is *Medical History of Contraception* by Norman Himes, first published in 1936, with a paperback edition in 1970. This is an exhaustive survey of contraception covering many cultures worldwide over 3,000 years. It is a masterful

collation of historical and anthropological evidence from preliterate societies to the early twentieth century.

In 1966, John T. Noonan wrote the superb *Contraception: A History
of Its Treatment by the Catholic Theologians and Canonists*. As stated in
the subtitle, it traces the very interesting history of contraception from the
pre-Christian era to the 1960s, with the heaviest concentration on the interpretation and reception of contraception in the Catholic Church.

The third major treatment is the more recent (2008) book by Robert
Jutte, *Contraception: A History*, published a few years earlier in German.
Jutte's book extends and updates much of the earlier work of Himes and
Noonan. All three books remind us that society's "attempts to control the
increase in numbers reach so far back into the dim past that it is impossible to discern their real origin. Some forms of limitation on the rate of
increase are undoubtedly as old as the life history of man" (Himes, [1936]
1970: 3).

Two other histories are also very useful, namely, McLaren's *History
of Contraception: From Antiquity to the Present Day* (1992), and Riddle's
Eve's Herbs: A History of Contraception and Abortion in the West (1999);
the latter is especially informative about the use of plant and herbal products to regulate fertility.

There are written records of contraceptive remedies and abortion techniques in Egyptian papyri (1900–1100 BC), in the Latin works of Pliny the
Elder (AD 23–79) and Dioscorides (AD 40–90), in the Greek writings of
Soranus (*c.* 100), and in works dealing with Arabic medicine in the tenth
century. The oldest surviving documents describing contraceptive methods
are the five Egyptian papyri dating from between 1900 BC and 1100 BC;
each provided different recipes for contraceptive preparations. According
to Noonan (1966: 9): "The Kahun Papyrus (mentions) pulverized crocodile
dung in fermented mucilage, and honey and sodium carbonate, to be sprin-
kled in the vulva…In the Ebers Papyrus it is said that pregnancy may be
prevented for one, two, or three years by a recipe of acacia tips, coloquin-
tida (a yellow lemon-sized bitter fruit sometimes used as a laxative), and
dates, mixed with honey, to be placed in the uterus." Until fairly recently,
most fertility control methods were relatively ineffective, with the exception
of induced abortion and **withdrawal**.

Virtually all of the contraceptive methods I review in this chapter,
except for the hormonally based methods, were available and used by the
end of the nineteenth century, some much earlier (Himes, [1936] 1970;
Jutte, 2008). Condoms date back to the seventeenth century. Indeed, James
Boswell, the famous diarist and author of *The Life of Samuel Johnson*,
wrote about "using a condom with a prostitute in London in 1763" (Potts,
2003: 96). Intrauterine devices (IUDs) were first developed in Germany in

the 1920s. However, owing to legal and other restrictions, it was not possible until much later to undertake IUD research in the United States. The manual vacuum-aspiration method of abortion was first described in England by Queen Victoria's gynecologist.

The physiological principles behind **oral contraceptives** were developed in the 1920s, "but the method made no progress, partly because of the lack of a cheap source of steroid and also because contraceptive research was not academically acceptable" (Potts, 2003: 96). Potts and Campbell (2002) have written about the vast historical disconnect between the acquisition of biological knowledge about birth control and its application.

In my presentation later in this chapter about the specific types of contraceptives, I will have occasion to mention the historical precedents for some of them. I turn next to a discussion of fertility control in the world today.

CURRENT PATTERNS OF FERTILITY CONTROL WORLDWIDE AND IN THE UNITED STATES

The Population Reference Bureau (2013) has published family planning and fertility control data from surveys conducted during the period from 2002 to 2013 by a host of national governments and international agencies. Fertility control data are presented for women between the ages of 15 and 49 who are married or in informal unions. These are the most comprehensive data currently available and portray a contemporary empirical picture of the reproductive revolution that has occurred in the world since the 1950s.

In Table 6.1 I present key data on percentages of married women using various family planning methods for the world and most regions. Observe in the table that data are lacking for Europe and Oceania. This is due to the paucity of family planning surveys conducted in the countries of those regions (see my discussion in Chapter 3 of the surveys that gather family planning data). Survey data are available, however, for a few European countries (e.g., Belgium, France, the Netherlands, the United Kingdom, Russia, Greece, Portugal, and Spain). For Oceania, data are available for Australia (the largest country in Oceania), but not for New Zealand and Papua New Guinea (the next two largest countries).

In the less developed countries of the world, the percentage of married women using family planning methods has increased from 9 percent in 1960, to 60 percent in 2007, to over 62 percent in 2012. According to data from the most recent surveys conducted in the various countries between 2002 and 2012, 63 percent of married women worldwide are using family planning methods: 72 percent of women in the developed countries and

Table 6.1 Percentage of Married Women Using Family Planning Methods: World and Most Major Regions, 2002–2012

	All methods	All modern methods	Pill	IUD	Injectables	Male condom	Sterilization Male	Female
World	63	57	8	13	5	8	3	18
More developed	72	63	–	–	–	–	–	–
Less developed	62	56	7	14	6	6	2	19
Least developed	34	29	10	1	11	2	–	3
Africa	33	27	9	4	9	2	–	2
Sub-Saharan Africa	26	21	5	1	10	2	–	2
North America	78	73	17	5	1	12	14	22
Latin America & the Caribbean	75	68	14	6	6	10	–	23
Asia	66	61	6	17	5	7	2	22
western Asia	56	36	8	15	–	8	–	5
central Asia	54	50	3	39	2	4	–	2
south Asia	54	47	7	2	–	6	1	29
southeast Asia	62	54	15	7	19	4	–	7
east Asia	82	81	1	37	–	11	5	26
Europe								
Oceania	63	–	–	–	–	–	–	–
Australia	72	68	30	2	2	15	9	7

Source: PRB (2013).

62 percent in the developing countries (see Table 6.1). Contraceptive use in the developing countries has now almost reached the level attained in the developed world. This has occurred even though the use of family planning methods in the developing world is quite uneven across the various countries; the percentage of married women using modern methods ranges from lows of 1 percent in South Sudan and Somalia and 2 percent in Chad to highs of 84 percent in the United Kingdom and China. The two countries with the highest percentages of married women using any family planning method, not just modern methods, are Norway at 88 percent and Portugal at 87 percent (PRB, 2013). The reproductive revolution is surely one of the most remarkable demographic stories of the past half-century.

The percentage data in Table 6.1 refer to users of family planning methods. If we subtract the user percentage for a country from 100, we get the percentage of women who are not using contraceptive methods. In Norway, the percentage of nonusers is 12 percent, whereas in South Sudan it is 99 percent.

Who is a nonuser of contraception? There are six categories of nonusers. Women in only one of the nonuser categories, the last category on the list I present below, are engaging in unprotected intercourse and are thus at risk of becoming pregnant. Here are the categories:

1. women who are surgically sterile via a **hysterectomy,** that is, the surgical removal of the uterus and sometimes the additional removal of the Fallopian tubes and the ovaries, or by some other noncontraceptive operation; these women would not be expected to be using contraception because they are sterile;
2. women who themselves or their male partners are nonsurgically sterile; these women would not be expected to be contraception users because they (or their partners) are sterile;
3. women who are pregnant or postpartum, that is, those who have just given birth; pregnant women are not expected to be using contraception; and for postpartum women, there is very little risk of pregnancy for several months after giving birth (recall my discussion of postpartum infecundability in Chapter 4);
4. women who are trying to become pregnant; they obviously would not be using contraception;
5. women who have never had intercourse or have not had intercourse in the past three months; if the women have never had intercourse, or have not had intercourse in the three months before the survey interview, then they are not considered to be sexually active;
6. women who have had intercourse in the last three months before the survey interview; it is women in this last category who are "sexually active" and hence are truly at risk of becoming pregnant (demographers define a "sexually active" woman as one who has had intercourse at least once in the past three months).

The data in Table 6.1 do not provide information for the various categories of nonusers. I noted, for example, that 63 percent, or almost two-thirds, of married women worldwide are using family planning methods; therefore, 37 percent of them are nonusers. But we cannot tell from the data in Table 6.1 how many of these nonusers are truly at risk of becoming pregnant involuntarily. That is, we do not know how many of the nonusers would fall into the sixth category of nonusers, as just described.

However, these types of nonuser data are available for women in the United States, and I shall describe them in more detail later. For example, I will show that 62 percent of all women aged 15–44 in the United States are using family planning methods; thus, 38 percent of them are not using contraceptive methods. I will report that of this 38 percent, only 8 percent who are not using contraceptive methods are sexually active; they are the

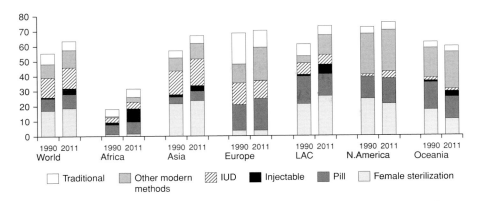

Figure 6.1 Percentages of Married or In-union Women Using Different Methods of Contraception: the World and its Regions, 1990 and 2011
Source: United Nations Department of Economic and Social Affairs (UNDESF, 2013: 1).

only ones who are truly at risk of an unintended pregnancy. But before looking at the contraceptive use of US women, allow me first to consider the worldwide use of specific methods of contraception.

The family planning use data I reported in the previous paragraphs pertain to all contraceptive methods, which may be divided into modern and traditional methods. The main modern methods of family planning are the oral contraceptive (i.e., the pill), the **intrauterine device (IUD)**, **contraception injection**, the **male condom**, and both **male and female sterilization**. Other modern methods include the **diaphragm**, **vaginal contraceptives**, including various foams and jellies, several kinds of contraceptive implant, the **female condom**, and "natural" family planning methods, also known as **fertility awareness** methods, such as the **Standard Days Method**® and the **Billings ovulation method**. Traditional family planning methods include less effective "natural" methods, such as the calendar **rhythm method** (i.e., periodic abstinence), coitus interruptus (i.e., withdrawal), long-term abstinence, and prolonged breast-feeding. I will discuss most of these and some other methods in the next section.

Table 6.1 also presents worldwide percentage data for married women using various types of family planning, as well as data for most of the major regions (only limited survey data are available for Europe); the data are from surveys conducted between 2002 and 2012. The differences in contraceptive use among the regions of the world are summarized in Figure 6.1.

Women in the different regions of the world vary in the principal contraceptive methods they use. But the patterns of their use have not changed much between 1990 and 2012. "Female sterilization remains common in Asia, Latin America and the Caribbean and North America, and the IUD continues to be important in Asia and Europe. The pill has the widest geographic distribution of any method" (UNDESF, 2013: 1). Regarding female sterilization, 18 percent of married women worldwide in the reproductive ages have been contraceptively sterilized. The next most popular methods, in order, are the IUD (13 percent), the oral contraceptive and the male condom (both at 8 percent), injectables (5 percent), and male sterilization (3 percent). The other modern methods, namely, hormonal implants, the diaphragm, and spermicides comprise a relatively small percentage of total use.

The traditional family planning methods noted above are employed by only around 6 percent of married women and men in the world. However, in Africa, where overall family planning use is very low, one in six married women using a method uses a traditional method, and in sub-Saharan Africa the number is one in five. Indeed, in many sub-Saharan African countries, traditional methods account for more than half of all methods used. To illustrate, 15 percent of women in Somalia use any family planning method, but only 1 percent use modern methods; 18 percent of women in the Democratic Republic of the Congo use a method, but only 5 percent use a modern method; 23 percent of women in Cameroon use any method, but only 14 percent use a modern method (PRB, 2013).

Of particular interest is the fact that among almost all the countries of the world, one or two contraceptive methods comprise half or more of "total contraceptive use among the married or in-union women" (UNDESF, 2013: 2). The pill is the dominant method in twenty countries, and traditional methods are dominant in eleven countries.

Having examined family planning methods worldwide, I turn now to a discussion of induced abortion. What are the current patterns worldwide of induced abortion?

An induced abortion is a pregnancy that has been terminated by human intervention with an "intent other than to produce a live birth" (Henshaw, 2003: 529). The most complete data on induced abortions are from countries where abortion is legal, but even here the quantity and quality of the data vary considerably. In Table 6.2, I show estimates of the numbers of induced abortions, and the **abortion rates**, for the world and its major regions for 1995, 2003, and 2008. In 2008, there were an estimated 44 million induced abortions worldwide, a decline from the approximately 46 million in 1995, but a slight increase from the 42 million in 2003. But the abortion rate (number of abortions per 1,000 women aged 15–44) has decreased from 35/1,000 in 1995, to 29 in 2003, to 28 in 2008. For every

Table 6.2 Global and Regional Estimates of Induced Abortion, 1995, 2003, and 2008

Region and subregion	Number of abortions (millions)			Abortion rate*		
	1995	2003	2008	1995	2003	2008
World	45.6	41.6	43.8	35	29	28
Developed countries	10.0	6.6	6.0	39	25	24
excluding eastern Europe	3.8	3.5	3.2	20	19	17
Developing countries**	35.5	35.0	37.8	34	29	29
excluding China	24.9	26.4	28.6	33	30	29
Region						
Africa	5.0	5.6	6.4	33	29	29
Asia	26.8	25.9	27.3	33	29	28
Europe	7.7	4.3	4.2	48	28	27
Latin America	4.2	4.1	4.4	37	31	32
North America	1.5	1.5	1.4	22	21	19
Oceania	0.1	0.1	0.0	21	18	17

* Abortions per 1,000 women aged 15–44.
** The developing countries are those in Africa, the Americas (excluding Canada and the United States), Asia (excluding Japan), and Oceania (excluding Australia and New Zealand).
Source: Guttmacher Institute (2012).

1,000 women in the childbearing ages in the world, 28 had an induced abortion in 2008 (Guttmacher Institute, 2012). Most of the abortions in the world in 2008 occurred in developing countries (38 million) rather than in developed countries (6 million). But this differential reflects the uneven distribution of the population in the two groups of countries. Indeed, the abortion rates for 2008 are much closer, namely, 29 in developing countries and 24 in developed countries.

Between 1995 and 2008, the abortion rates in the major regions of the world either declined or remained pretty much the same. The greatest decline occurred in Europe, from 48 in 1995 to 27 in 2008. Even though the abortion rates declined throughout Europe, it was, according to Cohen (2007: 2), "the precipitous drop in eastern Europe that drove the entire continent's decline and, by extension, literally moved the world's abortion rate downward" from 35 in 1995 to 27 in 2008.

Abortions do not occur more frequently in countries where they are legally performed versus in countries where they are not legally performed. To illustrate, the abortion data in Table 6.2 indicate that the rate in 2008 was 29 in Africa where abortion is, for the most part, illegal, but it was 27 in Europe where it is mostly legal.

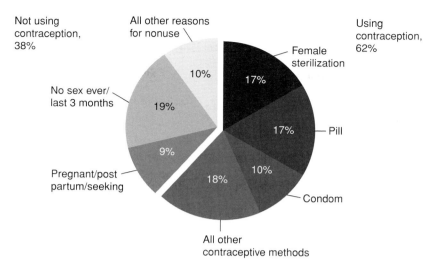

Figure 6.2 Percent Distribution of Women Aged 15–44, by Whether They are Using Contraception, and by Reasons for Nonuse and Methods Used, United States, 2006–2010
Source: Jones, Mosher, and Daniels (2012: 5).

An unsafe abortion is defined by the World Health Organization "as a procedure for terminating a pregnancy that is performed by an individual lacking the necessary skills, or in an environment that does not conform to minimal medical standards, or both" (Guttmacher Institute, 2012: 2). Abortions are far safer in countries where they are legally performed than where they are illegally performed. Worldwide, however, the rate of unsafe abortions did not change between 1995 and 2008, remaining right at about 14 abortions per 1,000 women in the childbearing ages. But the percentage of all abortions that were unsafe increased during the 1995–2008 period from 44 percent to 49 percent. In 2008, more than 97 percent of all abortions performed in Africa were deemed as unsafe. "In Asia, the proportion of abortions that are unsafe varies widely by subregion, from virtually none in Eastern Asia to 65 percent in South Central Asia" (Guttmacher Institute, 2012: 2).

There is a great disparity between the proportion of unsafe abortions in developed and developing countries. Almost all abortions in countries of the developed world are safe, but this is not at all the situation in the countries of the developing world. In East Asian countries abortions are very safe, but they are very unsafe in African countries.

I now turn my attention to the contraceptive behavior of US women. Table 6.3 and Figure 6.2 present data on the use and nonuse of contraception by US women aged 15–44, for the 2006–2010 period of time.

Table 6.3 Women Aged 15–44, by Current Contraceptive Status and Method Used: United States, 2006–2010

	All women 100.0%
Using contraception (contraceptors)	62.2
Female sterilization	16.5
Male sterilization	6.2
Pill	17.1
Other hormonal methods	4.5
Implant, Lunelle®, or patch	0.9
Three-month injectable (Depo-Provera®)	2.3
Contraceptive ring	1.3
IUD	3.5
Male condom	10.2
Periodic abstinence, calendar rhythm	0.6
Periodic abstinence, natural family planning	0.1
Withdrawal	3.2
Other methods*	0.3
Not using contraception	37.8
Surgically sterile – female (noncontraceptive)	0.4
Nonsurgically sterile – female or male	1.7
Pregnant or postpartum	5.0
Seeking pregnancy	4.0
Other nonuse	
Never had intercourse	11.8
No intercourse in 3 months before interview	7.3
Had intercourse in past 3 months before interview	7.7

* Includes diaphragm (with or without jelly or cream), emergency contraception, female condom or vaginal pouch, foam, cervical cap, Today sponge, suppository or insert, jelly or cream (without diaphragm), and other methods.
Source: Jones, Mosher, and Daniels (2012: 14).

These data were gathered via the NSFG (see my earlier discussion of this survey in Chapter 3).

In Figure 6.2 we see that 62 percent of US women were using contraception in the 2006–2010 period, and, thus, 38 percent were not. The most popular method for US women is the pill (17.1 percent) with female sterilization close behind (16.5 percent) (Table 6.3). The male condom is the third most popular method (10.2 percent), with male sterilization (6.2 percent) fourth. Unlike the situation worldwide, for US women the IUD is one of the least favored, not one of the most favored methods.

What about the nonusers of contraceptives. I noted in the previous paragraph that 38 percent of women were not using contraception. The

Table 6.4 Percentage Distributions of Women Using Contraception Aged 15–44, by Contraceptive Method, according to Marital or Cohabiting Status: United States, 2006–2010

	All marital statuses	Currently married	Currently cohabiting	Formerly married, not-cohabiting	Never married, not-cohabiting
All Methods	100.0	100.0	100.0	100.01	100.0
Female sterilization	26.6	30.2	24.0	55.5	10.2
Male sterilization	10.0	17.1	4.0	6.1	0.6
Pill	27.5	18.6	32.2	16.5	46.6
Male condom	16.4	15.3	15.8	7.7	22.0
Other hormonal methods*	7.2	3.9	10.1	7.3	12.0
IUD	5.6	7.1	5.9	3.6	3.0
Periodic abstinence**	1.2	1.7	1.4	–	–
Other methods	5.7	6.1	6.6	3.1	5.4

* Also includes Implanon, one-month injectable (Lunelle), contraceptive patch, and contraceptive ring.
** Includes calendar rhythm, natural family planning (NFP), cervical mucus test, and temperature rhythm.
Source: Jones, Mosher, and Daniels (2012: 17).

data in the bottom panel of Table 6.3 refer to women who are nonusers of contraception. Of the nearly 38 percent of all US women who are not currently using any form of contraception, over 2 percent of them are sterile (surgically or nonsurgically) and 9 percent are pregnant, just gave birth, or are trying to become pregnant. Almost 12 percent of the women have never had intercourse. Only 7.7 percent of the women who are nonusers of contraception are sexually active (defined by demographers as having had sexual intercourse at least once in the three months prior to being interviewed in the survey). Thus, most of the 38 percent who are not using contraceptives are women who are either sterile, pregnant, seeking to become pregnant, postpartum, never had intercourse, or not sexually active; only one in five of the nonusers of contraception are sexually active and do not fall into one of the other categories; it is only the sexually active group of women that is truly at risk of an unintended pregnancy.

I noted above some basic facts about the contraceptive methods used by all US women. To get a better and more comprehensive picture of the family planning method use of US women, I present in Table 6.4 method-specific data for all women according to their current marital status: married, cohabiting, formerly married (not now cohabiting), and never married (not now cohabiting). The data in this table apply only to women who are using contraception; the data do not apply to all women.

Among all women using contraception aged 15–44 (first column of data in the table), the leading contraceptive method is the oral contraceptive. Over 27 percent were using the pill in the 2006–2010 period. The second most popular method is female sterilization, at 26.6 percent. These two methods have been the most popular contraceptive methods among US women since 1982.

How do these patterns of contraceptive use differ for the four groups of women according to marital status? Among currently married women and formerly married women, the most popular method is female sterilization; over 30 percent of married women have been contraceptively sterilized, and over 55 percent of formerly married women have been sterilized. But among cohabiting women and among **single** (never married) women who are not cohabiting, the most popular method is the pill. Almost 47 percent of single women who are contraceptive users are using the oral contraceptive.

Among the married women and formerly married women who are using contraception, the second most popular method is the oral contraceptive. But for cohabiting women, the second most popular method is sterilization, and for single women the second most popular method is the male condom.

I noted earlier that the second most popular method worldwide is the IUD. Among US women, the IUD is not one of the most favored methods. The IUD is used by only 7 percent of married women, 6 percent of cohabiting women, 4 percent of formerly married women, and 3 percent of single women.

Here are some additional observations about the patterns of contraceptive use and nonuse of US women that are not reflected in the data I have shown in the above tables and the figure. Among users of contraception, the most popular method for young women is the pill; 49 percent of women aged 15–24 who are contracepting are using the pill. The percentage of pill users drops to 33 percent for contraceptors in their late 20s and to 10 percent for those in their early 40s. In contrast, 51 percent of all users aged 40–44 have been contraceptively sterilized; this percentage drops to 30 percent for contracepting women aged 30–34 and to 3 percent for contracepting women aged 20–24 (Jones, Mosher and Daniels, 2012: 17).

Among contracepting women in the United States, those with less education tend to rely on female sterilization, while those with more education use the pill. Only 11 percent of contracepting women without a high school education use the oral contraceptive, compared with 35 percent of

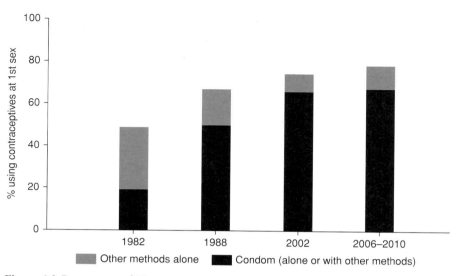

Figure 6.3 Percentage of Teenagers Using Contraceptives at First Sex: United States, 1982 to 2006–2010
Source: Guttmacher Institute (2014a: 2) (reprinted with permission of the Guttmacher Institute).

contracepting women holding at least a four-year college degree (Jones, Mosher, and Daniels, 2012: 19).

About 90 percent of US women in the childbearing ages report having engaged in sexual intercourse prior to marriage. Women on average have their first intercourse at age 17, but do not marry until the mid-20s. By age 20, over 70 percent of US women have had sexual intercourse and almost all are not married. I thus ask here about the use or nonuse of contraception in a woman's first premarital intercourse. This is an important question because the first premarital intercourse "marks the beginning of exposure to the risk of nonmarital pregnancy and birth and sexually transmitted infections" (Mosher et al., 2004: 5). Also, teenagers who do not use a contraceptive method the first time they have sex are twice as likely to become pregnant and have a baby compared with teenagers who do use a method the first time they have sex.

I show in Figure 6.3 for four different time periods the percentages of US females in their teens who reported using contraceptives at their first sexual experience. Among US teenage women who had their first intercourse in 1982, less than half (only 48 percent) used a method. This percentage has risen steadily over the years, reaching 75 percent for women whose first premarital intercourse occurred in 2002, and 78 percent for those whose first intercourse occurred in the 2006–2010 period. Also, the older the woman

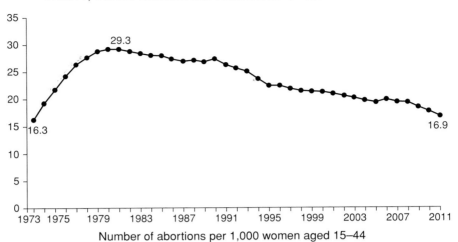

In 2011, the US abortion rate reached its lowest level since 1973

Number of abortions per 1,000 women aged 15–44

Figure 6.4 Number of Abortions per 1,000 Women Aged 15–44, by Year: United States, 1973–2011
Source: Guttmacher Institute (2014b) (reprinted with permission of the Guttmacher Institute).

at first nonmarital intercourse, the greater the likelihood she used a contraceptive method (Guttmacher Institute, 2014a).

What is known about abortion in the United States? Between 1973 and 2011, around 53 million legal abortions were performed in the United States. In 2011, there were just over 1 million legal abortions, a decrease from the 1.2 million abortions in 2008, which was a decrease from the 1.3 million performed in 2000. "The proportion of women expected to have an abortion by age 45 has declined substantially, from 43 percent in 1992 to 30 percent in 2008 ... Still, that almost one-third of women are anticipated to have had an abortion by age 45 suggests that it is not an uncommon procedure" (Jones and Kavanaugh, 2011: 1365). About one in five pregnancies in the United States ends in abortion; thus, abortion is now one of the most common surgical procedures experienced by US women. Discussion of its incidence and trends, I hold, is of major demographic and societal importance.

I show in Figure 6.4 abortion rates for US women from 1973 to 2011. The rate in 2011 of 16.9 abortions per 1,000 women aged 15–44 is the lowest the rate has ever been since the early 1970s. The rate was at its low of 16.3 in 1973, the first year in which abortions were legally permitted. It increased to a high of 29.3 in 1981 and has dropped steadily thereafter to its low value of 16.9 in 2011.

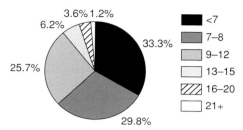

When women have abortions*
One-third of abortions occur at six weeks of pregnancy or earlier;
89% occur in the first twelve weeks, 2010

*In weeks from the last menstrual period.

Figure 6.5 Percentage of Abortions to US Women, by Time Period of Occurrence, 2010
Source: Guttmacher Institute (2014b) (reprinted with permission of the Guttmacher Institute).

Of the women having abortions in 2011, more than half of them (57 percent) were in their 20s; this breaks out with women aged 20–24 obtaining 33 percent of all abortions and women aged 25–29, 24 percent. In 2011, 30 percent of all abortions were obtained by NH-black women, 36 percent by NH-white women, 25 percent by Hispanic women, and 9 percent by women of other races. Regarding the religions of women having abortions in the United States in 2011, 37 percent of them were Protestants and 28 percent were Catholics. Women who have never married and are not presently cohabiting obtained 45 percent of all abortions, and women with one or more children had about 61 percent of the abortions (Guttmacher Institute, 2014b).

Abortions became legal in the United States in 1973 when the Supreme Court in the *Roe* v. *Wade* decision declared that "women, in consultation with their physician, have a constitutionally protected right to have an abortion in the early stages of pregnancy, that is, before the fetus is viable, free from government interference" (Guttmacher Institute, 2008: 2).

Figure 6.5 presents data on the time during their pregnancies when US women had abortions in 2010. The data indicate that 63 percent of all legal abortions were to women in the first eight weeks of their pregnancies, and 26 percent to women in the ninth through the twelfth weeks of their pregnancies. Thus, around 89 percent of all abortions performed in the United States in 2010 were to women in the first twelve weeks of their pregnancies, with only 1 percent performed in the twenty-first or later week of their pregnancies.

Having reviewed the patterns of family planning and abortion use and nonuse worldwide and in the United States, I turn in the next section to a discussion of each of the main methods of family planning. There are many kinds of family planning methods; some are controlled by females and others by males. This male–female categorization is "generally determined by which partner's body is most affected by the device's use" (Shepard, 1980: 72).

There are several ways to categorize contraceptives. One way is whether or not the contraceptive serves as a barrier to keep the man's sperm from entering the woman. Another category is whether the contraceptive contains hormones. And another is whether the contraceptive requires continuous input (e.g., the pill or the condom) or whether it is long-lasting (e.g., IUDs and implants). Still another way is to categorize or rank them on the basis of their efficacy in preventing pregnancy. This is the approach I will follow. In the next section, I first discuss the concept of contraceptive effectiveness and failure, and show how failure rates are measured and determined and what they mean. I then review each of the major contraceptive methods.

METHODS OF FAMILY PLANNING

The effectiveness of family planning methods may be measured in two ways, namely, in terms of **theoretical effectiveness** and in terms of **use effectiveness**. Theoretical effectiveness refers to the "efficaciousness" of the method when it is used "consistently according to a specified set of rules" and used all the time (Trussell, 2004: 91). In other words, it is the degree of effectiveness in preventing pregnancy that would occur with "perfect" use. Alternately, use effectiveness measures the effectiveness of the method taking into account the fact that some users do not follow the directions and the rules perfectly or carefully and/or may not use the method all the time; use effectiveness data tell us how effective the method is in **typical use**.

In Table 6.5, I report contraceptive failure percentage rates based on both use effectiveness and theoretical effectiveness data (the data are from Trussell and Guthrie, 2011: table 3-2). Use effectiveness data are empirical data gathered in surveys conducted in the past decade or so that studied the contraceptive and fertility behavior of women, mainly in the United States. Couples were surveyed about their use of specific family planning methods for specific periods of time, usually a year. The percentage of couples "typically" using a specific method and experiencing accidental pregnancies over the course of a year is the **failure rate** for that method according to use effectiveness data. One needs to keep in mind that typical use is broadly defined. In many of the surveys generating contraceptive use data, a woman is stated to be "using" a particular contraceptive method if "she considers herself to

Table 6.5 Contraceptive Failure Rates (Percentage of Women Experiencing an Unintended Pregnancy during the First Year of Use), by Contraceptive Method, according to Use (i.e., Typical) Effectiveness and Theoretical (i.e., Perfect) Effectiveness, United States, post-2000

Method	Use effectiveness	Theoretical effectiveness
No method	85	85
Spermicides*	28	18
Fertility awareness methods	24	–
Standard Days Method®	–	5
two-day method	–	4
ovulation method	–	3
symptothermal method	–	0.4
Withdrawal	22	4
Sponge		
parous women	24	20
nulliparous women	12	9
Female condom**	21	5
Male condom**	18	2
Diaphragm†	12	6
Combined pill & progestin-only pill	9	0.3
Ortho Evra patch	9	0.3
Vaginal ring, NuvaRing	9	0.3
Injectables, Depo-Provera	6	0.2
IUD		
ParaGard	0.8	0.6
Mirena	0.2	0.2
Female sterilization	0.5	0.5
Male sterilization	0.15	0.10
Implanon	0.05	0.05

Notes: * foams, creams, gels, and vaginal suppositories; ** without spermicides; † with spermicidal cream or jelly.
Source: Trussell and Guthrie (2011: ch. 3, table 3-2).

be using that method. So, typical use of the condom could include actually using a condom only occasionally" (Trussell, 2004: 91). Or "a woman could report that she is 'using' the pill even though her supplies ran out several months ago" (Trussell and Guthrie, 2011: 53). Thus, we need to keep in mind that "typical use is a very elastic concept" (Trussell, 2004: 91). It includes imperfect use and is not a measure of the "inherent efficacy of a contraceptive method when used perfectly, correctly and consistently" (Kost et al., 2008: 11).

The contraceptive failure rates based on theoretical effectiveness refer to pregnancies that would be experienced if a particular method was used under ideal, perfect conditions, that is, if the method was always used and used exactly according to the instructions and the rules.

I begin by first asking how many pregnancies will occur if no contraception is used. The failure rate for the nonuse of contraception is based on studies of "populations in which the use of contraception is rare, and on couples who report that they stopped using contraceptives because they want to conceive" (Trussell, 2011: 780). The failure rate for nonuse is 85 percent. This means that if 100 sexually active couples were to use no contraception (i.e., were to engage in unprotected intercourse) over the course of a year, 85 percent of the women on average would experience an accidental pregnancy. The nonuse of contraception, obviously, has the highest pregnancy (or failure) rate.

Alternately, the contraceptive with the lowest failure rate, determined by both theoretical effectiveness data and use effectiveness data, is the implant. The popular implant brand of Implanon has a failure rate of 0.05 percent (later I will discuss this method in more detail). This means that for every 10,000 women using an Implanon implant, five would experience an unintended pregnancy in the course of one year of use.

Failure rates are shown in Table 6.5 for all the major types of contraceptives according to use effectiveness and theoretical effectiveness. I have ranked them from the highest failure rate to the lowest failure rate according to use effectiveness data.

Vaginal spermicides are the least effective contraceptive method based on use effectiveness, but they are more effective than no contraception. Spermicides are contraceptive creams, jellies, and foams that are inserted into the vagina prior to the onset of genital contact and sexual intercourse. They are "commonly marketed for use with a diaphragm, but they can also be used alone for contraception" (Cates and Harwood, 2011: 395). They should be placed in the vagina several minutes before sexual activity commences. To be maximally effective, they should cover the vagina mucus and cervix. Some spermicides require the use of an applicator for correct insertion. The spermicide needs to be reapplied before each coitus. In addition to creating a physical barrier to the movement of sperm, many spermicides contain the sperm-killing chemical nonoxynol-9 (N-9), which further reduces the chance of conception (the beginning of pregnancy) by damaging and killing sperm in the vagina.

The idea of vaginal contraceptives is very old. Aristotle described the use of oil of cedar and frankincense in olive oil to block the cervical entrance. During the Middle Ages, rock salt and alum were frequently used as vaginal contraceptives (Himes, [1936] 1970: 80). Much later, a sponge moistened with diluted lemon juice and inserted into the vagina was described as an "effective" contraceptive. During the 1920s and 1930s, numerous vaginal suppositories and foam tablets were developed and sold widely.

Vaginal spermicides are available in pharmacies and supermarkets in the United States without a prescription under such brand names as Advantage-S, Conceptrol, Crinone, Delfen Foam, Emko, Encare, Endometrin, Gynol II, Prochieve, and Today Sponge, among several others. Despite their large-scale accessibility and small expense, they are not very effective from the vantage of either use effectiveness or theoretical effectiveness. Under typical use, the failure rate is 28 percent, and 18 percent under perfect use. Moreover, the effectiveness of a spermicide depends on the particular type. Aerosol foams and creams tend to be more effective than jellies and foam tablets. Foam compares favorably with the effectiveness of the **calendar rhythm method** (see subsequent discussion), but as indicated by the failure rate data just mentioned, produces more failures than most other methods.

Their relative ineffectiveness is the major disadvantage of vaginal spermicides. Also, as already noted, the preparations must be administered several minutes before intercourse, which will thus tend to interrupt foreplay and is often inconvenient. They must be inserted high into the vagina to be most effective, and some women may do this only reluctantly or not at all. On the other hand, their use does not require medical supervision. There are no known adverse side effects except for mild burning, which can be experienced by both females and males, and vaginal irritation, which can often be corrected by switching to some other type of preparation. A positive side effect is that spermicides provide some vaginal lubrication.

A very small number of US women use spermicides as their regular contraceptive method, less than one-half of 1 percent. Their number is so small that they are included in the "Other methods" category in Table 6.4.

Fertility awareness methods refer to several so-called natural family planning methods that employ an awareness of information about the woman's menstrual cycle to predict the time of the month when the probabilities are high that she will become pregnant. They "depend on identifying the 'fertile window,' or the days in each menstrual cycle when intercourse is most likely to result in a pregnancy" (Jennings and Burke, 2011: 417). In general, most of these methods are just slightly more effective than spermicides and a little less effective than withdrawal (based on use effectiveness).

These methods require that a woman refrain from having intercourse during the time when the probabilities are high that she will become pregnant. Some of the fertility awareness methods are classified as "modern" and some as "traditional." The more effective ones use various kinds of symptomatic information about the woman and her menstrual cycle.

The traditional and least effective fertility awareness method is the calendar rhythm method, known also as periodic abstinence or continence. There are several calendar methods, the first of which was developed independently in 1920 by a Japanese scientist, Kyusaka Ogino, and by an Austrian scientist, Hermann Knaus. It was based on the idea that a women can avoid pregnancy if she refrains from intercourse around the time of ovulation, when the egg is produced. Generally, only one egg is produced per menstrual cycle, and it is potentially fertilizable for around twenty-four hours after ovulation. The sperm is believed to be viable in the female tract for as many as six or seven days (Ryder, 1993: 723; Segal, 2003: 171) and is thus capable of fertilizing an egg several days after intercourse occurs. Theoretically, couples who avoid intercourse during the period when the egg and sperm are viable should be able to avoid conception. The trick is finding out the exact time interval during which to avoid intercourse, which is not an easy task.

The notion that females cannot conceive during most of the menstrual cycle is very old (Himes, [1936] 1970), but some of the early ideas on which part of the cycle was not "safe" were incorrect. For instance, Knaus held that ovulation would always occur fourteen days prior to the start of the next menstrual cycle (Jutte, 2008: 204), a fact we now know not to be true. Others held that the woman was most likely to conceive immediately after her menstrual period ended; thus, the rest of the cycle was considered safe because she was thought to be sterile during that time. Frequently, women following these principles became pregnant, and the calendar rhythm method gained a poor reputation. For instance, there is the joke I often tell my demography students that persons practicing the rhythm method are known as parents. Since the method was defined as "natural" and not "artificial," it was deemed to be acceptable by the Roman Catholic Church, and hence sometimes came to be called "Vatican roulette" or "calendar love."

The calendar rhythm method is typically applied as follows. The woman records the length of her menstrual cycles for a time period of a year or more. The presumed time of ovulation is then determined for the shortest and longest cycles. Nineteen is subtracted from the shortest and ten from the longest. These calculations inform the woman when it is safe and not safe to engage in intercourse. For example, if a woman determines that her menstrual cycles range in length from thirty-one to thirty-five days, it would be safe for her to have intercourse for the first through the twelfth days of the cycle ($31 - 19 = 12$), not safe on the thirteenth through the

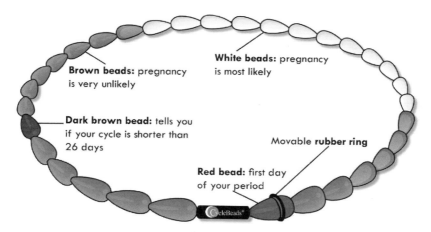

Figure 6.6 Standard Days Method® Necklace
Source: Institute for Reproductive Research, Georgetown University, Washington, DC, available at: http://irh.org/standard-days-method, last accessed July 1, 2015 (reprinted with permission of the Institute for Reproductive Research).

twenty-fourth days, and safe again starting on the twenty-fifth day (35−10 = 25) (Kipley and Kipley, 1996). Whereas few US women report using the calendar rhythm method (0.6 percent), there are no acceptable failure rate data available because "no well-designed prospective studies have been conducted, and no data are available from national surveys" (Jennings and Burke, 2011: 419). Thus, no data are shown for this method in Table 6.5.

Another fertility awareness method, the Standard Days Method®, also involves "counting the days in the menstrual cycle to identify the fertile days" (Jennings and Burke, 2011: 418). It is easy to use for women with menstrual cycles that last between twenty-six and thirty-two days. It is a variant of the calendar rhythm method just described, but is more effective (based on theoretical effectiveness data) and easier to learn and use. Developed by researchers at the Institute for Reproductive Health at Georgetown University, it is based on the principle that "women with regular menstrual cycles lasting 26–32 days can prevent pregnancy by avoiding unprotected intercourse on days eight through 19. This 12-day fertile window takes into account the variability in the timing of ovulation and the viability of sperm in the woman's reproductive tract" (Arévalo, Sinai, and Jennings, 1999; Gribble, 2003: 188). Thus, for pregnancy prevention, it is safe to engage in intercourse for the first seven days of the cycle, not safe from the eighth through the nineteenth days, and safe again from the twentieth day until the end of the cycle.

CycleBeads®, a string of color-coded beads to indicate fertile and infertile days, may be used by a woman to keep track of the days in her menstrual cycle (see Figure 6.6). The beads are colored either red, brown, or white;

the white beads are designed to glow in the dark. There is one red bead on the necklace, and it is used to mark the first day in the woman's menstrual cycle (i.e., the day she starts her menstrual period). Six brown beads follow the one red bead, and they signify the days when it is safe to have intercourse. Twelve white glow-in-the-dark beads follow the brown beads, and they signify days when it is not safe to have intercourse. They are then followed by brown beads signifying safe days until the menstrual period restarts, at which time the woman begins again by moving the ring to the red bead.

The woman is instructed to move a black marker ring each morning from one bead to the next (see Figure 6.6). Prior to engaging in intercourse, she checks the color of the bead; if it is white and glowing in the dark, it is not a safe day, if she wants to prevent a pregnancy.

The Standard Days Method® has been introduced in many developing countries to young women who are using contraceptives for the first time, many of whom find the method appealing. According to Gribble (2003: 188): "In trials conducted in El Salvador and India, up to one-half of women who adopted the method had never before practiced family planning, in large part because of concerns about side effects and a perceived threat to future fertility." There are no failure rate data available based on use effectiveness for the Standard Days Method®. Its failure rate based on theoretical effectiveness data is 5 percent (Table 6.5).

The other fertility awareness methods involve the "actual observation of fertility signs such as presence or absence of secretions, changes in characteristics of cervical secretions, or changes in basal body temperature" (Jennings and Burke, 2011: 418). The estimated time of ovulation may be calculated by use of a **basal body temperature** (BBT) chart. It is based on the principle that ovulation produces a rise in the basic metabolic rate, causing a corresponding increase in body temperature of between 0.3 and 0.9°C (between 0.5 and 1.6°F). The time of one's ovulation may thus be determined by reading and recording one's temperature daily. This technique greatly reduces the length of abstinence as required in the calendar rhythm method, but there are drawbacks. For instance, changes in body temperature are slight and easily misinterpreted, and the principle of an increase in temperature at the time of ovulation may not necessarily apply to all women (Shepard, 1980).

Another way for determining the time of ovulation is based on the association between the presence of cervical mucus and ovulation. Vaginal mucus tends to become more moist and cervical secretions more watery as the body prepares for ovulation. By slipping her finger into her vagina on a daily basis and checking on the moistness of the mucus and the consistency of the secretions, a woman, with appropriate training, can detect when ovulation is about to occur and when it has passed.

In Table 6.5, failure rate data based on theoretical effectiveness are presented for four different fertility awareness methods. I have already discussed the Standard Days Method® and its failure rate of 5 percent. The **two-day method** and the ovulation method (sometimes known as the **Billings ovulation method**) are based on the presence or absence of cervical secretions, and follow the research undertaken by John Billings, Evelyn Billings, and others starting in the 1950s (Billings, 1984; Billings et al., 1972; Billings and Westmore, 2000).

The rules for using the two-day method are easier than the rules for the ovulation method (Jennings and Burke, 2011: 426–429), but the two-day method has a slightly higher failure rate (4 percent) than the ovulation method (3 percent); keep in mind that both of these failure rates are based on theoretical effectiveness.

The last fertility awareness method shown in Table 6.5 is the **symptothermal method**. It is a "combined, or symptothermal, approach (using) both cervical secretions and basal body temperature" to identify the times when pregnancy is likely. The rules for its use are more involved than those for the ovulation method (Jennings and Burke, 2011: 429–431), but its failure rate (based on theoretical effectiveness data) is the lowest of all the fertility awareness methods at 0.4 percent.

Except for the pregnancies that result from method failures, no known serious side effects are associated with any of the fertility awareness methods I have just reviewed. No special equipment is necessary (except, perhaps, for a calendar, or a thermometer, or a set of beads, or a chart). Their use does not require the interruption of sexual foreplay or the application of mechanical or chemical devices, and all these methods are acceptable to the Roman Catholic Church. However, their effective use requires a high degree of motivation by both partners and the ability to estimate accurately the day of ovulation. There is also a mental disadvantage, that is, the extra worry some users may experience knowing in advance the probability of failure. The various fertility awareness methods have very low use rates among US women (Table 6.3).

The next method I discuss is withdrawal, also known as coitus interruptus and as the pull-out method. With coitus interruptus, "the couple may have penile–vaginal intercourse until ejaculation is impending, at which time the male partner withdraws his penis from the vagina and away from the external genitalia of the female partner. The man must rely on his own sensations to determine when he is about to ejaculate" (Kowal, 2011: 410). Coitus interruptus may be distinguished from a similar method with the same end result, namely, **coitus reservatus**, also known as **amplexus reservatus**. With the coitus reservatus method, the male enters his partner, does not ejaculate, and endeavors to remain at the plateau phase of sexual intercourse and excitement, thus prolonging and sometimes intensifying pleasure. It differs from coitus interruptus in that ejaculation does not occur or is delayed indefinitely.

Coitus interruptus is one of the oldest known contraceptive practices (Jutte, 2008). It is mentioned in the Old Testament (Genesis 38), and its use has been reported by field researchers in many parts of the world. In fact, demographers believe that withdrawal played a major role in the fertility decline that was part of the demographic transition in France during the nineteenth century (Ryder, 1959; Shepard, 1980: 74). As I will mention later in Chapter 12, the changes in the social and economic structure that accompanied industrialization rewarded smaller families and made large families much more costly. Modern contraceptives had not yet been developed, and withdrawal was a culturally acceptable method that was known and available. This illustrates nicely, I believe, how social, economic, and cultural factors affect the use of birth control methods.

To be used effectively, withdrawal requires a tremendous amount of self-control and trust. The male must have near-complete control of his sexual sensations and know exactly when he is about to reach the time of sexual excitement when ejaculation cannot be stopped or delayed; he must pull his penis out of the woman before this time occurs. But even if he withdraws his penis in time, the pre-ejaculate fluid often picks up enough sperm in the urethra from a previous ejaculation that an unintended pregnancy will still sometimes occur. Thus, the man should urinate between ejaculations to rid his urethra of leftover sperm. Even if the male withdraws his penis in time, but deposits the ejaculate or pre-ejaculate on or near the woman's vagina, pregnancy will sometimes occur (Segal and Nordberg, 1977).

The Roman Catholic Church objects to the use of withdrawal on moral grounds, owing to the belief that every act of intercourse must have the possibility of resulting in conception (Jutte, 2008; Noonan, 1966). And some believe that withdrawal is a physically and psychologically damaging technique, although there is no solid evidence to support this view. However, the method does require the complete cooperation of the male partner, as well as practice and considerable motivation. Obviously, coitus interruptus is not a good method for males who tend to ejaculate prematurely. Also, it is not recommended for males with little or no sexual experience because a lot of experience is required before a male can predict with a reasonable amount of certainty that ejaculation is about to occur. On the positive side, there is no financial expense associated with the use of withdrawal, and it requires no special preparation or equipment.

Withdrawal has a high failure rate according to use effectiveness data at 22 percent (Table 6.5). Only a small percentage of all US women (3.2 percent) report this as their method of contraception (Table 6.3).

I next discuss the **contraceptive sponge**, a vaginal spermicide designed for a single use. It is a "small, pillow shaped polyurethane sponge" that contains 1 gram of spermicide. "The concave dimple on one side is designed to fit over the cervix and decrease the chance of dislodgement during intercourse . . . The other side of the sponge incorporates a woven polyester loop to facilitate removal." The woman moistens it with water and inserts it deep into her vagina. It protects for twenty-four hours "no matter how many times intercourse occurs" (Cates and Harwood, 2011: 395–396). Its failure rates are different for parous and nulliparous women. For **parous women** (parous women are those who have previously given birth) the failure rate based on use effectiveness is 24 percent. For **nulliparous women** (those who have not previously given birth), the failure rate is half as high (Table 6.5).

Another barrier method is the condom, for both males and females. The male **condom** was not popularized until the late nineteenth century. However, it was first mentioned as far back as 1564 in the posthumous writings on syphilis of the Italian anatomist Gabriele Falloppio (who also described the Fallopian tubes, which were named after him). Falloppio recommended that condoms be used to prevent venereal disease (Jutte, 2008: 96). **Female condoms**, on the other hand, made a much later appearance; they were invented and popularized by the Danish medical doctor Lasse Hessel and launched worldwide in 1991. Under the brand name Reality, female condoms were first marketed in the United States in 1992.

The male condom is a mechanical barrier that fits snugly over the penis and prevents the ejaculated sperm from entering the vagina. Condoms have many names, for example, rubber, prophylactic, safe, raincoat, sheath, and jimmie. Himes has written that "the French call the condom 'le capot anglais' or English cape; the English have returned the compliment; to them it is the 'French letter'" (Himes, [1936] 1970: 194).

The condom's first recorded appearance was in the sixteenth century when it was recommended as a prophylactic against venereal disease. Its contraceptive effects at that time were incidental. Condoms were made of linen and were not very effective. Those made from sheep intestines first appeared in the eighteenth century. Tietze, among others, has noted that this innovation "has been attributed to an Englishman named Cundum, sometimes identified, although erroneously, as a physician at the court of Charles II" (Tietze, 1965: 70; see also Bernstein, 1940; and Himes, [1936] 1970: 191–194). But it was not until the vulcanization of rubber in the mid-nineteenth century that condom use became possible on a large scale. The introduction of liquid latex in the mid-1930s greatly facilitated the production of condoms with greater tensile strength, allowing them to last longer before decaying.

Driven by both the need for a safe and relatively effective contraceptive method and the important role that condoms now play in HIV intervention, the global condom market is forecasted to approach a value of US $5.2 billion by 2018 (Companies and Markets, 2015).

Condoms are moderately effective. Almost all failures result from nonuse and/or incorrect use rather than from defects in the condoms themselves. The rules for perfect condom use are not few in number (see Warner and Steiner, 2011: 382–384). The failure rate for male condoms based on use effectiveness is 18 percent (Table 6.5). Male condoms, especially when used with vaginal spermicides, are more effective than most of the other methods I have so far discussed. However, the male condom requires some interruption of sexual foreplay. An even larger drawback is decreased sensitivity for some males. Its major advantages are its effectiveness and the fact that it has no medical side effects. Condoms are easy to buy and store, and their use requires no special training. Medical examination, supervision, and follow-up are not necessary. Most important, in addition to providing visible postcoital evidence of effectiveness, condoms offer effective protection against venereal disease. More than 10 percent of all US women in the childbearing ages report that the male condom is their main method of contraception (Table 6.3).

The female condom is a female-initiated barrier method and its failure rate of 21 percent is only slightly higher than that of the male condom. It has many of the advantages of the male condom, but fewer of its disadvantages. It is a soft and strong transparent polyurethane sheath about the same length as a male condom (around 6.5 inches), with a flexible ring at each end. It is inserted into the vagina prior to intercourse. The inner ring at the closed end of the condom is used to insert it into the vagina; the ring then moves into place behind the pubic bone. The outer ring at the open end of the condom is soft and remains outside the vagina. Since its use does not depend on the male having an erection, it usually does not interrupt the spontaneity of the sex act. Moreover, unlike the male condom, it does not need to be removed immediately after ejaculation. Because it lines the vagina loosely, not tightly, some persons, particularly males, find the female condom more satisfying sexually than the male condom.

There is a very informative YouTube film (just over 3 minutes long) produced by the Women's Collective about the female condom, its use, directions and rules. You may view it at: www.youtube.com/watch?v=NQ5N6WJFHMQ. The distribution of the female condom has increased worldwide since first becoming available at a reduced cost in the mid-1990s, but it has nowhere near the impact on the world market as the male condom.

Two more vaginal barrier methods are the diaphragm and the **cervical cap**. The vaginal diaphragm is a device that erects a barrier between the sperm and the ova. It is a soft rubber vaginal cup with a metal spring reinforcing the rim. It should be inserted into the vagina at any time from one to two hours before sexual activity and should be left in place for six to eight hours after the last ejaculation. It functions mainly to block the access of sperm to the cervix (the opening to the uterus) and is held in place by the spring tension rim, the woman's vaginal muscle tone, and the pubic bone. Although the diaphragm acts as a barrier to most of the sperm, it usually does not fit tightly enough to prevent passage of all of the sperm. Thus, diaphragms should be used with a spermicidal cream or jelly.

A cervical cap is a small, thimble-shaped cup that also serves as a barrier contraceptive by fitting over the cervix. The first modern cervical caps were developed in 1838 by the German gynecologist Friedrich Wilde when he prepared custom-made rubber molds of the cervix for his patients (Himes, [1936] 1970: 211). Today, caps are made of latex or silicone. They provide a more effective mechanical block against sperm than diaphragms. Thus, spermicidal mixtures are not as necessary with cervical caps as they are with diaphragms, but they are still recommended. Cervical caps are much more effective when used by nulliparous women than by parous women.

Diaphragms and cervical caps were first developed for contraceptive use during the nineteenth century. The diaphragm was popularized in the early twentieth century by Margaret Sanger (I will have more to say about her when I discuss later the oral contraceptive). However, it lost favor "with the advent of non-event-related methods such as the IUD and oral contraceptive" (Shepard, 1980: 75). In combination with a contraceptive jelly or cream, the diaphragm and cap were the methods most often recommended by physicians in private practice and by birth control clinics throughout the United States and Europe during the 1930s and 1940s (Peel and Potts, 1969: 62–63). About one-third of American couples who tried to plan their families during the 1940s used diaphragms or cervical caps.

Even when properly used with a spermicide, the diaphragm has a relatively high failure rate of 12 percent according to use effectiveness, although lower at 6 percent according to theoretical effectiveness (Table 6.5). It is only somewhat more effective than spermicides and some other methods. In addition to nonuse because of insufficient motivation, diaphragm failures are due to lack of knowledge regarding proper insertion, an improper fit, displacement during intercourse, and defects in the diaphragm itself. So few women report using the diaphragm or cervical cap that these two methods are included in the "other methods" category in Table 6.3.

There are no known serious physiological side effects for either the diaphragm or cervical cap. They do not require the cooperation of the male partner and are used only when needed. Hence, they are both convenient methods for women who engage in sexual intercourse infrequently and do not need continuous protection. Using a spermicidal cream or jelly also produces additional vaginal lubrication during intercourse. However, since the diaphragm or cervical cap should be inserted several hours before intercourse, as already mentioned, its use requires the user to know in advance when she will have intercourse; otherwise, she will have to interrupt sexual foreplay to insert the device. Regular use requires considerable motivation. Some women do not like the process of insertion, and other women view it as messy because of the spermicide.

Diaphragms and cervical caps must be fitted by trained personnel, who teach the user the proper insertion techniques. Both seem particularly ill-suited for use in many developing countries, where there is often a lack of privacy for insertion and removal, as well as a convenient source of clean water for washing the devices after use. Moreover, there tends to be a shortage of medical personnel available for fitting the devices, and the need for a constant supply of spermicidal creams or jellies makes this barrier method relatively expensive (Wortman, 1976).

The next most effective and modern type of contraceptives are hormonal-based methods, of which the oral contraceptive, that is, the **birth control pill**, or "the pill," is the most popular. I will first review how hormonal methods work. The first oral contraceptives marketed in the 1960s were known as "combined" pills because they contained the two hormones similar to the estrogen and progesterone produced by the ovary and governed by the pituitary gland. When a woman ingests the hormones contained in the pill, one might say that her pituitary is "fooled" into thinking that she is already pregnant. Thus, there is no need for the pituitary "to send out hormones to stimulate the ovaries [into egg production] if there are already [in the woman] high levels of ovarian-type hormones" (Guillebaud, 2005: 7). The combined birth control pill containing both estrogen and progestin (a type of progesterone) thus prevents conception primarily by preventing ovulation. There are two additional factors that contribute to its contraceptive effect. Because ovulation does not occur, the consistency of the cervical mucus is maintained in a state that the sperm cannot easily penetrate. Also, because the full secretory pattern is not reached, the inner lining of the uterus is usually not suitable for implantation of the fertilized egg.

Today, there are several different hormonal methods, and they differ according to the type of hormone(s) in the contraceptive, the amount of the hormone(s) in the contraceptive, the way the woman receives the hormone(s), and whether the exposure to the hormone(s) is continuous or periodic. As already noted, the hormones are estrogen and progestin, and they may be received by the woman orally or via a patch, injected under her skin, implanted into a tissue, or placed into her vagina.

The first hormonal-based method was the oral contraceptive. Margaret Sanger (1879–1966) of the Planned Parenthood Federation of America, with funds from Katherine McCormick (1875–1967), a suffragist and philanthropist from Massachusetts, supported a reproductive physiologist, Gregory Pincus (1903–1967), who was the Director of the Worcester Foundation for Experimental Biology in Shrewsbury, Massachusetts, and John Rock (1890–1984), who was a Professor of Gynecology and Obstetrics at the Harvard Medical School in Cambridge, to develop a simple and effective oral contraceptive. Their story and collaboration are recounted in a lively, extremely interesting and fun book to read, by Jonathan Eig, *The Birth of the Pill: How Four Crusaders Reinvented Sex and Launched a Revolution* (2014). I recommend it highly.

In 1953–1954, Pincus and his collaborators tested a steroid for ovulation inhibition. Pincus and Rock then began work formulating a birth control pill at the Worcester Foundation. Pincus headed the science side of the research, and Rock directed the clinical trials to show that this new pill was safe and effective. The pill was first tested on some of Rock's patients in Boston, but systematic trials could not be performed because it was a felony in Massachusetts at that time to dispense contraceptives. The tests were moved to Puerto Rico, and later to Haiti, Mexico, and Los Angeles. The work of Pincus and Rock led eventually to G. D. Searle and Company marketing the oral contraceptive in the United States in 1960 as Enovid-10®.

Also playing a part in these efforts was Carl Djerassi, a chemist, who in 1951 led a research team in the first synthesis of a steroid oral contraceptive (see chapter 5 in his autobiography [Djerassi, 1992] for an interesting account of this discovery). Pincus, Rock, and Djerassi are sometimes referred to as the "fathers" of the oral contraceptive, although Djerassi referred to himself as its "mother" (Marks, 2001: 11). I would argue, however, that it is Margaret Sanger who is the "mother" of the pill.

John Rock was a devoted and devout Roman Catholic who believed that the newly invented birth control pill should and would be approved by the Roman Catholic Church. He compared the birth control pill to the calendar rhythm method, which had been approved earlier in 1951 by Pope Pius XII. Like the rhythm method, the pill did not kill sperm or obstruct the passage of sperm into the female tract. It suppressed ovulation with a combination of estrogen and progestin, much like a woman's body suppressed ovulation during pregnancy. Rock's landmark book published in 1963, *The Time Has Come: A Catholic Doctor's Proposals to End the Battle over Birth Control*, was a conscientious and honorable effort to justify the pill as a natural method of birth control. Although ghost-written by professionals of the Planned Parenthood Federation of America, the book clearly represented Rock's views and opinions (Tentler, 2008). The book noted that "the pills, when properly taken, are not at all likely to disturb menstruation, nor do they mutilate any organ of the body, nor damage any natural process. They merely offer to the human intellect the means to regulate ovulation harmlessly, means which heretofore have come only from the ovary, and during pregnancy, from the placenta" (Rock, 1963: 169).

Rock was deeply disappointed in 1968 when Pope Paul VI published his encyclical *Humanae Vitae* (Latin for "Of Human Life") declaring that oral contraceptives and all other so-called artificial methods of birth control were immoral. The papal declarations in *Humanae Vitae* were exactly the opposite of the recommendations of the majority report of a papal committee, that is, the Papal Birth Control Commission, which was established by the Vatican to study and make recommendations regarding oral contraception (the Commission, by the way, had two demographers among its members). Robert McClory's *Turning Point* (1995) is a dramatic story of the workings of the Commission. Margaret Marsh and Wanda Ronner's biography of John Rock, *The Fertility Doctor* (2008), is "a balanced portrait of a twentieth-century medical giant" (Tentler, 2008: 24) and describes in detail the kind of conflicts that Dr. Rock had with his Catholic Church.

Once introduced in the United States and other countries in 1960, the oral contraceptive became extremely popular, and remains so today. It is known simply as "the pill." If a woman informs her male friend that she forgot to take her "pill" for the past several days, he does not think to himself, "I wonder if she is referring to an aspirin or a sleeping pill or a vitamin pill or some other kind of pill." He knows exactly and right away that she is referring to the birth control pill.

I reported earlier (see Tables 6.1 and 6.3) that 8 percent of married women worldwide and 17 percent of women in the United States are using the oral contraceptive. Almost 8 million women in the United States use the oral contraceptive, as do around 104 million women worldwide (Guttmacher Institute, 2015).

When the oral contraceptive was first introduced in the early 1960s, its major disadvantage was adverse side effects. Some of them were nuisances, such as headaches, weight gain, and morning nausea, but many users found them so discomforting that they discontinued using the pill. Some of the side effects were life-threatening. Thromboembolic (blood-clotting) disorders are but one example. Although the more common superficial leg thromboses (or phlebitis) are not very dangerous, cerebrovascular diseases (strokes that are also thrombic) are potentially fatal. The estrogen content of the pill was primarily responsible for the thromboembolic problems. Other negative side effects included increased blood pressure and vaginal dryness (Guillebaud, 2005). There is also a demonstrated interaction between cigarette smoking and pill use and the incidence of heart disease. However, the oral contraceptives produced today "contain less than one-twentieth of the dose of the original pills, which results in a lower incidence of side effects" (Segal, 2003: 171).

Other side effects of the pill have been shown to be beneficial, such as those associated with the physical and emotional aspects of menstruation. These include decreased incidence of menorrhagia (heavy bleeding), dysmenorrhea (cramps), iron deficiency anemia, and premenstrual tension. Hence, for many women, oral contraceptives produce more regular menstrual cycles that are shorter in duration, produce less bleeding and abdominal discomfort, and are accompanied by less premenstrual tension than is normally the case (Potts, Diggory, and Peel, 1977: 38). There are several additional noncontraceptive health benefits, namely, "decreased risk of endometrial and ovarian cancer, decreased risk of colon cancer...and maintenance of bone density" (Segal, 2003: 171).

The modern oral contraceptive is either a combined pill containing estrogen and progestin, known as the **combined oral contraceptive**, or a pill containing only progestin, known as the **progestin-only pill**, or sometimes as the **mini-pill**. The combined pill is monophasic, biphasic, or triphasic, referring to the amounts of estrogen and progestin provided each day. A monophasic pill provides a constant amount of estrogen and progestin every day, while the other two types provide varying amounts (Nelson and Cwiak, 2011: 256–257). Depending on the manufacturer (there are around forty different combination pills produced), most combination pills come in either twenty-one- or twenty-eight-day packages. With the former, the woman takes a pill each day for twenty-one days and no pill for seven days when menstruation occurs, and then the process is repeated. With the twenty-eight-day packet, the hormonal medication is present in the pills for the first twenty-one days, and the pills for the last seven days are placebos.

The progestin-only pill, or the mini-pill, the other type of oral contraceptive, was first marketed in the United States in 1973. It consists of a small dose of progestin, which is taken daily, even during menstruation. It reduces the side effects of the combined pill, and it also makes available an oral contraceptive for women who breast-feed their children or who should avoid estrogen for health reasons. The mini-pill does not include estrogen; therefore, it does not always result in the suppression of ovulation. Thus, many of the menstrual periods of progestin-only pill users are natural. The mini-pill functions as a contraceptive mainly "by interfering with the passage of sperm through the mucus at the entrance to the uterus" (Guillebaud, 2005: 176), whether or not an egg has been released. In this sense, the mini-pill acts more like a barrier method of contraceptive, albeit one that is taken orally. The mini-pill also prevents pregnancy; since the **endometrium** (the lining of the uterus) is altered, the result is that a fertilized egg is not being implanted, if indeed ovulation does occur (Raymond, 2011b: 237). The mini-pill is not as popular as the combined pill; currently there are a half dozen or so brands on the market, for example, Camila, Errin, Heather, and Jolivette.

Both the combined oral contraceptive pill and the mini-pill are very effective. The data in Table 6.5 show that according to use effectiveness data, the combined pill and the progestin-only pill have a failure rate of 9 percent and a much lower rate of 0.3 percent according to theoretical effectiveness. Most of the pregnancies that occur to pill users result from the failure to take it regularly. The major advantages are its high effectiveness and the fact that its use does not interfere with the sexual act in any way. It is not necessary to interrupt foreplay or to conclude sexual activity right after coition. Moreover, the pill allows the female to use contraception independently of any cooperation by the male (or even of his knowledge). Over 17 percent of all US women use either the combined pill or the mini-pill. Among contracepting women in the United States, the pill is the most popular method for cohabiting women and for single women who are not cohabiting; almost 47 percent of contracepting women who are single and not cohabiting are using the pill (Table 6.4).

I noted previously that hormonal contraceptives need not only be administered orally. There are several other hormonal contraception delivery systems, one of which is the transdermal **contraceptive patch**. It was "approved by the U.S. Federal Drug Administration (FDA) in 2002. It is a thin, flexible, $20cm^2$ patch with three layers: a beige outer protective polyester layer; a middle medicated adhesive layer; and a clear liner" (Nanda, 2011: 343). The patch is about the size of a 50-cent piece that is placed on the buttocks, arm, or stomach. It works like the combination pill just discussed, except that instead of requiring the user to engage in a daily regimen, it is based on a weekly regimen. A new patch is placed on the skin once every seven days. The two hormones are released from the patch at a constant and continuous level each day. After three weeks, no patch is used for one week, to allow menstruation to occur. The one brand of birth control patch now on the market is Ortho-Evra. It has the same effectiveness numbers as the combined pill and mini-pill. A very small percentage of US women use the patch (Nanda, 2011).

A woman may also receive the contraceptive hormones by inserting into her vagina a **vaginal ring**, under the brand name NuvaRing®. It was approved by the FDA in 2001. It is a thin, transparent, flexible ring and is similar to the combined pill; it contains both estrogen and progestin, which are released on a continuous basis into the woman's body. It is inserted by the woman into her vagina usually during the first five days of her menstrual period and remains in place for three weeks. She then withdraws it, throws it away, and does not use a ring for a week, during which time menstruation occurs. A new ring is then inserted after seven days. Since the vaginal ring is not a barrier method like the diaphragm or cap or female condom, the exact and precise placement of the ring in the vagina is not a major issue. The vaginal ring has the same effectiveness numbers as the pill and the patch (Nanda, 2011).

Another way for women to receive hormonal contraception is through contraception injection. The most commonly used brand in the United States is Depo-Provera® and is similar to the progestin-only pill; it "prevents pregnancy primarily by inhibiting ovulation ... (it) also prevents pregnancy by thickening and decreasing cervical mucus ... (which) prevents sperm penetration" (Bartz and Goldberg, 2011: 210). Another brand, Lunelle®, similar to the combined pill, was previously available in the United States, but was withdrawn in 2002. Depo-Provera is administered via an injection by a health professional once every twelve weeks in the arm, buttocks, upper thigh, or abdomen. The economic cost is about the same as the birth control pill (Bartz and Goldberg, 2011).

Depo-Provera has a low use-effectiveness failure rate of 6 percent (Table 6.5). When failures (pregnancies) occur, they will mainly be due to the fact that the woman did not have her shots at the prescribed intervals. The failure rate based on theoretical effectiveness is a mere 0.2 percent. A woman typically stops having periods altogether after one year of use.

Still another way for the woman to receive hormonal contraception is via a **subdermal contraceptive implant**. The first implant was developed in the 1980s under the brand name of Norplant® (Sivin, Nash, and Waldman, 2002). It consisted of six small silicone capsule-type rods, each containing progestin, placed subdermally in the woman's upper arm, to remain in effect for five years. The implants were usually visible and resembled small veins. The Norplant implant has been phased out in favor of implants with fewer capsule rods. The main implant now available in the United States is Implanon®, containing one rod with protection for three years (Sivin, Nash, and Waldman, 2002; Raymond, 2011a). However, as of the writing of this chapter (July 2015), the manufacturer of Implanon, Merck, is phasing out

Implanon and replacing it with Nexplanon®. Both are single rod implants and are nearly identical, except that the insertion of Nexplanon has been simplified.

An obvious advantage of the implant is that a single visit to a clinic once every three years for an implant is substituted for the daily consumption of birth control pills, or the weekly employment of a patch, or the triweekly insertion of a vaginal ring, or the monthly or trimonthly birth control shot. The major advantage of the implant, however, is its effectiveness. It is the most effective of all contraceptives, including male and female sterilization. According to both use and theoretical effectiveness data, the failure rate for Implanon® is a miniscule 0.05 percent (Table 6.5) (Raymond, 2011a: 195; Ramchandran and Upadhyay, 2007). This means that after a year of usage, five pregnancies will occur, on average, for every 10,000 users of Implanon®.

Actually, Raymond has noted that "to date [that is, as of 2011 when her research was published], no pregnancies have been observed in prospective or retrospective cohort studies of Implanon, which included a total of more than 4,500 women and more than 7,000 women-years of exposure" (2011a: 195). There have been a few failures reported to medical authorities to women not included in statistically representative surveys; but most of the few failures were due to the "non-insertion of the implant" or to the fact that the pregnancies had been conceived "before the women had Implanon inserted" (Raymond, 2011a: 195).

All the aforementioned family planning methods that I have just reviewed are reversible; that is, a woman and her partner may use any of them and then decide later to stop using them if a pregnancy is desired.

The next method I discuss, **surgical sterilization** performed for contraceptive purposes, is rarely reversible. Surgical sterilization may be performed on both males and females. In the female, the sterilization is known as tubal ligation (tying of the tubes). It consists of cutting, tying, and removing a portion of the oviduct, that is, the Fallopian tubes. Female sterilization may be performed in one of several ways.

Laparoscopic sterilization is a sterilizing procedure using a laparoscope (from the Greek words *lapara*, meaning flank; and *skopein*, meaning to examine; the word thus means "look inside the abdomen"). It requires general anesthesia, during which a small incision is introduced near the woman's belly button and a second incision may be made right above the pubic hairline. A laparoscope, that is, a telescope-like device, is then inserted through the first incision so that the physician or operator can view the Fallopian tubes. Rings or clips are then inserted through the second incision (or if there is no second incision, through the first) and used to close the Fallopian tubes.

Minilaparotomy is a surgical sterilization procedure performed on a woman a few days after she delivers a baby. A general anesthesia is required. The operator makes a small incision in the woman's abdomen and then cuts and removes a piece of each of the Fallopian tubes (Roncari and Hou, 2011: 450–451)

Hysteroscopic sterilization, also known as the **Essure® procedure**, is performed using only a local anesthesia. A tiny coil insert is introduced into each of the Fallopian tubes through the vagina and uterus. The introduction of the Essure mechanism in each tube causes the development of scar tissues over a three-month period, resulting in both tubes becoming sealed (Conceptus, Inc., 2010).

Female sterilization is very effective. It has a failure rate of only 0.5 percent based on both use and theoretical effectiveness data. It frees the woman and her partner from ever again having to worry about an accidental pregnancy. But since it is a permanent form of contraception, it is not an appropriate method for persons who wish to delay a pregnancy to a later time or who are not completely certain that they wish to have no more (or no) children. Almost 17 percent of all US women have been sterilized. Also it is the most popular form of family planning worldwide (Table 6.1).

Quinacrine sterilization (QS) is an interesting method of nonsurgical female sterilization currently being researched and evaluated. The renowned family planning researcher and scholar, Malcolm Potts, former President of Family Health International and now Professor of Population and Family Planning at the University of California Berkeley, has noted that "QS is the most important new method of family planning since the Pill" (Donald A. Collins, pers. comm. with Leon F. Bouvier, May 26, 2008).

QS is a sterilization method that most women worldwide can afford because each application is manufactured for around US$1.00. The woman receives two treatments, one month apart, of seven tiny quinacrine pellets. They are placed into the uterus through the vagina using the same kind of inserter employed with IUDs. The pellets dissolve and flow into the openings of the Fallopian tubes where they cause a minor swelling that results in scar tissue, which closes the tubes. It is similar in concept to the Essure procedure, except that it is easier to administer, far cheaper, and less taxing on the patient (Collins, pers. comm. with Bouvier, 2008).

But the QS method is not without controversy (Schwartz and Gabelnick, 2011: 527). Its side effects are not fully known, and research continues with regard to this method (Whitney, 2003).

Male sterilization is known as **vasectomy**. It involves cutting, tying, and removing a portion of the spermatic duct, that is, the vas deferens. There are several ways the surgery may be performed. I will discuss two approaches. The traditional vasectomy is a minor procedure that occurs under local anesthetic. The surgeon makes one incision in the skin on each of the two sides of the scrotum to expose the tubes of the vas deferens from each testicle. The vas deferens tube is lifted from the scrotum, cut, and tied, or sometimes cauterized. The separated tubes are then returned to the scrotum and a few stitches are used to close the two incisions. After having a vasectomy, a man is still capable of ejaculating semen, but the semen no longer contains sperm.

A second approach to male sterilization is the **no-scalpel vasectomy** (also known as **keyhole vasectomy**). It was devised in 1974 by a surgeon in China, Li Shunqiang, and is now employed worldwide. It has been used in the United States since 1988. In this method, as its name indicates, no scalpel is employed, but there is still the need for a small opening to be made in the scrotum. The doctor applies a local anesthetic (which may be introduced without a needle) and then uses his or her hand to find the vas deferens under the scrotal skin. A very small set of pointed forceps then works to separate the scrotal tissue and to create a keyhole-type opening in the skin. Then, as with the traditional vasectomy procedure, the tubes of the vas deferens are lifted from the scrotal sac, cut, and tied, or sometimes cauterized, and then placed back into the scrotum. Because the scrotal skin opening is so small, it may not need to be closed with sutures (Roncari and Hou, 2011: 468–471)

Male sterilization is a very effective contraceptive method. Its failure rates of 0.15 percent and 0.10 percent based, respectively, on use effectiveness data and theoretical effectiveness data (Table 6.5) are even lower than those for female sterilization. Moreover, compared with female sterilization, male sterilization is faster to perform, requires only a local anesthetic, is less expensive, and presents less risk of complications. Finally, although sterilization reversal is a difficult operation and does not have high rates of success, it is sometimes a little easier to reverse a male sterilization than a female sterilization.

Overall, the effectiveness of sterilization varies according to the technique used by the physician and the gender of the patient. According to the failure rates just noted, there are very few failures. Most failures result from inadequate surgical procedures or because the tubes grow back together. Some men who obtain vasectomies have unprotected intercourse too soon after the operation. If this occurs before all the sperm-containing semen already stored in the reproductive tract has been expelled, then pregnancy could result. However, this is a short-term problem that is easily avoided.

Because a sterilization is only performed once, this method does not require continuous motivation. It does not interfere with sexual enjoyment in any way. But it is difficult to reverse, so it is not suitable for persons who might change their minds about not wanting more children. Although the development and use of microsurgical techniques have greatly increased the chance of reversibility among vasectomy patients, most physicians still consider surgical sterilization a permanent form of contraception.

Surgical sterilization does not lower the sexual drive or capabilities of the male or female. Indeed, males with vasectomies often report increased enjoyment of sex, which is usually attributed to freedom from anxiety about their partners becoming pregnant. The male partners of over 6 percent of contracepting women in the United States have been sterilized (Table 6.3).

The IUD, a device with or without hormones that is placed in the uterus, is the most widely used reversible contraceptive method in the world. The idea of placing devices in the uterus to prevent conception is fairly old. Giacomo Casanova, the eighteenth-century Italian adventurer and libertine, recommended the use of a gold ball for this purpose (Himes, [1936] 1970: 180). The antecedent of the modern IUD was the **stem pessary**, developed in the late 1860s. This was a small button or cap that covered the opening of the cervix and was attached to stems extending into the cervical canal. In the 1920s, a German, Ernst Grafenberg, developed a silver ring that was placed in the uterus. In 1934, a Japanese scientist, Tenrei Ota, introduced a gold ring. Neither was accepted widely until the late 1950s (Peel and Potts, 1969: 128–129; Tietze, 1965: 79). The Lippes Loop was a popular type of IUD in the 1960s, as were several other types of plastic IUDs.

Research on modern IUDs was initiated at about the time oral contraception research was in its final stages. But, as has been noted by Segal, "despite intensive research, scientists (still) do not fully understand why the presence of a foreign body in the uterus prevents pregnancy. The evidence clearly indicates that the IUD is a pre-fertilization method: the presence of fertilized eggs in IUD users cannot be demonstrated" (2003: 173).

The two types of IUDs available in the United States today are both flexible polyethylene devices shaped like a "T." One has copper wire twisted about it and is known formally as Copper T 380A, or sometimes as the Copper T; the brand marketed in the United States is the **ParaGard® IUD**. Adding copper wire to the device increases its contraceptive effectiveness significantly, "although it is not known why the release of copper in the uterus is so effective in preventing pregnancy" (Segal, 2003: 173).

The other "T"-shaped IUD is formally known as Levonorgestrel IUD; the brand marketed in the United States is the **Mirena IUD**. It contains 52 mg of levonorgestrel (a second-generation progestin hormone), "which is released directly into the endometrial cavity" (Dean and Schwarz, 2011: 149).

Either type of IUD is placed in the uterus by a healthcare provider. Small strings extend from its end into the vagina, where they may be checked periodically by the woman to make sure that the IUD has not been ejected. If the IUD is going to slip out of the uterus, this will most likely occur during the first several months of use and/or during the days of the menstrual period. The ParaGard IUD should be replaced after ten–twelve years of use, and the Mirena IUD after five years (Dean and Schwarz, 2011:164, 183).

The ParaGard is nonhormonal, as were most earlier types of IUDs; that is, it does not contain the female hormones used to suppress ovulation. The Mirena is hormonal. I referred earlier to the vaginal ring, for example, the NuvaRing, which is also a foreign body placed in the uterus that contains hormones to be released into the woman's system. The NuvaRing contains both estrogen and progestin, unlike the Mirena IUD, which contains only progestin. Also, the NuvaRing needs to be replaced monthly, whereas the Mirena IUD remains effective for up to five years.

IUDs are very effective. The ParaGard has failure rates of 0.8 percent and 0.6 percent, based on use effectiveness data and theoretical effectiveness data, respectively. The Mirena has even lower failure rates, 0.2 percent according to both types of effectiveness. The undetected expulsion of these devices is the most common cause of pregnancy, a major disadvantage. The major advantages are that insertion is necessary only once every ten–twelve years for the ParaGard and once every five years for the Mirena. Also, the IUD does not interfere with intercourse in any way.

IUDs that are expelled involuntarily may usually be reinserted successfully by medical-care professionals. Young women with no or few previous births may have higher rates of expulsion and pregnancy than older women with more births.

In addition to the risk of involuntary expulsion, IUDs sometimes need to be removed for medical reasons, particularly, menstrual bleeding and pain. Another disadvantage is that, unlike the case with vaginal rings, trained medical personnel are necessary for the insertion of IUDs. In the United States today, 3.5 percent of contracepting women use the IUD.

I discuss now a special type of contraception, the **emergency contraceptive pill** (ECP), also known as the **morning-after pill**. ECPs are contraceptive medications taken after unprotected intercourse and are designed to prevent pregnancy by interfering with the implantation of the fertilized ovum in the uterine lining. This is a different strategy from that of oral contraceptives and the other kinds of hormonal contraceptives that I discussed earlier; they prevent pregnancy primarily by preventing ovulation. The designation of "morning-after" is actually a misnomer. ECPs are licensed for use for up to seventy-two hours after an unprotected intercourse.

There are three types of ECPs now available for use in the United States: **Plan BOne-Step**®, a single 1,500 mcg levonorgestrel (a progestin hormone – see above) white pill, approved by the FDA in 2009; **ella**®, a single

30 mg ulipristal (an antiprogestin) white pill approved in 2010; and **Next Choice**®, a generic version of Plan B, taken as two peach pills, approved in 2009. Plan BOne Step and Next Choice are available without prescription to persons aged 17 and over, but a prescription is required for ella (Trussell and Schwarz, 2011: 113–114).

Plan BOne Step and Next Choice are progestin-only medications taken as either two doses twelve hours apart or as a single dose; the progestin acts to suppress ovulation and to thicken the cervical mucus so to immobilize the sperms. The ella ECP works in another way; it contains ulipristal which acts to suppress ovulation for up to five days. ECPs are not to be confused with abortifacients, that is, abortion pills (I discuss them next). ECPs are meant to function after fertilization has occurred but before the fertilized egg has settled into the uterine environment. Because ECPs have their effect prior to implantation, the International Federation of Gynecology and Obstetrics considers them legally and medically to be contraceptives. However, not all researchers and medical practitioners agree with this categorization.

These postcoital methods of birth prevention are particularly convenient for women who have sexual intercourse infrequently, and/or who did not have an opportunity to use contraceptives before intercourse, or who used a contraceptive that failed in the process, for example, a condom that broke open during use.

ECPs are regarded as a very effective means of preventing an accidental pregnancy. Those pregnancies that do occur result from (1) failure of an already established implantation, (2) an excessive lapse of time between unprotected intercourse and taking the ECP, (3) inadequate dosages, (4) regurgitation of the pill, or (5) failure of the drug itself. The major advantages of ECPs are effectiveness and suitability for use among women who had unexpected and unprotected sexual contact, particularly in situations of rape. The most common short-term side effects are nausea, headaches, menstrual irregularities, and breast tenderness (Trussell and Schwarz, 2011).

Finally, I consider **abortifacients**, which are pharmaceutical medications that cause the termination of an early pregnancy by interfering with the viability of an already implanted zygote (fertilized egg). A synthetic steroid compound with antiprogestational effects, known as RU-486, was discovered in 1982 by the French reproductive physiologist Etienne-Emile Baulieu and other researchers at the Roussel Uclaf Company in France, the eventual designer of the drug (hence, the designation "RU"). Since it contains antiprogestational agents, and the medication works in a way opposite to that of progesterone, which functions to prepare and maintain the uterine environment for the fertilized egg. The generic name of the drug is mifepristone, and it is marketed in the United States under the trade name Mifeprex®. Mifepristone "blocks the action of progesterone, which is necessary to establish and maintain placental attachment" (Paul and Stein, 2011: 706). It is produced in China and has been approved by the US Federal Drug Administration as a drug to terminate an implanted zygote of up to forty-nine days' gestation. A 600 mg dose of mifepristone is administered by a physician, and is followed two days later by a large dose of a prostaglandin, misoprostol, to induce contractions (Paul and Stein, 2011; Spitz et al., 1998).

SUMMARY

A thorough understanding of a population's level of fertility requires knowledge of the extent to which people endeavor to limit family size. Whether or not a person uses a birth prevention method, and how effectively that method is used, depend on the person's motivation and the availability of the various methods. These, in turn, are influenced by social, economic, and religious factors.

The chief means by which people attempt to limit their family size are contraceptive techniques and devices, surgical sterilization, and induced abortion. Some methods are more effective than others. However, there is no perfect method of birth prevention. Each involves risks of failure or adverse effects.

Although the use of birth prevention methods is sometimes associated with medical risks (occasionally including mortality), these are usually much smaller than the mortality risks associated with pregnancy and giving birth. Generally, they are also smaller than the mortality risks associated with many widely accepted activities of daily life.

7 Mortality

As population actors, our last and final behavior on this earth is our death. When this demographic event occurs, it will be at least the second time for many of us that we have had our name mentioned in the local newspaper. When we were born, our name was probably listed in the local paper along with the name of our mother and maybe that of our father. But not much else was reported about us when we were born because there was not much to report. However, when we die, not only will our name be listed (again), but also other information will likely be provided in a story, an **obituary**, about our life. Our obituary might include when and where we were born, our surviving family members, and perhaps something about our main occupation while we were alive, our education, and other items of interest.

The *Oxford English Dictionary* defines "obituary" as an "announcement of a death (in a newspaper)...usually comprising a brief biographical sketch of the deceased" (Simpson and Weiner, 2000: X, 640). What other time will a biographical sketch about you be written and published for everyone to read? Perhaps never. Our death is not only the last event in our life, but, indeed, one of the most important events in our life.

Every one of us has been born, and every one of us will die. This is a certainty. No one escapes death. In fact, all species are born and all species die. But we humans are the only species to actually think about and contemplate the act of dying.

Death will not occur at the same time for everyone. Some of us will die sooner than others. On average, death will come earlier to males than to females, and earlier to members of most racial minority groups than to members of the majority. However, if you are Latino, death will likely come later, not earlier. If you live in the United States and are a Latino female, you will have the longest average **longevity** (length of life). You will have the shortest longevity if you are an African American male. According to 2010 life tables, Latino women in the United States may expect to live, on average, 83.8 years from the day they were born, compared with 71.4 years for black males (Arias, 2014: 3).

We ourselves play an important role in deciding when we will die. In Chapter 1 in my discussion of our roles as population actors, I noted that our individual decision-making is more obvious and apparent, say, with regard to fertility than with regard to mortality. We had absolutely no control over when or where we were born; our birth was the decision or decisions of our biological parents. But we do have a lot of control and influence over whether, when, and where we ourselves produce children. Our dying is a similar kind of demographic act. We may exercise many options that result in extending or shortening our lives. While death is a certainty, the length of time we will live depends on many factors. Over some of them (e.g., our sex and race) we have no control, but over other factors we have a lot of control. Further, we have some influence not only on the timing and characteristics of our own death, but also on the deaths of some others.

The impact of mortality varies significantly according to social and demographic characteristics. People in higher social classes live longer than those in the lower classes. Richer people live longer than poorer people. Married people live longer than single, separated, or divorced people. I discuss some of these issues later.

Mortality and its effects are best discussed from the vantage point of the society. Demographers often consider all individuals together as members of a single society (or state or country) and inquire about the factors that contribute to differences among them in their average length of life. For instance, in 2013, a baby girl born in Japan had a life expectancy of 86 years; this means she could expect to live, on average, for about 86 years from the time she was born; a baby girl born in Singapore, Spain, Switzerland, or France had a life expectancy of about 85 years; these life expectancies of 86 and 85 are the highest in the world. By comparison, a baby girl born in 2013 in Lesotho (in southern Africa) could expect to live on average for about 45 years from the time when she was born, and a baby girl born in Sierra Leone (in western Africa), about 46 years (PRB, 2014). Why do baby girls born in Lesotho or Sierra Leone have such a low average life expectancy compared with baby girls born in Japan or in Singapore, Spain, Switzerland, or France? Levels of development, medical conditions, and a host of other factors are involved, and I discuss some of these later.

There have been major changes over the historical record in the main causes of death. People used to die mainly of infectious and parasitic diseases, but the major causes of death today in developed countries like the

United States are heart disease, cancer, and stroke. However, these days, the major causes of death are not always the same in countries with high and low levels of life expectancy. This topic, too, is covered in a later section.

This chapter has several sections. After addressing various issues of measurement, I will consider mortality and longevity from an international point of view. Then I will discuss the major causes of death in developed and developing countries and how these have changed over time. Another section is concerned specifically with changes in mortality in the United States, followed by a discussion of a special kind of mortality, that which occurs in infancy. I will also speculate about the future course of mortality and improvements in life expectancy. I now discuss the measurement of mortality.

MEASUREMENT OF MORTALITY

The quantification of mortality is central to demography. The measurement of mortality dates back to John Graunt (1620–1674) and his analyses of the "Bills of Mortality" (see my discussion of Graunt in Chapter 3, Box 3.2). Mortality refers to the relative frequency of death in a population.

Demographers use two different concepts when referring to mortality, namely, the **life span,** which is the numerical "age limit of human life" (Kintner, 2004: 307); and life expectancy, which is the average expected number of years of life to be lived by a particular population at a given time. An exact figure for the human life span or for the life span of any species is not known (Carey, 1997). However, demographers often use the "maximum recorded age at death" as an accepted operational definition of the human life span (Kintner, 2004: 307). As of the final writing and editing of this book in the year 2016, the longest known and verified life span is 122 years and 164 days, lived by the Frenchwoman Jeanne Louise Calment (see Box 7.1). The concept of life expectancy, which is used by demographers much more than the concept of the life span, is considered later.

Crude Death Rate

An easily understood and interpreted method for quantifying mortality, the **crude death rate** (CDR), is the number of deaths in a population in a given year per 1,000 members of the population. It is expressed as

$$\text{CDR} = \frac{\text{deaths in the year}}{\text{population at midyear}} * 1{,}000 \qquad (7.1)$$

BOX 7.1   THE LONGEST KNOWN LIFE SPAN (122+ YEARS)

At the time of writing, in 2015, the longest known and verified life span is 122 years and 164 days, lived by the Frenchwoman Jeanne Louise Calment, who was born in Arles (a city in southern France) on February 21, 1875. She died in a retirement home there on August 4, 1997. In the later years of her life, Mme Calment reportedly made the following observations:

"I've been forgotten by our good Lord."

"I took pleasure when I could. I acted clearly and morally and without regret. I'm very lucky."

"I've only got one wrinkle, and I'm sitting on it."

"If you can't do anything about it, don't worry about it."

(See obituary of Mme Calment by Craig Whitney, 1997, in the *New York Times*.)

As an illustration, using data for the United States for 2013, equation (7.1) becomes

$$\text{CDR} = \frac{2{,}596{,}993}{316{,}497{,}531} * 1{,}000 = 8.2 \tag{7.2}$$

This means that in the United States in 2013, there were just over 8 deaths for every 1,000 persons in the population.

CDRs for the countries of the world in 2014 ranged from a low of 1 in the United Arab Emirates (UAE) and Qatar to a high of 21 in Lesotho (PRB, 2014). The range of CDRs is narrower than that for the CBRs (discussed in Chapter 4).

However, CDRs must be interpreted with special caution. When CDRs are compared among countries, differences are sometimes due to differences in age composition. The fact that the UAE has a CDR of 1 and the United States has a CDR of 8 means that there are eight times more deaths per 1,000 people in the United States than there are in the UAE.

Why is the CDR of the United States eight times higher than that of the UAE? Why are there so many more deaths per 1,000 people in the United States than in the UAE? The main reason is that the UAE is much younger in average age than is the United States, and younger people have lower death rates than older people. In other words, countries with large proportions of young people and small proportions of old people will usually have lower

CDRs than countries with small proportions of young people and large proportions of old people.

   CDRs also should not be used to compare the death experiences of the same population at different points in time, particularly if the population's age structure has changed over time. Thus, it would be incorrect to compare the CDR of the United States, say, in 1960, when it was 9.5/1,000, with the CDR of the United States, say, in 2014, when it was 8.2/1,000, and conclude that the mortality experience in the United States only changed slightly in that fifty-four-year period. This would not be a correct statement because the United States became much older in the period between 1960 and 2014; its **median age** (the age that divides a population into equally younger and older groups) increased from 29 in 1960 to 37 in 2014. At the same time, the mortality experience in the United States (as measured by the **standardized death rate** (SDR) – see later discussion) dropped by more than 30 percent, but the CDR hardly changed at all. Much of the reduction in the mortality experience in the United States in the fifty-four-year period was offset by the fact that the population became older. The CDR is not capable of differentiating between these experiences.

   The CDR is referred to as crude because its denominator comprises the entire population, the members of which are not all equally at risk of experiencing death. This is so because the risk of death varies by age, sex, race/ethnicity, socioeconomic status, and many other characteristics. Thus, although it is true that all persons in the denominator of the CDR will eventually experience death, they are not all equally exposed to the risk of death.

   Death rates vary considerably by age. They are very high in the first year of life, but even then, the likelihood of death is not the same from month to month and day to day. Indeed, in the first year of life, deaths are much higher in the first month of life than in the remaining eleven months, much higher in the first day than in the remaining days of the month, much higher in the first hour than in the remaining twenty-three hours of the first day, and much higher in the first minute than in the remaining fifty-nine minutes of the first hour. This is the main reason why demographers who study mortality give such special attention to the study of **infant mortality** (Frisbie, 2005), a topic I cover later in this chapter.

Age-Specific Death Rate

Because death varies so considerably with age, demographers use **age-specific death rates** (ASDRs) as a more precise way to measure mortality. ASDRs are sometimes referred to as "M" rates. The ASDR (or $_nM_x$) is the number of deaths to persons in a specific age group per 1,000 persons in that age group. Its formula is:

$$_nM_x = \frac{\text{deaths to persons aged } x \text{ to } x + n}{\text{persons in the population who are aged } x \text{ to } x + n} * 1,000 \quad (7.3)$$

where the subscripts n and x refer, respectively, to the width of the age group and to the initial year of the age group. For instance, the ASDR for age group 15–19 is referred to as $_5M_{15}$.

The ASDR is not crude because deaths to persons in the age group x to $x + n$ are examined in relation to the total number of persons in the age group x to $x + n$.

I have noted already that death rates vary by age. They are high in the initial year of life, then drop precipitously; they begin increasing again at around age 40 or so (although in societies highly affected by HIV/AIDS, they tend to increase more so at the younger adult ages). ASDRs are very low for young persons after the first year or so of life. So if I were to plot a schedule of $_nM_x$ values, I would produce what demographers refer to as the **age curve of mortality**. Remember in Chapter 4, the chapter on fertility, when I referred to the age curve of fertility as a chart of the ASFRs? You will recall that when I plotted the seven ASFRs, an inverted "U" curve was formed.

Now were I to plot the age-specific death rates from the ASDR at the youngest age to the ASDR at the oldest age, a "U" curve would be formed.

In Figure 7.1, I present an illustration of the age curve of mortality for the United States. The figure displays the ASDRs, that is, the $_nM_x$ values, starting at age <1 (less than 1 year of age), then 1–4, 5–9, and all the way to 85+. The death rate in the United States at age <1 is not reached again until age 55–59; from there the death rates increase rapidly, and even more rapidly after age 75–79. The ASDR for 5–9 year olds is the lowest on the chart, and the ASDR for persons of age 85+ is the highest. Over 72 percent of all deaths in the United States in 2007 occurred to persons of age 65 and older, and almost 30 percent of all the deaths occurred to person of age 85 and older.

Standardization

ASDRs, and not CDRs, should be used to compare the mortality experiences of countries with known differences in age composition. I will elaborate this point with an example. The United States in 2006 had a CDR of 8, while Venezuela had a CDR of 4. This means that there were twice as many deaths per 1,000 people in the United States in 2006 than there were in Venezuela. But does this necessarily mean that young people, and

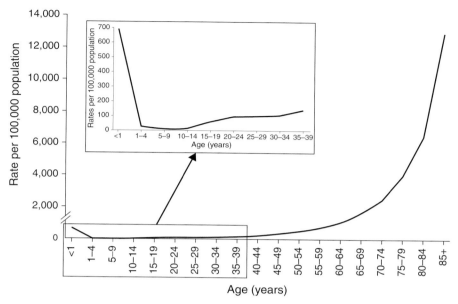

Figure 7.1 Age-specific Death Rates, United States, 2007
Source: Minino et al. (2009: 2).

middle-age people, and old people in the United States all die at higher rates than they do in Venezuela? To answer this question, I need to look at ASDR data and not CDR data.

In Table 7.1, I present ASDRs for the United States and for Venezuela for 2006. Observe the ASDR data in columns 2 and 4 of the table. At every age, except one, the United States has lower ASDRs than Venezuela. But I just mentioned in the preceding paragraph that the United States has a CDR twice as high as Venezuela's. How can this be? Why is Venezuela's CDR half that of the United States, while all but one of its ASDRs are higher than those of the United States?

The answer is shown in columns 3 and 5 of Table 7.1, namely, the proportions of people by age groups in the two countries. Venezuela has proportionately many more people in the younger age groups than the United States. For instance, the population of age 10–14 comprises 10.2 percent of Venezuela's total population, versus 7.2 percent of the US population. The opposite holds true with regard to people in the middle and older ages, with higher proportions in the United States than in Venezuela. Starting at age 35–39, the age-specific proportions become larger in the United States than in Venezuela. The population 65–69 is 3.4 percent of the United States versus 1.8 percent of Venezuela. The population in the age group 85–89 comprises 1.1 percent of the United States, compared with 0.2 percent of Venezuela. The United States is an "older" country than Venezuela,

Table 7.1 Age-specific Death Rates and Age-specific Proportions of the Population: United States and Venezuela, 2006

Age group	United States		Venezuela	
	ASDR	Proportion of population	ASDR	Proportion of population
<1	0.00654	0.0139	0.01623	0.0219
1–4	0.00029	0.0548	0.00064	0.0800
5–9	0.00014	0.0675	0.00032	0.1038
10–14	0.00018	0.0719	0.00041	0.1023
15–19	0.00064	0.0724	0.00146	0.1012
20–24	0.00091	0.0702	0.00238	0.0925
25–29	0.00090	0.0671	0.00221	0.0842
30–34	0.00106	0.0679	0.00203	0.0726
35–39	0.00153	0.0706	0.00215	0.0688
40–44	0.00231	0.0766	0.00289	0.0630
45–49	0.00341	0.0757	0.00411	0.0515
50–54	0.00493	0.0675	0.00568	0.0437
55–59	0.00742	0.0575	0.00775	0.0346
60–64	0.01150	0.0437	0.01173	0.0251
65–69	0.01780	0.0339	0.01877	0.0180
70–74	0.02771	0.0284	0.02838	0.0136
75–79	0.04350	0.0248	0.04270	0.0097
80–84	0.06958	0.0187	0.07531	0.0053
85–89	0.11056	0.0107	0.12769	0.0024
90–94	0.17477	0.0045	0.20820	0.0007
95–99	0.27656	0.0013	0.32576	0.0001
100+	0.43892	0.0003	0.48975	0.0001

Source: US Bureau of the Census, International Data Base. Calculations by DLP.

that is, the United States has more older people proportionately than does Venezuela. In contrast, Venezuela is a much "younger" country than the United States. Because younger people die at lower rates than older people, many (but not all) "young" countries have lower CDRs than "old" countries.

Demographers have a method for taking into account such a factor as age composition when they compare death rates among different countries. It is known as **standardization**. I focus here on age standardization, the most popular form. Young populations tend to have low CDRs, and old populations have high CDRs. One way to consider this issue is to observe that the CDR can be viewed as the sum of the ASDRs weighted by the size of the population in each age group. In other words, the CDR may be thought

Table 7.2 Age Data for a Hypothetical Population			
Age	Midyear population	Deaths	ASDR
0–34	2,000	40	20/1,000
35+	1,000	80	80/1,000
Total	3,000	120	40/1,000

Source: Palmore and Gardner (994: 15–16).

of as the "weighted mean of the death rates at each age, the weights used being the numbers at each age in the population being studied" (Pollard, Yusuf, and Pollard, 1981: 71–72).

I presented earlier in formula (7.1) the formula for the CDR. The numerator of the formula, deaths in the year, or D, is nothing more than the sum of each of the ASDRs multiplied by the size of the population in the age group. Consider, therefore, the following formula for the CDR as an alternative to that shown in formula (7.1):

$$CDR = \sum ASDR_x \left(\frac{nPx}{P} \right) * 1,000 \qquad (7.4)$$

where: P = total population; $_nP_x$ = population in age group x; and $ASDR_x$ = ASDR for age group x (Palmore and Gardner, 1994: 15).

Here is a very simple way to better understand formula (7.4). Imagine a hypothetical population with a CDR of 40. This population is divided into two broad age groups, 0–34 and 35+. Table 7.2 contains age data for this hypothetical population.

The data in Table 7.2 may be arranged using formula (7.4) as follows:

$$CDR = \frac{D}{P} * 1,000 = \frac{120}{3,000} * 1,000 = 0.04 * 1,000 = 40 \qquad (7.5)$$

Next, consider the CDR as a weighted sum of the ASDRs, and arrange the data in Table 7.2 using formula (7.4) as follows:

$$CDR = \left[\frac{2,000}{3,000} * 20 \right] + \left[\frac{1,000}{3,000} * 80 \right] = \left[\frac{2}{3} * 20 \right] + \left[\frac{1}{3} * 80 \right] \qquad (7.6)$$

$$CDR = \frac{40}{3} + \frac{80}{3} = \frac{120}{3} = 40 \qquad (7.7)$$

This example shows nicely and exactly how the CDR is a sum of the weighted (by population) ASDRs.

Now I will compare the mortality experiences of two or more populations. If a population such as the United States has more persons in the older age groups than in the younger age groups, then the death rates of the older groups (where there is more mortality) will be more heavily weighted than the death rates of the younger groups (where there is less mortality), and vice versa for a country such as Venezuela that has more persons in the younger age groups than in the older groups. This is seen clearly in the ASDRs in Table 7.1 for the United States and Venezuela. In other words, "if two populations of quite different age distributions are being compared, the weights used are quite different, and this method (i.e., the CDR) could give very misleading results" (Pollard, Yusuf, and Pollard 1981: 72). Hence, demographers need to control for age composition.

Actually, there are other features of population composition, namely, sex, that also need to be considered, that is, controlled, when comparing the death experiences of two populations. If one population has an excess of females and another an excess of males, and if the age compositions of the two are similar, the latter will have a higher CDR than the former because of the heavier representation of males. A similar statement may be made with regard to race composition, where the majority race usually has lower mortality rates than the minority group. Also, as I have already noted, it is not correct to compare the CDRs of the same population for different points in time, particularly if the age structure of the population has changed over the time periods under consideration.

Although my discussion here is restricted to standardization for age composition, the basic techniques of standardization are easily extended to sex composition, as well as to any other aspects of composition that the demographer believes could be influencing the death rates.

There are many statistical software programs available that demographers use to execute the statistical calculations for standardizing mortality rates for age composition. I prefer the Stata Statistical Software Program (StataCorp, 2015), although many other statistical software packages also have standardization programs based on formula (7.4). I have used Stata's direct standardization program to standardize Venezuela's death rate by assigning to Venezuela the age composition of the United States. Recall that Venezuela has a CDR of 4 and the United States has a CDR of 8. The result of the standardization exercise is that Venezuela has a directly SDR of 11.1. This means that if Venezuela had the age composition of the United States, while retaining its own ASDRs, it would have a CDR of 11.1, and not its actual CDR of 4. The fact that Venezuela has such a low CDR of 4 compared with the US CDR of 8 is due to its much younger age composition. Thus, if I assign to Venezuela the same age composition of the United States,

Venezuela ends up having a directly SDR of 11.1, which is higher than that of 8 for the United States.

The Life Table

One of the most important and elegant measures of the mortality experiences of a population is the life table. It dates back to John Graunt (1620–1674) and his "Bills of Mortality" (see Chapter 3, Box 3.2). The life table starts with a population (a radix) of 100,000 at age 0. Setting the radix at 100,000 is arbitrary but conventional. From each age to the next, the population is decremented according to age-specific mortality probabilities until all members have died. The mortality schedule is fixed and does not change over the life of the population. The basic life table consists of seven columns, including the probability of dying between age x and age $x + n$ ($_nq_x$), the number of survivors at each age x (l_x), and life expectancy at each age (e_x). In Box 7.2, I discuss and develop in more detail a life table for the US population for the year 2010.

Life expectancy, a statistic gleaned directly from the last column of the life table (see table in Box 7.2), is a primary indicator of quality of life. In 2013, life expectancy at birth in the world was 69 for males and 73 for females. In more developed countries, it was 75 and 82, and in less developed countries (excluding China), 65 and 69. Japan is the country with the highest life expectancy at birth, 80 for males, 86 for females. The lowest life expectancies were in Lesotho (42 for males, 45 for females), and Sierra Leone (45 for males, 46 for females) (PRB, 2014).

BOX 7.2   THE LIFE TABLE

Demographers use the life table to determine life expectancy, not only at birth but at any age. Like the TFR (see my discussion of the TFR in Chapter 4), the life table is a synthetic or hypothetical measure. It tells us many things about a population. One of the most important questions it answers is the following: how many years of life, on average, may a person expect to live if the person during his or her lifetime is subjected to the age-specific probabilities of dying of a particular country or population at a given time? Thus, when we say that the population of the United States in 2010 had a life expectancy at birth of 78.7 years, we mean that if a cohort of 100,000 persons, throughout the years of their life, were subjected to the ASDRs, that is, the $_nM_x$ rates, of the total population in the United States in 2010, they would live, on average, 78.7 years.

In the table below, I show an abridged life table for the US population for the year 2010. It is referred to as an abridged life table because it is calculated, for the most part, for five-year age groups, rather than for single-year age groups.

Life Table for the Total Population, United States, 2010						
(1)	(2)	(3)	(4)	(5)	(6)	(7)
Age range	$_nq_x$	l_x	$_nd_x$	$_nL_x$	T_x	e_x
<1	0.006123	100,000	612	99,465	7,866,027	78.7
1–4	0.001071	99,388	106	397,294	7,766,561	78.1
5–9	0.000573	99,281	57	496,250	7,369,267	74.2
10–14	0.000708	99,224	70	495,989	6,873,017	69.3
15–19	0.002463	99,154	244	495,240	6,377,028	64.3
20–24	0.004317	98,910	427	493,529	5,881,789	59.5
25–29	0.004791	98,483	472	491,249	5,388,260	54.7
30–34	0.005497	98,011	539	488,744	4,897,011	50.0
35–39	0.006913	97,472	674	485,753	4,408,267	45.2
40–44	0.009979	96,798	966	481,758	3,922,514	40.5
45–49	0.016044	95,833	1,538	475,584	3,440,756	35.9
50–54	0.024343	94,295	2,295	466,066	2,965,173	31.4
55–59	0.035106	92,000	3,230	452,347	2,499,106	27.2
60–64	0.049847	88,770	4,425	433,348	2,046,759	23.1
65–69	0.074406	84,345	6,276	406,912	1,613,411	19.1
70–74	0.112315	78,069	8,768	369,612	1,206,499	15.5
75–79	0.174782	69,301	12,113	317,694	836,886	12.1
80–84	0.274384	57,188	15,692	248,038	519,193	9.1
85–89	0.430820	41,497	17,878	162,723	271,155	6.5
90–94	0.615282	23,619	14,532	79,720	108,432	4.6
95–99	0.783397	9,087	7,119	24,670	29,212	3.2
100+	1.00000	1,968	1,968	4,542	4,542	2.3

Source: Arias (2014: 62).

A life table starts with a population of 100,000 persons born alive at age 0 (see the figure of 100,000 at l_0 in column 3). This initial group of 100,000 persons is then subjected to the probabilities of dying at each age, until all 100,000 are dead. I will now examine each of the seven columns of the life table for the total US population in the year 2010.

Column 1 refers to the age intervals of each group. The age groups shown here refer to the range of years between two birthdays. To illustrate, the age group 5–9 refers to the five-year interval between the fifth and the tenth birthdays.

Column 2 reports for each age group the probabilities of dying; these probabilities are designated as $_nq_x$. This is the most basic column of the life table. The $_nq_x$ values represent the probabilities that persons who are alive at the beginning of an age interval will die during that age interval, before they reach the start of the next age interval. While it is the case that the $_nq_x$ rates resemble the $_nM_x$ rates, there is an important difference between them. The difference has to do with their denominators; the denominator of the $_nM_x$ rates is the midyear population, whereas the denominator of the $_nq_x$ rates is the population alive at the beginning of the age interval. In most cases, the $_nq_x$ rates may be estimated from the $_nM_x$ rates with a straightforward transforming equation (Kintner, 2004)

At the oldest age category (100+ in the life table that I show here), the value of $_nq_x$ must equal 1.0 because all people alive at the start of that age interval must die. For a few age groups, namely, those less than 1, 1–4, and 100+, different formulas are used (see Kintner, 2004: 312).

Column 3 shows values for the number of people alive at the beginning of the age interval; this column is designated as the l_x column of data and is sometimes known as "the little l column." It is calculated by subtracting the $_nd_x$ value (column 5) from the l_x value in the age interval immediately preceding the one being calculated. For example, of the 99,224 people alive at the beginning of the age interval 10–14 (i.e., l_{10}), 70 of them die during the age interval between their tenth and fifteenth birthdays (i.e., $_5d_{10}$). Thus, for the next age group, those aged 15–19, there are 70 fewer people; therefore, the value of l_{15} is 99,154 (i.e., 99,224 minus 70).

Column 4 shows the number of people who die during a particular age interval and is designated as $_nd_x$. It is arrived at by multiplying l_x by $_nq_x$. Thus, for the number of people who die during the age interval of 40–44, the $_5d_{40}$ value is 966; this equals the $_5q_{40}$ value of 0.009979 times the l_{40} value of 96,798.

Column 5 reports for each age interval the total number of years lived by all persons who enter that age interval while in the age interval. It is designated as $_nL_x$ and is sometimes referred to as "the big L column" of data. For instance, the life table shows that 98,011 persons are alive at the beginning of age interval 30–34 (i.e., the l_{30} value). If none of those persons died during that age interval, they would have lived 490,055 years during the period of time between their thirtieth and thirty-fifth birthdays, or 98,011 times 5. But we know that some of them died during the age interval of 30–34, namely, 539 died (see the $_5d_{30}$ value of 539). Demographers assume that these 539 deaths are roughly distributed during the five-year period for many of the age intervals. But this assumption does not apply to the first few age intervals. With regard to the first year of life, I noted earlier in this chapter that it is erroneous to assume that deaths are evenly distributed throughout the first year.

There are several formulas that may be used to produce the $_nL_x$ value for the first few age groups (see Kintner, 2004: 313–315). At the other age extreme, 100+ in the life table, another formula is used (see Kintner, 2004: 314).

Column 6 reports the total number of years lived by the population in that age interval and in all subsequent age intervals; this column of data is designated as T_x. To determine the values of T_x for each age interval, one sums the $_nL_x$ from the oldest age backwards, using this formula:

$$T_x = \sum_{i=x}^{w} L_i$$

where: L_i = entry i in the $_nL_x$ column, and $\sum_{i=x}^{w}$ = the sum of the $_nL_x$ column starting at entry x through the last $_nL_x$ entry, namely, w.

I will calculate T_{95} from the life table for the US population in 2010, as follows:

$$T_{95} = {}_5L_{95} + {}_5L_{100}$$
$$T_{95} = 24{,}670 + 4.542 = 29{,}212$$

Column 7 presents the average number of years of life remaining at the beginning of the age interval. This column of data, known as e_x, provides life expectancy at any age; it is calculated by dividing column 7 by column 4. I noted earlier that the total US population in 2010 has an average life expectancy at birth of 78.7 years. This refers to the e_0 value of 78.7 in the life table and is calculated as T_0 (7,866,027) divided by l_0 (100,000) = 78.7. If I wanted to know the average number of years of life remaining for the US population in 2010 who had reached their twenty-fifth birthday, I would use the e_{25} value of 54.7 in the life table; it is calculated as T_{25}(5,388,260) divided by l_{25} (98,483) = 54.71. This means that persons aged 25–29 can expect to live an additional 54.7 years if they are subjected to the age-specific probabilities of dying of the total US population in 2010.

Life tables are used for many purposes other than studying human mortality. Examples include estimating the failure rates of contraceptives, tracing the progress of a population of freshmen through college, and measuring marital formation and dissolution. Regarding the second example, one would take the number of freshmen entering college as the radix of the life table and then subject them to age-specific probabilities of dying, of dropping out of college, and of graduating from college. One could then determine, for example, the average number of years of college life for, say, male freshmen who entered four-year public colleges in the state of Texas in the fall semester of 2010, and compare this value of e_x with that for male freshmen who entered four-year private colleges in the state of Texas in the fall semester of 2010. Is the average number of years of college life larger or smaller for male freshmen in public versus private colleges? An educational life table would give us the answer.

We need to be aware of the fact, however, that when considering life expectancy at birth, e_0, infant mortality plays a very important role. When e_0 is low, as in Lesotho or in Sierra Leone, for example, a major reason is their very high infant mortality rate. When comparing values of life expectancy at birth across countries, especially developing countries, therefore, we should not think of e_0 as, strictly speaking, a modal age at death.

Whereas John Graunt is referred to by most demographers as the founder of demography, many refer to Alfred Lotka (1880–1949) as the person most responsible for the development of modern demography. Lotka used life tables in the development of his **stable population theory**. The concept of a stable population was actually first set forth by Leonhard Euler ([1760] 1970), but its current development stems from the work of Lotka, who first introduced the concept in a brief note in 1907. Later, Sharpe and Lotka (1911) proved mathematically that if a population that is closed to migration experiences constant schedules of age-specific fertility and mortality rates, it will develop a constant age distribution and will grow at a constant rate, irrespective of its initial age distribution. I discuss this important demographic concept in more detail in Chapter 10.

Having covered some of the methodological issues involved in the study of mortality, I turn now to substantive issues. In the next section, I review briefly the history of mortality in the world and also cover the three positive checks of Malthus. Next, I discuss the major causes of death in developed and developing countries and how they have changed over time.

A SHORT HISTORY OF MORTALITY IN THE WORLD AND THE MALTHUSIAN CHECKS OF FAMINES, EPIDEMICS, AND WARS

Our knowledge of mortality levels and conditions prior to the Industrial Revolution is limited. We know that mortality then was high, but the availability and completeness of death data leave many questions unanswered. A life table for ancient Greece prepared from burial records shows a life expectancy at birth, e_0, of about 30 years (Dublin, Lotka, and Spiegelman, 1949). Age data from census records of Roman Egypt indicate an average life expectancy at birth in the first to third centuries AD of between 22 and

25 years, a finding that has been corroborated by data on tombstones in Roman North Africa (Scheidel, 2003: 45). A life table developed by John Graunt (see Chapter 3) reported that more than 35 percent of babies born in seventeenth-century London were dead by age 6. By comparison, according to a US life table for 2010, less than 1 percent of the US population born is dead at age 6 (see table in Box 7.2). Graunt's life table showed that by age 56, 94 percent of those born were dead, while the respective figure for the US population in 2010 was around 8 percent. We are living quite a bit longer these days compared to Londoners four centuries ago. Thank goodness.

As late as the eighteenth century, life expectancy ranged from only 30 to 40 years in much of Europe and the United States (Dublin, Lotka, and Spiegelman, 1949). As recently as 1901, the year my father was born, US males had a life expectancy at birth of 47.9 years and females, 50.7 years (US Department of Commerce, 1921) (my father died in 1977 at age 75, so he exceeded by 27 years the e_0 value when he was born).

Also, mortality levels in past centuries were not constant from year to year. There were short-term fluctuations caused principally by changes in the major causes of high mortality, namely, famines, epidemics, and wars. These are the "positive checks" noted by Malthus that kept the death rate high (Malthus, [1803] 1989) (see my earlier discussion of Malthus in Chapter 2). Poor living conditions in urban areas also contributed to high levels of mortality (Johnson, 2006).

Famines

I now consider famines as a cause of death. Populations in preindustrial times had much less control over their food supply than we do today. Agricultural output was severely limited by the inefficiency of manual labor, by plagues of rodents and insects, and by plant diseases. Abundant harvests usually could not be exploited owing to inadequate food storage facilities. Transportation technology and roadways were underdeveloped. Hence, isolated areas with food shortages were unable to import surplus food from other areas. Thus, famine was a major problem.

The demographic consequences of famines were often disastrous. Because famines have almost always taken place in rural and in poor populations, the precise nature of their toll is not easy to measure (O'Grada, 1999, 2001, 2003a). There were serious declines in population in much of Europe during the famine years of 1315–1317. In the 1690s, one-sixth of the population in some Swedish provinces died after severe crop failures.

The Irish potato famine of 1846–1851, known in Ireland as the Great Famine, killed around a million people, although some estimates place the number as high as 1.5 million (Foster, 1988: 324; Miller, 1985: 284). This is a huge number of deaths when one recalls that the total population of Ireland in the early 1840s was just over 8 million. As an Irish priest at the time observed, "Truly, the Angel of death and desolation reigns triumphant in Ireland" (Miller, 1985: 285). We also must not forget that these deaths do not include "averted births or allow for famine-related deaths in Britain and farther afield" (O'Grada, 2003b: 391; O'Grada, 1999).

The last major famine in Europe was the Finnish famine of 1868 (O'Grada, 2001). Also, it is likely that as many as 19 million persons perished in India between 1891 and 1910 as a result of famines (Davis, 1951; Wrigley, 1969).

One of the most destructive famines in the demographic record occurred in China between 1958 and 1961. As industrial and grain production dropped to low levels, the standard of living declined, and the birth rate dropped to near replacement levels (Peng, 1987). First there were food shortages, followed by famine, and, to make matters worse, food was exported, often from areas in China with food shortages. It is estimated that between 30 and 40 million Chinese died as a direct result of the famine, with 12 million of the deaths to children under the age of 10 (Ashton et al., 1984; MacDonald, 2003). The main cause of the famine stemmed from the ill-conceived and overly ambitious "Great Leap Forward" program, initiated in 1958 by Mao Zedong and designed to "involve a revolutionary struggle against nature to realize the great potential of agriculture by maximizing the advantages of the collective economy" (Aird, 1972: 278). The economic crisis and famine that followed were due to natural disasters, such as floods, plant diseases, and drought, as well as to bureaucratic inefficiency and improper management (Ashton et al., 1984; Dikotter, 2010; Yang, 2012).

Throughout human history, unless famines occur in very small populations, they seldom result in the deaths of more than a few percent of the people. As disastrous as was China's famine, it killed "at most 2 to 3 percent of the total population" of the country (O'Grada, 2003a: 383). An exception was Ireland's Great Famine, which killed between 12 and 18 percent of the population. I turn next to a consideration of epidemic diseases.

Epidemic Diseases

Diseases may be classified as endemic or epidemic. An **epidemic** is a major increase or upswing of an infectious disease in an area that results in a large number of deaths, followed then by a decline. Many infections and contagious diseases have become epidemic, including scarlet fever, chicken pox, measles, influenza, and cholera, among others. If a disease is maintained at a fairly constant level, it is called an endemic (Caldwell, 2006). Epidemic diseases "break out, reach a peak, and subside; endemic diseases cause a relatively constant amount of illness and death over time" (Johansson, 2003: 303). Epidemics typically start out on a local level and are then diffused to nearby areas. If an epidemic strikes several countries or continents, it is known as a **pandemic**. Pandemics are much more disruptive demographically, economically, and socially than are epidemics.

Caldwell (2006) has written that epidemics were important to the development of modern demography because it then became obvious that the tracking of deaths was necessary and important. For instance, the Spanish 'flu epidemic (see my later discussion) resulted in the establishment of the Growth Surveillance System by the League of Nations.

One of Europe's worst epidemics, the Black Death, was a virulent outbreak of a disease that likely originated in Central Asia, moved to the Mediterranean via the Silk Road, and then entered Europe between 1347 and 1352, mainly via rats on inbound ships, ultimately spreading into northern Europe. It resulted in the death of around one-third of the continent's population (Caldwell, 2006; Herlihy, 1997; Martin, 2007). Subsequent epidemics were so frequent and intense throughout Europe that the population was reduced by nearly 50 percent, and demographic recovery took more than two centuries (Johansson, 2003). The estimated number of deaths caused by the Black Death ranges from as low as 25 million up to a high of 60–75 million. A middle-range value is around 40–50 million deaths. This is an astounding value given that the entire population of Europe in the fourteenth century likely numbered around 80–90 million inhabitants.

The Great Plague that hit London in the 1660s had continuing outbreaks for several decades thereafter, but its toll was lower than that of the Black Death. It was once believed to have been a bubonic plague, but many now hold that it was a disease similar to a viral fever (Caldwell, 2006). The "Bills of Mortality" analyzed by John Graunt (see Chapter 3) were produced during the era of the Great Plague.

In the nineteenth century, Britain was subjected to four cholera epidemics. In 1854, when the epidemic was again sweeping through England and Wales, the mystery of the transmission of cholera was solved by "an ingenious physician named John Snow [whose discovery also] helped eliminate cholera from Britain and eventually from the Western world" (Epstein, 2007a: 41). In London, Snow showed that certain wells were yielding contaminated water, and that the people drinking water from these sources were mainly the ones who were dying. He mapped the wells and the incidence of cholera for various areas of London, a map that some refer to today as "one of the most famous documents in the history of science" (Epstein,

2007a: 42). He convinced the local officials to remove the handle from the water well that was yielding much of the contaminated water; they did, and the incidence of cholera dropped precipitously. This was one of the first times that a **geographic information system** (GIS) was ever used to shape a policy that led to the closing of certain wells (Swanson and Stephan, 2004). Steven Johnson's book *The Ghost Map* (2006) is a delightful, fascinating, and riveting account of Snow's pioneering work.

Today in London, there is a John Snow Pub located on Broadwick Street. It stands exactly where the bad well was located. Visit the pub the next time you are in London and salute and toast John Snow, who is recognized today as the father of epidemiology.

A more recent epidemic was the Spanish 'flu epidemic, so named because Spain was the first European country infected. It spread throughout Europe in 1918 and then to the rest of the world. Epidemiologists Niall Johnson and Juergen Mueller (2002) have estimated that the epidemic resulted in the deaths of around 50 million people; others place the toll even higher (Barry, 2004). The Spanish 'flu may well have infected almost 1 billion people, or nearly half of the population of the world at that time. Some believe that large numbers of influenza deaths went unreported in less developed countries. By the time the epidemic had run its course in North America, nearly 700,000 had died in the United States and around 50,000 in Canada. Some small villages in Quebec and Labrador were almost wiped out entirely. The most common victims of this epidemic were young adults, 20–40 years of age (Barry, 2004; Caldwell, 2006; Crosby, 2003; Kolata, 1999). If one examines month-specific death rates in the United States for the years 1911–1917 and for 1918, the impact of the Spanish 'flu is particularly apparent in the last quarter of 1918, and especially in the month of October.

Few cities in the United States, or perhaps even worldwide, were as affected by this epidemic as severely as my hometown of San Francisco, where "in only a few short months, the city recorded more than 50,000 cases and...3,500 deaths (Espey, 2014:1). The situation was so serious that a law was passed in the city in 1918 requiring residents to wear masks when venturing outside the home to visit public places, and this slogan was promulgated by the city's Health Department: "Wear a Mask and Save Your Life! A Mask is 99% Proof Against Influenza" (available online at: www.pbs.org/wgbh/americanexperience/features/general-article/influenza-san-francisco). Some evidence suggests, however, that the wearing of masks was not that effective (Espey, 2014: 3, 24).

Among the victims living in San Francisco and nearby were three of my grandparents and one aunt. I show in Figure 7.2 a copy of the actual death certificate of one of them, my maternal grandmother, Annie Kara. She died

Figure 7.2 Death Certificate of Annie Kara, Victim of the 'Flu Epidemic, San Francisco, 1918

on December 20, 1918, at age 42, of "influenza" and was buried the next day in Holy Cross Catholic Cemetery in Colma, a small town south of San Francisco. My mother, Kathryn Kara, who was then 9 years old, also contracted the Spanish 'flu in San Francisco in the fall of 1918, but, thankfully, she survived. In 1936, she married my father Dudley Poston, Sr., and gave birth to me in 1940, and to her daughter Kathleen in 1943. Kathryn Kara Poston, who died in San Francisco at age 69 in 1979, had a tremendous influence on the lives of her children and grandchildren during her lifetime. So powerful and long-lasting was her influence on my daughter Nancy that Nancy named her first daughter Kara after her great-grandmother. Had the vagaries of mortality and the 1918 'flu epidemic operated in another way, and had Kathryn Kara died in 1918 along with her parents and sister and 3,500 other residents of the San Francisco area in what Barry (2004) has referred to as the deadliest plague in human history, many persons named in this paragraph would not have been born, this demography textbook would not have been written, and the lives of countless others would be very different today.

Before leaving my discussion of the Spanish 'flu epidemic, let me mention two references deserving your attention. First, I have read several books about the 1918 'flu epidemic. In my opinion the best and the most readable one is Crosby's (2003) *America's Forgotten Pandemic*. It is fascinating reading and may well be the most thorough exploration of the epidemic. Second, the novelist Katherine Anne Porter's 1939 book *Pale Horse, Pale Rider* consists of three novellas. The third is the eponymous "Pale Horse, Pale Rider" and is about a newspaper woman and a soldier and their relationship. She contracts the 'flu, and he does also, and he may have caught it from her. It is a gripping story, only sixty pages long, and well worth reading. Porter herself was stricken by the 'flu, so the story is somewhat autobiographical. Alfred Crosby (see above) considered this short piece of fiction to be such an exceptional work that he dedicated his *America's Forgotten Pandemic* "To Katherine Anne Porter, who survived" (Crosby, 2003: v).

In the preceding paragraphs I noted that the Black Death resulted in around 50 million deaths, although this number might be too low; and the Spanish 'flu epidemic also resulted in around 50 million deaths, although this number also might be too low. Today, a disease of epidemic proportions is ravaging the world. I am referring to the HIV/AIDS epidemic, which could soon be responsible for more deaths than the combined 100 million toll of the Black Death and Spanish 'flu epidemics.

As of 2015, when I was writing this book, the world was more than thirty-five years into the HIV/AIDS epidemic. **Acquired immune deficiency syndrome** (AIDS) was first noticed in the United States in 1981, initially among gay men (Shilts, 1987). Hemophiliac cases of AIDS were first reported in 1982. The human immunodeficiency virus (HIV) causing AIDS was isolated in 1983 at the Pasteur Institute in Paris, and by the late 1980s and into the 1990s, HIV/AIDS had been identified in every region of the world. HIV is spread person to person via contact with body fluids. As Zaba (2003: 37) has written, "this may occur during sexual intercourse, or as a result of mother-to-child transmission during pregnancy, delivery, or breastfeeding. The virus may also be transferred in blood used for transfusions…[Also] it can be spread by unsterilized hypodermic needles and surgical instruments." The virus is mainly spread by having sex with someone with HIV, and secondly by sharing needles and syringes with someone who has HIV.

As of the start of 2014, the World Health Organization estimated that 74 million people worldwide had been infected since the virus was first recognized in 1981; of these, 39 million have died, and most of the 35 million living with HIV will likely die of HIV-related causes. In 2013 alone, 1.5 million people died of HIV-related causes. Each year in the world, there are more than 2 million new HIV cases. This means that in another fifteen or so

Total: 35.0 million [33.2 million – 37.2 million]

Figure 7.3 Adults and Children Estimated to be Living with HIV, 2013

years, perhaps around the year of 2030, there will have been more than 100 million HIV cases worldwide, almost all of whom will die of HIV-related causes. This number could surpass the 100 million deaths estimated to have resulted from the Black Death and Spanish 'flu epidemics.

Of the 35 million now living with HIV, 25 million reside in sub-Saharan Africa. Moreover, 70 percent of the global total of new HIV infections occur in sub-Saharan Africa (WHO, 2014). Figure 7.3 is a map of the world showing the numbers of children and adults in 2013 living with HIV in each major region of the world. The confidence intervals are shown in brackets. The map shows clearly that the region with the most cases in 2013 was sub-Saharan Africa with almost 25 million of the 35 million cases.

One reason for the very high levels of HIV infection in sub-Saharan Africa is partner concurrency, the practice of men and women having more than one partner concurrently, that is, simultaneously. A man might have a wife and one or two steady girlfriends, all at the same time. A woman might simultaneously have a husband and a couple of boyfriends. This pattern adds significantly to the risk of contracting the virus (Epstein, 2007b).

Although sub-Saharan Africa is by far the most affected region in the world, epidemics are also underway in Central Asia and in eastern Europe. Also, there is an enormous potential for a massive HIV/AIDS epidemic in China owing to the 30–40 million excess males already born in China who will not be able to find Chinese brides (Poston, Conde, and DeSalvo, 2011; Tucker et al., 2005; Tucker et al., 2009). These bachelors will likely live in the big cities and be dependent on sex workers.

It is clear that the HIV/AIDS epidemic has had, and continues to have, an enormous impact on the populations of many countries of the world. As I noted above, an estimated 39 million people have already died of AIDS, and another 35 million persons or so are living with HIV (Lamptey, Johnson, and Khan, 2006). In its 2012 revision of the *World Population Prospects*, the United Nations (2013d) reported that HIV prevalence is estimated to be 2 percent or higher among the population aged 15–49 in the thirty-nine most highly affected countries of the world, thirty-six of which are in Africa. Four very large countries with HIV prevalence rates below 1 percent, namely, Brazil, China, India, and the United States, should also be considered in this discussion because of their large absolute number of persons currently living with HIV.

Nine countries, all in sub-Saharan Africa, have astoundingly high rates of HIV. In Swaziland, 25 percent of its population aged 15–49 is infected with HIV, followed by Lesotho at 23 percent, Botswana at 22 percent, South Africa at 19 percent, Zimbabwe at 15 percent, Namibia at 14 percent, Mozambique at 11 percent, and Malawi at 10 percent. The next eight highest rates, from 7 percent in Uganda to 4 percent in Guinea-Bissau, are also in sub-Saharan African countries. Outside sub-Saharan Africa, no other country has an HIV prevalence rate higher than the 3 percent rate of the Bahamas or the 2 percent rate of Haiti (Central Intelligence Agency, 2015).

The HIV/AIDS epidemic has resulted in several African countries actually recording increases in past years in their levels of mortality. AIDS has had a devastating toll, for sure. Life expectancy in some of the most affected countries has actually declined. To illustrate, in Botswana, "life expectancy has fallen from 64 years in 1985–1990 to 47 years in 2005–2010...In Southern Africa as a whole, where most of the worst affected countries are, life expectancy has fallen from 61 to 52 years over the last 20 years" (United Nations, 2013d: 18).

I now turn next to a discussion of wars, the last of the Malthusian positive checks.

Wars

The demographic consequences of war with respect to mortality are not easy to determine. For one thing, there is the issue of definition. What is a war? Some military historians and archeologists define war as all kinds of conflict involving more than two combatants. But this is an unrealistic approach. Scholars now tend to define war in terms of the number of deaths that have occurred. Wilkinson (1980) developed a register of wars since 1820 that includes 315 engagements where the number of deaths exceeded 300 (see also Etherington, 2003). In addition to the number of recorded military deaths, there is also the issue of civilian losses that occur as a consequence of war, including infection by diseases carried by the soldiers, killings associated with plunder, famine following the destruction of farmland, and hardships occurring as a result of economic and social disorganization.

Mortality data from war are best documented for activities in the twentieth century compared with previous eras. The greatest number of deaths, unquestionably, occurred during the first part of the last century. The range of estimates is considerable, but "plausible sizes of the military and civilian death toll would be around 8.5 million in World War I and 40 million in World War II" (Etherington, 2003: 964). Often, the number of civilian deaths exceeds the number of military deaths. To illustrate, it is likely that during the Second World War in Russia, 60 percent of the deaths were civilian (Petersen, 1975: 269).

In the United States, the Civil War resulted in the largest number of deaths to Americans of any war ever experienced by the country, before or after. An estimated 620,000 men, roughly half from the North and half from the South, died during the four years of fighting between 1861 and 1865. This is about the same number of Americans lost in all of the country's other wars, from the Revolutionary War through the Korean War (Faust, 2008). The 620,000 Civil War deaths needs to be considered relative to the US population of around 31 million people at the time; approximately 2 percent of the country's total population died. This would be the equivalent of around 6.4 million people in terms of the US population today in 2015.

MORTALITY TRENDS AND CAUSES OF DEATH IN DEVELOPED AND DEVELOPING COUNTRIES

The eminent demographer Donald Bogue has noted that in many ways "it is superficial to treat death as a single unitary force…In reality death is an event brought about by one or a combination of a great variety of causes, or diseases, and a full understanding of mortality requires an understanding of the trends in each of the major causes of death" (1969: 578).

Even today, data on causes of death are far from complete. Some deaths around the world are not even registered. In many countries, a large proportion of deaths occurs outside the presence of physicians, and the causes are either unknown or incorrectly diagnosed. Sometimes, socially unpopular causes of death, such as suicide, syphilis, and HIV/AIDS, are misrepresented or camouflaged.

Moreover, international comparisons of cause-of-death data are difficult because countries often differ in terminology, method of certification, diagnostic techniques, and the quality of the coding and data collection system. Nevertheless, some generalizations are possible about the general structure of the causes of death.

In the world today, most national governments classify causes of deaths according to the **International Classification of Diseases** (ICD) as developed by the World Health Organization (WHO) (WHO, 1992). This classification undergoes periodic revision. The tenth revision of the classification (ICD-10) is currently undergoing revision; the release date for ICD-11 is 2017. Causes of death in the United States have been classified according to ICD-10 since 1999.

In ICD-10 (adapted in 1992), the causes of death are classified under twenty-two major headings. I list these headings, along with a few examples of specific causes for some of them (see WHO, 1992, for more details), as follows:

I. Certain infectious and parasitic diseases (tuberculosis; viral infections; HIV).
II. Neoplasms (cancers).
III. Diseases of the blood.
IV. Endocrine, nutritional, and metabolic diseases (malnutrition; diabetes).
V. Mental and behavioral disorders (schizophrenia; mental retardation).
VI. Diseases of the nervous system (meningitis).
VII. Diseases of the eye (glaucoma).
VIII. Diseases of the ear.
IX. Diseases of the circulatory system (ischemic heart diseases; cerebrovascular diseases).
X. Diseases of the respiratory system (influenza; pneumonia).
XI. Diseases of the digestive system (diseases of liver; hernia).
XII. Diseases of the skin and subcutaneous tissue.
XIII. Diseases of the musculoskeletal system (disorders of muscles; disorders of bone density).
XIV. Diseases of the genitourinary system (diseases of male genital organs; disorders of breast).
XV. Pregnancy, childbirth, and the puerperium.
XVI. Certain conditions originating in the perinatal period (birth trauma).
XVII. Congenital malformations, deformations, and chromosomal abnormalities (spina bifida; cleft palate).
XVIII. Symptoms, signs, and abnormal clinical and laboratory findings, not elsewhere classified (sudden infant death syndrome; unattended death).

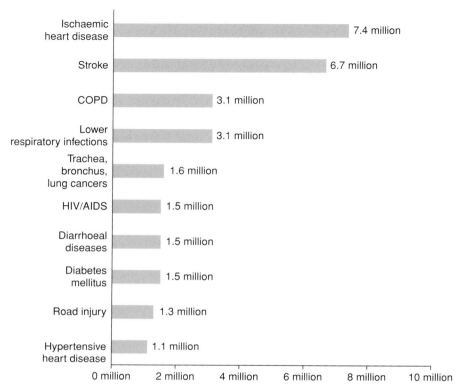

Figure 7.4 The Ten Leading Causes of Death in the World, 2012
Source: WHO, available at: www.who.int/mediacentre/factsheets/fs310/en, last accessed April 29, 2016.

XIX. Injury, poisoning, and certain other consequences of external causes (injuries to the head; frostbite).

XX. External causes of morbidity and mortality (traffic accidents; suicide).

XXI. Factors influencing health status and contact with health services.

XXII. Codes for special purposes (provisional assignment of new diseases of uncertain etiology).

This listing provides extensive detail about the structure of causes of death. Its presentation makes the general point that death is a complex behavior, and that there are literally many thousands of different ways to die. But some causes of death occur more frequently than others.

To illustrate, in 2012, there were approximately 56 million deaths in the world. In Figure 7.4, I show data from the WHO for the ten leading causes of death in the world in 2012. The top cause was heart disease at 7.4 million deaths; stroke was next at 6.7 million deaths; chronic obstructive pulmonary disease (COPD), a lung disease that interferes with normal breathing, accounted for 3.1 million deaths. The ten causes shown in the figure accounted for over half of all deaths in the world in 2012.

People do not all die of the same major causes, however. There are differences in causes of death, and these are largely due to the socioeconomic levels of the countries. The WHO (2011) has produced an illustrative example that makes this point very clear. Consider a hypothetical population of 1,000 persons to represent all the women, men, and children of the world who died in 2008. Of these 1,000 decedents, 159 will have come from rich countries, 677 from middle-income countries, and 163 from poor countries. For each group of countries, I examine the distribution of deaths according to the top ten causes. These are neither identical nor are they ranked the same in the three groups of countries.

Concerning the 159 people from the rich countries (chiefly in North America and Europe), more than two-thirds of them live beyond age 70 and die mainly of chronic diseases. Also, slightly more than half experienced death according to one of the WHO's top ten causes. Coronary heart disease is the cause of twenty-five of the 159 deaths, stroke the cause of fourteen, and lung cancer the cause of nine. HIV/AIDS is not one of the top ten causes of death in this group of countries (Figure 7.5).

In the middle-income countries, nearly half of the people lived to age 70, and the major causes of death were the chronic diseases, just as in the rich countries. However, included among the top ten causes for this group of countries are HIV/AIDS, road traffic accidents, and tuberculosis; these three causes were not included among the top ten causes in the rich countries. Of the 677 people who died from the middle-income countries, ninety-three died from heart disease and eighty-six from stroke.

In the poor countries (many located in sub-Saharan Africa), less than one in five people attained the age of 70, and more than a third of all deaths were to children under 15. Of the 163 people from these countries dying in 2008, eighteen died from lower respiratory infections (the top cause of death) and thirteen from diarrheal diseases. HIV/AIDS was the third leading cause of death responsible for the deaths of thirteen of the 163 decedents (WHO, 2011).

There is considerable variation around the world in causes of death. Life expectancy also varies considerably. I noted earlier that in 2013, a baby girl born in Japan, on average, could expect to live for about 86 years; in contrast, a baby girl born in Lesotho could expect to live, on average, 45 years.

Earlier, I mentioned that in the past, mortality was much higher. In its *World Population Prospects: The 2012 Revision*, the United Nations (2013d) noted that the twentieth century was the era characterized by the most rapid decline in mortality in human history. In the early 1950s, life

Low-income countries

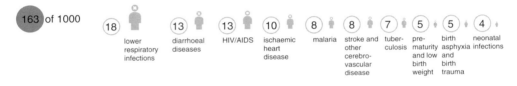

Middle-income countries

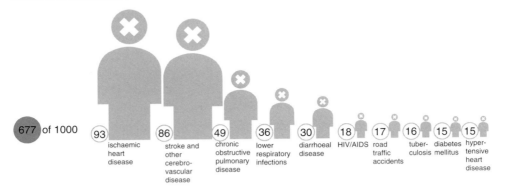

High-income countries

Figure 7.5 Top Ten Causes of Death: Low-, Middle-, and High-Income Countries of the World, 2008
Source: WHO (2011).

expectancy in the world was only 46 years, but reached 69 years by 2010. Figure 7.6 shows the estimated levels of life expectancy for the world and the three major development regions for the period 1950–2100.

The UN has projected that in 2050, life expectancy for the world will reach 76 years. It will reach 82 years by 2100. Life expectancy in the developed world in 1950 was already high, at 65 years; by 2010 it was 77, and is projected to be 83 years in 2050, and 89 years in 2100. In contrast, the forty-nine least developed countries, twenty of which have been severely impacted by HIV/AIDS, had a life expectancy of only 35 years in 1950; it reached 58 years in 2005–2010; is projected to 70 in 2050; and 77 by 2100.

The increases in life expectancy just noted for the more developed and the less developed countries tend to hide the variation in these changes among the world's major areas. The countries of Asia, Latin America and the Caribbean, North America, and Oceania have been experiencing

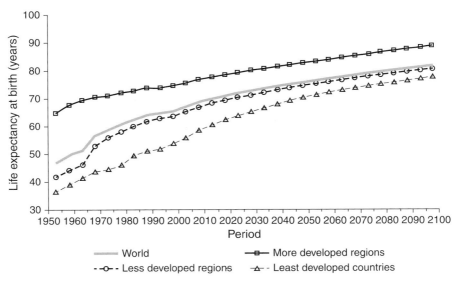

Figure 7.6 Life Expectancy at Birth: World and More Developed, Less Developed, and Least Developed Regions, 1950–2100
Source: United Nations (2013d: 16).

increases in life expectancy at a steady pace, but the countries of Europe for the most part have experienced a slowdown beginning in the late 1960s through the late 1980s. This is due to "severe reductions in life expectancy in countries of eastern Europe, particularly in the Russian Federation and the Ukraine. The remaining regions of Europe have had increasing life expectancies, which are currently equal to or higher than that of Northern America" (United Nations, 2013d: 15).

Unlike the situation in the other regions of the world, increases in life expectancy since the late 1980s in Africa have been slowing down. "While this trend is due in large part to the HIV/AIDS epidemic, other factors have also played a role, including armed conflict, economic stagnation, and resurgent infectious diseases such as tuberculosis and malaria. The recent negative developments in many countries of Africa represent major setbacks in reducing mortality. [But life expectancy is expected to begin rising again]...provided that efforts to reduce the expansion of the HIV/AIDS epidemic and to treat those affected by it succeed" (United Nations, 2013d: 17).

I turn next to a consideration of trends in mortality and longevity in the United States.

MORTALITY AND LONGEVITY IN THE UNITED STATES

The mortality declines that have taken place in the United States are consistent with DTT (as I have already described in Chapter 2). Mortality started dropping gradually in response to changes in the social and economic conditions and the environment that were part of societal modernization. Much of the mortality reduction started to occur before the initiation of any appreciable public health measures.

The Decline in Mortality

Mortality data for the United States are limited until about the middle of the 1800s. In fact, systematic information on US mortality has only been available since 1933 (see Chapter 3). It is believed that CDRs during the colonial period were moderate, ranging from 20 deaths per 1,000 per population to just under 40 (recall, however, my earlier discussion about problems in using CDRs comparatively). Life expectancy certainly did not exceed age 40, and was much lower in many places. In New Hampshire and Massachusetts, life expectancy was about 35, and had increased to around 40 by 1850 (Kitagawa and Hauser, 1973). Indeed, for the states of the United States reporting data as of 1850, life expectancy at birth for whites averaged just over 39 years and for blacks only 23 years. Infant mortality was very high.

Since around 1850, some of the mortality decline has resulted in part from "improvements in public health and sanitation, especially better water supplies and sewage disposal. The improving diet, clothing, and shelter of the American population over the period since about 1870 also played a role. Specific medical interventions beyond more general environmental public health measures were not statistically important until well into the twentieth century" (Haines, 2007). I noted earlier that death rates were often high in the urban areas of Europe. The same was true in the United States. However, in the 1890s, many of the larger US cities initiated "public works sanitation projects (such as piped water, sewer systems, filtration and chlorination of water) and public health administration" (Haines, 2007). As a result of these efforts, the death rates dropped and rural–urban differences in mortality disappeared. Still, white–black differences remained, as they do to this day.

Life expectancy in the United States increased dramatically from 46 for males and 48 for females in 1900 to its levels in 2013 of 76 for males and 81 for females. Most of the improvements occurred from 1900 to 1950. The advances were due to the increased recognition of the **germ theory** of disease, resulting in the identification and control of many infectious and parasitic diseases, particularly among infants and children (Preston and Haines, 1991; Shrestha, 2006). The germ theory led to such interventions for the control of infectious disease as "boiling bottles and milk, washing hands, protecting food from flies, isolating sick children, ventilating rooms, and improving water supply and sewage disposal" (Shrestha, 2006: 3). Today, these preventative behaviors are taken for granted and practiced by nearly everyone.

Improvements in life expectancy since mid-century have been due mostly to the increased prevention and control of the chronic diseases that affect adults, particularly heart disease and stroke.

Life expectancy has not increased uniformly at all ages. Most of the gains have occurred in the younger age groups. To illustrate, a boy born in 1900 could expect to live to the age of 46 and a girl to 48. By 2010, a boy infant could anticipate living for 76 years and a girl infant for 81 years. These are gains of thirty years for baby boys and thirty-three years for baby girls. For people in the older ages, the increases in the past century have not been as striking. A 60-year-old male in 1901 could expect to live for fourteen more years and a female of the same age for fifteen more years (Glover, 1921: 57, 61). In contrast, by 2010, a 60-year-old male could anticipate twenty-two more years of life and a 60-year-old female, twenty-four more years (Arias, 2014: 3). These are gains during the 110-year period of seven years for 60-year-old males and nine years for 60-year-old females. As noted, the greater gains at the younger ages occurred because we can now pretty much control the various infectious diseases that in the past resulted in the deaths of infants and young children. But we do not yet have control of the chronic diseases that cause death among older persons.

Race and Ethnic Differences

Despite the improvements in life expectancy in the twentieth century, a sizable racial difference remains. The gap has narrowed, but there are still differences between the races. Whites had a much higher life expectancy at birth than blacks at the start of the last century. In 1900, a white female infant could expect to live fifty-one years, compared with thirty-five years for a black female infant. A white male infant had a life expectancy in 1900 of forty-eight years, compared with thirty-three years for a newborn black male. So the white advantage for female infants in 1900 was sixteen years, and for male infants it was fifteen years.

I move forward now to 2010. Whites still had a longevity advantage over blacks, but the advantage had narrowed. By 2010, the life expectancy advantage for white females over black females had fallen to three years, and the advantage for white males over black males had dropped to almost five years. These gains are impressive, but the racial differences are still present. Blacks still live, on average, fewer years than whites. The racial differential in mortality in the United States has been studied and analyzed by medical and social scientists for many decades, but the differences have remained.

A major reason for the racial differential is the socioeconomic consequences of life-long poverty. Among other possible factors are low birth weight and low levels of childhood nutrition. Factors operating in midlife include the lack of access to health insurance provided by one's employer, "the strain of physically demanding work, and exposure to a broad range of toxins, both behavioral (e.g., smoking) and environmental (e.g., workplace exposures)" (Shrestha, 2006: 17). In addition, one cannot discount the unfortunate experiences of racial discrimination, which not only have serious and adverse psychological and physiological effects, but also, in a most important way, limit the potential quantity and quality of healthcare available (Shrestha, 2006).

Of particular interest in any analysis of majority–minority group differences in mortality is the very consistent finding that Hispanics in the United States, particularly Mexican Americans, have a life expectancy similar to, and sometimes higher than, Anglos (i.e., NH-whites) (Rogers et al., 1996; Rogers, Hummer, and Nam, 2000). This is a demographic situation exactly the opposite that of blacks. Mexican Americans and African Americans "are more likely to be unemployed, poor, and without a high school degree and...have [also] experienced a long history of discrimination" (Rogers, Hummer, and Nam, 2000: 55; see also Bean and Tienda, 1987). But Mexican Americans compared with Anglos are not at all disadvantaged with regard to life expectancy and other measures of longevity – in fact, they are advantaged, but African Americans are disadvantaged.

Several hypotheses have been offered to account for this so-called Hispanic **epidemiological paradox** (Markides and Coreil, 1986), also referred to as the Latino mortality paradox (Abraido-Lanza et al., 1999) and the **Hispanic paradox** (Palloni and Morenoff, 2001), that is, the empirical finding that Hispanics, especially those of Mexican origin, have death rates of about the same magnitude as, and sometimes lower than, Anglos (Markides and Eschbach, 2011; Riosmena et al., 2015). The hypotheses may be subsumed into three groups, namely, data artifacts, migration effects, and cultural effects. Under data artifacts are such reasons as the possible underreporting of Hispanic-origin identification on death certificates (Palloni and Arias, 2004; Rosenberg et al., 1999) and the misstatement of age, perhaps overstatement, at the older ages (Rosenwaike and Preston, 1983). There are two principal migration effects: First is the **healthy migrant effect**, which states that the longevity advantage is due to the facts that many Mexican Americans in the United States were born elsewhere (Rogers, Hummer, and Nam, 2000: 56) and that migration is known to be selective of persons in better physical and mental health (Palloni and Morenoff, 2001; Rosenwaike, 1991) (see my discussion of migration selectivity in Chapter 9). Second is the **return migrant effect**, also known as the **salmon bias**, which states that Mexican Americans in poor physical health often return to Mexico at

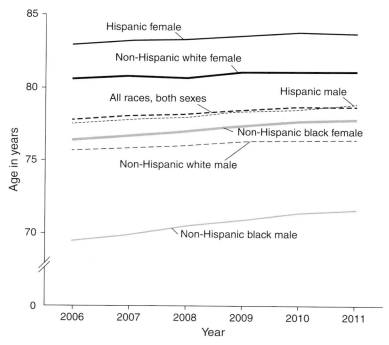

Figure 7.7 Life Expectancy at Birth, by Race and Hispanic Origin, United States, 2006–2011
Source: Hoyert and Xu (2012: 3).

old ages to live out the rest of their lives and, thus, that their deaths are not counted in the US statistics (Abraido-Lanza et al., 1999; Palloni and Arias, 2004). Third are various cultural effects, including the better dietary practices of Latinos compared with other US residents and the stronger family obligations and relationships among Latinos compared with non-Latinos (LeClere, Rogers, and Peters, 1997; Markides and Coreil, 1986; Scribner, 1996; Scribner and Dwyer, 1989).

One way to examine the Hispanic paradox is with data on life expectancy. In Figure 7.7, I show data on life expectancy at birth for the United States for the years of 2006–2011 for Hispanic males and females, NH-white males and females, and NH-black males and females. In every year, 2006–2011, Hispanic females have higher life expectancy than any of the other race/ethnic sex groups, with a life expectancy at birth, e_0, in 2011 of 83.7 years. Non-Hispanic-white females are next with an e_0 value of 81.1. And next are Hispanic males with a value of e_0 in 2011 of 78.9. NH-black females are next with an e_0 of 77.8, next are NH-white males at 76.4, and last are NH-black males with an e_0 of 71.6.

If the paradox were not operating, we would expect among females to see the following order with respect to their e_0 values: NH-white females, and then Hispanic females and NH-black females. For males we would expect the same ordering. But we see in the figure that Hispanic females have e_0 values for every year greater than those of NH-white females and NH-black females, and we see that Hispanic males have e_0 values for every year above NH-white males and NH-black males. This is a paradox because the orderings do not follow what we would assume to be the negative effect of socioeconomic disadvantage and discrimination on life expectancy. Socioeconomically disadvantaged groups, for example, blacks and Hispanics, should not live as long as socioeconomically advantaged groups for the socioeconomic reasons I addressed above, as well as for the effects of poverty and discrimination.

Some research has found limited support for the salmon bias and the healthy migrant effects (e.g., Palloni and Arias, 2004). But other analyses (e.g., Turra and Elo, 2008) find little support for these effects, particularly that involving the salmon bias.

The paradox has also been studied with cause of death data. Hispanics, especially those of Mexican origin, have lower death rates compared with NH-whites for nine of the fifteen leading causes of death (Dominguez et al., 2015). For instance, the prevalence of smoking is lower among Hispanics compared with NH-whites, which could contribute to lower Hispanic mortality.

And the paradox has also been analyzed by focusing on the presence of sexually transmitted infections (Obregon, 2015) and the prevalence of criminal behavior (Martinez, 2010, 2014; Martinez and Valenzuela, 2006; Romero, 2014). The presence of sexually transmitted infections (STIs) should be associated with socioeconomic status (SES), that is, the higher the SES the less the presence of STIs. But Obregon's analysis demonstrated that Mexican origin birth-giving women have lower odds of having STIs than NH-blacks.

My student Fabian Romero conducted research showing that neighborhood crime rates, especially murder, were higher for blacks living in segregated neighborhoods, but this relationship did not hold for Hispanics living in segregated neighborhoods. Dr. Romero's analyses indicated that the return to crime for residentially segregated blacks was much higher than it was for residentially segregated Hispanics, particularly for violent crimes (Romero, 2014: 107).

Thus, research shows that Latinos have an advantage over blacks, and in some cases over whites, with respect to higher life expectancy and lower death rates for most of the main causes of death. Mexican origin women have a much lower likelihood of contracting sexually transmitted infections compared with black women. And Hispanic men living in segregated neighborhoods have crime rates significantly lower than those of black men living in segregated neighborhoods. This research points to a Hispanic advantage

Table 7.3 Expectation of Life at Ages 70, 80, 90, and 100, by Sex, Race and Hispanic origin: United States, 2010

Age	Hispanics		NH-whites		NH-blacks	
	Males	Females	Males	Females	Males	Females
70	15.4	18.0	14.2	16.4	12.8	15.7
80	9.0	10.8	8.1	9.6	7.8	9.6
90	4.5	5.4	4.0	4.8	4.4	5.2
100	2.3	2.6	2.0	2.3	2.5	2.8

Source: Arias (2014: table A).

on several dimensions. This is an unexpected finding given the lower levels of socioeconomic status for Hispanics, their higher rates of poverty, and the decades of discrimination directed against them by the majority population.

I have reviewed some of the hypotheses that have been set forth to account for the Hispanic paradox. No analyses to date provide a definitive explanation. If I were pressed for a reason for the Hispanic advantage, I would lean toward the cultural effects explanation. It seems to me that the strong social support networks in the Hispanic community and their demonstrably better health habits should play a key role. But no one has the final answer. The paradox remains a topic of considerable interest among demographers.

There is another racial difference in mortality that deserves our attention. I showed earlier in this chapter that life expectancy at birth, e_0, is the lowest for blacks compared with Hispanics and whites. Indeed, for most of the years of their lives, blacks have higher death rates than Hispanics and whites. But the situation changes at the very oldest ages. By late life, death rates for blacks become lower than those for whites, and in some cases lower than those for Hispanics. This is what is known in demography as the **racial mortality crossover**.

I have extracted life expectancy data from a 2010 US life table (Arias, 2014) and present them in Table 7.3. The table shows values of life expectancy for ages 70, 80, 90, and 100 for Hispanic males and females, for NH-white males and females, and for NH-black males and females. Looking first at males at age 70, Hispanics have an expectancy value of 15.4 years, NH-whites, 14.2 years, and NH-blacks, 12.8 years. And the same pattern holds for females at age 70. This is the pattern we see throughout most of the life table, that is, Hispanics live the longest, then NH-whites, and last, NH-blacks.

But observe what happens at age 80. Among females at age 80, NH-blacks and NH-whites have the same value, 9.6 years. At age 80, the racial crossover is beginning to occur for females. But it has not yet started for males. Among males at age 80, Hispanics still live the longest, then NH-whites, and last, NH-blacks, the same pattern observed in most of the life table.

At age 90, NH-black males and NH-black females show a life expectancy advantage over NH-white males and females. And at age 100, NH-black males and NH-black females now have the higher life expectancy values compared with NH-white males and females and to Hispanic males and females.

The racial crossover has been studied extensively by demographers and other social scientists (Corti et al., 1999; Dupre, Franzese, and Parrado, 2006; Eberstein, Nam, and Heyman, 2008; Johnson, 2000; Manton, Poss, and Wing, 1979; Manton and Stallard, 1997; Nam, Weatherby, and Ockay, 1978; Sautter et al., 2012; Wing et al., 1985), and the findings have been rather consistent, showing results for the United States much like those I reported above in Table 7.3. Moreover, other analyses have found evidence of a racial mortality crossover in different time periods and in different parts of the world (Nam, 1995).

The issue, thus, is not whether the crossover exists. Clearly it does. The question is why. Specifically, why do blacks at the oldest ages have higher life expectancies than whites? Demographers have set forth two main explanations: age misreporting on death certificates and "population heterogeneity in frailty" (Sautter et al., 2012).

With respect to the first reason, Sautter and her colleagues (2012) have noted that "age misreporting (i.e., overstatement of age) on death certificates occurs and is more common among blacks; this error can bias mortality estimates downward at the oldest ages. However, some analyses show that . . . crossovers are postponed to later ages rather than eliminated when data are adjusted for age misreporting" (Sautter et al., 2012: 1566).

The second reason, "population heterogeneity in frailty," refers to the fact that socioeconomically disadvantaged groups, such as blacks in the United States, will suffer higher death rates throughout most of their lives, compared with the majority population, for the reasons I discussed earlier in this chapter. This ends up producing in the surviving elderly black population "a more robust group of disadvantaged individuals." As their age increases, the likelihood of dying is now "weighted toward the robust members of the disadvantaged subgroup who now exhibit lower mortality than the advantaged subgroup (i.e., the whites), who experience an acceleration of mortality at older ages" (Sautter et al., 2012: 1566). In a sense this is a "survival of the fittest" argument. The more frail blacks die before they are age 80 or 90, and this produces a more robust group of blacks that has survived the previous 70–80 or so years, and hence live longer than

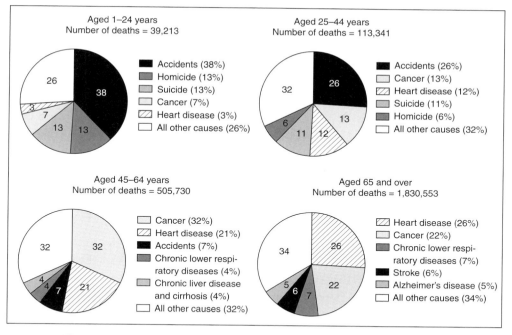

Figure 7.8 Percent Distribution of Five Leading Causes of Death, by Age Group: United States, 2011
Source: Minino (2013: 4).

the majority. The racial mortality crossover is certainly a phenomenon of considerable interest to demographers. Like the Hispanic paradox reviewed earlier, it is an area that will continue to be debated and analyzed by demographers in the decades ahead.

Prevailing Causes of Death

Changes in causes of death in the United States are somewhat predictable. Many decades ago mortality from infectious and parasitic diseases decreased as major causes of death in the United States, and mortality from degenerative diseases increased. The main causes of death in the United States today are associated with degenerative and chronic diseases. In the United States in 2011, the five top causes of death (heart disease, cancer, chronic lower respiratory diseases, stroke, and accidents) accounted for over 60 percent of all deaths.

However, this "general profile of leading causes varies substantially based on a decedent's age" (Minino, 2013: 4). Figure 7.8 shows percentage distributions of the five leading causes of death in the United States in 2011, for four broad age groups.

The three leading causes of death for persons aged 1–24 years are all external causes, that is, accidents, homicide, and suicide; they account for 64 percent of all deaths in this youngest age group. These three external causes of death are among the top five for decedents aged 25–44, accounting for 43 percent of all deaths in this age group. Among 45–64-year-olds, only one external cause, accidents, is among the five main causes for middle-aged decedents; most of the deaths in this age group are due to chronic conditions, namely, cancer, heart disease, chronic lower respiratory diseases, and chronic liver disease; they account for 61 percent of deaths to persons in this age group. Among the oldest group of decedents, those aged 65 and over, the five main causes of their deaths do not include any external causes; instead, they caused are heart disease, cancer, chronic lower respiratory diseases, stroke, and Alzheimer's disease; these account for 66 percent of all deaths to these elders. So not only does mortality vary by age (remember the "age curve of mortality"), but causes of death also vary by age.

Alzheimer's disease (AD) is in the fifth rank for elders. One of my students, Mary Ann Davis, pointed out in her doctoral research the very interesting fact that males are less likely to die of AD than females at all ages, and that the gap increases among the oldest-old. Why? She noted that women live longer than men and thus are more likely to die of chronic and degenerative diseases such as AD (Davis, 2008).

Socioeconomic Differentials in Mortality

Generally, the higher the socioeconomic status (SES), the lower the mortality. This relationship is found whether or not SES is measured in terms of income, occupation, or education (Stockwell, Wicks, and Adamchak, 1978). This inverse association is found in US data from the earliest times to the present, as well as in most other countries (Krieger et al., 1993; Rogers, Hummer, and Nam, 2000; Williams and Collins, 1995).

Two extensive and well-known studies of socioeconomic differentials deserve special mention. The first is the analysis of Evelyn Kitagawa and Philip Hauser (1973), *Differential Mortality in the United States*. In this very important and path-breaking book, the authors examined a sample of US 1960 death certificates matched with 1960 census data. They showed that income and education have strong negative relationships with mortality, particularly for persons in the 25–64 age group. This was one of the very first analyses reporting the relationship between socioeconomic status and mortality.

A more recent and very noteworthy analysis is by Richard Rogers, Robert Hummer, and Charles Nam (2000), *Living and Dying in the USA*. In this invaluable study of adult mortality, the authors used two matched data sets to analyze the effects of social factors on mortality. One data set, the

National Health Interview Survey (NHIS), was based on annual interviews of US residents about their health and sociodemographic characteristics. Data from the NHIS for persons aged 18 and older for several years in the late 1980s and early 1990s were then matched with death certificate data for persons who were included in the NHIS, but who subsequently died between 1986 and 1995. Rogers and his colleagues were able to relate a host of socioeconomic characteristics of persons interviewed in the NHIS with whether or not they died in the period through the mid-1990s. They showed statistically and concretely that mortality rates are not the same for all adults. The force of mortality is "stronger for the poor, the less educated, the unemployed and the uninsured rather than for the rich, the highly educated, and the insured...[Mortality is higher] for those who rarely attend religious services...than for those who frequently attend...[And mortality is higher] for those who smoke, drink heavily, and are inactive [compared with those] who have never smoked, who drink moderately, and exercise regularly" (Rogers, Hummer, and Nam, 2000: 321). The data and results reported in their book provide solid evidence that we are indeed population actors and that our personal choices and decisions throughout our lifetime on a number of socioeconomic and behavioral dimensions have dramatic effects on our longevity.

INFANT MORTALITY

An aspect of mortality that receives special consideration from demographers is infant mortality. This is due to at least two considerations. First, as Frisbie has written, "few, if any, human experiences are more tragic or emotionally devastating as the death of an infant or child" (2005: 251). Second, as I observed earlier, the death rate in the first year of life is much higher than in the succeeding several decades. Indeed, in high-mortality populations, the death rate in the first year of life is not reached again in the society until age 70 or later. And in some high-mortality populations, the highest death rate is in the first year of life.

Infant Mortality Rate

The **infant mortality rate** (IMR), the most common measure of infant death, is the number of deaths in a year to children under age 1 per 1,000 babies born in the year. It is expressed as

$$\text{IMR} = \frac{\text{deaths in the year to persons under age 1}}{\text{live births in the year}} * 1,000 \quad (7.8)$$

Infant mortality rates of 200 or more per 1,000 births were the rule as late as 1800, even in countries of the developed world. This means that around one in every five babies born were dead before reaching their first birthday. IMRs were even higher in countries prior to their completing the demographic transition. During those early periods, "IMRs were probably on the order of 260 to 370 per 1,000 live births" (Frisbie, 2005: 260). As late as the 1870s, the IMR in European countries varied from 100 in Norway to nearly 300 in southern Germany (United Nations, 1973: 124). Infant mortality in China in the early 1900s was likely around 300. Indeed, China probably did not reduce its IMR countrywide to around 200 until the founding of the People's Republic in 1949 (Banister, 1992: 167).

High IMRs led to the cultural practice in China and Korea and in many other Asian societies of not giving a newborn baby a name until it had lived for several months and showed signs of continued viability. In Korea, for instance, even to this day, a small feast is prepared on the 100th day after a baby is born. Rice, red bean cakes, and wine are served. This day was originally celebrated as a feast in honor of the child's surviving the first few months of life, the most difficult period of time for survival. In ancient times, the child was not given his or her name until the 100th day celebration. It made little sense to invest emotionally in a newborn by assigning it a name if the chances were only around four in ten that it would survive for a year.

During the latter part of the nineteenth century and into the twentieth century, most countries in the developed world experienced decreases in their IMRs. The transition to lower levels of infant mortality in the Western countries, as well as to lower child and adult mortality, was due in large part to reductions in infectious and parasitic diseases. Indeed, prior to the third and fourth decades of the twentieth century, "the role played by physicians and drug therapy in the reduction of mortality was relatively slight" (Frisbie, 2005: 260; McKeown, 1976).

In the United States in 2013, the IMR was 5 deaths per 1,000 live births. In earlier years and decades, it was much higher. The IMR in the United States was more than 100 in 1915–1916, dropping to 26 by 1960 and to 13 by 1980 (US Bureau of the Census, 2004). Figure 7.9 shows trends in the IMR in the United States by race and by Hispanic origin of the mother, from 2000 to 2010.

The US IMR dropped from 11 deaths per 1,000 births in the 1980s, to 9 in the 1990s, to 7 in 2000, to 6 in 2010. Black infant mortality is the highest of the major race/ethnic groups; Hispanics and Anglos (i.e., NH-whites) have IMRs that are very similar, just over 5 in 2010. Black infant mortality declined from under 14 infant deaths per 1,000 live births in 2000 to just over 11 in 2010. But black infant mortality in 2010 is still twice as high as infant mortality for Hispanics and NH-whites.

Infant mortality in the contemporary world varies considerably from country to country. In general, the more modernized the country, the lower

Table 7.4 Countries with the Highest and the Lowest Infant Mortality Rates in the World, 2013			
Highest infant mortality rates		Lowest infant mortality rates	
Central African Republic	116	Iceland	1.8
Congo, Democratic Republic of	109	Finland	1.8
Chad	96	Japan	1.9
Angola	96	Singapore	2.0
Guinea-Bissau	94	Estonia	2.1
Sierra Leone	92	Sweden	2.3

Source: PRB (2014).

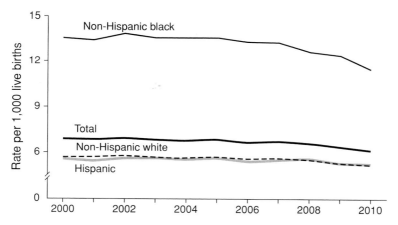

Figure 7.9 Infant Mortality Rates, by Mother's Race and Hispanic Origin, United States, 2000–2010
Source: Mathews and MacDorman (2013: 1).

its IMR. The IMR of the world in 2013 was 38 infant deaths per 1,000 live births. This means that in the world in 2013, on average, about one baby died before reaching the age of 1 year for every twenty-six born. The IMR was 5 in the more developed countries and 42 in the less developed countries (PRB, 2014).

I list in Table 7.4 the six countries with the highest IMRs in 2013 and the six with the lowest.

The Central African Republic had the highest IMR in the world in 2013: 116 infant deaths per 1,000 live births. The Democratic Republic of the Congo is not far behind, with an IMR of 109; the next highest IMRs are in Chad, Angola, Guinea-Bissau and Sierra Leone. In 2013, five more countries had IMRs of 80 or higher (i.e., Burundi, Mozambique, Somalia, Equatorial Guinea, and Lesotho) (PRB, 2014). These are astoundingly high levels of infant mortality. Although great success in lowering infant mortality has been achieved in the last century, these benefits have not been fully realized by the countries just mentioned.

The countries with the lowest IMRs in the world in 2013 were Iceland (1.8 infant deaths per 1,000 live births), Finland (1.8), and Japan (1.9). IMRs of 2 and 3 are about as low as will ever be attained.

The IMR in the United States in 2013 was 5.4. Although this is certainly low compared with the IMRs in many other countries, it is higher than the average IMR of 5/1,000 for the developed world. Most developed countries in the world and many developing countries had IMRs in 2013 lower than the IMR of the United States. Indeed, according to data from *The World Factbook* produced by the US Central Intelligence Agency (2015), fifty-four countries and territories had estimated IMRs for 2014 lower than that of the United States. The actual countries, ordered by how close their IMR is to the IMR of the United States are as follows: Serbia's is the closest; the next closest countries are Lithuania, Croatia, Bosnia and Herzegovina, Faroe Islands, Guam, Northern Mariana Islands, New Caledonia, Slovakia, Hungary, French Polynesia, Greece, Canada, Cuba, New Zealand, San Marino, Wallis and Fortuna, Taiwan, Portugal, the United Kingdom, Australia, Liechtenstein, Luxembourg, Belgium, Isle of Man, Austria, Denmark, Slovenia, Israel, South Korea, Jersey, Ireland, Switzerland, Andorra, the Netherlands, Belarus, Malta, Guernsey, Germany, Anguilla, Finland, Spain, France, Italy, Iceland, Macao, Hong Kong, Czech Republic, Sweden, Singapore, Bermuda, Norway, Japan, and Monaco.

Why was the US IMR higher than the IMRs of these fifty-four other countries? Part of the reason is statistical. The United States counts as a live birth an infant showing any sign of life (see my discussion and definition of a live birth in Chapter 3), whereas many other countries are not as stringent. Dr. Bernadine Healy, the former director of the US National Institutes of Health and director and chief executive officer of the American Red Cross, argued that it is incorrect to "compare US infant mortality with reports from other countries. The United States counts all births as live if they show any sign of life, regardless of prematurity or size. This includes what many other countries report as **stillbirth**. In Austria and Germany, fetal weight must be at least 500 grams (1 pound) to count as a live birth; in other parts of Europe, such as Switzerland, the fetus must be at least 30 centimeters (12 inches) long. In Belgium and France, births at less than 26 weeks of pregnancy are registered as lifeless. And some countries do not reliably register babies who die within the first 24 hours of birth. Thus, the United States is sure to report higher infant mortality rates" (Healy, 2006).

However, statistical adjustments that attempt to take into account these differences in definitions still do not move the US IMR to the low levels of Japan and Sweden (Haub and Yanagishita, 1991). Also, if one used only the IMR for the US Anglo (NH-white) population, the Anglo IMR would still be twice as high as that of the low IMR countries.

One reason for understanding why the United States fares so poorly is the powerful influence of the mother's socioeconomic status on the likelihood of the infant surviving. The leading cause of infant mortality in developed countries such as the United States is congenital malformations, a cause of infant death that can be reduced, if not eliminated, with good nutritional intake and prenatal vitamins. However, poor mothers, especially those in poverty, often lack the needed socioeconomic resources required to obtain these benefits. They also may be forced to forego full prenatal care, which could result in maternal complications at birth, another prime cause of infant mortality. Many countries in the developed world have socialized medical plans that provide universal healthcare to the entire population, and many of these countries have lower IMRs than the United States.

The further reduction of infant mortality in the United States has been and continues to be a major goal. One of the objectives of *Healthy People 2010*, a set of health initiatives being pursued by several federal agencies such as the National Institutes of Health, the Food and Drug Administration, and the Centers for Disease Control and Prevention, was to reduce the US IMR in 2010 to 4.5 infant deaths per 1,000 live births. Well, the goal was not reached; the 2010 IMR was slightly over 6 (see my above discussion).

In the United States and in most countries of the developed world, around two-thirds of infant deaths occur in the first month after birth and are due in large part to "health problems of the infant or the pregnancy, such as preterm delivery or birth defects" (Federal Interagency Forum on Child and Family Statistics, 2007: 61). Deaths to infants during the first month of life are frequently analyzed separately from those that occur after the first month but during the first year of life.

Neonatal Mortality Rate and Postneonatal Mortality Rate

The IMR may be thought of as the sum of two rates, namely, the **neonatal mortality rate** (NMR), that is, deaths of babies aged 28 days or less per 1,000 live births, and the **postneonatal mortality rate** (PMR), that is, deaths of babies aged between 29 days and 1 year per 1,000 live births. These two rates are expressed as follows:

$$\text{NMR} = \frac{\text{deaths of babies 0 to 28 days old}}{\text{live births in the year}} * 1{,}000 \qquad (7.9)$$

$$\text{PMR} = \frac{\text{deaths of babies 29 days to 365 days old}}{\text{live births in the year}} * 1{,}000 \qquad (7.10)$$

Table 7.5 Neonatal Mortality Rates and Number of Neonatal Deaths, by Major Development Regions of the World, 1990 and 2013

Region	Neonatal mortality rate (deaths per 1,000 live births)			Number of neonatal deaths (thousands)	
	1990	2013	Decline (%) 1990–2013	1990	2013
Developed regions	8	3	55	118	48
Developing regions	36	22	40	4,554	2,714
North Africa	30	13	56	109	53
Sub-Saharan Africa	46	31	32	977	1,066
Latin America and the Caribbean	22	9	58	255	101
Caucasus and Central Asia	26	15	42	51	26
eastern Asia	25	8	69	784	150
excluding China	12	8	35	11	7
southern Asia	51	30	42	1,940	1,086
excluding India	49	30	39	578	338
southeastern Asia	27	14	47	321	160
western Asia	28	14	50	111	67
Oceania	26	21	19	5	6
World	*33*	*20*	*40*	*4,672*	*2,763*

Source: UNICEF (2014: 13).

According to UNICEF (2014), there were almost 2.8 million neonatal deaths in the world in 2013; this amounts to over 60 percent of the approximately 4.6 million infant deaths that occurred in that year worldwide. I show in Table 7.5 NMRs for the developed world and the various regions of the developing world for 2013 and for 1990. Worldwide in 2013, the NMR was 20 neonatal deaths per 1,000 live births; it was 30 in 2000 and 33 in 1990. In countries of the developed world in 2013, it was 3 (in the United States it was 4), and 22 in the countries of the developing regions. In other words, the NMR of the developing regions in 2013 was more than seven times greater than the NMR of the developed world.

According to UNICEF estimates, "around two-thirds of all neonatal deaths occurred in just ten countries, with India accounting for more than a quarter and Nigeria for about a tenth" (UNICEF, 2014: 1).

The main, but not the only, causes of neonatal deaths are **endogenous conditions**, "such as congenital malformations, chromosomal abnormalities, and complications of delivery, as well as...low birthweight" (Pebley,

2003: 534). These are usually related to genetic disorders of the birth process itself. It was long thought that neonatal mortality was due primarily to endogenous causes. Research has shown, however, that the endogenous causes dominate infant mortality principally in the early days of life, and not for the entire first month of life (Bouvier and van der Tak, 1976; Poston and Rogers, 1985).

The PMR for the world in 2013 was 18, with a low value of 2 in the countries of the developed world. Deaths in the postneonatal period, as well as in the first few years of life, are often due mainly to exogenous causes, such as infectious disease, accidents, and injury. In countries experiencing declining death rates, their PMRs tend to decline much more rapidly than their NMRs. The main reason is that "improved living standards, better healthcare, and public health programs have greater effects on exogenous causes of death than on endogenous causes" (Pebley, 2003: 534). An **exogenous cause of death** is due mainly to environmental or external factors, such as infections or accidents. An **endogenous cause of death** in an infant can occur because of genetic issues or conditions associated with fetal development or the birth process.

Stillbirth Rate

Demographers are also interested in the rate at which **stillbirths** (also known as miscarriages or fetal deaths) occur. A stillbirth is a fetus not born alive. It is thus not registered as a death because it was not born. However, stillbirths are often identified in hospital reports dealing with obstetric procedures. A fetus may die prior to the onset of labor, that is, *in utero*, because of pregnancy complications or various maternal diseases. Or a fetus may be alive at the onset of labor but die during the process and, thus, emerge from its mother in a dead state. The WHO has reported that it "is therefore important to know at what point before birth the [fetus] died, so that appropriate interventions can be planned accordingly . . . Where women receive good care during childbirth, [these] deaths represent less than 10 percent of stillbirths due to unexpected severe complications" (2006: 3). The formula for the **stillbirth rate** (SBR), sometimes referred to as the **fetal death rate**, is the following:

$$\text{SBR} = \frac{\text{stillbirths}}{\text{live births plus stillbirths in the year}} * 1{,}000 \qquad (7.11)$$

Not all countries report data on stillbirths, so demographers rely on estimates produced by the WHO (2015a). According to the WHO, there were an estimated 2.6 million stillbirths in the world in 2009. Worldwide, the SBR in 2009 was 18.9 stillbirths per 1,000 live births plus stillbirths (remember that the denominator for the SBR comprises live births plus still-births). SBRs ranged from lows of 2 in Finland and Singapore to highs of 47 in Pakistan, 42 in Nigeria, 36 in Bangladesh, and 34 in Djibouti.

By far the most stillbirths occur in the countries of the developing world. And almost half of all stillbirths occur when the woman is in labor. The major causes are complications during the birthing process, maternal infections, and maternal disorders, especially diabetes and hypertension. Most stillbirths are preventable, according to the WHO (2015a).

Perinatal Mortality Rate

Another indicator of mortality at early life and before birth is the **perinatal mortality rate** (PeMR). Because the "endogenous causes of mortality in the first week after birth are similar to the causes of stillbirths . . . the two may be combined into the PeMR, which refers to deaths in the period immediately before and after birth" (Rowland, 2003: 202). The PeMR is a measure of what demographers refer to as "pregnancy wastage" because it reflects the number of wasted pregnancies, wasted because they either did not result in a live birth (they were fetal deaths) or resulted in a live birth of an infant who lived for only seven days or less. The PeMR is expressed as

$$\text{PeMR} = \frac{\text{stillbirths} + \text{deaths to babies 0 to 7 days old}}{\text{live births plus stillbirths in the year}} * 1,000 \quad (7.12)$$

The PeMR for the United States was 6.5 in 2006 and dropped slightly to 6.3 by 2011. More recent PeMR data for countries of the world are not available. In 2000, the PeMR for the world was 47 per 1,000 live births plus stillbirths; it was 10 in the developed world and 50 in the less developed regions (WHO, 2006: 18). The rates ranged from highs of 111 in Mauritania, 104 in Liberia, 96 in both Afghanistan and Côte d'Ivoire, and 90 in Sierra Leone, to lows of 4 in the Czech Republic and Singapore, and 5 in Italy, Martinique, and Sweden. The PeMR distribution worldwide indicated that as of the year 2000, the highest rates by far were in sub-Saharan Africa, a story that has been told time and time again in this chapter.

Maternal Mortality Ratio

A final measure, the **maternal mortality ratio** (MMR), gauges the extent to which mothers die immediately before, during, or after giving birth because of a problem or problems associated with the pregnancy or childbirth. The WHO has defined a **maternal death** as "the death of a woman while pregnant or within 42 days of termination of pregnancy, irrespective of the duration or site of pregnancy, from any cause related to or aggravated by the pregnancy or its management, but not from accidental or incidental causes" (Maine and Stamas, 2003: 628). The MMR is the number of deaths in a year of women dying as a result of complications of pregnancy, childbirth, and the puerperium (i.e., the condition of the woman immediately following childbirth, usually ending when ovulation begins again), per 100,000 births occurring in the year. Sometimes the deaths (the numerator) are referred to as deaths due to puerperal causes. The formula for the MMR is the following:

$$\text{MMR} = \frac{\text{deaths in the year due to puerperal causes}}{\text{live births in the year}} * 100,000 \quad (7.13)$$

Observe that the MMR is multiplied by a constant of 100,000 because since 1940, maternal deaths have become increasingly rare in the developed world (Loudon, 1992, 2000). However, as I show in the following paragraph, the same may not be said about countries in the developing world.

The WHO (2015b) reported that there were an estimated 313,000 maternal deaths in the entire world in 2015, which is a sizable reduction from the estimated number of 529,000 reported for the year 2000 (WHO, 2004). Developing regions accounted for almost 99 percent of all the maternal deaths in 2015, with the sub-Saharan Africa region alone accounting for 66 percent, or 201,000 maternal deaths, followed by the southern Asia region with 66,000 maternal deaths. The MMR for the world for 2015 was estimated to be 216 per 100,000 live births and was the highest in sub-Saharan Africa (546). The country with the highest MMR in the world in 2015 was Sierra Leone with an MMR of 1,360 maternal deaths per 100,000 births. An additional eighteen counties, all in sub-Saharan Africa, had very high MMRs in 2015, including the Central African Republic (an MMR of 881), Chad (856), Nigeria (814), and South Sudan (789). Sierra Leone's MMR in 2015 of 1,360 means that in Sierra Leone in 2015, 14 mothers died in the birthing process for every 1,000 babies born

The lowest MMRs are 2 maternal deaths per 100,000 live births in Estonia, 3 in Greece and Singapore, and 4 in Belarus, Italy, Sweden, and Austria. These are very low levels of maternal mortality. The MMR for the United States is 21, the same MMR value as Iran and Hungary (Central Intelligence Agency, 2015).

The WHO has noted, however, that the number of maternal deaths reported for many of these developed countries are likely understated owing to the misclassification of maternal deaths, and should be inflated by a factor of around 1.5 (WHO, 2004: 11). Regarding the MMR value of around 21 in the United States, the *Healthy People 2020* program is endeavoring to reduce it to a value of 11.4 by the year 2020.

Maternal deaths in earlier centuries were very common, even in Europe and the United States. Reliable data on maternal mortality were not collected in the Western world until the mid-nineteenth century. Loudon has noted that the levels were quite high until the 1930s: "The risk of women dying in childbirth in (England) in the 1920s and 1930s was still as high as it had been just after Queen Victoria came to the throne in the 1850s. Today, however, the risk of women in England and Wales dying is between 40 and 50 times lower than it was 60 years ago" (Loudon, 2000: 241S).

The two most important factors leading to maternal deaths are age and **parity** (the number of times a woman has given birth; it also refers to **birth order**, e.g., a second-born child, who would be a second-parity child). Very young women and older women are more likely to die during pregnancy or childbirth than are women in their 20s and 30s. High-parity women and women with short birth intervals are also at high risk: "Underlying these [factors] are such conditions as chronic disease and malnutrition, poverty, unwanted pregnancies, inadequate prenatal and obstetric care, and lack of access to a hospital" (Lamb and Siegel, 2004: 352).

THE FUTURE COURSE OF MORTALITY

Declining mortality has numerous social and economic implications. The efficiency and productivity of the labor force are increased because healthier adults are able to work better and for far longer. More surviving children translate into more potential and hopefully productive workers. Improved childhood survival often weakens and reduces the importance of some of the social, economic, and emotional rationales for high birth rates. At the same time, declining mortality has the direct effect of increasing rates of population growth, unless fertility rates fall as well; the mortality reductions will thus influence the population's age structure. Owing to these social, economic, and demographic implications, there is considerable speculation about the future levels of mortality (Bongaarts, 2006).

I will now discuss future mortality trends in terms of life expectancy. I noted earlier the high levels of life expectancy attained in the past 10–15 years by many of the countries of the developed world. In 2013, the developed world as a whole had a life expectancy at birth of 79 years (75 years for males, 82 for females). Japan's life expectancy of 83 years (80 for males, 86 for females) was the highest in the world, followed closely by Australia, Spain, Sweden, and Singapore, all at 82 years (PRB, 2014).

So I now ask, is it likely that mortality rates will continue to fall, resulting in even higher levels of life expectancy than those attained by these countries? There are two positions: one argues for a limit, and the other argues against it.

A major advocate for an upper limit to human life expectancy is James Fries, who predicted in 1980 that humans have a maximum potential life expectancy averaging about 85 years (Fries, 1980; see also 1983). In a paper published in 2000, he commented on the increases in life expectancy that have occurred since 1980 when he made his stark prediction of 85 years, noting that life expectancy may increase a little beyond his earlier proclaimed average of 85 years, but not by much.

Jay Olshansky and Bruce Carnes (2001) support the contention of Fries and have noted that all living organisms are subjected to a "biological warranty" period. Arguing against an average life expectancy of, say, 100 years, they have written that "if most humans are capable of living to 100, there should be little evidence of significant functional decline and pathology" of older people today who reach ages older than 80. But they noted that there is no such evidence. Indeed, "there is substantial decline in functioning of all human biological systems by age 80" (Sonnega, 2006: 2). They have also contended that human life expectancy in the United States is not likely to exceed 90 years at any time in this century (Olshansky et al., 2005).

The major proponent on the other side, proclaiming the real possibility of future and continued mortality declines, is the very distinguished demographer James Vaupel. He has observed that every time a maximum life expectancy number is published, it is soon surpassed. He and his colleagues, particularly James Carey, have noted that death rates in human and many nonhuman populations do not continue to increase with increasing age, but that there is a slowing or deceleration of mortality at the oldest ages (Carey, 2003; Carey and Vaupel, 2005; Carey et al., 1992).

Vaupel and his colleague Jim Oeppen have examined what they refer to as "best practice life expectancy" data. They have gathered and graphed data for every year from 1840 to 2000 for the six countries of the world with the highest recorded life expectancy (i.e., Australia, Iceland, Japan, New Zealand, Norway, and Sweden). Their analysis allowed them to conclude that "the gap between the record [highest life expectancy] and the national level is a measure of how much better a country might do at current states of knowledge and demonstrated practice" (Oeppen and Vaupel, 2002: 1029). They showed that female life expectancy has increased linearly by about three months per year (or 2.5 years per decade) between 1840 and 2000. They have extrapolated from this linear trend and predict that if it continues, the average life expectancy at birth for females could well reach 100 years by the year 2060. Follow-up analyses have been undertaken by Shkolnikov, Jdanov, Andreev, and Vaupel (2011) with rather similar results.

I am inclined to take a position closer to that of Vaupel and his associates than to that of Olshansky and his associates. Vaupel and Olshansky have been debating for over twenty years whether life expectancies will continue to rise. I have read a great deal of the research conducted by them and their colleagues, some of which I have cited above. As Couzin-Frankel (2011: 549) wrote several years ago, they have been "trying to answer a question that is essentially unanswerable: whether the future will resemble the past. Vaupel says it will, with life expectancies at birth rising unabated by about 3 months a year in countries where residents live the longest. Olshansky counters that sober realities, such as widespread obesity, will cut life spans short." My review of the arguments and the data in an extensive body of literature leads me to conclude against a fixed biological maximum life expectancy. I hold that at the global level, life expectancy will surely increase in the decades of this century. Whether female life expectancy reaches 100 years by 2060 is not as important as the expectation that it will not stagnate at just above 85.

In the developing world, there will certainly be increases in life expectancy. Many of the developing countries still have high rates of infant mortality and general mortality, including maternal mortality. Infectious diseases remain a dominant cause of death in many of these countries. Modern medical and public health techniques will surely bring about further reductions in mortality from these causes. The developing countries have a very young age structure, and the young, more so than the old, have benefited and will continue to benefit from reductions in infectious and parasitic diseases. Consequently, further declines in mortality can surely be expected in many developing countries.

I should temper my appraisal with the realization that progress in reducing the force of mortality in some countries of the world has stalled and has even reversed direction. This phenomenon of **mortality reversals** is a relatively new occurrence in demography. When I first began teaching demography to undergraduate students in 1970, any evidence of significant mortality reversals was for the most part unknown. Demographic transition theory proposed, and it was widely believed, that once death rates in a country began to fall, they would never change direction and start to increase (see my discussion of DTT in Chapter 2).

Since the early 1980s, however, we have seen more and more evidence of mortality reversals, first in some of the countries of eastern Europe and later in sub-Saharan Africa. Russia and many of the countries of the former Soviet Union experienced mortality reversals in the 1980s and 1990s. Life expectancy for males in 2000 in Russia was 59 years, below its value of 60 in the mid-1950s. Meanwhile, other Western countries have increased their life expectancy in the decades of the last century. Life expectancy at birth (both sexes) in the United States increased from around 70 years in 1960 to 79 in 2013.

What is causing the mortality reversals in eastern Europe? Possible factors include the "lack of preventative health programs and inadequate quality of medical services; smoking and alcohol abuse; [and] general neglect of individual health." These were caused by "a lack of life choices under the former Communist regimes, [as well as by] unemployment, relative deprivation, and inability to cope with the economic challenges of post-Communist times" (Shkolnikov, 2003: 677).

In many sub-Saharan African countries, there have been drastic increases in mortality and consequent declines in life expectancy since the mid-1980s. An analysis by Ashford (2006) examined mortality rates in the early years of the 2000–2010 decade for children under age 5 per 1,000 live births for the countries of Lesotho, Namibia, South Africa, Swaziland, and Zimbabwe, along with what the death rates would have been had there been no deaths to children via HIV/AIDS. The differences are striking. The mortality rates for young children are way above what they would have been without HIV. In Swaziland, the rate was 143 deaths to children under age 5 per 1,000 live births, but without the presence of HIV/AIDS, the rate would have been 73. In Lesotho, it was shown that 123 children under age 5 die for every 1,000 births, but without the presence of HIV/AIDS this rate would have been 71. In sub-Saharan Africa, "one-third of children who are born infected with HIV (transmitted through their mothers) die before their first birthday, and about 60 percent die by age 5" (Ashford, 2006: 2).

The AIDS epidemic has halted or reversed gains in life expectancy in many sub-Saharan African countries: "For example, in Lesotho, where one-fourth of adults were estimated to be living with HIV/AIDS in 2005, life expectancy was nearly 60 years in 1990–1995" (Ashford, 2006: 2), but has dropped to 44 for the year 2013 (PRB, 2014). Lesotho's life expectancy should have been approaching 69 years in this decade had the HIV/AIDS epidemic not hit the country. Instead, Lesotho's life expectancy will be considerably lower. The epidemic has taken a devastating toll on these countries.

Degenerative diseases are the major causes of death in the developed world. It is expected that there will be future improvements in the treatment of these diseases in the next decades. However, only a breakthrough in the area of the physiological process of aging will bring a substantial increase in the length of time people in the developed world will live. Even the total elimination of a specific degenerative disease, say, heart disease or cancer, would not greatly increase life expectancy.

The increases in life expectancy resulting from the elimination of a specific degenerative disease are small mainly because these diseases occur principally in the older ages. The elimination of one degenerative disease will shift the cause of death from one degenerative disease to another, resulting in a gain in life expectancy of perhaps one or two years. I have already noted that the two leading causes of death in the developed world are heart disease and cancer. If heart disease were eliminated as a cause of death in the United States, life expectancy at birth would increase only by a few years. If cancer were eliminated, life expectancy would increase by only three years (Arias, Heron, and Tejada-Vera, 2013: 5).

However, this does not necessarily mean that people will not live longer. They will live progressively longer as new medical advances occur and are implemented. But major medical advances, such as a cure for cancer, will not result in huge gains in life expectancy. Instead, it will result only in a modest improvement, as I showed in the previous paragraph, of about three years. This is because of a phenomenon known in demography as the **Taeuber paradox**, named after the demographer Conrad Taeuber, who pointed out many years ago that if a cure is found for one degenerative disease, this will provide the opportunity for death to occur from another. Or, in the words of Nathan Keyfitz, the demographer responsible for attributing the paradox to Taeuber, "Everyone dies of something sooner or later, so that, when the effects of the eradication of cancer had shaken down, the same number of deaths would occur as before, and the only benefit would be the substitution of heart and other diseases for cancer. A cure for cancer would only have the effect of giving people the opportunity to die of heart disease. [Thus] all that this particular medical advance would do would be to increase the options: one could choose to die of heart disease rather than cancer" (Keyfitz, 1977b: 412; see also Rogers, Hummer, and Krueger, 2005).

Few demographers would claim there will be no future improvements in life expectancy. Although some countries have experienced setbacks, mainly in eastern Europe and in sub-Saharan Africa, they will hopefully be of short duration.

I close this chapter with a pithy and optimistic observation advanced by Rogers, Hummer, and Krueger (2005: 305): "The question seems to be not whether mortality will improve in the future, but by how much it will improve, and what age, sex, race/ethnic, socioeconomic and geographical groups will reap the greatest benefits. Overall, continued improvements in health behavior, medical technology, and overall quality of life bode for a generally bright future, most likely with steady but deliberate increases in average length of life accompanied by an increasingly healthy population."

8 Internal Migration

In earlier chapters, I discussed two of the three ways that populations change their size. People are added to a population through fertility and are taken away through mortality. I now turn to the third and last way that populations change their size, namely, **migration**. Persons may be added to a population by moving into it or be subtracted from it by moving away from it. Unlike a birth and a death, which occur to each of us once and only once, migration may occur on multiple occasions, or we may never experience migration.

There are two main types of migration, namely, within a country and between countries. The former is **internal migration**, and the latter, **international migration**. The dynamics of the two kinds of migration differ significantly, and many of their concepts and theories are also different. Although their theories are more or less governed by "push" and "pull" factors (as I have mentioned in Chapter 2), they differ in their emphasis and focus. In this chapter, I cover internal migration. In Chapter 9, I cover international migration.

Internal migration is the change of permanent **residence** within a country, involving a geographical move that crosses a political boundary, usually a county or county-type geographical unit. However, not all changes in residence are migrations. Indeed, demographers distinguish between **movers** and **migrants**. Any person who changes residence, whether the change involves moving across the street or moving from Maine to Hawaii, is a mover. A migrant is a person whose residential move involves the crossing of a political boundary. The US Bureau of the Census defines migration occurring within the United States as residential "moves that cross jurisdictional boundaries (counties in particular)" (Mateyka, 2015: 3). This definition of an internal migrant is generally the definition used worldwide; any persons who change residence by moving from one county (or county-type unit) to another is a migrant. Bear in mind that all migrants are movers, but not all movers are migrants.

Virtually all of us, at least once in our lives, will be migrants. And usually this happens early in our lives, not later. In modern industrialized countries such as the United States, nearly everyone experiences migration. My dear friend and (now deceased) colleague Leon Bouvier wrote with me the first edition of this book. As of 2010 when the first edition of our book was published, he and I had taught demography courses to over 8,000 undergraduate and graduate students in a half-dozen different universities. Of these students taught by Leon and myself, we found that fewer than a dozen had not yet migrated by the time they took our courses. And, if we broaden the concern from migration to **residential mobility**, the two of us remembered teaching only a couple of students who had never ever moved; that is, they had never moved from the homes in which they lived as infants. Residential mobility and migration affect and will continue to affect virtually all of us.

Migration is a significant event not only for persons, but also for communities. Migration from one area to another has the effect of decreasing the size of the population in the **area of origin** and increasing it in the **area of destination**. Concerning the dynamics of population growth for communities, internal migration is the single most important of the three demographic processes (i.e., fertility, mortality, and migration). Differences in birth rates and death rates between communities of the same country are usually small compared with differences between the communities in migration. Migration is the major method for redistributing the population within a country (Bogue, 1969; Poston and Frisbie, 2005; Poston, Luo, and Zhang, 2006).

Let me start with a few facts about movers and migrants in the United States. Since 1970, the US Bureau of the Census has asked questions in the decennial censuses and the CPSs, and more recently in the ACSs, about each person's place of residence five years earlier. These data over time show between 35 and 45 percent of the population living in a different place five years earlier. The five-year mover rate in 2010 was just over 35 percent, the lowest since the data were first gathered in 1970 (Ihrke and Faber, 2012). Data have also been gathered by the Census Bureau on one's residence in the previous year. In the 1950s, around 20 percent of the population changed residences each year, but now the rate is down to around 12 percent (Ihrke, 2014). This means that presently about one in eight Americans moves each year from one house to another. And about one in twenty-five persons each year are migrants, that is, they move from one county to another. And almost one-half of the migrations involve the crossing of state boundaries (Ihrke, Faber, and Koerber, 2011).

The cumulative effect of this mobility is striking. Census Bureau demographers have estimated that a person in the United States can expect to move around twelve times in his or her lifetime. At age 18, a person can expect to move another nine times, and by age 45, still another three times (US Bureau of the Census, 2015c). The internal migration rates in the United States are comparable with those in Canada and Australia, but are much higher than those in many other developed countries like Sweden, Ireland, and Japan. Of course, these latter countries are smaller geographically than the United States, Canada, and Australia.

The next sections of this chapter cover the basic concepts and definitions used in analyses of internal migration. I conclude the chapter with detailed discussions of domestic migration in the United States and of temporary, that is, "floating" internal migration in China.

CONCEPTS AND DEFINITIONS

Over the years, demographers have developed a standard set of concepts and definitions for studying internal migration. The most basic distinction, as I have already mentioned, is between migration and **local movement**. Local movement is the short-distance change of residence within the same community that does not involve crossing a county jurisdictional boundary. Migration is the geographical movement resulting in the permanent change of residence that involves crossing a county boundary. Migration differs from local movement in that a migrant leaves his or her community and moves to a new community. Such a move typically involves other changes: in one's school, job, church, doctor, dentist, library, pub, shopping center, nightclub, automobile mechanic, and the other institutional aspects of daily life. In contrast, a local change in residence does not involve changing the main institutions in the mover's daily life. "It is customary to define migration as intercounty mobility" because county units, most of the time, "correspond most nearly to the average size of a community" (Bogue, 1969: 756). A person's residential move from one county to another will most likely also involve changes in his or her institutions of daily life. A migration, but not necessarily a local movement, is a sociological event of major magnitude.

A residential move, be it a local move or a migration, is necessarily defined as a "change in permanent residence, typically of a year or more in duration" (Frey, 2003: 545). Most countries have few or no restrictions on the internal movement of its peoples. In the United States, for example, we are free to move to wherever we wish and whenever we wish. However, in China and in a few other countries, for example, North Korea, internal migration is tightly controlled. In these few countries, therefore, internal migrants may be classified as either permanent migrants or temporary migrants.

A permanent migrant in China is the same as a permanent migrant elsewhere; the migration involves a permanent change in residence and the crossing of a county boundary. The difference in China is that the permanent migration must first be approved by the government. A temporary migrant in China, and in the few other countries where internal migration is heavily controlled, is one whose residential move does not have governmental approval. In other words, the temporary migrant moves without permission. However, in many, if not most, cases, the migration is not temporary but becomes permanent, or relatively permanent. Nevertheless, it is a migration that is not officially sanctioned. Later in this chapter, I discuss in more detail this phenomenon of temporary migration in China, referred to by the Chinese as "floating" migration. It is particularly important because its volume is so large. The 2010 census of China counted more than 220 million temporary internal migrants in the country (Liang, Li, and Ma, 2014). The internal migration of "floaters" to China's cities is the largest stream of peacetime mobility in recorded human history (Roberts, 1997).

Other concepts used by demographers in their studies of internal migration are the following: **in-migration** refers to the residential migration of persons to an area of destination; **out-migration** refers to the migration of persons from an area of origin. The area of origin is the area or community where the migration began, and the area of destination is the area or community where the migration ended. **Return migration** is the migration of persons back to their area of origin at some time after their initial out-migration.

Net migration refers to the migration balance of an area, consisting of the number of in-migrants minus the number of out-migrants; the net balance may be positive (representing a net population gain to the area), or negative (representing a net loss), or, conceivably, zero (Poston, Luo, and Zhang, 2006). Every time we migrate, we are simultaneously an in-migrant and an out-migrant. But we are never a net migrant. The concept of net migration applies only to populations and geographic areas, not to individuals. In contrast, the concepts of in-migration, out-migration, and return migration apply to both persons and geographic areas.

Like the concept of net migration, several other migration concepts apply only to geographic areas. **Gross migration** is the sum of migration for an area and is comprised of the in-migration into the area plus the out-migration from the area. **Migration efficiency** is an area's net migration divided by its gross migration. Migration in an area may be efficient or inefficient. For example, if there has been a lot of in-migration and little out-migration (i.e., most of the migrants have moved in and very few have moved out), then the migration is positively efficient. This is a case with little turnover of people, that is, not much milling around. In contrast, the migration could be negatively efficient if there has been very little in-migration and a lot of out-migration. Migration is not effective (it is inefficient) for an area when there are about the same number of persons migrating into the area as there are persons migrating out of the area (Shryock, 1964; Thomas, 1941). High negative migration efficiency often characterizes areas of economic hardship, whereas high positive efficiency is usually found in areas experiencing economic expansion (Bogue, 1969: 784).

A **migration stream** is a body of migrants departing from a common area of origin and arriving at a common area of destination during a specified time interval. A **migration counterstream** is the migration stream, smaller in size, going in the opposite direction during the same time interval.

A **migration interval** refers to the time period during which the migration occurs. Because migration is a process that occurs over time, its analysis requires that time be broken into intervals, so that migration data may be assembled separately for each interval. Time intervals of one year, five years, or ten years are commonly used in studies of internal migration. Irrespective of the length of the intervals chosen by the researcher, they need to be consistent in the analysis: "Two or more sets of migration statistics that have been collected for unequal intervals of time are therefore not fully comparable" (Bogue, 1969: 757).

Differential migration refers to the study of differences in migration according to the demographic, social, and economic characteristics of the population. This is also known as **migration selectivity** and points to the fact that some persons are more likely to migrate than others. The strongest selectivity factor associated with both migration and local movement is age: "The incidence of making each kind of move is highest for persons in their early to middle twenties and then declines precipitously during the thirties and forties, with a sometimes small upturn in the early retirement years" (Frey, 2003: 546).

I show in Figure 8.1 the age-specific percentages of persons, and of households, in the United States who changed residences between 2008 and 2009. The overwhelming importance for residential change of persons in the young adult years is striking. Americans aged 18–24 have the highest annual rates of residential change, followed by those aged 25–29. "These ages cover busy points in the life course because several major events (college, employment, and marriage) typically occur during these years" (Ihrke, Faber, and Koerber, 2011: 4). The percentage rates are the lowest for older persons.

Another influential factor in the decision to migrate is education. Among migrants, there is "strong educational selectivity in movement.

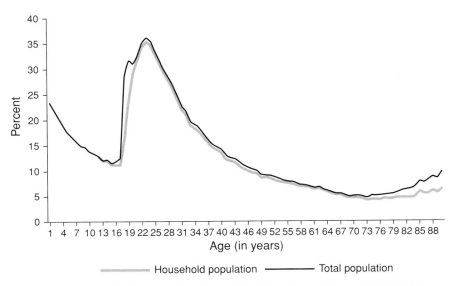

Figure 8.1 Age-specific Rates of Residential Mobility, United States, 2008–2009
Source: Ihrke, Faber, and Koerber (2011: 4).

College graduates, who are likely to be in a national labor market, show higher (migration) rates...than do those with lesser educational attainment" (Frey, 2003: 546). Homeownership is also important. Homeowners are much less likely to engage in local moves than are renters. I discuss migration selectivity in more detail later in this chapter in the context of domestic migration in the United States.

Many of these concepts are used by demographers in the different ways they measure migration. In the next section, I consider some of the issues involved in measuring migration.

MEASURES OF MIGRATION

There are inherent difficulties in measuring migration that are not generally encountered when analyzing fertility or mortality. Births and deaths are registered at the time of occurrence, but in most countries the residential move of a person is not. A few countries, for example, China and the Scandinavian countries, require people to register with government officials when they move from one place to another. However, in most countries, including the United States, there are no such requirements. Hence, it is necessary to rely on other types of data for measuring migration.

The US Bureau of the Census has used two items in its decennial censuses prior to the 2010 census that are now included in the ACS. These are of particular benefit to demographers who use them to measure migration, namely, one's state of birth and one's place of residence five years prior to the date of the census or survey. The Census Bureau also uses administrative data, namely, IRS tax returns data, for this same purpose. By comparing one's state of birth with one's place of residence at the time of enumeration, it is possible to divide people into the following categories: (1) those living in a given state and born there; (2) those living in a given state but born somewhere else; and (3) those born in a given state but living in some other state.

People in the first category are referred to as nonmigrants, or natives. People in the second and third categories are classified as lifetime migrants. A caveat is needed here. Just because a person was born in Texas and was living there in 2010 does not necessarily mean that the person did not leave Texas between the time he or she was born and the enumeration date of 2010; the person could have moved from and back to Texas several times between birth and 2010. The same caution applies to measuring migration five years prior to the enumeration date.

Data concerning people in these categories can be used to estimate the presence (and size) of migration streams. It is also possible to estimate the proportion of a state's population that was born elsewhere. The "holding power" of a state (or region) can be estimated by calculating the percentage of the people born there who still live there when the survey or census is taken.

Having information about one's residence five years before the enumeration date makes possible the determination of the proportion of a state's population that moved into the state within the past five years. People in this category are known as recent migrants.

Measures of migration are usually developed as rates that show empirically the relative frequency of a certain kind of migration. Four of the migration concepts presented above lead directly to rates, and one leads to a ratio, as follows:

$$\text{in-migration rate (IMR)} = (I/P) * 1,000$$
$$\text{out-migration rate (OMR)} = (O/P) * 1,000$$
$$\text{net migration rate (NMR)} = [(I - O)/P] * 1,000$$
$$\text{gross migration rate (GMR)} = [(I + O)/P] * 1,000$$
$$\text{migration efficiency ratio (MER)} = [(I - O)/(I + O)] * 100$$

where: I refers to the number of in-migrants moving into an area during a certain time interval (usually one, five, or ten years); O refers to the number of out-migrants moving out of an area during a certain time interval; and P is the denominator and refers to the midyear or average size of the population of the area.

Table 8.1 State-to-State Domestic Migration between 2004 and 2005: California, Nevada, New York, and Texas

State	Migration flows			
	In-migrants	Out-migrants	Gross migrants	Net migrants
California	448,718	717,121	1,165,839	−268,403
Nevada	129,957	103,482	233,439	26,475
New York	226,065	465,913	691,978	−239,848
Texas	503,251	378,709	881,960	124,452

State	Migration measures				
	IMR	OMR	GMR	NMR	MER
California	12.9	20.5	33.4	−7.7	−23.0
Nevada	56.4	44.9	101.3	11.5	11.3
New York	12.2	25.1	37.3	−12.9	−34.7
Texas	23.4	17.6	41.0	5.8	14.1

IMR = in-migration rate; OMR = out-migration rate; GMR = gross migration rate; NMR = net migration rate; MER = migration efficiency ratio.
Source: Koerber (2007). Calculations by DLP.

Determining the statistically correct denominator in calculating migration rates can be troublesome. Ideally, every individual in the denominator of a rate should have an equal chance to perform the event in the numerator. Obviously, this is not the case with respect to domestic IMRs, where, strictly speaking, the denominator should be the entire US population, excluding the resident population in the area of destination. In order to be able to compare the migration rates more straightforwardly, demographers use as the denominator for all migration rates the resident population of the area for which the rate is being calculated. As indicated, the four rates are usually multiplied by a constant of 1,000, and the migration efficiency ratio by a constant of 100.

Bogue (1969: 758) noted many years ago that the OMR is analogous to the CDR, and the IMR to the CBR. The parallel to the NMR is the rate of natural increase/decrease. All these rates may be computed not only for the total population, but also for specific subgroups of the population, for example, sex groups, age groups, race/ethnic groups, and so forth. They may also be calculated for specific education groups and occupational groups.

I now present examples of these migration measures for a few selected states of the United States.

Table 8.1 presents domestic migration data for California, Nevada, New York, and Texas for the period 2004–2005. The upper panel of the table shows the migration flow data for each of the four states, and the lower panel, the five migration measures. Between 2004 and 2005, California received over 448,000 migrants from other states; for every 1,000 persons in California's population in 2005, almost 13 were in-migrants. By comparison, during the same time period, over 717,000 persons departed from California for other states, or nearly 21 persons per 1,000 population. The total number of migrants entering and leaving California during this period, that is, gross migration, was almost 1.2 million. Finally, California lost through migration 268,000 more persons than it gained; that is, between 2004 and 2005, over 268,000 more persons departed from California for other states of the United States than entered California from other states. California's net migration rate (NMR) was −7.7, indicating that for every 1,000 persons in the population in 2005, there was a loss of almost 8 persons through net migration. California's MER was −23.0. For every 100 migrants to and from California during the period, there was a loss of almost 23 migrants.

Of the four states shown in the table, Nevada had the highest positive NMR; it gained almost 12 persons through net migration for every 1,000 members of its population. Arizona, a state not shown in the table, had the highest positive net migration rate of all the states in the United States, a rate of 23.7.

Of the states shown in the table, New York had the largest negative NMR, losing nearly 13 persons during the 2004–2005 period for every 1,000 members of its population. The state with the largest negative NMR of all the US states (not shown in the table) was Alaska, with a NMR of −34.6. The District of Columbia and Louisiana also had very high negative NMRs of −25.1 and −22.8, respectively (Koerber, 2007).

Regarding migration efficiency, of the four states shown in Table 8.1, Texas reported the highest positive efficiency ratio of 14.1, and New York the highest negative efficiency ratio of −34.7. Migration was considerably more efficient in New York than it was in Texas, but in New York the efficiency was negative, and in Texas it was positive. The MER for Nevada was the lowest for the states in the table, a ratio of 11.3. In other words, for Nevada there was a lot of coming into and leaving the state, which produced a net gain of only 11 persons for every 100 migrants. Migration was not that much more efficient in Texas. There was a lot of milling around, that is, coming and going, that ended up in small net gains for both states.

Having discussed the major concepts, definitions, and measures used in the analysis of internal migration, I next focus on internal migration trends and patterns in the United States.

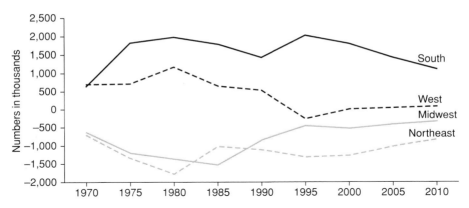

Figure 8.2 Five-Year Domestic Net Migration, by Region, 1970–2010
Source: Ihrke and Faber (2012: 9).

DOMESTIC MIGRATION IN THE UNITED STATES

Overall Trends

In Chapter 14 on population distribution, I will note that the major inter-regional flows of internal migrants in the United States have been from east to west and from north to south. During the nineteenth and early twentieth centuries, there was a steady movement westward as new areas beyond the Mississippi River were settled. With the exception of California, migration into the western states diminished during the first half of the twentieth century. Since then, it has accelerated considerably. Between 1970 and 1978, the western region of the United States had a net in-migration of 1.4 million people; that is, 1.4 million more people entered the region than left it. This was sufficient to account for almost half of the population increase in that area during that time period.

The southern region of the country has long been an exporter of people, from late in the nineteenth century until well into the 1960s. Long the most underdeveloped and rural area of the nation, the South lagged behind as industrialization surged in the North (Biggar, 1979). The movement from south to north is an excellent example of rural to urban migration. Blacks often left behind limited economic opportunities in rural areas of the South when they moved to the big cities of the North to find jobs (Hamilton, 1964). The adjustment problems facing those migrants were enormous as they tried to adapt to big-city norms of living. The move also contributed to the development of the urban ghetto and its attendant problems.

In the past four decades (since 1970), the trend of movement out of the South has been reversed. I show in Figure 8.2 five-year net migration data from 1970 to 2010 for the four regions of the United States. (The states comprising the four regions are shown in Figure 8.3.) For every five-year period from 1970 to 2010, the South has been the only region in the United States to have continuously experienced positive net domestic migration. The Midwest and Northeast regions have continuously had negative net migration, and the West region has vacillated from positive to negative.

Between 1970 and 1975, both the South and the West gained more persons than they lost through migration, although only the South had a net gain of 1 million or more. The Northeast and the Midwest each lost more than 1 million in this period. In each of the next seven five-year periods up to 2000–2005, the Northeast lost more than 1 million persons through migration than it gained. In the 2005–2010 period the Northeast region also lost more migrants than it gained, but the loss was less than 1 million. The Midwest also lost more migrants than it gained in all the periods up to 2010, but its losses, since 1990, were less than those of the Northeast.

In all eight of the five-year periods from 1970 to 2010, the South experienced positive net migration, with numbers in each period always over 1 million, and in the 1990–1995 period, 2 million. Except for the 1990–1995 period, the West gained more migrants than it lost in all the other periods, although its gains in the most recent time periods have been very small.

The entire southern region is gaining migrants. Previously, only the large numbers of migrants into Florida offset net out-migration from the rest of the region. Between 1990 and 2000, and again between 2000 and 2010, states like North Carolina, South Carolina, Georgia, Virginia, and Texas have experienced significant amounts of positive net migration. While the West region shows positive net migration, it is now mainly because of the rapid growth in the states in the Mountain division. The Pacific division has lost population through net migration between 1990 and 2010 primarily because of the very large domestic out-migration from California (also shown in Table 8.1).

Demographers are especially interested in the migration patterns of the college educated population. Virtually all the cities, states, and regions of the country wish to increase the migrations to their areas of college graduates because a well-educated labor force is vital everywhere. Migration data of the population categorized by levels of education show that between 2005 and 2010, "the South and West were popular destinations among graduate degree holders 25 years and over with net gains of 89,000 and 104,000, respectively. The Northeast had a net loss of 124,000 professional or graduate degree holders" (Ihrke and Faber, 2012: 8).

In sum, at this broad geographic level, the pattern is one of net out-migration from the Northeast and the Midwest and net in-migration to the South, and less so to the West. Within the Northeast, the New England

Census Regions and Divisions of the United States

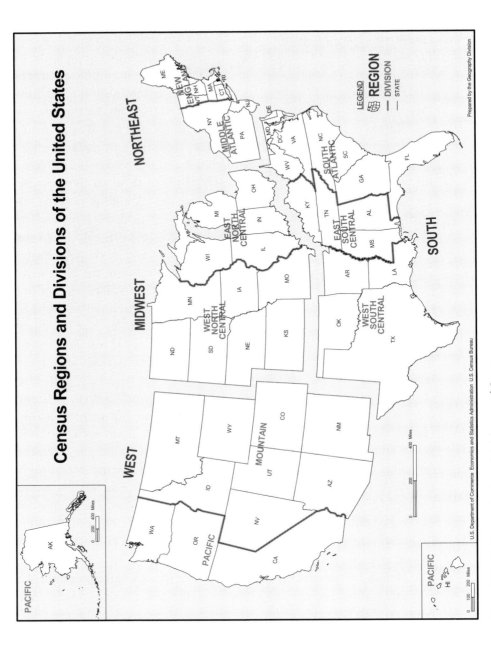

Figure 8.3 US Census Regions, Divisions, and States
Source: US Bureau of the Census, available at: www2.census.gov/geo/pdfs/maps-data/maps/reference/us_regdiv.pdf, last accessed April 29, 2016.

states continued to experience net out-migration between 2000 and 2010, but at lower levels than during the 1990s. In the West, there was net in-migration to the Mountain division and net out-migration from the Pacific division. In both cases, these trends moderated the pace of the 1990s. The South continued to have the most net in-migration of any region.

Migration Selectivity

I noted earlier the concept of migration selectivity. This refers to the fact that migrants are not all alike. For example, migration is selective on the basis of age, race, sex, and socioeconomic status. I have also mentioned that young adults between the ages of 20 and 29 were more likely to move than anyone else. Those between 20 and 29 leave their family home to seek employment or to attend college. This is also a time when couples get married, which generally involves at least one residential move, if not two. The somewhat higher levels of residential movement beyond age 29 differ a bit from previous decades. These days, people are getting married at later ages and divorces are more and more common. Also, more people are switching jobs. The level of residential movement is also high among the very young. This, of course, reflects the fact that the young are moving with their parents, who themselves are relatively young. Beginning at around age 40, levels of residential mobility and migration drop considerably. The older the people, the less likely they are to move. There used to be a slight surge at around the retirement age of 65, but this trend is not reflected in Figure 8.1 (above). The lack of an increase in residential mobility at the age of retirement is in part owing to the fact that more and more people today continue working beyond the age of 65. (At age 75 I am still teaching classes at Texas A&M University. And my deceased co-author, Leon Bouvier, was teaching classes at Old Dominion University at the time of his death at the ripe old age of 88.)

Generally speaking, the higher a person's education, the more likely he or she will migrate. Indeed, the farther the move, the stronger the role that education plays in the decision to move. White-collar workers are the most migratory occupational group. Manual workers tend to be as mobile, but their moves are more likely to be local. Farm and service workers are the least mobile occupational group. People not in the labor force have high mobility. This, of course, is attributed in part to the fact that many are looking for a position in the labor force.

A few decades after the end of the Civil War, blacks started to out-migrate from the South, to the Midwest and Northeast and the Pacific coast. Between 1910 and 1970, over 6 million blacks moved out of the South. This is known as the **Great Migration**. In 1900, almost nine out of ten African

Americans lived in the South. By 1970, the states of New York, Illinois, and California had the most African Americans in the country. As recently as 1965–1970, the number of blacks leaving the South was 2.3 times greater than the number coming into the South. But the migration started to reverse itself in the early 1970s and turned into a dramatic turnaround. The reversal "began as a trickle in the 1970s, increased in the 1990s, and turned into a virtual evacuation from many northern areas in the first decade of the 2000s. The movement is driven largely by younger, college-educated, and soon to be retiring baby boomer blacks, from both northern and western places of origin" (Frey, 2015: 107). The cities and metro areas of Atlanta, Dallas, and Houston are among the destinations benefiting the most from the reversal. These places "are in the midst of new immigrant growth and white in-migration, which are shaping a region that is welcoming to blacks as well as new immigrant minorities" (Frey, 2015: 107). Of particular interest is the fact that the states that were the destinations of most of the Great Migration migrants, namely, New York, Illinois, Michigan, and California, are now among the several states sending the most blacks to the South. However, there is one big difference between the migration patterns of those blacks who participated in the Great Migration and those now participating in its reversal. The blacks who left the South were largely from rural areas, whereas those now migrating to the South are "younger and privileged migrants (who) are moving to a more prosperous and post-civil rights South that was unknown to their forebears" (Frey, 2015: 125).

In summary, migration is not a random event. Certain kinds of people are more likely to move than others; some move short distances and others move long distances. Whatever the nature of the moves, there are certain consequences for the areas involved. I now consider some of them.

Consequences of Domestic Migration

Contrary to fertility and mortality, migration affects two areas: the place of origin and the place of destination. In addition, moving affects the individual lives of movers and nonmovers alike. Often, the consequences for the individual migrant differ from those of the aggregate population. For example, with increased immigration to the United States from Latin America into cities not generally prepared for such newcomers, the experience can be difficult for both the newcomers and the long-time residents of the cities. Allow me to consider some of these influences at both the origin and destination.

One way that migration affects the area of origin is by reducing its potential for population growth. This usually happens in two ways. People who move out of an area represent negative entries in the demographic

---

BOX 8.1   ESTIMATING NET MIGRATION

In Chapter 1 in formula (1.1), I presented the demographic equation:

$$P_2 - P_1 = (B - D) + (I - O)$$

Suppose for the area you are studying you only have information about the size of its population at two points in time and the number of births and deaths that occurred in the area in the interval between the two points in time. Using the above equation, here is how you would use the population size and vital statistics data to estimate the amount of net migration for the area:

$$(I - O) = P_2 - P_1 - (B - D)$$

where P_1 is the population size at an earlier date (T_1); P_2 is the population size at a later date (T_2); B is the number of births that occurred during the interval between T_1 and T_2; D is the number of deaths that occurred during the interval between T_1 and T_2; I is the number of in-migrants that entered the area between T_1 and T_2; O is the number of out-migrants that left the area between T_1 and T_2; $B - D$ = natural increase/decrease; $I - O$ = net migration; thus, net migration = population growth minus natural increase/decrease.

---

equation that I discussed earlier in Chapter 1. (I show in Box 8.1 how to use the demographic equation that I discussed earlier in Chapter 1 to estimate net migration.) This loss may at least partially compensate for any reproductive increase that occurs. However, as I have already mentioned, those who move out of an area tend to be in the young childbearing ages, which thus tends to reduce the reproductive potential of the population at origin.

Most large cities in the United States owe their population declines to out-migration, and not to an excess of deaths over births. The area of origin is affected as well by the type of people who migrate. The question of who migrates depends in part on whether the migration is a response to push or pull factors. Migrants responding to pull factors at the place of destination tend to be positively selected, and migrants responding to push factors in the area of origin tend to be negatively selected. That is, for instance, the migrants responding to the pull factors tend to be of higher socioeconomic status than those responding to the push factors.

With regard to the area of destination, migration tends to increase the population in two ways, that is, directly and indirectly. The net number of in-migrants constitutes the direct effect. The number of children born to the in-migrants after their arrival is the indirect effect. The magnitude of the direct effect depends on the relative size of the migrant and the receiving populations. For instance, adding ten people via in-migration to Harris County, Texas (the third largest county in the United States with a population of just over 4 million in 2010) has far less of an impact on the area of destination than adding ten people to Loving County (a county in West Texas with a population of 82 in 2010, the least populous county in the United States).

The magnitude of the indirect effect depends on the relative levels of reproductive behavior of the migrants and the receiving population. If the in-migrants have more children than those already living in the area of destination, then there will be a larger impact on that area.

Each person added to the population means an additional individual who must be fed, clothed, housed, educated, transported, and given at least occasional medical care. Massive in-migration can put a severe strain on the receiving area to deliver these services. This is particularly true if the original population size of the area is relatively small. The extent to which the strains become real problems depends on the socioeconomic characteristics of the in-migrants and the extent to which the labor force can absorb them.

In-migration affects the size of the labor force in two ways. First, because of the (usually) younger age composition of the migrants, in-migration may increase the ratio of the economically active persons to the total number of persons. To be sure, there are exceptions, especially in retirement areas where the rapid growth of the elderly population presents special issues. Second, within the same-age categories, the in-migrants may have higher rates of labor force participation than the receiving population. Both these effects depend on the socioeconomic characteristics and the occupational skills of the in-migrants.

When people with different cultural and linguistic backgrounds migrate to a particular site, some cultural heterogeneity may develop. Cultural factors certainly have an impact on the tolerable levels of in-migration. Only a certain number of newcomers can be absorbed without the receiving population feeling that their social institutions and value systems may be threatened. I turn now to the impact of migration on the individual migrant.

Impact on the Individual Migrant

One important consequence for the migrant is the opportunity to live in an environment with the social, economic, political, or physical characteristics that he or she believes to be preferable to those of the old environment. Whether or not this is the case depends on the accuracy of the migrant's perceptions of the circumstances in both the old and the new environments, as well as the migrant's ability to use the advantageous features of the new environment. The latter, in turn, depends on whether the migrant possesses useful skills, and how rapidly he or she is assimilated into the prevailing culture.

In general, the difficulty that migrants experience in being acculturated depends on how different they are from the receiving population. Nonwhite groups (and I am referring here to blacks, Hispanics, and Asians) have found it much more difficult to be "accepted" into mainstream American life than their white counterparts. Some are now beginning to be accepted by the whole society, but this is not yet the case in some isolated heavily white areas.

While immigrants to America perhaps face more daunting problems, the native-born individuals moving within the country must also adapt to new situations as they join the residents of a new urban or rural area or leave the Northeast for the South or West. Customs vary somewhat from region to region, and some "assimilating" is usually necessary if a newcomer is to adjust to the unfamiliar surroundings. Despite the "nationalization" emanating from television and the Internet, many Americans still "speak funny" to other Americans.

In the preceding pages, I have discussed various aspects of domestic migration in the United States. I turn now to a consideration of domestic migration in China, particularly the so-called temporary internal migration.

TEMPORARY ("FLOATING") MIGRATION IN CHINA

Unlike the process of internal migration in most countries, "migration" in China is not defined merely as changing a residence from one location to another while crossing a geographical (county-level) boundary. To be allowed to migrate in China, one needs first to obtain permission to officially transfer one's household registration (known in Chinese as the *hukou*) from the origin location to the destination location. People in China who move without permission are known as "floaters." These are people "who have crossed over some territorial ... boundary, [who] have not altered their permanent registration (*hukou*), and, [who] at least in theory, 'flow in and out'" (Solinger, 1999: 15; see also Fan, 1999; Liang and Ma, 2004). In China, thus, there are two types of internal migration: a move that is an officially permitted permanent change in the person's place-of-household registration; and a move without such official sanction (Poston and Mao, 1998; Poston and Zhang, 2008).

In 1948, China enacted the *hukou*, or household registration system. Urban residents were entitled to subsidized housing, social insurance, medical care, and, for the most part, employment. These rights and entitlements were denied to those holding rural *hukous*. In the late 1970s, Deng Xiaoping, the key Chinese leader who succeeded Mao Zedong, established the economic reforms that changed the *hukou* controls. At about the same time, the state relaxed the rules; for instance, these days, one no longer needs coupons to buy grain in stores in China's cities. The economic reforms also resulted in a tremendous requirement for manpower in the cities in low-level construction and manufacturing jobs and, more recently, in many kinds of household service and related jobs. Concurrently, the incentives of Deng's so-called Household Responsibility System, whereby a household can keep much of what it produces, resulted in the release of millions of farmers who in the past, during the communal regime, were inefficiently employed in agriculture (see Nolan, 1991; Oi, 1999). There has existed in China for the past several decades a huge agricultural labor surplus that continues to grow because of the implementation of technology that increases even further the efficiency of agriculture (A. Mason, 1997).

So what happens to this agricultural labor surplus? Much of it ends up migrating to the cities to the newly available low-level construction, manufacturing, and household service jobs; these migrants are the so-called **floating migrants**. The bulk is absorbed in the construction sector; others find jobs in manufacturing, services, and light industry: "The predominance of construction jobs is one reason men migrate more often than women. In areas where light assembly jobs dominate, however, female workers...outnumber males ... " (World Bank, 1997: 55).

The size of the floating population in China is enormous. More than 220 million floaters were counted in the 2010 census, and there were an estimated 250 million floaters in 2012. On average in China, for every one interprovince permanent (i.e., legally permitted) migrant, there are between twelve and thirteen interprovince floating migrants (Poston and Mao, 1998). The growth of the floating population in Beijing has paralleled the growth of the floating population in the country (Poston and Duan, 2000). In Beijing in the early 1950s, the floating population was very "efficiently controlled" and, hence, quite small in size. But by the late 1980s, the number of floaters had reached more than 1.3 million, and by 1994 almost 3.3 million, or almost one-third of its then population of about 11 million. By 2000, the official number was 2.6 million, and it reached over 7 million by 2010 (Liang, Li, and Ma, 2014). Floaters in Guangdong Province, in southern China, numbered over 34 million in 2010.

Who are the floating migrants? They are mainly young and unmarried males and females seeking employment in blue-collar, service, and household jobs. According to the World Bank (1997: 55), the "average [floating] migrant is less educated than the general population but more educated than the rural population. Few [floating] migrants come from the ranks of the absolute poor, who lack even the few years of schooling and basic Mandarin [Chinese language] required for most migrant jobs" (see Yang, 1994, 1996).

Using data from China's 2010 census, Liang, Li, and Ma (2014) noted that there are over 220 million floating migrants in China; of these, around 171 million are intercounty migrants; most are in the big cities and hail from rural areas. The proportions of floaters in the resident populations of China's large cities typically range from one-third to one-fourth of the total population. Shanghai's is even larger; 42 percent of Shanghai's total population is comprised of floaters, that is, there are over 11 million floaters in Shanghai. The growth trends of the floaters in most of China's cities parallel those noted for Beijing. Floaters comprise around 40 percent of the country's total urban population. The internal migration of floaters to China's cities constitutes the largest stream of peacetime mobility in recorded human history (Roberts, 1997). This is the main reason why this particular migration is so important.

But there is another reason. Many could become international immigrants and leave China, mainly as undocumented migrants. Here is how and why this might happen. The floating migrants in China's big cities earn wages that are several times greater than the wages earned by their countrymen in their home villages in the rural areas, and they send as much as half of their salaries back to their home villages. This occurs even though the floaters' wages are quite a bit less than those of the permanent urban workers, as much as 20 to 40 percent less. Usually, up to half of a floater's wage is sent back to the home village. In the rural counties of some provinces (e.g., Sichuan and Anhui Provinces), urban remittances from floaters account for almost half of household cash income (World Bank, 1997: 56–57).

If and when the floaters are unable to find jobs, or lose their jobs, in the cities of China, some may well look elsewhere, likely outside China, where there are jobs and where there are already established Chinese networks. In future years, there will be more rural surplus workers in China, as well as more floaters. Moreover, indications point to increases in unemployment in China's cities in the future. Liang (2001: 693) has written that the "likelihood of competition for jobs between internal migrants [i.e., the floaters] and unemployed workers [among the permanent residents of the cities] is clear . . . Some members of the floating population and unemployed workers [may be pushed] onto the market for illegal transnational migration."

When floaters lose their jobs in the Chinese cities, some will not wish to return home to their rural villages, to which they have been sending remittances. Returning home unemployed would result in tremendous embarrassment and loss of "face." Many floaters may well look elsewhere, most likely outside China, to countries such as the United States and many

European countries. It is not inconceivable that there could well be between 25 million and 50 million floaters looking for jobs outside China in the next decade. The prominent demographer and migration scholar, Douglas Massey, has written that "China's movement towards markets and rapid economic growth may contain the seeds of an enormous migration...that would produce a flow of immigrants [to the United States] that would dwarf levels of migration now observed from Mexico" (1995: 649).

My colleague Peter Morrison and I, in a short piece we wrote a few years ago for the *Houston Chronicle*, noted that the United States, in particular, could be a popular destination for the floaters. "The Chinese in the U.S. today form a potent interest group of Chinese-Americans of more than 3.3 million nationwide...(These ties could well) draw several million of them to Chinese-American enclaves in Texas, California and elsewhere in the U.S." (Poston and Morrison, 2011). Morrison and I then asked what this possible shift of human resources might mean for Americans. "Opponents of immigration – including, understandably, jobless American workers – may not welcome more foreign newcomers. Nevertheless, established immigration networks anchored by longstanding family ties to particular destinations in Texas, California, New York and other states will facilitate their arrival, surreptitiously or otherwise" (Poston and Morrison, 2011).

SUMMARY

Migration is a permanent shift of residence of such duration and distance that a change in the physical and social environment occurs. It is usually measured as a change of residence across political boundaries, generally between counties. I showed in this chapter that there is a great deal of geographic mobility in the United States, much of it created by people who move repeatedly. On average, every year one person in eight changes residence. One person in twenty-five migrates by moving from one county to another. Until about 1950, a large part of the interregional migration was from east to west and south to north. Since then, the latter flow has reversed. Both whites and blacks are now moving into the South.

There are marked differences among those who migrate in terms of age, race, and socioeconomic status. Young adults are the most likely to move, as are young children, who move with their parents. Whites are more likely to migrate than blacks, although the latter move locally more often. There is a positive relation between education and the possibility of moving: the better educated tend to migrate more often than the less educated.

In this chapter, I also considered the case of internal migration in China, where population movement is tightly controlled by the government. This is referred to as temporary, or floating, migration. Floating migrants are not expected to remain permanently in their areas of destination even though, in fact, most do. In 2012, there were more than 250 million floating migrants in China.

Migration is seldom explained in terms of the characteristics of only one place or factor. In any move, a decision has been reached that the area of destination offers advantages that outweigh the disadvantages of moving. Generally, it may be stated that people move "to better their lot" in life. This is happening today and will continue to happen as long as people believe that opportunities and living conditions are better elsewhere. Humankind is indeed peripatetic and will most likely always be so.

9 International Migration

The first "international" migration of humans began around 60,000 years ago, and the migrations continue to this day. Of all the demographic topics presented in this book, none is discussed today by both laypeople and social scientists as frequently and as forcefully as international migration. **International migration** is migration that occurs between countries. Its dynamics differ from those of internal migration, that is, migration within the geographical boundaries of a single country. Thus, a separate chapter is devoted here to international migration.

I begin this chapter by considering some of the definitions and concepts used in the study of international migration. I next cover world immigration patterns over time. This is followed by a discussion of immigration to the United States. I then consider some of the positive and negative economic issues pertaining to international migration. Considerations of legal and unauthorized immigration are next reviewed. I conclude the chapter with a discussion of the meaning of the concept of zero net international migration.

DEFINITIONS AND CONCEPTS

Similar to the study of internal migration, demographers have developed a fairly standard set of concepts and definitions for studying international migration. The first distinction is between **immigration** and **emigration**. **Immigration** refers to the movement of people to a new country for the purpose of establishing permanent residence; an **immigrant** is a person who moves to a new country to reside there and crosses an international boundary in doing so. These concepts are analogous in the study of internal migration to in-migration and in-migrant. Conversely, **emigration** refers to the permanent departure of people from a country; an **emigrant** is one who migrates away from a country with the intention of establishing a permanent residence elsewhere. The analogous internal migration concepts are out-migration and out-migrant.

In every international migration, a migrant is simultaneously an immigrant and an emigrant. The key element in the definition of an immigrant is the establishment of a permanent residence in the new country. This usually means residence in the destination country for at least one year, and is referred to as **long-term immigration**. The number of long-term immigrants in the world has increased considerably in recent decades, from 75 million in 1965, to 120 million in 1990 (Martin, 2001), to 190 million in 2006 (United Nations, 2006) to 232 million in 2013 (United Nations, 2013c). Approximately 3.2 percent of the world's population in 2013 were long-term immigrants. Although this is a relatively small percentage, it is a very large number, that is, 232 million persons.

Re-migration refers to the migration of international migrants back to their original countries of origin. A **re-migrant** is an international migrant who moves back to and re-establishes permanent residence in his or her original country of residence. Sometimes international migrants return to their countries of origin in their later years of life (see the last section of this chapter). For example, say, a person leaves China and moves to the United States. This person is an emigrant from China and an immigrant to the United States. If at some later point in time the person decides to leave the United States and move back to China, we would refer to him or her as a re-migrant. The analogous concept with respect to internal migration is return migrant.

I have already noted that international migration is the permanent movement of people from one country to another. International migrants are distinguished from **tourists** and visitors because tourists and visitors return home without establishing permanent residence in the destination country. People who travel to a foreign country as tourists, or to work for a short period, for example, diplomats, are not regarded as international migrants (Münz, 2003). However, this demarcation is not always an easy one to make in practice.

Immigrants in past decades to the major destination countries of the world (e.g., the United States, Russia, Germany, Saudi Arabia, the United Arab Emirates, and the United Kingdom, among other countries) may be grouped into four broad categories: refugees/asylees; migrants from former colonies; economic migrants; and "ethnic privileged" migrants (Münz, 2003).

A **refugee** or an **asylee** is one who involuntarily emigrates from his or her native country because of persecution, threat of violence, or extreme deprivation; often going to a neighboring country. Postcolonial migration began in the 1950s as a result of the decolonization of mainly southern nations. Indigenous peoples moved from former colonial countries to the European countries that had colonized them to pursue better living conditions or to escape political persecution.

Economic migrants are voluntary migrants motivated by economic aspirations; this flow is more likely to occur from the less to the more developed countries (the latter group typically includes the United States and Canada, all the countries of Europe, plus Australia, New Zealand, and Japan). Most international migration is economically motivated. More than half of international migrants these days are moving to the more developed countries. Of the 232 million long-term immigrants in the world in 2013, 136 million, or almost 60 percent of them, resided in more developed countries (United Nations 2013b).

Massey presents a slightly different set of international migrant categories, on the basis of whether the migration is voluntary or involuntary, and whether the migrants "are well or poorly endowed with human capital" (2003: 549).

Most of the people of the world never engage in international migration; "most live and die near their place of birth" (Martin and Zurcher, 2008: 3). Those that do engage in international migration often move between countries that are geographically close together. For the United States, this means that most immigrants come from Mexico and Central America. Some countries, however, attract migrants from longer distances. For instance, many international migrants to Germany hail from Turkey, a country around 1,500 miles away from Germany.

Recently, a large number of migrants have entered the United States from China. Even though China is geographically distant from the United States (over 7,000 miles away), making migration difficult and expensive, the push and pull factors of China and the United States are strong (Cortes and Poston, 2008; Poston and Luo, 2007;). Indeed, between 2012 and 2013, more international migrants moved to the United States from China than from Mexico, 147,000 from China versus 130,000 from Mexico (Oppenheimer, 2015).

In 2013, over half of the international migrants in the world resided in just ten countries (see Figure 9.1). The largest number, 46 million, or one-fifth of all the international migrants in the world in 2013, resided in the United States. Also, in the years 2010, 2000, and 1990, the United States had more international migrants residing within its borders than any other country in the world. The data shown in Figure 9.1 indicate clearly that the United States receives more migrants than any other country in the world.

Other countries in 2013 with large numbers of international migrants are the Russian Federation with 11 million, Germany with 10 million, Saudi

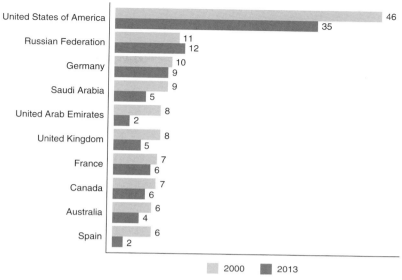

Figure 9.1 Ten Countries with the Largest Number of International Migrants (in millions), 2000 and 2013
Source: United Nations (2013c).

Arabia with 9 million, and the United Arab Emirates and the United Kingdom with 8 million each (United Nations, 2013b: 5). Of all the countries of the world, the United States gained the largest number of international migrants in the 2000–2013 period, a net gain of 11 million in the period, equal to just under 1 million each year.

PATTERNS OF WORLD IMMIGRATION OVER TIME

The residential movement of large numbers of people spanning great distances goes far back into human history, way before the beginning of the establishment of nations. The first "modern" humans emerged in sub-Saharan Africa, as many as 195,000 years ago, and lived there for the first two-thirds of their history. By 35,000 years ago, humans "thrived at opposite ends of Eurasia, from France to Southeast Asia and even Australia" (Goebel, 2007: 194). One of the greatest "untold stories in the history of humankind" is how humans went about colonizing "these and other drastically different environments during the intervening 160,000 years" (Goebel, 2007: 194). Humans began to migrate out of Africa around 50,000–60,000 years ago, first to southern Asia, China, and Java, and later to Europe. Evidence suggests that humans began migrating to the Americas around 14,000 years ago ("Before the Exodus," 2008: 101; Goebel, Waters, and O'Rourke, 2008; Meltzer, 2009). These "first Americans used boats, and the [west] coastal corridor would have been the likely route of passage...Once humans reached the Pacific Northwest, they...continued their spread southward along the coast to Chile, as well as eastward...possibly...to Wisconsin" (Goebel, Waters, and O'Rourke, 2008: 1501).

Years later, movements were often across land areas and over short sea routes. The migration of a population was often preceded by an invasion of its armies. Sometimes the invaders would occupy the new lands permanently, perhaps intermarrying with the subdued population. The Norse peoples from Scandinavia illustrate this principle. They carried out numerous raids in Europe until the ninth century and then settled in England, Ireland, and France (where they were known as Normans). Occasionally, the invaders would occupy the new lands only briefly, and later return to their original territory, leaving some of their members in the occupied region.

Prior to the 1400s, many of the international migrations leading to invasion and the conquering of new territory did not involve oceanic crossings. The invasions of the Mongols in the fourteenth century, led by Tamerlane, seeking to conquer all of Eurasia, were the last time in human history when massive international migrations and invasions did not cross oceans. Thereafter, international migrations/invasions were transoceanic (Darwin, 2008).

Sometimes the international migrations/invasions were accompanied by the enslavement of the defeated peoples and their **forced migration** to the land of the conquerors. For example, a single Roman military campaign could bring in as many as 50,000 prisoners. During the height of the Roman Empire, it is thought that the population of Rome reached 1 million people, a large number of whom were slaves who had immigrated involuntarily. Earlier, during the fifth century BC, the population of Athens included between 75,000 and 150,000 slaves, from both Africa and Asia, representing around 25–35 percent of the population (Davis, 1974: 95).

Exploration also played a role in the dynamics of human migration in the thirteenth century from China, and in the fifteenth and sixteenth centuries from Europe. Zheng He, Marco Polo, Columbus, Magellan, and others led large naval expeditions to other parts of the world to both satisfy the curiosity of their governments, and to explore parts of the world unknown to them. They brought back treasures and stories about the new lands. Some settled in the new parts of the world then and later. For example, the Portuguese started colonies in Africa; the Spaniards, English, Dutch, and French in the Americas; the Chinese in southeast Asia; and the English in Australia and New Zealand (Davis, 1974; Dreyer, 2007; Menzies, 2003).

The greatest period of European migration overseas occurred between 1840 and 1930 when around 52 million people emigrated from European countries, primarily to North America. This number equaled around one-fifth of the population of Europe in 1840 and exceeded the number of Europeans already abroad after more than 300 years of settlement (Davis, 1974: 98). Haines has estimated that the transatlantic migration stream from Europe to the western hemisphere, from the beginning of colonization around 1500 until 1940, numbered 60 million and was "the greatest and probably the most consequential population movement in modern human history" (Haines, 2003: 942).

Compared with the massive movements out of Europe, intercontinental migration from Asia before the Second World War was not quite as large. Asian Indians went to such places as British Guiana, East Africa, Fiji, Mauritius, and Trinidad. Japanese and Filipino migrants went to Hawaii; some Japanese settled in Brazil; and many Chinese migrated to the United States (Poston, Mao, and Yu, 1994).

Intercontinental migration from Africa differed from the preceding movements. The mass outpouring of Africans to other continents was mostly involuntary. Around 9.6 million enslaved Africans were taken to the New World between 1650 and the nineteenth century, when slavery there was abolished. During these sea voyages, mortality was high, with as many as 25 percent who began the voyage dying before reaching the Americas. Thus, the total number of Africans taken from Africa was likely well over 11 million. This was the largest slave migration in recorded human history in terms of distance and numbers moved (Curtin, 1969).

These massive migrations have had a number of consequences for the world. One reason for the increase in world population after 1750 was that emigration was partly responsible for relieving the pressures of the population on land and resources, postponing an inevitable change in birth and death rates. Certainly, there are exceptions, but in general, the greater the rate of emigration from a European country, the later the decline of its birth rate. In France, a country characterized by low levels of emigration during this period, the birth rate began to fall as early as the mid-eighteenth century. In Italy, a country with sizable levels of emigration, conversely, a significant fertility decline did not occur until early in the twentieth century. In the countries of destination, the immigrants often exhibited high birth rates. Indeed, some of the highest birth rates ever recorded were in French Canada in the latter part of the seventeenth century. Crude birth rates were as high as 65 per 1,000 among some of the immigrant groups to the New World (Bouvier, 1965; Sabagh, 1942).

Another consequence of these international migrations was the geographic redistribution of the global population. Between 1750 and 1930, the population of the main areas of destination of European emigrants increased in size by fourteen times, while the population of all the other areas of the world little more than doubled. In 1750, these areas of destination of European emigrants comprised less than 3 percent of the population of the world; by 1930 they comprised 16 percent. The geographic distribution of the races also changed dramatically. By 1930, about one-third of all whites no longer lived in Europe, and more than one-fifth of all blacks no longer lived in Africa (Davis, 1974: 99).

There have been several major international migration movements since the 1930s and the period of unrest preceding the Second World War to the present. Most of these migrants were refugees and asylum seekers.

First, during Adolf Hitler's rise to power in the 1930s, large numbers of Jews and political refugees fled Germany. At the end of the Second World War, there were compulsory large-scale transfers of the European population as a result of repatriation. The uprooting of more than 20 million eastern and central Europeans via flight, expulsion, transfer, or population exchange represented a drastic solution to the presence of ethnic minorities in these regions (Bouvier, Shryock, and Henderson, 1977).

Second, after the end of the Second World War, about 3 million Japanese were returned by decree to Japan from other Asian nations. Third, in 1947, after the partition of India and Pakistan, more than 7 million Muslims fled from India to Pakistan, and a comparable number of Hindus fled from Pakistan to India. In the Punjab area of Pakistan alone, the refugees who fled made up more than two-thirds of the population.

Fourth, in 1948, thousands of Palestinians were displaced from the territory that is now Israel, which is the classic example of an immigrant country drawing a population from dozens of other countries. The United States is another such example; indeed the United States is the *ne plus ultra* of immigrant nations.

Fifth, in the 1970s, millions of southeast Asians were uprooted owing to political and economic upheavals, resulting in one of the largest and most tragic refugee migrations in history. In 1971, 10 million refugees migrated from what had been East Pakistan (now Bangladesh) to northern India. Subsequently, millions of Asians escaped from Cambodia, Vietnam, and Laos into Thailand and elsewhere (Patrick, 2003).

Sixth, an often overlooked international migration is that involving refugees fleeing Afghanistan following the Soviet invasion in 1979. There were as many as 6.5 million Afghan refugees between 1988 and 1991, and another 5 million from the early 1990s to 2000. By the early part of the twenty-first century, it is estimated that one in four Afghans were refugees (Patrick, 2003: 827).

Finally, the modern refugee era began at the end of the Cold War in around 1991, when "many, mostly developing countries found themselves embroiled in often violent conflicts after they lost support of their superpower backer" (Patrick, 2003: 827). Several million additional refugees resulted from the US invasion of Iraq in 2003. The numbers of refugees and asylum seekers are astoundingly high. From around 2001, there were almost 3.6 million Afghans alone in Pakistan and Iran (Patrick, 2003: 828).

The United Nations High Commissioner for Refugees (UNHCR) estimates there were 46.3 million refugees in the world in 2014. The countries sending out the largest numbers of refugees are Syria, Afghanistan, Somalia, Sudan, and South Sudan. The countries receiving the largest numbers are Pakistan, Lebanon, Iran, Turkey, and Jordan. For more than three decades Afghanistan was the origin country of the largest number of refugees; its peak year was 1990–1991 when more than 6 million refugees hailed from there. But by mid-2014, with more than 3 million registered refugees, Syria has become the country producing the largest number. "Syrians had overtaken Afghans as the largest refugee population under UNHCR's mandate, a reflection of the continuous conflict and violence in the country" (UNHCR, 2015: 4).

IMMIGRATION TO THE UNITED STATES

Nearly all the current residents of the United States, more than 98 percent, are immigrants or are the descendants of immigrants. In 2010, only 4.2 million people, or just about 1.5 percent of the population, identified themselves as American Indians, Alaska Natives, or Native Hawaiians (Norris, Vines, and Hoeffel, 2012), and were hence neither immigrants to the United States nor descendants of immigrants. The American Indians were by far the largest of these three groups; they lived in North America for thousands of years before the arrival of the first immigrants. Later, many coexisted with European settlers until the eighteenth century, when most were eliminated through either disease or war. These conflicts continued through the late 1800s, when only a fraction of Native Americans remained (Cortes and Poston, 2008; Purcell, 1995; Snipp, 1989).

The United States receives the most immigrants of all the countries in the world. In 2013, 46 million US residents, or over 14 percent of the total population, were born in foreign countries (Figure 9.1). This is the largest number of immigrants residing in any country of the world.

Some countries have larger percentages of foreign-born residents than the United States, but they have many fewer people; their foreign-born residents are mainly migrant workers and are seldom citizens of the host countries. For example, in 2013, 84 percent of the United Arab Emirate's total population of 9.4 million residents was foreign-born; this is the largest percentage of foreign-born residents in any one country. Three more countries with very large percentages of foreign-born persons in 2013 were Qatar at 74 percent, Kuwait at 60 percent, and Bahrain at 55 percent

(United Nations, 2013b). These Gulf countries "tend to extend few rights to migrants; it is very hard for a guest worker to win immigrant status and naturalize . . . " (Martin and Zurcher, 2008: 8).

One country, the Vatican City State (known officially as the Holy See), has a total population of just over 800 people, and nearly all are foreign-born. Its population consists of the Pope, priests and other members of religious orders, and laypeople (and their families) who work at the Vatican. Citizenship is given to people (and their families) who work there and is revoked when they are no longer employed there. Thus, not only are almost all the residents foreign-born, there are no permanent residents. The Vatican City State is the smallest country in the world with respect to both population size and land mass; it comprises less than one-fifth of a square mile (less than one-half of a square kilometer) and is completely surrounded by the city of Rome. The country is so small that it does not have street addresses (Central Intelligence Agency, 2015).

I now review the history of immigration to the United States. Immigration has played a crucially important role in the American narrative. The sociologist and political scientist Seymour Martin Lipset (1997) once wrote about the "exceptional" character of the United States. He noted that when the thirteen colonies emerged from the American Revolution as a new nation, they relied on a broadly shared ideology based on human liberty, egalitarianism, populism, individualism, and republicanism. This made America exceptional, and Lipset referred to this as "American exceptionalism."

I hold that there is a demographic aspect of American exceptionalism that needs to be mentioned. This feature results from America growing the population of the country with peoples from everywhere. Prior to, and after, the founding of America, virtually everyone and anyone was permitted to immigrate to the country. As I noted in a previous paragraph, over 98 percent of the population of the United States today comprises either immigrants or the descendants of immigrants. In my view, this reliance on international migration has been crucial for the development of an "exceptional" America.

Why is this so? Because international migration is selective of the very best peoples from other countries. Persons without motivation and without a striving for advancement and improvement, persons with few socioeconomic skills and talents, persons not willing to take risks and chances – these persons will more often remain at home where they were born and not immigrate abroad.

Moreover, international migrants to the United States, both legal and undocumented, are less likely to commit serious crimes and are less likely to be imprisoned, compared with the native US-born population. Moreover,

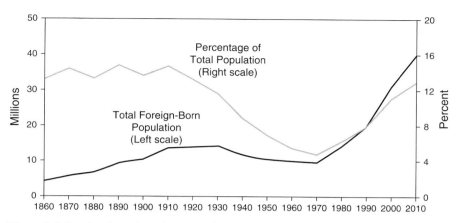

Figure 9.2 Foreign-born Population in the United States, 1860–2010
Source: Congressional Budget Office (2013).

periods of high levels of immigration in the United States are associated with low levels of criminal behavior. Extensive demographic and sociological research has shown the lack of any relationship between immigration and crime. This holds "true for both legal immigrants and the unauthorized, regardless of their country of origin or level of education. In other words, the overwhelming majority of immigrants are not 'criminals' by any commonly accepted definition of the term" (Ewing, Martínez, and Rumbaut, 2015: 1).

It is unfortunate that US immigration policy is too often written more on the basis of fear and stereotype than on the empirical evidence provided by demographers and other social scientists. Consequently, "immigrants have the stigma of 'criminality' ascribed to them by an ever-evolving assortment of laws and immigration-enforcement mechanisms. Put differently, immigrants are being defined more and more as threats" when there is little if any evidence for such a designation. Despite the overwhelming evidence that "immigration is not linked to higher crime rates, and that immigrants are less likely to be criminals than the native-born, many US policymakers succumb to their fears and prejudices about what they imagine immigrants to be" (Ewing, Martínez, and Rumbaut, 2015: 2).

International migration is selective, for the most part, of the very best people. If America is indeed as exceptional as many have argued, we cannot and should not overlook the crucial role played by international migration.

The number of immigrants residing in the United States have varied greatly over time. Figure 9.2 shows the number and percentage of immigrants living in the United States from 1860 to 2010; the number of immigrants reached almost 40 million in 2010, and, as shown in Figure 9.1,

46 million in 2013. The number of 46 million immigrants in 2013 is the largest absolute number of immigrants ever recorded in the United States. It comprises around 13 percent of the population, which is the largest share of foreign-born persons in the United States since 1920. In the decades from 1860 to 1910, persons living in the United States who were born elsewhere comprised between 13 and 15 percent of the country's population. The percentage started to decline in 1910, reaching 7 percent in 1950 and less than 5 percent in 1970, at which time the trend reversed. In the forty years between 1970 and 2010, the foreign-born population increased from 9.6 million to almost 40 million. Population policies played a major role in these trends, and I discuss them later in Chapter 15.

The migration streams to the United States from China and Mexico are among the largest and most important, both historically and currently. Thus, in later paragraphs, I give them special attention.

In 1598, Spaniards first came to what would later become the United States. They exploited the land and persecuted the indigenous peoples, but they differed from earlier explorers in that many remained permanently in the areas known today as the southwest and Florida (Purcell, 1995).

The first really large stream of European immigrants to what is now the United States hailed from England, and they settled mainly in the present state of Virginia (Purcell, 1995). The first permanent settlement was Jamestown, established in 1607. These immigrants largely lived off tobacco crops, which proved to be a profitable but labor-intensive product. This sustenance activity eventually led to the immigration of British indentured servants and African slaves. The arrival of the pilgrims on Plymouth Rock in 1620 marked the beginning of a large migration stream of English people moving to the New World for religious freedom. These early immigrant groups "of the 1600s and 1700s established the basic context of American society. English was the dominant language in America; English legal and government documents were the norm; and culture was for two centuries copied after English literature, drama, and art" (Purcell, 1995: 5). This model of American society set the standard and foundation during the next two centuries for the future discrimination and exclusion of certain immigrants and for the acceptance of others (Cortes and Poston, 2008).

In a previous section, I noted the sizable involuntary migrations of Africans that also occurred during this period. The first enslaved Africans were purchased in exchange for food provisions from a Dutch-flagged ship in Jamestown in 1619. The white-imposed slavery of Africans was relatively slow to develop in the colonies because Native Americans and white indentured servants were being used for cheap labor. However, by 1690, there were more African slaves than white indentured servants (Purcell,

1995). The Act Prohibiting the Importation of Slaves, a federal law passed on March 2, 1807, that took effect in 1808, officially ended slave trade. But slavery persisted until the end of the Civil War. However, to this day, the system of racism upon which slavery was founded is engrained in the United States and remains a major hurdle for African Americans and other racial and ethnic minorities seeking socioeconomic success in America (Bonilla-Silva, 2013; Feagin, 2006, 2014).

The Dutch came to America in the 1600s and claimed much of present-day New York (Purcell, 1995). Swedish immigrants also came to the New World, but were less successful than the British and the Dutch. Scots-Irish immigrants came for economic reasons and settled mainly in Pennsylvania. The seventeenth century also saw a considerable migration of German peoples who were motivated to leave Germany by economic factors and by political and religious oppression. They were the largest non-British and non-English-speaking immigrant group to come to America. The cultural and linguistic differences of the Germans led to their being one of the first European immigrant groups to experience discrimination by earlier settlers in the country (Cortes and Poston, 2008). According to recent data from the ACS, there were over 46 million people residing in the United States in 2013 claiming German ancestry, making Germans the largest ancestry group in the country.

Before 1830, the contribution of immigration to US population growth was minimal. Between 1821 and 1825, for example, the average number of immigrants every year was only about 8,000; this increased to almost 21,000 between 1826 and 1830. From 1841 to 1845, each year immigrants numbered more than 86,000. In the eight years between 1850 and 1857, the total number of immigrants to the United States was 2.2 million. In sum, between 1790 and 1860, the number of immigrants to the United States was almost 5 million, and most of them were from Europe (Cortes and Poston, 2008; Taeuber and Taeuber, 1958).

Starting on January 1, 1892, many immigrants, mainly from Europe, were processed through the portal of Ellis Island, a small island in New York Harbor. There were other ports of immigrant entry into the United States located in Boston, Philadelphia, Baltimore, San Francisco, Savannah, Miami, Galveston, and New Orleans, but Ellis Island was the major one. The Immigration Act of 1924 resulted in far fewer immigrants coming to the United States and also permitted the processing of immigrants at overseas embassies. By the time Ellis Island finally closed in 1954, more than 12 million immigrant steamship passengers had been processed into the United States through this port of entry (Coan, 2004: xiii). The National Park Service (2015) has estimated that around 40 percent of America's population today traces its ancestry to immigrants who entered the United States through Ellis Island. The immigrants had left behind their history, homeland, and people to come to the United States in search of a new and better life.

The first immigrant to enter the United States through Ellis Island when it first opened on January 1, 1892, was Annie Moore, a young woman from County Cork, Ireland. She and her two brothers had traveled alone across the Atlantic Ocean to be reunited with their parents, who had emigrated from Ireland two years earlier (Coan, 2004: xxiv). Annie Moore (1874–1924) has been immortalized in the popular song "Isle of Hope, Isle of Tears," written and composed by Brendan Graham and performed by, among others, the Celtic Woman and the Irish Tenors. Listen to the song (see at: www.youtube.com/watch?v=yluUCjH6Ons). The first two verses, and the chorus, illustrate well the hopes, fears, dreams, and courage of so many of the immigrants to the United States, feelings and attributes that continue to characterize immigrants to this day. To illustrate, one verse speaks of "her dreams for the future in the land of liberty." Keep in mind, however, that for most of the transatlantic and transpacific immigrants who came to the Americas a century or more ago, once they departed from their home countries they were unlikely ever to return home again. The song makes this point with the verse "the Isle (of home) you'll never see again…is always on your mind."

When you listen to the song, you will learn that on January 1, 1892, when Annie Moore entered Ellis Island, she was 15 years old. As an aside, Brendan Graham, the author of "Isle of Hope, Isle of Tears," informed me in a personal communication (October 8, 2009) that Annie Moore was actually 17 years old when she moved from Ireland to the United States, not 15 as stated in his song. Years after writing and publishing the song, Graham obtained a copy of her birth certificate reporting her year of birth as 1874. It was then that he learned that she apparently lied about her age and claimed to be 15. If she was 15, she could remain with her two younger brothers in the "family section" of the ship, but if she was 17 she would have to travel in the "adult section" of the ship and be separated from her brothers.

The last person to pass through Ellis Island was a Norwegian merchant seaman, Arne Petersson, who was processed on November 12, 1954 (Coan, 2004: xxiv).

In the 1800s, the combination of pro-immigration campaigns and the reduced cost of transcontinental transportation increased considerably the numbers of immigrants to the United States. Later, there was a second influx of German and Irish immigrants. Germans found work in several established industries, aiding in the overall development of US commerce. The Irish immigrants, mostly Catholics, suffered severe discrimination that reached a peak in the mid-1850s with the emergence of the Know-Nothings, an anti-Catholic organization dedicated to maintaining the dominance of Anglo-Saxon Protestants. Between the early seventeenth century and the 1920s, an estimated 7 million people left Ireland for North America (Miller, 1985: 3). Data from the 2013 ACS indicate that in 2013 there were 33.3 million people in the United States claiming Irish ancestry; this is the second largest ancestry group in the United States, after the Germans at 46 million. US residents claiming Irish ancestry are almost six times larger in size than the total of the two large Irish populations in Europe, that is, the Republic of Ireland (4.6 million) and Northern Ireland (1.8 million).

The end of the nineteenth century also saw immigration from some Scandinavian countries. These immigrants sought land for farming and developed the mostly unsettled Midwest (Cortes and Poston, 2008).

The Chinese have a long history of immigration to the United States. They first came to the United States after the beginnings of the California Gold Rush in 1849. An estimated 288,000 Chinese came during this period, although many returned to China before 1882 (Black, 1963; Poston and Luo, 2007). Like most immigrants, the Chinese came as laborers in search of work and wages. Their port of entry was San Francisco, which is where they hoped to become rich and realize their dreams. To this day, the Chinese name for San Francisco is "Jiu Jin Shan," or "Old Gold Mountain."

The Chinese were subjected to hostile discrimination because many American workers were threatened by the low wages they were willing to take. The passing of the Chinese Exclusion Act of 1882 ended the first period of Chinese immigration; it tapered off, eventually stopping by the end of the nineteenth century (Pedraza and Rumbaut, 1996; Poston and Luo, 2007).

The next period of Chinese immigration began in 1882 and extended to 1965. The Chinese Exclusion Act was renewed in 1892, was made permanent in 1902, and was not repealed until 1943. For all practical purposes, Chinese immigration to the United States during this period was banned. The only exceptions were diplomats, merchants, and some students, as well as their dependants, but these were very small in number. The Chinese Exclusion Act resulted from a concern about the large numbers of Chinese who had come earlier in response to the need for inexpensive labor, particularly to help with the construction of the western part of the transcontinental railroad. Competition with American workers and a growing nativism brought pressure for restrictive action, beginning with the Chinese Exclusion Act. Passed by the 47th Congress on May 6, 1882, this law suspended the immigration of Chinese laborers for ten years. However, it permitted Chinese who were in the United States in 1880 to stay, travel abroad, and return, but it prohibited their naturalization.

The next significant exclusionary legislation was the Act to Prohibit the Coming of Chinese Persons into the United States of May 1892, better known as the Geary Act. It allowed Chinese laborers to travel to China and reenter the United States, but its provisions were more restrictive than the preceding immigration laws. The Geary Act required Chinese to register and secure a certificate as proof of their right to be in the United States. Those failing to do so could be put into prison or deported. Other restrictive immigration acts affecting citizens of Chinese ancestry followed. The ban continued in force until 1943, at which time an annual quota of 100 immigrants was assigned to Chinese who wished to enter the United States (King and Locke, 1980; Poston and Luo, 2007).

In 1943, President Franklin D. Roosevelt signed the Act to Repeal the Chinese Exclusion Acts, mainly because China and the United States were allies during the Second World War. The Act of 1943 also lifted restrictions on naturalization. However, until the Immigration and Nationality Act of 1965, various laws continued to restrict Chinese immigration. Chinese already in the United States were confined to highly segregated Chinatowns in major cities, for example, San Francisco and New York, and in isolated regions in rural areas. Because the Chinese were deprived of their democratic rights, they sometimes made extensive use of the courts and diplomatic channels to defend themselves.

The US Civil Rights movement of the 1960s, particularly the enactment of the Civil Rights Act of 1964 and the Immigration and Nationality Act of 1965, began a new period of Chinese immigration, covering the years from 1965 to the present. The new laws restored many of the basic rights denied earlier to Chinese Americans. Since the 1980s, thousands of Chinese people have come to the United States each year. For instance, during the twenty-three years between 1980 and 2002, the volume of permanent Chinese immigration to the United States numbered more than 911,000, almost seven times the number between 1891 and 1979. It is during this latest period that the number of Chinese student immigrants increased substantially; in many cases, however, students are not included in the count of permanent immigrants (Poston and Luo, 2007). In the United States today there are around 4 million people who identify as Chinese, over 60 percent of whom were US-born. In Chapter 15, I will discuss immigration laws and regulations in more detail and will cover some of the points I have mentioned above.

Overlapping with early Chinese immigration to the United States were population movements from eastern and southern Europe. These immigrants were not as welcome as the previous European immigrants because the "old" immigrants thought that these "new" immigrants would take their jobs (Purcell, 1995). They were mainly Italians, Greeks, Poles, and

Slavs who spoke different languages and had slightly different physical features to those of the western Europeans. They were subjected to discrimination, but were able to assimilate into white American culture with passing generations (Cortes and Poston, 2008).

Currently, the largest numbers of immigrants to the United States are from certain Asian and Central American countries, particularly Mexico. These immigrants come for many of the same reasons that the European immigrants came in earlier decades. Population booms and increased industrialization, combined with the economic opportunities of the United States, created the push and pull factors that increased emigration from Asia. Many Asians move directly into ethnic enclaves where they find jobs and homes with people from their countries of origin. However, they are often criticized for not assimilating into "mainstream" white American culture (Portes and Rumbaut, 1990).

The end of the twentieth century to the beginning of the twenty-first century has seen the immigration of millions of Mexicans to the United States. There is a long-standing social, economic, and geographical relationship between the two countries. As Massey and his colleagues have written, "the USA has invaded Mexico three times; it annexed one-third of its territory; it is the primary source of capital for Mexican investment; it is Mexico's largest trading partner; and Mexico is the second most important trading partner for the USA" (Massey et al., 2005: 67). Like most other newcomers to the United States, Mexicans are seeking better working conditions and higher wages than are available in their home country. They are subjected to the same discrimination as earlier immigrant groups. Americans of Mexican descent vary in their levels of assimilation, based mostly on how long they or their ancestors have been in the United States (Cortes and Poston, 2008).

The first major migration of Mexicans took place after the Mexican Revolution (1910) and was motivated in large part by labor requirements in the southwestern United States (Donato, 1994). This migration was maintained until the immigrants became subjected to unfair treatment and were deported in large numbers during the 1930s. At about this time, the Immigration Act of 1924 was passed, which gave preference to northern and western Europeans. However, there was again a need for agricultural labor, so large-scale Mexican migration was resumed (Donato, 1994; Garcia, 2011).

Mexican migration to the United States may be categorized into three major periods: the *bracero* (i.e., guest worker) period (1942–1964); the post-bracero period (1965–1986); and the post-Immigration Reform and Control Act (IRCA) period (1987–present) (Donato, 1994; Durand, Massey, and Parrado, 1999). The **bracero program** (1942–1964) began as a response to the requirement for temporary agricultural labor. Attitudes toward immigration were tolerant during this twenty-two-year period. Mexicans were brought in on a temporary basis, and they maintained ties with their home country. Very little legal and unauthorized migration occurred during this period (Reichert and Massey, 1980). The bracero period is important because it established a precedent for Mexican migration to the United States, as an opportunity to obtain earnings in the form of remittances, and for the dynamic of a seasonal migration pattern (Garcia, 2011).

When the bracero program was terminated in 1964, around 200,000 of these guest workers lost their jobs, "leading to a buildup of social unrest" (Plankey Videla, 2008: 592). Several immigration regulations were then put into effect. Only a person with family ties to a **green card** holder was allowed to work in the United States (Reichert and Massey, 1980). Thus, persons without such associations would need to use undocumented migration as a means to gain US employment, and more and more Mexican immigrants were women and children (Reichert and Massey, 1980). Unauthorized migration also increased because of the caps placed on migration from Europe. In fact, Mexican migrants could enter and leave the United States without much difficulty, and employer sanctions for hiring undocumented workers were minimal.

In the latter part of this period, however, the American public began discussing and debating the issue of unauthorized migration (Bean, Telles, and Lowell, 1987). Durand and his colleagues have written that "after 1973, wages stagnated, unemployment rates rose, income inequality grew, and the distribution of wealth became progressively more skewed" (Durand, Massey, and Parrado, 1999: 520). Some felt that the United States was losing control of its borders. These and other concerns resulted in the passage of the 1986 Immigration Reform and Control Act (IRCA) (Garcia, 2011; Warren and Passel, 1987).

The IRCA was designed to drastically reduce unauthorized migration from Mexico (Durand, Massey, and Parrado, 1999; White, Bean, and Espenshade, 1990), mainly by imposing strict employer sanctions, providing amnesty to long-term residents of the United States, and instituting stricter border control. The act was successful in reducing undocumented migration. But, as Passel (2006) has noted, rates began to increase in the early 1990s and continued to do so until around 2010 (see also Garcia, 2011). Since 2010 or so the numbers of immigrants from Mexico have decreased, and net international migration from Mexico has even been negative in some years.

The period following the IRCA is known as the new era of migration (Durand, Massey, and Parrado, 1999). The immigrant population is

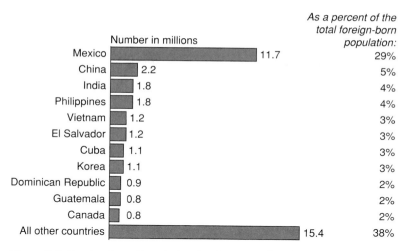

Figure 9.3 Foreign-born Population by Country of Birth, 2010
Source: US Bureau of the Census, available at: www.census.gov/newsroom/pdf/cspan_fb_slides.pdf, last accessed June 14, 2015.

no longer temporary, seasonal, geographically concentrated, and predominantly male, but is now rather long-term, urbanized, and geographically dispersed. In the past two decades, there has been an increase in nativist sentiment (Espenshade and Hempstead, 1996), due in large part to a stagnating economy, a perceived threat to national security, particularly since the tragedy of 9/11, and the mistaken belief that immigrants, especially Mexicans, are taking jobs from permanent residents, even though extensive research indicates this is not true (Garcia, 2011).

The number of unauthorized Mexicans estimated to be residing in the United States in 2012 was about 5.9 million of the roughly 11.2 million total number of unauthorized immigrants, lower than the high of 6.8 million in 2008 (Passel and Cohn, 2014). I discuss this issue in more detail later in this chapter.

I show in Figure 9.3 data on the percentage distribution of the foreign-born population of the United States in 2010. By far the largest share is Mexican, at 29 percent; China is second with 5 percent; and India and the Philippines are tied for third place with 4 percent each. The other top countries are from Latin America, North America, and Asia. Only 12 percent of the US foreign-born population in 2010 was born in Europe (Grieco et al., 2012).

The character of US immigration has indeed changed since the mid-1800s; that is, the origin locations of immigrants to the United States have changed dramatically. Allow me to put this issue into more perspective. In Figure 9.4, I show the numbers of the foreign-born population of the United States, from 1960 to 2010, according to their major regions of birth.

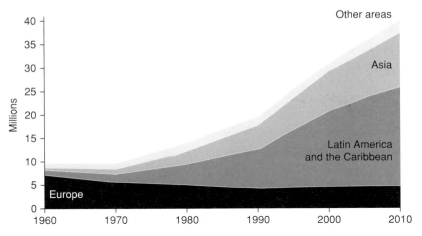

Figure 9.4 Foreign-born Population by Region of Birth, 1960–2010
Source: US Bureau of the Census, available at: www.census.gov/newsroom/pdf/cspan_fb_slides.pdf, last accessed June 14, 2015.

In 1960, three-quarters of the US foreign-born were born in Europe. By 2010, the European percentage had declined to only 12 percent. In the mid-1960s, as I will discuss in Chapter 15, a major immigration law was passed which resulted in the character of US immigration changing from a policy preferring Europeans to one preferring Asians and Latin Americans. This was another change in the character of US immigration. What were these changes about, and when did they occur?

In an earlier section of this chapter, I discussed the history of immigration to the United States. I noted that the first immigrants were mainly from northern and western Europe. Indeed, in 1850 and 1860 over 90 percent of the foreign-born persons in the United States were born in northern and western Europe. The share of the foreign-born from northern and western Europe was 87 percent in 1870 and 79 percent in 1890 (Gibson and Jung, 2006). Immigration to the United States began with immigrants from northern and western Europe, which lasted up to the 1870s. In those times northern and western Europeans defined US immigration.

However, this began to change in the 1880s. I showed earlier in Figure 9.2 that the number of foreign-born persons started to increase from 6.7 million in 1880, to over 9 million in 1890, to over 10 million in 1900. These increases in the foreign-born were due almost entirely to increases in immigration. For instance, after the depression in the United States in the 1880s, the number of immigrants increased from 3.5 million in the 1890s to over 9 million in the first decade of the new century. By 1910, immigrants from southern and eastern Europe comprised over 70 percent of persons entering the United States; the US foreign-born population in 1910 was now one-third southern and eastern European (Gibson and Jung, 2006). During this period from the 1880s through the 1910s, southern and eastern Europeans defined US immigration. The character of US immigration had changed.

Immigration numbers fell off considerably in the latter years of the 1910s because of the First World War. Population policies were passed in the 1920s that seriously restricted immigration to the United States, especially immigration from southern and eastern Europe. The numbers of foreign-born persons in the United States began declining in 1930 (Figure 9.2), reaching lows of less than 10 million in 1960 and 1970 (Figure 9.4). Then, in the 1970s and 1980s, the character of immigration changed again. The passage of the Immigration and Nationality Act in 1965 opened up US immigration to peoples from Latin America and Asia, so that by 2010 US immigration was no longer defined by Europeans, but by Latin Americans and Asians (Figure 9.4).

So the character of US immigration was first based on northern and western Europeans, then changed in the 1880s to one based on southern and eastern Europeans, and then changed in the late 1960s to one based on Latin Americans and Asians.

ECONOMIC EFFECTS OF INTERNATIONAL MIGRATION

I noted at the start of this chapter that no demographic topic is discussed these days by laypeople and social scientists alike as frequently, as emotionally, and as forcefully as international migration. Surveys of US residents conducted in recent years point to increasing levels of negativity about immigrants. A survey conducted in 2008 in Houston, for instance, found that "residents increasingly carry negative views about immigrants, saying they burden tax-supported services including schools and hospitals, while contributing to crime" (Pinkerton, 2008). A more recent article in the *Texas Observer* makes similar points (Hooks and Rahman, 2014). Houston residents are not unlike the residents of other big cities in the United States regarding their negative views about immigration and immigrants.

These negative sentiments are reflected in numerous popular books published in the United States about international migration. In 2002, Patrick Buchanan published *The Death of the West* and in 2007 he published *State of Emergency*. Other recently published books with alarmist views are *In Mortal Danger* by Tom Tancredo (2006), *Immigration's Unarmed Invasion* by Frosty Wooldridge (2004), *Fighting Immigration Anarchy* by Daniel Sheehy (2006), and *Alien Nation* by Peter Brimelow (1996). I could go on and list another half dozen or more polemics with gloomy alarmist views about international immigration. Fewer books show the positive contributions of international migration. Some include Philippe Legrain's *Immigrants, Your Country Needs Them* (2006), Dowell Myers' *Immigrants and Boomers* (2008), and Goldin, Cameron, and Balarajan's *Exceptional People* (2011).

There is a wealth of published literature by demographers and other social scientists dealing with the positive and negative aspects of international migration, considered from many different vantage points. These include economic effects, cultural effects, environmental effects, health effects, and security effects, to list several of the dimensions that have been surveyed. In this section, I draw on this literature and undertake a review of some of the positive and negative characteristics of international migration. My focus is on the economic effects: what is good and what is not good economically about international migration?

In general terms, there are two basic perspectives on international migration: one permitting it, and one denying it. Organizations and bodies such as the Catholic Church and the World Bank argue for more and freer international migration because "people should not be confined to their countries of birth by national borders, and that more migration would speed economic growth and development in both sending and receiving countries" (Martin and Zurcher, 2008: 4). An opposite approach is espoused by organizations in almost every developed country of the world, arguing for reductions in the numbers of international immigrants. In the United States, two such bodies are Negative Population Growth (NPG) and the Federation for American Immigration Reform (FAIR). FAIR argues that "unskilled newcomers hurt low-skilled U.S. workers, have negative environmental effects, and threaten established U.S. cultural values" (Martin and Zurcher, 2008: 4).

The economic arguments about the costs and benefits of international migration, on which I concentrate here, are usually the main ones cited when scholars and laypeople argue for or against immigration. There is an impressive and extensive literature, and it is complex and diverse. I summarize some of this literature in the paragraphs below.

From the vantage point of the receiving (host) countries, there are several related concerns: are immigrants taking away jobs from the local population, are immigrants driving down wages, and are immigrants a burden on the welfare system of the host country? Most analyses in western Europe and the United States indicate that the impact of immigration on jobs and wages is weak or nonexistent. Immigrants often wind up in the "three Ds jobs"; these are the "dirty, difficult and dangerous (or demeaning) jobs...shunned by local workers" (Ghosh, 2005: 168).

Evidence shows little, if any, competition in these and in many other type of jobs between immigrants to a country and the local residents. There is a wealth of literature on this topic, and no correlation is found between immigration and employment. Immigrants are often the first to be fired, and they are also "found to earn less than local workers in comparable jobs" (Ghosh, 2005: 169–170). As Brown, Bean, and Bachmeier (forthcoming) have noted, research on immigration's labor-market effects finds very little if any evidence that immigrants harm the employment or wages of similar natives (also see Holzer, 2011).

There is some literature showing how immigration can have a negative impact on the labor market. This would be the situation in industries or geographic areas with large concentrations of foreign workers; sometimes this results in "pressure on jobs and working conditions of the local labor force" (Ghosh, 2005: 169; see also Borjas, 2003; Borjas, Freeman, and Katz, 1997).

Regarding wages, some believe that even if immigrants do not take jobs from local workers, they will depress wages. Research from numerous studies in Europe and the United States are mixed, with most indicating little, if any, depressing impact on local wages. Those showing negative effects of immigration on wages report a very small effect, on the order of −0.3 to −0.8 percent. In a study of US workers, Brucker (2002) found that a 10 percent increment in the number of immigrants has essentially a zero effect on non-immigrant wages. Other analyses actually show that the presence of immigrants tends to increase local wages, especially those of the highly skilled.

What about the effect of immigration on social welfare costs? Studies in the United Kingdom show that immigrants contributed the equivalent of US$4 billion more in personal and employment taxes than they received in welfare benefits. Recent analyses conducted in the United States reach similar conclusions. Much depends on the degree to which immigrants depend on welfare. This varies from high levels in many western European countries, sometimes higher than those of the local people, to levels in other European countries and in Canada where the welfare dependence of immigrants is lower than that of citizens. Immigrants to the United States, particularly in their early years in the new country, do add to some welfare and education costs. But, eventually, the immigrants and their descendants end up paying taxes that result in a net positive contribution (Ghosh, 2005: 171).

There is a real economic gain for many countries in admitting skilled workers. European Union member states, particularly Germany and the United Kingdom, are experienced users "of highly skilled foreign nationals, [and] are leading the way in selecting qualified workers from abroad" (Papademetriou, 2003: 571).

One study showed that there are approximately 400,000 engineers and scientists from countries of the developing world, representing 30–50 percent of the total stock, who work in developed countries in research and development industries. Immigrants to the United States from developing countries have roughly twice as much education than their countrymen remaining at home: "An extreme case is that of Jamaica in 2000, when there were nearly four times more Jamaicans with tertiary education in the U.S. than at home. [Also], more Ethiopian doctors are practicing in Chicago than in Ethiopia" (Ghosh, 2005: 173).

Of all the developed countries, the United States has gained the most with respect to attracting skilled immigrants. In 2000, the United States had admitted more than 10.5 million highly skilled immigrants, while losing just over 431,000 graduates to other countries, for a net gain of 10 million (Legrain, 2006: 95). Skilled immigrants from developing nations play a very important role in the economic activities of developed nations, a point often overlooked by those less accepting of international migrants.

Skilled immigrants have another type of impact on the economies of the host countries. Research has shown, for example, a positive association between the presence of foreign-born workers in California and exports from California to the home country. Specifically, "a one percent increase in the number of first generation immigrants generated a 0.5 percent increase in exports from California to the respective country" (Iredale, 2005: 224).

I turn next to the economic effects that migrants have on the sending countries. Does international migration help or hinder the economic development of the origin countries? On the one hand, emigration is a safety valve, temporarily, on job losses and labor restructuring in the process of industrial development. But since emigrants involve only a small share of the labor force of the sending countries, no more than 2–3 percent at best, their departure does not appear to have much of a real and long-term impact on unemployment. In many developing countries, labor emigration does not result in a rise in wages because these countries "generally suffer from a large backlog of unemployed and underemployed; this is one reason why employers normally do not oppose labor emigration" (Ghosh, 2005: 173).

Another economic effect I wish to consider is the contribution of remittances to the economies of the origin countries. (A **remittance** is a transfer of money by a foreign immigrant worker from the host country to an individual in his or her home country.) The many millions of migrants living outside their countries of birth send billions of dollars home each year. The total amount of remittances (in US$ billions) worldwide have risen from just under $200 billion in 2000 to $511 billion in 2013. "The economic importance of remittances is larger in poorer countries than in richer ones" and account for 8 percent of the "gross domestic product in low-income nations" (Connor et al., 2013: 6). Remittances worldwide are so large and are growing so rapidly that they are "among the fastest growing international financial flows" (Martin and Zurcher, 2008: 18).

Remittances are valuable, for one reason, because their recipients have been shown to have a high propensity to save the funds. The remittances also result in credit that may be used as investment capital. Small business ventures grow via remittances. The remittances aid local community development and businesses, and they are an important and sometimes sizable addition to the gross national product (GNP) (i.e., the total dollar value of all goods and services produced for consumption in the society during a particular time period). However, one needs to be careful and not overestimate the effect of remittances on business development. "Businesses established through remittances cannot necessarily rely on their continued flow for sustainability" (Skeldon, 2005: 263).

Studies have also shown a positive association between remittances and poverty reduction. "A 10 percent increase in the share of remittances in country Gross Domestic Product (GDP) [leads] to a 1.2 percent decrease in the percentage of persons living on less than US$1.00 per day, and also reduces the depth or severity of poverty" (Ghosh, 2005: 179). Remittances are indispensable for the economic survival of many developing countries (Skeldon, 2005: 260).

As an aside, let me distinguish between GDP and GNP. GDP refers to goods and services produced in the country, whereas GNP refers to goods and services produced by companies of a country irrespective of their location. For instance, US GNP refers to goods and services produced by American companies everywhere, whereas US GDP refers to goods and services produced in the United States.

What is the economic cost to the origin countries when they lose skilled personnel via emigration? Is emigration always a "brain drain" that "can act as a serious brake on development and poverty alleviation?" (Laczko, 2005: 287). Actually, in nursing and teaching jobs, the international departure of residents, followed by their return, enables the migrants to obtain new skills, "and in many cases plays a useful role in exposing migrants, as well as the host societies, to new ideas and ways of doing things" (Laczko, 2005: 289). Research on the net effects of return international migration, that is, re-migration, shows that the origin countries derive the greatest benefit when the skilled immigrants return home in, say, ten to fifteen years after their departure (Laczko, 2005: 289).

The literature on the effects of international immigration is extensive. I have discussed here only a small amount of the relevant research, and have focused only on economic effects. Although there are, indeed, some important economic costs to international migration, on balance there are many more benefits, and this generalization may be made with regard to both the host countries and the sending countries.

UNAUTHORIZED INTERNATIONAL MIGRATION

International migrants are often categorized as either legal or illegal. The main adjectives I use in this book to refer to international migrants who are not legally residing in a country are unauthorized and undocumented. What does this mean? An **unauthorized** (or **undocumented**) **immigrant** is a person who immigrates into a host country "through irregular or extralegal channels" (Armbrister, 2003: 512). More specifically, an unauthorized immigrant is an international migrant who resides in the host country of destination, but who is not a citizen of the host country, who has not been admitted by the host country for permanent residence, "and is not in a set of specific authorized temporary statuses permitting longer-term residence and work" (Passel, 2006: 1; see also Passel, Van Hook, and Bean, 2004). An international migrant is classified as unauthorized if (1) during the process of migrating to the host country, the person "avoided inspection by crossing borders clandestinely or . . . traveled with fraudulent documents, e.g., a falsified visa or counterfeit passport" – such persons are referred to as **entries without inspection** (EWIs); or (2) the migrant "overstayed the time limit of a legally obtained non-immigrant temporary visa" – such persons are referred to as **visa overstayers** or **visa overstays** (Armbrister, 2003: 512).

The United States used to be unique among all the countries of the world regarding the most common type of unauthorized immigration. The most frequent type in almost every country of the world is one who arrives legally in the host country often "as a non-immigrant (e.g., tourist, student, or temporary laborer), and [stays] beyond the legally sanctioned period" (Armbrister, 2003: 512), that is, a visa overstayer. Previously, the majority of unauthorized immigrants in the United States "entered without inspection over land borders with Mexico and Canada" (Armbrister, 2003: 512); they are EWIs, and most are from Mexico. It was estimated that, in 2005, among the unauthorized immigrant population in the United States, 25–40 percent were visa overstayers and the balance, the majority, were the so-called EWIs (Passel, 2006: 16). However, the percentage of visa overstayers has increased in recent years, and in 2012 was estimated at around 50 percent (Warren and Kerwin, 2015: 93). Now, in the United States, unauthorized immigrants are pretty much split into two more or less equally sized groups, EWIs and visa overstayers.

Whereas most of the unauthorized migrants entering the United States as EWIs are from Mexico, the same may not be said about visa overstayers.

Demographers Susan Brown and Frank Bean remind us that "visa-overstays do not come predominantly from any one country" (2005: 369). Also, they differ markedly from EWIs. They most frequently enter the United States by air and are usually more socioeconomically advantaged than EWIs. At a minimum they need to possess resources to obtain a valid passport and a US visa.

Regarding the volume of unauthorized immigrants worldwide, the International Organization for Migration (2010: 29) estimates the number to be between 30 and 35 million persons, constituting around 15 percent or so of the estimated total number of 232 million international migrants. Most unauthorized immigrants go mainly to a few developed countries, and they mainly hail from developing countries. Visa overstayers in countries of the developed world are now believed to constitute a significant proportion of unauthorized immigrants.

During the 1990s, the volume of unauthorized immigrants increased significantly. Worldwide, most were between the ages of 18 and 35, and more than half were male, although this percentage has decreased in recent years: "With large numbers of women in developed countries working outside the home, opportunities for employment in domestic work and child-care have attracted women from developing countries, swelling both legal and unauthorized migrant numbers" (Armbrister, 2003: 513).

In the major regions of the world, certain countries serve as magnets for unauthorized immigrants. In Africa, South Africa in the post-apartheid era has become the major destination for unauthorized immigrants from other African countries. In Asia, most of the unauthorized immigrant streams are to Japan, South Korea, and Malaysia. In Europe, the major destination countries used to be the United Kingdom, Germany, France, Belgium, the Netherlands, and Switzerland, but in the 1990s, these countries introduced strict immigration laws. The unauthorized immigrant streams then moved south to Italy, Spain, and Portugal.

In the western hemisphere, the United States is the magnet country for unauthorized migrants. The numbers have increased considerably in past decades. In the United States, the estimated number of unauthorized immigrants grew from roughly 3.5 million in 1990, to around 8.6 million in 2000, and to about 12.2 million in 2007; the number declined to 11.2 million in 2012 (Figure 9.5). Mexico has maintained its position as the prime source of unauthorized immigrants to the United States. The estimated number of unauthorized migrants from Mexico to the United States grew from 4.5 million in 2000 to 6.9 million in 2007, and then declined remarkably to 5.9 million in 2012 (Figure 9.6). "The sudden reversal of a long trend of growth in the number of Mexican unauthorized immigrants probably results from both a marked decline in new arrivals and an

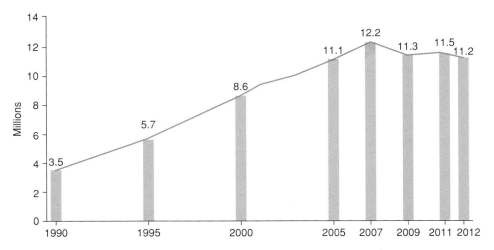

Figure 9.5 Unauthorized Immigrant Population in the United States, 1990–2012
Source: Passel and Cohn (2014: 13). Figure prepared by Huanjun Zhang and DLP.

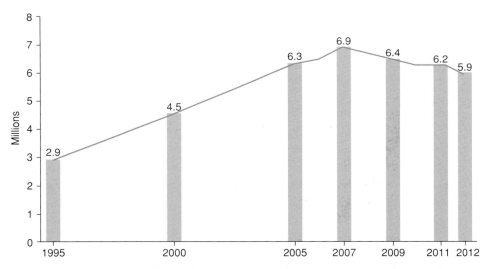

Figure 9.6 Unauthorized Immigrant Population in the United States from Mexico, 1995–2012
Source: Passel and Cohn (2014: 9). Figure prepared by Huanjun Zhang and DLP.

increase in departures (from the U.S. back) to Mexico" (Passel and Cohn, 2014: 19).

Countries sending the next largest numbers of unauthorized immigrants to the United States in 2012 were El Salvador (675,000), Guatemala (525,000), India (450,000), and Honduras (350,000).

Where in the United States do the unauthorized immigrants reside? An estimated 2.5 million, or 22 percent, of all the unauthorized migrants in the

United States in 2012 were in California. Texas is the next leading state, with 1.7 million, and Florida is the third largest with 925,000.

The geographical distribution of the unauthorized immigrant population in the United States became more diversified between 2000 and 2012. In seven states – Florida, Idaho, Maryland, Nebraska, New Jersey, Pennsylvania, and Virginia – the unauthorized population increased in size. Conversely, the counts declined in fourteen states – Alabama, Arizona, California, Colorado, Georgia, Illinois, Indiana, Kansas, Kentucky, Massachusetts, Nevada, New Mexico, New York, and Oregon. Passel and Cohn hold that the declines in all these states, except for Massachusetts, "was due to decreases in unauthorized immigrants from other countries" (Passel and Cohn, 2014: 12).

A most interesting fact is that most of the children of unauthorized immigrants are themselves legal residents. Nearly 4.5 million of the 5.5 million children of unauthorized immigrants in 2010 were born in the United States, and thus are themselves legal residents of the United States.

I conclude this chapter by introducing a demographic concept that is very important in discussions of international migration and migration policy, **zero net international migration**. This concept is not as easily understood as it should be, and is often used incorrectly.

ZERO NET INTERNATIONAL MIGRATION

Net international migration and natural increase (the difference between births and deaths) are the demographic processes that determine the amount of growth or decline in a nation's population. In many European countries that are today characterized by low levels of fertility and mortality, the contribution of net international migration to overall population change overshadows the contribution of natural increase. Some hold that international migration to the United States is too large, and thus argue for **zero net international migration**. They state that if the number of people who leave the country each year is the same as the number who enter each year, then the effect of net international migration will be zero. For example, proponents of negative population growth (NPG) have stated that the United States should place a ceiling on annual immigration so that it is balanced by emigration, and thus will not contribute to overall population growth (Mann, [1992] 2015). In this last section of the chapter, I draw on my earlier research with Leon Bouvier and Nanbin Zhai (Bouvier, Poston, and Zhai, 1997) that shows why this reasoning is incorrect.

Zero net international migration should not be confused with no (i.e., zero) international migration. The former is characterized by the same numbers of persons immigrating into a country as emigrating from it. In the latter, there is no international migration. The two concepts are not the same.

Zero net international migration is at least theoretically possible. Indeed, such has always been the intent behind temporary worker programs – whether in Europe, or in the Middle East, or in the Persian Gulf. Workers are allowed to enter the country for a specified period of time and then later are expected to return to their homelands.

Allow me here to assume that zero net international migration could become a reality even in a country like the United States. If this were to occur, and if each year a number, say, 200,000, were to immigrate to the United States, and 200,000 were to emigrate from the United States, does this mean that immigration will no longer be a main contributor to population growth, as the NPG proponents conclude?

The answer is no. Even with zero net international migration, the impact of the immigration and emigration movements that produce it would result in considerable population increases in receiving countries, such as the United States, and substantial population losses in sending countries, such as Mexico.

In considering the direct impact of zero net international migration, I first need to note that immigrants to a country are usually always younger than re-migrants from that country. Immigrants often arrive in their countries of destination when they are in their 20s and early 30s; conversely, re-migrants usually depart the host countries either fairly soon after their arrival, or much later when they are in their 60s or older when they reach retirement.

To simplify my hypothetical illustration about patterns of immigration to and re-migration from the United States, I will assume that all immigrants enter the country at age 15, and that all re-migrants leave the country at age 65. Thus, the immigrants tend to spend most of their adult lives in the United States, their country of first destination, for an average of about fifty years.

In this illustration, net international migration each year would be zero because 200,000 people would immigrate in each year and 200,000 would leave each year. I will use the life table (already discussed in Chapter 7) as a way of keeping track of the immigrants and re-migrants. For most people, the life table indicates how many additional years a person can expect to live, on average, after having attained a specific age. If 200,000 people enter the United States at say, age 15, and leave at say, age 65, the total number of person-years spent in the country for any one of these cohorts of 200,000 persons would be 10 million (200,000 immigrants times fifty years) minus the person-years that would have been lived in the United States by those who died there before reaching age 65. If 200,000 persons immigrate to the United States at age 15, stay for fifty years, and then depart at age 65, this one cohort of 200,000 persons will have lived there for more than 9.5 million person-years (see my discussion in Chapter 7 of the "big L" column in the life table). Even though 200,000 persons leave the United States each year (at age 65) and 200,000 enter each year (at age 15), there is nevertheless a sizable direct effect of zero net international immigration. In the hypothetical case that I have constructed here, the direct effect of the net international migration involving 200,000 emigrants and 200,000 immigrants each year is in excess of 9.5 million person-years lived in the United States for each cohort of 200,000 immigrants who enter at age 15. Therefore, one must not confuse the two concepts of zero net international migration and zero (or no) international migration; they are very different from one another. The direct impact of zero net international migration can be quite substantial.

SUMMARY

This chapter focused on the demographic dynamics of international migration. No demographic topic is discussed by laypeople and social scientists as frequently, as forcefully, and as emotionally as international migration. Having considered in Chapter 8 the topic of internal migration and now, in this chapter, international migration, it is certainly the case that the dynamics of the two differ significantly.

I began this chapter by reviewing the definitions and concepts used by demographers in their analyses of international migration. World immigration patterns over time were next addressed, followed by a discussion of immigration to the United States. I next turned to a discussion of the positive and negative economic issues pertaining to international migration, followed by a consideration of legal and unauthorized immigration. I concluded the chapter with a section on the concept of zero net international migration.

This chapter completes my presentation in this book of the three demographic processes of fertility (Chapter 4), mortality (Chapter 7), and migration (Chapters 8 and 9). In the next chapter, I focus on the two most important characteristics studied by demographers, namely, age and sex. These are so relevant for demography that they are often referred to as *the* demographic characteristics.

10 Age and Sex Composition

Of all the characteristics of human populations, age and sex are the most important and relevant for demographers. They are so important for demographic analysis that they are sometimes referred to as *the* demographic variables. The demographic processes of fertility, mortality, and migration produce the population's age and sex structure (Horiuchi and Preston, 1988), and the age and sex structure influences the demographic processes. I have already shown in Chapter 1 the very close relationship between the **demographic variables** and the **demographic processes**.

The importance of age and sex extends considerably beyond demography. The division of labor in traditional societies is based almost entirely on age and sex. In fact, age and sex differences of one form or another are found in all known human societies (Davis, 1949; Murdock, 1949).

At the individual level, age and sex are of such tremendous importance in our daily life that we usually do not realize that we are observing them. Whenever you walk across campus or on the streets where you live, what are the first two characteristics you recognize about an approaching person? The person's presentation of gender from which you infer his or her sex, and a rough notion of his or her age, that is, whether the person is a baby, an adolescent, a young adult, a middle-aged person, or a senior. We make these determinations mainly on the basis of outward appearances, and we make them so automatically that they are done subconsciously.

The determination of a person's sex is usually the first item of information we obtain, and this is based mainly on how the person presents themselves. Also, it is often the case that the person's given name tells us his or her sex. If you inform your mother that you have just met someone with the name Nancy, Jane, Bethany, or Rachel, she will certainly know that the person you met is female. If the person you have just met has the given name David, Daniel, Richard or Mark, your mother will recognize this person to

266

be male. However, if you tell your mother that you have just met someone with the given name Pat, Jordan, Leslie, Chris, Jean, or Ryan, the first question your mother will almost certainly ask you is, "Is your new friend a man or a woman?" Try speaking to someone about another person who has an androgynous name, such as those just mentioned. Your conversation will not get very far until the other person knows the sex of the person being discussed.

Actually, my Texas A&M colleague Melanie Hawthorne told me after she read an earlier draft of this chapter that the knowledge of one's biological sex may well be one of the last things we generally learn about another person, and in most cases, it could be something we never learn about most people. "We almost never see their genitals, never mind find out what their chromosomes or hormones are. We assume and infer those things from the way the people present themselves, from social cues like clothes, and most of the time it's not a particularly problematic assumption." When we ask about or discuss someone's sex we are really referring to how the person represents him- or herself socially, and not to how the person is defined biologically (pers. comm. between author and Melanie Hawthorne, August 8, 2015). My doctoral student Cheryl Rollman-Tinajero made a similar observation to me about the real importance of distinguishing between biological sex and gender performance and behavior (pers. comm. between author and Cheryl Rollman-Tinajero, December 6, 2015).

In addition, when a person marries, or dies, or achieves some important recognition, and these events are written up in stories in local newspapers, the given name usually tells us the person's sex. If the person's name is androgynous, the use of sex-specific pronouns inform the reader of the person's sex. Following the first mention of the person's full name, there appears, almost always, the person's age. We seem to need or want to know not only the person's sex but also the person's age. Indeed, people have a remarkable curiosity about the age of other people when reading about their achievements or recognizing their contributions. Why is this so? Rowland has noted that this curiosity "reflects a pervasive interest in comparing the timing of events with our expectations or social timetables" (Rowland, 2003: 77; see also Neugarten and Hagestad, 1976: 35).

Changes in the age distribution of a population have consequences for educational, political, and economic life (Keyfitz and Flieger, 1971). A society's age and sex distribution has important implications for socioeconomic and demographic development (Keyfitz, 1965), as well as for labor-force participation and gender relations (South and Trent, 1988). Indeed, "almost any measurement that can be taken of human beings, or of groups of human beings, will show substantial variation by sex and age" (Bogue, 1969: 147).

In this chapter, I first consider the definition of age and sex. Age is easy to define because it is based on temporal change. Some may think that sex is also easy to define, but it is not. There are many issues to consider in determining one's sex. They are involved and complex, and I spend several pages discussing them. Next, some of the theoretical issues in demography dealing with age and sex structure are reviewed, especially those pertaining to what demographers refer to as stable population theory. I then cover some of the methods and approaches demographers use to represent age and sex structure. This is followed by discussions of two key areas of age and sex structure, namely, the **sex ratio at birth** (SRB) and **population aging**. I conclude the chapter with a discussion of cohorts and generations.

CONCEPTS OF AGE AND SEX

Definition of Age and Sex

To a certain extent, the classification, definition, and enumeration of persons by age and sex are more straightforward compared with the situation with most other characteristics of human populations. For instance, the characteristics of race, marital status, and occupation "involve numerous categories and are subject to alternative formulation as a result of cultural differences, differences in the uses to which the data will be put, and differences in the interpretations of respondents and enumerators" (Shryock, Siegel, and Associates, 1976: 105). Still, the classification and definition of age and sex, especially sex, can be problematic.

Age is defined more straightforwardly than most demographic variables. Age is an ascribed, yet changeable, characteristic. It is usually defined in population censuses in terms of the age of the person at his or her last birthday. The United Nations (1998: 69) defines age as "the estimated or calculated interval of time between the date of birth and the date of the census, expressed in complete solar years" (see also Hobbs, 2004). In most censuses, the respondent is asked to give his or her current age, as well as the date when he or she was born. Adjustments are then introduced by census-editing procedures if the respondent's current age does not correspond to the age denoted by the date of birth. This tends to minimize the phenomenon of age heaping, an issue I discuss later (Poston, 2005).

Sex is also an ascribed characteristic and, for most people, unchangeable. Although there are some who do indeed change their sex, for most people, sex is fixed at birth. When a baby is born, its sex is determined on the basis of his or her genital tubercle. On average, boys are born with penises ranging in length from 2.9 to 4.5 centimeters (1.2–1.8 inches) (Flatau et al., 1975). For girls, clitoral length at birth ranges from 0.2 to

0.9 centimeters (0.08–0.33 inches) (Fausto-Sterling, 2000: 60; Sane and Pescovitz, 1992). When the length of the tubercle is somewhere between the range for penis length and the range for clitoral length, sex determination is open for discussion and decision-making by the parents and medical workers. But even in such extreme situations (one or two cases per 1,000 live births), sex assignment is made soon after birth (Money, 1988). The census definition of sex, therefore, is not usually problematic because everyone knows his or her sex. The question, however, is how one's sex is determined.

There are several biological and social considerations regarding the determination of one's sex. When demographers identify the sex of a person or its distribution in a population, they almost always rely on the social definition of self-identification. That is, when a person's sex is listed on a census questionnaire or survey or certificate, its designation is based on the person's self-identification of his or her sex, and not on biological considerations, such as the person's chromosomes or external genitals. However, sex is determined biologically, in five ways, discussed next.

Biological Definitions of Sex

The first biological definition of sex is based on chromosomes, which are structures containing genetic material. Males have an X chromosome and a Y chromosome, and females have two X chromosomes. The X chromosome is larger than the Y chromosome and carries more genetic material (Tavris and Wade, 1984: 135). Chromosome distribution is determined by one's biological parents. The ovum of the female and the sperm of the male each contain twenty-three chromosomes. When the sperm and the ovum come together in one of the woman's Fallopian tubes, they produce a fertilized egg, known as an embryo. It consists of forty-six chromosomes aligned in twenty-three pairs. One of these constitutes the sex of the embryo. An X chromosome is contributed by the mother and either an X or a Y chromosome is contributed by the father.

The second biological definition of sex is based on gonads, that is, testes in males and ovaries in females. If the embryo is chromosomally male, one theory asserts that a gene on the Y chromosome produces male gonads (testes) at about the sixth week after conception. If the embryo is chromosomally female, female gonads (ovaries) appear a few weeks later. Scholars are not entirely sure how this occurs.

The gonads produce the sex-specific hormones, which are the basis for the third biological definition of sex. Androgens are a class of hormones, found mainly in males, though also in females, of which testosterone is the most important. Testosterone is responsible for the differentiation of male and female primary sex characteristics at about the seventh week of fetal life. "On average men…have about ten times the testosterone level that women have, but the range among men varies greatly, and some women have levels higher than some men" (Kimmel, 2004: 40). Without the release of testosterone and other androgens, the male fetus will not develop male external genital organs. Males also receive major surges of testosterone at puberty, so that the task of sex differentiation can be completed. Estrogen surges also occur at puberty in females.

Every embryo contains "two sets of ducts, one of which will become the internal reproductive structures appropriate to the embryo's sex" (Tavris and Wade, 1984: 137). These internal sexual properties constitute the fourth biological definition of sex. In males, these tissues are referred to as Wolffian ducts, and they result in the internal male accessories, namely, the vas deferens, the seminal vesicles, and the prostate. In females, they are known as Mullerian ducts, and they become the "Fallopian tubes, the uterus, and the inner two-thirds of the vagina. In each sex, the ducts that do not develop eventually degenerate, except for traces" (Tavris and Wade, 1984: 137; see also Kimmel, 2004: 39–40).

The sex-specific internal sex structures of the fetus lead finally to the development of sex-specific external genitals, namely, a penis and scrotal sac for males and a clitoris and vagina for females. The external sex structures are the basis for the fifth biological definition of sex. Moreover, it is this fifth definition that results in the assignment of sex at the birth of the baby.

Intersex

Most embryos are consistent on the above five biological definitions of sex. Usually, if an embryo is chromosomally a male, it will also be a male gonadally and hormonally, and will possess male internal and male external sex structures; similarly for females. But this is not always the case. In around 23/10,000 births, these five definitions of sex are not consistent, resulting in what is referred to as an intersexed birth.

There are numerous types of **intersex**. I discuss below some of the major ones; the prevalence statistics I report are approximations. But before doing so, I note that the definition of intersex is not without controversy. I am using the term here to refer to any inconsistency in the five biological definitions. Some have questioned whether a chromosomal anomaly (I will mention below several of them) should be classified as intersex when externally there is no observable ambiguity (Dreger, 1998a, 1998b).

In my view, a good definition of intersex, indeed one of the best I have read, is that of the United Nations Office of the High Commissioner for Human Rights: "An intersex person is born with sexual anatomy, reproductive organs, and/or chromosome patterns that do not fit the typical definition of male or female. This may be apparent at birth or become so later in life. An intersex person may identify as male or female or as neither. Intersex status is not about sexual orientation or gender identity: intersex people experience the same range of sexual orientations and gender identities as non-intersex people" (UNOHCHR, 2013: 1).

One intersex category is chromosomal. Occasionally, chromosomal inconsistencies occur, sometimes during sperm production, resulting in what Renzetti and Curran (1999: 34) have referred to as an "abnormal complement of sex chromosomes." If the sperm fails to divide properly, that is, if what is called nondisjunction occurs, one kind of sperm produced will have neither an X nor a Y chromosome. If this sperm fertilizes a normal egg, the offspring will have only an X chromosome. This type of intersex is known as **Turner's Syndrome**. The person appears to be a female because although that person lacks ovaries, they do possess some external female characteristics. This condition is estimated to occur in about 4/10,000 live births (Fausto-Sterling, 2000: 53).

Another case of nondisjunction is a sperm produced with both an X and a Y chromosome, or two Y chromosomes, resulting in the XXY and XYY chromosome combinations. The XXY is referred to as **Klinefelter's Syndrome** and occurs in roughly 9/10,000 live births (Fausto-Sterling, 2000: 53). A person born with this chromosomal characteristic has the height of a normal male, with long legs, an absent or weak sex drive, "feminized" hips, some breast development, and a small penis and testes (Money and Ehrhardt, 1972). The XYY is referred to as **Jacob's Syndrome** and occurs in about 1/2,000 births. A person born with this chromosomal characteristic is an anatomical male with no physical abnormalities, except for slightly unusual height. The extra Y chromosome does not result in the person's having more androgens than an XY male. Such persons appear to be able to reproduce successfully and rarely come to the attention of investigators, except through large-scale screening of newborns.

The other chromosomal type is the person with three X chromosomes, which is known as the XXX Syndrome, or **Triple X Syndrome**, or Trisomy X. This too occurs roughly in 1/2,000 live births. People born with this chromosomal characteristic are anatomically females and show few visible signs of abnormality, although they tend to be taller than XX females and have a slightly higher incidence of learning disorders (Renzetti and Curran, 2003: 36).

These examples of intersex are chromosomal combinations other than the XY male or the XX female. The designation of the sex of these persons at birth is usually based on external sexual organs. There are other forms of intersex in which the persons are chromosomally male (XY) or female (XX), but the sexual distinctions occur at the level of hormones.

One such example is when an XX fetus receives an excessive amount of androgens. This is known as the **adrenogenital syndrome** (AGS), also referred to as **congenital adrenal hyperplasia** (CAH). Renzetti and Curran (2003: 37) have estimated the incidence of AGS at between 1/5,000 and 1/15,000 live births. Untreated females with AGS have normally functioning ovaries and normal internal female sexual organs, but a masculinized external appearance. This can vary from a slightly enlarged clitoris to a nearly normal-size penis with an empty scrotum. If treated with cortisol from birth on, these chromosomally females will have a later menarche than normal, but will be able to conceive, lactate, and deliver babies normally (Money and Ehrhardt, 1972).

Another type of intersex at the hormonal level is a fetus that is chromosomally male, but is unable to absorb androgen; it often has genitals that are ambiguous or that look more like a clitoris than a penis. This condition is known as **androgen insensitivity syndrome** (AIS). It cannot be treated by administering androgen after birth because the cells remain incapable of responding to androgen. At puberty, AIS persons develop breasts and a feminine body shape, and identify as females. Blackless and her colleagues (2000) have estimated the incidence of AIS to be around 1/13,000 live births.

These are a few of several examples of intersex occurrences. Such persons are inconsistent on the five biological definitions of sex. But the designation of their sex at birth is most always based on their external organs, that is, the presence or lack thereof of a penis. Sexual consistency on the five biological conditions is not a requirement for sex designation. Indeed, I noted earlier that more than 23/10,000 live births are inconsistent on the five biological definitions.

Several well-known individuals are alleged to be/have been intersexed. These include the historical figure Joan of Arc (Gordon, 2000), and such Hollywood celebrities as Mae West, Greta Garbo, Marlene Dietrich, and Jamie Lee Curtis (Young, 2002). A search on the Internet of "intersex" will bring up these and many more names of historical and contemporary figures. In most of these instances, however, medical verification, for example, in the form of chromosomal data, is lacking.

The case of Joan of Arc is of particular interest. Joan may be "the one person born before 1800, with the exception of Jesus Christ, that the average Westerner can name" (Gordon, 2000: xix). In writings, movies, and plays about her, she is often referred to as a "girl/boy." She reportedly had, what Gordon refers to as, "beautiful" breasts, yet was not known to have ever menstruated (Gordon, 2000: 144, 145, 169). These two observations are also made by Castor in her new and highly acclaimed *Joan of Arc: A History* (2015). Both characteristics are consistent with those of persons with AIS.

The sociologist Georgiann Davis has written a captivating book about intersex titled *Contesting Intersex: The Dubious Diagnosis* (2015). Part autobiographical, Professor Davis was diagnosed at age 13 with AIS, but she was not told she was AIS with undescended testes. Instead, the medical doctors informed her that she had underdeveloped ovaries that needed to be surgically removed. She had the surgery and did not learn until she was age 19 that she had an intersex trait. In her book she writes about how best to respond to these naturally occurring conditions of intersex. She describes in detail how intersex is defined, experienced, and contested in the United States today. It is a groundbreaking book, astute and very readable. I recommend it highly.

Transgender

I noted earlier that once sex assignment is made, it is usually permanent. However, there are instances of persons who change their sex. These persons are usually consistent on the five biological definitions but voluntarily decide, usually during adulthood, to change their sex. These persons are referred to as **transsexuals**. (Note that sometimes the term "transsexual" is spelled with one *s* rather than with two, as "transexual." This is done because if the term has a single *s*, this removes the medical connotation that tended to dehumanize the situation; see Shultz, 2015.)

According to the American Psychological Association's Committee on Lesbian, Gay, Bisexual, and Transgender Concerns, the "term transsexual refers to people whose gender identity is different from their assigned sex" (American Psychological Association, 2014: 1). Often, transsexual people alter their bodies via hormonal therapy, surgery, and other means to make them more congruent with their identities. "This process of transition through medical intervention is often referred to as sex or gender reassignment, but more recently is also referred to as gender affirmation" (American Psychological Association, 2014: 1).

Another term, and the one I used as the title for this section of the chapter, is **transgender**. Transgender is an umbrella term referring roughly to all persons whose gender identities, expressions, or behaviors do not conform to the sex to which they were assigned at birth, which, as I have already noted, is based on the fifth biological definition, that is, that dealing with external sexual accessories. It includes any persons who have transitioned surgically, medically, or socially; it includes any persons who assert their gender in a nonconforming manner; and it includes anyone who does not fit into the masculine/feminine, male/female categorizations. It also includes cross-dressers or transvestites (people who wear clothing stereotypically worn by members of the other sex and/or who live as the opposite sex, whether or not they have had sex-change surgery or hormonal therapy), drag queens (males who dress as women so to entertain others at bars and other venues), drag kings (females who dress as men for purposes of entertainment), and genderqueer persons, sometimes referred to as nonbinary persons (those who identify their sex as outside the binary male and female constructs) (American Psychological Association, 2014; Shultz, 2015).

One of the first identifiable and recorded recipients of sex reassignment surgery was Lili Elbe (1882–1931) who had her surgery in Germany around 1930. She was born a male with the name of Einar Wegener and wrote at length about her life as a transsexual. After her death, a friend, Niels Hoyer, collected her writings and edited them into Elbe's autobiography, *Man Into Woman: The First Sex Change* ([1933] 2004). Her story is the centerpiece of Tom Hooper's movie, *The Danish Girl*, first released in 2015 and featuring Eddie Redmayne and Alicia Vikander.

Christine Jorgenson (1927–1989) was the most well-known transsexual in her day. George Jorgenson was a former GI and professional photographer who had sex reassignment surgery in Denmark in 1952. Thereafter Christine Jorgenson "entered the public spotlight and became the catalyst for other would-be transsexuals, many of whom went to Europe for surgery" (Haskell, 2013: 33). She also was a patient of Harry Benjamin (see below), the endocrinologist and sex researcher.

Later, in 1965, sex-change surgery became possible for the first time in the United States with the establishment of the Johns Hopkins Gender Identity Clinic at the Johns Hopkins Hospital in Baltimore, Maryland. The co-founder of the clinic was Howard W. Jones, Jr., who when learning that Christine Jorgenson had her surgery in Denmark, stated "that if the Europeans can do it, he could too" (Epstein, 2015). The clinic was closed in 1979.

In the mid-1970s the ophthalmologist and professional tennis star Richard Raskind underwent sex reassignment surgery and took the name Renee Richards. The New York Supreme Court later ruled that she was eligible to play in the US Open Tennis Tournament as a woman. She chose the name because "Renée" is French for "reborn."

In June 2015 when I was writing this chapter, the magazine *Vanity Fair* published a lead cover story in its July 2015 issue titled "Call Me Caitlyn," featuring the Olympic icon Bruce Jenner who had transitioned to Caitlyn Jenner. She had earlier announced formally her male-to-female transition in a television interview on April 24, 2015, with Diane Sawyer in which she discussed her life-long struggle with gender identity. In early February

2016, the American Society of Magazine Editors named *Vanity Fair*'s "Call Me Caitlyn" cover story the Cover Story of the Year 2015.

I mentioned Harry Benjamin (1885–1986) in an earlier paragraph. He is believed to be the first to have used the term "transsexual." He was a medical doctor concentrating in hormonal research. He became acquainted with the sexuality researcher Alfred Kinsey, who introduced him to his first transgendered patient. Benjamin's young patient was anatomically male, but claimed to be female (Rudacille, 2005: 81–82). Benjamin labeled the condition "transsexualism" and devoted much of his career to studying and treating such individuals. His book *The Transsexual Phenomenon* (1966) became the definitive exposition of the subject (Poston, DeSalvo, and Kincannon, 2009).

Benjamin attempted to define and differentiate among the several concepts dealing with sex. He defined transvestism as the desire to dress as a member of the opposite sex, although as I noted above, a transvestite is not the same as a transsexual. Regarding transsexuals per se (male or female), he observed that such persons were upset by the fact that they were born in what they considered to be the wrong sex and hence they rejected their natural sexual anatomy. This condition, he observed, had nothing in common with conditions of intersex (see my earlier discussion). Transsexuals are biologically and physically normal (i.e., they are consistent on all five biological definitions of sex), but are disconcerted by their assigned sex. Benjamin noted that some may mollify their unhappiness by cross-dressing, but such behavior tends to be an incomplete and short-lived solution to the problem. Benjamin wrote that transsexuals believe they were born in the wrong sex and desire to realize themselves as members of the opposite sex both physically and socially (Benjamin, 1966).

According to Benjamin, few people are as unhappy (before the sex change) as transsexuals. Drug and alcohol abuse, self-mutilation, and suicide are common outcomes of their depression and frustration. Self-mutilations occurred among some of Benjamin's own patients. He stated that some of these self-mutilations were performed in despair, while others were deliberate attempts to pressure the surgeon into finishing the sex change despite his or her initial resistance (Benjamin, 1966; Poston, DeSalvo, and Kincannon, 2009).

A female-to-male (FTM) transsexual, also referred to as a "trans man," is a genetic female who thinks of himself as a male, and has "taken social, medical, or surgical steps to physically or socially masculinize his gender expression or body" (Shultz, 2015: 200). In a similar way, a male-to-female (MTF) transsexual, that is, a "trans woman," is a genetic male consistent on all five biological definitions who thinks of herself as a female, and has "taken social, medical, or surgical steps to physically or socially feminize her gender expression or body" (Shultz, 2015: 200–201). When a transsexual opts for sexual reassignment, this may be done with hormonal therapy, and sometimes also through surgery in which the external genitals are changed.

There may be more MTF than FTM transsexuals (Haskell, 2013), although there are no reliable data on the numbers. Many transsexuals report that they felt they were in the wrong body as far back as they can remember, and that even as preschoolers they often preferred the clothes, toys, and so forth of children of the opposite sex (Boylan, 2013a, 2013b; Brevard, 2001; Haskell, 2013; Hoyer, [1933] 2004; Jorgensen, 1967; Khosla, 2006; McCloskey, 2000; Morris, 1974; Shultz, 2015).

I mentioned earlier the umbrella term, transgender. What is the prevalence of transgender persons in the population? The demographer Gary Gates, who in my view has conducted some of the very best quantitative research on the lesbian, gay, bisexual and transgender (LGBT) populations, estimates that around 0.3 percent of adults in the United States are transgender; this would mean that as of around 2010, there were almost 700,000 transgender adults in the United States (Gates, 2011).

Transgender persons are often linked with lesbians, gay males, and bisexuals in the LGBT so-called group of differences. Sometimes, intersex persons are added to the group listing, LGBTI. In my opinion it is a mistake to link transgender persons and intersex persons with lesbians, gay males, and bisexuals. Homosexuals and bisexuals are not persons with issues of sexual identity, nor are they likely to be persons with atypical combinations of the physical attributes commonly used to distinguish males from females biologically. Homosexuals and bisexuals are grouped together owing to their sexuality or sexual orientation (see my earlier discussion of sexuality in Chapter 5). Indeed, sexual orientation per se varies among transgender individuals and among intersex persons. One therapist has stated that "one-third of male-to-female transsexuals become man-desiring heterosexuals, a third homosexual (i.e., lesbian), and another third asexual" (Haskell, 2013: 37). Also, the sexual orientations varied among the sixty-five intersex persons interviewed by the sociologist Georgiann Davis (2015) in her fascinating book on intersex that I mentioned earlier.

Sex Determination, Self-Identification, and the Olympic Games

When demographers measure the sex composition of a population, they almost always rely on self-identification. The census or survey questionnaires contain an item asking about one's sex (or gender). If the person self-identifies as male, that person is counted as a male, and similarly if the person reports her sex as female. Demographers do not base their classification of sex on any one or combination of the five biological definitions reviewed earlier in this chapter, only on the social definition of self-identification. Indeed, there is no demographic research of which I am aware that has examined whether males and females who are and who are not consistent on the five biological definitions of sex vary with respect to their fertility, mortality, and migration.

The International Olympic Committee (IOC) has been struggling for many years with the issue of sex determination. In the Olympic Games in the 1960s, female competitors were required to submit themselves for an inspection or examination of their genitalia (Fausto-Sterling, 2000: 3), that is, the fifth biological definition of sex (in the list of definitions I presented earlier in this chapter). In later games, chromosomal verification of sex was required (XX equals female, XY equals male), that is, the first biological definition of sex. The IOC decided in 2003 to abandon both kinds of sex testing. For the most part, self-identification of one's sex became the criterion for determining sex for Olympic competition.

With regard to Olympic competitors who are transsexuals, however, such persons must have undergone surgery transforming their genitals to those of the assigned sex and, moreover, there must be verification of the administration of hormonal therapy appropriate for the assigned sex.

In 2014, the IOC issued a statement modifying the above position, and it became effective at the 2014 Winter Olympic Games in Sochi, Russia. This modification seems to be moving toward the third definition of sex, that is, the category based on hormones. According to the new guidelines, if testing shows that a female athlete has higher than average levels of natural testosterone (referred to as "female hyperandrogenism"), she is deemed to have an unfair advantage over her competitors, and could thus be disqualified from participating in the competition. According to the IOC guidelines, "If, in the opinion of the Expert Panel (consisting of a gynecologist, an endocrinologist and a genetics expert), the investigated athlete has female hyperandrogenism that confers a competitive advantage, because it is functional and the androgen level is in the male range, the investigated athlete may be declared ineligible to compete" (International Olympic Committee, 2014: 5). But the IOC does not specify quantitatively what is meant by "the male range." Nevertheless, in the words of the anthropologist Barbara J. King, "excluding athletes who have trained and competed as women from the Olympics on the basis of naturally occurring hormones in their blood inappropriately reduces athletic ability to hormone levels, and gender to biology" (King, 2012: 1).

Moreover, there is no mention in the IOC guidelines regarding the testing of male athletes. I would think that if a male athlete was shown to have higher than average male levels of natural testosterone, then he too should be disqualified because this would give him a competitive advantage over males with normal, that is, lower levels.

I suspect that the 2014 IOC statement was a response to sex identification controversies that emerged in 2006 and 2009. In 2006, a middle distance woman runner from India, Santhi Soundarajan, won a silver medal in the women's 800 meters race at the 2006 Asian Games in Doha, Qatar. Some doubted she was female, so she was required to undergo sex testing, even though she was raised as a female and self-identified as a female. It was determined she had the intersex condition known as AIS – see my above discussion. She was stripped of her silver medal. She returned home to her village in India very depressed and later attempted to commit suicide.

In 2009, a middle distance runner from South Africa, Caster Semenya, won the women's 800 meters race at the 2009 International Association of Athletics Federations (IAAF) World Championships in Berlin, Germany. Many claimed she had a masculine appearance and questioned her gender. The IAAF required she undergo a gender test, not because they suspected her of cheating, but because they wanted to determine whether she had a medical condition giving her a competitive advantage. The IAAF did not release the results of the gender tests for reasons of privacy. She was allowed to continue to compete and did not lose her medals. I have read several reports about Ms. Semenya. Some state she has both external female genitalia and undescended testes. She was raised as a female and identifies as a female. But it appears from the several reports about her that she is intersex, that is, she is not consistent on the five biological definitions of sex.

The question here is the definition of sex to be employed that determines if persons pass the sex test to be eligible to compete athletically. Must a person be consistent on the five biological definitions as a female (or as a male) to be classified as a female (or as a male)? Are intersex persons or transgender persons not eligible to participate in the competitions?

The IOC in its 2014 statement has taken the position that the important criterion is hormones, the third biological definition of sex. If a person claiming to be female has too much testosterone, even if it is produced naturally in her body, then she runs the risk of disqualification because too much testosterone means you are male. The cases of Ms. Soundarajan and Ms. Semenya are a symptom of the debate about what counts as "passing" or "not passing" the sex test. Does "passing" the gender test depend on chromosomes, gonads, hormones, internal accessories, or external genitals? The IOC seems to have taken the position it is hormones that count.

After I had finished drafting this section of Chapter 10 in mid-July 2015, there was a major change in the above position. An athletics governing body based in Switzerland, the Court of Arbitration for Sport, declared on July 27, 2015, that they were questioning the so-called advantage to female athletes of high levels of testosterone. They thus suspended "the practice of 'hyperandrogenism regulation' by track and field's governing body, the International Association of Athletics Federations. It gave the . . . I.A.A.F. two years to provide more persuasive scientific evidence linking 'enhanced testosterone levels and improved athletic performance' . . . If sufficient evidence is not presented within two years, the hyperandrogenism regulation will be declared void" (Branch, 2015: A1).

Sex versus Gender

I have already noted that sex, for the most part though not always, is an ascribed variable whose designation (male or female) is based on biology. In the social sciences, therefore, the concept of *sex* is often used when discussing biological differences between males and females, for example, fertility and mortality differences. The concept of *gender* is most often used when discussing nonbiological differences between males and females, for example, differences in socioeconomic status.

However, demographers tend to use the term *sex* when discussing both biological and nonbiological differences owing, perhaps, to demography's major focus on fertility and mortality. I do not wish to suggest that demographers are uninterested in nonbiological differences between the sexes. Differences between males and females in migration, marriage and divorce, and labor-force participation, to name but a few, are nonbiological differences of significant interest to demographers (Poston, 2005; Riley, 2005). But even when demographers study these nonbiological behaviors, they often retain the use of the term *sex* (for a broader discussion, see Riley, 2005).

THEORETICAL AND SUBSTANTIVE ISSUES OF AGE AND SEX

The age and sex structure of a population is an important piece of information because in many ways it is a map of the demographic history of the population. Persons of the same age constitute a group or cohort of people who were born during the same period, and therefore have been exposed to similar historical facts and conditions. These experiences often also differ according to sex. For instance, military personnel who participate in wars are usually restricted to a narrow age range and comprise more males than females. For decades after the cessation of fighting, one will observe heavier attrition among the male cohorts owing to war casualties. Major events in a population's immediate history, say, those that occurred within the previous eight decades, are easily recognized when only the population's current data on age and sex are examined.

Social scientists in particular are interested in the age and sex composition of populations. The numerical balance between the sexes affects many social and economic relationships, not the least of which is marriage. Later, I will describe how the severely imbalanced SRBs in China since the mid-1980s are affecting and will continue to affect the marriage market for the next few decades.

Age is also important theoretically and substantively. Bogue (1985: 42) has written that "almost any aspect of human behavior, from states of subjective feeling and attitudes to objective characteristics such as income, home ownership, occupation, or group membership, may be expected to vary with age." Populations with large proportions of young members differ in many ways from those with large proportions of elders.

Age and Sex and the Demographic Processes

The demographic processes themselves vary significantly by age and sex. With regard to fertility, more males are born than females, usually around 105 males for every 100 females. The fecundity and, hence, the childbearing years of females and males occur within certain ages, for females between the ages 15 to 49 and for males usually a few years later and up to age 79. This is "usually" the situation for males, because while "in polygamous populations a man's fertility can remain high well into his fifties and sixties…in controlled fertility societies, it peaks…with a mode in the mid-twenties" (Coleman, 2000: 41). This is due in part to low fertility norms in Western societies, as well as to a small average age difference of about two to three years between men and women in first marriages (Poston, 2005).

Regarding mortality, females have lower death rates than males at every age of life. Death rates are high in the first year of life and then drop to very low levels. In modern populations, they do not again attain the level reached in the first year of life for another five to six decades. Also, as I noted earlier in Chapter 7, cause-specific mortality is often age-related.

The sex difference in mortality deserves additional discussion. Females live longer than males. This differential has been observed through the centuries and may be attributed to both behavioral and genetic causes. Regarding behavioral factors, males are more prone than females to engage in risk-taking behaviors, and they also engage more than females in cigarette smoking. Regarding genetic factors, the sex chromosomes and hormones, such as testosterone and estrogen, increase longevity for females, but decrease it for males. Research by the actuary Barbara Blatt Kalben (2003) has shown that "the primarily female hormone, estrogen, is protective for females, while the primarily male hormone, testosterone, is detrimental. Estrogen protects the heart and blood vessels. Testosterone, in contrast, tends to promote higher blood pressure, suppress the effectiveness of the immune system, and increase thrombosis" (2003: 45). Kalben's research provides some evidence for both explanations, but the major determining component of the female advantage, she has argued, are the differing chromosomes and hormones between the sexes.

That the genetic factor is the major reason for the physical superiority of women over men was also a conclusion of Madigan (1957) in his classic and very interesting study of the mortality patterns of Roman Catholic nuns (sisters) and brothers, all of whom were teachers in Catholic grammar schools and high schools. Madigan's subjects were similar in most all behavioral characteristics, and none were married. The daily regimes of both the "brothers and sisters (were) extremely similar as regards time for sleep, work, study, and recreation, and with respect to diet, housing, and medical care" (Madigan, 1957: 204). Their major difference was their sex.

Madigan found that the "sisters consistently exhibited greater expectations of life, and the brothers shorter expectations" (1957: 210). The title of his research paper was "Are Sex Mortality Differentials Biologically Caused?" He answered in the affirmative: "Biological factors played by far the chief part in differentiating the death rates" of the brothers and the sisters (Madigan, 1957: 221).

Migration also differs by age and sex. Traditionally, males and females have not migrated to the same places in equal numbers. Long-distance migration has tended to favor males, and short-distance migration, females; and this has been especially the case in developing countries. However, with increasing gender equity in a society, migration rates of females tend to approximate those of males. Migration is also age-selective, with the largest numbers of migrants found among young adults (Benetsky et al., 2015; Stone, 1978; Tobler, 1995). Goldscheider has observed that "given different political, social, economic, cultural and demographic contexts, age remains as a critical differentiation of migration ... [These contexts] determine the specifics of age and mobility" (1971: 311).

Finally, the age and sex structure of human populations sets important limits with respect to sustenance organization. The characteristics of age and sex define a biological entity to which the population's sustenance organization is or must be adapted. The esteemed demographer Amos Hawley observed that the demographic structure (of age and sex) contains the possibilities and sets the limits of organized group life (1950: 78). The age and sex structure of a population at "any given time constitutes a limiting factor on the kinds of collective activities [it] may engage in ... In effect, the organization of relationships in a population is an adaptation to its demographic [i.e., age and sex] structure. And to the extent that the [sustenance organization] is differentiated, the adaptation to its demographic features must be precise" (Hawley, 1950: 144). The degree to which a population's age and sex structure limits the kinds and varieties of sustenance activities in which the collectivity may be engaged is an important analytical issue, but one not well explored or understood (Poston and Frisbie, 2005; Poston, 2015).

Demographic Theories of Age and Sex

Demographers are well known for their formal theories and have developed some of the most mathematically elegant theories in the social sciences. Age and sex, particularly age, comprise the centerpiece of most formal theory in demography. Examples of formal age models include Ansley Coale's (1971) development of marriage patterns by age, Andrei Rogers' (1975) elaborate presentation of migration patterns by age, and Louis Henry's (1961) description of fertility patterns by age in the absence of voluntary fertility control. But the most powerful and elegant formal mathematical theory in demography that incorporates a population's age and sex structure, particularly age, is stable population theory. Many claim this theory to be the most important aspect of the entirety of the mathematics of population (Pollard, Yusuf, and Pollard, 1990; Yusuf, Martins, and Swanson, 2014).

I have already mentioned stable population theory in Chapter 7. I noted that if a population closed to migration experiences constant schedules of age-specific fertility and mortality rates, it will develop a constant age distribution and will grow at a constant rate, irrespective of its initial age distribution. Its mathematical bases and foundation are laid out and discussed in many places, one of the best expositions being Coale's masterpiece, *The Growth and Structure of Human Populations* (1972) (see also Keyfitz, 1977a; Pollard, Yusuf, and Pollard, 1990; Preston, Heuveline, and Guillot, 2001; Schoen, 1988; Yusuf, Martins, and Swanson, 2014).

The age distribution of the stable population depends on two items, namely, the underlying age-specific mortality rates and the rate of growth: "The higher the mortality, the more rapidly the age distribution falls with increasing age; and also the higher the rate of growth, the more rapidly the age distribution falls with age" (Pollard, Yusuf, and Pollard, 1990: 106).

An important point to remember about a stable population is that it eventually converges to a constant age distribution, irrespective of the age distribution with which it began. Thus, demographers sometimes state that "stable populations forget their past." In other words, when fixed fertility and mortality rates have prevailed, a stable population eventually ends up with an unchanging age structure that will be completely independent of its form at any earlier time.

Actually, Coale (1957) demonstrated that all human populations, not just stable populations, forget their past: "The age distribution of France is no longer much affected by the excess mortality and reduced numbers of births experienced during the Napoleonic wars, and the age distribution of Greece is no longer affected at all by the Peloponnesian Wars" (Coale, 1987: 466). Obviously, when fertility and mortality schedules constantly change, the age structure constantly changes. Thus, following Coale, one may state that all populations, whether or not stable, have forgotten the past. But the stable population, in addition, has a fixed form, and fixed birth and death rates.

This theorem is very nicely illustrated by Etienne van de Walle and John Knodel (1970) in their demographic simulation known as "The Case of Women's Island," an exercise that reports quantitatively the "story" of 1,000 young women marooned with five men on an island that is forever closed to migration. After 100 years have elapsed, "one cannot find any evidence that the initial population (of the island was so)…distorted in both its [initial] age and sex composition" (van de Walle and Knodel, 1970: 436). This is an interesting demonstration of the statement that a population, stable or not, "forgets" its past and "stabilizes itself in due time with a structure that is entirely dependent on fertility and mortality levels" (van de Walle and Knodel, 1970: 436).

Stable population theory has many implications for age and sex distribution. One is that changes and fluctuations in fertility cause far greater change in a population's age distribution than do changes and fluctuations in mortality. Coale and Demeny (1983) have shown that populations closed to migration that have near stable fertility rates but differ only in their mortality schedules will have similar age and sex structures (see also Hinde, 1998; Yusuf, Martins, and Swanson, 2014).

I have limited my discussion here of the stable model to the **closed population,** that is, a population in which migration does not occur. However, it has also been shown mathematically that even when migration is taken into consideration, a stable population (indeed, a **stationary population,** that is, one with the same birth and death rates) can eventually be reached. As long as fertility is below replacement levels, a constant number and age distribution of in-migrants (with fixed fertility and mortality rates) will lead to a stationary population. Neither the level of the NRR nor the size of the in-migration stream will affect this conclusion; a stationary population will eventually emerge (Espenshade, Bouvier, and Arthur, 1982).

I turn now to a consideration of some of the basic methods that demographers use to represent the age and sex structure of populations.

METHODS FOR ANALYZING AGE AND SEX DISTRIBUTIONS

The age and sex structure of a population may be examined and portrayed along several dimensions. The two characteristics of age and sex may be analyzed separately, and a summary evaluation may be conducted of age cross-classified by sex. I first consider the **population pyramid**.

The Population Pyramid

The age and sex structure of a population at a given moment of time may be portrayed as an aggregation of cohorts born in different years. A graphic representation of the age–sex structure of the population is the age–sex pyramid, or population pyramid; it shows for a specific point in time the different surviving cohorts of persons of each sex. A population pyramid is one of the most elegant ways of graphically presenting age and sex data (Poston, 2005).

A population pyramid is nothing more than two ordinary **histograms** (bar graphs), representing the male and female populations in, usually, one- or five-year age categories, placed on their sides and back to back. The base of the pyramid, representing the size of each of the age–sex population groups, is presented in either absolute numbers or in percentages. When using percentages as the metric, one must be sure to "calculate the percentages on the basis of the grand total for the population, including both sexes and all ages" (Hobbs, 2004: 162).

Figure 10.1 is a population pyramid for the United States in 2015, presented in absolute numbers. Note first the larger numbers of women, compared with men, at the older ages, an illustration of the fact that women survive longer than men at every age. Look also at the larger numbers of males and females between the ages of 45 and 64. Many of these persons, especially the older ones, were born during the "baby boom" years after the Second World War, when the TFR in the United States reached its peak level of 3.7 children per woman in the late 1950s. Observe as well the slightly larger cohorts of ages 20–34 years. These are mainly the babies of parents born during the baby boom, that is, the babies of the baby boom babies. We see, thus, an echo of the baby boom one generation later, the so-called **echo effect**.

Figure 10.2 is an age–sex population pyramid for France in 2006 and "reflects various irregularities associated with that country's special history" (Hobbs, 2004: 164). This pyramid was constructed with data for individual years of age. There are five special aspects of the pyramid worth mentioning, and they are identified at the bottom of the pyramid. The first represents the very small birth cohorts born in France during the First World

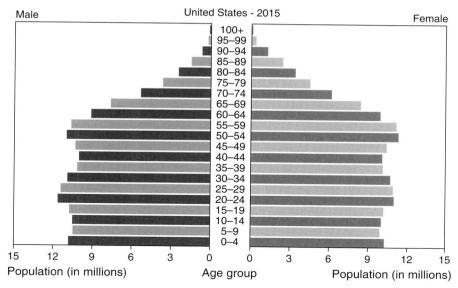

Figure 10.1 Age–Sex Pyramid, United States, 2015
Source: US Bureau of the Census, International Data Base.

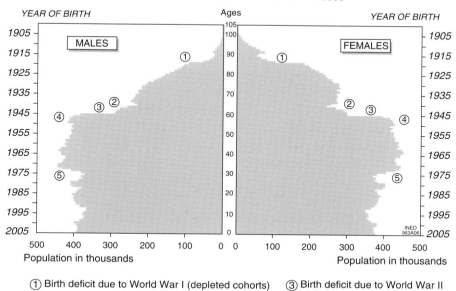

① Birth deficit due to World War I (depleted cohorts)   ③ Birth deficit due to World War II

② Depleted cohorts reach reproductive age   ④ Baby boom

                                                         ⑤ End of baby boom

Figure 10.2 Age–Sex Pyramid, France, 2006
Source: Pison (2006: 3) (reprinted with permission of Institut National d'études Démographiques (INED)).

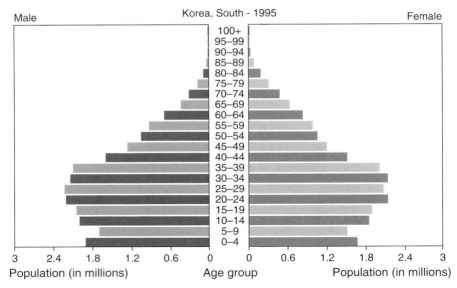

Figure 10.3 Population Pyramid, South Korea, 1995
Source: US Bureau of the Census, International Data Base.

War. One also sees at the older ages of the pyramid the larger number of females than males; this latter consideration characterizes all national populations, not only France. The second special feature of the pyramid points to the smaller number of persons born during the First World War who reached the reproductive years in 1940. The third feature worthy of note follows closely behind the second and refers to the smaller numbers of babies born in France during the Second World War. After the Second World War, France, too, experienced a baby boom, and this is shown in the fourth mark on the pyramid. The fifth and last special aspect of the French pyramid refers to the smaller numbers of babies born after the end of the baby boom. I noted earlier that knowledge of the age and sex structure of the population tells us a great deal about its history. This is certainly the case for France.

Figure 10.3 is a pyramid for the Republic of Korea in 1995. The bottom bars of the pyramid show the effects of the fertility reduction in South Korea since the 1970s. In 1995, less than 12 percent of Korea's population was male aged 0–14 (compared with more than 21 percent in 1970), and also less than 12 percent was female aged 0–14 (more than 20 percent in 1970). The lower bars also indicate the much larger numbers of males, compared with females, born in Korea since the mid-1980s. The lowest two bars of the pyramid indicate that the sex ratio for Koreans in 1995 in the age group 0–4 was 113.4; this suggests a much higher SRB than that regulated by biology and is evidence of son preference (also see Poston, 2002; Poston

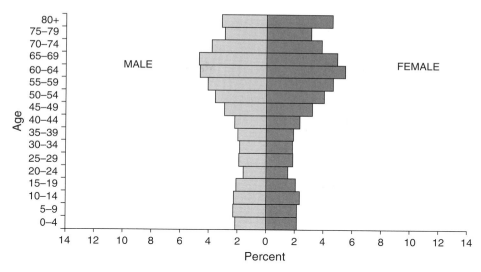

Figure 10.4 Population by Age and Sex, Llano County, Texas, 2013
Source: US Bureau of the Census. Figure prepared by DLP.

et al., 1997; Poston et al., 2000; Poston et al., 2003; Zeng et al., 1993). Also shown in the South Korean pyramid is a relatively smaller number of men between the ages of 65 and 74. This is the special population who suffered the most, that is, was heavily depleted through mortality, during the Korean War.

In some subnational populations, usually counties, states, or provinces, their sustenance and livelihood bases may be so restrictive in terms of persons of just one sex, or of just one or a few age groups, that they will often overwhelm the area's demography. Their principal ecological organization and function may be inferred by viewing their population pyramid. Figures 10.4 and 10.5 are pyramids for two counties in Texas in 2013, namely, Llano County and Brazos County.

Llano County (Figure 10.4), located in the Highland Lakes area of central Texas, is demographically a very old county, with over 41 percent of its population age 60 or older. It is a prime destination of inter- and intrastate elderly migrants and is demographically top-heavy because elderly people have moved into the county and young people have moved out. Llano County's population pyramid is typical of the pyramids of the so-called retirement counties in Texas, Florida, Arizona, and California.

The major sustenance and economic activity of Brazos County, Texas (Figure 10.5) is higher education. Texas A&M University is located in Brazos County. With a student population on the main campus in College Station of almost 55,000, Texas A&M University in 2015 was the fourth largest institution of higher learning in the United States and the largest in

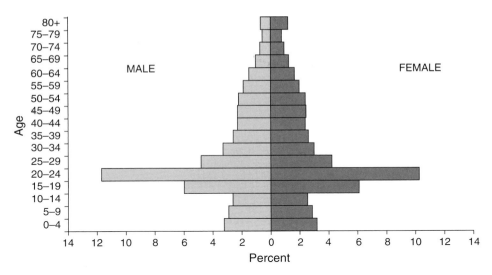

Figure 10.5 Population by Age and Sex, Brazos County, Texas, 2013
Source: US Bureau of the Census. Figure prepared by DLP.

Texas. Also located in Brazos County is the Bryan campus of Blinn College, a community college with a student body population in 2014 in Bryan of almost 14,000. Because most of the students attending Texas A&M University and Blinn College live in Brazos County, they overwhelm the county's demography. Nearly one-quarter of the county's population is in the age group 20–24, the ages of most of the Texas A&M and Blinn students. Younger undergraduates at Texas A&M and at Blinn comprise a part of the preceding age group 15–19, which is over 12 percent of the county's population. Many of the approximately 11,000 Texas A&M graduate students are in the 25–29 age group, which comprises more than 9 percent of the county's population.

Despite their descriptive utility, however, population pyramids give only a graphic representation of age and sex structure at a particular point in time. I will now discuss several indexes that may be used to examine patterns of age data and patterns of sex data, considered separately.

Age Dependency

One may analyze the age distribution of a population in many ways (cf. Arriaga and Associates, 1994; Hobbs, 2004). A popular measure of age structure is the **dependency ratio** (DR). The DR is the ratio of the dependent-age population (both young – persons 0–14 years old – and old – persons 65 years of age and older) to the working-age population (persons 15–64 years old). The DR is usually multiplied by a constant of 100. The higher the ratio,

Table 10.1 Values of Youth-Dependency Ratio, Old-Age-Dependency Ratio, and Total Dependency Ratio, Selected Countries of the World, 2014

Country	Youth-DR	Old-Age-DR	Total DR
Macao	13.6	9.9	23.5
South Korea	21.6	13.5	35.1
China	20.5	16.4	36.9
Russia	22.5	18.3	40.8
Spain	22.4	26.9	49.3
United States	28.4	20.9	49.3
Mexico	42.4	9.1	51.5
Italy	21.5	32.3	53.8
Japan	21.3	42.6	63.9
Nigeria	83.0	5.7	88.7
Gambia	88.5	3.8	92.3
Uganda	96.0	4.0	100.0
Chad	100.0	4.1	104.1
Niger	106.4	6.4	112.8

Source: PRB (2014).

the more people each worker has to support; the lower the DR, the fewer the number of dependants. Demographers usually split the DR into the **youth-dependency ratio** (YDR or Youth-DR) and the **old-age-dependency ratio** (Old Age-DR), also known as the **aged-dependency ratio** (ADR or Aged-DR); both have the same denominator, namely, the population aged 15–64. The numerator of the Youth-DR is the population aged 0–14 and the numerator of the Old Age-DR is the population aged 65+. The Youth-DR plus the Old-Age DR equals the DR.

An index analogous to the Old-Age-DR is a measure of elderly support, known as the **parent support ratio**. It takes the number of persons 80 years old and older, per 100 persons aged 50–64 (Wu and Wang, 2004). It represents the relative burden that the oldest-old population, that is, the elderly parents, has on the population aged 50–64, that is, the children of the elderly parents. Later, the ratio is illustrated with data for the United States and for China.

Presented in Table 10.1 are values of the Youth-DR, the Old Age-DR, and the **total dependency ratio** (Total DR) for fourteen countries of the world. I selected these countries because they have low or high values of Total DR, and low or high values of the component DRs. The countries are ranked according to their Total DR values, from lowest to highest. Macao (strictly speaking, not a country – it is a Special Administrative

Region [SAR] of China) and South Korea and China have Total DRs that are among the lowest in the world. For every 100 persons in the economically producing ages (15–64) in Macao and China, there are twenty-four and thirty-five persons, respectively, in the dependent ages that the producers must support; and more of them are young people (younger than age 15) than old people (65+ years of age). The United States and Spain both have Total DRs of 49.3, indicating that for every 100 persons in the producing population, there are more than 49 dependants. But in the United States 42 percent of the dependants are old dependants, whereas in Spain, 55 percent of the dependants are old persons. At the other extreme are the five African countries of Nigeria, Gambia, Uganda, Chad, and Niger, with Total DRs that are the highest in the world. For every 100 persons in the economically producing ages in Chad and Niger, there are 113 and 104, persons, respectively, in the dependent ages that the producers must support; and virtually all of these dependants are young people. Compare Macao and Niger, the countries with the lowest and highest Total DRs in the world. The producers in Niger are supporting almost five times as many dependants as are the producers in Macao.

Age Heaping

Demographers sometimes use single years of age data to determine whether there are irregularities or inconsistencies in the data. If a population tends to report certain ages (say, those ending in 0 or 5) at the expense of other ages, this is known as **age heaping**.

Age heaping tends to be more pronounced among populations or population subgroups with low levels of education: "The causes and patterns of [age heaping] vary from culture to culture, but preference for ages ending in '0' and in '5' is quite widespread" (Hobbs, 2004: 136), particularly in the Western world. In Korea, China, and some other countries in east Asia, there is sometimes a preference for ages ending in the numeral "3" because the number "3" sounds like the word or character for "life."

In some cultures, certain numbers and digits are avoided; for example, "13" is frequently avoided in the West because it is considered unlucky. The number "4" is avoided in Korea and in China because it has the same sound as the word or character for "death." For example, hotels in the United States and in some Western countries sometimes do not have floors designated as 13. Similarly, many hotels in China, South Korea, and some other east Asian countries do not have floors designated as 4.

Age heaping is easily detected using graphs and indexes. Figure 10.6 is a graph of single years of age for females in South Korea in 1995. Aside from some heaping on ages 43, 53, and 63 (note the preference for ages ending in

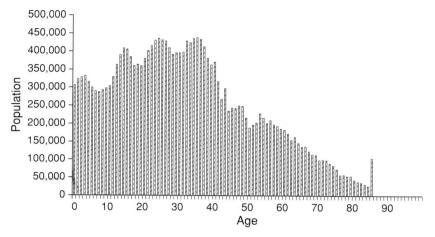

Figure 10.6 Single Years of Age, Female Population, Republic of Korea, 1995
Source: US Bureau of the Census, International Data Base. Figure prepared by DLP.

the numeral 3), there is little evidence elsewhere of age heaping. Compare the situation of females in South Korea in 1995 with that of males in Pakistan in 1981 (Figure 10.7). In Pakistan in 1981, there was an astounding amount of age heaping on ages ending in 0 and 5.

The extent of age heaping may be ascertained more precisely with indexes. A popular one is **Whipple's Method (WM)**, an index designed to reflect preference for the terminal digits of "0" and "5," usually in the age

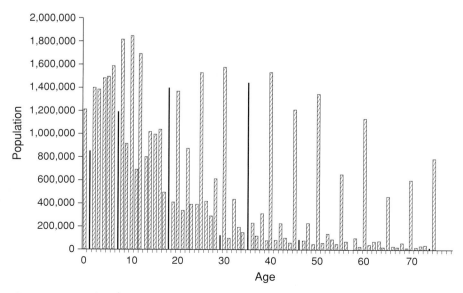

Figure 10.7 Single Years of Age, Male Population, Pakistan, 1981
Source: US Bureau of the Census, International Data Base. Figure prepared by DLP.

range 23–62 (cf., Hobbs, 2004). WM varies from 0 (when the digits 0 and 5 are not reported in the census data) to 100 (when there is no preference for 0 or 5 in the census data) to a maximum of 500 (when only the digits 0 and 5 are reported in the census data). The United Nations (1990) has noted that if the values of Whipple's Index are less than 105, then the age distribution data are "highly accurate." If the WM values are between 105 and 109.9, the age data are "fairly accurate"; if between 110 and 124.9, "approximate"; if between 125 and 174.9, "rough"; and if 175 or more, "very rough" (United Nations, 1990: 18–19). WM is calculated as follows (Hobbs, 2004: 138):

$$\text{WM} = \frac{\sum (P_{25} + P_{30} + \cdots + P_{55} + P_{60})}{1/5 \sum (P_{23} + P_{24} + P_{25} \cdots P_{60} + P_{61} + P_{62})} * 100 \quad (10.1)$$

The UN has reported that "although Whipple's Index measures only the effects of preferences for ages ending in 5 and 0, it can be assumed that such digit preference is usually connected with other sources of inaccuracy in age statements, and the indexes can be accepted as a fair measure of the general reliability of the age distribution" (1990: 20).

The decision in the Whipple's Index to focus on the age range 23–62 is partly an arbitrary one. The ages of early childhood and old age are excluded because, frequently, they are more influenced by other types of errors and issues than digit preference; also, "the assumption of equal decrements from age to age is less applicable" at the older ages (Hobbs, 2004: 138).

The WM value for South Korean females in 1995 (see Figure 10.6 above) is 100.1; the WM value for Pakistani males in 1981 (see Figure 10.7 above) is 330.8. Among Korean females in 1995, the WM Index indicates virtually no age heaping on digits ending in 0 and 5. This means that in South Korea, the numbers of females counted in 1995 at ages ending in 0 and 5 overstate an unbiased population, that is, one in which there is no age heaping on 0 or 5, by a mere 0.1 percent. Conversely, in Pakistan in 1981, males counted at ages ending in 0 and 5 overstate an unbiased population by almost 231 percent.

To illustrate the range of WM values, I have calculated WM scores for three more developed countries, namely, Japan in 1985, Denmark in 1988, and Hong Kong in 1995; and for two developing countries, namely, Iran and Mexico, both in 1988. Their WM scores are 98.4 for Japan, 101.5 for Denmark, and 101.7 for Hong Kong, versus 122.7 for Iran and 133.4 for Mexico. The WM values for the developed countries, as expected, are lower and closer to 100 than those for the developing countries.

Several other summary indexes of age heaping and digit preference have been developed by Myers (1940), Bachi (1951), Carrier (1959), and

Ramachandran (1967). These differ only slightly from one another and from the WM as general indicators of heaping.

Sex Structure

Demographers use several methods to index sex composition: (1) the masculinity proportion, (2) the ratio of the excess or deficit of males to the total population, and (3) the sex ratio. The masculinity proportion is frequently used in nontechnical discussions of sex composition (Hobbs, 2004) and is calculated by dividing the number of males in the population by the number of males and females and multiplying the result by 100.

The ratio of the excess, or deficit, of males to the total population is obtained by subtracting the number of females from the number of males, dividing by the total number in the population and multiplying by 100.

The sex ratio (SR), by far the most popular index of sex composition in demographic and other scholarly analyses, is defined as the number of males per 100 females, as follows:

$$\mathrm{SR} = \frac{P_m}{P_t} * 100 \tag{10.2}$$

An SR above 100 indicates an excess of males and an SR below 100 indicates an excess of females. In some eastern European countries and in India, Iran, Pakistan, Saudi Arabia, and a few other countries, the SR is calculated as the number of females per 100 (or per 1,000) males. But the SR definition just shown in formula (10.2) is used by most demographers and by international bodies such as the United Nations (Poston, 2005).

In general, "national sex ratios tend to fall in the narrow range from about 95 to 102, barring special circumstances, such as a history of heavy war losses (less males), or heavy immigration (more males); national sex ratios outside the range of 90 to 105 should be viewed as extreme" (Shryock, Siegel, and Associates, 1976: 107).

Most societies have SRBs between 104 and 106, that is, 104–106 boys are born for every 100 girls. This so-called biologically normal SRB is likely an evolutionary adaptation to the fact that females have higher survival probabilities than males (see Clarke, 2000, for another discussion). Since at every year of life males have higher ASDRs than females, slightly more males than females are required at birth for there to be around equal numbers of males and females when the groups reach their marriageable ages.

If the biologically normal SRB is between 104 and 106 in most human populations, what might be the average value of the sex ratio at conception (SRC)? Clearly, it is not possible to obtain a valid figure for the SRC, although much of the literature estimates the SRC to be between 110 and

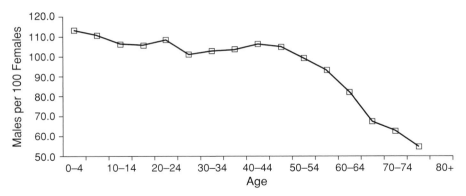

Figure 10.8 Sex Ratios by Age Group, Republic of Korea, 1995
Source: US Bureau of the Census, International Data Base. Figure prepared by DLP.

120 (Carey and Lopreato, 1995; Hassold, Quillan, and Yamane, 1983; Matthiessen and Matthiessen, 1977). A recent study, however, suggests that the SRC may be even, that is, a value of 100, meaning that 100 males are conceived for every 100 females (Orzack et al., 2015). These authors suggest that the proportion of males increases relative to the proportion of females mainly during the first trimester, and that female mortality exceeds male mortality throughout the pregnancy. Their arguments need additional theoretical justification and empirical support. For now, I am inclined to set the SRC in the range of 110–120.

Biology dictates that the age-specific SR will be highest at the very young ages, starting around 104–106 at age 0, and should then decline with age, attaining a value of around 100 for persons in their late 20s and continuing to decline to levels around age 50 or 60 in the oldest ages.

Barring extreme forms of human intervention and disturbance, these types of SR patterns by age will occur in most populations. One such intervention would be a major war, such as the Korean War, which would reduce significantly the numbers of males in their 20s and 30s. Another would be high amounts of immigration and/or emigration. International migration is usually driven economically when, typically, males depart one country and enter another in search of employment. Such disturbances in some countries can be extreme, as I show later for some of the oil-producing countries in the Middle East. Another intervention would be female-specific abortion, resulting in an SRB well above 105.

One way to describe a population's sex structure is to examine sex ratios for each of its five-year age groups. Figure 10.8 is a graph of the age-specific SRs for South Korea in 1995. The figure shows SRs at the very young ages that are much higher than would be expected biologically. These are the result of human interventions, namely, prenatal sex identification,

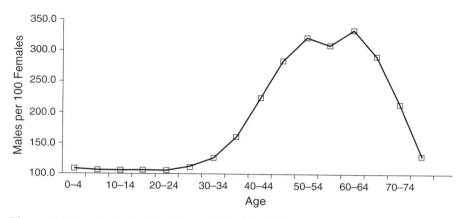

Figure 10.9 Sex Ratios by Age Group, United Arab Emirates, 2000
Source: US Bureau of the Census, International Data Base. Figure prepared by DLP.

followed by female-specific abortion (Poston, 2002, 2005). The SRs for age groups 0–4 and 5–9 are 113.4 and 110.6. Other than the higher-than-expected SRs at the very young ages, the declining trend in SRs in 1995 shown in Figure 10.8 for the remaining ages is pretty much as expected.

Some national populations have extreme imbalances by sex in certain age groups. The United Arab Emirates (UAE) is a good example. The UAE is one of several countries in the region of the world known as the Cooperation Council of the Arab States of the Gulf, originally and still colloquially, the Gulf Cooperation Council: the other member countries are Kuwait, Saudi Arabia, Qatar, Bahrain, and Oman. Most of these countries have very large percentages of foreign-born residents, often over 70 percent. Many of the foreigners are in the young working ages and are heavily male. They hail from Asia and other countries in the Middle East, and are brought to the UAE and the other Gulf countries to work in the oil fields and in construction; these labor migrants are infrequently accompanied by family members (McFalls, 2007). These high concentrations of foreigners have a major impact on the demography of countries that are not large in population size. For instance, Qatar's 2014 population numbered 2.3 million residents and the UAE, just over 9.4 million. The immigration patterns that favor young working-age males result in extremely unbalanced distributions of SRs by age.

Figure 10.9 is a graph of the age-specific SRs for the UAE in 2000. The SR is balanced at the younger ages, and then at age 25 starts to climb above 100. At age 35, there are around 150 males per 100 females, and more than 200 by age 40. By age 50, there are more than 300 males per 100 females. It is not until the SR is considerably above 300 at age 65 that it begins to decline. These tremendous sex imbalances are concentrated in around thirty

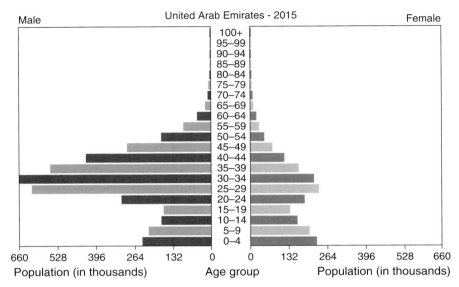

Figure 10.10 Population by Age and Sex, United Arab Emirates, 2015
Source: US Bureau of the Census, International Data Base.

years or so of the population's age structure. These sex ratio imbalances are clearly seen in its population pyramid. I show in Figure 10.10 a UAE population pyramid for 2015. The age-specific sex ratio imbalances shown in the previous chart (Figure 10.9), even though the data were for the year of 2000, continue to be manifested in the age–sex pyramid produced with data for 2015. Not many national populations, other than the few Gulf countries just mentioned, have an age and sex population pyramid like that of the UAE in 2015.

I turn now to a specific example of the centrality of age and sex structure. I first discuss the unbalanced SRBs now being experienced in China and Taiwan, and a few other countries such as India. I next focus on the process of demographic aging in the United States and China and note its implications for the provision of elderly care that will be required during the next few decades. Both of these are relevant and challenging exemplars of the importance of age and sex composition in human societies.

SEX RATIO AT BIRTH

I have already noted that most societies have SRBs of around 105; that is, 105 boys are born for every 100 girls. Figure 10.11 shows time-series data for the SRB for China, Taiwan, and the United States for the individual years from 1980 to 2010. The United States follows the normal SRB pattern, but China and Taiwan do not.

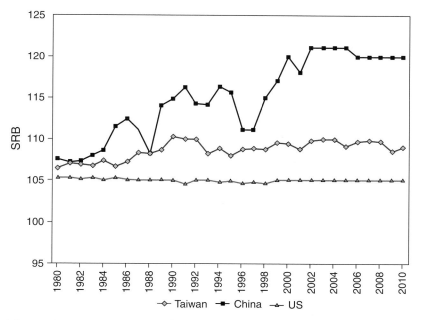

Figure 10.11 Sex Ratios at Birth, Taiwan, China, and the United States, 1980–2010
Figure prepared by DLP.

The SRB in the United States is invariant, at about 105 for every year. This is expected when there are no human interventions operating to disturb the biology. I should note, however, that the SRB in the United States is slightly above 105 for some groups, and slightly below 105 for other groups. For instance, the older the mother, the lower the SRB. The higher the birth order, the lower the SRB. Also, SRBs vary slightly by race and ethnicity. Chinese and Filipinos have SRBs a little higher than 105, and blacks and most Hispanics have SRBs a little lower. Across the entire US population, the SRB averages out each year at around 105, as shown in Figure 10.11.

In contrast, whereas in 1980 China and Taiwan had SRBs only slightly above 107, they began to increase in the late 1980s, reaching values in 1990 of 116 in China and 110 in Taiwan. Taiwan's SRB has not risen above its 1990 value of 110, but China's SRB rose to 120 by the year 2000, increased to 122 a few years later, and was back at around 120 for the years of 2006–2010. Its SRB in 2014 (not shown in Figure 10.11) was 118.

As I have already noted, if there are no human interferences with the biological processes, the SRBs will range from 104 to 107, with an average of around 105. What are the kinds of human intervention that might disturb the biological processes?

China, Taiwan, South Korea, India, and several other Asian countries have been reporting abnormally high SRBs since the 1980s (Arnold and Liu,

1986; Eberstadt, 2000; Goodkind, 1996, 2002; Gu and Roy, 1995; Hudson and den Boer, 2002, 2004; Jha et al., 2006; Kim, 1997; Poston, Conde, and DeSalvo, 2011; Sheth, 2006). What are the immediate causes of these abnormally high SRBs? China, Taiwan, and the other countries just mentioned all showed or are still showing, in varying degrees, the same kind of interventions leading to abnormally high SRBs. A main intervention is prenatal sex identification followed by gender-specific abortion, and another intervention, particularly in China, is the underreporting of daughters (Chu, 2001; Goodkind, 2011, 2015; Hull, 1990; Johansson and Nygren, 1991; Poston, Conde, and DeSalvo, 2011; Tucker and Van Hook, 2013).

Why would countries such as China and Taiwan resort to an intervention such as gender-specific abortion that would produce higher than biologically normal SRBs? The immediate cause is China's and Taiwan's dramatic fertility declines. Why would rapid fertility reductions lead to abnormally high SRBs?

One reason is that China and Taiwan have a Confucian patriarchal tradition where son preference is strong and pervasive (Poston et al., 1997). Female subordination is a major characteristic of Confucianism and was exemplified in such behaviors in China as female foot-binding (from the tenth century onward) and the modification of feminine clothing.

A preference for sons is a part of Chinese history and culture. But when fertility was high, the chances that a boy would be born were good (Pison, 2004). When Chinese women were having six children on average, the probability was very low (less than 2 percent) that none of the six children would be male. By comparison, when women have only two children, the probability that neither will be a son is much higher (around 25 percent). When women have only one child, the probability that it will not be a son is just under 50 percent.

Birth-planning policies, as well as social, economic, and industrial transformations in China and Taiwan, have been responsible for the number of babies born per woman falling below replacement levels, and doing so quickly (Poston, 2000). Couples now have fewer children than they had just a couple of decades ago. However, the deeply rooted cultural influences of son preference still make it important for many families to have at least one son. Thus, many families implement strategies and interventions to ensure that they will have a son (Gu and Roy, 1995; Zeng et al., 1993).

Since the late 1980s, ultrasound technology enabling the prenatal determination of sex has been widely available. Recently, China proposed a ban on the practice and launched a "pro-girl" campaign to help mediate the strong son preference (China Daily, 2004). This campaign, however, is not believed to have had much of an impact. Similar campaigns in Taiwan and South Korea had similar outcomes.

There is little evidence of female infanticide causing the high SRBs (Banister, 2004; Chu, 2001; Eberstadt, 2000; Zeng et al., 1993). The human interventions that disturb the SRB are mainly due to norms and traditions among Chinese families to have sons, within a more recent policy as well as a normative context to have fewer births.

How many excess boys will there be in China who will be unable to find brides from their counties? I have already mentioned in Chapter 1 that my students Drs. Eugenia Conde and Bethany DeSalvo, and I, have taken data for every year from 1978 to 2010 and have calculated the numbers of males and females born every year, as well as the SRBs for each year. Using data from life tables (see Chapter 7), we next survived the boys born each year to the age of 29 and the girls to the age of 27, which are, or are near, the average ages that boys and girls now marry in China. We estimated that there have already been born in China more than 41 million Chinese boys who, when they reach their mid-20s and are looking for brides, will not be able to find Chinese girls to marry (Poston, Conde, and DeSalvo, 2011). Our number does not take into account the likelihood of some daughters at birth being underreported (Goodkind, 2011), so the figure of over 40 million may be a little too high.

Nevertheless, there will not be enough Chinese women in the marriage market for the excess boys to marry. What will these 30 to 40 million young men do when they cannot find brides? Here are some speculations.

While it is true that throughout history, especially in western Europe, "bachelorhood was an acceptable social role, and the incidence of never-marrying bachelors in the total population was high" (Eberstadt, 2000: 230; see also Hajnal, 1965), China throughout its thousands of years of history has never been so characterized. Unless in the next few decades China is "swept by a truly radical change in cultural and social attitudes toward marriage [it is] poised to experience an increasingly intense, and perhaps desperate, competition among young men for the nation's limited supply of brides" (Eberstadt 2000: 230).

China could well turn to a more authoritarian form of government to better control the bachelors. In such a scenario, its progress toward democracy could be stalled, if not halted. China could modify the magnitude of the potential unrest of these millions of unmarried young men by dispatching them to public works and construction projects thousands of miles away from the big cities.

When confronted with large numbers of excess males during the Middle Ages, Portugal sent them off to wars in North Africa (Hudson and den Boer, 2002, 2004). With many millions of bachelors in the big cities, all within twenty years of age, bellicose Chinese leaders might be tempted to "kill two birds with one stone"; they could reduce the tensions caused by the bachelors in the cities by sending the excess manpower to pick a fight with or participate in an invasion of another country. What better country with which to engage in such activities than their "renegade province," Taiwan, located less than 100 miles across the Taiwan Straits from the southern province of Fujian.

One solution to the problem would be the immigration into the country of Chinese brides from other countries. This is unlikely for China because most of its bachelors will be poor rural workers unable to afford "mail order brides" (Eberstadt, 2000). But even if this kind of marriage immigration were to occur, it would need to be of a substantial magnitude to even begin to offset the gender imbalances of marriage-age males that are expected in the first two decades of this new century. Of course, it would cause shortages of many millions of females in the areas of origin. So if China gains brides, other countries will lose them.

An even less likely solution would be increases in levels of homosexuality. This is an unlikely alternative because most scientific evidence on the origins of homosexuality argues in favor of a strong biological foundation (LeVay, 1991, 1996; also see Murray, 2000, for other views and arguments). I do not believe it is at all likely that when Chinese males are unable to find females to marry they will turn to homosexual relationships as an alternative to (heterosexual) marriage. On the other hand, homosexual behavior could well become more acceptable, so that closeted homosexuals would be freer to openly declare their orientation.

The most likely possibility, of course, is that these Chinese bachelors will never marry and will have no other choice but to develop their own lives and livelihoods. They will likely resettle with one another in "bachelor ghettos" in Beijing, Shanghai, Tianjin, and other big cities where commercial sex outlets will likely be prevalent. The possible implications of large numbers of bachelors using commercial sex workers need also to be addressed, particularly with regard to the worldwide AIDS epidemic.

The heterosexual transmission of HIV is currently the fastest growing avenue for the transmission of HIV/AIDS in China, with commercial sex workers accounting for as much as one-fifth of new cases (Poston, Conde, and DeSalvo, 2011). The statistical analyses by Tucker and his colleagues (2005) have shown that the HIV risk for surplus men is bolstered by several factors that make them likely to engage in sex with prostitutes, such as migration and low education. The number of HIV cases in China in the next decade and later, owing to the bachelors and other factors (e.g., the extremely large "floating," i.e., rural to urban migrant, population in China – see my discussion in Chapter 8), could well rival the number of HIV cases in sub-Saharan Africa. As I have already noted in Chapter 7, in sub-Saharan Africa in 2013, there were 25 million adults infected with

HIV, which is more than 70 percent of the total number of 35 million adult infections worldwide. Moreover, nearly three-quarters of the global total of new HIV infections occur in sub-Saharan Africa (WHO, 2014). China could well rival, if not exceed, these numbers by 2030.

There is some historical precedent behind an expected growth of bachelor ghettos. In the nineteenth century, many thousands of young Chinese men immigrated to the United States to work in the gold mines and help build the transcontinental railroad. When the work projects were completed, many stayed in the United States and resettled in Chinese bachelor ghetto areas in New York, San Francisco, and a few other large US cities (Kwong, 1988; Zhou, 1992). The sex ratios of the Chinese in these areas were extraordinarily high.

If these Chinese men do not marry, sociological research suggests that they will be more prone to crime than if they married (Laub and Sampson, 2006). This possibility has alerted some to the potential increases in crime in China's future, and perhaps political ramifications resulting from these excess males (Hudson and den Boer, 2002, 2004).

No one, of course, knows what this excess number of young Chinese males will do. Several possibilities have been entertained. The only fact known for sure is that in China there have already been born many, many millions more baby boys than there are girls for them to marry. This issue needs the immediate attention of research scholars and policymakers.

POPULATION AGING

China is the largest country in the world, with a population, in 2015, of more than 1.3 billion. The United States is the third largest country in the world (after China and India), with a population of more than 320 million. China has a land mass just slightly less than that of the United States (China has a surface area of 9.6 million km^2 compared with the United States with 9.8 million km^2), but has a population more than four times larger than that of the United States.

Of even greater interest is the size of the older and oldest-old populations in China and the United States. In this section of the chapter I follow the practice of the US Bureau of the Census (Velkoff and Lawson, 1998) and refer to the older population as persons aged 60 and older, and the oldest-old as those aged 80 and older. In the world in 2010, there were almost 772 million older persons and more than 106 million oldest-old. Of the world's older population in 2010, more than 22 percent (or more than 171 million) lived in China, compared with 7.4 percent (or more than 57 million) in the United States.

If the older population of China in 2010 were a single country, it would be the seventh largest country in the world, outnumbered only by the non-elderly population of China and the populations of India, the United States, Indonesia, Brazil, and Pakistan.

Of the 106 million oldest-old in the world in 2010, 18.5 percent lived in China compared with 10.6 percent residing in the United States. In the early 1970s, China came to grips with the burgeoning size of its population and established a nationwide fertility control program that stressed *later* marriages, *longer* intervals between children, and *fewer* children. However, the large numbers of children born during China's baby boom in the early 1960s caused China's leaders in the middle to late 1970s to become increasingly worried about demographic momentum and the concomitant growth potential of this extraordinarily large cohort. Thus, in 1979, they launched the One-Child Campaign, with a goal of eliminating all births above or equal to three per family, and encouraging most families to have no more than one child, especially those living in urban areas. These two policies, along with increasing levels of socioeconomic development, resulted in a drastic decline in China's fertility rate, from levels greater than six children per woman in the early 1950s, to less than two in the late 1990s, to around 1.5 in 2015. These policies are discussed in more detail later in Chapter 15.

The United States has also experienced a fertility reduction, although not as dramatic as China's. Since I have already discussed the US fertility reduction in Chapter 4, I will not repeat it here. Suffice it to state that the United States experienced a sustained fertility decline starting in the nineteenth century (Sternlieb and Hughes, 1978). The TFR (for whites) dropped to 4.5 in 1870 and to 3.5 in 1900 (US Bureau of the Census, 1975). By 1920, just after the First World War, the white TFR had declined to 3.2. In the late 1950s, at the height of the baby boom era, the TFR reached its peak at 3.7. In 1972, the US TFR dropped for the first time below the replacement level of 2.1 (Kahn, 1974). The fertility declines experienced in China and the United States have produced, and will continue to produce, unprecedented increases in the proportions of older populations.

It is important to remember that the relatively large numbers of the older and oldest-old populations of China and the United States in 2010 are numbers that were generated during demographic regimes in which fertility and mortality rates declined. A consequence of these transitions, and especially unanticipated in China, are the extremely large older and oldest-old populations projected for the decades of this new century.

Table 10.2 shows population projections of the total populations, the older populations, and the oldest-old populations of the World, China, and the United States for the decennial years 2020–2050. (A population projection is a systematic calculation of the future population size of an area given certain assumptions about the behavior in the projection years of

Table 10.2 Total Population, Older Population (aged 60+), and Oldest-Old Population (aged 80+), World, China, and the United States, 2010 and 2020–2050

World			
Year	Total	Older (60+)	Oldest-Old (80+)
2010	6,866,054,000	771,641,000	106,177,000
2020	7,631,072,000	1,047,071,000	148,476,000
2030	8,315,758,000	1,403,525,000	209,296,000
2040	8,896,845,000	1,741,939,000	315,576,000
2050	9,376,417,000	2,082,998,000	446,610,000
China			
Year	Total	Older (60+)	Oldest-Old (80+)
2010	1,330,141,000	171,050,000	19,658,000
2020	1,384,545,000	245,028,000	28,729,000
2030	1,391,491,000	349,324,000	42,482,000
2040	1,358,519,000	411,150,000	70,138,000
2050	1,303,723,000	459,525,000	113,890,000
United States			
Year	Total	Older (60+)	Oldest-Old (80+)
2010	309,326,000	57,466,000	11,301,000
2020	333,896,000	76,986,000	13,163,000
2030	358,471,000	92,228,000	19,459,000
2040	380,016,000	98,962,000	27,615,000
2050	399,803,000	106,087,000	30,942,000

Source: US Bureau of the Census, International Data Base.

the demographic processes of fertility, mortality and migration.) The projections were produced by the US Bureau of the Census and are middle range or average projected numbers about the future size of the populations. They assume a stabilization of fertility rates and a modest decline in mortality over the projection years. International migration is based on a continuation of past levels (Kinsella and He, 2008).

In 2020, there are projected to be more than 1 billion older persons in the world. Almost one-quarter of them (245 million) will be in China and almost 10 percent in the United States. By 2020, there is projected to be almost 149 million oldest-old people in the world, with more than 19 percent living in China and almost 9 percent in the United States.

By the midway point of this century (in 2050), there are projected to be just over 2 billion older persons in the world out of a total population of 9.3 billion. Of these more than 2 billion older persons, almost 460 million

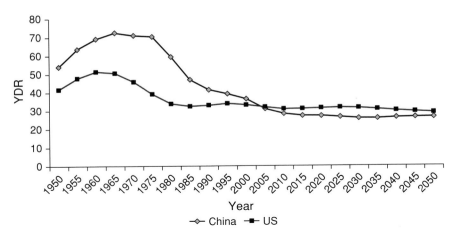

Figure 10.12 Youth-Dependency Ratios, China and the United States, 1950–2050
Source: US Bureau of the Census, International Data Base. Figure prepared by DLP.

(more than 22 percent) will be residing in China and 106 million (5 percent) in the United States.

This projected number of almost 460 million older persons in China in 2050 is a remarkably large number. The number of older persons alive in the entire world in 2000 (591 million) is only 131 million more than the total number of older persons projected to be living in China in 2050.

In the world in 2050, there are projected to be more than 446 million oldest-old people (persons aged 80+), with 25.5 percent living in China and almost 7 percent in the United States. The almost 114 million oldest-old projected to be living in China in 2050 is nearly 1.7 times larger than the total number of 68 million oldest-old living in the entire world in 2000.

A large number of elderly persons in a population is not problematic if at the same time there exists in the population a large number of producers. It is only when the ratio of elderly to producers becomes high that a host of economic, social, and related problems occur. I will now show empirically the degree of the dependency burden in China and the United States in 2010, and how much worse these burdens will become in the years ahead.

Earlier in this chapter, I described the measures of total dependency, youth dependency, and old-age dependency. Figure 10.12 presents the YDRs for China and the United States for every five years from 1950 to 2010 and projected to 2050. Between 1950 and 2010, the YDRs dropped for both countries. In 1950, the YDRs were 54 in China and 41 in the United States. By 2010, they had declined to just about 30 in both countries. Note, however, the increases in the YDRs for both countries during their baby boom years in the 1950s and 1960s. The YDRs of the two countries in 2010 are modest compared with those of other countries. Recall the much

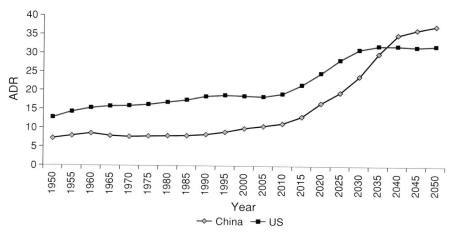

Figure 10.13 Aged-Dependency Ratios, China and the United States, 1950–2050
Source: US Bureau of the Census, International Data Base. Figure prepared by DLP.

higher YDRs for several countries that I discussed earlier in this chapter (see also Table 10.1 above), namely, Chad at 100 and Niger at 106.

The YDRs in China and the United States are not projected to change significantly between 2010 and 2050. The data shown in Figure 10.12 indicate that in China, the YDR will drop from 30 in 2010 to 26 in 2050. The United States is projected to experience little change in its YDR between 2010 and 2050.

Figure 10.13 shows old-age (aged-)dependency ratios (ADRs) for China and the United States for every five years from 1950 to 2010 and projected to 2050. Unlike the situation with respect to the YDR, in which both the United States and China experienced major decreases between 1950 and 2010, there have been modest increases in the ADR. In China, the ADR increased from 7 in 1950 to 11 in 2010. The ADR for the United States increased from 13 in 1950 to almost 20 in 2010.

China's ADR in 2010 is a little higher than average but not appreciably so. The ADR for the United States in 2010 is 9 points higher than in China. But these are not excessively high ADRs. Japan, the oldest country in the world, has an ADR over 42 (Table 10.1).

The aged-dependency situation changes remarkably when we skip ahead forty years to 2050. China will have become much older by 2050. China's ADR is projected to increase from 11 aged dependants per 100 producers in 2010 to 37 aged dependants per 100 producers in 2050. The United States also is projected to have grown older; its ADR will increase from around 20 in 2010 to 32 in 2050.

By 2050, China is expected to have made the transition to a demographically very old country. The United States also will have become quite old, but not as old as China. In the forty years after 2010, the two countries will have become demographically top heavy. In 2050, more than 35 percent of China's population (over 459 million people) will be 60 years of age or older. The oldest country in the world today, Japan, is not quite as old as China is projected to be in 2050. In 2015, Japan's older population (persons aged 60+) comprised 33 percent of its population (although this figure for Japan is projected to be 46 percent in 2050). In 2050, China will be older than the United States, the latter in 2050 with "only" one-quarter of its population (more than 106 million people) of age 60 or older.

By 2050, China will have grown to be one of the oldest populations in the world, and a country with one of the heaviest aged-dependency burdens of any population in the world. The United States will be close behind. What are the implications of this very old population, particularly for China?

Traditionally in China, the support of one's elder parents has been the responsibility of the sons. Often the parents lived with the oldest son and either with or nearby the other sons. The eldest son and his brothers were the ones responsible for providing the parents with economic support. The sons would rely on one of their sisters, or sometimes on one or more of their wives, to provide their parents with emotional support. These norms have been adjusted or modified in past decades, especially since the founding of the People's Republic in 1949, and particularly among urban residents. Nevertheless, the provision of economic and emotional support to one's parents has seldom been a major burden. As one might expect in a population with modestly high levels of fertility, there have usually been many more producers in the Chinese population than aged dependants. Similar traditional norms have not governed the US family to the same extent as in China.

However, given the very low levels of fertility in contemporary China, as well as a highly unbalanced SRB since the 1980s, the provision of elder care will be a major concern in the years of this new century. For one thing, as I have already noted, there are projected to be many more aged dependants per producer in China in the years ahead. In 2010, there were 11 aged dependants per 100 producers in China; in 2030, there are projected to be 24 aged dependants per 100 producers, and by 2050 there are projected to be 37 per 100 producers. This is an astonishingly high number of old persons per 100 producing members in the population. The number of aged dependants per 100 producers in China in 2050 is projected to be 3.4 times larger than China's number in 2010. This ADR for 2050 will likely be one of the highest of any country in the world.

When we couple this very high ADR for the year 2050 for China with the abnormally high SRBs in China (Poston, Conde, and DeSalvo, 2011), the issue of elder-care provision in the years ahead becomes even more complex. I have previously noted that there have already been born in China 30 to 40 million boys who will be unable to find Chinese brides when they reach the marriageable ages. And if the higher SRBs continue to 2030 and 2040, an enormously large number of Chinese males will find it difficult if not impossible to meet Chinese females to marry. Many of these single males will have the responsibility for providing both the economic and emotional support for their parents. Since they are not likely to marry, they will have no sons or daughters to take care of them. Since many of them will be only children, they will have no siblings with whom to grow old.

Unlike the case in past decades in China, where there have usually been several married sons, along with their sisters, available to care for the elderly parents, the situation in the next thirty to forty years will be different: there will be many, many more elderly parents and aunts and uncles requiring care than has been the situation in the recent past. Moreover, many of the providers will be sons, perhaps only-born sons, without wives. The care of the elderly in China in the decades after 2010 and 2020 will not be without problems.

COHORTS AND GENERATIONS

The last topic I discuss in this chapter is that of the cohort. Demographers define a **cohort** as a group of persons who "have in common the fact that they all experienced a given event during a given time interval" (van Imhoff, 2003: 155). Birth cohorts are of special interest to demographers; that is, groups of persons born during the same time interval. Birth cohorts are sometimes referred to as generations. Many of you reading this book are college undergraduates and likely are members of the birth cohort of 1983–2001; that is, you were born in one of the years between 1983 and 2001. Demographers have given this cohort the name "New Boomers." But the cohort has other names, such as "Millennials," "Generation Y," and the "Boomerang Generation"; this latter name is due to the trend of many members of the 1983–2001 birth cohort living with their parents for longer periods of time than did members of previous cohorts (Farris, 2016).

As I mentioned earlier in Chapter 1, I am a member of the birth cohort born between 1929 and 1945 (I was born in 1940). My birth cohort is often referred to as the **Lucky Few** cohort. We have this name because there were many fewer of us born compared with the much larger number of persons in the cohort immediately following us, those born between 1946 and 1964, the **Baby Boomer** cohort. There were around 44 million "Lucky Few" births versus 76 million baby boomer births (Carlson, 2008: 25). My cohort is not only smaller than the cohort following us, we are also very lucky. Our smaller size has enabled us to enjoy higher employment rates and a greater variety of social opportunities than members in the preceding or following cohorts.

One of the very best books written about birth cohorts is Elwood Carlson's *The Lucky Few: Between the Greatest Generation and the Baby Boom* (2008). This is one of my favorite demography books, and I highly recommend it to you. In his very engaging book, Carlson discusses the seven birth cohorts born between 1871 and 2001: (1) the "New Worlders" (1871–1889); (2) the "Hard Timers" (1890–1908); (3) the "Good Warriors" (1909–1928); (4) the "Lucky Few" (1929–1945); (5) the Baby Boomers (1946–1964); (6) "Generation X" (1965–1982); and (7) the New Boomers (1983–2001).

The New Worlders is Carlson's first birth cohort; it is so named because a large number of its members immigrated to the United States, the so-called new world, from other countries. The Hard Timers, the second cohort, is so named because its members lived during the years that "included a world war, a disastrous economic depression, and then another world war, a string of calamities that all but smothered their adult lives" (Carlson, 2008: 18). The third birth cohort, the Good Warriors, received its name "because this one generation essentially did all the fighting for the United States in the Second World War" (Carlson, 2008: 20). I have already mentioned the fourth birth cohort, the Lucky Few. The fifth, the Baby Boomers, is so named because there was a "boom" in the number of births during the years after the Second World War when birth rates skyrocketed, reaching a high of 3.7 births per woman. Almost 76 million baby boomers were born in the United States between 1946 and 1964, "nearly double the 44 million Lucky Few births" (Carlson, 2008: 25). The sixth cohort, "Generation X," has its name because, according to Carlson (2008: 27), "perplexed marketing specialists who couldn't think of any other name simply took to calling these people Generation X, and that label with all its implications of confusion and alienation has persisted." Finally, the seventh cohort, the New Boomers, began to be born in 1983. Its number of births was large because the parents of its members, namely, the Baby Boomers, were very large in number. So when the Baby Boomers began to have their babies, there were a lot of them having babies, thus producing the large number of New Boomers born between 1983 and 2001.

In Figure 10.14, the number of persons in each of the seven birth cohorts are graphed according to their size in each of the US decennial censuses of 1900 to 2010 in which they were enumerated. The oldest cohort, the New Worlders, appears first on the left side of the figure, followed by the next cohort, the Hard-Timers, and so forth up to the last and youngest cohort, the New Boomers. Each cohort "changes in size as successive censuses count its members over the course of their lives" (Carlson, 2008: 12).

not larger than, the New Boomers, which is already the largest generation in US history.

Regarding the name of this birth cohort that began in 2002, it could well be based on its diversity of backgrounds. Also its members will likely be increasingly fragmented by more and more personally customized media that will have different content from one member to another. Dr. Carlson suggested to me that maybe the name of "Divergents" will be used for this generation born in 2002 and thereafter (pers. comm., June 2, 2015).

SUMMARY

In this chapter, I first discussed the definition of age and sex. The definition of sex is not as straightforward as one might imagine; there are many complex issues involved in determining one's sex. I next discussed some of the key theoretical issues in demography dealing with age and sex structure, particularly stable population theory. I then described the major methods and approaches used by demographers to measure age and sex structure. Data reflecting the age and sex structure of South Korea, China, the United States, and some other countries were used to illustrate these methods. I then presented detailed discussions of two key features of age and sex structure: the SRB and population aging. I concluded the chapter with a discussion of cohorts and generations.

11 Race and Ethnicity

This chapter deals with the demography of race and ethnicity. I am mainly concerned here with demographic issues pertaining to race and ethnicity, their implications and consequences. I first discuss why demographers are interested in race and ethnicity. I then review briefly the history of categorizing people according to race and ethnicity. I follow with a discussion of how in the United States the statistical concepts of race and ethnicity evolved over time, from the 1790 census to the 2010 census, resulting in the five race/ethnic categories used today in the US federal government system. I then examine current patterns of race and ethnicity in the United States. Finally, given that the United States is a nation of immigrants and that the future growth of the US population is due directly and indirectly to immigration, I conclude the chapter with a detailed discussion of some of the sociological and demographic perspectives that have been used to discuss racial and ethnic adaptation. In my mind, adaptation is a key concern for Americans, particularly as by the mid-2040s, the United States will have become a majority-minority country, that is, a country where the NH-white population will no longer be the majority.

WHY DO DEMOGRAPHERS STUDY RACE AND ETHNICITY?

Very early in Chapter 1 of this book, I wrote that one of the concerns of demography is with "how populations are composed according to age, sex, race, marital status, and other characteristics." My interest in the present chapter, and in the previous chapter, is with features of population composition. In Chapter 10, I focused on two very important aspects of composition, age and sex. In this chapter, I cover yet another feature of population composition, race and ethnicity. So why are demographers so interested in the race and ethnicity of human populations? What is it about race and ethnicity that is so important for demography?

Do you remember in Chapter 1 my discussion of the basic demographic equation? It will be worth our time for me to spend a few paragraphs here discussing it again. The basic demographic equation (noted as equation (1.1) in Chapter 1) states that the change in the size of a population that occurs between two points in time, say, between times t and $t + 1$, is due to the changes in the levels of fertility, mortality, and migration that occur in the interval between times t and $t + 1$.

So suppose we wish to analyze population change in the United States in the period between April 1, 2010 and July 1, 2014, when the US population grew by 10.1 million from 308.8 million residents in 2010 to 318.9 million residents in 2014. To figure out how this change came about, we need to examine that number of 10.1 million and determine how it occurred via the three demographic processes of fertility, mortality, and migration. In doing so, we would find out that there were 16.8 million babies added to the population, 10.7 million decedents were subtracted from the population, and a net gain of 4 million international migrants added to the population, to equal the overall population change of 10.1 million.

Race and ethnicity enter into consideration because the different race and ethnic groups do not contribute in the same way to the three demographic processes. Hispanics have higher birth rates and lower death rates than NH-whites, blacks, and Native Americans. And Hispanics and Asians have higher international migration rates than either NH-whites, blacks, or Native Americans.

So, for instance, if we wanted to figure out how and why there were 16.8 million births in the United States between 2010 and 2014, we would need to take into account the proportional representation of the race and ethnic groups in the US population because each has a different birth rate. As Saenz and Morales (2005: 169) have written, "race and ethnicity are important dimensions in understanding the demography of the United States, for racial and ethnic groups vary tremendously with respect to population composition (and) population processes." Saenz and Morales (2005: 176–179) have written a detailed and excellent discussion of the differential impacts of race and ethnic groups on the three demographic processes.

BRIEF HISTORY OF RACE AND ETHNIC CATEGORIES

The concepts of race and ethnicity are often used interchangeably by demographers, but they are really two different terms. "The former is associated with physical characteristics, and the latter is related to behavioral or cultural attributes" (Saenz and Morales, 2005: 171). The questionnaire instruments of the US census and the ACS (see Chapter 3) contain two questions dealing with race and ethnicity (see Figure 3.1 in Chapter 3). One question asks whether the person is of Hispanic, Latino, or Spanish origin. The second question asks about the person's race. Respondents are required to answer both questions on the census and ACS forms. Demographers typically use the answers to these two questions to develop population counts for the five major race/ethnic groups. How is this done?

The demographer Rogelio Saenz has recommended a procedure to classify people into the various race/ethnic categories using the answers to the above two questions, an approach which most demographers now follow. I refer to it as "the Rogelio Rule" because for the past two or more decades Saenz has been a strong proponent of this approach (Saenz, 2010).

According to Saenz, "Because Latinos (i.e., Hispanics) can be of any race, in doing comparative analysis, one should first place all persons who identify as Latino into a specific group and subsequently place all others (non-Latinos) into specific categories based on their own race. This assures that the groups are mutually exclusive and that, for example, the white category does not include Latinos who identify themselves racially as white" (pers. comm. between author and Rogelio Saenz, July 8, 2015).

The large residual group, then, is composed of non-Hispanics; they are separated by their answers to the race question into the four non-Hispanic race groups of NH-whites, NH-blacks, NH-Asians, and NH-Native Americans (i.e., American Indians).

Hispanics may be further subdivided into Cubans, Mexicans, Puerto Ricans, and Other Hispanics. Similarly, Asians may be further subdivided into several Asian groups, for example, Chinese, Korean, Japanese, Filipino, Vietnamese, Asian Indians (to distinguish them from American Indians), and Native Hawaiians (see the listing in Figure 3.1 for all the groups).

But how did these race/ethnic categories come about?

Carl Linnaeus (1707–1778) (also known as Carl von Linne) was a Swedish scientist and is recognized as the father of **taxonomy** (the branch of science concerned with classification). He published the first edition of his *Systema Naturae* (*System of Nature*) in 1735; it was only twelve pages long. By the time it reached its tenth edition in 1758, it classified over 4,000 species of animals and over 7,000 species of plants. According to Prewitt (2013: 15), the book "offered the first authoritative, systematic classification of human variation . . . it favored skin color as the distinguishing trait . . . (the colors were) reddish, sallow, black and white," and they represented, according to Linnaeus, the categories of Americanus (i.e., American Indian), Asiaticus, Africanus, and Europeaeus. Although neither a psychologist nor an anthropologist, Linnaeus claimed that temperament, behavior, and character varied significantly among these color groupings. Racial essentialism, that is, "the idea that there are characteristics that any member of a given race must possess," became an accepted tenet with Linnaeus.

Henceforth, "race, more or less as we know it today, entered the scientific canon as a fact of nature" (Prewitt, 2013: 15).

Other natural scientists followed Linnaeus in the eighteenth and nineteenth centuries, proposing other "rudimentary human classification scheme(s) that conflated color and culture" (Prewitt, 2013: 16). Foremost among them was Johann Blumenbach (1752–1840), a German physician and naturalist, who, in 1775, published his *De Generis Humani Varietate Nativa* (*On the Natural Varieties of Mankind*) in which he "offered the first explanation for the presumed superiority of the white race … (attributing it) to the influence of climate, diet, and living habits" (Prewitt, 2013: 16). In the second edition of the book published in 1776, he added a fifth category to the four categories of Linnaeus, and he ranked the five in order of their superiority, namely, "Caucasian, Mongolian, Malay, American Indian, and Negro (Ethiopian). This taxonomy bequeathed to Western science and culture the all-too-familiar color-denominated racial pentagon: white, yellow, brown, red and black" (Prewitt, 2013: 17). These are the same five race/ethnic group categories used today by the US federal government to cross-classify virtually all the micro data produced by the government, from birth and death and marriage and divorce records, to educational and income data, and residence, and military records; moreover, these categories are part and parcel of federal and state laws, policies, and regulations.

(Blumenbach's five categories did not include, specifically, one for Latinos/Hispanics. His "brown" race referred to "Malays," that is, persons from Malaysia, the Philippines, Brunei, and certain other southeast Asian areas, plus Polynesians and other Pacific Islanders. Hollinger [2006] and Hochschild and Powell [2008] use Blumenbach's "brown" category to refer to Latinos/Hispanics. I also follow their approach in this chapter.)

THE CATEGORIES OF LINNAEUS AND BLUMENBACH ARE EMBEDDED IN US RACIAL CATEGORIES

The racial categories first set out in 1735 and in 1775/76 by Linnaeus and by Blumenbach still exist today in the US government's census enumeration procedures. Race has been part of every census since the first census conducted in 1790. Recall in Chapter 3 that the 1790 census had items on its questionnaire differentiating the population according to whether they were free "white" males and free "white" females, other free persons who were not white, and persons who were neither free nor white, namely, slaves. "Various racial distinctions and taxonomies came and went over the next twenty-two censuses, but never was there a census without a racial classification" (Prewitt, 2013: 20). Waters has further stated that the racial and ethnic categories used by the US federal government are "subject to a great deal of flux and change, both intergenerationally, over the life course and situationally" (Waters, 2002: 25).

Here are some examples of race questions in the various censuses. In the 1830 census there was a new question about white persons who were foreign-born and not yet naturalized. In the 1850 census the enumerators were instructed to identify free persons with different designations depending on their color: the "color" column on the census questionnaire was left blank if the person was white, was scored "M" if the person was **Mulatto,** and "B" if the person was black. In the 1870 census two more race codes were added to the above question, "C" if the person was Chinese, and "I" if the person was American Indian. In the 1890 census, some of the different east Asian groups were distinguished, for example, Japanese. The 1890 census was also the first census to actually use the term of "race" on the questionnaire. Among the racial categories the census enumerators could write in were "White," "Black," "Mulatto," **"Quadroon," "Octoroon,"** "Chinese," "Japanese," or "Indian" depending on the perceived race of the respondent. The term "Mulatto" was taken out of the 1900 census, but appeared again in the 1910 census (US Bureau of the Census, 2014b).

In the 1930 census, the term "Mulatto" was removed again. Enumerators were required to report the race of mixed-race persons as "Negro," no matter the fraction of the racial categories. This was the beginning of the so-called "one-drop rule," where a mixed-race person was to be recorded as "black" irrespective of how small the black lineage might be. Also in this census for the first and only time, "Mexican" was added as a racial category. In the 1940 census, the race category of "Mexican" was removed and Mexican-origin persons were assigned the race of "white." In the 1950 census the term "color" was removed from the race question, but it was added back in the 1960 census (US Bureau of the Census, 2014b).

In the 1970 census, a question pertaining to Hispanic/Latino origin was added for the first time; it was a separate question from the race question. Since then, a similar question has remained on all decennial censuses and ACSs. Specifically, on the 5 percent sample questionnaire of the 1970 census, here is the new question that was added:

Is this person's origin or descent:

- Mexican
- Puerto Rican
- Cuban
- Central or South American
- Other Spanish
- None of these

The 1970 census was also the first census to be conducted as a mail-out, mail-back enumeration system. Census enumerators were only used to visit households who had not returned their questionnaires and those in smaller areas (US Bureau of the Census, 2014b).

In the 1980 census more options were added to the race question, including Vietnamese, Guamanian, and Samoan. And the Hispanic/Latino origin question (above) was moved to the 100 percent census questionnaire (i.e., the questionnaire that everyone in the population answers) where it has remained to this day (the race question has always been included on the 100 percent questionnaire). In the 1990 census, persons who wrote in a multi-race response to the "other" category on the race question were assigned the race of the first part of their response; thus someone who wrote in white-Asian was coded as "white," whereas someone who wrote in Asian-white, was coded as "Asian." The 2000 census was the first to allow persons to check more than one category on the race question (see question No. 9 in Figure 3.1, in Chapter 3). The race question and the Hispanic/Latino ethnicity question on the 2010 census are pretty much the same as they were on the 1990 and 2000 censuses; the major difference from the 1990 census is that now persons have the option of checking more than one response on the race question (US Bureau of the Census, 2014b).

In the 2010 census, 2.9 percent of the US population selected two or more races, an increase from the 2.4 percent choosing two or more races in the 2000 census (Jones and Bullock, 2012).

I have reviewed some of the key changes pertaining to the census classification of race and ethnicity starting in the 1790 census up to and including the 2010 census. The principal race/ethnicity categories used today by the Bureau of the Census are pretty much the same categories developed by Blumenbach in 1775 and 1776, namely, the five I specified above: Hispanics, and the four non-Hispanic race groups of NH-whites, NH-blacks, NH-Asians, and NH-Native Americans (or American Indians). These represent the same all-familiar color groupings of brown, white, black, yellow, and red.

In Kenneth Prewitt's (2013: 8) words: "Today, nearly two and a half centuries (after a German doctor divided the human species into five races), these are the same five races into which the U.S. Census divides the American population, making America the only country in the world firmly wedded to an eighteenth-century racial taxonomy ... (in which) there were not just different races but superior and inferior races." There have been a lot of changes in the statistical categorization of race and ethnicity in the United States since 1790, but despite all the many changes, we are still using today pretty much the same racial categories that were first developed in 1776.

PATTERNS OF RACE AND ETHNICITY IN THE UNITED STATES

According to the 2010 census, the NH-white (i.e., Anglo) population comprised less than 64 percent of the nation's population – the lowest ever recorded. The white population in the United States has always exceeded 80 percent of the total population, from the date of the first census in 1790 when whites comprised 81 percent of the total. The white percentage reached 90 percent in 1920 and remained at or above 90 percent until 1950. By 2000, the white percentage had dropped to 75 percent, and to 72 percent by 2010.

But here we run into a classification issue with the statistical data. Up until 1970 when a question was added to the census pertaining to Hispanic/Latino origin (see my discussion above), persons of Hispanic origin were usually counted as white. Therefore, the white percentages I just mentioned almost always included persons of Hispanic origin. It was not until 1980, and certainly by 1990, that demographers began to distinguish among the various race groups (white, black, Asian, and Indian) by whether they were Hispanic or non-Hispanic (recall my earlier discussion of "the Rogelio rule"). This is especially important with regard to whites, since the white race group, by itself, includes the greatest number of Hispanics.

The percentages of the white race group in the US population for the years of 1990, 2000, and 2010 are, respectively, 80 percent, 75 percent, and 72 percent. The percentages of the white race group who are not Hispanic, that is., the NH-white group, for 1990, 2000, and 2010 are, respectively, 76 percent, 69 percent, and 64 percent. Thus, irrespective of how whites are counted, their representation in the US population has been declining since 1950.

Table 11.1 reports percentage data for the US population for the non-Hispanic race groups and for Hispanics for 2000 and 2010. The NH-white percentage, as just noted, declined between 2000 and 2010 from 69 percent to 64 percent. The black percentage has remained about the same at 12 percent. The Asian percentage has increased slightly. The percentage of persons checking two or more races has also changed a little. It is the Hispanic population where there has been the largest increase of the US total, from 12.5 percent in 2000 to 16.3 percent in 2010.

The two major population trends in the United States between 2000 and 2010 are a declining NH-white population and an increasing Hispanic population. Or put another way, the majority population is declining, and the minority population (Hispanics, blacks, Asians, and Indians) is increasing. Between 2000 and 2010 the size of the US population increased by 27.3 million, from 281.4 million in 2000 to 308.7 million in 2010 (Table 11.1). In the United States, racial/ethnic "minorities accounted for

Table 11.1 US Population, by Non-Hispanic and Hispanic Population Groups, 2000 and 2010

Population group	Number (thousands) 2000	% 2000	Number (thousands) 2010	% 2010
Total	281,422	100.0	308,746	100.0
Non-Hispanic				
White	194,553	69.1	196,818	63.7
Black	33,948	12.1	37,686	12.2
Asian	10,123	3.6	14,465	4.7
Native Hawaiian and Other Pacific Islander	354	0.1	482	0.2
American Indian and Alaska Native	2,069	0.7	2,247	0.7
Some other race	468	0.2	604	0.2
Two or more races	4,602	1.6	5,966	1.9
Hispanic	35,306	12.5	50,478	16.3

Source: Mather, Pollard, and Jacobsen (2011: 7) (table reprinted with permission of the PRB).

92 percent of the total U.S. population growth during the…decade, and Hispanics accounted for over half of the increase" (Mather, Pollard, and Jacobsen, 2011: 7).

Between 2000 and 2010 the minority population in all fifty states grew faster than the majority population. Among all the states, Nevada's minority population grew the fastest, 78 percent, compared with 12 percent for the majority NH-whites. Only in the District of Columbia did the minority population decrease in size. In 1980, as many as twenty-one states had minority populations comprising less than 10 percent of their populations, by 2000, the number had dropped to six, by 2010 the number was down to only four (Maine, New Hampshire, Vermont, and West Virginia).

In 1980, only Hawaii and the District of Columbia had more than 50 percent of its population minority; they were the so-called **majority-minority populations**, that is, over 50 percent of their populations comprised minorities. By 2000, California and New Mexico had joined Hawaii as majority-minority states. In 2000, Texas was 48 percent minority, but became a majority-minority state in 2004. As of 2010, therefore, four states and the District of Columbia were majority-minority: 77 percent of Hawaii was minority, as well as 60 percent of New Mexico, 60 percent of California, 55 percent of Texas, and 65 percent of the District of Columbia. Eight states in 2010 had minority populations of more than 40 percent (Nevada 46 percent, Maryland 45 percent, Georgia 44 percent, Arizona 42 percent,

Florida 42 percent, Mississippi 42 percent, New York 42 percent, New Jersey 41 percent); they are next in line to become majority-minority states (Humes, Jones, and Ramirez, 2011: 18–19).

Of the 3,143 counties in the United States, 348 of them, or more than 10 percent of all counties, were majority-minority counties in 2010. The majority-minority counties are located "along the East coast from Massachusetts to Florida and in…the Gulf Coast states of Alabama, Mississippi, and Louisiana. (They are also located)…across the southwest through the states lining the U.S.–Mexico border" (Humes, Jones, and Ramirez, 2011: 22).

Just over 38 percent of all US counties are heavily majority, that is, they are 90 percent or more comprised of NH-whites. These counties are "located in Appalachia, in the upper Northeast, and in the central and upper Midwest (Humes, Jones, and Ramirez, 2011: 19–21).

In 2008, the US county with the highest percentage minority was Starr County, Texas (98 percent), followed by Maverick County, Texas (97 percent) and Webb County, Texas (95 percent). The bulk of the minority populations of these three counties is Hispanic. Nationwide in 2008, there were forty-eight majority-minority Hispanic counties, and the ten largest were in Texas. There were seventy-seven majority-minority African American counties, and all were in the South. The only majority-minority Asian county in 2008 was Honolulu County, Hawaii, with 58 percent of its population Asian. Ten US counties in 2008 were majority-minority American Indian and Alaskan Natives (AIAN) counties, the largest being Shannon County, South Dakota, with 88 percent AIAN.

I have discussed the Hispanic/Latino population in many places throughout this chapter. Allow me here to specify in greater detail the ethnic composition of this population group. I will answer here the question, who are the Hispanics?

Figure 11.1 presents information about the US Hispanic population in 2010 according to their place of origin. By far the greatest proportion of Hispanics in 2010 was Mexican (63 percent); this is an increase from 58 percent in 2000. The next largest Hispanic group was Puerto Rican, at 9.2 percent, which is a slight drop from the 10 percent in 2000. Cubans comprised around 4 percent of the Hispanic population in 2010, which is about the same as in 2000. These three groups, Mexicans, Puerto Ricans, and Cubans, accounted for around three-quarters of the US Hispanic population in 2010. Other relatively large Hispanic groups residing in the United States in 2010 were Salvadorans (3.3 percent), Dominicans (2.8 percent), and Guatemalans (2.1 percent)

Regarding geographic distribution in 2010, more than three-quarters of the Hispanic population were residing in the south and west regions of

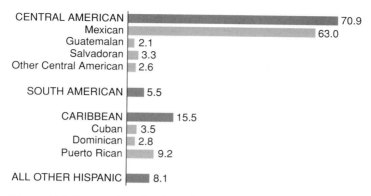

Figure 11.1 Percent Distribution of the Hispanic Population by Origin in the United States, 2010
Notes: The "Other Central American" group includes Costa Rican, Honduran, Nicaraguan, etc.; the "South American" group includes Argentinean, Bolivian, Chilean, Colombian, etc.; the "All Other Hispanic" group includes people who responded "Spaniard," "Hispanic," "Latino," etc.
Source: Ennis, Rios-Vargas, and Albert (2011: 5).

the United States, with over half of them living in just three states, California (14 million), Texas (9.5 million), and Florida (2.8 million). Hispanics comprised the majority population in eighty-two of the 3,143 counties in the United States. They comprised "the majority in 51 counties in Texas and one (Miami-Dade) in Florida ... Hispanics were the majority in 12 counties in New Mexico and nine counties in California" (Ennis, Rios-Vargas, and Albert, 2011: 11).

In Chapter 13 on "Population Change in the United States," I examine and discuss population projections for the United States to the year of 2060. I will show that the United States is projected to become more racially and ethnically diverse by the year 2060 compared with the present. The NH-white population of the United States, the "majority" race/ethnic group today, is projected to fall gradually to 44 percent of the US population by 2060; it is projected to drop below 50 percent in around 2044. At that time, the United States will have become a majority-minority country; no race/ethnic group will have a majority share of the population, and the United States will have become a "plurality of racial and ethnic groups" (Colby and Ortman, 2015: 9).

The major changes in racial and ethnic composition in the United States and some other countries are the result directly and indirectly of immigration. Immigration has a direct effect because the immigrants are added to the population; it has an indirect effect because the immigrants have children in the host country and the children are then added to the population (Lichter, 2013). This indirect effect is increasingly important if the immigrants have higher birth rates than the native population, as is the case with Hispanics, but not with Asians. What is likely to occur in the United States and certain European countries in the process of their becoming majority-minority countries? How will the populations interact? What will be the result of these race/ethnic changes? In the last part of this chapter, I explore some of the issues of group adaptation.

CONCEPTUAL AND THEORETICAL ISSUES OF ADAPTATION

Some new form of interaction necessarily follows whenever one group migrates into an area already inhabited by another group. Both groups must adapt to a new situation. Humankind has been faced with the challenges of group adaptation ever since international migration began many thousands of years ago. In the United States and elsewhere, some form of adaptation typically begins whenever a new group of immigrants arrives. The immigration of Europeans into what is now the United States during the seventeenth and eighteenth centuries forced a kind of adaptation by them and their hosts. The earliest immigrants were Native Americans, who first arrived in North America about 14,000 years ago (see my discussion in Chapter 9). They coexisted with European immigrants until the eighteenth century, when a large number of them were eliminated through disease and war. These conflicts continued throughout the late 1800s, after which only a fraction of Native Americans remained (Cortes and Poston, 2008; Purcell, 1995; Snipp, 1989). Admittedly, this adaptation was brutal, but it was nevertheless a form of cultural adaptation. The adaptation is again occurring and will be repeated as long as immigration to this country persists. I will now discuss cultural adaptation and its variants in more detail.

Residents of and newcomers to an area must adapt to a new social situation that results from group interaction. At one extreme is **cultural separatism**. Here, the newcomers are socially isolated from the residents either through their own volition or through separatist practices of the host society. The slave–free person relationship exemplifies cultural separatism at its most extreme. Another example is the relationship between the dominant American society and a religious group such as the Amish or the Fundamentalist Church of Jesus Christ of Latter-Day Saints (FLDS).

At the other extreme lies **cultural amalgamation**. Here, a new society and culture result from the massive intermingling and intermarriage between two or more groups. The racial blending that occurred in nineteenth-century Latin America between the Spanish newcomers and the indigenous groups resulted in the emergence of the **mestizos**. (A mestizo is a person of mixed blood, the result of this racial blending.) A slightly different result occurred in China over the centuries and during many dynasties. Alien groups would conquer and dominate parts of the country, intermingle and intermarry, eventually becoming Chinese. The Chinese have a saying reflecting this form of cultural amalgamation: "Just as all water becomes salty when it flows into the sea, so everyone who comes to China becomes Chinese" (Kimball, 2000).

Between these extreme processes of cultural adaptation are **pluralism**, **assimilation**, and the so-called **melting pot**. In pluralism, the society allows its constituted ethnic groups to develop, each emphasizing its own cultural heritage. Assimilation assumes that the new groups will take on the culture and values of the host society and gradually discard their own. The sociologist Milton Gordon (1964) distinguished between cultural assimilation (or acculturation), where a subordinate (minority) group takes on many of the characteristics of the dominant (majority) group; and structural assimilation, where the subordinate group gains access to the principal institutions of the society.

In the melting-pot process, the host and immigrant groups share one another's cultures and, in the process, a new group emerges. Consequently, the melting-pot concept differs somewhat from that of pure assimilation. While early US advocates of the melting-pot theory encouraged newcomers to "assimilate" into American society, that society was not intended to be totally dominated by Anglo-Saxons, but rather was to be a new society formed by the blending of the various groups, albeit with a strong Anglo-Saxon influence.

Throughout American history, immigrants as well as nonimmigrant residents have adjusted to one another. A process of cultural adaptation was necessary if the society was to survive.

ASSIMILATION VERSUS PLURALISM

At the beginning of the twentieth century, the Anglo majority favored the total assimilation of the new European groups into an Anglo-dominated society. But on the other hand, it was taken for granted – indeed, it was ordered – that Mexicans, Asians, and blacks would remain culturally separate. Cultural pluralism and even the melting pot were adamantly opposed. President Theodore Roosevelt felt nothing but disdain for the "hyphenated American," and President Woodrow Wilson actually stated that "any man who thinks of himself as belonging to a particular national group in America has not yet become an American" (cited in Adams, 1983: 111).

Assimilation

"Americanization" was in full vogue in the early decades of the twentieth century. It was assumed that all European immigrants would become Americanized. Anglo-conformity was encouraged – indeed, demanded – for all the new immigrants. More than thirty years ago, the sociologist Nathan Glazer (1983: 335–336) wrote that "the ideal, i.e., Americanization, was the full assimilation of all immigrant groups to a common national type, so that ethnicity would play a declining role in individual consciousness, groups would not be formed around ethnic interests, 'hyphenated Americans' would be a thing of the past, and the United States would be as homogeneous in its Americanness as the nations of the old world were once in their Englishness, their Frenchness."

Cultural Pluralism

Aligned against total assimilation were the cultural pluralists, who urged a new type of nation in which the various national groups would preserve their identity and their cultures, uniting in a world federation in miniature (Bourne, 1916). With this approach, immigrants would assimilate into the American culture while maintaining and taking pride in the important characteristics of their native culture.

Melting Pot

The melting-pot theory was a compromise between cultural pluralism and assimilation. The first recorded mention of this idea is attributed to Hector St. John de Crevecoeur in 1782 when he noted that "here in America, individuals of all nations are melted into a new race of men" ([1782] 1997: 25). The 1909 play *The Melting Pot* by Israel Zangwill (1864–1926) brought this idea to the attention of many people and made the term more widespread. But the historian Frederick Jackson Turner probably did more than anyone to popularize the concept with his remark that "the tide of foreign immigration . . . has risen so steadily that it has made a composite American people whose amalgamation is destined to produce a new national stock" ([1893] 1920: 190). In one sense, the melting pot is a form of assimilation in that emphasis is on the formation of an American culture. Nevertheless, its determination not to overemphasize Anglo-conformity makes it a different type of assimilation than that emphasized by the "Americanization" movement.

RECENT PATTERNS OF CULTURAL ADAPTATION

Looking back at the twentieth century, it is clear that the attempt to Americanize everyone to Anglo-conformity through total assimilation did not succeed. Most European groups retained some semblance of ethnicity over the years, while at the same time adapting to their new surroundings.

Neither has cultural pluralism been particularly successful among European immigrants and their descendants in the United States, despite efforts on the part of some of its advocates to maintain ethnic identities.

By the 1940s, the melting pot was beginning to work fairly well for immigrants from southern and eastern Europe. But it may have been working in different ways than had been anticipated. A new population was in the process of forming the "unhyphenated American." In addition, the power elite, historically almost exclusively white Anglo-Saxon Protestant (WASP), was being replaced by one in which persons of non-WASP heritage were commonplace. Finally, the melting pot, although only among Anglos (NH-whites), was coming to a boil.

Consider several examples of such success, namely, Lee Iacocca, a successful American corporate executive, and A. Bartlett Giamatti, the president of Yale University, who later became the commissioner of Major League Baseball. In the 1968 election, both major parties offered second-generation American vice presidential candidates: Spiro Agnew, of Greek parentage; and Edward Muskie, of Polish parentage. Among those mentioned as possible presidential candidates in 1988 were second-generation Italians, Greeks, and Basques. Most important was the fact that the voting public was apparently not that concerned with the diversity of the candidates. Who would argue that Michael Dukakis was less American than George H. W. Bush?

Finally, in 2008, Barack Hussein Obama, formerly the junior senator from the state of Illinois, became the forty-fourth president of the United States. Obama was born in Hawaii to a Kenyan father and an American mother. He lived in Hawaii for most of his childhood and adolescent years, but also lived for four years in Jakarta, Indonesia, with his mother and Indonesian stepfather. Is Barack Obama any less American than the Republican Party's candidate for president in 2008, John S. McCain, born at the Naval Air Station in Panama to an American father and mother?

While the melting pot has worked fairly well among Americans of European ancestry, there are islands of dissent. In the minds of a few, some hesitancy still remains about accepting "ethnics" as truly American, even though the nation has come a long way with its population of European ancestry. However, we need to recall that this encouraging process has been limited to Anglos. Blacks, Hispanics, and Asians have mostly remained out of the mainstream.

We are now into the second decade of the twenty-first century, and new adaptation challenges are facing the nation. Today, well over 80 percent of immigrants come from either Latin America or Asia. As I noted earlier in this chapter, by around 2044 in the United States, there will be no race/ethnic numerical majority. We will all be minorities. What kind of a nation will emerge? While interracial marriages used to be a relatively rare occurrence, they have been increasing in past years. A recent analysis by demographers at the Pew Foundation reported a "record 14.6% of all new marriages in the United States in 2008 were between spouses of a different race or ethnicity from one another. This includes marriages between Hispanics and nonHispanics…(Also) among all newlyweds in 2008, 9% of whites, 16% of blacks, 26% of Hispanics, and 31% of Asians married someone whose race or ethnicity was different from their own" (Passel, Wang, and Taylor, 2010: ii). Interracial marriages have been legal since 1967 in all US states. Indeed, the great African American sociologist W. E. B. Du Bois ([1903] 1921: 21–22) predicted that "some day, on American soil, two world races may give each to each those characteristics both so sadly lack." Du Bois called for the maintenance of racial purity only "until this mission of the Negro people is accomplished, and the ideal of human brotherhood has become a practical possibility."

Another factor to consider in my discussion of the mode of cultural adaptation for today's American society is that the current immigration pattern is not a wave. Earlier immigration movements were actual waves; that is, there was a beginning and an end to the immigration movement. This explains to a large degree the success of the newcomers from eastern and southern Europe. Once the wave ended, they were more likely to Americanize than to remain ethnically separated. Today, this does not appear to be the case. There is a continuing movement of people to the United States from Latin America and from Asia. However, as I note later in Chapter 13, the number of immigrants to the United States from Mexico has reduced in recent years.

We must thus ask whether the relative success achieved during the twentieth century in the adaptation of southern and eastern European immigrants and their descendants into a new kind of America will be duplicated with the current and future mix of racially and ethnically diverse groups. The question of how the United States is to maintain a unified country composed of people from all over the world cannot be ignored.

It seems unlikely that a repetition of the successful melting-pot process will occur given the situation in 2015–2025 as compared with 1900–1910. The differences in the economic structure, in the increasing trends in interracial marriages, in the increasing emphasis on group rights, and particularly in the levels of immigration are far too great to envision a new interracial melting pot in the near future. What then are the alternatives?

I hope that cultural separatism is a phenomenon of the past. The nation is well past that period when the various race and ethnic groups were deliberately separated. Neither does the total cultural assimilation of the new minority groups (i.e., the complete surrender of immigrants' cultures and values and their absorption into the core culture) seem to be a realistic goal. In the United States in less than four decades from now, there will no longer be a majority in which to assimilate. Indeed, I noted earlier in this chapter that right now in four US states and the District of Columbia, the Anglo population is not the majority; moreover, eight more states are rapidly approaching majority-minority status.

The first US population consisting of the original thirteen colonies was comprised almost entirely of persons from England. Today, according to data from the ACS, less than 10 percent of the US population was born English or has ancestors from England.

The racial- and ethnic-identity consciousness that has emerged during the past few decades, together with the growth of large enclaves of new immigrants in certain parts of the country, preclude any substantive assimilation into a dominant Anglo culture. Furthermore, there is considerable doubt as to whether the new groups desire total assimilation and, for that matter, whether the majority favors it.

The choices lie between cultural pluralism and what I have called here pluralistic assimilation. Whatever direction the nation follows will determine the kind of America that will evolve in this century.

A benign form of cultural pluralism has always been part and parcel of American life. Ethnic enclaves are still present in major cities. Diverse religious and cultural holidays remain on the calendars of many Americans. However, cultural pluralism took on a different meaning in the 1960s. To some people, "cultural pluralism implies the conscious pursuit of a national order in which Americans find their identity primarily as members of ethnic and/or religious groups and only secondarily as individuals engaged in carving out a position in the greater society" (Christopher, 1989: 20). A harder-edged version of cultural pluralism seems to be currently in vogue. The focus is on the contention that the United States is a compact between what some are beginning to lump together as a "Euro-American" population and a limited set of minority groups made up principally of African Americans, Hispanics, and Asians (Archdeacon, 1990: 18). The non-European immigrants and long-time minorities tend to rely more and more on in-group cohesiveness and cultural reassertion as the only effective means to combat racial/ethnic discrimination.

Too often, Americans confuse the fact that we are a pluralistic nation with an acceptance of cultural pluralism. America is pluralistic in the fact of having many religious groups and ethnicities represented in its population. Nevertheless, it has constantly striven to achieve an overall unity in its basic interests and ideals. A motto of the United States and included on the official seal of the country, *E Pluribus Unum* ("Out of Many, One"), succinctly describes the "ideal" American nation. If cultural pluralism were but a supplement to these common interests and ideals, it would be appropriate. However, cultural pluralism, as currently conceived, nonetheless argues for the primacy of the homeland language and culture. Indeed, as Theodore White once commented, "some…have made a demand never voiced by immigrants before, that the United States, in effect, officially recognize itself as a bicultural, bilingual nation" (1982: 367).

PLURALISTIC ASSIMILATION

The challenge to the nation is to find a way to assure that all of its residents, of whatever background, have equal access to all avenues of success, and in the process are able to adapt to American culture while contributing to its ever-changing content. At the same time, they need also to have the choice of maintaining their own subculture within the broader American society. As the nation becomes more and more multiracial and multiethnic, it is particularly important that it accepts a form of cultural adaptation that takes the best of cultural pluralism and assimilation, while at the same time maintaining the American culture and assuring its acceptance.

The sociologist J. Milton Yinger and the historian John Higham both addressed this issue some years ago and suggested new forms of adaptation that would take into account pluralism as well as assimilation. Yinger (1981: 261) wrote that some sort of integration that falls short of assimilation may be the right compromise. Higham (1975: 265) stated that "pluralistic integration" does not eliminate ethnic boundaries, but upholds the validity of a common culture. However, neither Yinger nor Higham envisioned the possibility of a truly multiracial society where no one group clearly predominates, a situation that will characterize the United States by around 2044. The concept of pluralistic assimilation, while derived from these earlier models, looks at a truly multiracial society.

Pluralistic assimilation would be appropriate if the goal of the society is to be united, insofar as possible, given the population's composition. All groups would be assimilated, both culturally and structurally, into the already diverse mainstream American society. This is neither "Anglo-conformity" nor "white American conformity." This is really *assimilation among* rather than *assimilation into* and reflects the changing demographic picture and the fact that no one ethnic group predominates. It is a "New Americanization."

The inclusion of structural assimilation suggests that all groups will have equal access to power, whether economic or political. Pluralistic, conversely, reflects the fact that the society is no longer dealing with groups of the same race or ethnicity. These multiracial and multiethnic groups may maintain their identity at the same time that they become assimilated into the ever-changing mainstream American society (Bouvier, 1992).

Some form of pluralistic assimilation may have been implied in Benjamin Franklin's first version of the shield for the nation. That shield represented the six European nations that comprised the white population of the new country. In that context, *E Pluribus Unum* was a recognition that the survival of the new government depended on its ability to forge a nation from a population in which ethnic diversity was the norm (Archdeacon, 1990: 11).

The success of Japanese Americans, despite the horror of the concentration camps during the Second World War, and of Chinese Americans, despite the outright discrimination directed against them as written into early immigration laws (see my discussions in Chapters 9 and 15), provide us with a working model of pluralistic assimilation. While the Japanese and the Chinese gradually became assimilated, both culturally and structurally, into the mainstream American society, they have remained as identifiable racial groups even though interracial marriages have increased. Perhaps part of their success can be attributed to the fact that immigration from Japan and China to the United States was practically nonexistent until the 1980s, except for the rather small streams that entered the country in the nineteenth century. This eases the adaptation process. It would be naive to pretend that prejudice toward Japanese Americans or Chinese Americans does not exist. Pluralistic assimilation is an ongoing process, and its eventual success requires the cooperation of all groups. Nevertheless, the fact that Japanese Americans and Chinese Americans are often cited as an example of the achievement of a New Americanization is evidence of the powerful integrative forces at work in American society.

Numerous factors must be present if pluralistic assimilation is to succeed.

First, American society must provide the means to make economic and social advancement possible for *all* Americans. This necessarily involves easy and inexpensive access to higher education and to technical training. It necessitates a revamping of the nation's educational institutions to allow for the better preparation of *all* Americans for the occupations of the future. Given the rapid change in the process of information through the Internet and email and other forms of social media, this goal is especially vital. A new kind of structural mobility must be developed for the US economy of the twenty-first century. Should these plans fail and blacks and Latinos find themselves overwhelmingly in lower-paying jobs while Asians and whites are dominant in the higher-paying positions, conflict will be inevitable and pluralistic assimilation will fail.

Second, future immigrants must demonstrate their desire to become "one of us," changing the meaning of "us" in the process. Just as most eighteenth- and early-nineteenth-century immigrants wanted to become American, so too should those of the present era. If the nation is to retain *E Pluribus Unum*, there can be no room for cultural separatism or for irredentist movements on the part of newcomers.

Third, all forms of discrimination must end. This is a strong challenge. The United States is still a racist society (Bonilla-Silva, 2013; Feagin, 2006, 2014), and this must change if pluralistic assimilation is to succeed. If pluralistic assimilation is truly desired as the ideal mode of adaptation for the future, Americans must cease thinking of the newest immigrants as "inferior" foreigners. The newcomers need to be accepted wholeheartedly and without reservation. These motivated individuals are not a "mob at the gates"; Americans need to show them that the United States is a benevolent community eager to welcome newcomers into their society (Waltzer, 1981: 10). Every effort must be made to assist the newest residents to participate fully and equally in this dynamic society.

This applies *a fortiori* to long-time American minorities. The Civil Rights legislation of the 1960s, as well as no less than the US Constitution, promised a nation in which all persons would be treated equally. This goal still remains distant on the horizon. Even relations among minorities are fragile. With the newest immigrants' share of the population growing (by 2060, almost one in five Americans will have been born outside the United States [Colby and Ortman, 2015]), it is vital for the survival of the American society that a mechanism be found for all groups to know and understand one another.

Pluralistic assimilation, forms of interaction, cultural assimilation, the melting-pot theory, cultural amalgamation, and group integration are all examples of terms and concepts that sociologists, demographers, and other social scientists have developed to better understand the relations in a society between members of different groups. Basically, these terms emphasize the fact that whenever one person or group moves into an area inhabited by another person or group, both must adapt to a newly defined situation.

While I have concentrated in this chapter on the United States, the process of cultural adaptation is at work whenever and wherever two different groups find themselves sharing the same land. Indeed, in some ways, the situation in Europe is more challenging than that in the United States. There, as I have already shown in Chapter 4, the fertility of the resident population is so low that without immigration some European countries could well disappear as economic forces. Yet most of these countries are not familiar with massive movements of individuals from other races and cultures, as is the United States. There, too, some significant modes of cultural adaptation are called for. To date, the prospects for peaceful relations between the residents and the newcomers do not look particularly favorable. All the various modes of cultural adaptation that I have discussed in this chapter may be tried, but as of now, it is too early to determine the eventual result.

SUMMARY

In this chapter on the demography of race and ethnicity, I first discussed why demographers are interested in race and ethnicity. Next, I reviewed briefly the development of racial categories, as set forth principally by Linnaeus and Blumenbach. I next discussed how the statistical issues of race and ethnicity evolved in the United States, resulting in the five basic categories used today by the US federal government. I then examined some of the current patterns of race and ethnicity in the United States. And I concluded the chapter with a detailed discussion of some of the different sociological and demographic concepts and perspectives pertaining to adaptation.

12 World Population Change over Time

I have already discussed the three demographic processes in Chapters 4, 7, 8, and 9. I am now in a position to put them all together and analyze overall population change. This chapter deals with the dynamics over time of population change in the world, and the next chapter (Chapter 13) with US population change.

To help better understand the issues I will present in the chapter, I will first review, albeit briefly, the main theory of population change, namely, demographic transition theory (DTT) (please look over my more detailed discussion of this theory, and other writings on population change, in Chapter 2). Then, I will look specifically at the dynamics of world population change, taking both a long and a short view. I will conclude this chapter with a discussion of the future of the world's population.

How large right now is the population of the world, and how rapidly is it growing? The population clock of the US Bureau of the Census estimated that the population of the entire world numbered almost 7.4 billion people in late October 2015, the date when I was writing some revisions for this chapter. The CBR was around 20/1,000, and the CDR about 8/1,000. Thus, the rate of annual growth was about 1.2 percent. So, if these birth and death rates were to continue unchanged into the future, the size of the population of the world would double about every fifty-eight years (see my discussion of doubling time later in this chapter). Of course, such astronomical numbers are unlikely to occur. Either the birth rate will fall or the death rate will rise, and it will most likely be the former, not the latter.

There were an estimated 7.4 billion people on the Earth in October 2015. I have already mentioned in Chapter 9 that the first humans emerged in sub-Saharan Africa as many as 195,000 years ago, and lived there for the first two-thirds of their history. But given that we humans first appeared on Earth nearly 200,000 years ago, I wondered how many people have ever been born, that is, how many people have ever lived on Earth. Carl Haub, a demographer at the PRB in Washington, DC, first addressed this question back in the 1990s because at the time there was a factoid circulating claiming that 75 percent of persons ever born in the world were now alive. This seemed to Haub to be a ridiculous statement, and I agree with him, it certainly was. Haub answered the question in 1995, updated it in 2002, and again in 2011 (Haub, 2011).

To obtain an estimate of the number of people ever born, Haub needed to estimate the levels of the birth rate at the various eras since humans first appeared on Earth. He began the human race with two people 50,000 years ago with a birth rate of 80/1,000, dropped the rate to 60 starting in 1200 AD, and continued dropping the rate until the year 2011 when it was 23/1,000. He then did the calculations and determined that as of 2011 there had been 108 billion people ever born on this Earth. Thus, the 2011 population of the Earth was just 6.5 percent of all people ever born, a much more realistic figure than the 75 percent factoid.

Since evidence indicates that the first "modern" humans emerged as many as 195,000 years ago (see Chapter 9), I have revised Haub's estimate by starting the first two humans 195,000 years ago. I have also extended his analysis from 2011 up to 2015. As an aside, I note that it is probably not the case that we humans descended from a single pair of individuals (see "All About Adam" [2013] and Fagundes et al. [2007] for discussion). I will nevertheless begin the human population with two people because it makes my demographic model less complicated.

I set the birth rate at 80/1,000 for the period 195,000 to 50,000 years ago, and this results in an estimate of around 8 billion births for that period (remember that Haub assumed humans began 50,000 years ago, so I first needed to estimate how many babies were born for those first almost 150,000 years of our existence). I show later in this chapter that there was very little growth in the human population then and for most of its history. Yes, birth rates were high, around 80/1,000, but so were death rates.

Next, I needed to extend Haub's analysis by four years from 2011 to 2015. Around 130–140 million babies are born in the world each year, so I added another 520–560 million births to carry us up to the present.

My revised answer to Carl Haub's question of "How many people have ever lived on earth?" from their beginnings 195,000 years ago up to the year of 2015, is around 117 billion. The present population of the earth of 7.4 billion is just 6.3 percent of all persons ever born.

Livi-Bacci (2012: 26) also developed an answer to the question of how many people have ever lived on the Earth, with slightly different assumptions about when the human population began and the levels of its birth

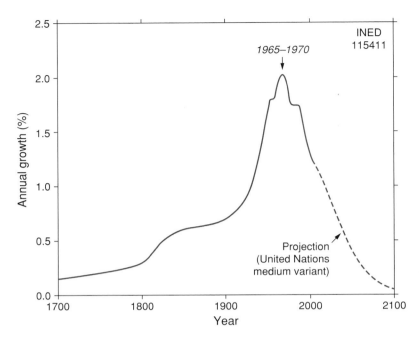

Figure 12.1 World Population Growth Rates, 1700–2100
Source: Pison (2011) (reprinted with permission of Institut National d'études Démographiques [INED]).

and death rates over time. He comes up with a number of 82 billion, a little less than my number of 117 billion that I developed from Haub's calculations. We will never know for sure which number is the closest to the true number.

The PRB has prepared a five-minute video of Carl Haub discussing the above question and showing us how he developed his answer. I encourage you to spend a few minutes and observe a demographer at work addressing and answering a very interesting question (see at: www.prb.org/Multimedia/Video/2011/distilled-demographics-how-many-ever-lived.aspx).

Figure 12.1 presents the growth rates of the world's population from 1700 to the present, and then projected to 2100. The author of the chart, Gilles Pison (2011), reminds us that there was very little growth in the population of the world up until around 1700. Birth rates and death rates were both very high, and there was little growth in the population. This was the first stage of the demographic transition, as I discussed earlier in Chapter 2. The current growth rate of the world's population of about 1.2 percent has not been constant in past years. Pison's chart (Figure 12.1) indicates that the annual rate of world population growth started going up around 1700, reached a rate of around 0.25 percent by 1800, continued increasing to 1.5 percent in 1950, and then to a high rate of just slightly above 2 percent in the mid- to late 1960s. Then the rate started to decline around 1970, reaching 1.2 percent currently. Pison uses projection data from the medium-variant of the United Nations to show us that by around 2100 the world population growth rate will be back at about the same zero rate of increase that characterized the world prior to 1700.

Some demographers, myself included, believe that the period in the late 1960s when the world started seeing a decreasing growth rate (dropping below 2 percent) may well be the most important demographic date in human history. It marks the start of the movement to eventual no population growth in the world, which is projected to occur around 2100, maybe a little later.

The increases and decreases in the world's population growth rates have not always been steady. Indeed, the slowing down for a few years of the growth rate in the late 1950s to the early 1960s was due almost entirely to events in China, namely, the natural disasters and decreased agricultural production there that resulted in a great famine following the calamitous years of the Great Leap Forward (I discussed this famine earlier in Chapter 7). This means that the notion of a "world population" may be misguided because there is not really a "world society." Changes and trends in world demographic behavior result from the differential demographic behaviors of the major world regions. This point is made more apparent later in this and in other chapters.

DEMOGRAPHIC TRANSITION THEORY

I have already written in some detail in Chapter 2 about the most prominent explanation of population change, namely, the theory of demographic transition. The theory has four stages of mortality and fertility change that occur in the process of societal modernization (Figure 12.2). The first stage is the pre-transitional or pre-industrialization stage. It lasted worldwide for thousands and thousands of years when the world was characterized by high birth and death rates and stable population growth. Because of the high birth rates that occurred during this stage, it is sometimes referred to as the stage of high growth potential because of the great potential for population growth if mortality were ever to fall. No countries in the world today are located in the first stage.

The pre-transitional stage is followed by the first transitional stage, known as Stage 2. Stage 2 likely started worldwide around 1700 or so. The forces of modernization and industrialization were responsible for moving countries of the world from Stage 1 to Stage 2, and the first effect was a reduction in mortality. This intermediate stage resulted in rapid rates

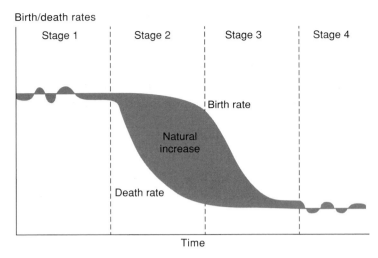

Birth/death rates

| Stage 1 | Stage 2 | Stage 3 | Stage 4 |

Birth rate

Natural increase

Death rate

Time

Figure 12.2 The Classic Stages of Demographic Transitions
Source: McFalls (2007: 27) (reprinted with permission of the PRB).

of population growth because fertility remained high after mortality had declined. During Stage 2, the rate of population growth was high. Examples of some of the countries today in Stage 2 are Guatemala, Iraq, and several in sub-Saharan Africa.

The next stage (Stage 3) was characterized by decreasing population growth due to lower birth and death rates. It was during this stage that fertility began to decline. Some of the countries today in Stage 3 would be India and Malaysia.

In the final stage (Stage 4), called incipient decline, both fertility and mortality are low. During this stage, however, there are often slight fluctuations in fertility; thus both natural increase and natural decrease will occur owing to these fluctuations. Brazil, Germany, and Japan are examples of countries in Stage 4. The world is projected to reach Stage 4 by around the year 2100 (Figure 12.1 above).

Demographic transition theory is the most popular of the demographic theories of population change. But be sure you keep in mind the revisions of the theory, discussed already in Chapter 2, particularly those resulting in the "second" and the "third" demographic transitions.

Doubling Time and Halving Time

How fast or how slow is the world's current population growth rate of 1.2 percent? I noted in the first part of this chapter that in the 1960s, the world was growing at around 2 percent, and now it is growing at around 1.2 percent. Demographers sometimes use the **Rule of 69.3** to gain an idea about whether a population's growth rate is fast or slow. Where did the Rule of 69.3 come from? What does it mean?

One way to determine the significance or relevance of a population's rate of growth is through the concept of **doubling time**. That is, if a population maintains its present birth rates and death rates year after year after year, how long would it take to double its size? The answer may be presented with the use of natural logarithms. The **natural log** of 2 is 0.693. I multiply 0.693 by 100 to equal 69.3.

To illustrate, if I divide 69.3 by the population's positive growth rate expressed as a percentage, the answer tells me how many years it will take for the population to double its size if it were to maintain its current birth and death rates. The world's CBR in 2015 was 20/1,000 and its death rate was 8/1,000, giving a difference between the two of 12/1,000, or 1.2 percent, that is, 1.2/100. Dividing 69.3 by 1.2 equals 57.8, which is the number of years it would take the world population to double its size from 7.25 billion to 14.5 billion if it kept its birth and death rates steady. If its present birth and death rates were maintained, the world would number 14.5 billion in 2073, and 29 billion in 2131. A population growth rate of 1.2 percent is a very high rate of growth, leading to a doubling of the population every fifty-eight years. As I will show below, even though this growth rate of the world today of 1.2 percent is not as high as it was in the 1960s when the world was growing at 2 percent (a doubling time of almost thirty-five years), population growth rates greater than 1 percent have not been common in the world until just a few centuries ago (see Figure 12.1).

If you are wondering about how many years it would take a population to triple its size if its birth and death rates did not change, then use the natural log of 3 (which is 1.10), multiply it by 100, and divide it by the percent growth rate. How long will it take the world to triple its current size of 7.25 billion to 21.75 billion? Divide 110 by 1.2, equals 91.7. This means that in around ninety-two years from now (in 2015), that is, in around the year 2107, if the world maintained a growth rate every year of 1.2 percent, by around 2107 the population size of the world would be approximately 21.8 billion.

I will now compare the population growth rates of two countries of about the same size with very different rates of growth. The west African country of Niger had a mid-year 2014 population numbering just over 18 million, with a CBR of 50 and a CDR of 11, equaling a growth rate of 3.9 percent. The European country of the Netherlands had a mid-year 2014 population of just under 17 million people, with a CBR of 10 and a CDR of 8, resulting in a population growth rate of 0.2 percent (PRB, 2014).

Here are two countries with populations of nearly the same size, around 17–18 million. Their growth rates are 3.9 percent and 0.2 percent.

How different are these growth rates? The difference between the two, one might say, is only 3.7 percent; this is not very much.

But it is a very large difference, a huge difference, if one answers the question in terms of doubling time. If Niger were to maintain its current birth and death rates, its population would double in size in less than eighteen years, that is, 69.3 divided by 3.9 equals 17.8. If the Netherlands were to maintain its current birth and death rates, its population would double in size in almost 347 years.

Keep in mind that the doubling time concept does not necessarily reflect what will actually happen in the future because a country's birth and death rates hardly ever remain the same from year to year. But the doubling time concept does allow us to appraise the relevance or significance of a particular percentage rate of population change.

What happens if the difference between the population's crude birth and death rates is not positive but is negative? May we still use the Rule of 69.3 to tell us about the significance or relevance of a negative rate of growth? Yes, we may.

For example, Germany in mid-year 2014 had a population of 80.9 million people; its birth rate was 8/1,000 and its death rate 11/1,000, for a percentage rate of population change of -0.3 percent (PRB, 2014). If we divide this negative percentage rate into 69.3, the answer is −231. This means that if Germany were to maintain its current birth and death rates, its population would become half as large in 231 years (i.e., a **halving time**). I noted earlier that many countries, most of them in Europe, are experiencing population decline because of their low birth rates. Germany is certainly one of them.

I turn next to a discussion of population change in the world. I look first at population growth before 1650 and then since 1650.

WORLD POPULATION GROWTH

Population Growth before 1650

If we go back in time to around 65,000 BC, the world population then was estimated to number between 400,000 and 500,000 people. For thousands of years, the world grew very slowly. By about 35,000 BC, the population of the world numbered around 4 million. By about 8,000 BC, it was about 6 million. That was about the time, give or take a thousand years, when the first Agricultural Revolution got underway. With settled agriculture and the domestication of animals, it was possible to support a denser population. There were long periods of stationary growth, that is, no growth, until around the time of Christ, when the world's population numbered around 250 million (Biraben, 2003). The population did not double again until about AD 1600. The annual rate of growth then was a mere 0.04 percent. To be sure, the growth patterns were uneven. The population would grow fairly rapidly for a few years, and this was followed by epidemics or plagues, and the population would then decline in size. Indeed, the size of the world population apparently declined a little between 1300 and 1400 because of the Black Death (see my discussion in Chapter 7). Overall, death rates were very high, and birth rates had to be at least as high if the population was to grow even very slowly.

These stationary conditions of near zero to very low population growth rates continued until the period of around 1650–1700, when the population of the world numbered around 650 million. During these many thousands of years, the world's population was kept small in size by the various **Malthusian checks** I mentioned earlier in Chapter 2. Death rates were high because of the positive checks of plagues, famines, and poor living conditions. Generally, populations had high birth rates to compensate for the high death rates. If the birth rates were not high, the human population would have become extinct.

Population Change since 1650

The world's population grew from around 650 million in 1650 to 1 billion by 1850. It then took less than eighty years to double again in 1927 (Pison and Belloc, 2005). As the Agricultural Revolution resulted in more density, so too did the Industrial Revolution. People began to leave their farms and move to cities where factories and mills were humming. An urban revolution occurred along with the Industrial Revolution. This made it possible for density to increase as well. Figure 12.3 portrays changes in the size of the world population from 1950 to the present, with projections to 2050.

Much of the growth was attributable to lower death rates while birth rates remained high. The improved standards of living eventually resulting from industrialization help to explain the declining death rates. However, death rates rose slightly before they fell.

The onset of the Industrial Revolution was not especially kind to the individuals who joined the urban labor force. Indeed, their situation was a major concern of Karl Marx, who saw this as an attempt by the bourgeoisie to force the proletariat to accept incredibly poor working conditions (Marx and Engels, [1848] 1935). Only later did conditions improve somewhat, and this was accompanied by a lower death rate. With birth rates remaining high, the result was massive population growth. A latent function of that growth was international migration away from the highly populated European countries to the underpopulated Americas and elsewhere (see my discussion in Chapter 9).

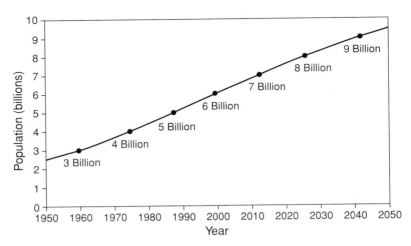

Figure 12.3 World Population, 1950–2050
Source: US Bureau of the Census, International Data Base, June 2011 Update.

The rapid population growth during this period was limited to western Europe. In the other regions of the world, where the Industrial Revolution had not fully taken hold, death rates remained high, as did birth rates. It was only later that death rates began to fall rapidly in the developing regions.

The decline in mortality in the developed nations was later followed by a decline in fertility. By the 1930s, growth rates were coming down. Whereas throughout most of history, until the eighteenth century, population growth was very slow because of high fertility and high mortality, this time population growth slowed down because of low fertility and low mortality.

The political and economic challenges from these demographic shifts in distribution are considerable. Will the massive numbers of poor people in the developing regions rise up against the far fewer rich in the developed nations? Will it be necessary for the rich to increase their contributions to the poor of the world? The lists of questions are endless.

The declines in both fertility and mortality warrant explanations. As I have already noted, the Industrial Revolution eventually created a healthier society. With better transportation, food supplies were improved and famines occurred less frequently. New foods were introduced from the colonies in the Americas and elsewhere. Also, better housing was constructed, and better clothing became available as cotton was plentiful. In the nineteenth century, sanitary behavior began to be practiced by the people, and public-health movements were appearing. Medical improvements did not really contribute too much to declining mortality until the twentieth century (see my more detailed discussion of these changes in Chapter 2).

Death rates remained very high in the developing regions. It was not until after the Second World War that there were significant improvements there in longevity. Then, death rates in many countries fell rapidly. These areas benefited from the knowledge learned in the more advanced nations a decade or two earlier. By then, too, medical knowledge had increased, and the residents were the benefactors of this information.

The decline in fertility is not as easily understood as that for mortality. Note that individual decisions were not as important when it came to lowering mortality. The social system, for the most part, was the major contributing factor. When it came to fertility, however, individual decisions were necessary if the rates were to be lowered. But even those decisions depended on the social situation. As urbanization and industrialization began to occur, the family became less important as an economic unit of production. When most people resided in rural areas, having large families was important. The children, as they grew up, participated in the daily household chores. Having another child was economically feasible since families lived mainly off the land. With the move to the city, impersonal systems like the factory took over the allocation of jobs. Those moving from the farm to the city often found themselves living in tenement houses, often with only one or two bedrooms. It was soon concluded that children who were useful as a cheap supply of labor in farming families were not as useful in industrial working-class urban families. Furthermore, child labor laws were soon passed and formal education became mandatory. Hence, children did not contribute as much to the family economy as they did prior to the initiation of these changes.

Another factor in the process of declining fertility was the fall in infant mortality. Along with overall mortality declines, there was also a decrease in infant deaths. Prior to the Industrial Revolution, families would often have nine, ten, or more children, perhaps subconsciously realizing that only three or four would survive to adulthood. Now, most survived; the solution, thus, was to limit fertility.

Returning to my earlier point, individual decisions had to be made with reference to limiting family size. (I have already discussed birth prevention measures in Chapter 6.) Such decisions were long in the making. For centuries, the culture virtually dictated that women should have as many offspring as possible. Consider how dramatic this shift in sexual behavior was for those couples. It was not at all surprising that it took more than one generation for smaller families to become the norm. This was a major cultural change in familial behavior.

The decline in fertility among people in the developing regions has been slow. With mortality falling swiftly, this slow decline in fertility began in the 1960s and resulted in large increases in the size of the population. This, in turn, led to a growing concern about overpopulation (Connelly, 2008). The fairly esoteric topic of demographic growth took on a new meaning in the United States and elsewhere with the publication in the 1960s of several high-profile books: Frederick Osborn's *This Crowded World* was written in 1960; it was followed in 1967 by William and Paul Paddock's *Famine, 1975*, and in 1968 by Paul R. Ehrlich's best-seller, *The Population Bomb*. These treatises, sometimes referred to as **neo-Malthusian**, "were designed to be alarmist in tone, and Ehrlich and his wife Ann went on to advocate the need for incentives bordering on coercion to induce couples to have fewer children" (Bouvier and Bertrand, 1999: 64; see also Connelly, 2008).

Since then, however, there have been several success stories among the countries of the developing world that were not predicted by the neo-Malthusians. Bangladesh, one of the poorest countries, has seen its TFR fall from 7 births per woman in 1970 to 2.2 births per woman in 2013. Iran's fertility rate declined from 6.4 in 1970 to 1.8 in 2013. Mexico's rate has fallen significantly in the same period, from 6.7 to 2.2. And India, the country that Paul Ehrlich highlighted in *The Population Bomb* as the place where he first began to experience "the feel of overpopulation" (Ehrlich, 1968: 16), dropped its fertility rate from 5.5 in 1970 to 2.4 in 2013. There are numerous other examples of evolving success. Indeed, pretty much the only countries today with high birth rates are in sub-Saharan Africa, but even some of these are beginning to experience fertility declines (PRB, 2014). The alarmist predictions of the neo-Malthusians, for most of the world, were well off the mark.

The *New York Times* recently produced a very informative "retro-report" film, "The Population Bomb?" (note the question mark), about Paul Ehrlich, his book, his doomsday predictions, and today's reality. This short thirteen-minute film may be accessed at: www.nytimes.com/2015/06/01/us/the-unrealized-horrors-of-population-explosion.html?_r=0. I encourage you to view it.

Let me mention here the situation in sub-Saharan Africa. In many African countries, especially in western and eastern Africa, fertility rates remain above 5 births per woman, and above 6 births per woman in some middle African countries, for example, Angola and Chad. But these high rates were even higher in 1970. To illustrate, both Ethiopia's and Ghana's fertility rates were 7 in 1970, but dropped to 4.1 and 4.3, respectively, by 2013. Kenya's was 8.1 in 1970, but declined to 4.3 by 2013 (PRB, 2014). Will the fertility rates in the sub-Saharan African countries all fall to lower levels? Projections by the United Nations (see my discussion below) assume they will. So do I.

THE FUTURE POPULATION OF THE EARTH

Before gazing into the future, allow me to reexamine world population growth of the last few decades. Recent demographic trends can be described without exaggeration as revolutionary, a virtual discontinuity with all of human history. When one realizes that it was not until about 1850 that world population reached the first billion and that it is now at 7.4 billion, it becomes altogether clear that for most of the time that *Homo sapiens* has been on this planet, growth has been infinitesimal. This point was made most clearly in Figure 12.3.

The population projections I now present suggest that such a demographic balance will necessarily take place again in the not-too-distant future as population approaches the ultimate carrying size of the planet.

Note that I have used here and elsewhere in this book the word projection rather than "prediction" or "forecast." Predictions of things to come are best left to seers and psychics. Forecasts are best left to meteorologists. Demographers usually do not make population forecasts or population predictions. They make population projections. A **population projection** refers to the number of people who will comprise the population of an area at some future point in time according to clearly stated demographic assumptions about the demographic processes of fertility, mortality, and migration.

A population projection is intended to answer the question, "What if...?" It need not necessarily be realistic. In fact, population projections are sometimes used to demonstrate the impossibility of maintaining certain rates of growth. For example, Coale (1974) once stated that if the then-current rate of world population growth continued indefinitely, in less than 700 years there would be one person for every square yard of the earth's surface. Coale's calculation was definitely not intended to be a prediction. Rather, it was meant to illustrate rather vividly that the planet cannot maintain such a rate of population growth indefinitely.

Such examples are extreme, yet they demonstrate what demographer Peter Morrison (1977: 12) meant when he wrote that "the purpose of projecting population is not exclusively, or even primarily, to make accurate predictions. Rather, it is to identify and chart the likely effects of influences and contingencies that will determine future population size."

Most projections, however, are intended to be realistic. The assumptions generally reflect what appears to be reasonable at a given point in time. Populations rise and fall because of shifts in fertility, mortality, and migration. Assumptions are thus made about the future levels of such demographic behavior. The person making the assumptions must be clear about the intent of the effort. Are the projections realistic, or are they intended to show the absurdity of the assumptions? Far too many projections are reified. Looking for quick and easy answers, analysts not well versed in demographic research too often ignore the assumptions and only emphasize the projections.

In this chapter, I use world population projections prepared recently by the Population Division of the United Nations (2013d). It is my view that these reflect reasonable assumptions about future demographic behavior. Nevertheless, they are just that, namely, projections that indicate what the population of the world will be according to stated assumptions. In no way should they be seen as predictions, nor should they be considered the final word. The United Nations is continuously revising its assumptions based on the latest data available.

Another issue with projections is the length of time for which they are made. The longer the period of time into the future, the less reliable the projection. Short-term projections are usually grounded in a detailed analysis of current trends. These projections amount to statements of a sort about the near-term future, as long as the underlying trends do not change substantially. Of course, these trends can affect the future, and ultimately falsify themselves, by alerting policymakers to the need for policies to thwart an undesirable future.

Fluctuations have occurred and will continue to occur in the future. The projections that I set forth here extend to the year 2100. Confidence in the first fifty years is far greater than in the latter part of the century.

What do the numbers tell us? The world population was estimated to number 7.2 billion in 2013; it is projected to reach 8.1 billion in 2025, 9.6 billion in 2050, and 10.9 billion in 2100 (United Nations, 2013d).

You may be asking about the assumptions that the UN demographers used to arrive at these figures, and you are correct in asking such a question. Whether it is the United Nations or the US Bureau of the Census making the projections, alternate projections are usually prepared, namely, a high one, a low one, and one in the middle. In this chapter, I am using the middle projection that "assumes a decline of fertility for countries where large families are still prevalent as well as a slight increase of fertility in several countries with fewer than two children per woman on average" (United Nations, 2013d: xv). As for mortality, the middle range projections see gradual improvements in life expectancy, especially among the developing nations. Since I am considering here the projected population numbers for the entire world, there is obviously no need to make assumptions about migration.

I show in Figure 12.4 a world population growth chart through the year 2100 prepared by demographers at the United Nations. You will observe a single line showing the population growth of the world from 1950 to 2010; then four lines are shown from 2010 to 2100, each reflecting the future population of the world from 2010 to 2100, depending mainly

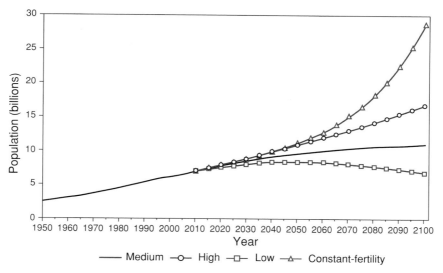

Figure 12.4 Population of the World, 1950–2010, according to Different Projections and Variants
Source: United Nations (2013d: xv).

on assumptions with regard to fertility behavior. I have already described above the assumptions behind the medium-variant projection. The high-variant assumes each woman will have one-half more child than projected under the medium-variant, and the low-variant assumes each woman in the world will have one-half less child than assumed under the medium-variant. The line showing the greatest increase in the world's population is the upper line, reflecting "constant fertility," that is, a continuation to 2100 of the actual levels of fertility in 2010. If the levels of fertility in the countries of the world in 2010 were to be maintained until the year 2100, the population of the world would number around 29 billion people. This is quite different from the population size of the world projected for 2100 under the medium-variant, namely, almost 11 billion.

Frankly, I consider the assumptions governing the medium-variant, especially about fertility, to be a little conservative. I suspect the fertility behavior of the women in the countries of the world between 2010 and 2100 could well be closer to that assumed by the low-variant (see Wattenberg [2004], for more discussion of this point). Yet, by using the medium-variant projections of the UN, no one will ever accuse me of being an alarmist. It is always better to err on the conservative side in matters like population growth projections.

The middle or medium scenario I am using here indicates that world population will continue to grow, but, I repeat, this is a rather conservative projection.

How large can a population grow? Or, to borrow the question from Cohen's (1995) book, How Many People Can the Earth Support? Unfortunately, Cohen never gives a direct answer, but he does identify the variables that must be considered before arriving at one. For example, at what standard of living will the people of the Earth live? Will it be that of the United States, France, or Niger? He states the following: "The human population of the Earth now travels in the zone when a substantial fraction of scholars have estimated upper limits on human population size. These estimates are no better than the present understanding of humankind's cultural, economic, and environmental choices and constraints. Nevertheless, the possibility must be considered seriously that the number of people on the Earth has reached, or will reach within a half century, the maximum number the Earth can support in modes of life that we and our children and their children will choose to want" (Cohen, 1995: 76).

It may seem contradictory to project such momentous increases while the growth rate itself is falling. Three factors account for this apparent anomaly. First, the population itself is expanding. Even though the growth rate is falling, it is based on an ever-growing population. Consider the parallel situation in banking, where one's bank account continues to grow in size despite falling interest rates.

Second, infant and childhood mortality rates have fallen rapidly in many developing countries during the past few decades. The result is a sort of baby boom attributable not to higher fertility, as in the United States, but rather to lower mortality. This baby boom has contributed to a third factor. In any young population, there is a built-in momentum for growth. Looking at the world, and particularly its developing regions, the numbers of young people are enormous, proportionally speaking. Even if these people all decide to lower their fertility, the number of births will increase because there are more and more women of reproductive age who are available to have children. This is called population momentum (see my earlier discussion in Chapter 4).

The conclusion is apparent. Despite recent declines in fertility, population growth is likely in store for the world for the foreseeable future. However, different regions and countries will exhibit different demographic behaviors, resulting in a growing proportion of the world's population residing in the developing areas.

Today, major portions of Malthus' line of reasoning are suspect, particularly his doubts concerning people's ability (and willingness) to practice "moral restraint." His rejection of contraception and abortion as immoral (although the latter view is still held today by some persons and organizations) is clearly not in line with the thinking of a majority of the inhabitants of the world. Yet his concern about a sufficient supply of food for a growing population remains an issue to this very day. I will have more to say on this issue of available resources in Chapter 16.

CONCLUSION

Through most of the human time on Earth, the population has grown very slowly. High birth rates and high death rates prevailed. It was not until about 1650 or so that population growth began to accelerate when death rates began to decline. By the early twentieth century, births had fallen; growth in the developed regions had slowed and have recently reached an almost "no-growth" situation. This has not been the case with developing nations, particularly those in sub-Saharan Africa. There, the death rates did not fall until the twentieth century and birth rates are still fairly high, although there are many examples of lower birth rates in some of these African countries.

The world continues to grow at about 1.2 percent annually. The possibility of a world population between 10 and 11 billion by the end of this century is real. This growth contributes to several problems in many countries: massive malnutrition, pressures on nonrenewable resources, and low standards of living. Stopping growth would not completely solve these problems, but it would make it easier to deal with them.

Eventually, the world's population must stop growing because we inhabit a finite space. Turning once again to Malthus, we can accomplish that goal by high death rates that balance high birth rates, or it may be accomplished by a combination of low birth rates and low death rates. The latter alternative is definitely preferable.

13 Population Change in the United States

INTRODUCTION

The United States is the third most populous country in the world after the two demographic billionaires, China and India. In 2015, the population of the United States numbered 321 million inhabitants, compared with 1.36 billion in China and 1.29 billion in India (PRB, 2015). When the first census was conducted in the United States in 1790, the population size of the country (as then defined geographically) was just under 4 million, which is about the size today of the metropolitan area of Phoenix, Arizona. In 220 years, the United States has increased tremendously in size, from 3.9 million inhabitants in 1790, to just under 309 million in 2010 (Figure 13.1), to more than 321 million in 2015. In this chapter, I trace the patterns of population growth of the United States from colonial times to the present and then examine some projections of the US population for the future.

HISTORY OF POPULATION CHANGE IN THE UNITED STATES

The Precolonial Period

Estimates for the precolonization period of the size of the population in the land now known as the United States are not easy to obtain, and they vary considerably: "There is probably no single figure that can be accepted as the 'best' estimate of the late fifteenth century North American population" (Snipp, 1989: 9). According to Zinn, "The Indian population of [around] 10 million that lived north of Mexico when Columbus came would ultimately be reduced to less than a million. Huge numbers of Indians would die from diseases introduced by the whites. A Dutch traveler in New England wrote in 1656 that 'the Indians ... affirm, that before the arrival of the Christians and before the smallpox broke out amongst them, they were ten times as numerous as they now are, and that their population had been melted down by this disease, whereof nine-tenths of them have died'" (2003: 16).

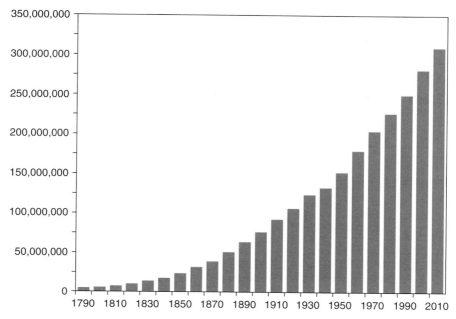

Figure 13.1 US Population, 1790–2010
Source: State of Wyoming Economic Analysis Division (2015) (reprinted with permission of the State of Wyoming).

The number of Native Americans continued to decline over the next centuries and totaled between 125,000 and 150,000 by 1900 (Thornton, 1990: 42). This decline resulted in part from attrition during the continual warfare in which they participated in the defense of their tribal lands, as well as from unusual hardships and, as just noted, from diseases introduced by the European settlers. At the beginning of the twentieth century, "there were so few Indians left in America that it was widely believed that they would eventually disappear" (Snipp, 1989: 23).

For many decades up through the 1950s, the American Indian population hardly grew at all, reaching just over 500,000 in the 1960 census. But by 2013, the number of persons in the United States self-identifying as American Indians or Alaskan Natives was roughly 5.3 million, representing around 2 percent of the US population. This growth from just over 500,000 to well over 5 million is demographically impossible without a massive amount of immigration or without a change in the manner in which the data were collected. It is the latter factor that has been largely responsible for this extraordinary growth.

Beginning in the 1970 decennial census, population counts of the American Indian and Alaskan Native populations have been based on self-identification. The demographer Jeffrey Passel has noted that "persons answering the census choose their response to the race question. A person choosing the American Indian racial response did not have to provide any substantiation or documentation of this identification. There was no requirement that an 'American Indian' be enrolled as a member of a recognized tribe or that any tribal group recognize the respondent as a member, and there was no 'blood quantum' requirement. This method of identification differs from that of previous censuses, in which a person's racial identification tended to be assigned by an enumerator, usually based on observation, local knowledge, or custom" (Passel, 1996: 80).

Demographers have undertaken considerable research on the phenomenal growth since 1970 of the American Indian population (Passel, 1976, 1996; Eschbach, 1993; Passel and Berman, 1986; Snipp, 1989). They have shown that at least through the 1990s, the dramatic growth of the American Indian population "was achieved through changing patterns of racial self-identification on the part of people with only partial or distant American Indian ancestry, coupled with relatively high fertility and improving mortality" (Passel, 1996: 79).

Another issue responsible for the growth of the American Indian population in recent decades is a recent change in definition that recognized Mexican, Central American, and other Latin American backgrounds/tribes as part of the American Indian population. This has led to increasing the number of American Indians, and has also increased the percentage of the Indian population that is Hispanic (pers. comm. between author and Jeffrey Passel, August 11, 2015).

Of the over 5.3 million persons today identifying themselves as American Indians or Alaskan Natives, nearly one-half are multiracial, that is, they selected two or more races (see my discussion in Chapter 11 of the multirace option on the census and ACS questionnaires). Almost two-thirds of the multiracial American Indians/Alaskan Natives selected "white" as their second race; 12 percent selected "black"; and 10 percent selected both "white" and "black" (Norris, Vines, and Hoeffel, 2012). The multiracial option when answering the census questionnaire also contributed to the increase in the population of American Indians between 2000 and 2010.

The Colonial Period, 1607–1790

On May 14, 2007, the town of Jamestown, Virginia, celebrated the 400th anniversary of its first settlement. At its founding in 1607, Jamestown had just over a hundred colonists. By 1610, Virginia counted 350 settlers. The non-Native American population of the colonies numbered more than 2,000 in 1620 and likely reached 50,000 by 1650. By 1790, when the first census of the United States was taken, almost 4 million people were enumerated. The eightyfold increase from 1650 to 1790 is surely one of the

Figure 13.2 The Bottom Page of the "1790 Census Act"
Source: US Bureau of the Census (2015a).

most spectacular examples of population growth in human history (Weller and Bouvier, 1981: 52–53).

Immigration was the main contributor to growth in the decades immediately following settlement. Later in the colonial period, natural increase became as important as, if not more important than, immigration. The pattern of population growth in that era follows closely the phases of the demographic equation. At the end of the eighteenth century, the CBR was estimated at about 55 per 1,000 and the CDR at about 25 per 1,000 (Thompson and Whelpton, 1933). This rate of growth alone would increase the population by 3 percent annually. Massive immigration compounded this growth.

The first population census in the United States was conducted in 1790; the official census day was August 1. The "1790 Census Act" authorizing the first census was signed into law on March 1, 1790. I show in Figure 13.2 the bottom page of the "1790 Census Act" with the names of George Washington, the President of the United States, and John Adams, the Vice-President of the United States and President of the Senate, among others. The marshals of the US Judicial Districts were responsible for conducting the census. They were required to visit every household, and ensure that completed census schedules were posted in "two of the most public places within [each jurisdiction], there to remain for the inspection of all concerned . . . " and that "the aggregate amount of each description of persons" for every district be transmitted to the president (US Bureau of the Census, 2015a: 1).

As I noted at the start of this chapter, the population of the United States was just under 4 million at the time of the first census in 1790. However, the census count included only the populations of the original thirteen states, along with the districts of Kentucky, Maine, and Vermont, as well as the so-called Southwest Territory, that is, what is now Tennessee (Gauthier, 2002: 5). The actual census questionnaire was quite short. I reported in Chapter 3 that the first census counted people only according to whether they were free white males aged 16 years and older, free white males younger than 16 years of age, free white females, slaves, and "other" persons. Most of the Native American population was not included in the enumeration.

About 80 percent of those counted were white. Most were either English or Scots-Irish; others came from Holland, Sweden, Spain, and France. The majority of the remaining 20 percent of the population was black. Most were slaves who had been brought involuntarily to the United States from Africa. Their forced migration began slowly in the seventeenth century and increased in the eighteenth and early nineteenth centuries. The settlement of blacks was concentrated in the South (Taeuber and Taeuber, 1971: 5).

The Nineteenth Century

The United States grew rapidly between 1790 and 1860. The US population numbered 3.9 million in 1790, 5.3 million in 1800, 12.9 million in 1830, and 31.4 million in 1860. The size of the population increased approximately 30 percent per decade from 1790 to 1860, which was amazing considering that the growth rate in Europe at the same time was less than half as much. The numbers of the US population more than quadrupled between 1800 and 1850. The combination of high levels of immigration and a high rate of natural increase explains this phenomenal growth in just half a century. For example, the TFR in 1800 was more than 7.0 and dropped only to 5.4 by 1850 (US Bureau of the Census, 1975).

I just mentioned that in addition to high fertility, the other component of this population increase was immigration (Hughes and Cain, 2002). Before 1830, the contribution of immigration to overall population growth in the United States was small. Between 1821 and 1825, for example, the average number of immigrants each year totaled only about 8,000. This number increased to almost 21,000 between 1826 and 1830. From 1841 to 1845, immigrants to the United States each year numbered more than 86,000. In the eight years between 1850 and 1857, the number of immigrants was 2.2 million. In sum, between 1790 and 1860, the total number of immigrants to the United States was almost 5 million, and most of these were from Europe (Taeuber and Taeuber, 1958).

Of course, I need also mention that the country grew geographically as well as demographically. The land area of the United States, according to the first census, comprised only 889,000 square miles. The Louisiana Purchase in 1803 nearly doubled the land area. The accession of Florida in 1819 added still more land. Between 1840 and 1850, the territory of the United States was increased by two-thirds through the annexation of Texas in 1845, and Oregon in 1846, as well as the cession by Mexico in 1848 (Taeuber and Taeuber, 1958). The addition of these new states brought with them vast increases in the number of people.

Most of the population growth between 1800 and 1850 occurred on the Atlantic seaboard. Yet, despite the geographic growth to encompass the forty-eight contiguous states, the population density (i.e., the number of persons per unit of land) actually grew from 6.1 persons per square mile in 1800 to 7.9 persons per square mile in 1850. The newly acquired western part of the United States remained relatively underpopulated, except for the Native Americans, who were not counted systematically in the decennial censuses until 1890. After 1850, the rate of population growth slowed down somewhat, although the population still managed to triple in size by 1900 when the 1900 census counted about 76 million inhabitants (Figure 13.1). By then, there were 25.6 persons per square mile.

The first major slowdown in the population growth rate in the United States started during the Civil War years in the 1860s. Compared with a 32–36 percent increase in each decade between 1790 and 1860, the increase from 1860 to 1890 was around 26–27 percent per decade.

Despite this decline in the rate of population growth, the Industrial Revolution had a major impact on the American population during the second half of the nineteenth century. Urbanization intensified, and the CBRs and CDRs both fell. By 1900, the CBR was 32.2 and the CDR was 17.2. Here again we see the demographic transition in action.

By the beginning of the twentieth century, almost 40 percent of the people lived in urban areas, compared with only 15 percent in 1850. The nation was also becoming increasingly heterogeneous. Until the middle of the nineteenth century, most of the population was of white Anglo-Saxon ancestry. These people, along with the African Americans and the Native Americans, comprised the bulk of the nation's population. However, during the second half of the century, new waves of immigration brought people from southern Europe and Asia, particularly China and Japan. By 1900, the nation could no longer be classified as predominantly white Anglo-Saxon and Protestant (WASP).

The African American population increased from around 1 million in 1800 to 8.8 million in 1900. Yet the percentage of the total population that was African American fell from almost 19 percent to 12 percent during the period. One reason for the decline was that the mortality rate for African Americans was higher than that for whites. Another reason was that large numbers of whites immigrated to the United States from Europe, while few blacks came from Africa, particularly after the slave trade was abolished in 1808.

The Twentieth Century

I noted above that the first major decline in the population growth rate of the United States occurred during and after the years of the Civil War. The second decline occurred between 1890 and 1910, when the rate of population growth dropped to about 20 percent per decade. The third major decline was in the decade between 1910 and 1920, when the growth rate dropped to about 15 percent, largely due to the First World War. During the war years, immigrant flows were interrupted, fertility rates declined, and death rates rose. The increase in death rates was also due to the influenza epidemic of 1918–1919, a topic I have already discussed in Chapter 7. Although there was a little rebound in the next decade, the population growth rate in the 1930s dropped to a new record low of 7.2 percent, which was less than half of the lowest decennial increase in earlier decades (Taeuber and Taeuber, 1958). This very low rate of increase resulted mainly from the Great Depression of the 1930s, which caused a sharp drop in births (Kahn, 1974). The decline of the 1930s did not continue into the 1940s and 1950s, however. The baby boom after the Second World War ended in the 1960s, and the population growth rate began to decline, dropping to almost 10 percent in the 1980s.

Although the size of the US population increased more than fourfold in the next 110 years, from 76 million in 1900 to almost 309 million in 2010 (Figure 13.1), the rate of population growth slowed slightly. The population merely doubled between 1900 (76 million) and 1950 (151 million).

Two demographic events greatly affected the growth of the population. First, the baby boom began in 1946. Fertility rates rose to levels unanticipated in any industrialized nation. In the late 1950s, at the height of the baby boom era, the TFR reached its peak of more than 3.7 children per woman. This high fertility following the Second World War was promoted by the need to compensate for population losses during the war, as well as to rehabilitate the economy and production. The demographic effects were startling. About 30 million people were added to the population between 1950 and 1960, compared with only 19 million during the 1940s.

The second demographic surprise, the **baby bust**, came in the late 1960s and early 1970s when fertility declined sharply. Many factors came together to influence the decline, such as increases in living expenses, the extension of education, increases in voluntary childlessness, and more women employed in the labor force. Cheap and easily accessible contraceptives and abortions, permitting greater control over births, were an added factor. In 1972, the country's TFR dropped for the first time below the replacement level of 2.1. Total population increase in 1972 was only 0.7 percent, almost half the average annual increase during the 1960s (Kahn, 1974). Fertility in the United States kept declining, although not as rapidly as in earlier years. Since 1990, the TFR each year has been at around 2.1, some years slightly below and other years slightly above.

People continued to settle in and around cities during the first half of the century. By the time of the Second World War, about two-thirds of the population lived in urban areas, compared with only 40 percent in 1900. Immigration had dwindled after the First World War, slowing the pace of heterogeneity. However, as I have already mentioned in Chapter 9, immigration soared after the Second World War, reaching its largest levels ever. Once again, heterogeneity became a part of American society.

THE US POPULATION: TODAY AND TOMORROW

The 2010 census counted more than 309 million residents in the United States. This absolute numerical increase between 2000 and 2010 of 27.3 million people was less than the 32.7 million increase in population size between 1990 and 2000.

In 2015, the estimated US population was 321 million. More than 83 percent of the population resided in one of the nation's 366 metropolitan areas, and 10 percent in one of the country's 576 micropolitan areas. Although the population living in metropolitan areas, on average, has grown more rapidly than the populations residing in micropolitan areas and in areas neither metropolitan nor micropolitan (Mackun and Wilson, 2011), the inner cities of many of the larger metropolitan areas have been losing population. I will cover these issues in greater detail in the next chapter on population distribution.

Two important phenomena warrant noting here. First, heterogeneity has been on the increase. According to the 2010 census, the NH-white (i.e., Anglo) population represented less than 64 percent of the nation's population – the lowest ever recorded. African Americans comprised 13 percent and Hispanics over 16 percent (Humes, Jones, and Ramirez, 2011). Early in 2003, the Hispanic percentage became larger than that of African Americans, so that Hispanics are now the nation's largest minority. I have covered these issues already in Chapter 11.

Second, the United States has become an older population. In 2010, more than 40 million elderly (defined as anyone aged 65 and older) were enumerated. This is by far the largest number of elders ever recorded in the United States. As with growing heterogeneity, aging in America is just beginning.

The US Bureau of the Census prepares projections of the nation's population every few years. I will now discuss the 2014–2060 projections that were developed in 2015 (Colby and Ortman, 2015). I noted in earlier chapters that a population projection is a systematic calculation of the future population size of an area given certain assumptions about fertility, mortality, and migration. Thus, I will first focus on the assumptions generating the 2014–2060 projections. "Total fertility rates were projected to 2060 by assuming a linear convergence in the year 2100 of the ... fertility rates of all

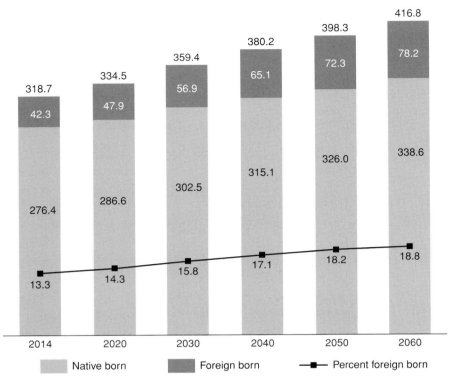

Figure 13.3 US Population by Nativity, 2014–2060 (population in millions)
Source: Colby and Ortman (2015).

five nativity, race, and Hispanic groups to ... a value of 1.86" (US Bureau of the Census, 2014a: 5). Regarding mortality, the projections are based on the assumption that by 2060, life expectancy at birth will be 84.6 for NH-white and Hispanic males and 81 for black males, and 87.5 for NH-white and Hispanic females and 85 for black females. With regard to net international migration, Hispanic levels are assumed to be the highest, at about the mid-500,000 for each year through 2060, with Asian levels the next highest, increasing to 400,000 in 2043 and remaining at that level until 2060. NH-white levels are projected to grow from 224,000 in 2014 to 277,000 in 2060. Black levels are assumed to rise from 109,000 in 2014 to 246,000 in 2060 (US Bureau of the Census, 2014a).

Figure 13.3 illustrates the projected population of the United States up to 2060. There are projected then to be well over 416 million people living in the country, which is an increase of just under 100 million compared with the size of the population in 2014. The foreign-born population of the country is projected to increase from 42.3 million in 2014 to 78.2 million in 2016, an increase from 13.3 percent of the population in 2014 to

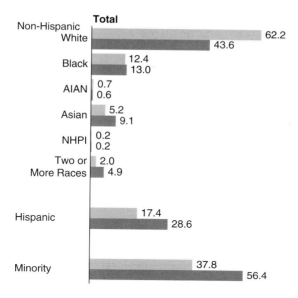

Legend: upper bar = 2014
         Lower bar = 2060

Figure 13.4 Percentage Distribution of the US Population by Race and Hispanic Origin, 2014 and 2060
Source: Colby and Ortman (2015).

18.8 percent in 2060. The projected foreign-born percentage of 18.8 percent would be the highest ever for the United States.

Figure 13.4 shows the population of the United States by race and ethnicity in 2014 and projected to 2060. By 2060, the United States is expected to be more racially and ethnically diverse. The NH-white proportion of the US population, the "majority" race/ethnic group in 2014 in the United States at 62.2 percent, and once well over 80 percent of the US total population, is projected to fall gradually to 44 percent of the population by 2060. "The point at which the non-Hispanic White population will comprise less than 50 percent of the nation's total population (is the point at which the country) … becomes a majority-minority nation" (Colby and Ortman, 2015: 9); this is projected to occur in 2044. At that time, no race/ethnic group in the United States will have a majority share of the population, and the country will have become a "plurality of racial and ethnic groups" (Colby and Ortman, 2015: 9).

The Asian share will also increase, from over 5 percent in 2014 to over 9 percent by 2060. The African American population, while increasing numerically, will see its percentage share grow very little – from 12.4 percent to 13 percent. Persons identifying themselves with two or more races will increase from 2 percent in 2014 to nearly 5 percent by 2060. The Hispanic population is projected to grow from 55 million (17.4 percent of the total) in 2014 to 119 million (28.6 percent) in 2060. The minority population of the United States, that is, all race/ethnic groups except for NH-whites, is projected to comprise 56.4 percent of the total population in 2060. The nation can thus expect major shifts in its population composition between now and 2060.

The aging of America is another major challenge for today and for the future. In 2014, there were over 46 million elderly in the United States, representing nearly 15 percent of the population. By 2030, there are projected to be over 74 million elderly (around 21 percent of the population). By 2060, the projected number of elderly will be over 98 million (almost 24 percent of the population). By 2060, almost one in four inhabitants of the United States is projected to be 65 years of age or older. Between 2014 and 2060, the total US population is projected to increase by almost 31 percent, whereas the elderly population is expected to increase by over 112 percent.

What is causing this enormous growth in the numbers of the elderly? Life expectancy among older citizens is increasing; that is, more people are living longer. More important is the effect of the baby boom. Those babies born during its peak years, between 1950 and 1960, will be reaching retirement age in about 2020–2030. The huge baby boom cohort of the population that has "haunted" the United States since the late 1940s remains with us and will continue to be with us for some time to come, culminating in, as these data show, a gigantic **senior boom**.

The rather dramatic changes that I have noted are the result of variations in demographic behavior. Indeed, any change in the basic demographic processes will affect population size as well as population composition. There have been significant changes in fertility and mortality, and these have contributed to the size and composition of the nation. I now consider some of these changes.

FERTILITY

Fertility was high during the colonial period. Women averaged eight to ten births, resulting in a CBR of about 55 per 1,000. Fertility then began to decline slowly. By 1850, when the CBR was 44, women were averaging 5.5 live births. In 1900, the CBR was around 30 and the TFR was 3.6. This drop in fertility continued until after the Great Depression in the 1930s. In 1937, the CBR was 17 and the TFR was 2.2. This change in fertility mostly mirrors the DTT model I have already discussed in Chapter 2 and elsewhere in this book.

The birth rate began to increase during the mid-1940s. The period after the Second World War was characterized by large increases in fertility; as was to be expected. Historically, fertility has always increased at the conclusion of a war during demobilization as men return home and renew the process of family formation that was interrupted during wartime. However, the fertility rate was not expected to remain high for so long a period. Instead of dropping just a few years after the war ended, fertility climbed steadily for more than a decade. The CBR of 25 in 1957 was the highest recorded in the United States since the 1920s. The TFR in 1957 was 3.7, a figure 60 percent higher than the rate in 1940. What caused this unexpected baby boom?

It can be partially explained by the "catching up" of veterans after the Second World War. It can be partially explained by the end of the severe economic conditions during the 1930s. But other factors were also at work. Weller and Bouvier (1981: 57) have suggested the following factors as being instrumental: (1) the proportion of women in their childbearing years was greater than normal, as a result of the high fertility rates of the 1920s relative to that of the 1930s; (2) the percentage of women who remained single dropped significantly during this period; (3) voluntary childlessness declined to a new low; (4) the three- or four-child family became the norm, as people moved to the suburbs and had more space, time, and money to raise children; (5) the prosperous postwar economic situation encouraged parents to have an extra child; and (6) the average age at marriage decreased, and people began having their children sooner after marriage and closer together.

Together, all these factors contributed to the baby boom. The people born in that period have represented and will continue to represent a bulge in the age and sex composition of the nation's population throughout their lives. This will be happening again as soon as they become the senior boom (Carlson, 2008).

Fertility fell rapidly after the baby boom. By 1961, the CBR was 24; by 1968, it was 18. By the 1970s, the United States was experiencing a baby bust. The CBR reached a new low of 15 in 1975. The TFR also fell spectacularly from its high level of 3.7 in 1957. By 1968, it had fallen to 2.5 and reached 2.1 in 1972. It fell even more to 2.0 in 1972. Since then, it has hovered around 2.1 and 2.2, occasionally dropping below 2.0.

The rapid shift in behavior from the baby-boom period to the baby-bust period was amazing. Admittedly, fertility could not stay high. Sooner or later, it was bound to fall. However, it took only a short time to accomplish this shift. What are some of the causes of such a change in behavior?

Perhaps the unsettled economic conditions that began in the late 1960s were a factor that led people to postpone marriage or childbearing. Perhaps people felt that they could not afford another baby. Morgan and Hagewen (2005: 233–234) have noted that "the factors include 'structural' changes in the way we live and work that make children costly (in economic terms and in terms of foregone opportunities). Secular forces also include ideologies of self-actualization and individualism that could become even more powerful and pervasive antinatalist ideologies." In a word, the declines in fertility that occurred in the United States, Europe, and Japan may be explained by "modernity."

Predicting the future course of fertility is difficult, if not impossible. Norms could change; economic booms could occur. Conversely, it is quite likely that we will continue our current pattern of low fertility, and that the two-child (or even smaller) family norm will be sustained as modernity becomes ever more meaningful in the twenty-first century. I discussed some of these issues in Chapter 2 in the context of what demographers refer to as "the second demographic transition."

MORTALITY

Death data for the early years of the United States are scant at best. Nonetheless, Irene and Conrad Taeuber (1971: 495) have written that "the mortality of the early American population was low in comparison with that in many areas of the world at that time." It is estimated that the CDR averaged about 25 per 1,000 between 1800 and 1820. From that high level, the rate dropped quite steadily, and by 1900 it was 17. Newly born Americans could expect to live on average for about 47 years. In 1940, the CDR was 11, and it dropped even more to 9 in 1980 (Table 13.1). A better measure of mortality is life expectancy. When I was born in 1940, a newborn male could expect to live, on average, 60.8 years, and a newborn female, 65.2 years. In 1950, the life expectancies increased to 65.6 years and 71.1 years, respectively. And as I show in Table 13.1, life expectancy has continued to increase. The latest data (for 2013) indicate that men can expect to live 76 years from their birth, and women 81 years. Yes, it is true: women live longer than men! I have already discussed in Chapter 10 the main reasons for the female advantage.

Some molecular biologists are convinced that we are on the verge of major new discoveries that will increase life expectancy to more than a hundred years in the not-too-distant future, and this has been a topic of discussion for many years (Endres, 1975). No one can say for certain that this will not occur. Some argue it will not. First, there is little evidence that dramatic improvements in disease elimination will come to pass. Cases of heart disease and cancer remain high, and we now have the tragedy of AIDS

Table 13.1 Mortality in the United States, 1940–2013

| Year | CDR | Life expectancy at birth | |
		Male	Female
2013	8.0	76.0	81.0
2000	8.5	74.3	79.7
1990	8.6	71.8	79.8
1980	8.8	70.0	77.4
1970	9.5	67.1	74.7
1960	9.5	66.6	73.1
1950	9.6	65.6	71.1
1940	10.8	60.8	65.2

Sources: NCHS (2001, 2002); PRB (2014).

to consider. Second, the demographic effects of the elimination of a specific disease will be rather small. For example, the noted demographer Nathan Keyfitz (1977b: 411–418), estimated that totally eliminating cancer deaths would increase life expectancy at birth by just 3 percent. This is because deaths from other causes would increase, and the major causes of death are clustered largely in the same age groups. I discussed this already in Chapter 7.

INTERNATIONAL MIGRATION

Admittedly, there is a lot of guesswork and conjecturing involved when examining data on international migration. The US Citizenship and Immigration Services (USCIS), formerly the Immigration and Naturalization Service (INS), did not begin gathering immigration data until a few decades into the 1800s. These data revealed nothing about undocumented immigration because for all practical purposes, there was no undocumented immigration at that time; there were not even any immigration laws in existence then. Moreover, there are few reliable estimates about emigration, that is, the number of people leaving the United States to live elsewhere.

Around 80 million people are believed to have immigrated to the United States since its independence; three-quarters of them remained. We do know that between 1819 and 1850, about 2.5 million people moved to the United States. These newcomers came mostly from England, Ireland, and Germany. Between 1850 and 1900, there were about 17 million more immigrants. By 1890, the emphasis had shifted from northern and western

Europe to southern and eastern Europe, particularly Italy, Poland, and Greece. It was at that time, too, that immigration from Asia, especially from China and Japan, began to rise. Tensions arose between the older immigrants (mostly WASPs) and these newer immigrants, who were less likely to speak English and were more likely to be Catholic or Jewish rather than Protestant.

The volume of immigration reached what was a historic peak in the first decade of the twentieth century. A total of 6.3 million immigrants came to the United States between 1900 and 1910. Immigration then dropped sharply, in part because of the First World War and the Great Depression of the 1930s. Only 2.5 million came in the 1910–1920 decade. Just about 100,000 came during the 1930s. In some years, more people left the United States than came in (Taeuber and Taeuber, 1971: 97).

After the Great Depression and the Second World War, immigration increased dramatically to levels not seen previously: 3 million came during the 1950s, 4 million during the 1960s, and almost 5 million in the 1970s. During the 1990s and to this day, more than 1 million immigrants enter the United States almost every year. "The United States received a historical high of over 1 million legal immigrants annually in the 2000s ... " (Iceland, 2014: 112). Again, there has been a shift in the sending countries. Now, a large majority of all immigrants come from either Latin America or Asia. The largest-sending country, by far, has been Mexico, although the streams from Mexico have dropped in size in recent years. Indeed according to recent data from the 2013 ACS, there were more immigrants to the United States in 2013 from China and India than from Mexico. Specifically, "China was the top sending country with 147,000, followed by India with 129,000, and Mexico with 125,000" (Jensen, 2015). The 125,000 Mexican immigrants to the United States in 2013 was a considerable reduction from the 400,000 Mexican immigrants in 2000 (see Figure 13.5).

Undocumented (also referred to as unauthorized or irregular) immigration movements, especially across the country's southern border with Mexico, are significant, although it is difficult to be precise about the numbers. There were as many as 11.2 million undocumented immigrants residing in the United States in 2012, with 5.9 hailing from Mexico (Passel and Cohn, 2014).

Future levels of immigration are difficult to forecast. The levels of immigration into the United States depend on economic conditions in the sending country, as well as those in the United States. More importantly, they depend to a considerable extent on legislation passed by Congress determining the number of immigrants who will be allowed to enter in any given year and the countries from which these immigrants may come.

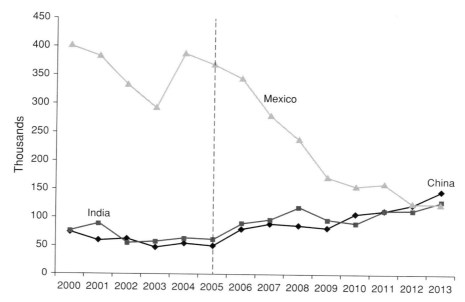

Figure 13.5 Foreign-Born Population Whose Residence One Year Ago was Abroad by Selected Places of Birth, 2000–2013
Note: The ACS did not include the group quarters population until 2006. The time series from 2000 to 2005 represents immigration for the household population, while the time series from 2006 to 2013 represents immigration for the resident population.
Source: Jensen (2015).

SUMMARY

Since the first census was taken in 1790, the population of the United States has increased from just below 4 million to more than 308 million in 2010 (Figure 13.1). The proportion that is urban has grown from 5 percent to well over 75 percent. The US population has aged during the years and will continue to do so in future decades. The population is increasingly heterogeneous and is projected to become even more heterogeneous in future years. The twenty-first century will be an era of major shifts. Americans need to be aware of these changes and be prepared to adapt to them.

Birth rates and death rates fell steadily during the nineteenth and twentieth centuries. The death rate is unlikely to fall too much more; the birth rate is another story. As I have shown, it has fluctuated wildly during the twentieth century, highlighted by the baby boom and the baby bust. Currently, the TFR is hovering at around 2.1, in some years slightly above, in some years slightly below. Although the United States has the highest fertility rate of all the developed countries in the world, the population is just barely replacing itself through "natural increase."

The population of the United States will continue to grow during the twenty-first century, but likely at rates below those of the 1950s and 1960s. How large the population will be in 2100 depends on the demographic behavior not only of Americans born in the United States, but also of immigrants coming to the country.

14 Population Distribution

Whether looking at the planet Earth, Africa, or the United States, it is clear that the population is far from being equally distributed. The distinguished demographer Mark Fossett has written that "structured patterns in spatial distribution are evident from the highest levels of macrospatial scale...to 'fine-grained' patterns in metropolitan areas...and nonmetropolitan hinterlands" (2005: 479).

Most know that China's population is more than 1.3 billion, and that the population of the United States is around 321 million. However, many may not be aware that China and the United States are very close in geographic size. China has 9.6 million km^2 of surface area compared with the United States with 9.8 million km^2. But the populations in both countries are not distributed randomly. Most of the people in both countries live in the eastern regions. However, the distribution in China is far more concentrated in the eastern half of the country, where 90 percent of the population resides. A night-time satellite map for the United States (Figure 14.1) shows that much more than 10 percent of the US population resides in the western half of the country, unlike the situation in China.

In some countries, people are more likely to be rural than urban dwellers. Generally, however, there is an urbanization movement throughout the world: "Without question, the dominant feature of spatial distribution in the United States and other developed countries is the concentration of population in densely settled urban areas" (Fossett, 2005: 479). For that matter, the way in which cities have evolved is a quite interesting phenomenon. In this chapter, I examine how the inhabitants of the world are distributed, and how most of us have become **city** dwellers rather than cave dwellers, as was the case thousands of years ago.

Figure 14.1 Night-time Satellite Map of the United States
Source: National Aeronautics and Space Administration, available at: http://geology
.com/articles/satellite-photo-earth-at-night.shtml, last accessed June 15, 2015.

DISTRIBUTION OF THE POPULATION OF THE WORLD

Only about one-third of the Earth's land is permanently inhabited. Areas
such as the Arctic and the Antarctic, as well as the vast deserts such as the
Sahara, have very few people. The situation is similar where rugged mountains make it almost impossible for humans to survive. The geographic
distribution of the global population is shown in Table 14.1. South Asia
(mainly India) and east Asia (mainly China) are the most populated of the
world regions, and Oceania (primarily Australia) is the least.

Today, five countries have populations that exceed 200 million, and
they are led by China and India. Table 14.2 lists the top ten countries by
current population size (as of 2014), and projected to 2050.

Back in 1930, Great Britain, France, Germany, and Italy were among
the ten largest nations in the world. Changes that have occurred in past
decades reflect the rapid growth in developing nations and the slow and
even declining growth in many of the developed nations. Peering into the
future, Table 14.2 informs us that by 2050, India will likely have surpassed
China as the most populated nation in the world, and this will mainly be the
result of the lower fertility of the Chinese and the fact that India's current
RNI is three times China's, that is, 1.5 percent versus 0.5 percent (PRB,
2014). Actually, this crossover when India will have the largest population
in the world will probably occur around the year 2025.

Note also the two countries projected to be newcomers to the list of the
ten most populated countries in 2050: Congo (i.e., the Democratic Republic
of the Congo, formerly Zaire) and Ethiopia will replace Japan and Russia.

Table 14.1 Distribution of the World's Population by Major Area and Region, 2014	Estimated midyear population (millions)
World	7,238
Africa	1,136
North Africa	217
western Africa	339
eastern Africa	378
middle Africa	142
southern Africa	61
Americas	972
North America	353
Central America	165
Caribbean	43
South America	410
Asia	4,351
western Asia	255
central Asia	67
south Asia	1,806
southeast Asia	621
east Asia	1,601
Europe	741
western Europe	190
northern Europe	102
eastern Europe	294
southern Europe	154
Oceania	39

Source: PRB (2014).

Again, their entry into the top ten is a reflection of the major population increases projected for the African continent and the very low fertility rates in most of the developed nations.

Earlier, I noted that China and the United States are quite similar in areal size, although the former is four times larger in population. Thus, regional or national population figures do not fully take into account differences in the size of the areas. A better descriptive measure that demographers use is **population density**, that is, the number of persons per square mile (or square kilometer; a mile equals about 1.6 kilometers).

The world's population density in 2014 was 53 persons per square kilometer. The density of the United States was 33, and China's was 143. Countries with densities of between 1,000 and 2,000 persons per square

Table 14.2 The World's Ten Most Populous Countries, 2014 and 2050			
2014		**2050**	
Country	Population (millions)	Country	Population (millions)
China	1,364	India	1,657
India	1,296	China	1,312
United States	318	Nigeria	397
Indonesia	252	United States	395
Brazil	203	Indonesia	365
Pakistan	194	Pakistan	348
Nigeria	178	Brazil	226
Bangladesh	159	Bangladesh	202
Russia	144	Congo, Dem. Rep.	194
Japan	127	Ethiopia	165

Source: PRB (2014).

kilometer include Bahrain at 1,901, Malta at 1,351, the Maldives at 1,241, and Bangladesh at 1,101. Countries with densities higher than 2,000 persons per square kilometer are usually city-states, such as Monaco at 37,000 and Singapore at 8,034.

Western Europe is much more densely settled than western Asia, although the latter population has more people (see Table 14.1); and east Asia is the most densely settled, and the most populated, of all the regions in the world. Of course, considerable variation in population density exists among countries in the same region, and even greater differences exist within any particular country. In the United States, vast portions of the Mountain states are sparsely inhabited compared with the Northeast and parts of the West Coast (Figure 14.2).

The measure of population density I have been using is a crude measure because it divides the number of persons in the population by the number of square kilometers (or miles) of territory in the country or area. An alternative, and perhaps a more meaningful and accurate, measure uses the amount of arable land area as the denominator. One such measure is **physiological density**; it is calculated by dividing the number of persons in the country by the country's quantity of arable land (in square kilometers or miles) (Fellmann, Getis, and Getis, 1999: 125; Plane, 2004: 96).

I will illustrate this concept with data for the countries of Bangladesh and Japan. Bangladesh had a population density in 2014 of 1,101 persons per square kilometer of land, versus Japan's 336, indicating that Bangladesh

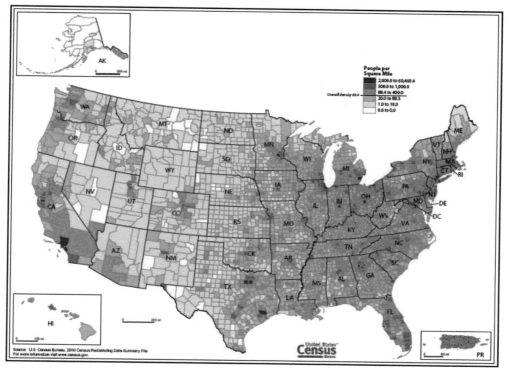

Figure 14.2 Population Density by County or County Equivalent, 2010
Source: US Bureau of the Census, available at: www2.census.gov/geo/pdfs/maps-data/
maps/thematic/us_popdensity_2010map.pdf, last accessed June 15, 2015.

was three times more densely populated than Japan. However, since land in Bangladesh is much more devoted to agricultural activity than is the case in highly urbanized Japan, Japan's physiological density is 2,136 persons per square kilometer of arable land, versus 2,924 for Bangladesh. The difference between the two countries in physiological density is nowhere near as striking as the difference between the countries in the conventional measure of population density. The United States had a physiological density value in 2014 of 193 persons per square kilometer of arable land.

Many factors influence the distribution of the population, including geographic factors, such as climate, terrain and soils, and natural resources; economic, social, and political factors, such as the type of economic activity and the form of social organization; and demographic factors, mainly the rates of population change due to the three processes of fertility, mortality, and migration. These factors continue to contribute to the distribution of the world's population, some more than others. In the sections that follow, some of these factors are considered and their impacts addressed.

RESIDENTIAL DISTRIBUTION AND URBANIZATION

When looking at population distribution, whether for the world or for the United States, it is customary for demographers to examine the percentages of the populations living in rural and urban areas. More than simple numbers are involved here. The economy of rural areas tends to be overwhelmingly agricultural. The economy of **urban areas** tends to be diversified and nonagricultural. Sociologists have long pointed out that lifestyles differ in rural and **urban places**. For example, Émile Durkheim ([1893] 1984) labeled the lifestyles as "mechanical" and "organic," that is, in rural areas, behavior and relationships more or less follow mechanical rules and approaches; roles are not complex and are few in number. In contrast, in urban areas the roles are many, and there is a division of labor leading to an "organic" lifestyle, that is, one with increasing complexities and differences.

Typically, there are also sharp demographic differences between rural and urban areas. For example, fertility has usually been higher in rural than in urban areas, and educational attainment has been lower. But in industrialized nations, many of these differences have been reduced, largely through the pervasiveness of modern media, namely, radio, TV, the Internet, cell phones, and other forms of social media. As a result of these means of rapid communication, distinctions between rural and urban areas have often become blurred. The differences, however, are still apparent in the developing nations of the world.

Throughout most of history, humans have been rural dwellers. Even after the Industrial Revolution, many people were still "living on the farm." They had simply stopped wandering in search of food and shelter. It was really not until the Industrial Revolution that true urbanization began to occur, especially in the countries of western Europe and their colonies. True, there were exceptions, such as the ancient cities of Chang'an (in China, now known as Xi'an), Rome, Athens, and several others. These housed governments and religious headquarters, but were not urban in the modern meaning of the word. Thus, large-scale **urbanization** – or changes in the proportion of the population that dwells in cities – is a modern development. It should not be confused with **urbanism**, which is a reflection of lifestyle and is a sociological, not a demographic, term.

China is the country with the longest urban tradition of any country in the world. Cities made their first appearance in China more than 2,000 years ago. By AD 100, the city of Luoyang had reached a population size of 650,000, a number equal at the time to that of Rome, another **metropolis** (United Nations, 1980: 6). Ancient Chang'an (the present city of Xi'an, the capital of Shaanxi Province) attained a population size of 1 million residents in AD 700, the first million-plus city on record in the whole of Asia (Chandler and Fox, 1974: 291). Indeed, between 600 and 900, no capital in the Western world could compete with Chang'an "in size and grandeur" (Fairbank and Goldman, 2006: 78). For most of the 1,000 years between 800 and 1800, China was unsurpassed by any country in the world in both the number and size distribution of its cities.

Three conditions must always be present for cities to develop. First, there must be a surplus of farm products, that is, farmers must produce more than is needed for their own subsistence. Second, there must be a means of transporting these products to the urban areas, where they are processed into items of food, clothing, and shelter. Third, there must be a sufficiently developed technology in the urban areas to use the farm products and to provide employment for the urban dwellers. Mills and factories thus emerge in urban areas where the products coming from the farms are developed into cotton, machinery, and the like.

The United States serves as an example of how the impacts of the Industrial Revolution contributed to the growth of cities. It is especially important to concentrate on the mode of transportation available at any point in time. Here, I am assuming that the farm regions of the nation are producing a sufficient amount of goods to export to the cities. I am also assuming that the mills and factories are being developed to handle such products. How do they get there? Early in the nineteenth century, water was the main source of transportation. Horses and wagons are not really capable of moving large amounts of material.

The first large and important cities, thus, were all water-based, namely, Boston, New York, Baltimore, and Charleston, South Carolina. The latter was one of the ten largest cities in the nation in 1800, due primarily to the cotton industry and the slave trade. A little later, Chicago and Detroit emerged, mainly because of their locations on the Great Lakes. New Orleans was another early city, the result of its location near the mouth of the Mississippi River.

Then came the railroad era in the nineteenth century, opening up more areas for **urban growth**. Atlanta, Denver, and Indianapolis, among others, emerged as major urban centers. The automobile and the construction of the interstate highway system also contributed to this urban growth. Another recent contributor is the airline system with its hubs. On a smaller dimension, consider that wherever two interstate highways intersect, fast-food restaurants and hotel chains open for business and more residents move in. These may not be particularly great in number but, nevertheless, are examples of how growth follows the transportation modes. Indeed, Garreau (1991) has written about the so-called **edge cities**. These are new "cities" that are actually formed at the edges of metropolitan areas to better serve those residing more remotely from the central cities (a **central city** is the largest city in a metropolitan or micropolitan area).

Returning to my discussion of world urbanization, in 1800 only 3 percent of the population of the world was classified as urban. Later, as technological and economic changes made possible large agricultural surpluses, people began moving to the cities in search of jobs in the factories. Consequently, massive urbanization was soon underway. By 1950, 29 percent of all residents in the world lived in urban places. In 2014, 54 percent of all the world's inhabitants were classified as urban. The United Nations projects that this figure will be 60 percent in 2030 and 66 percent in 2050 (United Nations, 2014b).

Recent urbanization has been especially marked in the developing regions of the world. Some concern has been expressed over this growth as faceless migrants multiply in and near metropolitan areas like Mexico City and Mumbai (in India, formerly known as Bombay). There, millions of homeless migrants from rural areas live in slum conditions with little hope of securing employment. This is also true of other large cities such as Lagos in Nigeria and Harare in Zimbabwe.

Is this phenomenon urbanization or is it simply urban growth? I will distinguish between the two. As mentioned earlier, urbanization refers to an increase in the percent of a region's or country's population living in urban areas; urban growth refers to an increase in the number of people living in urban areas. This is not to minimize the problems exhibited in today's large cities in developing countries; however, it may well be that the rural populations are also growing.

The enormous growth of large urban areas is a recent development. Large cities existed in ancient times – I already mentioned Chang'an, Rome, and a few others – but such cities were not common. In 1800, only one city in the world, London, had more than a million residents (LeGates, 2006).

Starting in 1900, however, there began a very rapid urbanization in many parts of the world. "Globally, more people live in urban areas than in rural areas. In 2007, for the first time in history, the global urban population exceeded the global rural population, and the world population has remained predominantly urban thereafter. The planet has gone through a process of rapid urbanization over the past six decades. In 1950 . . . 70 per cent of people worldwide lived in rural settlements and . . . 30 per cent in urban settlements. In 2014, 54 per cent of the world's population is urban. The urban population is expected to continue to grow, so that by 2050, the world will be one third rural . . . and two-thirds urban . . . roughly the reverse of the global rural-urban population distribution of the mid-twentieth century" (United Nations, 2014c: 7).

Rank	Urban agglomeration	Nation	Population (millions)
	Table 14.3 World's Twenty Largest Urban Agglomerations, 2014		
1	Tokyo	Japan	37.8
2	Delhi	India	25.0
3	Shanghai	China	23.0
4	Mexico City	Mexico	20.8
5	São Paulo	Brazil	20.8
6	Mumbai	India	20.7
7	Osaka	Japan	20.1
8	Beijing	China	19.5
9	New York-Newark	United States	18.6
10	Cairo	Egypt	18.4
11	Dhaka	Bangladesh	17.0
12	Karachi	Pakistan	16.1
13	Buenos Aires	Argentina	15.0
14	Kolkata	India	14.8
15	Istanbul	Turkey	14.0
16	Chongqing	China	12.9
17	Rio de Janeiro	Brazil	12.8
18	Manila	Philippines	12.8
19	Lagos	Nigeria	12.6
20	Los Angeles*	United States	12.3

* Refers to the Los Angeles–Long Beach–Santa Ana urban agglomeration.
Source: United Nations (2014b: 26).

Table 14.3 presents population data for the twenty largest urban agglomerations in the world; all have populations larger than 12 million. The United Nations (2014c) defines an **urban agglomeration** as an urban area of at least 1 million inhabitants, including all inhabitants in the surrounding territory living in urban levels of residential density. With almost 38 million residents in 2014, Tokyo is the most populous of the world's urban areas. Tokyo in 2014 had more residents than the country of Canada. Delhi and Shanghai with 25 million and 23 million residents, respectively, follow Tokyo. Next come Mexico City and São Paulo, each with 20.8 million (United Nations, 2014c: 26).

In addition to the twenty urban agglomerations in the world in 2014 with more than 12 million residents, there were twenty-eight with more than 10 million residents. And there were forty-three agglomerations with between 5 and 10 million residents, and 417 with between 1 million and 5 million residents (United Nations, 2014c: 13). As I have already noted, today more than half (54 percent) of the world's population lives in urban areas.

ECONOMIC DISTRIBUTION

Another way to consider the distribution of the world's population is to classify people according to the level of **economic development** of their country of residence. Economic development is not an easily defined concept. Two common measures are (1) per capita income, and (2) per capita energy consumption. Each yields similar results with respect to population distribution. Less than 20 percent of the population of the world resides in the more economically developed regions.

The small proportion of one-fifth of the world's population living in the more economically developed regions is expected to decline in future years. By 2050, it may be below 15 percent. This is projected to occur because the rates of population growth are much higher in the developing than in the developed nations. For example, in Africa, the annual rate of population growth via fertility and mortality now stands at 2.5 percent (PRB, 2014). That means that the population of Africa would increase from 1.1 billion in 2014 to over 2.2 billion by 2042 if the difference between its birth and death rates in 2014 did not change. Conversely, the population of Europe, with an annual growth rate of 0.0 percent would see no change in its 2014 population of 741 million as long as the difference between its birth and death rates did not change. These examples suggest why a significant shift in the proportion of people living in developed and developing regions is now occurring and will continue in the coming decades.

Massive migration from developing regions into the developed ones is unlikely because of political barriers erected by the latter to prevent such international movements. However, as I noted in Chapter 9, despite many and varied limitations, quite a large number of people, around 30–35 million, are estimated to be moving from one country to another without official documents. These migrants are sometimes referred to as undocumented, irregular, illegal, or unauthorized immigrants; the adjective *illegal* carries considerable emotional baggage, so I recommend not using it. As already mentioned, most undocumented immigrants are moving from the developing countries of the world to the developed and richer countries.

DISTRIBUTION OF THE US POPULATION

Over history, several trends have occurred to shape the distribution of the population of the United States. Generally, there has been a long-time movement westward. After the end of the Civil War, a migration out of the South also occurred. However, in more recent decades, there has been a resurgence

	2010 Population (thousands)	2010 % of total	1970 Population (thousands)	1970 % of total
Table 14.4 Population of the United States by Region, 1970 and 2010				
Region				
Northeast	55,317	17.9	49,061	24.1
Midwest	66,927	21.7	56,589	27.8
South	114,556	37.1	62,812	30.9
West	71,946	23.3	34,838	17.1

Sources: US Bureau of the Census (1994); Mackun and Wilson (2011).

of population movement into the South. Table 14.4 shows population data for each of the four geographic regions of the United States for 1970 and 2010. (Figure 8.3 in Chapter 8 shows the four census regions, as well as their divisions, and the individual states comprising them.) In the forty years since 1970, the shares of the US population living in the South and the West have increased, and they have declined in the Northeast and the Midwest.

The United States is divided into four regions and nine divisions (Figure 8.3, above). The nation's population is concentrated in the eastern third of the land area. Vast proportions of the land are sparsely populated (see Figure 14.1). Nevertheless, the long-term trend in geographic distribution has been westward.

Figure 14.3 is a map showing the approximate center of the United States population for each decade from 1790 to 2010. The **center of population** "is determined as the place where an imaginary, flat, weightless, and rigid map of the United States would balance perfectly if all residents were of identical weight" (US Bureau of the Census, 2007: 11). In 1790, the center of population was located in the upper portion of the Chesapeake Bay. A gradual movement westward followed. By about 1820, the entire middle section of the United States started its growth as agricultural and grazing lands were developed west of the Mississippi. The West began to grow around 1850 as the frontier became more accessible to settlers, rich ore deposits were located, and cheap land became scarcer in the East. As a result of this expansion, the center of population moved farther west with each census. By 1970, the center was located in St. Clair County, Illinois. Since then, the center has continued its movement west and by 1980 had crossed the Mississippi River for the first time. As the map shows, by the time of the most recent census in 2010, the center of the population of the United States was in Texas County, Missouri; this is about 23 miles southwest of the location of the center of population in 2000.

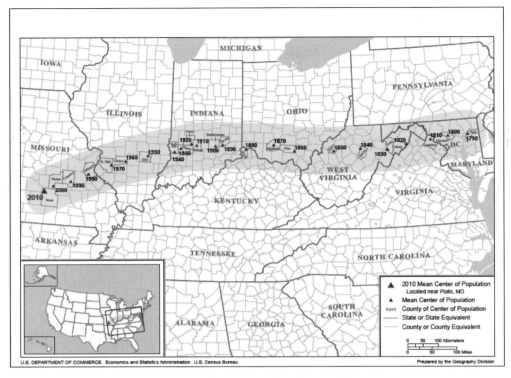

Figure 14.3 Mean Center of Population for the United States, 1790–2010
Source: US Bureau of the Census, available at: www2.census.gov/geo/pdfs/reference/cenpop2010/centerpop_mean2010.pdf, last accessed June 15, 2015.

In the past, most changes in US population distribution resulted from migration movements from one part of the country to another. Historically, there has been a movement out of the South into the East, then the Midwest, and finally the Far West. In more recent decades, people have been moving into the South from other regions. Especially notable has been the massive migration of retirees into the states of Florida, Arizona, and Texas. As a result, there is a **concentration** of elderly in these states.

In an earlier chapter, I mentioned the situation of a metropolitan area in Florida, The Villages, where despite the fact that deaths outnumbered births, The Villages was the most rapidly growing metropolitan area in the United States between 2012 and 2013, and between 2013 and 2014. Since about 1970, however, the United States has witnessed a substantial increase in international migration, especially from Latin America and Asia. Many of these newcomers have settled in a few states, namely, Florida, California, New York, and Texas. This, too, has contributed to shifts in population distribution (see my earlier discussions in Chapters 8, 9, and 13).

METROPOLITANIZATION AND MICROPOLITANIZATION

Even more important than the western and southern shifts in the nation's population has been the rapid concentration in urban areas, or **metropolitanization**. First, I need to define an urban area. In the United States, one type of urban area is known as an **urbanized area (UA)**; it consists of a densely settled core of census blocks and block groups that meet minimum population-density requirements, along with adjacent, densely settled surrounding census blocks that together encompass a population of 50,000 people, at least 35,000 of whom live in an area that is not part of a military installation. In contrast, an **urban cluster (UC)** is a densely settled core of blocks and block groups, along with adjacent densely settled surrounding blocks that together encompass a population of at least 2,500 people, but fewer than 50,000 people, or greater than 50,000 people if fewer than 35,000 of them live in an area that is not part of a military installation. Strictly speaking, any place that is not in an urban area or urban cluster is defined as rural.

Within these broadly defined urban areas, I will now consider the concepts of a **metropolitan area** and a **micropolitan area**. The US Bureau of the Census defines them as follows: metropolitan and micropolitan areas are "collectively known as core based statistical areas (CBSAs). A metropolitan area contains a core urban area population of 50,000 or more. A micropolitan area contains a core urban area population of at least 10,000 (but less than 50,000). Each metropolitan or micropolitan area consists of one or more counties and includes the counties containing the core urban area, as well as any adjacent counties that have a high degree of social and economic integration (as measured by commuting to work) with the urban core" (Mackun and Wilson, 2011: 4).

In 1900, there were sixty-one areas that would qualify under the above metropolitan area definition. By 1970, the number had grown to 202. The proportion of the US population living in such areas increased from about one-third in 1900 to two-thirds in 1970. This increase was caused both by actual population increase and redefinitions of these areas as urban living styles spread beyond what had been the traditional city borders. By the 1990s, there were 331 metropolitan areas in the United States, and they contained around 83 percent of the nation's population. By 2010, there were 366 metropolitan areas, containing almost 84 percent of the US population.

The micropolitan area is a new spatial concept that was introduced in 2003. In 2010, there were 576 micropolitan areas in the United States, and they contained 10 percent of the country's population.

In 2013, new metro areas were added when some micro areas grew to become metro areas. As of 2013, there were 381 metropolitan areas

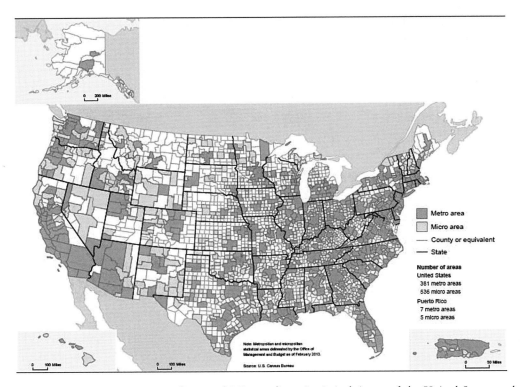

Figure 14.4 Metropolitan and Micropolitan Statistical Areas of the United States and Puerto Rico, 2013
Source: US Bureau of the Census, available at: www.census.gov/population/metro/files/ metro_micro_Feb2013.pdf, last accessed June 15, 2015.

(85 percent of the population) and 536 micropolitan areas (9 percent). This leaves 1,355 rural counties (6 percent) that are neither metro nor micro. Figure 14.4 is a map of the metropolitan and micropolitan areas of the United States as of 2013. The dark areas are metro, the light gray are micro, and the white areas are rural. If you live in the United States, or are attending school there, or have a favorite US state, you may wish to download the map at: www.census.gov/population/metro/files/metro_ micro_Feb2013.pdf, enlarge it, and then look at the metro and micro areas in your state.

Table 14.5 presents data on population change between 2000 and 2010 in the ten largest and ten fastest-growing metropolitan areas of the United States. The already noted patterns of population movement westward and southward can be seen in the data in this table. Note how the metro areas have kept growing, and also that many of the older metropolitan areas of the Northeast and Midwest (e.g., Cincinnati and Pittsburgh, to mention

Table 14.5 Population Change for the Ten Most Populous and Ten Fastest-growing Metropolitan Statistical Areas, 2000–2010

Metropolitan statistical area	Population		Change	
	2000	2010	Number	%
Most populous				
New York–Northern New Jersey–Long Island, NY–NJ–PA	13,323,002	16,697,109	574,107	3.1
Los Angeles–Long Beach–Santa Ana, CA	12,365,627	12,328,837	463,210	3.7
Chicago–Joliet–Naperville, IL–IN–WI	9,098,316	9,461,105	362,789	4.0
Dallas–Fort Worth–Arlington, TX	5,161,544	6,371,773	1,210,229	23.4
Philadelphia–Camden–Wilmington, PA–NJ–DE–MD	5,667,147	5,965,343	278,196	4.9
Houston–Sugar Land–Baytown, TX	4,715,407	5,946,800	1,231,393	26.1
Washington–Arlington–Alexandria, DC–VA–MD–WV	4,796,183	5,532,170	785,987	16.4
Miami–Fort Lauderdale–Pompano Beach, FL	5,007,564	5,564,635	557,071	11.1
Atlanta–Sandy Springs–Marietta, GA	4,247,981	5,268,860	1,020,879	24.0
Boston–Cambridge–Quincy, MA–NH	4,391,344	4,552,402	161,058	3.7
Fastest growing				
Palm Coast, FL	49,832	95,696	45,864	92.0
St. George, UT	90,354	138,115	47,761	52.9
Las Vegas–Paradise, NV	1,375,765	1,951,269	575,504	41.3
Raleigh–Gary, NC	797,071	1,130,490	333,419	41.3
Cape Coral–Fort Myers, FL	440,888	618,754	177,866	40.3
Provo–Orem, UT	376,774	526,810	150,036	39.3
Greeley, CO	160,926	252,826	71,899	39.7
Austin–Round Rock–San Marcos, TX	1,249.763	1,716,289	466,526	37.3
Myrtle Beach–North Myrtle Beach–Conway, SC	196,629	269,291	72,662	37.0
Bend, OR	115,367	157,733	42,366	36.7

Source: Mackun and Wilson (2011: 6).

only two) are not included among the ten largest or fastest growing. The fastest-growing metro areas are all located in the West and the South. Fifty years ago, the big cities in the Northeast and Midwest would have been included.

All ten of the largest metro areas in the table increased in size between 2000 and 2010, with Houston, Atlanta, and Dallas–Fort Worth growing the fastest and all three growing by over 20 percent. The population growth in the Atlanta metro area accounted for over 54 percent of the population growth in all of Georgia between 2000 and 2010. The Houston and Dallas–Fort Worth metro areas together comprised nearly one-half of the population of all of Texas and almost 57 percent of the state's growth between 2000 and 2010 (Mackun and Wilson, 2011: 4).

What about the micropolitan areas of the United States? "Many of the fast-growing micro areas are located near fast-growing metro areas. Likewise, many of the micro areas that are slow-growing or declining are located near slow-growing or declining metro areas" (Mackun and Wilson, 2011: 5).

MEGALOPOLIS

A new community form has been emerging in recent decades, namely, the **megalopolis**. The term is taken from the Greek words *mega* (μέγς), meaning "large," and *polis* (πόλις), meaning "city," or "great (or large) city." The geographic term was first introduced by Patrick Geddes (1915), then by Oswald Spengler ([1918] 1991), and then by Lewis Mumford ([1938] 1970). The French geographer Jean Gottmann (1961) used the term to refer specifically to the chain of metropolitan areas extending along the northeastern coast of the United States. Generally, the term megalopolis describes any densely populated social and economic entity encompassing two or more cities and the increasingly urbanized space between them.

One can often drive the entire area of a megalopolis, going from one city to another, with barely any break in nongreen spaces. This vast concentration of people, goods, and services functions as an "economic hinge" for the United States. It links the North American continent with the foreign markets accessible via the Atlantic.

In particular, this urban phenomenon came to describe the urbanized region of the northeastern United States that arose in the second half of the twentieth century. *Boswash* is a well-known megalopolis, having around 52 million people in 2010. Stretching between the metropolitan areas of Boston on the northeast side to Washington, DC on the southwest side, it includes the metropolitan areas of New York City, Philadelphia, Baltimore, and the District of Columbia. There are other megalopolitan areas in the United States, such as the *Chi–Pitts* megalopolis, with around 59 million people. It is located in the Great Lakes area and comprises the metropolitan areas of Chicago, Pittsburgh, Detroit, Cleveland, Milwaukee, Buffalo, and some others.

The *Texas Triangle* is another megalopolis, so named because its three main metro areas of Dallas–Fort Worth, San Antonio, and Houston are linked together by interstate highways 45, 10, and 35, which, when connected, form a triangle. Other metro areas in the Texas Triangle are College

Station–Bryan, Killeen–Temple–Fort Hood, Waco, and Austin. The Texas Triangle contains five of the twenty largest cities in the United States (Houston, San Antonio, Dallas, Austin, and Fort Worth) and is home to over 70 percent of the population of Texas.

The largest megalopolis in the world is the *Taiheiyo Belt* in Japan comprising the linked metropolises on the country's western shores. The Belt includes over 83 million residents and consists of Tokyo, Okayama, Hiroshima, Osaka, Yokohama, and some other large cities in Japan.

In an earlier paragraph I mentioned the megalopolis of *Boswash*. It begins with the northern suburbs of Boston, which extend into southern New Hampshire. To the south, the Boston suburbs extend toward the northern suburbs of Providence, Rhode Island. Then it follows to New London–New Haven, Connecticut, and the large cities that approach New York. It continues on through New Jersey to Philadelphia, Baltimore, and Washington, and then into the southern suburbs of Washington into northern Virginia. Indeed, as suburbs continue to grow, one could make a case that *Boswash* extends to Richmond, Virginia and its suburbs.

However, does a megalopolis have the essential characteristics of a community? It has one such characteristic, namely, a common geographic area that is distinguishable from other areas. To be a community, its people must be linked in a system characterized by a division of labor, increased differentiation of economic activity, and functional interdependence. Without such a pattern of interaction, it is difficult to conceive of a megalopolis as anything other than a grouping of contiguous metropolitan areas sharing a common, heavily populated geographic area.

TRENDS TOWARD DECONCENTRATION

At the same time that the population has become concentrated into metropolitan areas, there has also occurred a **deconcentration** in metropolitan areas, that is, **suburbanization**. This represents a shift from the higher-density central cities to the lower-density areas beyond the traditional city limits. Another form of deconcentration is the shift from metropolitan to nonmetropolitan areas.

Since 1900, the proportion of the US population living in metropolitan areas has increased and, by 2013, 85 percent was residing in metropolitan areas. However, since 1930, the proportion living in the central cities of the metropolitan areas has been falling. Thus, while most metropolitan areas have experienced population growth, much of that growth has been taking place in the suburban portions. This does not mean that the population of central cities has necessarily declined; rather, it means that it has grown more slowly than the suburban portions.

Indeed, some of the growth that has occurred in central cities in past decades can be explained by annexation, that is, by placing outlying areas under the jurisdiction of the central cities for one reason or another. Jacksonville, Florida, annexed all of Duval County, much of which is actually quite rural. Similarly, Nashville, Tennessee, has annexed all of Davidson County. Houston, Texas, is another example of a city that has grown by leaps and bounds, partly by gradually annexing all of Harris County: "The city of Houston grew by 29 percent during the 1970s – one of the most rapidly growing large cities in the country. But the city also annexed a quarter of a million people. Without the annexation, the city would have grown only modestly" (Miller, 2004: 31).

A number of older US cities have shown population declines in recent decades. For example, Detroit's population has been reduced by over 60 percent since 1950. The US Bureau of the Census estimates the population of Detroit in 2013 to be less than 700,000 persons. Detroit had a population in 1950 of over 1.8 million. These older cities are unable to annex contiguous lands because those territories are already incorporated; there are no more unincorporated sections ready to be grabbed by the larger central cities.

Although the city of San Francisco, my home town, has gained population since 1970, increasing from just over 715,000 in 1970 to more than 805,000 in 2010, none of this growth occurred through annexation. San Francisco is bounded on the west by the Pacific Ocean, and on the north and east by San Francisco Bay, and on the south by the small cities of Daly City and Brisbane. There is no available contiguous territory anywhere for San Francisco to annex, a situation not unlike that of many other older US cities. San Francisco is not too much larger in population today than it was when I was growing up there in the 1940s and 1950s; its population size in 1950 was just over 775,000.

Social reasons also help explain the declining populations of many central cities. One is the so-called **white flight**. The large movement of poorer, often nonwhite, residents into the central cities has contributed to the massive out-migration to the suburbs of the mostly white middle and upper classes. The production of large, relatively moderate housing developments in the suburbs after the end of the Second World War also contributed to this movement away from the cities. Admittedly, some of the white flight is a matter of out-and-out racism and takes place to avoid sending children to the same schools as people of color or living in the same neighborhoods with them. But the attractiveness of living in the suburbs, that is, owning a piece of land, having a yard, and leading a middle-class life, is difficult to overcome. More recently, middle-class minority families have also taken advantage of such benefits. Indeed, the declining populations of the central cities cannot be ascribed solely to racial fears in view of the fact that black migration to the suburbs has been accelerating for many years. The negative side of this movement is that the central cities have been left to the poor and to the underclass.

International migration must also be considered when discussing population distribution. Whether from Europe or Asia, in the late nineteenth and early twentieth centuries, immigrants were most likely to settle in the poor downtown areas of the big cities. Later, these immigrants (and their children) started moving to the suburbs. A recent upsurge in immigration represents a new growth for many downtown areas. It is difficult to determine the exact contribution made by such movements. It is clear, however, that these newcomers tend to reside near and in close contact with one another, usually in the bigger cities.

However, there are exceptions. For example, certain middle-size cities with a need for low-wage workers often attract undocumented immigrant workers. This has been especially true in some sections of North Carolina and Alabama, such as Winston–Salem and Huntsville.

There was a time when internal migration was overwhelmingly from nonmetropolitan to metropolitan areas. This has changed. Today, people are more likely to move from the suburb of one area to the suburb of another. In other words, the traditional move "to the city" is now being bypassed. Those who move within a metropolitan area are often more likely to move from the city to the suburbs, and increasingly to the **exurbs**, that is, geographic areas beyond the beltways that circle the metropolitan areas. Furthermore, those who make these moves are apt to be young adults, along with their children. Thus, an area experiencing net in-migration gains population in two ways: (1) through the net number of movers; and (2) through the number of children born to those movers after the migration has occurred.

Summing up my discussion of population deconcentration in the United States, there was first a movement from rural to urban areas. This was followed by a movement from the urban centers to the inner suburbs. Now there is beginning to be movement even farther away from the historic downtowns into the exurbs. This, in turn, leads to the development of edge cities, which then typically contribute to growth ever farther from the "downtown."

The New England Patriots of the National Football League (NFL) are an interesting example of what has been happening in recent decades. Originally, they were called the Boston Patriots. When the size of the population and, hence, the fan base declined in Boston, and the suburbs grew rapidly, the team moved from Boston to Foxboro, Massachusetts. But Foxboro is not just a suburb of Boston. It lies in the center of a triangle composed of

Boston, Worcester, and Providence. Since other New England states are geographically close to this area, the team wisely chose "New England" as its official name, a truly regional name for a professional football team. Similar statements may be made about the regional appeal, and name, of another NFL team, the Tennessee Titans, as well as at least two Major League Baseball teams, the Texas Rangers and the Colorado Rockies.

CONSEQUENCES OF POPULATION DISTRIBUTION

I have alluded briefly to some of the problems related to the geographical movements of people. One consequence is that particular types of economic activity have relocated to the ring portions of metropolitan areas. This tends to remove important sources of tax revenues and jobs from the central city. Also, the composition of the population of central cities has changed radically. The out-migrating middle class has been replaced by relatively disadvantaged segments of the population, often poor minority groups, the chronically unemployed, the aged, and the socially disadvantaged.

The significance of this concentration of economically and socially disadvantaged persons in the central cities is twofold. First, the increasing proportion of such persons has added to the demand for related social services, namely, welfare, health, public housing, sanitation, and police protection, to name but a few. At the same time, the economic status of the resident population is lowered because more families tend to move out of the central cities than move in, and because the average income of the out-migrants tends to be higher than that of the in-migrants. The lowered economic status of the resident population and the loss of industry and business activity through deconcentration combine to reduce the tax base. This subsequently leads to declines in the financial ability of the central city governments to support the increased need for services brought about by the spatial concentration of the disadvantaged. Thus, many central cities, especially the older ones, are confronted with a financial crisis. Demands for services are increasing at the same time that taxable resources are diminishing. To meet the demands, the central city often responds by increasing the property tax rate, which has the effect of forcing more homeowners and industries to move out of the central city, further lowering the tax base. It is a vicious circle.

In recent years, however, **gentrification**, that is, the migration of middle-class and affluent people into the once poorer areas of cities, has been taking place in some older central cities. People have begun to move back "downtown" from the outer suburbs as the cities offer new opportunities. New condominiums are being built in many of the areas in the city that were once considered depleted. Other rundown sections have been renovated. New office towers have sprung up as businesses begin to realize that there is much to be said about being "downtown." These movements back into the cities usually involve older, and sometimes retired, whites, as well as gay men and lesbians, many of them without children (Bradley and Longino, 2009). Whether this will result in sustained population growth in central cities remains to be seen.

SUMMARY

The terms **population explosion** and **population implosion** appear contradictory. Yet they are both occurring these days throughout the world. I have already written about the population growth that occurred during the twentieth century (see especially my discussions of world population growth in Chapter 12). But, as an earlier table illustrates, the growth of metropolitan areas has been enormous, while rural areas have lost population. The demographers Avery Guest and Susan Brown have given us an example of this double phenomenon in their very interesting sentence about population distribution in the United States. They noted that "the Las Vegas metropolitan area tripled between 1980 and 2000, while 46 of the 53 counties in the state of North Dakota lost population" (2005: 59). We can only speculate as to whether this will be the direction of population distribution in the twenty-first century not only in Nevada and North Dakota, but all over the world.

15 Population Policy

A **population policy** is a deliberately constructed arrangement or program "through which governments influence, directly or indirectly, demographic change" (Demeny, 2003: 752). These arrangements, typically, are "legislative measures, administrative programs, and other governmental actions intended to alter or modify existing population trends in the interest of national survival and welfare" (Eldridge, 1968: 381). The demographer John May has written that "population policies are designed to regulate and, if possible, mitigate the problems [of too rapid growth or decline] by adjusting population size and structure to the needs and aspirations of the people" (2005: 828; 2012).

Population policies usually represent strategies for governments or sometimes, albeit less frequently, nongovernmental organizations (NGOs) to attain specific goals. The procedures or programs are put into place to ensure that the policy goals are attained. A policy is generally intended to either reduce or increase population levels. Policies are developed "in the interest of the greater good ... in order to address imbalances between demographic changes and other social, economic and political goals" (May, 2005: 828).

I have mentioned in earlier chapters of this book that many countries in the world today have high rates of population growth, that many have negative or near-negative rates of growth, and that many have fertility rates below replacement levels. In 2013, for instance, seventy-nine countries had TFRs below 2.1; in 1970, there were only ten such countries (PRB, 2014). Countries exhibiting demographic conditions of too-high growth or too-low growth sometimes develop policies whose goals are aimed at trying to restore the demographic balance.

Whether the issue is severe or minor, demographic behavior is of interest to all governments. In the United States, the onset of the baby boom in the mid-1940s resulted in major changes in governmental action in many areas. And, of course, some governments actually installed stated government policies, several of which I will review in this chapter.

As I have noted in this book time and time again, there are only three ways to change the size of a population, namely, through births, deaths, and migration. Therefore, any policies aimed at restoring demographic balance must be oriented toward one, two, or all three of these demographic processes. But not all of the options are used as the bases for policies.

To illustrate, a policy with the goal of increasing mortality to lower population growth would be unethical and not considered to be a viable means for solving an issue of population growth. This is not to say that governments have not developed policies to explicitly raise the mortality levels of groups or subgroups in their countries. One need only recall the explicit policies in the not-too-distant past of the Nazi government in Germany and the Khmer Rouge government in Cambodia to raise the mortality levels of subgroups in their populations.

Population policies dealing with mortality are usually intended to reduce, not increase, its levels. Reducing mortality, however, is not as popular or as prominent a strategy of population policy. Most policies focus on manipulating fertility and/or migration. They will receive most of my attention in this chapter.

How do governments affect the demographic processes? Generally, they influence the demographic behavior indirectly. Governments typically find ways to persuade people to act voluntarily in a "desired" manner. But often, mere legislation and propaganda are insufficient to attain the intended goal. Then governments act directly, say, to either raise or lower fertility levels or to force people to move or not to move.

The task of formulating a population policy is complicated by the fact that sometimes there is no consensus on the appropriate size of the population and/or its fertility or migration rates. There may be some disagreement as to the magnitude of the problem (if, indeed, there is a problem) of population growth or decline. More frequently, a "laissez-faire" attitude evolves as opposed to a "let's do something about it now" position. For example, today in the United States there is widespread disagreement as to whether levels of immigration should be reduced or increased. Some groups argue for the former, others the latter.

Furthermore, not everyone agrees on the true meaning of a population policy. Here are some questions pointing to possible issues of disagreement among demographers as well as non-demographers:

1. Must there be an explicit statement by a government that a policy exists? The United States has no official population policy. Nevertheless, the US government finances and sponsors programs designed to

eliminate unwanted childbearing and to make contraception available to certain target populations.

2. Does there have to be a planned course of action or program? Sometimes doing nothing is a policy. In 2014, US fertility was below the replacement level of 2.1 children per woman. But the US government does not appear to be at all concerned about raising its level of fertility, or lowering it, to compensate for increases to the population via immigration.

3. Must the goals of a policy be demographic, or may they be social and economic? In other words, do the goals have to be direct or indirect? For example, it is well known that, on average, increased educational attainment of women results in lower fertility; the higher the education of women, the fewer, on average, the number of children born to them. If a developing country decides to improve the educational levels of its female youth, is this a population policy? Yes, but only indirectly. Similarly, opening job opportunities for women tends to result in lower fertility. This is another example of an indirect population policy.

My point of raising these questions is to illustrate that there are no "correct" answers. Governments may differ in their definitions and in the formulation of population policies, and it is sometimes difficult to decide whether a specific country has a population policy. My concern here is not to make judgments about objectives. My purpose is to address the question: in what ways may a government influence levels of fertility, mortality, and migration?

THE THREE WORLD POPULATION CONFERENCES

The issue of human population growth as a problem or concern is really a twentieth-century phenomenon. However, as I mentioned in Chapter 12, the concern with overpopulation is not new. Indeed, during the eighteenth century, Malthus declared that overpopulation was bound by nature to occur. He and others wrote about population growth and its problems (see my discussions of Malthus and others in Chapter 2). But it was not until the 1960s and the early 1970s that the public became acutely aware of them. Several high-profile books, such as *The Population Bomb* (Ehrlich, 1968), *The Limits to Growth* (Meadows et al., 1974), and *Small is Beautiful* (Schumacher, 1975) brought the issue of overpopulation to the attention of millions of readers. Unlike Malthus, however, many of these authors gave special attention to the degradation of the environment by larger and larger numbers of humans (Poston, DeSalvo, and Meyer, 2009; Russell and Poston, 2008). To this day, there is still some discussion of the issue of overpopulation. Friedman (2005) has noted, for instance, that aspects of these themes of overpopulation and environmental degradation are reflected in the contemporary antiglobalization movement.

Starting in the 1970s, there was considerable debate in academic circles with many advocating voluntary family planning. The position among the so-called birth controllers and many population specialists was that inducing women in developing countries to practice contraception would simultaneously improve their social and economic situation and alleviate the societal problems of their countries (Connelly, 2008; Hodgson and Watkins, 1997). Affluent countries such as the United States, along with private foundations and other organizations, provided large amounts of financial assistance to the population-control movement and the worldwide endeavor to limit population growth.

In 1965, President Lyndon Johnson established an Office of Population in the Department of State and the US Agency for International Development (USAID). The goal of USAID was to convince governments in developing countries to foster contraceptive usage among its citizens. In many instances, this was a politically charged issue that ran counter to traditional pronatalist cultural norms (those advocating increases in fertility). The USAID sent teams of demographers and other specialists to countries all over the world to inform their leaders and officials about the impacts of continued rapid population growth. My deceased colleague and co-author of the first edition of this book, Leon Bouvier, made such presentations in several Francophone African countries in the early 1980s.

The attempts by the United States to promote family planning overseas in countries not yet "ready" for this message inevitably met with cries of imperialism. Officials in the host countries often asked why the United States was promoting family planning instead of addressing, according to their way of thinking, more pressing needs like assistance in relieving the millions of people suffering from malaria (Connelly, 2008). In part to defuse this issue, the United States worked with the United Nations to help create in 1969 the **United Nations Fund for Population Activities** (UNFPA). UNFPA served as a major source of funds for population initiatives in developing countries.

Since the United Nations came into existence in 1945, it has sponsored and conducted three world population conferences, held in 1974, 1984, and 1994. These conferences pretty much framed the story of international family planning that has unfolded since the 1970s (Bouvier and Bertrand, 1999).

The first World Population Conference was held in Bucharest, Romania, in 1974. It was an attempt to bring together government officials from around the world and to illustrate for them the facts and consequences of rapid population growth. It was expected by the developed nations in attendance that the rest of the world would recognize the so-called population problem and join the growing movement to curb population growth. To the surprise of many, there was no such endorsement. Rather, most developing nations stressed their preoccupation with the importance of socioeconomic development, both in its own right and as a catalyst for lowering fertility. They called for a "New Economic Order," whose position was encapsulated in the expression "Development is the best contraceptive."

The second conference was held in Mexico City in 1984. During the ten years since the first conference, many developing countries had changed their opinions about population growth and were now interested in assistance directed toward their fledgling family planning programs. (A **family planning program** is a systematic effort to promote modern fertility control.) African countries, especially, were seeing the benefits of more widespread family planning programs, if not for demographic reasons, then at least for the health of women and children. However, by this time, the political atmosphere in the United States had changed dramatically. The official US delegation under the administration of President Ronald Reagan asserted that "population is a neutral phenomenon" in the development process, and that excessive state control of the economy was more responsible for economic stagnation than population growth (Hodgson and Watkins, 1997). James Buckley, the brother of the late conservative scholar, editor, and journalist William F. Buckley, headed the US delegation.

This unexpected US position stunned the delegates. Instead of rallying the world community behind population issues, the United States introduced to the world its controversial Mexico City policy. The US administration, over strong Congressional objection, decided to police the actions of developing countries with respect to abortion services by refusing to fund the family planning activities of local organizations that also provided abortion, even if abortion was legal in that country and paid for by private funds (Bouvier and Bertrand, 1999).

I note here that one of the first acts of President Bill Clinton's administration when he took office in 1993 was to reverse this policy of President Reagan. But when the administration of George W. Bush came into power in 2001, the Reagan policy was once again restored. With the inauguration of Barack Obama in 2009, the Bush–Reagan policy was changed back to the policy of the Clinton administration regarding the providing of funds for family planning. When President Obama reversed the Bush–Reagan policy on January 23, 2009, he remarked that "for the past eight years [the Bush–Reagan restrictions] have undermined efforts to promote safe and effective voluntary family planning in developing countries. For these reasons it is right for us to rescind this policy and restore critical efforts to protect and empower women and promote global economic development" (Filteau, 2009: 1).

The 1994 International Conference on Population and Development (ICPD) was held in Cairo, Egypt. This conference radically altered the international population movement. Its major outcome was a new definition of population policy, giving prominence to reproductive health and downplaying the demographic rationale for population policy (McIntosh and Finkle, 1995). Two radically diverse groups, feminists and neo-Malthusians, joined forces to create a new manifesto that included the following stipulations: (1) population stabilization is a desirable, ultimate goal, although not one warranting the use of compulsion; (2) national programs enhancing access to contraception are justified in terms of individual human rights, not in terms of their development advantages for populations; and (3) the empowerment of women is a prerequisite for the enduring low fertility that population stabilization requires (Hodgson and Watkins, 1997).

The Cairo conference was considered to be very successful, mainly because it allowed historically opposed and oppressed groups to identify a unified position. Later, however, many officials and scholars working on population matters were surprised that, apparently, discussions of aggregate demographic concerns were being seen as politically incorrect. Indeed, some argued that "programs that are demographically-driven, and are intended to act directly on fertility, are inherently abusive of women's rights to choose the number and timing of their children" (McIntosh and Finkle, 1995: 260). Others argued that there is nothing inherently abusive or intrusive about demographically driven population policy (Presser, 1997).

In sum, Cairo "stressed the importance of individual choices and the necessity to further empower women" (May, 2005: 830). An action program was prepared with the consensus and support of 179 governments that "individual human rights and dignity, including the equal rights of women and girls and universal access to sexual and reproductive health and rights, are a necessary precondition for sustainable development" (UNFPA, 2014: iii). More recent international conferences have largely agreed with this preoccupation. It was the main theme of follow-up meetings of the International Conference on Population and Development, "which included a meeting in the Netherlands and a meeting of the U.N. General Assembly in 1999" (May, 2005: 830)

One might ask why there was no world population conference in 2004. After three conferences in 1974, 1984, and 1994, a conference was indeed planned for 2004. But when the United States, under the administration of President George W. Bush, withdrew its funding of the UNFPA, it was decided to simply incorporate the goals of earlier conferences for the present and the immediate future.

In 2014, twenty years after the Cairo conference, the United Nations reviewed the action program just mentioned and stated that achievements since 1994 have been remarkable. Noted in particular were the world-wide "gains in women's equality, population health and life expectancy, educational attainment, and human rights protection systems," along with the fact that "an estimated 1 billion people (have been moved) out of extreme poverty" (UNFPA, 2014: iii). Also emphasized was the improvement around the world in the dignity of women and adolescent girls, especially their empowerment "to exercise their reproductive rights." Moreover, it was stressed that "sexual and reproductive health and rights and understanding the implications of population dynamics are foundational to sustainable development" (UNFPA, 2014: iii).

POLICIES AFFECTING FERTILITY

It is most interesting to note that in all three of the world population conferences, fertility was the only major topic on the agenda. Reductions in mortality were alluded to only briefly in the demand for assistance in combating malaria; issues of international migration were never mentioned. Yet immigration has become an important phenomenon in recent decades in many parts of the world. In this section of the chapter, I turn attention to actual policies affecting fertility behavior, whether direct or indirect, that is, whether to raise or lower its levels. Immigration policies are covered in a later section.

A Brief History

Prior to the twentieth century, most fertility policies were concerned with increasing population growth, that is, they were pronatalist. These policies were usually of three types: pronatalist propaganda; measures related to the family, such as family allowance programs; and restrictions on the distribution and use of contraceptives and abortion.

Some of the earliest known population policies were those of the Roman Emperor Augustus, enacted between 18 BC and AD 9. Inheritance laws and rules concerning eligibility for office penalized the childless and favored parents. During the medieval period, high mortality caused by plague, especially the Black Death (see Chapter 7), encouraged the development of pronatalist views and policies. In France, tax exemptions and other privileges were used in the latter part of the thirteenth century to encourage fertility. A Spanish edict in 1623 granted tax exemptions to those who married young and who raised large families (Glass, 1940).

It is important to recall that Marxist leaders long believed that population problems in their countries were social and economic rather than demographic. They believed that if matters deteriorated, a social revolution would occur. Thus, in their view, population growth was seen as a spur for the revolution necessary to achieve social, economic, and political change. I discuss this issue later when I address fertility policies in China.

In the twentieth century during the years between the First and Second World Wars, the pronatalist movement reached its peak in Germany, Italy, and Japan. Intensive pronatalist propaganda, cash payments to families with children, the restriction of access to contraceptives, and the enactment of so-called eugenic laws aimed at encouraging the reproduction of some genetic traits and discouraging others, reflected the attempts of governments to have larger and racially "pure" populations. Such measures were adopted because power and prosperity were equated with large numbers of people (Eldridge, 1968: 382; Teitelbaum, 2005).

Countries such as France and Romania adopted pronatalist policies at various times after the First World War. These policies represented a reaction to the low fertility that accompanied modernization. France, Romania, and other nations feared that their national economic and political well-being would decline unless their populations continued to grow.

Sometimes countries have policies that have both pronatalist and antinatalist effects. France is a good example. In 1920, France prohibited the distribution of birth-control propaganda and devices. The Law of 1920 stipulated that it was illegal to distribute contraceptives or information on fertility control, not unlike the Comstock Act in the United States, which was passed in 1873 and overturned by the US Congress in 1971. In 1932, in France, laws prohibiting abortion were tightened. In 1939, the French government adopted a *Code de la Famille*, which incorporated existing family welfare and pronatalist measures. Allowances were extended to all economically active persons. Marriage loans, premiums on the birth of a first child, and other forms of aid for parents were provided (Glass, 1940). The code was strengthened after 1945 when the CBR was less than 15/1,000.

However, in 1967, France legalized the distribution of contraceptives in response to public demand. By 1974, a new statute was passed that provided for the distribution of free contraceptives, and another law lifted the prohibition on abortion. These measures were adopted to achieve the social goal of voluntary parenthood, but they also illustrate how social policies with antinatalist effects can exist in countries with pronatalist population policies (Bouvier and Bertrand, 1999: 139–140).

It does not appear that pronatalist measures in industrialized countries have ever been very effective. In 1979, the CBR in France was still under

15/1,000; it is even lower today. Total fertility rates in 2013 in all the countries of Europe were below the level needed to replace the population. Only France, Kosovo, and Ireland have TFRs of 2.0; all other countries have rates below 2.0, with ten below 1.4 (PRB, 2014). Pronatalist policies have not been sufficient to offset the antinatalist aspects of social and economic policies.

As programs began to develop, the administrators were cautious in the face of legal barriers. Indeed, the Law of 1920 (just discussed) proved to be a serious impediment to the reduction of fertility in Francophone African countries. Most African countries successfully removed the law from their statutes by the late 1980s, and it is not upheld in the few countries where it still exists. However, this law unquestionably has had a dampening effect on family planning promotion.

Singapore is another example of a country reversing its policies regarding population growth. Its determination to reduce growth through lowered fertility was very successful. These efforts included indirect measures such as better facilities for health and education. "The initial effort on family planning combined with demographic investments ... and other productive investments have probably accelerated the transformation of Singapore into a new industrialized country (fertility dropped to sub replacement levels in 1986)" (May, 2005: 843). Its rate of population growth fell from 2.3 to 1.3 percent in the ten-year period between 1968 and 1978. In 2013, its TFR was 1.2.

Recently, the government has expressed grave concerns over this small country's very low fertility and is encouraging certain groups (especially Singapore citizens of Chinese ancestry) to elevate their fertility. Indeed, the government organized a commission to devise ways to bring single adults together (Crosette, 1997). A back-to-work program was also introduced to support the goals and activities of women. Today the Singapore government spends over $1 billion annually in programs to raise its moribund birth rate. One program set aside an evening known as "National night" for citizens to specifically allow their patriotism to "explode" and in so doing help raise the birth rate. The government has also limited the number of small one-bedroom flats. Moreover, a couple receives $15,000 for each child along with tax incentives and extended maternity leave. In 2012, the government of Singapore enhanced the country's Marriage and Parenthood Package to "(a) enable couples to get housing faster and more easily, so that they can marry and start families earlier; (b) provide support for conception and delivery costs; (c) further defray child-raising costs, including healthcare costs; (d) enhance work–life measures to help working couples balance work and family commitments; and (e) signal to fathers to play a bigger role through paternity and shared parental leave" (National

Population and Talent Division, 2013: 4). Yet, as I noted in the previous paragraph, Singapore's TFR remains very low at 1.2, and is one of the lowest in the world.

Similarly, South Korea and Taiwan have both adopted incentive programs to increase the number of children per household. There is, however, little evidence of any success in raising fertility, and TFRs remain much below the replacement level. In 2013, South Korea's TFR was 1.2 and Taiwan's 1.1 (PRB, 2014).

Abortion has long been a method used in some countries to reduce fertility. Restricting access to abortion may result in a sharp increase in fertility. Such was the case in Romania in the 1950s. By 1956, the birth rate had fallen to 24 births per 1,000 population, primarily due to the widespread use of illegal abortion (David and Wright, 1971). In 1957, the government legalized abortion to allow women to decide whether and when to have children, as well as to reduce the incidence of illegal abortion (Mehlan, 1965). However, the government did not encourage the use of contraception. As a result, induced abortion became the socially accepted means of birth prevention. The CBR fell from 23 in 1957 to 14 in 1966 (Teitelbaum, 1972: 405).

The Romanian government became concerned about its low birth rate and in November 1966 revised its abortion policy. It restricted legal abortion only to cases involving risk to the mother's life, risk of congenital malformation, evidence of rape, pregnancy in women older than 45 years of age, women supporting four or more living children, and a rigorously defined set of physiological conditions, as well as several other limiting social and economic circumstances (Teitelbaum, 1972).

The results of this dramatic change in Romanian population policy were astounding. The CBR tripled in just nine months from 13 per 1,000 in December 1966 to 40 in September 1967. Since then it has declined steadily, and fertility is now well below replacement; the TFR in Romania in 2013 was 1.3. Apparently, the decline has occurred because of a strong preference for small families. However, it took a little time for Romanian couples to make the sudden transition from a primary reliance on legal abortion to other methods of birth prevention, including the use of coitus interruptus, condoms, illegally imported contraceptives, and illegal abortion (David and Wright, 1971). In that interval, the birth rate increased substantially.

Thus far, I have concentrated on policies aimed at increasing fertility, although in some instances, the policies have tended to be redirected as the situation demanded. Now I examine a few antinatalist policies, both direct and indirect. The two basic approaches are government-sponsored family planning programs and various nonfamily planning approaches.

Antinatalist Policies

Mexico is an example of a country in which the two approaches have been pursued simultaneously. In the early 1970s, the Mexican government engaged in a historic reversal of its pronatalist policies, embarking on an aggressive family planning initiative. Four branches of the public sector were enlisted to implement this strategy. The program also received additional and important support from two private sector organizations: the Mexican affiliate of the International Planned Parenthood Federation (MEXFAM) and the Mexican Federation of Private Health Associations and Community Development (FEMAP). Between the early 1970s and 2000, the TFR fell from 6.5 to 2.8. In 2013, the TFR in Mexico was 2.2, just slightly above the replacement level.

There have been other family planning successes leading to dramatic reductions in population growth. Bangladesh, despite its incredible poverty, finances a third of the costs of its very active family planning program (Bouvier and Bertrand, 1999: 109). Other countries with active family planning programs include Colombia, the Dominican Republic, Egypt, El Salvador, India, Indonesia, Jamaica, Peru, Tunisia, and Vietnam.

I have been concentrating to this point on family planning efforts to reduce population growth. But I need to go "beyond family planning" to get a more complete picture of population policies intended to reduce growth. Generally speaking, increased education and increased labor force participation for females contribute to lowering fertility, albeit, as noted earlier, indirectly. But there are other less opaque methods that have been used to achieve this purpose. India provides a good example.

In the 1950s, India was the first country to introduce incentives to influence childbearing behavior. They were targeted at three groups: (1) acceptors, that is, women and men complying with the government family planning policy; (2) providers, that is, physicians and other healthcare personnel; and (3) promoters, that is, individuals in the community who influenced the acceptors to adopt family planning. Payment was usually in the form of cash to the providers, and cash, services, or gifts to the acceptors and promoters (Freedman and Isaacs, 1993). For example, men received gifts such as radios, traditional garments, and money for undergoing sterilization. However, it should be noted that such incentives are sometimes linked to abuses of human rights. For example, in the 1970s, India not only provided incentives to individuals but also penalized local officials for not reaching assigned quotas. Problems arose when public officials allegedly used force on low-status individuals to meet their quotas. This, in turn, created a backlash, contributing to the defeat of Indira Gandhi's government in 1977, as well as setbacks for family planning in India (Gillis et al., 1996).

China undoubtedly has had one of the most stringent population policies in human history (Poston and Yaukey, 1992: 397–398). Indeed, one reason why China is such an interesting and intriguing country for demographers to study is precisely because of its fertility policies. Another reason, as noted by Keyfitz (1984: 45), is that in China the political leaders are "able to control the annual number of births with considerable precision." An important point to make in this regard is that family planning in a socialist country like China differs dramatically from family planning as we know it in the West. In China, "births are planned by the state to bring the production of human beings in line with the production of material goods" (Greenhalgh, 2008: 46). The numbers of babies produced are heavily controlled by the country.

In the period between 1949, when Mao Zedong and the Chinese Communists assumed control of the country and established the People's Republic of China (PRC), and the early 1970s, China's fertility policy was characterized as "on-again-and-off-again." During the early years of the PRC, there was very little attention given to the size of the population. But when the 1953 census data were made public, many leaders expressed anxiety about the size and growth trends of the country. Accordingly, by the summer of 1956, a birth control campaign was underway. However, this fledgling campaign lost its momentum and importance with the introduction in 1958 of communes and the nationalized movement in the country known as the Great Leap Forward, which was intended to move China to the status of an industrialized society. The Leap proved to be a disaster, and as I have already noted in Chapter 7, there was a tremendous increase in mortality; an estimated 30–40 million people died as a result of famine (Ashton et al., 1984; Dikotter, 2010; Yang, 2012). China soon recovered and the fertility rate skyrocketed to a TFR in the early 1960s of more than 6.0. In early 1962, China resumed its family planning program, mainly via the publication of propaganda encouraging family size limitation. But this second campaign lasted only until the beginning of the Great Proletarian Cultural Revolution in 1966, at which time all birth-control efforts in the country were interrupted.

In 1971, China introduced its third family program, the so-called *wan-xi-shao* program, a campaign stressing *later* marriages (*wan*), *longer* intervals between children (*xi*), and *fewer* children (*shao*). However, the large numbers of children born during China's baby boom in the early 1960s caused government leaders and officials in the middle to late 1970s to be concerned about demographic momentum and the concomitant growth potential of this huge cohort. Population projections for China developed by two scientists, Song Jian and Yu Jingyuan, and their associates showed that under the *wan-xi-shao* program, China would greatly exceed its goal of a population size of 1.2 billion by the year 2000 (Song, Tuan, and Yu, 1985; Song and Yu, 1988). Hence, with arguments and data from Song and his colleagues (Greenhalgh, 2008), the government of Deng Xiaoping approved the "one child is best" norm and intensified its already strong family planning program by launching, in 1979, the so-called One-Child Campaign. Its principal goal was to eliminate births above or equal to three per family, and to encourage families to have no more than one child, especially those in the urban areas. In practice, because of the many exceptions to the policy allowing some couples to have more than one child (Scharping, 2003), China's fertility policy came to be best defined as a one-and-a-half-child policy (usually one in the cities and sometimes two in the countryside). China's TFR has dropped from over 6.0 in the early 1970s to below replacement levels today.

It would be a mistake, however, to attribute the dramatic reduction in China's fertility rate solely to the policies. Yes, the *wan-xi-shao* and the one-child policies likely had impacts in the 1970s and 1980s. But the policies were in force at the same time that China was modernizing and moving toward becoming an industrial and urbanized society. Societal modernization has many components, not the least of which are increased and enhanced educational and occupational opportunities for women. Demographers have argued for at least two decades that China's socioeconomic development must not be overlooked when appraising its remarkable fertility reduction (Cai, 2010; Poston, 2000; Poston and Gu, 1987; Wang, Cai, and Gu, 2013). As demographer Yong Cai noted a few years years ago, "structural changes brought about by socioeconomic development and ideational shifts accompanying the new wave of globalization played a key role in China's fertility reduction" (Cai, 2010: 419).

On October 29, 2015, the government abandoned the policy, permitting all couples in China to have two children. The "announcement of the new policy came on the last day of a meeting of top party leaders known as the Fifth Plenum, where they charted out China's economic and social plan for the next five years" (Burkitt, 2015). The government has become concerned about its increasing numbers of elderly and small numbers of children. Many leaders believe that "an aging population with fewer young people could drain resources" (Burkitt, 2015) making more difficult the intended shift in the country toward economic policies focusing more so on consumer spending and services.

I do not expect that this policy change will result in any dramatic increases in China's fertility rate. At best the TFR might go up over the next decade by 0.1 or 0.2. This is so because most of China's fertility reduction in recent decades has been largely voluntary and was more a result of China's modernization than its fertility control policies. We also need to be aware of what demographers refer to as the "low fertility trap," that is, the hypothesis advanced by Lutz (2006) and others that for several reasons once a country's fertility rate drops below 1.5 or 1.4, it is very difficult to increase it by a significant amount. The Chinese government places its fertility rate at around 1.7, but the true rate is likely to be closer to 1.4 or so (Guo and Gu, 2014). Despite the concerns of some that this change in China's family planning policy will soon produce a baby boom in the country, I doubt seriously that one will occur now or in the next few years or decades.

China's fertility policies have been characterized by some as especially coercive. For instance, Aird (1990) wrote that the policy follows a cycles-of-coercion model of family planning: the Chinese central authorities enforce an unpopular birth control policy by exhorting the local authorities to coerce the people and to force them to accept the program's mandates. The pressure continues until opposition becomes so strong that a relaxation of the policy occurs, which itself leads to more new births than can be allowed, thus leading to another wave of coercion. This causes the kind of fluctuations one sees in China's vacillating fertility rates, especially in the 1980s and early 1990s.

An alternate view espouses a linear model in which over time, the mandates of an unpopular policy are relaxed and the mechanisms for enforcing the regulations are weakened; more and more couples, especially rural ones, are permitted to have more children. A linear model does not necessarily assume that all of the political directives in China are top-to-bottom in direction, but that cadres (the approximate equivalent in China of civil servants) at the local level have considerable influence in not only enforcing, but also developing fertility plans and policies (Greenhalgh, 1986, 1990a, 2008).

Pronatalist Policies

I now move away from India and China, countries characterized by fertility policies designed to reduce population growth, and direct attention to countries with policies encouraging population growth. The current situation in virtually all the countries of the developed world is one with fertility rates well below the level needed to replace the population. Such low rates over a long period of time have many consequences, not the least of which is a dramatic aging of the population and, later, a reduction in the size of the population. Thus, there is much concern about below replacement fertility in the countries of the developed world and in some other countries, for example, South Korea, Singapore, and Taiwan, to mention only three. The concern is not solely about population decline, but also about the aging of the population as a result of the very low fertility. This kind of ramification of a below replacement fertility rate in place for several decades will challenge social security and healthcare systems and may even hinder productivity and global competitiveness (Lutz, O'Neil, and Scherbov, 2003).

Development of pronatalist policies in countries these days is difficult to promote. Today, family policies seem to be based on an equal opportunities rationale and aim to help women combine childrearing with employment (Lutz, O'Neil, and Scherbov, 2003).

Different countries have developed different types of policies to encourage increased fertility. I have already mentioned France. In recent years, France has employed numerous policies with two purposes, namely, reconciling family life with work and reversing declining fertility. According to the Rand Corporation, "To accomplish the first goal, France instituted generous child-care subsidies. To accomplish the second goal, families have been rewarded for having at least three children. Sweden, by contrast, reversed the fertility declines it experienced in the 1970s through a different mix of policies, none of which had the specific objective of raising fertility. Its parental work policies during the 1980s allowed many women to raise children while remaining in the workforce. The mechanisms for doing so were flexible work schedules, quality child care, and extensive parental leave on reasonable economic terms" (Rand Corp., 1995: 1–4).

Other countries have implemented fertility policies involving financial remittances for each child born, liberal parental leave benefits, and guaranteed child care and schooling for children. One of the most expansive and generous fertility policies has been enacted in Australia, where remittances per child per year exceeded US$3,000 (Balter, 2006). The efforts to increase the country's fertility rate have been extensive. The TFR actually increased between 2001 and 2008 from 1.73 to 1.96. An appraisal of the effects of the policies on this small increase suggest that components of the program known as the "Baby Bonus" and the "Child Care Rebate" have had only a very slight effect. Most of the small fertility increase has been attributed to indirect effects, such as increased levels of education and income (Parr and Guest, 2011).

In Russia, efforts to increase fertility have focused on an aggressive pronatalist policy involving financial incentives, medals for "baby-making," and an array of other awards (Rodriguez, 2009; see also Eberstadt, 2009). However, the effectiveness of these fertility incentives is hotly debated. Some argue that incentives are beneficial in easing the financial burdens caused by additional children, making families more willing to increase their childbearing. Others emphasize that any increases due to these policies will be small, as was the case in Australia. While financial resources may make it easier for families to pay for the children they already want to have, they are unlikely to raise fertility to the level necessary to stave off population decline (Howden and Poston, 2008).

To be sure, even if successful, these are long-term goals that will take decades to come to fruition. In the meantime, many countries with below replacement fertility rates are faced with another population-related dilemma: whether they should continue losing population or begin accepting more immigrants. Some have suggested that declining populations and the resulting dramatic imbalances in population age structure can be corrected through increases in migration. Since many developing countries are still experiencing high birth rates and population growth, immigration originating in these countries can supplement small working-age cohorts in other countries (Wattenberg, 2004). While international migration may be beneficial in the redistribution of national populations, immigration policies encouraging migration from developing countries remain the least-favored policies of countries experiencing population declines (Howden and Poston, 2008). I will focus on immigration policy in a later section.

In sum, fertility policies vary across the world, and they have for decades. In some regions, birth rates are high; in others, they are low. Both governmental and nongovernmental agencies have been and are involved in attempting to restore some demographic balance in their respective societies.

POLICIES AFFECTING MORTALITY

Some demographers hold that mortality-related policies should not be considered to be direct population policies. The reduction of mortality should be the goal of governments, even those wishing to reduce their rates of population growth. Thus, measures taken by governments that deal with mortality may only be viewed as indirect population policies as long as they have a demographic effect. For example, most industrialized countries subsidize medical care. Often, medical clinics provide free healthcare to the public. While these can be said to be examples of health policies, their overall effect is to increase life expectancy. I look now at some examples of how indirect policies can affect mortality by causing either increases or decreases in the number of deaths.

Mortality policies receiving the most attention are those supporting the development of medical knowledge with the potential to expand life expectancy, as, for example, through the development of new wonder drugs or the facilitation of organ transplants. Beginning in the eighteenth century, there was considerable scientific work in this area of medical knowledge. The work of scientists like Edward Jenner (1749–1823), Louis Pasteur (1822–1895), and Alexander Fleming (1881–1955) all contributed to the reduction of mortality in western Europe and elsewhere. "Before the Second World War, colonial powers as well as independent governments in Latin American and Asia had enacted public health measures, launched sanitation and disease vector control programs, and organized targeted campaigns to bring down high mortality levels, notably in cities" (May, 2005: 838).

The demographer Massimo Livi-Bacci (2012) has noted that programs to eradicate malaria in Sri Lanka (formerly known as Ceylon) were successful as early as the 1940s, and the successes were mainly attributable to the use of dichloro-diphenyl-trichloroethane or DDT. For centuries, mosquitoes had been major killers in Ceylon and elsewhere, where the parasite would afflict "more than half of the population with anemia and chronic fatigue" (Connelly, 2008: 116). In the mid-1940s, public health officials sprayed more than half a million homes in Ceylon with DDT: "Within two years the total number of malaria cases had been cut by three-quarters, and six years later life expectancy had increased from 46 years to 60, largely because of the decline in infant mortality" (Connelly, 2008: 116).

Government policies can directly contribute to lower mortality. Every developed country in the world, with the exception of the United States, offers free or subsidized healthcare to all its citizens. This is reflected in comparative levels of life expectancy, as discussed earlier in Chapter 7. Government policies aimed at reducing the incidence of specific diseases are clearly related to mortality. In 1972, then President Richard Nixon declared a "War on Cancer," and millions of dollars have been spent for this purpose with much success. Thousands of lives are saved each year as a result of government regulations requiring installation of safety features, such as seat belts in new vehicles.

Perhaps the most publicized health policy that affects mortality relates to the use of tobacco. The US National Institutes of Health have for many years cited studies showing a strong positive relationship between smoking and the risk of lung cancer and certain cardiovascular diseases. Even second-hand smoke is detrimental. Today, smoking is banned in most public buildings, including restaurants and bars in some states. Again, these efforts were not directly intended to increase life expectancy; their intent was to improve health.

If we accept the fact that some existing government measures or policies contribute to declining mortality, we must also accept the fact that some government policies can lead to increased mortality. Measures that endanger health, although unintentionally, will eventually raise mortality. Just as there are policies that decrease mortality, there are also policies that raise it.

International warfare is the most obvious mortality-related governmental policy. Hundreds of millions of people have been killed as a result of humans declaring war on one another. I noted in Chapter 7 that the greatest number of deaths due to wars occurred during the first part of the last century: "Plausible sizes of the military and civilian death toll would be around 8.5 million in World War I and 40 million in World War II" (Etherington, 2003: 964). The number of civilian deaths due to wars usually exceeds the number of military deaths. For instance, it is likely that during the Second World War in Russia, 60 percent of the deaths were to civilians (Petersen, 1975: 269). The Civil War resulted in the most number of deaths to Americans of any war ever experienced by the United States, before or after. Around 620,000 men died during the four years of fighting between 1861 and 1865 (Faust, 2008).

Government policies are sometimes deliberately aimed at increasing mortality. I noted earlier the practice of genocide in Nazi Germany as an example. Sadly, the world has witnessed more and more genocides in recent decades, for example, in Rwanda where Hutus tried to eliminate Tutsis, and in Darfur where religious hatred led to millions of deaths.

In far less revolting ways, governments frequently, albeit indirectly, affect mortality. Even while state and federal agencies are speaking out against smoking, they continue to subsidize tobacco growers and benefit from cigarette tax revenues. Indeed, cigarette advertising is still allowed in all media except broadcasting. Cigarette smoking, however, is but a minor contributor to air pollution.

For decades, the growth policies of most developed countries have resulted in increased degrees of smog and dangerous chemicals, which pollute the environment, both air and water. Epidemiologists have found relationships between polluted air and water and the prevalence of certain respiratory and gastrointestinal diseases. Nicholson (1976) found in the mid-1970s that due to the use of asbestos fibers textile workers who had worked for twenty years in the industry had more than four times the risk of cancer of the respiratory system as the general population.

Perhaps the strongest example of failure on the part of the US government to do everything possible to improve health and longevity is its policy on medical assistance. For at least half a century, there has been a growing demand for a national health program. According to an observation written more than sixty years ago, but still applicable today, the United States remains "the only great industrial country without a compulsory nationwide program for health insurance or sickness benefits . . . There is ample evidence, however, of a shift of public opinion toward handling medical care as a predictable and insurable risk and responsibility" (Woytinsky and Woytinsky, 1953: 238).

The United States has instituted the Medicare and Medicaid programs to help the poor and the aged. Assistance has been provided to the elderly for pharmaceutical expenses. An almost nationwide program of health insurance in the United States known as the Affordable Care Act, colloquially as Obamacare, was signed into law by President Barack Obama on March 23, 2010, and upheld by the US Supreme Court on June 28, 2012, and again on June 22, 2015. The Affordable Care Act has surely raised the insurance coverage levels of the population, but, still, not everyone, around 20–25 million Americans, is covered.

For its degree of modernization, the United States has a poor showing on various health indexes, such as life expectancy and infant mortality, an issue that I have already discussed in Chapter 7. Perhaps the failure to institute a national health program that would provide subsidized medical care to everyone in part explains this poor showing.

Thus far, I have concentrated on policies related to natural population change. I now turn to policies related to immigration.

POLICIES AFFECTING INTERNATIONAL MIGRATION

Throughout most of human history, people have been free to move about in search of a better life. I noted in Chapter 9 that human populations began their migrations out of Africa around 50,000–60,000 years ago, first going to southern Asia, China, and Java, and later to Europe. There were no legal encumbrances then that made such moves difficult or impossible. To a considerable extent, however, such freedom of international movement has been significantly restricted since late in the nineteenth century. Many countries have introduced laws that infringe on the freedom to engage in international migration. In some instances, people have not been permitted to enter a country and, in other instances, people have not been permitted to enter certain parts of a country.

At the same time, some governments have taken measures to encourage movement into some areas and out of others. There have been instances of policies involving both nations and areas within a nation. Policies regarding international migration are much more common and pervasive than those pertaining to internal migration. An example of the latter is China's prohibition on most rural residents' freedom to migrate to urban areas, an issue I have already discussed in Chapter 8. In this section, I restrict my discussions to policies related to international migration.

Some countries encourage immigration in order to increase the size of their population. This was true of the United States during the eighteenth and nineteenth centuries. Immigration from other countries was necessary for the United States to grow in population. Canada, Australia, and New Zealand also fall into this category. Indeed, most of the current residents of these countries are immigrants or the descendants of immigrants. I noted earlier that in the United States, less than 2 percent of the resident population, around 4.2 million people, identified in the 2010 census as American Indians, Alaskan Natives, or Native Hawaiian or Pacific Islanders. That is, more than 98 percent of the US population is comprised of immigrants or the descendants of immigrants. The United States, Canada, Australia, and New Zealand, all of which owe their heritage to immigration, are no longer encouraging large numbers of people to immigrate there.

Today, Israel is one of the few countries that actively seeks immigrants. In fact, immigration is considered the lifeblood of the country. Other nations, faced with rapid population growth, view emigration (movement out of a country) as a safety valve to relieve population pressures; some of the Caribbean countries are examples. In actuality, there are no countries in the world today without some sort of immigration policy, for or against. Some seek immigration, and others, such as Japan, allow little if any immigration. In the few countries that permit modest amounts of immigration, such as the United States, there is often considerable discussion and even disagreement about the numbers and the policies and how those policies should be enforced.

In the developed world today, there are three main types of national immigration regimes. The first is the so-called traditional immigration regime. The United States, Canada, and Australia are the three most important and sizable traditional immigration countries: "Founded by European settlers, they have long experiences with immigration and [to this day] allow the acquisition of citizenship through naturalization or birth within their territory" (Freeman, 2003: 515). The number of people legally admitted into these three countries are categorized in terms of family unification, economic needs of the country, and refugees. The United States admits most of its immigrants under the family unification category, whereas Canada and Australia admit most of their immigrants under the skilled worker category. These three countries used to restrict immigrants on the basis of their national origins; persons from certain European countries were usually preferred. But "all three countries ceased to discriminate on the basis of national origin by the early 1970s" (Freeman, 2003: 515).

The second type of national immigration regime includes countries that mainly allow immigrants to enter as guest workers. In past decades these were primarily "European countries that recruited temporary labor (guest workers) or received substantial colonial migration during the post–World War II economic expansions" (Freeman, 2003: 516). The immigrants came from southern and eastern Europe, North Africa, Turkey, south Asia, and the West Indies for the most part. The receiving countries were mainly in northern and western Europe, particularly Germany, Great Britain, France, and the Netherlands. These immigrations stopped in the early 1970s, but not many of the guest workers ever returned to their home countries. Indeed, most of the workers brought members of their families into their new host destinations. As a consequence, by the 1980s, most of the northern and western European countries had large immigrant and foreign-born populations, as well as second-generation immigrants, many of whom were not citizens of these host countries. Today, many Gulf countries, for example, Qatar, the United Arab Emirates, and Kuwait, among others, fall into this second category.

The third type of immigration regime is the group of southern and eastern European countries "more likely to receive than to send immigrants" (Freeman, 2003: 516). The four countries most prominent in this category are Greece, Spain, Portugal, and Italy. These countries serve as entry points for undocumented immigrants from other countries who are seeking to enter the European Union. As a consequence, as of early 2013, there were more than 33.5 million people born in a non-European Union country living in one the twenty-seven member countries of the European Union (EU-27), or almost 7 percent of its population of 503 million (Eurostat, 2015). When one adds in the children of these immigrants, the foreign population becomes larger. As an example, in 2010 there were around 13 million Muslims residing in the European Union. The 4.8 million in Germany are themselves, or their ancestors were, mainly from Turkey. The 4.7 million in France are mainly from the former French colonies of Algeria, Morocco, and Tunisia (Hackett, 2015). Freeman (2003) has remarked about the difficulties that these countries have experienced in embracing multiculturalism. Their difficulties may be compared with the less difficult and problematic experiences of the United States, Canada, and Australia. To get an idea of the many and varied types of immigration policies, I turn in the next section to a discussion of the history of immigration policies in the United States.

US IMMIGRATION POLICIES

Immigration was not a concern in early America, and there were no formal laws or policies regulating immigration on a national level. But the new US Constitution did deal with the issue of naturalization, that is, the process by which an individual becomes a citizen (Purcell, 1995). The Articles of Confederation allowed aliens to naturalize as American citizens after two years' residence in the United States, something that was not previously allowed under British rule (Gabaccia, 2002). These policies, however, did not apply to white indentured servants or to blacks. The restrictions were particularly reflected in the Aliens Acts of 1798, which required aliens to register and allowed the president to deport any individuals deemed to be dangerous. The laws expired in 1801 when Thomas Jefferson became president, and the citizenship waiting period increased to five years (Cortes and Poston, 2008; Purcell, 1995).

One of the most notable laws restricting immigration to the United States was the Chinese Exclusion Act of May 6, 1882, which reflected the public concern about the large numbers of Chinese who had come to provide inexpensive labor for the construction of the transcontinental railroad. This law suspended the immigration of Chinese laborers for ten years; it permitted Chinese who were in the United States as of November 17, 1880, to stay, travel abroad, and return; it prohibited the naturalization of Chinese; and it created the so-called section 6 exempt status for Chinese teachers, students, merchants, and travelers who were admitted on the presentation of certificates from the Chinese government (Cortes and Poston, 2008).

The next significant exclusionary legislation was the Act to Prohibit the Coming of Chinese Persons into the United States of May 1892, better known as the Geary Act, and discussed earlier in more detail in Chapter 9. It allowed Chinese laborers to travel home to China and reenter the United States, but its provisions were very restrictive. Other restrictive immigration acts affecting citizens of Chinese ancestry followed (King and Locke, 1980). The Chinese Exclusion Act and later exclusionary laws were the first to use the concept of an illegal **alien** (Pedraza and Rumbaut, 1996).

The next major immigration policy was the 1917 Immigration Act that increased the head tax on immigrants to $8.00 and required incoming migrants to pass literacy tests. The Immigration Act also "established several new categories for exclusion, including vagrants, alcoholics, and the psychopathically inferior" (Purcell, 1995: 82). This law required the potential immigrant to be able to read a passage in English or in another language. It also extended the exclusion of Chinese and Japanese to all Asians (Cortes and Poston, 2008).

In 1921, further restrictions were passed that set quotas based on nation of origin. In 1924, Congress took this one step further by passing the National Origins Act, which restricted the total number of immigrants to 150,000; the division of the quotas reflected the American population enumerated in the 1890 census. This was done in an attempt to allow mainly immigrants from Great Britain, Scandinavia, and Germany, while reducing immigration from all Asian countries and severely restricting the immigration of Italians, Slavs, Jews, Greeks, and other southern and eastern Europeans (Purcell, 1995).

From the 1920s to the 1950s, immigration in the United States changed significantly. The Great Depression and the Second World War resulted in a period of slow and sometimes negative immigration, culminating in net losses in population size due to international migration. The only significant immigration was from Mexico under the bracero program, which admitted

Mexican male workers while Americans were overseas (see Chapter 9). In 1952, the Immigration and Nationality Act, also known as the McCarran–Walter Act, was passed, maintaining most of the quotas set forth in the National Origins Act of 1924 (Hay, 2001). It was introduced by Representative Pat McCarran of Nevada and Representative Francis E. Walter of Pennsylvania.

The next major US immigration policy was the Immigration and Nationality Act of 1965, also known as the Hart–Cellar Act; it became law in 1968. It was proposed by Representative Emanuel Cellar of New York and co-sponsored by Senator Philip Hart of Michigan. This act, signed by President Lyndon B. Johnson, ended the national origins quota system and allowed the immigration of family members of those already living in the United States, as well as individuals in certain occupations. It also ended the restrictions on Asian immigration, and it limited immigration from the western hemisphere as a whole to 120,000 (Hay, 2001). Iceland has noted that the most significant effect of the 1965 law "was that it spurred immigration from countries that had little recent history of sending immigrants to the United States, especially Asia and later Africa" (2014: 111).

Total permanent immigration to the United States has undergone many changes in recent years. The numbers increased from about 600,000 in 1986 and 1987 to over 1.8 million in 1991, and then fell back to around 660,000 in 1998. The number of immigrants increased to over 1 million in 2001 and 2002, dropped to under 1 million in 2003 and 2004, and then rose to over 1 million in the years up to 2012, falling back to just under 1 million in 2013 (US Department of Homeland Security, 2014, table 1).

The rise in the total number from 1987 to 1991 may be attributed in part to the Immigration Reform and Control Act (IRCA) of 1986, which granted legal status to undocumented immigrants who had been in the United States continuously since 1982. This Act has also been cited as a reason for the increased number of pending "adjustment of status" applications and the subsequent reduction in the number of approved applications.

Changes in the number of permanent immigrants to the United States from all countries in the world are also explained in part by the impact of the Immigration Act of 1990, which revised the annual ceiling on immigration and the preference categories used to regulate immigration. This Act, which became effective on October 1, 1991, increased the levels of employment-based immigration and allotted a higher proportion of visas to highly skilled immigrants.

The number of permanent immigrants from China to the United States has fluctuated since 1989. The IRCA, a one-time-only amnesty, does not appear to have had as dramatic an impact on Chinese permanent immigration as it had on total permanent immigration. Indeed, the Chinese immigration rate to the United States has been relatively stable since 1980, except for increases in 1993 and 1994. They were due in part to the influence of the Immigration Act of 1990 but, more important, to the Chinese Student Protection Act of 1992, a bill sponsored by Representative Nancy Pelosi of California, which granted permanent resident status to Chinese immigrants who were in the United States after June 4, 1989, and before April 11, 1990. Its stated purpose was to prevent the political persecution of Chinese students in the aftermath of the Tiananmen demonstrations and protests of 1989. One of its provisions was that permanent residency status slots granted to Chinese nationals under the Act would be subtracted from the immigration spaces available in later years. But, ironically, the primary beneficiaries of this act were reported to be undocumented immigrants from Fujian Province, China, who were not students at all (Poston and Luo, 2007).

From 2004 to 2013, the number of Chinese immigrants to the United States ranged from between 55,000 and 72,000 per year, resulting in China, along with Mexico and India, being the three countries sending the largest numbers of immigrants each year to the United States (US Department of Homeland Security, 2014, table 3).

In 1996, two laws were passed that impacted the levels of permanent immigration to the United States, namely, the Welfare Reform Act of 1996 and the Illegal Immigration Reform and Immigrant Responsibility Act of 1996. One eliminated the entitlement to support for poor families, requiring able-bodied persons who received government assistance to work (Espenshade, Baraka, and Huber, 1997). The other circumscribed the eligibility of immigrants for public benefit programs by creating a four-tier system: "The broadest eligibility is reserved for U.S. citizens; next come refugees and asylees; newly limited access is imposed on legal immigrants; and illegal immigrants remain ineligible for almost all social programs" (Espenshade, Baraka, and Huber, 1997: 771–772). Prior to its enactment, US citizens, legal immigrants, and refugees were all equally eligible for most public benefit programs.

The Illegal Immigration Reform and Immigrant Responsibility Act of 1996 was passed to strengthen the effects of the Welfare Reform Act that year by combating illegal immigration and creating higher standards of financial self-sufficiency for the admission of sponsored legal immigrants. This act focused in particular on immigrant access to public benefits by: (1) establishing measures to control US borders, protect legal workers through worksite enforcement, and remove criminal and other deportable aliens; (2) placing added restrictions on benefits for aliens; and (3) introducing miscellaneous limitation provisions, such as a limit on the ability of F-1 students to attend public schools without reimbursing those institutions.

Espenshade, Baraka, and Huber (1997) have argued that the combined effects of these two 1996 laws have had important consequences. The welfare reforms of 1996 led to a larger number of eligible legal immigrants becoming naturalized so that the actual cost savings attributable to benefits for immigrants were smaller than expected. In addition, the 1996 immigration and welfare reforms were expected to reduce the future volume of US legal immigration and to produce a legal immigrant stream with higher skill and income levels.

In 1998, the US Congress passed the American Competitiveness and Workforce Improvement Act. It was a response, in part, to the belief in the Congress that the United States was facing a severe shortage of workers qualified to perform skilled jobs in information technology, even though the evidence of a shortage was inconclusive. Under this Act, the annual ceiling of certain petitions valid for initial employment was increased from 65,000 to 115,000 in fiscal years 1999 and 2000 and to 107,500 in 2001.

The stated purpose of the act was to protect native-born American workers by preventing employers from hiring low-skilled aliens instead of native-born workers. Employers are required to take good-faith steps to recruit American workers for jobs that could potentially be performed by certain immigrants, and to offer the jobs to American workers who are equally or better qualified than the aliens.

The Enhanced Border Security and Visa Entry Reform Act of 2002 dealt with entry documents and data-sharing among government agencies. It was passed by Congress and signed into law by President George W. Bush on May 14, 2002, around eight months after the terrorist attacks of 9/11. It represented "the most comprehensive immigration-related response to the continuing terrorist threat" faced by the United States (Jenks, 2002: 1).

The Real ID Act of 2005 modified several federal laws pertaining to the issuance standards of drivers' licenses and identification cards accepted by the federal government for official purposes, such as entering federal buildings and boarding national and international air flights.

The preceding is a summary of many of the immigration and immigration-based laws passed in the United States since the late 1800s. The immigration laws, especially the more recent ones, are numerous and very complex in their meaning and interpretation. Attorneys specializing in immigration law are needed these days to facilitate the entry of immigrants into the United States, and this process, if it is successful, usually takes not months but years. Compare this long-drawn-out and complicated process of entering the country with that of many of our ancestors who entered the United States after undergoing a screening at Ellis Island of, at best, a few days (see Chapter 9).

REPLACEMENT MIGRATION

I noted earlier that in this new era of declining fertility and reductions in population size, countries might consider turning to immigration as a means of redressing the population losses occurring through declining fertility. In other words, migration could be used as a means of replacing the population lost through lower fertility. In this last section, I consider the concept of replacement migration (Keeley, 2009) and how it would work and be applied. I do so within the context of South Korea, a country with an extremely low fertility rate, that is, a TFR in 2013 of 1.2.

Population projections prepared for South Korea for the next several decades indicate that the absolute and relative numbers of the older population (persons aged 65+) will increase dramatically. By 2050, South Korea is projected to have made the transition to a top-heavy and demographically very old country. In 2050, almost 36 percent of its population is projected to be 65 years of age or older. In 2050, South Korea will be older than the United States, which in 2050 is projected to have 21 percent of its population aged 65 or older. What are some of the implications of this aging of South Korea's population?

One effect is the tremendous change that will occur in the extent to which the older members of the population will be able to be supported economically and emotionally by the younger members. To appraise quantitatively the extent of this age-structure imbalance, the United Nations (2001) developed a measure of elderly support, known as the **potential support ratio** (PSR). It represents "the extent that persons of working age [15–64] can be seen as supporting the older population [65 years or older], and is the ratio between the two" (United Nations, 2001: 7). The PSR value represents the number of persons in the population who "support" each old person in the population.

To illustrate, I show in Table 15.1 that in 1950 in South Korea, there were 11,257,000 persons aged 15–64 and 620,000 persons aged 65+. Dividing the former by the latter indicates the number of persons in the population who are available to support every one old person. In 1950, the PSR for South Korea was 18.2. The United States had a PSR in 1950 more than half that of South Korea because the US fertility rate at that time was considerably lower than that of South Korea. The values of the PSR for South Korea and for the United States for 1950, 2010, and 2050 are shown in Table 15.1.

In the last few decades in South Korea, "life expectancy at birth for both sexes combined increased from 47.5 years in 1950–55 to 70.9 years in 1990–95" (United Nations, 2001: 59). Increasing levels of life expectancy, along with a rapidly declining fertility rate, have resulted in the pace of

Table 15.1 Total Population, Population in Age Groups 0–14, 15–64, and 65+, and PSRs, South Korea and the United States, 1950, 2010, and 2050

	1950	2010	2050
South Korea			
Total population ('000)	20,357	48,636	43,368
Age group 0–14 ('000)	8,479	7,895	4,426
Age group 15–64 ('000)	11,257	35,349	23,364
Age group 65+ ('000)	620	5,392	15,579
Potential support ratio (15–64 / 65+)	18.16	6.56	1.50
United States			
Total population ('000)	152,271	309,326	399,803
Age group 0–14 ('000)	40,998	61,202	71,781
Age group 15–64 ('000)	98,876	207,648	244,284
Age group 65+ ('000)	12,397	40,477	83,739
Potential support ratio (15–64 / 65+)	7.98	5.13	2.92

Source: US Bureau of the Census, 2050 projection data from International Data Base. Calculations by DLP.

population aging in South Korea being one of the fastest in the world. The proportion of persons aged 65 and older in South Korea's population increased from 3.0 percent in 1950, to 4.0 percent in 1960, to 5.6 percent in 1995 (United Nations, 2001: 59), to 11 percent in 2010, and it is projected to be 36 percent in 2050.

Of even greater interest is the change in the PSRs. The PSR dropped from 18.2 in 1950 to 6.6 in 2010. Whereas in 1950 there were more than 18 "supporting" persons in the South Korean population for every one old person, this ratio declined in 2010 to less than 7 supporters for every one old person. During this sixty-year period, the PSR also decreased in the United States from 8 to 5. In 2010, the PSR of the United States was a little less than that of South Korea.

By 2050, however, the PSR in South Korea is projected to plummet to 1.5. That is, there are projected to be less than 2 South Koreans in the population available to support every one elderly South Korean. In South Korea in 2010, almost 7 persons were available to support every one elderly person; in 2050, there will be less than 2 supporting persons available for every one South Korean elder.

The United States is also projected to have a low PSR in 2050, a PSR of 2.9, almost twice that of South Korea. But, as noted, the United States had a PSR in 2010 of 5.1, a lower level of elderly support than in South Korea in 2010. Whereas in the United States in 2010 there were 5.1 supporting persons in the population for every one elder, in South Korea in 2010 there were 6.7 supporting persons for every one South Korean elder. The process of population aging in the United States has been less rapid than the process in South Korea.

Given the projected PSR of 1.5 for South Korea for 2050, one might ask what would need to be done to return to a higher PSR. Specifically, what would South Korea have to do demographically to have a PSR of 12 in 2050 instead of the projected PSR of 1.5? (I selected a PSR of 12 because it is midway between South Korea's PSRs of 18 in 1950 and 6 in 2010.) In other words, what would South Korea have to do to alter its demographic destiny of a highly imbalanced PSR of 1.50 for 2050? How could South Korea obtain more persons in the supporting population so as to offset its very low projected PSR for 2050?

One way would be to increase the fertility rate. South Korea's TFR of 1.2 in 2013 is one of the lowest in the world. Some countries have introduced population policies to raise their fertility rates, and I reviewed some of these earlier in this chapter. Although this is one approach, it would be demographically inefficient because it takes many years before a newborn becomes a supporting member of the population.

A quicker approach would be international migration, a strategy that would permit South Korea to bring supporting members into its population directly and immediately. How many international migrants would South Korea require if the end result would be to maintain, through the year of 2050, a PSR of around 12? That is, between 2000 and 2050, how many immigrants would South Korea need to admit into the country if it wished to maintain a PSR of 12? (I am using the interval here of 2000 to 2050 because this was the interval used by the United Nations when it published its calculations in 2001.)

The answer is an astonishingly high number of 5.1 billion immigrants! That is, for South Korea to maintain between 2000 and 2050 a PSR of 12 supporters for every one elderly, it would require a total of 5,128,147,000 immigrants, or an average of almost 103 million immigrants each year! The UN reports that this "number is enormous because the initial level of the PSR ... is relatively high" (2001: 60). This number of immigrants required between 2000 and 2050 is almost equal to the total population of the world. This unrealistic number also indicates that South Korea's current PSR "is transitional and will be considerably lower in the future, irrespective of migration flows" (United Nations, 2001: 60).

A less drastic scenario would ask how many immigrants would South Korea need if the end result was to not allow the PSR to ever fall below 3.0. I have already shown in Table 15.1 that South Korea's PSR in 2010 was 6.6

and is projected to be 1.5 in 2050. If South Korea's policymakers wish to avoid the PSR reaching the projected level of 1.5, but rather to stabilize at 3.0, how many immigrants would be needed?

To attain this objective, "no immigrants would be needed until 2035, and 11.6 million immigrants would be needed between 2035 and 2050, an average of 0.8 million new immigrants per year" (United Nations, 2001: 60). Under this scenario, South Korea would have a total population in 2050 of 65.7 million, of which "14 million, or 21 percent, would be post-1995 immigrants or their descendants" (United Nations, 2001: 60).

The provision of elder care in South Korea will be a major concern between now and the year 2050 and beyond. As I have mentioned above, in 2010, there were 6.6 South Koreans supporting every one South Korean elder, and this PSR is projected to drop precipitously to 1.5 by 2050. One way for South Korea to offset this dramatic decline in its PSR would be to develop population policies encouraging persons to immigrate to South Korea, that is, turn to international migration for demographic replacement. Although replacement migration is a more efficient strategy than increasing fertility, the number of replacement immigrants is so large that this approach may not be quite as easy as one might suspect. Nevertheless, I agree with Keeley that "replacement migration will probably continue to be a topic that is redressed from time to time as the demography of the last century and the demographic behaviors of the 21st century play out in a variety of social settings...Its salience, however, is unlikely to become very high" (2009: 403).

SUMMARY

Populations change in size, composition, and distribution via fertility, mortality, and migration. But these changes are not random in their occurrence. Many governments have passed laws and regulations that deal with their levels of fertility, mortality, and migration, particularly migration. Many of the laws represent direct effects to influence national rates of population change, and others involve indirect effects.

Regarding policies intended to influence levels of fertility, there are two main approaches. One is to provide birth control knowledge and services and related enhancements through massive government-sponsored family and family planning programs. The other is to change the social and economic environments so that people are motivated to have fewer, or more, children. Examples of these nonprogram efforts include modernization, payments for having or not having children, increased opportunities for the employment of women, population education, and maternal and paternal employment leave. The two approaches are often viewed as complementing each other.

Governments influence mortality mainly through their attempts to improve the health levels of the population. But there are several government practices (e.g., war) that serve to increase mortality rather than lower it. The failure of governments to enact remedial laws and programs, say, with regard to health insurance coverage, has also been shown to increase mortality.

Governments also have laws and policies influencing the number of people coming across their borders, and some have laws relating to persons departing. The United States receives the largest number of immigrants of any country in the world and, as a consequence, has a wealth of laws dealing with immigration, many of which I have reviewed and commented on in this chapter. At times, countries have expressed a concern in their immigration laws about the "quality" of the population. This was particularly the case with immigration laws invoked in many countries, including the United States, in the last two centuries with regard to the national origins of the immigrants. Quality restrictions are still found in the immigration laws of many countries today regarding the labor force, educational, and economic qualifications of potential immigrants.

With the increasing number of countries in the world today with below replacement fertility, we can expect to see more countries writing and implementing policies in an attempt to increase the numbers of babies born. With the growing socioeconomic gap between countries and the desire of persons from poorer countries to move to better-off countries, we can expect the receiving countries to continue to prepare policies and laws in an attempt to regulate and balance these streams of migrants from abroad. But the policies, whatever their intention and reason for their genesis, will never be successful unless they take into account the social, cultural, and economic milieu in which demographic behavior occurs, and unless they consider the indirect as well as the direct effects.

16 The Earth in the Twenty-first and Twenty-second Centuries

INTRODUCTION

You have now read through the first fifteen chapters of this book (I hope you have read all the chapters). You have learned a good deal about population and demography and the world in which we live. You now should know more demography than you did when you first started to read the book. I certainly hope so.

I have discussed the three demographic processes. I have discussed the basic population characteristics, especially age and sex, as well as the family and race/ethnicity. I have discussed population growth as well as population decline. In this final chapter, I look specifically at the population of the Earth, the number of inhabitants on our planet now and in the future. I will inquire how the world population now and in 2100 may be related to other major factors of life on Earth. I will consider the future of the Earth's population from the perspectives of ecology, sociology, and philosophy. Hence, this last chapter has less to do with demography per se and more to do with the influence of population in several other arenas.

In Chapter 12, I considered several different scenarios with respect to the size of the population of our world in the year 2100. I present here as Figure 16.1 the same figure I presented earlier as Figure 12.4. Let me consider the different scenarios to get an idea of what the size of the world's population might be in 2100.

In Chapter 12, I used world population projections prepared recently by the Population Division of the United Nations (2013d). I preferred them over projections prepared by other organizations because, in my view, the UN projections reflect the most reasonable assumptions about future demographic behavior. However, I remind you again, as I have already in Chapter 12, that these are projections about what the population of the world will be in 2100 according to stated assumptions. In no way should they be seen as predictions, nor should they be considered the final word. (Please look

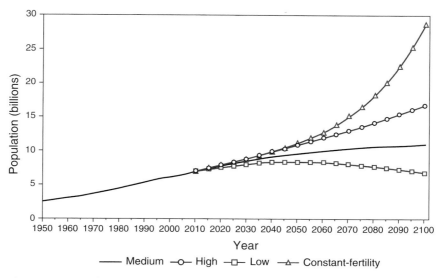

Figure 16.1 Population of the World, 1950–2010, According to Different Projections and Variants
Source: United Nations (2013d: xv).

back at Chapter 12 for my discussion of the assumptions that guided the development of these UN projections.)

What do the trend data in Figure 16.1 tell us? Observe first the single line in the figure showing the population growth of the world from 1950 to 2010; then four lines are shown from 2010 to 2100, each reflecting the future population of the world up to 2100 depending mainly on assumptions with regard to fertility behavior. The population of the world was 2.5 billion in 1950, 4.4 billion in 1980, and around 7 billion in 2010. It is from this point in time that the UN then set out four sets of projections about the future size of the world population up to the year 2100.

The medium-variant (the solid line) assumes that between now and 2100 a fertility decline will occur in those countries where large families are prevalent, and a slight increase in fertility will occur in those countries with fewer than 2 children per woman (United Nations, 2013d: xv). A projection based on these assumptions results in a world population of 9.6 billion in 2050, and 10.9 billion in 2100.

The high-variant projection assumes that each woman will have one-half more child than projected under the medium-variant. Under this projection, the population of the world will be 10.9 billion in 2050, and 16.6 billion in 2100 (see the second line from the top in Figure 16.1, the one with the small circles).

The low-variant projection assumes that each woman in the world will have one-half less child than assumed under the medium-variant. This projection will result in the population of the world numbering 8.3 billion in 2050 and 6.8 billion in 2100. (The 6.8 billion projected value for 2100 is not a typo; the low-variant projection results in a smaller population size by 2100 – see the bottom line in Figure 16.1 with the small squares.)

The projection showing the greatest increase in the world's population is the top line in Figure 16.1; it reflects "constant fertility," that is, a continuation to 2100 of the actual levels of fertility in existence in 2010. If the levels of fertility in the countries of the world in 2010 were to be maintained until the year 2100, the population of the world would be 11.1 billion in 2050 and 28.6 billion in 2100.

As I noted in Chapter 12, I used the numbers of the medium-scenario, but I thought that they might be a little too high. In other words, my personal take on the size of the world's population in 2100 would be a number in the range 9.5–10.5 billion, which is 0.5–1 billion less than the number emerging from the medium-variant projection.

So, according to these four UN projections, the world's population in 2050 would range from 8.3 billion, to 9.6 billion, to 10.9 billion, to a high of 11.1 billion. And the world's population in 2100 would range from 6.8 billion, to 10.9 billion, to 16.6 billion, to 28.6 billion (United Nations, 2013d: 2). Were you to press me for a world population count for 2100, I would set it at between 9.5 and 10.5 billion. (This expectation, of course, assumes there will be no major cataclysmic events such as catastrophic global warming, fresh-water shortages, a nuclear war, and so forth.) I will average out my number to be 10 billion in the year 2100.

What do these numbers mean, and what are their implications?

ECOLOGICAL CONSIDERATIONS

I look first at resources, pollution, and technology. What might be the impact of 10 billion inhabitants of the Earth were we to take an *ecological* view of the population? I will use here what demographers and human ecologists refer to as the ecological complex, that is, the interaction of population, organization, environment, and technology (POET) (Duncan, 1959; Hawley, 1950; Poston, 2015; Poston and Frisbie, 2005).

I believe that the world's population in 2100 will number around 10 billion, and could be higher. But an ever-growing proportion of that population will reside in the developing regions of the world. Around 1.3 billion of the world's population in 2100 will be in the developed countries. Thus, as much as 85 percent of the world's population in 2100 will be in countries we classify today as developing (the developed countries are the United States, Canada, all of Europe, Japan, Australia, and New Zealand). More than 95 percent of the projected growth in the world population between 2010 and 2100 is expected to occur in developing countries. And much of this population growth will come disproportionately from people on the margins, those with limited resources and life opportunities.

The US population now stands at 321 million and is likely to reach around 460 million by 2100. Like the situation with the world's population, the subpopulations in the United States that are increasing disproportionately are mainly those with limited resources and life opportunities.

Let me use these numbers and consider how they are related to resources, pollution, and technology. I first look at resources, specifically oil and water. To maintain any kind of ecological balance in a social system, there must be sufficient resources for the system to maintain itself. While it is not my intention here to delve deeply into resource issues, it is appropriate to point out that today the world is very much concerned about the availability of petroleum (Deffeyes, 2005; Juvkam-Wold and Dessler, 2009). A worldwide energy crisis is not beyond reason, and we already are aware of the growing tensions in the Middle East and elsewhere, in large part because of the need for oil.

But there is a problem with respect to distinguishing between resources and reserves. We have a fairly good idea of the extent of resources. Reserves are more plentiful, but the cost of mining/extracting these areas is so high as to question the economics of such undertakings.

A cause for optimism is the determination on the part of many countries both to foster limitations on petroleum use and to find alternative sources of energy. The Kyoto Protocol is an international treaty intended to bring countries together to reduce global warming and calling on nations to stabilize greenhouse gases in the atmosphere. Most of the developed countries of the world support the protocol; the few that do not include the United States, Canada, and Australia.

Another resource is water. To most readers of this book, water is probably taken for granted. Yes, we know of polluted water but, overall, "What's the problem?" First of all, I need to point out that water is a far more unreliable resource than oil. It is fundamental to life, human and otherwise. Indeed, it is a prerequisite for all living things. Second, there are no substitutes for most of its uses, unlike oil, which can be replaced with other forms of energy. Finally, while water is a renewable resource, it is also finite. In the twenty-first century, the scarcity of water may be the single greatest threat to global food production.

Sandra Postel, a leading authority on water resources, noted the following in her book about water and sustainability. Although she wrote this paragraph in the early 1990s, its insights are still considerable today: "We are entering an unprecedented period of water stress globally. In 2015, nearly 3 billion people – 40 percent of the projected world population – will live in countries that find it difficult or impossible to mobilize enough water to satisfy the food, industrial, and domestic needs of their citizens. How nations respond to this dilemma individually and collectively will have serious implications for food security, for the health of the aquatic environment, and for social and political stability. A new mindset for water policy and management is required if we are to meet the needs of 9 billion people while protecting the health of the aquatic environment that our economies and all life depend upon" (Postel, 1992: 12).

As population grows, there is increasing pressure to deplete our aquifers that are so essential to life. Aquifers are crucial to our water supplies. Consider aquifers as huge water-storage reservoirs. Whereas groundwater is a renewable source, the reserves replenish slowly. We put water in and we take water out. "Falling water tables have already curtailed irrigation from some aquifers, and the competition for water between irrigated agriculture and urban population growth has already led to a systematic diversion of water from agriculture to cities in Arizona and California" (Bouvier and Grant, 1994: 15). Increasing numbers of cities are beginning to experience water shortages: "Cities like San Antonio, El Paso, and Phoenix could run out of water in 10 to 20 years. San Diego's water company has resorted to a once-unthinkable option, namely, recycling toilet water for drinking" (Rubenstein, 2008/9: 5). Today in the United States, groundwater is utilized about four times faster than it is replaced naturally. The great Ogallala Aquifer that covers parts of eight states is gradually being depleted, but remains a primary source of water for much of the Great Plains. It is so important that attempts have been made by billionaire industrialists to purchase much of the land that covers the aquifer. The end result is more expensive water for ordinary users.

Again, as with petroleum, population growth is taken as unchangeable; it is a constant. In his usual pithy manner, Benjamin Franklin said it best: "When the well runs dry, we know the worth of water" (cited in Bartlett, 1968). I note here that a billion or so fewer inhabitants in the world in 2100 would at least postpone the water crisis that will likely be felt eventually. We should not take out more water than enters the system, although we already are doing just that. We should not see our aquifers dry up and disappear, but we do face that prospect. The water wars of the nineteenth century made famous, or infamous, by western movies could return to haunt us in the twenty-first century, if population growth continues unabated. This could, in turn, lead to food shortages and significant increases in the cost of food.

I turn next to considerations of the environment. What do we mean by environment? The term is extremely broad and vague. Hawley defined it as "whatever is external to and potentially or actually influential on a phenomenon under investigation" (1968: 330). Schnore wrote that it is "a set of limiting conditions, which may be narrow or broad, depending on the technological devices and modes of organization that prevail in a given population" (1958: 628). These definitions are useful in limiting the term. For my purposes here, however, the concept "social environment" is not really an environmental issue. Hence, I will limit my discussion to issues of the physical environment, namely, global warming and pollution, and the related problem of waste. These are environmental issues that are significantly related to the human population.

Global warming is the evidence of a rise in the Earth's temperature. It is sometimes referred to as climate change. There is an almost unanimous agreement among scientists that global warming is taking place. Furthermore, "most of the observed increase in globally averaged temperatures since the mid-20th century is very likely due to the observed increase in anthropogenic greenhouse gas concentrations" (IPCC, 2007: 8).

To be sure, other factors are involved, but greenhouse gases seem to be the prime cause of this momentous change in the Earth's temperature. There is already evidence near the Arctic Circle where Greenland is losing some of its ice foundation, causing massive increases in oceanic water to be sent in a southward direction.

My primary concern is with the contribution of population to the problem, not with an in-depth discussion of climate change. Carbon dioxide is a major contributor to greenhouse gas. Motor vehicles are a major contributor to carbon dioxide. As a general rule of thumb, we can add 700 motor vehicles for every 1,000 persons added to a population. This is true in developed nations, and also in China and India, although less so in the other regions of the world. Now let us add a billion or more inhabitants to the planet. You do the math and see what the result will be. So, once again, I point out that although reductions in population growth will not solve all these problems, they would be drastically alleviated if such reductions were at least discussed. In an otherwise excellent article several years ago in the *American Prospect*, Gelbspan (2007) failed to even mention population limitation as a possible aid to solving the planet's problems. He cited a report from the insurance giant Swiss Re in which it was noted that "there is a danger that human intervention will accelerate and intensify climate change to such a point that it will become impossible to adapt our socio-economic systems in time" (Gelb-span, 2007: 47). One wonders what he meant by the phrase "human intervention."

Pollution is closely related to global warming. There are, of course, numerous types of pollution, such as air, water, and noise. Here, I concentrate on air pollution that involves the release of chemicals into the atmosphere. Examples are carbon monoxide and nitrogen oxide, both of which are produced by industry and motor vehicles. Motor vehicle emissions are among the leading causes of air pollution. For decades, we have lamented the dense smog over such cities as London, Los Angeles, and Houston and, more recently, some of the major cities in China, particularly Beijing. The cause has overwhelmingly been the result of too many vehicles. As noted, adding 1,000 people to an area, especially in the industrialized world, results in around 700 more vehicles. Indeed, the ratio may be even more damaging given the increased number of automobiles per household in economically advanced nations. So, once again, I repeat my observation that limiting population growth could well reduce many of our problems; this time, it is pollution.

Of all the problems associated with continued rapid population growth, garbage and waste disposal may be among the most visible. Cities today in the developed world produce more solid waste than they did in the 1960s (Bouvier and Grant, 1994: 15). The problems associated with waste disposal are critical: "Because they were polluting, or simply full, the number of landfills has declined ... Cities have unsuccessfully tried to unload the waste on third world countries ... Eastern cities [in the United States] have been negotiating with rural counties as far away as New Mexico and Texas to accept the stuff. The nation is on a treadmill" (Bouvier and Grant, 1994: 16). The challenge of waste disposal continues, and some states today, for example, Virginia, are beginning to question the wisdom of accepting waste from northern cities.

I will sum up the overall environmental problems faced by the planet. These include "encroaching deserts, rising sea levels, deforestation, acid precipitation, resultant forest dieback, toxic contamination of food supplies, soil oxidation and pollution of water tables, ozone depletion, greenhouse gas buildup and climatic change" (Rees, 2004: 12). Population growth is a contributor, direct or indirect, to all these challenges for our planet.

SOCIOLOGICAL CONSIDERATIONS

Thus far, I have presented a rather dismal picture of population growth and its impact on the world. Allow me to present here a less dismal point of view, indeed an optimistic one, presented by two economists, Ester Boserup and Julian Simon.

Boserup, a deceased Danish economist, argued that population growth was a stimulus to social change (1965). To illustrate, it was population growth that contributed to the move from an agricultural to an industrial society. She also wrote that a society with a growing population is more likely to experience economic development than one where growth is limited or even nonexistent (Boserup, 1981).

Simon, the late American economist, was also demographically optimistic. Politically conservative, he was a major proponent of the argument that "population growth is neutral." This was the basis for the US position at the Second World Population conference in Mexico City (see my discussion in Chapter 15). Simon argued in his influential and very interesting book *The Ultimate Resource* (1981) that population growth and the ability to innovate go together. Indeed, the "ultimate resource" referred to more people. People innovate, and the more people there are, the more likely innovation will occur. In his later years, Simon paid less attention to population growth and more to the commercial market: "Misplaced attention to population growth has resulted in disastrously unsound advice being given to developing nations" (1992: xiii).

While the views of optimists such as Boserup and Simon may have had merit in the past, it is more difficult for such arguments to hold significant sway in a world with more than 7 billion inhabitants, which according to some projections could double in size by 2100. Perhaps one area where the optimists and the pessimists can agree is technology. The technological changes in the world, developed and developing, especially during the last half of the twentieth century, have been remarkable. One immediately thinks of the computer and the Internet. The computer chip has made communications incredibly rapid. A person in New York can be in contact with a person in Beijing in seconds. Recall, too, my earlier discussion of the interstate highway system. Consider how this has increased our ability to get almost anywhere in the United States faster than previously possible. Now we have more speed in our communications and in our travel capabilities. What will the future bring? What technological changes will take place in this century that might impact our lifestyles even more than have been observed in recent decades?

If one thinks that the recent advancements in technology were amazing, we have only seen the beginnings. We, as a species, are constantly evolving. This is nothing new. Auguste Comte, considered by many to be the father of sociology, believed that humanity progressed through three stages of thought and development: theological, metaphysical, and positivist (1853). Émile Durkheim saw a gradual evolving of society from what he called "mechanical" to "organic" ([1893] 1984). Herbert Spencer believed there to be "an inexorable tendency toward differentiation both in the case of organisms into species and in the case of societies into more differentiated structures" (Wallace and Wolf, 2005: 160).

Several years ago Anthony Giddens (2002: 7) remarked that "we live in a world of transformations, affecting almost every aspect of what we do. For better or worse, we are being propelled into a global order that no one understands, but which is making its effects felt upon all of us. Globalization may not be a particularly attractive or elegant word, but absolutely no one who wants to understand our prospects...can ignore it...The global spread of the term is evidence of the very developments to which it refers...[E]ven in the late 1980s the term was hardly used...It has come from nowhere to be almost everywhere."

Two of Thomas Friedman's recent books, *The World is Flat* (2005) and *Hot, Flat and Crowded* (2008), are additional examples of the rapid changes that are occurring as globalization intensifies and as Friedman finds himself communicating instantly from Boston to Bangalore and elsewhere.

PHILOSOPHICAL CONSIDERATIONS

Humankind is evolving. We see it in our behavior, in our changing activities, in the globalization of knowledge, and in our relationships. When do we stop evolving? One of my favorite theologians, the Jesuit priest and scientist, Pierre Teilhard de Chardin (1959, 1969b), argued that reaching the noosphere (or the Omega point) will mark the end of human evolution. Indeed, the noosphere could be easily interpreted as heaven for believers, although Teilhard made no such assertion. For others, perhaps Karl Marx's dictum, namely, "From each according to his abilities to each according to his needs," will mark the end of social evolution.

In the process of human evolution, our numbers have increased at an ever-increasing rate. I have made this point several times in earlier chapters in this book. Now allow me to bring back a term I used earlier, **exponential growth**. It is important to bear in mind the fact that the number of "items" doubles in size in every doubling time. Two exponential concepts will concern us as we look at the future of the world, namely, population, that is, human exponentialism, and noetic exponentialism.

I have already discussed **population exponentialism**. I referred to it in Chapter 12 as doubling time. I have mentioned earlier at several points in this book that the world is now increasing at a growth rate of 1.2 percent. At a rate of increase of 1.2 percent per year, a population doubles its size every 57.8 years, that is, 69.3 / 1.2 = 57.75. We cannot continue to double the size of the world population for very much longer, given the earlier discussion about resources: "Human society is presently breaching the bio-physical limits to growth, but this time on a global scale. As a result, the very qualities that once assured humanity's remarkable evolutionary success are threatening to do us in" (Rees, 2004: 11).

Exponentialism is present in many areas of human life. "Thought" is such an area. Our knowledge, be it technical, medical, philosophical, or scientific, grows exponentially. This is a result of human thinking. Consider all that has evolved over recent generations, not only with regard to computers and the Internet but also with respect to medicine, the genome project, and stem-cell research. Indeed, more has happened in the last generation (the last thirty to thirty-five years) than in earlier generations. This, too, is exponentialism.

We might, however, consider here the remarks made in 1981 by the biologist Lewis Thomas, namely, that "the greatest single achievement of science in this most scientifically productive of centuries is the discovery that we are profoundly ignorant; we know very little about nature and we understand even less...There is no limit to the ingenuity of the nature of this planet" (quoted in Gellerman, 2003: 1). This suggests that care is necessary in integrating human technologies with those of the natural world. It warns us about the challenges of noetic (i.e., thought and intellectual) exponentialism.

Humans rely on the knowledge acquired in previous generations and build on it. What, then, might transpire in the next generation? Our consciousness may improve, but one wonders about the growing complexity that will also occur. Will humankind be able to adapt to an exponentially growing availability of knowledge? With increasing complexity, will we be able to adjust to these rapidly growing challenges? Many of us elders are aware of a generational gap in computer knowledge, with children of elementary and high school age often knowing more about the basics than their parents and grandparents. When my spouse Patricia or I need help with our iPhones or iPads, we don't ask our daughter or son to help us; we ask our sixteen-year-old grandson Daniel Espey for assistance.

As both numbers and thoughts grow exponentially, what will happen to social interactions? We are already witnessing a significant decrease in the number of our actual face-to-face interactions, especially as a result of the computer and, more recently, email, the cell phone, and other forms of social media. On the pessimistic side, does this mean an end to social interactions? Will we lose the capability to simply "talk" to one another face to face? Will college professors, for example, be replaced by computerized lessons? On the more optimistic side, improved technology should allow us to communicate with more people, although much of that communication will be "artificial." Perhaps we are entering a new phase in the evolutionary process of humanity where, increasingly, social interactions will take place through ever-improving technologies. If so, we must all adapt to a new paradigm of communication.

Population exponentialism is also related to human evolution. For example, how are increasing numbers related to human interaction? Perhaps surprising to some demographers, my favorite theologian Teilhard de Chardin was seriously concerned about population growth. In his remarkable book *The Future of Man* he wrote that "after rising slowly until the seventeenth century, when it reached about 400 million, the earth's population began to shoot up again in an alarming fashion. It was 800 million by the end of the eighteenth century, 1.6 billion by 1900 and over 2 billion by 1940. At the present rate of increase, regardless of war and famine, we must expect a further 500 million in the next 25 years. This demographic explosion is closely connected with the development of a relatively unified and industrial earth. Clearly it gives rise to entirely new necessities and problems, both quantitative and qualitative" (Teilhard, 1969a: 242–243). He then asked, "How are we to prevent this compression of mankind on the closed surface of the planet from passing the critical point beyond which any increase in numbers will mean famine and suffocation?" (Teilhard, 1969a: 243).

Teilhard was clear in his concern about population growth interfering with the ultimate evolution of humankind. He anticipated the writings of the neo-Malthusians, some of whom I mentioned in Chapter 2 and elsewhere in this book. Indeed, it appears that he may well have been the first scholar to use the term population explosion, and he was not a demographer.

So here we are now, in 2016, faced with the challenge of adapting to both evolution and exponentialism. Will we be able to support 3–5 billion or more additional inhabitants on this small planet? These are questions that face us today, questions of which we must be aware if we are to handle the increasing complexity that comes with these types of exponentialism.

Furthermore, increasing complexity can be directly related to social interaction. What kind of social interaction can be expected in the kind of world foreseen for the twenty-first and twenty-second centuries? Virtually all sociologists note that without human social interaction, any group, or any nation for that matter, is bound to fail. Yet, as we continue into the twenty-first century and move toward the twenty-second, it is clear that actual face-to-face human interaction is declining. Electronic technology has contributed to this dangerous decline. This is not to say that these new technologies are not beneficial. The sociologist Robert Merton (1968) pointed out many years ago that there are manifest functions and there are latent functions. We know the manifest functions of these technologies, most of which are positive. But a latent function of them has been a serious decline in the real face-to-face interactions that must occur if the society is to prevail.

All of us must develop a "self" if we are to maintain some sort of identity. More than a hundred years ago, the social psychologist Charles Horton Cooley (1902) coined the term "looking glass self." To a certain extent, we develop a personal self by looking at how others react to us through social interaction. How will one develop a self if there is no longer a "looking glass?"

What can be done about this growing malaise, which could eventually get worse? Obviously, we cannot turn back the clock and bar all new technology. But perhaps we can all try just a little harder to talk more to friends and even strangers and, yes, even enemies. How much more difficult might this be with 10 or more billion people inhabiting the earth, rather than 7 billion?

In Chapter 1, I mentioned the phrase "demography is destiny." While journalists occasionally use it, some demographers tend to shy away from it. Upon reflection, however, there may be some truth to "demography is destiny," at least in the short term. For example, the world population will most likely grow to around 10 billion by the year 2100. The actual number may prove to be a little more or less, but the population of the world will grow. Here in the United States, we can forecast the problems associated with the baby boom now reaching its retirement ages. In that sense, demography *is* destiny. In a recently published book, *The Post-American World* (2008), the noted journalist Fareed Zakaria concluded that "as the industrial world ages, India will continue to have lots of young people – in other words, workers. China faces a youth gap because of its successful 'one-child' policies. India faces a youth bulge because, ironically, its own family planning policies of the past failed. If demography is destiny, India's future is secure" (Zakaria, 2008: 132).

CONCLUSION

In this final chapter, I looked broadly at the remaining years of the twenty-first century and the start of the twenty-second. In so doing, I considered the implications of a world population in 2100 of over 10 billion. Some, if not all, of these musings may appear dismal to many readers. Certainly, we are facing monumental population and environmental challenges. We are witnessing enormous advances in technology. Both population and noetic exponentialism are becoming ever more problematic. The era of the Industrial Revolution is long over. Now we are experiencing the Information

Revolution. Indeed, we are at the onset of dramatic transformations never before imagined. Population size and change are in the middle of this incredible phenomenon. In this looming era of globalization, we once again ask the question, "Will we all get along?" The answer depends on how we adapt to one another in this twenty-first century.

Glossary

abortifacients: pharmaceutical medications that cause the termination of an early pregnancy by interfering with the viability of an already implanted zygote; intended to terminate an implanted zygote of up to forty-nine days gestation.

abortion: termination of a pregnancy after the implantation of the fertilized egg in the uterine wall, but before the fetus is viable; includes both spontaneous and induced abortions.

abortion rate: the number of abortions in a given year per 1,000 women aged 15–44 (or sometimes 15–49).

acquired immune deficiency syndrome (AIDS): a disease of the human immune system caused by the human immunodeficiency virus (HIV); a person is said to have AIDS when the virus has weakened the immune system to the point that it is difficult to fight any type of infection.

adolescent fertility: the fertility of adolescents, usually referred to as women aged 15–19.

adolescent fertility rate: the age-specific fertility rate for women aged 15–19.

adrenogenital syndrome (AGS): characteristic of an XX fetus that receives an excessive amount of androgens; also known as congenital adrenal hyperplasia (CAH).

age composition: the composition of a population with respect to age (i.e., the distribution of a population among age categories).

age curve of fertility: a plot reflecting the changing values of the fertility of women over their childbearing ages; the plot is usually based on the age-specific fertility rates (ASFRs) from 15–19 to 45–49; most often the age curve is an inverted "U" form.

age curve of mortality: a plot that shows the changing values of mortality over the life course, best reflected with data from the full schedule of age-specific death rates (ASDRs); most often the age curve is a "U" form.

aged-dependency ratio (ADR or aged-DR): the ratio of persons 65 years of age and older to the working-age population (i.e., persons 15–64 years old), multiplied by 100; also known as old-age-dependency ratio.

age heaping: irregularities or inconsistencies in the age data for a population due to an overreporting of certain ages (e.g., those ending in 0 or 5) at the expense of other ages.

age-/sex-specific rate: a rate referring to the demographic behavior (e.g., regarding fertility), of a subset of the population categorized by age and sex.

age-specific death rate (ASDR): the number of deaths to persons in a specific age group per 1,000 persons in that age group; also known as "M" rate.

age-specific fertility rate (ASFR): births to women according to their age; ASFRs are usually calculated for women in each of the seven five-year age groups of 15–19, 20–24, and so forth to 45–49.

aging of a population: an increase in the average age of a population.

alien: a person living in a country who is not a citizen of that country.

American Community Survey (ACS): a survey conducted continuously by the US Bureau of the Census that gathers economic, social, demographic, and housing data.

amplexus reservatus: see coitus reservatus.

androgen insensitivity syndrome (AIS): a condition of fetuses that are chromosomally male with genitals that are ambiguous or look more like a clitoris than a penis.

area of destination: in the context of migration, the area where the migration ended.

area of origin: in the context of migration, the area where the migration began.

assimilation: the sociological concept that new groups to a society will take on the culture and values of the host society and gradually discard their own.

asylee: a person forced to leave his or her country of birth or nationality and move to another country seeking legal refugee status.

at-risk population: the set of people who could have produced a specified type of population event (e.g., a birth, a death, a migration); the at-risk population is usually the denominator of a rate.

audio computer-assisted self-interviewing (ACASI): an important technique for eliciting true answers to questions pertaining to private and personal information, where the respondent listens to questions through headphones, reads them on the computer screen, or both, and enters the response directly into the computer.

average: in statistical usage, the one value that best represents all cases in a set; one such measure is the *median*, the score above which and below which half the cases fall; another is the arithmetic *mean*, which is the total of all scores divided by the number of cases.

baby boom: the increase in fertility that occurred after the Second World War during the late 1940s and 1950s in most developed nations; more generally, a baby boom is any dramatic and extended increase in the birth rate.

baby boom cohort: those persons born in the United States during the high fertility years following the Second World War from 1946 to 1964.

baby bust: the decrease in fertility that occurred during the 1970s in most developed nations; more generally, a baby bust is any dramatic and extended decline in the birth rate.

balancing equation: the equation that shows that the size of the population of an area at the end of the time interval equals the size of the population at the beginning of the time interval plus the number of births and in-migrants, minus the number of deaths and out-migrants, occurring in the time interval; also sometimes known as the population equation.

basal body temperature (BBT): the lowest body temperature measured in the morning before walking and eating.

basal body temperature method: the contraceptive method based on the principle that ovulation produces a rise in the basic metabolic rate, causing a corresponding increase in body temperature of between 0.3 and 0.9°C (between 0.5 and 1.6°F); the reading and recording of one's basal body temperature on a daily basis may thus assist in determining the time of ovulation.

Billings ovulation method: a fertility awareness method based on the woman's knowledge of the presence or absence of cervical secretions.

biphasic pills: type of birth control pills containing different amounts of progestin and/or estrogen to be ingested during the menstrual cycle.

birth: "the complete expulsion or extraction from its mother of a product of conception, irrespective of the duration of pregnancy, which, after such separation, breathes or shows any other evidence of life, such as the beating of the heart, pulsation of the umbilical cord, or definite movement of voluntary muscles, whether or not the umbilical cord has been cut or the placenta is attached" (Shryock, Siegel, and Associates, 1976: 221).

birth control: deliberate measures taken to delay or avoid a birth, including contraception, sterilization, and induced abortion.

birth control pill: a contraceptive substance that is taken orally; also called an oral contraceptive and sometimes more generally "the pill."

birth order: the numerical order in which a person is born (e.g., first born, third born); also known as parity.

bracero program: an immigrant guest worker program established from 1942 to 1964, allowing laborers from Mexico to work temporarily in the United States.

calendar rhythm method: one of the least effective fertility awareness methods of contraception, also known as periodic abstinence or continence; it is based on the idea that a women can avoid pregnancy if she refrains from intercourse around the time of ovulation, when the egg is produced.

census: a complete count of every inhabitant in a given geographic entity at a specific point in time; censuses are typically conducted once every ten years or once every five years.

center of population: the geographical point or location in a country at which an imaginary flat, weightless, and rigid map of the country would balance perfectly if all persons distributed in the population were of identical physical weight.

central city: the largest city in a metropolitan area or micropolitan area.

cervical cap: a small, thimble-shaped cup used to prevent conception by blocking the cervix.

childbearing ages: the age range 15–49 usually marks the limits of the childbearing ages; however, sometimes, especially in developed countries, the childbearing ages refer to 15–44 because so few births occur to women older than age 44.

childlessness: the behavior of having no children, either voluntarily or involuntarily.

children ever born: number of children ever born.

city: a place that is incorporated and has been granted certain powers, as defined in its charter, by the state or country in which it is located.

closed population: a population in which migration does not occur.

cohort: a group of people who experience a major demographic event in the same time period (e.g., one- or five-year); e.g., a birth cohort (persons born in the same year or five-year period) or a marriage cohort (persons married in the same year or five-year period).

cohort analysis: examination of a cohort's demographic behavior over time (e.g., children ever born to a specific birth cohort or marriage cohort of women); this is in contrast to an examination of a demographic event at one point in time (i.e., a period or cross-sectional analysis).

coitus interruptus: also known as the "pull-out" contraceptive method; with this method, "the couple may have penile–vaginal intercourse until ejaculation is impending, at which time the male partner withdraws his penis from the vagina and away from the external genitalia of the female partner; the male must rely on his own sensations to determine when he is about to ejaculate" (Kowal, 2011: 410).

coitus reservatus: the behavior in which the male enters his partner, does not ejaculate, and endeavors to remain at the plateau phase of sexual intercourse and excitement; also known as amplexus reservatus.

combined oral contraceptive: a hormonally-based contraceptive containing estrogen and progestin.

components of population growth: the only events by which a population's size can be determined directly; these are births, deaths, and migrations.

concentration of the population: the clustering of population in areas of high population density surrounded by areas of low population density.

conception: the fertilization of an ovum by a sperm, marking the beginning of pregnancy, or gestation.

condom (male): a type of barrier to conception or disease, usually a male condom, a sheath designed to cover the penis during sexual intercourse; see also female condom.

congenital adrenal hyperplasia (CAH): see adrenogenital syndrome (AGS).

contraception: measures taken to prevent coitus from resulting in conception.

contraception injection: an injection containing hormones to prevent pregnancy; typically administered by a health professional once every three months or so in the arm, buttocks, upper thigh, or abdomen.

contraceptive patch: an adhesive device about the size of a 50-cent piece placed on the buttocks, arm, or stomach; it releases estrogen and progestin at a constant and continuous level each day to avoid pregnancy.

contraceptive sponge: a vaginal spermicide designed for a single use; it is a "small, pillow shaped polyurethane sponge" that contains 1 gram of spermicide (Cates and Harwood, 2011: 395).

cross-sectional: a one-point-in-time portrayal, for instance of the size, composition, and distribution of the population, as in a census.

crude birth rate (CBR): the number of live births in a given year per 1,000 total population at the midpoint of the given year.

crude death rate (CDR): the number of deaths in a given year per 1,000 total population at the midpoint of the given year.

cultural amalgamation: the theory that a new society and culture result from the massive intermingling and intermarriage of two or more groups.

cultural separatism: the theory that newcomers are socially isolated from the residents either through their own volition or through separatist practices of the host society.

Current Population Survey (CPS): a monthly nationwide survey conducted by the US Bureau of the Census for the Bureau of Labor Statistics to gather labor force data and other data about the civilian noninstitutional population.

death: "the permanent disappearance of all evidence of life at any time after a live birth has taken place; a death can occur only after a live birth has occurred" (Shryock, Siegel, and Associates, 1976: 221).

decedent: a person who has died.

deconcentration: a shift in population distribution from the higher-density central cities to the lower-density areas located beyond the traditional city limits; or a shift from metropolitan to nonmetropolitan areas.

de facto **population:** the population physically present in an area at a given moment in time, such as at the time the census was undertaken.

de jure **population:** the population that usually, habitually, or legally lives in an area.

Demographic and Health Survey (DHS): a survey carried out mainly in developing countries that gathers data dealing with fertility, population, health, and nutrition. Surveys have been carried out in ninety developing countries since 1984.

demographic characteristics: usually, the variables of age and sex.

demographic equation: the equation that states that the size of an area's population can change because of only three types of event: births, deaths, and migrations. It is also known as the demographic balancing or accounting equation.

demographic processes: the three processes of fertility, mortality, and migration that account for any change in the size of a population.

demographic transition theory (DTT): the theory that describes the transition from a situation in which fertility and mortality are high to a situation in which fertility and mortality are low.

demographic variables: the main and key demographic variables are age and sex.

demography: the scientific study of the size, composition, and distribution of human populations, and their changes resulting from fertility, mortality, and migration.

denominator: the bottom number in a fraction; the number below the line; the divisor.

dependency ratio (DR): the number of persons under 15 years of age and aged 65 and older, divided by the number of persons aged 15–64, multiplied by 100.

dependent variable: a variable whose value depends on one or more other variables known as independent variables; the dependent variable is also known as the outcome variable or the Y variable.

depopulation: the decline in the size of a country's or area's population.

developed countries: those countries that have higher levels of per capita income and modernization than other countries; according to the United Nations, the developed countries of the world, sometimes referred to as "more developed" countries, usually consist of all the countries of North America and Europe (including Russia), along with Japan, Australia, and New Zealand.

developing countries: those countries that have lower levels of per capita income and modernization than the developed countries; they include the 200 or so countries not classified as "developed" (see previous definition).

diaphragm: a contraceptive device consisting of a flexible disk that covers the uterine cervix.

differential migration: differences in migration behavior according to various demographic, social, and economic characteristics of the population; also known as migration selectivity.

division of labor: differences among members of a population in their work activities; the more complex the division of labor in a society, the more differentiated the members are in their work activities.

divorce: the marital status of currently nonmarried persons whose previous marriage has been legally dissolved.

doubling time: the number of years required for a population to double its size were it to maintain its present rate of natural growth (as long as the growth rate is positive); at a +1.0 percent rate of growth, the doubling time is 69.3 years; the numerator of the doubling time formula is the natural log of 2×100, i.e., 69.3; the denominator is the rate of natural increase (RNI); if the growth rate is negative, see halving time.

dual labor market theory: the theory that argues that migration stems from the demands of the economic structure of industrial societies.

echo effect: the tendency toward repetition, one generation hence, of any span of abnormally high (or low) fertility, which is caused by the effect of the initial fertility level on the age structure.

ecological theory of migration: the theory that focuses on characteristics of the population to predict the level of migration; individual attitudes and propensities do not play a role in this theory.

economic development: the level of economic activity in a population; two common measures are (1) per capita income, and (2) per capita energy consumption.

edge cities: new cities formed at the edges of metropolitan areas.

effectiveness (of family planning methods): there are two types of effectiveness, theoretical effectiveness and use effectiveness; theoretical effectiveness refers to the "efficaciousness" of the method when it is used exactly as prescribed; use effectiveness refers to the effectiveness of the method taking into account the fact that some users do not follow the directions perfectly, thus representing how effective the method is in "typical" use.

ella®: brand name of an emergency contraceptive pill containing ulipristal.

emergency contraceptive pill (ECP): a contraceptive medication taken after unprotected intercourse designed to prevent pregnancy by interfering with the implantation of the fertilized ovum in the uterine lining; also known as the morning-after pill.

emigrant: one who migrates away from a country with the intention of establishing a permanent residence in another country.

emigration: the permanent departure of people from one country to establish permanent residence in another country.

endogenous cause of death: a cause of death that originates from within the body or genetic make-up; endogenous causes of infant death typically include "congenital malformations, chromosomal abnormalities, complications of delivery, as well as ... low birth weight" (Pebley, 2003: 534).

endogenous conditions: conditions (usually of infant death) caused by factors within the organism or system, "such as congenital malformations, chromosomal abnormalities, and complications of delivery, as well as ... low birthweight" (Pebley, 2003: 534).

endometrium: lining of the uterus.

entries without inspection (EWIs): international migrants who during the process of migrating to the host country "avoid inspection by crossing borders clandestinely or ... traveling with fraudulent documents, e.g., a falsified visa or counterfeit passport" (Armbrister, 2003: 512).

epidemic: a disease that spreads and then disappears within a fairly short time, if it can be controlled. Where it appears in a large number of countries, it is sometimes called a pandemic.

epidemiological paradox: the empirical finding that Mexican Americans have death rates of about the same magnitude as, and sometimes lower than, Anglos; also known as the Latino mortality paradox or Hispanic paradox.

epidemiological transition theory (ETT): the theory that focuses on the societal-wide decline of infectious disease and the rise of chronic degenerative causes of death.

essentialism: the essentialist view with regard to sexuality is one of dimorphism; there is an "essential" biological or psychological characteristic or attribute that is common to all persons and that distinguishes them as either of one sexuality or not of that sexuality.

Essure® procedure: a female sterilization method performed using a local anesthesia; a tiny coil insert is introduced into each of the Fallopian tubes through the vagina and uterus; this causes the development of scar tissues over a three-month period, resulting in both tubes becoming sealed, in turn preventing pregnancy.

ethnic: refers to group distinctions based on shared cultural origins.

ethnic enclave: a community with distinctive cultural characteristics that can help migrants transition into life as immigrants by providing support and environments much like those in their mother countries.

exogenous cause of death: a cause of death that is external to the body or genetic makeup; exogenous causes of death include infectious disease, accidents, and injuries.

exponential growth: a constant rate of growth applied to a continuously growing population.

exurbs: geographic areas beyond the beltways that circle the metropolitan areas.

failure rate (of a contraceptive): the number of pregnancies per 100 person years of use of a birth control method.

family partnering: two opposite-sex persons or two same-sex persons living together in a family or family-type household.

family planning: attempts by couples to regulate the number and spacing of their births.

family planning program: a systematic effort, often government-sponsored, to provide the information, supplies, and services for modern fertility control.

fecund: capable of giving birth.

fecundity: the biological capacity or capability of a man, a woman, or a couple to produce a live birth.

fecundity indeterminate: referring to couples who meet the criteria for being semifecund, except that the wife sometimes reports douching "for cleanness only" soon after intercourse.

female condom: a female-initiated barrier to conception and disease. The female condom is a sheath about the same length as a male condom (around 6.5 inches) with a flexible ring at each end; the inner ring at the closed end of the condom is inserted into the vagina and remains in place behind the pubic bone; the outer ring at the open end is soft and remains outside the vagina during sexual intercourse.

female sterilization: a contraceptive sterilization procedure commonly known as tubal ligation (tying of the tubes), consisting of cutting, tying, and removing a portion of the oviduct, i.e., the Fallopian tubes. Female sterilization may be performed in one of several ways, including laparoscopic sterilization, minilaparotomy, and hysteroscopic sterilization.

fertility: the frequency with which a birth of either sex occurs in a population, i.e., the actual production of female or male births.

fertility awareness methods: several "natural" family planning methods, such as the Standard Days Method®, the Billings ovulation method, and others.

fetal death: the disappearance of life prior to live birth.

fetal death rate: the number of fetal deaths (i.e., stillbirths), divided by the sum of live births and stillbirths in the year, times 1,000; also known as the stillbirth rate.

fetus: the product of conception when it matures from being an embryo, after about twelve weeks (or three months) of intrauterine life.

first union: the first living or partnering arrangement an adult has with another adult that involves commitment, romance, and emotion.

floating migrant: in China, an internal migrant who moves from one place to another without government authorization.

forced migration: in the modern context, a kind of migration in which individuals are compelled by public authorities to move; includes flight or displacement and the creation of refugees (see refugee); historically, it would also include migration for slavery and involuntary indentured servitude.

foreign-born: referring to a person residing in one country but born in another; the foreign-born population of a country is that portion of the population born outside that country.

general fertility rate (GFR): the number of live births per 1,000 women aged 15–44 (or aged 15–49) in a given year.

gentrification: the migration of middle-class and other affluent people into the once poorer areas of cities.

geographic information systems: mapping of areas used to analyze data.

geographic mobility: any change of residence within a country, including both local movements and migration beyond specific boundaries.

germ theory: the identification of the microorganism as the cause of many infectious diseases, particularly among infants and children.

gestation: the carrying of a fetus in the uterus from conception to delivery.

Great Depression, the: refers to the severe and long-term economic downturn in the Western world from 1929 to 1939.

Great Migration, the: refers to the several decades in the United States after the Civil War when large numbers of blacks migrated out of the South to the North and West.

green card: an identification card documenting that the holder is a legal permanent resident of the United States. Known officially as a United States Permanent Resident Card, the green card is so called because its color was green between 1946 and 1964; although it was not green for almost fifty years, reverting back to green only in 2010.

gross migration: the sum of the number of in-migrants to an area and the number of out-migrants from the area.

gross migration rate (GMR): the sum of the numbers of migrants into and out of a given area in a given period of time, per 1,000 members of the population.

gross reproduction rate (GRR): the average number of daughters that would be born to a hypothetical group of 1,000 women if they completed their childbearing years following the age-specific rates for a given year at which women produced female births; similar to the total fertility rate but is restricted to female births.

halving time: the number of years required for the size of a population to become half as large were it to maintain its present rate of growth; this will occur if the growth rate is negative; at a −1.0 percent rate of growth, the halving time is 69.3 years; if the growth rate is positive, see doubling time.

healthy migrant effect: the hypothesis that states that the longevity advantage of Latinos compared with other minority groups (i.e., African Americans) occurs because many Latinos in the United States were born elsewhere, and that migration is known to be selective of persons in better physical and mental health.

Hispanic paradox: see epidemiological paradox.

histogram: a graphical representation of tabulated data frequencies shown as bars.

hormonal IUD: an intrauterine (contraceptive) device of flexible plastic, often shaped like a "T," that contains progestin, which usually blocks ovulation and thickens the woman's cervical mucus.

household: a group of individuals who reside together, whether related or not.

human ecological theory: a macro-level explanation of population growth and decline.

human immunodeficiency virus (HIV): the virus that causes AIDS; it destroys the T cells or CD4 cells that the body needs to fight infections.

hypothetical cohort: an imaginary set of people traced through a series of specified risks in order to detail the cumulative impact of those risks.

hysterectomy: the surgical removal of the uterus; it may also involve the additional removal of the Fallopian tubes and the ovaries.

hysteroscopic sterilization: see Essure® procedure.

immigrant: a person who enters a country with the intention of residing there permanently.

immigration: the migration of people into a new country from any other country for the purpose of establishing residence there.

independent variable: a variable that is believed to have an effect on the dependent variable; also known as an X variable and as a co-variate.

induced abortion: a pregnancy that has been terminated by human intervention with an intent other than to produce a live birth; an induced early fetal death, legal or illegal; specifically, the premature expulsion of the fetus at a time before it is viable of sustaining life.

infant mortality: the mortality of infants, i.e., persons less than one year of age.

infant mortality rate (IMR): the number of deaths among infants under one year of age per 1,000 live births in the same year.

infecundity: the physiological inability to produce a live birth.

infertility: the production of no children; also referred to as childlessness.

in-migration: the residential migration of persons into a specific political subdivision (e.g., a county or state) from another subdivision of the same country.

in-migration rate (IMR): the number of persons migrating into an area usually during a one- or five-year time interval, divided by the population of the area at the start of the interval, times 1,000.

internal migration: the geographical movement within a country for a permanent change of residence that involves the crossing of a county boundary.

International Classification of Diseases (ICD): the classification of diseases developed by the World Health Organization; the present classification (the tenth revision) was adopted in 1992 and categorizes causes of death under twenty-two major headings.

international migration: migration between countries.

intersex: referring to people with atypical combinations of the physical attributes (e.g., chromosomes, gonads, genitalia) that are commonly used to distinguish males from females.

intrauterine device (IUD): a small device that is inserted directly into the uterus to prevent conception.

in vitro **fertility:** the process whereby an ovum is fertilized by sperm outside the body.

Jacob's Syndrome: characteristic of a person born with an extra (i.e., third) sex chromosome, in the configuration of XYY.

keyhole vasectomy: alternate term for no-scalpel vasectomy, a male sterilization procedure.

Klinefelter's Syndrome: characteristic of a person born with an extra (i.e., third) sex chromosome, in the configuration of XXY.

labor force: the portion of the population that is employed or is actively seeking work.

laparoscopic sterilization: a female sterilization procedure using a laparoscope to view and then close the Fallopian tubes.

less developed countries (LDCs): countries with the lowest indicators of socioeconomic and human development, as classified by the United Nations.

life expectancy: the average number of years yet to be lived by people attaining a given age, according to a given life table; it is the value given by the value of "e," usually the last, column of data in the life table.

life span: the maximum number of years a person can expect to live; the numerical age limit of human life.

life table: a statistical table used for tracing the cumulative effect of a schedule of age/sex specific death rates over a lifecycle for a hypothetical cohort.

live birth: "the complete expulsion or extraction from its mother of a product of conception, irrespective of the duration of pregnancy, which, after such separation, breathes or shows any other evidence of life, such as the beating of the heart, pulsation of the umbilical cord, or definite movement of voluntary muscles, whether or not the umbilical cord has been cut or the placenta is attached" (Shryock, Siegel, and Associates, 1976: 221).

local movement: the short-distance change of residence within the same community that does not involve crossing a county jurisdictional boundary.

longevity: the length of an individual life; collectively, average length of life of a cohort.

long-form questionnaire: census questionnaire containing detailed questions regarding education, occupation, income, mobility, and several other topics; used in the 2000 census and administered roughly to one in six households.

long-term immigration: the movement of a person from one country to another for the purpose of establishing residence in the destination country for at least one year.

Lucky Few: the birth cohort born in the United States between 1929 and 1945. This cohort enjoyed higher employment rates and a greater variety of social opportunities than Americans in the preceding or in the following generations; and much of this was due to their small population size.

macro analysis: the study of the behavior of large population groups, e.g., countries.

male fertility: the production of children, i.e., fertility, by males.

male sterilization: a surgical procedure in which a portion of the spermatic duct is cut, tied, and removed; also known as vasectomy.

Malthusian checks: the two kinds of controls, preventive checks and positive checks, argued by Thomas Malthus as tending to check population growth; The major preventive check is "moral restraint"; the main positive checks are war, famine, and pestilence.

Malthusianism: the theory or belief, based on the writing of Thomas Malthus, that if left unchecked, the population tends to outstrip the means for its subsistence.

majority-minority population: a population, e.g., a county or state or country where more than 50 percent of its population comprises minorities.

maternal death: "the death of a woman while pregnant or within 42 days of termination of pregnancy, irrespective of the duration or site of pregnancy, from any cause related to or aggravated by the pregnancy or its management, but not from accidental or incidental causes" (Maine and Stamas, 2003: 628).

maternal mortality ratio (MMR): deaths in a year to women dying as a result of complications of pregnancy, childbirth, and the puerperium (the condition immediately following childbirth), per 100,000 live births occurring in the year.

median age: the age that divides a population into two equal groups, half younger and half older.

megalopolis: a term referring to any densely populated social and economic area encompassing two or more contiguous metropolitan areas and the increasingly urbanized space between them.

melting pot: the theory stating that the host and immigrant groups share each other's cultures and, in the process, a new group emerges.

menarche: the beginning of the female reproductive, or childbearing, period signaled by the first menstrual flow, i.e., period.

menopause: the end of the female reproductive, or childbearing, period signaled by the termination of menstruation.

mercantilism: an economic practice in which a population or country attempts to grow economically by trading with other countries and exporting more materials and goods than importing them.

mestizo: a person of mixed blood, the result of racial blending that occurred in nineteenth-century Latin America between the Spanish newcomers and indigenous groups.

metropolis: a very large and/or important city.

metropolitan area: a large concentration of population usually consisting of a central city (or cities) of at least 50,000 people and the surrounding settlements.

metropolitanization: the relative growth of the metropolitan area population, compared with other populations.

metropolitan statistical area (metro area or MSA): a geographic area containing a large population nucleus, together with adjacent communities with considerable economic and social integration with the core.

micro analysis: the study of the behavior of individuals.

micropolitan area: a geographic area that contains at least one urban cluster of between 10,000 and 49,999 people.

migrant: a person who changes his or her residence and the change involves the crossing of a political boundary, i.e., a county in the United States.

migration: the spatial movement of persons resulting in their permanent change of residence; if the movement is within a country, it is referred to as internal migration; if it is between countries, it is known as international migration.

migration counterstream: a body of migrants, smaller in size than its corresponding migration stream, going in the opposite direction during the same time interval.

migration efficiency: an area's net migration divided by its gross migration.

migration efficiency ratio (MER): the number of gross migrants divided by the number of net migrants, multiplied by 100.

migration interval: the time period, usually expressed as the number of years, during which the migration occurs.

migration network theory: the theory that focuses on networks, such as interpersonal ties that connect migrants, former migrants, potential migrants, and nonmigrants in the origin and destination countries.

migration selectivity: the fact that migrants are selected on the basis of age, race, sex, socioeconomic status, and other characteristics; in other words, some persons are more likely to migrate than others.

migration stream: a body of migrants departing from a common area of origin and arriving at a common area of destination during a specified time interval; compare with migration counterstream.

minilaparotomy: surgical sterilization procedure performed on a woman a few days after she has delivered her baby.

mini-pill: oral contraceptive containing only progestin.

Mirena IUD: an IUD brand marketed in the United States that contains a second-generation progestin hormone.

miscarriage: the spontaneous or accidental termination of fetal life that occurs early in pregnancy.

monophasic: type of birth control pill that provides a constant amount of estrogen and progestin every day.

morbidity: the prevalence of sickness in a population.

morning-after pill: a contraceptive medication taken after unprotected intercourse that is designed to prevent pregnancy by interfering with the implantation of the fertilized ovum in the uterine lining; also known as the emergency contraceptive pill.

mortality: the frequency with which death occurs in a population.

mortality reversal: the increase in mortality after a population has experienced a decrease in mortality.

mortality transition: that part of the demographic transition in which mortality declines from a high, variable, and relatively uncontrolled level, to a low, constant, and controlled level; see demographic transition theory.

mover: a person who changes his or her residence.

Mulatto: a racial classification term that was used at one time, e.g., in the 1890 US census, to refer to a person born of a black parent and a white parent; or to persons with two Mulatto parents.

National Longitudinal Study of Adolescent to Adult Health (Add Health): a longitudinal study of a nationally representative sample of adolescents in grades 7–12 in the United States in 1994–1995. This adolescent cohort has been followed on several occasions into young adulthood with in-home interviews.

National Survey of Family Growth (NSFG): a nationally representative US multistage survey of male and female respondents aged 15–44 that collects information on family life and reproductive health.

natural decrease: a negative change between two points in time in the number of births minus the number of deaths in a population.

natural increase: a positive change between two points in time in the number of births minus the number of deaths in a population.

naturalized citizen: a permanent immigrant who has been granted citizenship by the country into which he or she immigrated.

natural log: the natural logarithm of a number is the power to which e (an irrational constant approximately equal to 2.7182) would have to be raised to equal the desired number; thus, the natural log of 2 is 0.693; i.e., $e^{0.693} = 2$, or $2.7182^{0.693} = 2$.

neoclassical economic theory of international migration: the theory that migration is based on individual cost–benefit decisions to maximize expected incomes through geographic movement.

neo-Malthusianism: the belief (according to Thomas Malthus) in the tendency for populations, if left unchecked, to outstrip the means for their subsistence; also advocacy (but not by Malthus) of the promotion of birth control as a solution to this dilemma.

neonatal mortality rate (NMR): deaths to babies of 28 days of age or less, per 1,000 live births.

net international migration: immigration minus emigration.

net migration: the migration balance of an area, consisting of the number of in-migrants minus the number of out-migrants; the balance may be positive or negative.

net migration rate (NMR): the number of persons moving into an area minus the number of persons moving out of that area, divided by the population size of the area, times 1,000.

net reproduction rate (NRR): the average number of daughters that would be born to a female birth cohort if the mothers completed their childbearing years subject to the schedules of age-specific fertility and mortality rates of a given place and time.

new economics theory of migration: the theory that migration decisions are made not only by isolated individuals, but also by larger units, such as families and households.

Next Choice®: brand name of a progestin-only emergency contraceptive pill.

nonmarital fertility: the fertility of women who are not married.

no-scalpel vasectomy: a male sterilization procedure in which a small opening is made in the scrotum with local anesthetic, and then, as with the traditional vasectomy procedure, the tubes of the vas deferens are lifted from the scrotal sac, cut, tied, or sometimes cauterized, and then placed back into the scrotum. Because the scrotal skin opening is so small, it may not need to be closed with sutures; also known as keyhole vasectomy.

nosologist: a person who studies the classification and categorization of diseases and causes of death.

nulliparous women: women who have not given birth.

numerator: the number above the line, i.e., the top number, in a common fraction.

obituary: an announcement, or story, in a newspaper of a person's death that usually includes a brief biographical sketch.

Octoroon: a racial classification term that was used at one time, e.g., in the 1890 US census, to refer to a person with one black great-grandparent and seven white great-grandparents.

old-age-dependency ratio (ADR or Aged-DR): the ratio of persons 65 years of age and older to the working-age population (i.e., persons 15–64 years old), multiplied by 100; also known as aged-dependency ratio.

oral contraceptive (the pill): a pill containing both estrogen and progestin that is used to prevent conception primarily by preventing ovulation.

out-migration: the residential migration of persons out of a specific political subdivision (e.g., a county or state) into another subdivision of the same country.

out-migration rate (OMR): the number of persons migrating from an area usually during a one- or five-year time interval, divided by the population size of the area at the start of the time interval, times 1,000.

pandemic: an epidemic spreading throughout a large area, such as a continent, or even the world, and affecting a very large portion of the population.

ParaGard® IUD: a flexible plastic (contraceptive) device shaped like a "T" with copper wire twisted about it, placed into the uterus to prevent conception.

parent support ratio: the ratio of the number of persons 80 years of age and older per 100 persons aged 50–64; meant to represent the relative burden of the oldest-old population, i.e., the elderly parents, on the population 50–64, i.e., the children of the elderly parents.

parity: the number of times a woman has given birth; also refers to birth order.

parous women: women who have had one or more births.

partnering: the behavior of two persons living together, whether married or cohabiting.

parturition: the act or process of giving birth.

perinatal mortality rate (PeMR): the sum of the number of stillbirths and the number of deaths to babies aged 0–7 days, divided by the sum of the number of live births and stillbirths in the year, multiplied by 1,000; also known as pregnancy wastage.

period perspective: the viewing or studying of a population process cross-sectionally as the combined experience of population groups in a specified short period of time, normally one year.

period rate: a rate based on behavior occurring at a particular point or period in time, such as one year; also known as a cross-sectional rate.

physiological density: a population density measure calculated by dividing the number of persons in the country by the country's quantity of arable land (in square kilometers or miles); also known as nutritional density.

Plan BOne-Step®: brand name of a progestin-only emergency contraceptive pill.

pluralism: the concept that the host society allows its constituted ethnic groups to develop, each emphasizing its own cultural heritage.

political economic theory of fertility: an investigative framework used to study fertility in which several fields of knowledge are used, such as economics, politics, anthropology, sociology and psychology; the analysis combines both micro-level and macro-level perspectives.

polygyny: the marital union of a male to two or more females simultaneously.

population: a set of people residing in a given area at a specific time.

population aging: the increase in the proportion of the population that is old, usually defined as persons aged 60 and older, or as persons aged 65 and older.

population density: the relationship between the size of a population and the size of the area in which it lives, usually expressed as the number of persons per square mile (or kilometer) of land.

population equation: see balancing equation.

population explosion: a dramatic increase in population size.

population exponentialism: see doubling time.

population implosion: a dramatic decrease in population size.

population momentum: the growth of a population attributable to the high proportion of people in the childbearing years; the growth continues to occur even after replacement-level fertility has been attained. A negative version appears when the proportion of people in their childbearing years is proportionally small.

population policy: a deliberately constructed arrangement or program "through which governments influence, directly or indirectly, demographic change" (Demeny, 2003: 752); measures instituted by governments that influence demographic behavior.

population projection: a systematic calculation of the future population size of an area based on an assumed level of population growth and/or the assumed levels of fertility, mortality, and migration.

population pyramid: a conventional form of bar graph representing the age–sex structure of a population at a particular point in time.

population register: the continuous recording of population events for individual members of a population.

population replacement: replacing a group of females who have completed their childbearing ages with a new group of females beginning their childbearing ages; this occurs via the production of female births, known also as reproduction

positive checks: in Malthusian theory, the checks on population growth operating through increases in the death rate; these include war, famine, and pestilence.

postneonatal mortality rate (PMR): deaths to babies between the ages of 29 days and 1 year, per 1,000 live births.

postpartum infecundability: "Following a pregnancy a woman remains infecundable (i.e., unable to conceive) until the normal pattern of ovulation and menstruation is restored. The duration of the period of infecundity is a function of the duration and intensity of lactation" (Bongaarts, 1978: 107).

potential support ratio (PSR): a measure that represents the extent that people of working age can support the older population, calculated by dividing the number of persons of working age (15–64) by the number of older persons (65 years or older).

preventive checks: in Malthusian theory, those checks on population growth operating through the decrease in the birth rate; these include delayed marriage and abstinence.

primary demographic characteristics: age and sex are the primary, i.e., the most important demographic characteristics.

progestin-only pill: a hormonally-based contraceptive pill containing only progestin, sometimes also known as the mini-pill.

projection: see population projection.

pronatalist: referring to advocating an increase in fertility.

proximate determinants: the most immediate causes of a population process such as fertility; those biological and behavioral variables that are "intermediate" or "between" the broad social factors that influence fertility and fertility per se.

push and pull factors of migration: combination of factors pushing or not pushing the person from the area of origin and pulling or not pulling the person to the area of destination.

Quadroon: a racial classification term that was used at one time, e.g., in the 1890 US census, to refer to a person born of a Mulatto parent and a white parent.

quinacrine sterilization (QS): nonsurgical female sterilization in which a woman receives treatments of tiny quinacrine pellets placed into the uterus; the pellets dissolve and flow into the openings of the Fallopian tubes and cause a minor swelling resulting in scar tissues that close the tubes.

racial mortality crossover: the demographic finding that at the very oldest ages the death rates for blacks become lower than those for whites, and in some cases lower than those for Hispanics.

rate of natural increase (RNI): the percentage rate of change in a population due to births and deaths; usually calculated as (crude birth rate – crude death rate) / 10.

ratio: a comparison of the sizes of two categories in a series by dividing one by the other.

refugee: a person who has immigrated into a new country in response to strong pressure because his or her continued stay in the country of origin may have exposed that person to danger of persecution.

registration: the recording in a register of population events on a continuous basis for all members of a population.

registration system: a continuous recording of a population's demographic events (births and deaths and, in some places, migrations) as they occur.

re-migrant: an international migrant who moves back to and re-establishes permanent residence in his or her country of origin

re-migration: the international migration of persons back to their country of origin at some time after their emigration from that country.

remittance: a transfer of money by a foreign immigrant worker from the host country to an individual in his or her home country.

replacement-level fertility: the level of fertility at which a cohort of women, on average, has only enough children to replace themselves in the population, at current mortality levels; in low-mortality populations, replacement fertility equals around 2.1 children per woman.

reproduction: the production of female births (there is no demographic term to refer to the production of only male births); analogous to fertility, but only refers to female births.

residence: the location with which an individual is affiliated, where he or she usually or habitually lives.

residential mobility: the movement within and across geographic units that includes not only migration, but also residential moves not involving migration (e.g., a residential move within a county); all migrations are residential movements, but not all residential movements are migrations.

return migrant effect: the hypothesis that states that the longevity advantage of Latinos compared with other minority groups (i.e., African Americans) occurs because Latinos in poor physical health often return to Mexico at old ages to live out the rest of their lives and, thus, their deaths are not counted in the US statistics

return migration: the migration within a country of persons back to their area of origin at some time after their initial out-migration.

rhythm method: the method of contraception based on abstinence from coitus around the period when a woman is believed to be ovulating.

Rule of 69.3: a formula based on the natural logarithm of 2 to determine the length of time before the size of the population would become twice as large, or one-half as large, if its birth and death rates did not change; if the difference between the two is positive, it results in a doubling of the size of the population; if the difference is negative, a halving; the numerator of the doubling time/halving time formula is the natural log of 2×100, i.e., 69.3; the denominator is the rate of natural increase (RNI).

salmon bias: see return migrant effect.

second demographic transition (SDT): further fertility declines in a population after reaching the fourth stage of the (first) demographic transition; the demographic behaviors observed in the SDT include, but are not limited to, increasing age at first marriage, increases in cohabitation, increases in divorce, the emergence of same-sex partnerships and marriages, increasing rates of nonmarital childbearing, and voluntary childlessness.

semifecund: descriptive of couples who have married or cohabited for a relatively long time without using contraception, but have not conceived.

senior boom: the large number of baby boom babies born in the United States from the late 1940s to 1960 started reaching retirement age around 2010, resulting in a large increase in the number of seniors, i.e., a senior boom.

sex composition: the composition of a population with regard to sex.

sex ratio (SR): the number of males in a population divided by the number of females in the population, times 100.

sex ratio at birth (SRB): the number of males of age 0 divided by the number of females of age 0, times 100.

single: the never-married category of marital status.

social constructionism: with respect to sexuality, this view argues against essentialism and the notion of binary categories, i.e., that one either is or is not in a specific sexual category; instead, it argues for a continuum with varying degrees of the categories of sexuality

specific rate: any rate for some subset of the population (e.g., an age group) rather than for the total population.

stable population: a hypothetical population with an unchanging birth and death rate, rate of growth, and age composition.

stable population theory: the theory stating that a population closed to migration that experiences constant schedules of age-specific fertility and mortality rates will develop a constant age distribution and will grow at a constant rate, irrespective of its initial age distribution.

Standard Days Method®: the contraceptive method based on the principle that "women with regular menstrual cycles lasting 26–32 days can prevent pregnancy by avoiding unprotected intercourse on days eight through 19" (Gribble, 2003: 188).

standardization: a statistical technique that controls for the effects of factors (e.g., age and/or sex) that may contaminate the comparison of populations with respect to demographic processes such as mortality and fertility.

standardized death rate (SDR): a death rate that has been adjusted for age composition and, perhaps, other factors such as race and sex. If the death rates for two populations with different age structures are being compared, death rates standardized for age need to be used rather than crude death rates.

stationary population: a stable population in which the birth rate equals the death rate, resulting in no change in the size of the population, in the absence of migration.

stem pessary: antecedent form of the modern IUD, developed in the late 1860s.

sterility: infecundity.

sterilization: an operation or procedure performed on either a male or a female to prevent conception.

stillbirth: a late fetal death at 20–28 weeks or more of gestation.

stillbirth rate (SBR): number of miscarriages or fetal deaths (stillbirths) divided by the total number of live births plus stillbirths, times 1,000.

subdermal contraceptive implant: a device consisting of one or more small silicone capsule-type rods, each containing progestin, placed subdermally, usually in a woman's upper arm, to prevent conception.

subfecund: whereas fecund couples are capable of giving birth, subfecund couples have impairments of one sort or another making it difficult for them to produce children.

suburbanization: the process of population movement from the core city to the fringe area around and nearby the core city.

surgical sterilization: a procedure performed on either males or females to prevent conception; for females, known as tubal ligation (tying of the tubes); for males, known as vasectomy.

symptothermal method: the most effective of the fertility awareness methods of contraception; it uses both cervical secretions along with basal body temperatures to identify the times when pregnancy is most likely.

Taeuber paradox: the paradox, attributed to demographer Conrad Taeuber, that a cure found for one degenerative disease will provide the opportunity for death to occur from another.

taxonomy: the branch of science concerned with classification.

theoretical effectiveness (of a contraceptive): degree of effectiveness that would occur with "perfect" use of the contraceptive.

third demographic transition: the tendency, indeed perhaps the need, for countries with very low levels of fertility to rely on immigration to replenish their populations.

total dependency ratio (Total DR): aged-dependency ratio plus youth-dependency ratio.

total fertility rate (TFR): a usually cross-sectional estimate of the number of births that a hypothetical group of 1,000 women would have during their reproductive lifetime, if their childbearing followed the ASFRs for a given period; alternately, a cohort TFR is the actual fertility of a real (marriage or birth) cohort of 1,000 women, i.e., the actual number of children they produced during their childbearing years.

tourist: a person who travels to another country for a short-term visit; a visitor.

transgender: an umbrella term referring roughly to all persons whose gender identity, expression, or behavior does not conform to the sex to which they were assigned at birth.

transsexual: refers to people "whose gender identity is different from their assigned sex" (American Psychological Association, 2014: 1); often, transsexual people alter their bodies via hormonal therapy, surgery, and other means to make them more congruent with their identities.

Triple X Syndrome: characteristic of a person born with an extra (i.e., third) sex chromosome, in the configuration of XXX.

tubal ligation: female sterilization consisting of cutting, tying, and removing a portion of the oviduct (i.e., the Fallopian tubes).

Turner's Syndrome: where nondisjunction occurs, one kind of sperm produced will have neither an X nor a Y chromosome. If this sperm fertilizes a normal egg, the offspring will have only an X chromosome.

two-day method: a fertility awareness method based on the woman's knowledge of the presence or absence of cervical secretions.

typical use (of a contraceptive): broadly defined as the actual use in practice of a contraceptive; thus, it does not refer to the "inherent efficacy of a contraceptive method when used perfectly, correctly and consistently" (Kost et al., 2008: 11).

unauthorized/undocumented immigrant: an international migrant residing in the host country of destination who is not a citizen of the host country and has not been admitted for permanent residence, nor is "in a set of specific authorized temporary statuses permitting longer-term residence and work" (Passel, 2006: 1).

United Nations Fund for Population Activities (UNFPA): a major source of funding for population initiatives in developing countries, created in 1969.

urban agglomeration: according to the United Nations, an urban area of at least 1 million inhabitants, including all inhabitants in the surrounding territory living in urban levels of residential density.

urban area: a central city, or cities, and the surrounding closely settled territory.

urban cluster (UC): a densely settled core of blocks and block groups, along with adjacent densely settled surrounding blocks that together encompass a population of at least 2,500 people, but fewer than 50,000 people.

urban growth: an increase in the number of people living in urban areas.

urbanism: a lifestyle characteristic of urban places.

urbanization: the process of change in the proportion of the total population living in urban places.

urbanized area (UA): in the United States, a densely settled core of census blocks and block groups that meet minimum population density requirements, along with adjacent densely settled surrounding census blocks that together encompass a population of 50,000 people.

urban places: densely populated places; in the United States, incorporated and unincorporated places of 2,500 or more inhabitants.

use effectiveness (of a contraceptive): measure of the effectiveness of a method, taking into account the fact that some users do not follow directions perfectly or carefully, or may not use the method all the time. Use effectiveness data reflect how effective the method is in "typical" use.

utopianism: the goal of creating the perfect society in which all people are treated equally and with respect.

vaginal contraceptives: foams, jellies, or pastes that are inserted into the vagina to prevent conception by chemically immobilizing or destroying the sperm.

vaginal ring: a thin, transparent, flexible device similar in content to the combined oral contraceptive pill, which contains both estrogen and progestin that are released on a continuous basis into the woman's body to prevent conception.

vasectomy: male sterilization involving the surgical excision of a part of the vas deferens.

visa overstayers/overstays: a migrant who "overstayed the time limit of a legally obtained non-immigrant temporary visa" (Armbrister, 2003: 512).

vital statistics: the processed results of registrations of vital events; strictly speaking, vital events are deaths and births only, but the term is often broadened to include other population events such as marriages and divorces.

voluntary childlessness: having no children intentionally or voluntarily.

wealth flows theory: the theory that if the wealth flow runs from children to their parents, parents will want to have larger families; if the flow is from parents to children, they will want smaller families, or maybe even no children.

Whipple's Method (WM): an index of age data of a population designed to reflect preference for the terminal digits of "0" and "5."

white flight: the massive out-migration to the suburbs from the core cities of the mostly white middle and upper classes.

withdrawal: a birth control method that consists of removing the penis from the vagina before ejaculation; also known as coitus interruptus.

World Fertility Survey (WFS): one of a number of sample surveys conducted between 1974 and 1986 in sixty-two mainly developing countries, representing 40 percent of the world's population, to gather data on reproductive behavior and related social and psychological indicators.

world systems theory of migration: the theory arguing that international migration is the natural result of the globalization of the market economy.

youth-dependency ratio (YDR or Youth-DR): the number of persons under 15 years of age, divided by the number of persons aged 15–64, multiplied by 100.

zero net international migration: the equal number of persons immigrating into a country in comparison with the number emigrating from the country.

zygote: a fertilized egg, produced when the sperm of a male and the egg of a female are united.

References

Abma, Joyce C. and Gladys M. Martinez, "Childlessness Among Older Women in the United States: Trends and Profiles," *Journal of Marriage and Family*, 68 (2006), 1045–1056.

Abraido-Lanza, A. F., B. P. Dohrenwend, D. S. Ng-Mak, and J. B. Turner, "The Latino Mortality Paradox: A Test of the 'Salmon Bias' and Healthy Migrant Hypotheses," *American Journal of Public Health*, 89 (1999), 1543–1548.

Adams, Willi Paul, "A Dubious Host," *Wilson Quarterly* (New Year's), 1983, p. 110.

Aird, John S., "Population Policy and Demographic Prospects in the People's Republic of China," in *People's Republic of China: An Economic Assessment*, a Compendium of Papers Submitted to the Joint Economic Committee, Congress of the United States, May 18 (92nd Congress, 2nd Session) (Washington, DC: US Government Printing Office, 1972).

Slaughter of the Innocents: Coercive Birth Control in China (Washington, DC: AEI Press, 1990).

Aleccia, Jonel, "'The New Normal': Cohabitation on the Rise, Study Finds," *NBC News, Health News*, April 4, 2013.

"All About Adam," *The Economist*, November 23, 2013.

American Psychological Association, Committee on Lesbian, Gay, Bisexual, and Transgender Concerns, *About Transgender People, Gender Identity, and Gender Expression* (Washington, DC: American Psychological Association, 2014).

Anderson, Margo, "Census," in Paul Demeny and Geoffrey McNicoll (eds.), *Encyclopedia of Population* (New York: Macmillan Reference, 2003), vol. 1, pp. 122–126.

Archdeacon, Thomas J., "Melting Pot or Cultural Pluralism: Changing Views of American Ethnicity," *Revue Européenne des Migrations Internationales*, 6 (1990), 1–18.

Arévalo, Marcos, Irit Sinai, and Victoria Jennings, "A Fixed Formula to Define the Fertile Window of the Menstrual Cycle as the Basis of a Simple Method of Natural Family Planning," *Contraception*, 60 (1999), 357–360.

Arias, Elizabeth, "United States Life Tables, 2010," *National Vital Statistics Reports*, 63(7) (2014).

Arias, Elizabeth, Melonie Heron, and Betzaida Tejada-Vera, "United States Life Tables Eliminating Certain Causes of Death, 1999–2001," *National Vital Statistics Reports*, 61(9) (2013).

Armbrister, Adria N., "Immigration, Unauthorized," in Paul Demeny and Geoffrey McNicoll (eds.), *Encyclopedia of Population* (New York: Macmillan Reference, 2003), vol. 2, pp. 512–515.

Arnold, F., and Z. Liu, "Sex Preference, Fertility, and Family Planning in China," *Population and Development Review*, 12 (1986), 221–246.

Arriaga, Eduardo E. and Associates, *Population Analysis with Microcomputers, vol. 1: Presentation of Techniques* (Washington, DC: US Bureau of the Census, 1994).

Ashford, Lori S., "How HIV and AIDS Affect Populations," *Population Reference Bureau BRIDGE Policy Briefs* (Washington, DC: Population Reference Bureau, July 2006).

Ashton, Basil, Kenneth Hill, Alan Piazza, and Robin Zeitz, "Famine in China, 1958–61," *Population and Development Review*, 10 (1984), 613–645.

Aubrey, John, *Brief Lives, Chiefly of Contemporaries, set down by John Aubrey in 1669–1696*, ed. Andrew Clark (Oxford: Clarendon Press, 1898).

Bachi, R., "The Tendency to Round Off Age Returns: Measurement and Correction," *Bulletin of the International Statistical Institute (Proceedings of the 27th Session, Calcutta)* 33 (1951), 195–221.

Badenhorst, L. T. and Edward Higgins, "Fecundity of White Women in Johannesburg," *Population Studies*, 15 (1962), 279–290.

Balinski, Michael L. and H. Peyton Young, *Fair Representation: Meeting the Ideal of One Man, One Vote* (New Haven, CT: Yale University Press, 1982).

Balter, Michael, "The Baby Deficit," *Science*, 312(5782) (2006), 1894–1897.

Banister, Judith, "China's Changing Mortality," in Dudley L. Poston, Jr., and David Yaukey (eds.), *The Population of Modern China* (New York: Plenum, 1992), pp. 163–223.

"Shortage of Girls in China Today," *Journal of Population Research*, 21 (2004), 19–34.

Barrett, R. E., *Using the 1990 U.S. Census for Research* (Thousand Oaks, CA: Sage, 1994).

Barry, John M., *The Great Influenza: The Epic Story of the Deadliest Plague in History* (New York: Viking, 2004).

Bartlett, John, *Bartlett's Familiar Quotations*, 14th edn. (Boston, MA: Little, Brown, 1968).

Bartz, Deborah and Alisa B. Goldberg, "Injectable Contraceptives," in Robert A. Hatcher, James Trussell, Anita L. Nelson, Willard Cates, Jr., Deborah Kowal, and Michael S. Policar (eds.), *Contraceptive Technology*, 20th rev. edn. (New York: Ardent Media, 2011), pp. 209–236.

Baumle, Amanda K., D'Lane R. Compton, and Dudley L. Poston, Jr., *Same Sex Partners: The Demography of Sexual Orientation* (Albany, NY: SUNY Press, 2009).

Baumle, Amanda K. and Dudley L. Poston, Jr., "Apportioning the House of Representatives in 2000: The Effects of Alternative Policy Scenarios," *Social Science Quarterly*, 85 (2004), 578–603.

Bean, Frank D., Edward E. Telles, and B. Lindsay Lowell, "Undocumented Migration to the United States: Perceptions and Evidence," *Population and Development Review*, 13 (1987), 671–690.

Bean, Frank D. and Marta Tienda, *The Hispanic Population of the United States* (New York: Russell Sage Foundation, 1987).

"Before the Exodus," *The Economist*, 387, April 26, 2008, p. 101.

Belkin, Lisa, "70 Year-old Woman Gives Birth." *New York Times* , December 9, 2008.

Benetsky, Megan J., Charlynn Burd, and Melanie Rapino, "Young Adult Migration: 2007–2009 to 2010–2012," *American Community Survey Reports*, ACS-31 (Washington, DC: US Bureau of the Census, 2015).

Benjamin, Harry, *The Transsexual Phenomenon* (New York: Ace Books, 1966).

Bernard, Aude, Martin Bell, and Elin Charles-Edwards, "Life-Course Transitions and the Age Profile of Internal Migration," *Population and Development Review*, 40 (2014), 213–239.

Bernstein, E. L., "Who Was Condom?" *Human Fertility*, 5 (1940), 172–175, 186.

Biggar, Jeanne C., "The Sunning of America: Migration to the Sunbelt," *Population Bulletin*, 34 (March 1979).

Billari, Francesco C. and Hans-Peter Kohler, "Patterns of Low and Lowest-low Fertility in Europe," *Population Studies*, 58 (2004), 161–176.

Billings, Evelyn, John J. Billings, J. B. Brown, and H. G. Burger, "Symptoms and Hormonal Changes Accompanying Ovulation," *Lancet*, 1 (1972), 282–284.

Billings, Evelyn and Ann Westmore, *The Billings Method: Controlling Fertility without Drugs or Devices* (Toronto: Life Cycle Books, 2000).

Billings, John J., *The Ovulation Method: Natural Family Planning*, 5th edn. (Collegeville, MN: Liturgical Press, 1984).

Biraben, Jean-Noel, "The Rising Numbers of Humankind," *Population & Societies*, 394 (2003), 1–4.

Black, Dan A., Gary Gates, Seth G. Sanders, and Lowell J. Taylor, "Demographics of the Gay and Lesbian Population in the United States: Evidence from Available Systematic Data Sources," *Demography*, 37 (2000), 139–154.

Black, Isabella, "American Labour and Chinese Immigration," *Past and Present*, 25 (1963), 59–76.

Blackless, Melanie, Anthony Charuvastra, Amanda Derryck, Anne Fausto-Sterling, Karl Lauzanne, and Ellen Lee, "How Sexually Dimorphic are We? Review and Synthesis," *American Journal of Human Biology*, 12 (2000), 151–166.

Blake, Judith, "Can We Believe the Recent Data on Birth Expectations in the United States?" *Demography*, 11 (1974), 25–44.

Blank, Hanne, *Straight: The Surprisingly Short History of Heterosexuality* (Boston, MA: Beacon Press, 2012).

Blow, Charles M., "Black Dads are Doing Best of All, *New York Times*, June 8, 2015, p. A21.

Blumenbach, Johann, *On the Natural Varieties of Mankind* (New York: Bergman, [1775, 1776] 1969).

Bogue, Donald J., *Principles of Demography* (New York: Wiley, 1969).

The Population of the United States (New York: Free Press, 1985).

Bogue, Donald J. and James A. Palmore, "Some Empirical and Analytic Relations among Demographic Fertility Measures, with Regression Models for Fertility Estimation," *Demography*, 1 (1964), 316–338.

Bongaarts, John, "A Framework for the Proximate Determinants of Fertility," *Population and Development Review*, 4 (1978), 105–132.

   "The Fertility-Inhibiting Effects of the Intermediate Fertility Variables," *Studies in Family Planning*, 13 (1982), 179–189.

   "How Long Will We Live?" *Population and Development Review*, 32 (2006), 605–628.

Bongaarts, John and Robert G. Potter, *Biology and Fertility Behavior: An Analysis of the Proximate Determinants* (New York: Academic Press, 1983).

Bonilla-Silva, Eduardo, *Racism without Racists: Color-Blind Racism and the Persistence of Racial Inequality in the United States*, 4th edn. (Lanham, MD: Rowman & Littlefield, 2013).

Borjas, George J., "Benefits and Cost of Immigration," in Paul Demeny and Geoffrey McNicoll (eds.), *Encyclopedia of Population* (New York: Macmillan Reference, 2003), vol. 2, pp. 509–512.

Borjas, George J., Richard B. Freeman, and Lawrence F. Katz, "How Much Do Immigration and Trade Affect Labor Market Outcomes?" *Brookings Papers on Economic Activity* (1997), 1–67.

Borrie, W. D., "The Place of Demography in the Development of the Social Sciences," in *International Population Conference, Liège* (Liège: International Union for the Scientific Study of Population, 1973), pp. 73–93.

Boserup, Ester, *The Conditions of Agricultural Growth* (Chicago, IL: Aldine, 1965).

   Population and Technological Change: A Story of Long-Term Trends (University of Chicago Press, 1981).

Bourne, Randolph S., "Trans-national America," *Atlantic Monthly*, 118 (July 1916).

Bouvier, Leon F., "A Genealogical Approach to the Study of French-Canadian Fertility," *Sociological Analysis*, 26 (1965), 148–156.

   Peaceful Invasions (Lanham, MD: University Press of America, 1992).

Bouvier, Leon F. and Jane T. Bertrand, *World Population: Challenges for the 21st Century* (Santa Ana, CA: Seven Locks, 1999).

Bouvier, Leon F. and Lindsey Grant, *How Many Americans? Population, Immigration, and the Environment* (San Francisco, CA: Sierra Club Books, 1994).

Bouvier, Leon F., John J. Macisco, and Alvan Zarate, "Toward a Framework for the Analysis of Differential Migration: The Case of Education," in Anthony H. Richmond and Daniel Kubat (eds.), *Internal Migration: The New World and the Third World* (Beverly Hills, CA: Sage, 1976), pp. 24–36.

Bouvier, Leon F., Dudley L. Poston, Jr., and Nan Bin Zhai, "The Population Growth Impacts of Zero Net International Migration," *International Migration Review*, 31 (1997), 294–311.

Bouvier, Leon F., Henry S. Shryock, and Harry W. Henderson, "International Migration, Yesterday, Today, and Tomorrow," *Population Bulletin*, 30 (September 1977).

Bouvier, Leon F. and Jean van der Tak, "Infant Mortality: Progress and Problems," *Population Bulletin*, 31 (April 1976).

Boyd, Nan Alamilla, *Wide Open Town: A History of Queer San Francisco to 1965* (Berkeley, CA: University of California Press, 2003).

Boylan, Jennifer Finney, *She's Not There: A Life in Two Genders*, expanded 10th anniversary edn. (New York: Random House, 2013a).

Stuck in the Middle with You: A Memoir of Parenting in Three Genders (New York: Random House, 2013b).

Bradley, Don E. and Charles F. Longino, "Geographic Mobility and Aging in Place," in Peter Uhlenberg (ed.), *International Handbook of Population Aging* (Newark, NJ: Springer, 2009), pp. 319–339.

Branch, John., "A Win for Athletes Whose Sex was Questioned," *New York Times*, July 28, 2015, p. A1.

Brevard, Aleshia, *The Woman I Was Not Born to Be: A Transsexual Journey* (Philadelphia, PA: Temple University Press, 2001).

Brimelow, Peter, *Alien Nation: Common Sense about America's Immigration Disaster* (New York: Harper Perennial, 1996).

British Broadcasting Corporation (BBC) News, "Woman in India 'Has Twins at 70'," 2008, available at: http://news.bbc.co.uk/1/hi/world/south_asia/7491782.stm, last accessed July 8, 2008.

Brown, Susan K. and Frank D. Bean, "International Migration," in Dudley L. Poston, Jr. and Michael Micklin (eds.), *Handbook of Population* (New York: Springer, 2005), pp. 347–382.

Brown, Susan K., Frank D. Bean, and James D. Bachmeier, "Fertility and Socio-Demographic Change and the Shrinkage of the U.S. Born Less-skilled Workforce," in Dudley L. Poston, Jr., Samsik Lee, and Hangon Kim (eds.), *Low Fertility Regimes and Demographic and Societal Change* (New York: Springer, forthcoming).

Brown, Susan L., "Family Structure and Child Well-being: The Significance of Parental Cohabitation," *Journal of Marriage and the Family*, 66 (2004), 351–367.

Browning, Harley L. and Dudley L. Poston, Jr., "The Demographic Transition," in Rochelle N. Shain and Carl J. Pauerstein (eds.), *Fertility Control* (New York: Harper & Row, 1980), pp. 197–203.

Brucker, H., "Can International Migration Solve the Problems of European Labour Markets?" paper presented at the UNECE Economic Analysis Division's Spring Seminar "Labour Market Challenges in the ECE Region", Geneva, 2002.

Bryan, Thomas., "Basic Sources of Statistics," in Jacob S. Siegel and David A. Swanson (eds.), *The Methods and Materials of Demography*, 2nd edn. (San Diego, CA: Elsevier Academic, 2004), pp. 9–41.

Bryn, Mary and Morgan Holcomb, "Same Sex Divorce in a DOMA State," *Family Court Review*, 50 (2012), 214–221.

Buchanan, Patrick J., *The Death of the West: How Dying Populations and Immigrant Invasions Imperil Our Country* (New York: St. Martin's Griffin, 2002).

State of Emergency: The Third World Invasion and Conquest of America (New York: St. Martin's Griffin, 2007).

Burch, Thomas K., "Demography in a New Key: A Theory of Population Theory," *Demographic Research*, 9 (2003), 263–284.

Burkitt, Laurie, "China Abandons One Child Policy," *Wall Street Journal*, October 30, 2015.

Burnett, Kristin D., "Census Apportionment," *2010 Census Briefs*, C2010BR-08 (November) (Washington, DC: US Bureau of the Census, 2011), pp. 1–7.

Cai, Yong, "Social Forces behind China's below Replacement Fertility: Government Policy or Socioeconomic Development," *Population and Development Review*, 36 (2010), 419–440.

Caldwell, John C., "Toward a Restatement of Demographic Transition Theory," *Population and Development Review*, 2 (1976), 321–366.

"Epidemics," in David Lucas and Others, *Beginning Australian Population Studies* (Canberra: Australian National University, 2006), ch. 3a, available at: http://demography.anu.edu.au/Publications/Books/BAPS.php, last accessed July 18, 2007.

Carey, Arlen D. and Joseph Lopreato, "The Biocultural Evolution of the Male–Female Mortality Differential," *Mankind Quarterly*, 36 (1995), 3–28.

Carey, James R., "What Demographers Can Learn from Fruit Fly Actuarial Models and Biology," *Demography*, 34 (1997), 17–50.

Longevity: The Biology and Demography of Life Span (Princeton University Press, 2003).

Carey James R., P. Liedo, D. Orozco, and James W. Vaupel, "Slowing of Mortality Rates at Older Ages in Large Medfly Cohorts," *Science*, 258 (1992), 457–461.

Carey, James R. and James W. Vaupel, "Biodemography," in Dudley L. Poston, Jr., and Michael Micklin (eds.), *Handbook of Population* (New York: Kluwer Academic/Plenum, 2005), pp. 625–658.

Carlson, Elwood, *The Lucky Few: Between the Greatest Generation and the Baby Boom* (New York: Springer, 2008).

Carlson, Marcia, Sara McLanahan, and Paula England, "Union Formation in Fragile Families," *Demography*, 41 (2004), 237–261.

Carrier, N. H., "A Note on the Measurement of Digital Preference in Age Recordings," *Journal of the Institute of Actuaries*, 85 (1959), 71–85.

Castells, Manuel, *The Information City: Information Technology, Economic Restructuring, and the Urban–Regional Process* (Oxford: Blackwell, 1989).

Castor, Helen, *Joan of Arc: A History* (New York: HarperCollins, 2015).

Cates, Willard, Jr. and Byrna Harwood, "Vaginal Barriers and Spermicides," in Robert A. Hatcher, James Trussell, Anita L. Nelson, Willard Cates, Jr., Deborah Kowal, and Michael S. Policar (eds.), *Contraceptive Technology*, 20th rev. edn. (New York: Ardent Media, 2011), pp. 391–408.

Cavanaugh, Shannon, "An Analysis of New Census Data on Family Structure, Education, and Income," *Council on Contemporary Families Brief Reports* (Coral Gables, FL: Council on Contemporary Families, February 26, 2015).

Central Intelligence Agency, *The World Factbook* (Washington, DC: Central Intelligence Agency, 2015).

Central Statistical Office, Zambia, and the DHS Program, ICF International, *Zambia Demographic and Health Survey, 2013–2014, Preliminary Report* (Lusaka: Central Statistical Office, 2014).

Chandler, Tertius and Gerald Fox, *3000 Years of Urban Growth* (New York: Academic Press, 1974).

Chandra, Anjani, William D. Mosher, and Casey E. Copen, "Sexual Behavior, Sexual Attraction, and Sexual Identity in the United States: Data from the 2006–2008 National Survey of Family Growth," *National Center for Health Statistics, National Health Statistics Reports*, 36 (March 3, 2011).

Child Trends, "Births to Unmarried Women," *Child Trends Data Bank* (Washington, DC: Child Trends (March 2015).

China Daily, "China Bans Selective Abortion to Fix Imbalance," 2004, available at: www.chinadaily.com.cn/english/doc/2004-07/16/content_349051.htm, last accessed January 11, 2005.

Christopher, Robert C., *Crashing the Gates: The De-Wasping of America's Power Elite* (New York: Simon & Shuster, 1989).

Chu, J., "Prenatal Sex Determination and Sex-Selective Abortion in Rural Central China," *Population and Development Review*, 27 (2001), 259–281.

Clarke, J. I., *The Human Dichotomy: The Changing Numbers of Males and Females* (Amsterdam: Pergamon, 2000).

Cleland, John, "Demographic Data Collection in the Less Developed Countries," *Population Studies*, 50 (1996), 433–450.

Cleland, John and J. Hobcroft, *Reproductive Change in Developing Countries: Insights from the World Fertility Survey* (New York: Oxford University Press, 1985).

Cleland, John and C. Scott, *The World Fertility Survey: An Assessment* (New York: Oxford University Press, 1987).

Coale, Ansley J., "How the Distribution of Human Population Is Determined," *Cold Spring Harbor Symposium on Quantitative Biology*, 22 (1957), 83–89.

"Age Patterns of Marriage," *Population Studies*, 25 (1971), 193–214.

The Growth and Structure of Human Populations (Princeton University Press, 1972).

"The History of the Human Population," *Scientific American*, 231 (1974), 51.

"Stable Populations," in J. Eatwell, M. Milgate, and P. K. Newman (eds.), *The New Palgrave: A Dictionary of Economics* (London: Macmillan, 1987), vol. 4, pp. 466–469.

Coale, Ansley J. and Paul Demeny, *Regional Model Life Tables and Stable Populations*, 2nd edn. (New York: Academic Press, 1983).

Coale, Ansley J. and Susan Cotts Watkins (eds.), *The Decline of Fertility in Europe* (Princeton University Press, 1986).

Coan, Peter Morton, *Ellis Island Interviews: Immigrants Tell Their Stories in Their Own Words* (New York: Fall River, 2004).

Cohen, Joel, *How Many People Can the Earth Support?* (New York: W. W. Norton, 1995).

Cohen, Stephanie, "Retire to the Bedroom," *New York Post*, January 25, 2009.

Cohen, Susan A., "New Data on Abortion Incidence, Safety Illuminate Key Aspects of Worldwide Abortion Debate," *Guttmacher Policy Review*, 10 (2007), 2–5.

Colby, Sandra L. and Jennifer M. Ortman, "Projections of the Size and Composition of the US Population: 2014 to 2060," *Current Population Reports*, P25–114 (March) (Washington, DC: US Bureau of the Census, 2015).

Coleman, David A., "Male Fertility Trends in Industrial Countries: Theories in Search of Some Evidence," in Caroline Bledsoe, Susana Lerner, and Jane I. Guyer (eds.), *Fertility and the Male Life-Cycle in the Era of Fertility Decline* (Oxford University Press, 2000), pp. 29–60.

"Immigration and Ethnic Change in Low-fertility Countries: A Third Demographic Transition," *Population and Development Review*, 32 (2006), 401–446.

Companies and Markets, "Global Condom Industry," *Consumer Goods*, available at: www.companiesandmarkets.com/MarketInsight/Consumer-Goods/Global-Condom-Industry/NI8052, last accessed July 1, 2015.

Compton, D'Lane R., D. Nicole Farris, and Yu-ting Chang, "Patterns of Bisexuality in America," *Journal of Bisexuality*, 15 (2015), 1–17.

Comte, Auguste, *The Positive Philosophy of Auguste Comte* (New York: Calvin Blanchard, 1853).

Conceptus, Inc., *When Your Family is Complete, Choose Essure* (Mountain View, CA: Conceptus, Inc., 2010).

Conde, Eugenia, "Theoretical and Methodological Issues and Challenges in Analyses of Teen Fertility," PhD dissertation, Texas A&M University, College Station, 2011.

Congressional Budget Office, *A Description of the Immigrant Population*, update (Washington, DC: Congressional Budget Office, 2013).

Connelly, Matthew, *Fatal Misconception: The Struggle to Control World Population* (Cambridge, MA: Harvard University Press, 2008).

Connor, Phillip, D'Vera Cohn, Ana Gonzalez-Barrerra, and Russ Oates, "Changing Patterns of Global Migration and Remittances" (Washington, DC: Pew Research Center, 2013).

Cooley, Charles Horton, *Human Nature and the Social Order* (New York: C. Scribner's Sons, 1902).

Coontz, Stephanie, *The Way We Never Were: American Families and the Nostalgia Trap* (New York: Basic Books, 2000).

Marriage, A History: From Obedience to Intimacy or How Love Conquered Marriage (New York: Viking, 2005).

Copen, Casey E., Kimberly Daniels, and William D. Mosher, "First Premarital Cohabitation in the United States: 2006–2010 National Survey of Family Growth," *National Health Statistics Reports*, 64 (April 4, 2013).

Corijn, Martine and Erik Klijzing, *Transitions to Adulthood in Europe* (New York: Kluwer Academic, 2001).

Cortes, Rachel Traut and Dudley L. Poston, Jr., "Immigrants to North America," in William A. Darity (ed.), *International Encyclopedia of the Social Sciences*, 2nd edn. (Detroit, MI: Macmillan Reference, 2008), vol. 3, pp. 576–580.

Corti, Maria-Chiara, Jack M. Guralnik, Luigi Ferrucci, Grant Izmirlian, Suzanne G. Leveille, Marco Pahor, Harvey J. Cohen, Carl Pieper, and Richard J. Havlik, "Evidence for a Black–White Crossover in All-Cause and Coronary Heart Disease Mortality in an Older Population: The North Carolina EPESE," *American Journal of Public Health*, 89 (1999), 308–314.

Couzin-Frankel, Jennifer, "A Pitched Battle over Life Span," *Science*, 333 (2011), 549–550.

Cox, T. K. and G. Pendell, "Attitudes about Childlessness in the United States: Correlates of Positive, Neutral, and Negative Responses," *Journal of Family Issues*, 28 (2007), 1054–1082.

Crosby, Alfred W., *America's Forgotten Epidemic: The Influenza of 1918*, 2nd edn. (New York: Cambridge University Press, 2003).

Crosette, Barbara, "How to Fix a Crowded World," *New York Times*, November 2, 1997.

Curtin, Philip, *The Atlantic Slave Trade* (Madison, WI: University of Wisconsin Press, 1969).

Curtin, Sally C., Stephanie J. Ventura, and Gladys M. Martinez, "Recent Declines in Nonmarital Childbearing in the United States," *NCHS Data Brief* 162 (Hyattsville, MD: National Center for Health Statistics, August 2014).

Darwin, Charles, *Autobiography and Selected Letters*, ed. Francis Darwin (New York: Dover, [1887] 1958).

Darwin, John., *After Tamerlane: The Global History of Empire Since 1405* (New York: Bloomsbury, 2008).

David, Henry P. and Nicholas H. Wright, "Abortion Legislation: The Romanian Experience," *Studies in Family Planning*, 2 (1971), 205–210.

Davis, Georgiann, *Contesting Intersex: The Dubious Diagnosis* (New York: New York University Press, 2015).

Davis, Kingsley, *Human Society* (New York: Macmillan, 1949).

    The Population of India and Pakistan (Princeton University Press, 1951).

    "The Theory of Change and Response in Modern Demographic History," *Population Index*, 29 (1963), 345–366.

    "The Migrations of Human Populations," *Scientific American*, 231 (1974), 92–105.

Davis, Kingsley and Judith Blake, "Social Structure and Fertility: An Analytical Framework," *Economic Development and Cultural Change*, 5 (1956), 211–235.

Davis, Mary Ann, *Alzheimer's Disease Mortality: A Demographic Analysis of Alzheimer's Disease Deaths in the United States from 1998 to 2002* (Saarbrücken: VDM Verlag, 2008).

Dean, Gillian and Eleanor Bimla Schwarz, "Intrauterine Contraceptives (IUCs)," in Robert A. Hatcher, James Trussell, Anita L. Nelson, Willard Cates, Jr., Deborah Kowal, and Michael S. Policar (eds.), *Contraceptive Technology*, 20th rev. edn. (New York: Ardent Media, 2011), pp. 147–191.

de Crevecoeur, J. Hector St. John, "Letter III," in *Letters from an American Farmer*, ed. Susan Manning (New York: Oxford University Press, [1782] 1997).

Deffeyes, Kenneth, *Beyond Oil: The View from Hubbert's Peak* (New York: Hill & Wang, 2005).

Demeny, Paul, "Population Policy," in Paul Demeny and Geoffrey McNicoll (eds.), *Encyclopedia of Population* (New York: Macmillan Reference, 2003), vol. 2, pp. 752–763.

Dikotter, Frank, *Mao's Great Famine: The History of China's Most Devastating Catastrophe, 1958–1962* (New York: Walker & Co., 2010).

Djerassi, Carl, *The Pill, Pygmy Chimps, and Degas' Horse: The Autobiography of Carl Djerassi* (New York: Basic Books, 1992).

Dominguez, Kenneth, Ana Penman-Aguilar, Man-Huei Chang, Ramal Moonesinghe, Ted Castellanos, Alfonso Rodriguez-Lainz, and Richard Schieber, "Leading Causes of Death, Prevalence of Diseases and Risk Factors, and Use of Health Services among Hispanics in the United States, 2009–2013," *Morbidity and Mortality Weekly Report*, 64 (2015), 469–478.

Donato, Katharine M., "US Policy and Mexican Migration to the United States, 1942–92," *Social Science Quarterly*, 75 (1994), 705–729.

Dreger, Alice Domurat, "Ambiguous Sex – or Ambivalent Medicine," *Hastings Center Report*, 28(3) (1998a), 24–35.

  Hermaphrodites and the Medical Intervention of Sex (Cambridge, MA: Harvard University Press, 1998b).

Dreyer, Edward L., *Zheng He: China and the Oceans in the Early Ming Dynasty, 1405–1433* (New York: Pearson Longman, 2007).

Dublin, Louis, Alfred J. Lotka, and Mortimer Spiegelman, *Length of Life*, rev. edn. (New York: Ronald Press, 1949).

Du Bois, W. E. B., *The Souls of Black Folks* (Greenwich, CT: Greenwood Press, [1903] 1921).

Duncan, Otis Dudley, "Human Ecology and Population Studies," in Philip M. Hauser and Otis Dudley Duncan (eds.), *The Study of Population* (University of Chicago Press, 1959), pp. 678–716.

Dupre, Matthew E., Alexis T. Franzese, and Emilio A. Parrado, "Religious Attendance and Mortality: Implications for the Black–White Mortality Crossover," *Demography*, 43 (2006), 141–164.

Durand, Jorge, Douglas S. Massey, and Emilio A. Parrado, "The New Era of Migration to the United States," *Journal of American History*, 86 (1999), 518–536.

Durkheim, Émile, *The Division of Labour in Society*, trans. W. D. Halls (London: Macmillan, [1893] 1984).

Easterlin, Richard A., "Introduction," in Elwood Carlson, *The Lucky Few: Between the Greatest Generation and the Baby Boom* (New York: Springer, 2008), pp. xvii–xx.

Eberstadt, Nicholas, *Prosperous Paupers & Other Population Problems* (New Brunswick, NJ: Transaction, 2000).

  "Drunken Nation: Russia's Depopulation Bomb," *World Affairs*, 171 (2009), 51–62.

Eberstein Isaac W, Charles B. Nam, and K. M. Heyman, "Causes of Death and Mortality Crossovers by Race," *Biodemography and Social Biology*, 54 (2008), 214–228.

Edin, Kathryn and Maria Kefalas, *Promises I Can Keep: Why Poor Women Put Motherhood before Marriage*, 2nd edn. (Oakland, CA: University of California Press, 2007).

Ehrlich, Paul R., *The Population Bomb* (New York: Ballantine Books, 1968).

Eig, Jonathan, *The Birth of the Pill: How Four Crusaders Reinvented Sex and Launched a Revolution* (New York: W. W. Norton, 2014).

Eldridge, Hope T., "Population Policies," in David L. Sills (ed.), *International Encyclopedia of the Social Sciences* (New York: Macmillan, 1968), vol. 12, pp. 380–388.

Endres, Michael E., *On Diffusing the Population Bomb* (New York: John Wiley, 1975).

Ennis, Sharon R., Merarys Rios-Vargas, and Nora G. Albert, "The Hispanic Population: 2010," *2010 Census Briefs*, C2010BR-04 (May) (Washington, DC: US Bureau of the Census, 2011).

Epstein, Helen, "Death by the Numbers," *New York Review*, June 28, 2007a, pp. 41–43.

   The Invisible Cure: Africa, the West, and the Fight against AIDS (New York: Farrar, Straus & Giroux, 2007b).

Epstein, Randi Hutter, "Howard W. Jones Jr., a Pioneer of Reproductive Medicine Dies at 104," *New York Times*, July 31, 2015.

Eschbach, Karl, "Changing Identification among American Indians and Alaska Natives," *Demography*, 30 (1993), 635–652.

Espenshade, Thomas J., J. L. Baraka, and G. A. Huber, "Implications of the 1996 Welfare and Immigration Reform Acts for US Immigration," *Population and Development Review*, 23 (1997), 769–801.

Espenshade, Thomas J., Leon F. Bouvier, and W. Brian Arthur, "Immigration and the Stable Population Model," *Demography*, 19 (1982), 125–133.

Espenshade, Thomas J. and Katherine Hempstead, "Contemporary American Attitudes toward US Migration," *International Migration Review*, 30 (1996), 535–570.

Espey, David, "Spanish Influenza in San Francisco 1918–1919: A Case Study," unpublished Senior Thesis, Kenyon College, Gambier, Ohio, 2014.

Etherington, Norman, "War," in Paul Demeny and Geoffrey McNicoll (eds.), *Encyclopedia of Population* (New York: Macmillan Reference, 2003), vol. 2, pp. 963–966.

Euler, Leonhard, "General Research on Mortality and Multiplication," trans. Nathan Keyfitz and B. Keyfitz, *Theoretical Population Biology*, 1 ([1760]1970), 307–314.

Eurostat, *Migration and Migrant Population Statistics* (Brussels: European Commission, 2015).

Eversley, D. E. C., *Social Theories of Fertility and the Malthusian Debate* (Oxford: Clarendon Press, 1959).

Ewing, Walter A., Daniel E. Martínez, and Rubén G. Rumbaut, *The Criminalization of Immigration in the United States* (Washington, DC: American Immigration Council, 2015).

Fagundes, Nelson J. R., Nicolas Ray, Mark Beaumont, Samuel Neuenschwander, Francisco M. Salzano, Sandro L. Bonatto, and Laurent Excoffier, "Statistical Evaluation of Alternative Models of Human Evolution," *Proceedings of the National Academy of Sciences*, 104 (2007), 17614–17619.

Fairbank, John K. and Merle Goldman, *China: A New History*, 2nd enlarged edn. (Cambridge, MA: Belknap Press, 2006).

Fan, C. Cindy, "Migration in a Socialist Transitional Economy: Heterogeneity, Socioeconomic and Spatial Characteristics of Migrants in China and Guangdong Province," *International Migration Review*, 33 (1999), 954–987.

Farris, Demetrea Nicole, *Boomerang Kids: The Demography of Previously Launched Adults* (New York: Springer, 2016).

Farris, Demetrea Nicole and Dudley L. Poston, Jr., "Family Issues in Taiwan and China," in Dudley L. Poston, Jr., Wen Shan Yang, and D. Nicole Farris (eds.), *The Family and Social Change in Chinese Societies* (New York: Springer, 2014), pp. vii–xviii.

Faust, Drew Gilpin, *This Republic of Suffering: Death and the American Civil War* (New York: Alfred A. Knopf, 2008).

Fausto-Sterling, Anne, *Sexing the Body: Gender Politics and the Construction of Sexuality* (New York: Basic Books, 2000).

Feagin, Joe R., *Systemic Racism: A Theory of Oppression* (New York: Routledge, 2006).

   Racist America: Roots, Current Realities, and Future Reparations, 3rd edn. (New York: Routledge, 2014).

Federal Interagency Forum on Child and Family Statistics, *America's Children: Key National Indicators of Well Being, 2007* (Washington, DC: US Government Printing Office, 2007).

Fellmann, Jerome D., Arthur Getis, and Judith Getis, *Human Geography: Landscapes of Human Activities*, 6th edn. (New York: WCB McGraw-Hill, 1999).

Field, Layton and Dudley L. Poston, Jr., "Subnational Depopulation via Natural Decrease in the Countries of Europe and in the States of the United States in the Early 21st Century," paper presented at the XXVII International Population Conference, International Union for the Scientific Study of Population, Busan, South Korea, August, 26–31, 2013.

Filteau, Jerry, "Obama Rescinds Family-Planning Aid Restrictions," *National Catholic Reporter*, 45 (February 6, 2009), 1, 12–13.

Finer, L. B., "Trends in Premarital Sex in the United States, 1954–2003," *Public Health Reports*, 122 (2007), 73–78.

Fingerhut, Lois A., "Accidents," in Paul Demeny and Geoffrey McNicoll (eds.), *Encyclopedia of Population* (New York: Macmillan Reference, 2003), vol. 1, pp. 2–6.

Fischer, Peter A., Reiner Martin, and Thomas Straubhaar, "Should I Stay or Should I Go?" in Thomas Hammar, Grete Brochmann, and Kristof Tamas (eds.), *International Migration, Immobility and Development* (Oxford: Berg, 1997), pp. 49–90.

Flatau, E., Z. Josefsberg, S. H. Reisner, O. Bialik, and Z. Laron, "Penis Size in the Newborn Infant," *Journal of Pediatrics*, 87 (1975), 663–664.

Fossett, Mark, "Urban and Spatial Demography," in Dudley L. Poston, Jr. and Michael Micklin (eds.), *Handbook of Population* (New York: Kluwer Academic/Plenum, 2005), pp. 479–524.

Foster, R. F., *Modern Ireland: 1600–1972* (New York: Penguin Books, 1988).

Foucault, Michel, *The History of Sexuality, vol. 1: An Introduction* (New York: Vintage Books, 1978).

Freedman, Lynn P. and Stephen L. Isaacs, "Human Rights and Reproductive Choice," *Studies in Family Planning*, 24 (1993), 18–30.

Freedman, Mary Anne and James A. Weed, "Vital Statistics," in Paul Demeny and Geoffrey McNicoll (eds.), *Encyclopedia of Population* (New York: Macmillan Reference, 2003), vol. 2, pp. 960–962.

Freeman, Gary P., "Immigration Policies," in Paul Demeny and Geoffrey McNicoll (eds.), *Encyclopedia of Population* (New York: Macmillan Reference, 2003), vol. 2, pp. 515–519.

Frey, William H., "Internal Migration," in Paul Demeny and Geoffrey McNicoll (eds.), *Encyclopedia of Population* (New York: Macmillan Reference, 2003), vol. 2, pp. 545–548.

Diversity Explosion: How New Racial Demographics are Remaking America (Washington, DC: Brookings Institution Press, 2015).

Friedman, Benjamin M., *The Moral Consequences of Economic Growth* (New York: Knopf, 2005).

Friedman, Thomas L., *The World is Flat: A Brief History of the Twenty-First Century* (New York: Farrar, Straus & Giroux, 2005).

Hot, Flat and Crowded: Why We Need a Green Revolution, and How it Can Renew America (New York: Farrar, Straus & Giroux, 2008).

Fries, James F., "Aging, Natural Death, and the Compression of Morbidity," *New England Journal of Medicine*, 303 (1980), 130–136.

"The Compression of Morbidity," *Milbank Memorial Fund Quarterly*, 61 (1983), 397–419.

"Compression of Morbidity in the Elderly," *Vaccine*, 18 (2000), 1584–1589.

Frisbie, W. Parker, "Infant Mortality," in Dudley L. Poston, Jr. and Michael Micklin (eds.), *Handbook of Population* (New York: Kluwer Academic/Plenum, 2005), pp. 251–282.

Gabaccia, Donna R., *Immigration and American Diversity: A Social and Cultural History* (Malden, MA: Blackwell, 2002).

Garcia, Ginny E., *Mexican American and Immigrant Poverty in the United States* (New York: Springer, 2011).

Garreau, Joel, *Edge City: Life on the New Frontier* (New York: Doubleday, 1991).

Gates, Gary J., "How Many People are Lesbian, Gay, Bisexual and Transgender?" The Williams Institute, April 2011, available at: http://williamsinstitute.law .ucla.edu/wp-content/uploads/Gates-How-Many-People-LGBT-Apr-2011 .pdf, last accessed May 30, 2015.

"Geography of the LGBT Population," in Amanda K. Baumle (ed.), *International Handbook on the Demography of Sexuality* (New York: Springer, 2013), pp. 229–242.

Gates, Gary J. and J. Ost, *The Gay and Lesbian Atlas* (Washington, DC: Urban Institute Press, 2004).

Gauthier, Jason G., *Measuring America: The Decennial Censuses from 1790 to 2000* (Washington, DC: US Bureau of the Census, 2002).

Geddes, Patrick, *Cities in Evolution* (London: Williams & Norgate, 1915).

Gelbspan, Ross, "Two Paths for the Planet," *The American Prospect*, August 2007, pp. 45–47.

Gellerman, Jo, "Medical Ignorance Conference to Explore Timely Challenges and Questions," 2000, available at: http://uanews.org/node/8144, last accessed July 8, 2015.

Ghosh, Bimal, "Economic Effects of International Migration: A Synoptic Overview," in Irena Omelaniuk (ed.), *World Migration, 2005: Costs and*

Benefits on International Migration (Geneva: International Organization for Migration, 2005), pp. 163–184.

Gibson, Campbell and Kay Jung, "Historical Census Statistics on the Foreign-born Population of the United States: 1850 to 2000," Population Division, Working Paper 81 (Washington, DC: US Bureau of the Census, 2006).

Giddens, Anthony, *Runaway World: How Globalization is Reshaping Our Lives* (London: Profile Books, 2002).

Gill, Richard T., Nathan Glazer, and Stephen A. Thernstrom, *Our Changing Population* (Englewood Cliffs, NJ: Prentice-Hall, 1992).

Gillis, Malcolm, D. H. Perkins, M. Roemer, and D. R. Snodgrass, *Economics of Development*, 4th edn. (New York: W. W. Norton, 1996).

Gimenez, Martha E., "The Population Issue: Marx vs. Malthus," revised version of a paper presented at the annual meeting of the Pacific Sociological Association, Honolulu, 1971.

Glass, David V., *Population Policies and Movements in Europe* (New York: Augustus M. Kelley, 1940).

(ed.), *Introduction to Malthus* (New York: Wiley, 1953).

Glazer, Nathan, *Ethnic Dilemma* (New York: Hawthorne, 1983).

Glover, James W., *United States Life Tables, 1890, 1901, 1910, and 1901–1910* (Washington, DC: US Government Printing Office, 1921).

Goebel, Ted, "The Missing Years for Modern Humans," *Science*, 315 (2007), 194–196.

Goebel, Ted, Michael R. Waters, and Dennis H. O'Rourke, "The Late Pleistocene Dispersal of Modern Humans in the Americas," *Science*, 319 (2008), 1497–1502.

Goldin, Ian, Geoffrey Cameron, and Meera Balarajan, *Exceptional People: How Migration Shaped Our World and Will Define Our Future* (Princeton University Press, 2011).

Goldscheider, Calvin, *Population, Modernization and Social Structure* (Boston, MA: Little, Brown, 1971).

Goodkind, Daniel, "On Substituting Sex Preference Strategies in East Asia: Does Prenatal Sex Selection Reduce Postnatal Discrimination?" *Population Research and Policy Review*, 22 (1996), 111–125.

"Recent Trends in the Sex Ratio at Birth in East Asia," paper presented at the Conference on Chinese Populations and Socioeconomic Studies: Utilizing the 2000/2001 Round Census Data, Hong Kong University of Science and Technology, 2002.

"Child Underreporting, Fertility, and Sex Ratio Imbalance in China," *Demography*, 48 (2011), 291–316.

"The Claim that China's Fertility Restrictions Contributed to the Use of Prenatal Sex Selection: A Skeptical Reappraisal," *Population Studies*, 69 (2015), 263–279.

Gordon, Mary, *Joan of Arc* (New York: Penguin Putnam, 2000).

Gordon, Milton, *Assimilation in American Life* (New York: Oxford University Press, 1964).

Gottmann, Jean, *Megalopolis: The Urbanized Northeastern Seaboard of the United States* (Cambridge, MA: MIT Press, 1961).

Graunt, John, *Natural and Political Observations Made Upon the Bills of Mortality*, US edn. with Introduction by Walter F. Willcox, ed. Jacob B. Hollander (Baltimore, MD: Johns Hopkins University Press, [1662] 1939).

Greene, Margaret E. and Ann E. Biddlecom, "Absent and Problematic Men: Demographic Accounts of Male Reproductive Roles," *Population and Development Review*, 26 (2000), 81–115.

Greenhalgh, Susan, "Shifts in China's Population Policy," *Population and Development Review*, 12 (1986), 491–515.

"The Evolution of the One-Child Policy in Shaanxi, 1979–1988," *China Quarterly*, 122 (1990a), 191–229.

"Toward a Political Economy of Fertility: Anthropological Contributions," *Population and Development Review*, 16 (1990b), 85–106.

"Controlling Births and Bodies in Village China," *American Ethnologist*, 21 (1994), 3–30.

Just One Child: Science and Policy in Deng's China (Berkeley, CA: University of California Press, 2008).

Greenwood, Michael J., "Research on Internal Migration in the United States: A Survey," *Journal of Economic Literature*, 13 (1975), 397–433.

Gribble, James M., "The Standard Days Method of Family Planning: A Response to Cairo," *International Family Planning Perspectives*, 29 (2003), 188–191.

Grieco, Elizabeth M., Yesenia D. Acosta, G. Patricia de la Cruz, Christine Gambino, Thomas Gryn, Luke J. Larsen, Edward N. Trevelyan, and Nathan P. Walters, "The Foreign-Born Population in the United States: 2010," *American Community Survey Reports* ACS-19 (Washington, DC: US Bureau of the Census, 2012).

Grieco, Elizabeth M. and Monica Boyd, "Women and Migration: Incorporating Gender into International Migration Theory," Working Paper WPS98-139, Florida State University, Center for the Study of Population, Tallahassee, 1998.

Griffith, J., "Social Pressures on Family Size Intentions," *Family Planning Perspectives*, 5 (1973), 237–242.

Gu, Baochang and Krishna Roy, "Sex Ratio at Birth in China, with Reference to Other Areas in East Asia: What We Know," *Asia-Pacific Population Journal*, 10 (1995), 17–42.

Guest, Avery M. and Susan K. Brown, "Population Distribution and Suburbanization," in Dudley L. Poston, Jr. and Michael Micklin (eds.), *Handbook of Population* (New York: Kluwer Academic/Plenum, 2005), pp. 59–86.

Guillebaud, John, *The Pill and Other Hormonal Contraceptives*, 6th edn. (New York: Oxford University Press, 2005).

Guo, Zhigang and Baochang Gu, "China's Low Fertility: Evidence from the 2010 Census," in Isabelle Attané and Baochang Gu (eds.), *Analyzing China's Population: Recent Trends and Major Challenges* (New York: Springer, 2014), pp. 15–36.

Guttmacher Institute, "Facts on Induced Abortion in the United States," Guttmacher Institute, New York, 2008.

"Facts on Induced Abortion Worldwide," In Brief: Fact Sheet, Guttmacher Institute, New York, January 2012.

"American Teens' Sexual and Reproductive Health," Fact Sheet, Guttmacher Institute, New York, May 2014a.

"Induced Abortion in the United States," Fact Sheet, Guttmacher Institute, New York, July 2014b.

"Contraceptive Use in the United States," Fact Sheet, Guttmacher Institute, New York, June 2015.

Hackett, Conrad, "Five Facts about the Muslim Population in Europe," *FactTank: News in the Numbers* (Washington, DC: Pew Research Center, 2015).

Haines, Michael R., "Trans-Atlantic Migration," in Paul Demeny and Geoffrey McNicoll (eds.), *Encyclopedia of Population* (New York: Macmillan Reference, 2003), vol. 2, pp. 942–946.

"Fertility and Mortality in the United States," 2007, available at: https://eh.net/encyclopedia/fertility-and-mortality-in-the-united-states, last accessed June 26, 2015.

Haines, Michael R. and Avery M. Guest, "Fertility in New York State in the Pre-Civil War Era," *Demography*, 45 (2008), 345–361.

Hajnal, J., "European Marriage Patterns in Perspective," in D. V. Glass and D. E. C. Eversley (eds.), *Population in History* (London: Edward Arnold, 1965), pp. 101–143.

Hamilton, Brady E., Joyce A. Martin, and Stephanie J. Ventura, "Births: Preliminary Data for 2005," *National Vital Statistics Reports*, 55(11) (Hyattsville, MD: National Center for Health Statistics, 2007).

Hamilton, C. Horace, "The Negro Leaves the South," *Demography*, 1 (1964), 273–295.

Harris, J. R. and Michael P. Todaro, "Migration, Unemployment, and Development: A Two-Sector Analysis," *American Economic Review*, 60 (1970), 126–142.

Haskell, Molly, *My Brother, My Sister: Story of a Transformation* (New York: Penguin, 2013).

Hassold, T., S. D. Quillen, and J. A. Yamane, "Sex Ratio in Spontaneous Abortions," *Annals of Human Genetics*, 47 (1983), 39–47.

Haub, Carl, *How Many People Have Ever Lived on Earth?* (Washington, DC: Population Reference Bureau, 2011).

Haub, Carl and Machiko Yanagishita, "Infant Mortality: Who's Number One?" *Population Today*, 19 (1991), 6–8.

Hauser, Philip M. and Otis Dudley Duncan (eds.). *The Study of Population: An Inventory and Appraisal* (University of Chicago Press, 1959).

Hawley, Amos H., *Human Ecology: A Theory of Community Structure* (New York: Ronald Press, 1950).

"Human Ecology," in David L. Sills (ed.), *International Encyclopedia of the Social Sciences* (New York: Crowell, Collier, & Macmillan, 1968), pp. 328–337.

Hay, Jeff (ed.), *Immigration* (San Diego, CA: Greenhaven, 2001).

Healy, Bernadine, "Beyond the Baby Count," *US News and World Report*, September 24, 2006.

Henry, Louis, "Some Data on Natural Fertility," *Eugenics Quarterly*, 8 (1961), 81–91.

Henshaw, Stanley K., "Induced Abortion, Prevalence," in Paul Demeny and Geoffrey McNicoll (eds.), *Encyclopedia of Population* (New York: Macmillan Reference, 2003), vol. 2, pp. 529–531.

Herek, Gregory M., "Confronting Sexual Stigma and Prejudice: Theory and Practice," *Journal of Social Issues*, 63 (2007), 905–925.

Herlihy, David, *The Black Death and the Transformation of the West* (Cambridge, MA: Harvard University Press, 1997).

Higham, John, *Send These to Me* (New York: Athenaeum, 1975).

Hill, Reuben, J. Mayone Stycos, and Kurt Back, *The Family and Population Control: A Puerto Rican Experiment in Social Change* (Chapel Hill, NC: University of North Carolina Press, 1959).

Hillygus, D. Sunshine, Norman H. Nie, Kenneth Prewitt, and Heili Pals, *The Hard Count: The Political and Social Challenges of Census Mobilization* (New York: Russell Sage Foundation, 2006).

Himes, Norman E., *Medical History of Contraception* (New York: Schocken Books, [1936] 1970).

Hinde, Andrew, *Demographic Methods* (London: Arnold, 1998).

Hirschman, Charles, "Why Fertility Changes," *Annual Review of Sociology*, 20 (1994), 203–233.

Hobbs, Frank, "Age and Sex Composition," in Jacob S. Siegel and David A. Swanson (eds.), *The Methods and Materials of Demography*, 2nd edn. (San Diego, CA: Elsevier Academic, 2004), ch. 7, pp. 125–173.

Hochschild, Jennifer L. and Brenna Marea Powell, "Racial Reorganization and the United States Census, 1850–1930: Mulattoes, Half-breeds, Mixed Parentage, Hindoos, and the Mexican Race," *Studies in American Political Development*, 22 (2008), 59–96.

Hodgson, Dennis and Susan Watkins, "Feminists and Neo-Malthusians: Past and Present Alliances," *Population and Development Review*, 23 (1997), 469–523.

Hollinger, David, *Postethnic America: Beyond Multiculturalism* (New York: Basic Books, 2006).

Holzer, Harry J., *Immigration Policy and Less-Skilled Workers in the United States: Reflections on Future Directions for Reform* (Washington, DC: Migration Policy Institute, 2011).

Hooks, Christopher and Fauzeya Rahman, "Fear Dominates at Immigration Protests in Austin and Houston," *Texas Observer*, July 18, 2014.

Hopcroft, Rosemary L., "Sex Differences in the Relationship between Status and Number of Offspring in the Contemporary US," *Evolution and Human Behavior*, 36 (2015), 146–151.

Horiuchi, Shiro and Samuel H. Preston, "Age-Specific Growth Rates: The Legacy of Past Population Dynamics," *Demography*, 25 (1988), 429–441.

Horton, Hayward Derrick, "Critical Demography: The Paradigm of the Future?" *Sociological Forum*, 14 (1999), 363–367.

Howden, Lindsay and Dudley L. Poston, Jr., "Depopulation," in William A. Darity (ed.), *International Encyclopedia of the Social Sciences*, 2nd edn (Detroit, MI: Macmillan Reference, 2008), vol. 2, pp. 301–302.

Hoyer, Niels, *Man Into Woman: The First Sex Change* (Ashburn, VA: Blue Boat Books, [1933] 2004).

Hoyert, Donna L., and Jiaquan Xu, "Deaths: Preliminary Data for 2011," *National Vital Statistics Report*, 61 (October 10, 2012), available at: www.cdc.gov/nchs/data/nvsr/nvsr61/nvsr61_06.pdf, last accessed June 26, 2015.

Hudson, Valerie M. and Andrea M. den Boer, "A Surplus of Men, a Deficit of Peace," *International Security*, 26 (2002), 5–38.

  Bare Branches: Security Implications of Asia's Surplus Male Population (Cambridge, MA: MIT Press, 2004).

Hughes, Jonathan and Louis P. Cain, *American Economic History*, 6th edn. (Boston, MA: Addison-Wesley, 2002).

Hull, T. H., "Recent Trends in Sex Ratios at Birth in China," *Population and Development Review*, 16 (1990), 63–83.

Humes, Karen R., Nicholas A. Jones, and Roberto R. Ramirez, "Overview of Race and Hispanic Origin, 2010," *2010 Census Briefs*, C2010BR-02 (March) (Washington, DC: US Bureau of the Census, 2011).

Hummer, Robert A. and Elaine M. Hernandez, "The Effect of Educational Attainment on Adult Mortality in the United States," *Population Bulletin*, 68(1) (2013), 1–15.

Iceland, John, *A Portrait of America: The Demographic Perspective* (Oakland, CA: University of California Press, 2014).

Ihrke, David K., "Reasons for Moving, 2012–2013," *Population Characteristics*, P20–574 (Washington, DC: US Bureau of the Census, 2014).

Ihrke, David K. and Carol S. Faber, "Geographic Mobility, 2005–2010," *Population Characteristics*, P20–567 (Washington, DC: US Bureau of the Census, 2012).

Ihrke, David K., Carol S. Faber, and William K. Koerber, "Geographical Mobility, 2008–2009," *Population Characteristics*, P20–565 (Washington, DC: US Bureau of the Census, 2011).

Intergovernmental Panel on Climate Change (IPCC), *Climate Change, 2007: The Physical Science Basis* (Geneva: IPCC, 2007).

International Olympic Committee, *IOC Regulations on Female Hyperandrogenism* (Lausanne: International Olympic Committee, 2014).

International Organization for Migration, *World Migration Report 2010* (Geneva: International Organization for Migration, 2010).

Iredale, Robyn, "Balancing the Benefits and Costs of Skilled Migration in the Asia-Pacific Region," in Irena Omelaniuk (ed.), *World Migration, 2005: Costs and Benefits on International Migration* (Geneva: International Organization for Migration, 2005), ch. 11, pp. 221–237.

Issawi, C., *An Arab Philosophy of History: Selections from the Prolegomena of Ibn Khaldun of Tunis (1332–1406)* (Princeton University Press, 1987).

Jenks, Rosemary, "The Enhanced Border Security and Visa Entry Reform Act of 2002: A Summary of HR 3525," *Backgrounder 5-02* (Washington, DC: Center for Immigration Studies, 2002).

Jennings, Victoria H. and Anne E. Burke, "Fertility Awareness-based Methods," in Robert A. Hatcher, James Trussell, Anita L. Nelson, Willard Cates, Jr., Deborah Kowal, and Michael S. Policar (eds.), *Contraceptive Technology*, 20th rev. edn. (New York: Ardent Media, 2011), pp. 417–434.

Jensen, Eric, "China Replaces Mexico as the Top Sending Country for Immigrants to the United States," *Research Matters* (May 1) (Washington, DC: US Bureau of the Census, 2015).

Jha, P., R. Kumar, P. Vasa, N. Dhingra, D. Thiruchelvam, and R. Moineddin, "Low Male-to-Female Sex Ratio of Children Born in India: National Survey of 1.1 Million Households," *Lancet*, 367(9506) (2006), 211–218.

Johansson, S. Ryan, "Epidemics," in Paul Demeny and Geoffrey McNicoll (eds.), *Encyclopedia of Population* (New York: Macmillan Reference, 2003), vol. 1, pp. 302–307.

Johansson, S. Ryan, and O. Nygren, "The Missing Girls of China: A New Demographic Account," *Population and Development Review*, 17 (1991), 35–51.

Johnson, Kenneth M., Layton Field, and Dudley L. Poston, Jr., "More Deaths than Births: Subnational Natural Decrease in Europe and the United States," *Population and Development Review*, 41 (2015), 651–680.

Johnson, Kenneth M. and Daniel T. Lichter, "Natural Increase: A New Source of Population Growth in Emerging Hispanic Destinations," *Population and Development Review*, 34 (2008), 327–346.

"Growing Diversity among America's Children and Youth: Spatial and Temporal Dimensions," *Population and Development Review*, 36 (2010), 151–175.

Johnson, Nan E., "The Racial Crossover in Comorbidity, Disability, and Mortality," *Demography*, 37 (2000), 267–283.

Johnson, Niall and Juergen Mueller, "Updating the Accounts: Global Mortality of the 1918–1920 'Spanish Influenza Pandemic'," *Bulletin of the History of Medicine*, 76 (2002), 105–115.

Johnson, Peter D., "Population Censuses: Observations on the Past 50 Years and a Peek at the New Century," paper presented at the Workshop on Gridding Population Data, Columbia University, New York, 2000.

Johnson, Steven, *The Ghost Map: The Story of London's Most Terrifying Epidemic, and How it Changed Science, Cities, and the Modern World* (New York: Riverhead Books, 2006).

Jones, Jo, William Mosher, and Kimberly Daniels, "Current Contraceptive Use in the United States, 2006–2010, and Changes in Patterns of Use since 1995," *National Health Statistics Reports*, 60 (October 18, 2012).

Jones, Nicholas A. and Jungmiwha Bullock, "The Two or More Races Population: 2010," *2010 Census Briefs*, C2010BR-13 (September) (Washington, DC: US Bureau of the Census, 2012).

Jones, Rachel K. and Megan L. Kavanaugh, "Changes in Abortion Rates between 2000 and 2008 and Lifetime Incidence of Abortion," *Obstetrics & Gynecology*, 117 (2011), 1358–1366.

Jorgensen, Christine, *Christine Jorgensen: A Personal Autobiography* (New York: Paul S. Eriksson, 1967).

Jutte, Robert, *Contraception: A History*, trans. Vicky Russell (Malden, MA: Polity, 2008).

Juvkam-Wold, H. C. and A. J. Dessler, "Using the Hubbert Equation to Estimate Oil Reserves," *World Oil*, April 2009, pp. 107–115.

Kahn, E. J., *The American People: The Findings of the 1970 Census* (New York: Weybright & Talley, 1974).

Kalben, Barbara Blatt, *Why Men Die Younger: Causes of Mortality Differences by Sex*, Society of Actuaries (SOA) Monograph M-Ll101 (Schaumburg, IL: Society of Actuaries, 2003).

Kann, L., S. Kinchen, S. L. Shanklin, K. H. Flint, J. Hawkins, W. A. Harris, and S. Zaza, "Youth Risk Behavior Surveillance – United States, 2013," *Morbidity and Mortality Weekly Report, Surveillance Summaries*, 63(4) (2014).

Kasarda, John D., "Economic Structure and Fertility: A Comparative Analysis," *Demography*, 8 (1971), 307–317.

Keeley, Charles B., "Replacement Migration," in Peter Uhlenberg (ed.), *International Handbook of Population Aging* (Newark, NJ: Springer, 2009), pp. 395–403.

Kertzer, David I. and Dennis P. Hogan, *Family, Political Economy, and Demographic Change: The Transformation of Life in Casalecchio, Italy, 1861–1921* (Madison, WI: University of Wisconsin Press, 1989).

Keyfitz, Nathan, "Age Distribution as a Challenge to Development," *American Journal of Sociology*, 70 (1965), 659–668.

Applied Mathematical Demography (New York: John Wiley, 1977a).

"What Difference Would it Make if Cancer were Eliminated? An Examination of the Taeuber Paradox," *Demography*, 14 (1977b), 411–418.

"The Population of China," *Scientific American*, 250 (1984), 38–47.

Keyfitz, Nathan and W. Flieger, *Population: Facts and Methods of Demography* (San Francisco: W. H. Freeman, 1971).

Khosla, Dhillon, *Both Sides Now: One Man's Journey through Womanhood* (New York: Penguin, 2006).

Kim, D., "The Pattern of Changing Trends and the Regional Difference in the Sex Ratio at Birth: Evidence from Korea and Jilin Province, China," *Korea Journal of Population and Development*, 26 (1997), 19–24.

Kimball, Charles, "An Introduction to Chinese History," *A Concise History of China*, 2000, available at: http://xenohistorian.faithweb.com/china/ch01.html, last accessed July 7, 2015.

Kimmel, Michael S., *The Gendered Society*, 2nd edn. (New York: Oxford University Press, 2004).

King, Barbara J., "IOC takes Questionable Stand on Gender and Hormones at the Olympics," *Cosmos & Culture, Commentary on Science and Society*, June 5, 2012.

King, H. and F. B. Locke, "Chinese in the United States: A Century of Occupational Transition," *International Migration Review*, 14 (1980), 15–42.

Kinsella, Kevin and Wan He, "An Aging World, 2008," *International Population Reports*, P95/09-1 (Washington, DC: US Government Printing Office, 2009).

Kinsey, Alfred C., Wardell B. Pomeroy, and Clyde E. Martin, *Sexual Behavior in the Human Male* (Philadelphia, PA: Saunders, 1948).

Kinsey, Alfred C., Wardell B. Pomeroy, Clyde E. Martin, and Paul H. Gebhard, *Sexual Behavior in the Human Female* (Philadelphia, PA: Saunders, 1953).

Kintner, Hallie J., "The Life Table," in Jacob S. Siegel and David A. Swanson (eds.), *The Methods and Materials of Demography*, 2nd edn. (San Diego, CA: Elsevier Academic, 2004), pp. 301–340.

Kipley, Sheila K. and John F. Kipley, *The Art of Natural Family Planning*, 4th edn. (Cincinnati, OH: Couple to Couple League International, 1996).

Kiser, Clyde V., "The Indianapolis Fertility Study: An Example of Planned Observational Research," *Public Opinion Quarterly*, 17 (1953), 496–510.

Kiser, Clyde V. and Pascal K. Whelpton, "Resume of the Indianapolis Study of Social and Psychological Factors Affecting Fertility," *Population Studies*, 7 (1953), 95–110.

Kitagawa, Evelyn and Philip M. Hauser, *Differential Mortality in the United States* (Cambridge, MA: Harvard University Press, 1973).

Knodel, John, Aphichat Chamratrithirong, and Nibhon Debavalya, *Thailand's Reproductive Revolution: Rapid Fertility Decline in a Third-World Setting* (Madison, WI: University of Wisconsin Press, 1987).

Knodel, John and Etienne van de Walle, "Lessons from the Past: Policy Implications of Historical Fertility Studies," *Population and Development Review*, 5 (1979), 217–245.

Koerber, Kin, "Domestic Migration Flows for States from the 2005 ACS," paper presented at the annual meetings of the Population Association of America, New York City, March 29–31, 2007.

Kohler, Hans-Peter, Francesco C. Billari, and Jose Antonio Ortega, "The Emergence of Lowest-Low Fertility in Europe during the 1990s," *Population and Development Review*, 28 (2002), 641–680.

Kolata, Gina, *Flu: The Story of the Great Influenza Pandemic of 1918 and the Search for the Virus that Caused It* (New York: Farrar, Straus & Giroux, 1999).

Kost, Kathryn, Susheela Singh, Barbara Vaughan, James Trussell, and Akinrinola Bankole, "Estimates of Contraceptive Failure from the 2002 National Survey of Family Growth," *Contraception*, 77 (2008), 10–21.

Kowal, Deborah, "Coitus Interruptus (Withdrawal)," in Robert A. Hatcher, James Trussell, Anita L. Nelson, Willard Cates, Jr., Deborah Kowal, and Michael S. Policar (eds.), *Contraceptive Technology*, 20th rev. edn. (New York: Ardent Media, 2011), pp. 409–415.

Kraeger, Philip, "New Light on Graunt," *Population Studies*, 42 (1988), 129–140.

Krieger, N., D. Rowley, A. Herman, B. Avery, and M. Phillips, "Racism, Sexism and Social Class: Implications for Studies of Health, Disease and Well-Being," *American Journal of Preventive Medicine*, 9 (Supp. 1993), 82–122.

Kwong, Peter, *The New Chinatown* (New York: Hill & Wang, 1988).

Laczko, Frank, "Enhancing the Benefits of Return Migration for Development," in Irena Omelaniuk (ed.), *World Migration, 2005: Costs and Benefits on International Migration* (Geneva: International Organization for Migration, 2005), ch. 16, pp. 287–295.

Lamb, Vicki L., and Jacob S. Siegel, "Health Demography," in Jacob S. Siegel and David A. Swanson (eds.), *The Methods and Materials of Demography*, 2nd edn. (San Diego, CA: Elsevier Academic, 2004), pp. 341–370.

Lamptey, Peter R., Jami L. Johnson, and Marya Khan, "The Global Challenge of HIV and AIDS," *Population Bulletin*, 61(1) (2006), 1–28.

Landry, Adolphe, *Traité de Démographie* (Paris: Payot, 1945).

Laub, John H. and Robert J. Sampson, *Shared Beginnings, Divergent Lives: Delinquent Boys to Age 70* (Cambridge, MA: Harvard University Press, 2006).

Laumann, Edward O., John H. Gagnon, Robert T. Michael, and Stuart Michaels, *The Social Organization of Sexuality: Sexual Practices in the United States* (University of Chicago Press, 1994).

LeClere, Felicia, Richard G. Rogers, and Kimberley Peters, "Ethnicity and Mortality in the United States: Individual and Community Correlates," *Social Forces*, 76 (1997), 169–198.

Lee, Everett S., "A Theory of Migration," *Demography*, 3 (1966), 47–57.

LeGates, Richard, "Visualizing World Urbanization with GIS and Data Graphics," paper presented at the annual meeting of the Association of American Geographers, Chicago, 2006.

Legrain, Philippe, *Immigrants: Your Country Needs Them* (Princeton University Press, 2006).

Lesthaeghe, Ron J., "The Second Demographic Transition in Western Countries: An Interpretation," in Karen O. Mason and A. M. Jensen (eds.), *Gender and Family Change in Industrialized Countries* (Oxford: Clarendon Press, 1995), pp. 17–62.

"The Unfolding Story of the Second Demographic Transition," *Population and Development Review*, 36 (2010), 211–251.

Lesthaeghe, Ron J. and Lisa Neidert, "The 'Second Demographic Transition' in the U.S.: Spatial Patterns and Correlates," Population Studies Center Research Report No. 06-592 (March), University of Michigan, Ann Arbor, 2006.

"U.S. Presidential Elections and the Spatial Pattern of the American Second Demographic Transition," *Population and Development Review*, 35 (2009), 391–400.

LeVay, Simon, "A Difference in Hypothalamic Structure between Heterosexual and Homosexual Men," *Science*, 252 (1991), 1034–1037.

Queer Science: The Use and Abuse of Research into Homosexuality (Cambridge, MA: MIT Press, 1996).

Liang, Zai, "Demography of Illicit Emigration from China: A Sending Country's Perspective," *Sociological Forum*, 16 (2001), 677–701.

Liang, Zai, Zhen Li, and Zhongdong Ma, "Changing Patterns of the Floating Population in China, 2000–2010," *Population and Development Review*, 40 (2014), 695–716.

Liang, Zai and Zhongdong Ma, "China's Floating Population: New Evidence from the 2000 Census," *Population and Development Review*, 30 (2004), 467–488.

Lichter, Daniel T., "Integration or Fragmentation: Racial Diversity and the American Future," *Demography*, 50 (2013), 359–391.

Linnaeus, Carolus, *Systema Naturae*, 1st edn. (Leiden: Haak, 1735).

Lipset, Seymour Martin, *American Exceptionalism: A Double-Edged Sword* (New York: W. W. Norton, 1997).

Livi-Bacci, Massimo, *A Concise History of World Population* (Malden, MA: Wiley-Blackwell, 2012).

London, Bruce, "Ending Ecology's Ethnocentrism: Thai Replications and Extensions of Ecological Research," *Rural Sociology*, 52 (1987), 483–500.

London, Bruce and Kenneth P. Hadden, "The Spread of Education and Fertility Decline: A Thai Province Level Test of Caldwell's 'Wealth Flows' Theory," *Rural Sociology*, 54 (1989), 17–36.

Lotka, Alfred J., "Relation Between Birth Rates and Death Rates," *Science* (ns), 26(653) (1907), 21–22.

Analytical Theory of Biological Populations, trans. David P. Smith and Helene Rossert (New York: Plenum, [1934] 1998).

Loudon, Irvine, *Death in Childbirth: An International Study of Maternal Care and Maternal Mortality, 1800–1950* (Oxford: Clarendon, 1992).

"Maternal Mortality in the Past and its Relevance to Developing Countries Today," *American Journal of Clinical Nutrition*, 72 (Supp.) (2000), 241S–246S.

Lutz, Wolfgang, "Fertility Rates and Future Population Trends: Will Europe's Birth Rate Recover or Continue to Decline?" *International Journal of Andrology*, 29 (2006), 25–33.

Lutz, Wolfgang, Brian C. O'Neil, and Sergei Scherbov, "Europe's Population at a Turning Point," *Science*, 299 (2003), 1991–1992.

MacDonald, Alphonse L., "Famine in China," in Paul Demeny and Geoffrey McNicoll (eds.), *Encyclopedia of Population* (New York: Macmillan Reference, 2003), vol. 1, pp. 388–390.

Macisco, John J., Jr., Leon F. Bouvier, and Robert H. Weller, "The Effect of Labor Force Participation on the Relation between Migration Status and Fertility," *Milbank Memorial Fund Quarterly*, 48 (1970), 51–69.

MacKellar, F. Landis, "Homicide and Suicide," in Paul Demeny and Geoffrey McNicoll (eds.), *Encyclopedia of Population* (New York: Macmillan Reference, 2003), vol. 1, pp. 496–499.

Mackun, Paul and Steven Wilson, "Population Distribution and Change, 2000 to 2010," *2010 Census Briefs*, C2010BR-01 (March) (Washington, DC: US Bureau of the Census, 2011).

Madigan, Francis C., "Are Sex Mortality Differentials Biologically Caused?" *Milbank Memorial Fund Quarterly*, 35 (1957), 202–223.

Maine, Deborah and Katrina Stamas, "Maternal Mortality," in Paul Demeny and Geoffrey McNicoll (eds.), *Encyclopedia of Population* (New York: Macmillan Reference, 2003), vol. 2, pp. 628–631.

Malthus, Thomas R., *An Essay on the Principle of Population (with the Variora of 1806, 1807, 1817, 1826)*, 2 vols., ed. Patricia James (Cambridge University Press, [1803] 1989).

Mann, Donald, "Why We Need a Smaller US Population and How We Can Achieve It," *A Negative Population Growth Position Paper*, July 3 (Alexandria, VA: Negative Population Growth, [1992] 2015).

Manning, Wendy, "Trends in Cohabitation: Over Twenty Years of Change, 1987–2010," *National Center for Family and Research, Family Profile* (Bowling Green, OH: Bowling Green State University, 2013), pp. 13–22.

Manton, Kenneth G., Sharon Sandomirsky Poss, and Steven Wing, "The Black/White Mortality Crossover: Investigation from the Perspective of the Components of Aging," *The Gerontologist*, 19 (1979), 291–300.

Manton, Kenneth G. and Eric Stallard, "Health and Disability Differences among Racial and Ethnic Groups," in Linda G. Martin and Beth J. Soldo (eds.), *Racial and Ethnic Differences in the Health of Older Americans* (Washington, DC: National Academy Press, 1997), pp. 43–105.

Markides, Kyriakos S. and Jeannine Coreil, "The Health of Hispanics in the Southwestern United States: An Epidemiologic Paradox," *Public Health Reports*, 101 (1986), 253–265.

Markides, Kyriakos S. and Karl Eschbach, "Hispanic Paradox in Adult Mortality in the United States," in Richard G. Rogers and Eileen M. Crimmins (eds.), *International Handbook of Adult Mortality* (New York: Springer, 2011), pp. 225–238.

Marks, Lara V., *Sexual Chemistry: A History of the Contraceptive Pill* (New Haven, CT: Yale University Press, 2001).

Marsh, Margaret and Wanda Ronner, *The Fertility Doctor: John Rock and the Reproductive Revolution* (Baltimore, MD: Johns Hopkins University Press, 2008).

Martin, Joyce A., Brady E. Hamilton, and Michelle J. K. Osterman, "Births in the United States, 2014," *NCHS Data Brief*, 216 (September 2015).

Martin, Philip, "The Global Challenge of Managing Migration," *Population Bulletin*, 68 (2013), 1–16.

Martin, Philip, and Gottfried Zurcher, "Managing Migration: The Global Challenge," *Population Bulletin*, 63 (2008), 1–20.

Martin, Sean, *The Black Death* (Edison, NJ: Chartwell Books, 2007).

Martin, Susan F., "Global Migration Trends and Asylum," UNHCR, The UN Refugee Agency, Evaluation and Policy Analysis Unit Working Paper 41, April 30, 2001.

Martinez, Gladys, Casey E. Copen, and Joyce C. Abma, "Teenagers in the United States: Sexual Activity, Contraceptive Use, and Childbearing, 2006–2010 National Survey of Family Growth," *Vital and Health Statistics*, 23(31) (2011).

Martinez, Gladys, Kimberly Daniels, and Anjani Chandra, "Fertility of Men and Women Aged 15–44 Years in the United States: National Survey of Family Growth, 2006–2010," *National Health Statistics Reports*, 51 (April 12, 2012).

Martinez, Ramiro, Jr., "Policy Essay: Economic Conditions and Racial/ethnic Variations in Violence: Immigration, the Latino Paradox and Future Research," *Criminology & Public Policy*, 9 (2010), 707–713.

Latino Homicide: Immigration, Violence and Community, 2nd edn. (New York: Routledge, 2014).

Martinez, Ramiro, Jr. and Abel Valenzuela, *Immigration and Crime: Race, Ethnicity, and Violence* (New York: NYU Press, 2006).

Marx, Karl and Friedrich Engels, "The Communist Manifesto," *Selected Works* (London: Lawrence & Wishart, [1848] 1935), vol. 1.

Mason, Andrew D., "Dimensions of the Labor Market in China: Rural Labor Markets, and Rural, Urban, and Regional Linkages," Background paper, World Bank, Washington, DC, 1997.

Mason, Karen Oppenheim, "Explaining Fertility Transitions," *Demography*, 34 (1997), 443–454.

Massey, Douglas S., "International Migration and Economic Development in Comprehensive Perspective," *Population and Development Review*, 14 (1988), 383–414.

"The New Immigration and Ethnicity in the United States," *Population and Development Review*, 21 (1995), 631–652.

"International Migration," in Paul Demeny and Geoffrey McNicoll (eds.), *Encyclopedia of Population* (New York: Macmillan Reference, 2003), vol. 2, pp. 548–553.

Massey, Douglas S., Joaquin Arango, Graeme Hugo, Ali Kouaouci, Adela Pellegrino, and J. Edward Taylor, "Theories of International Migration: A Review and Appraisal," *Population and Development Review*, 19 (1993), 431–466.

"An Evaluation of International Migration Theory: The North American Case," *Population and Development Review*, 20 (1994), 699–751.

Worlds in Motion: Understanding International Migration at the Dawn of the Millennium (New York: Oxford University Press, 2005).

Mateyka, Peter J., "Desire to Move and Residential Mobility, 2010–2011," *Household Economic Studies*, P70–140 (Washington, DC: US Bureau of the Census, 2015).

Mather, Mark, *Fact Sheet: The Decline in U.S. Fertility* (Washington, DC: Population Reference Bureau, 2012).

Mather, Mark, Kelvin Pollard, and Linda A. Jacobsen, *Reports on America: First Results from the 2010 Census* (Washington, DC: Population Reference Bureau, 2011).

Mathews, T. J. and Marian F. MacDorman, "Infant Mortality Statistics from the 2010 Period Linked Birth/Infant Death Data Set," *National Vital Statistics Reports*, 62 (Hyattsville, MD: National Center for Health Statistics, December 18, 2013).

Matthiessen, P. C. and M. E. Matthiessen, "Sex Ratio in a Sample of Human Fetuses in Denmark, 1962–1973," *Annals of Human Biology*, 4 (1977), 183–185.

May, John F., "Population Policy," in Dudley L. Poston, Jr. and Michael Micklin (eds.), *Handbook of Population* (New York: Kluwer Academic/Plenum, 2005), pp. 827–851.

World Population Policies: Their Origin, Evolution and Impact (New York: Springer, 2012).

McClory, Robert, *Turning Point: The Inside Story of the Papal Birth Control Commission, and how Humanae Vitae Changed the Life of Patty Crowley and the Future of the Church* (New York: Crossroad, 1950).

McCloskey, Deirdre N., *Crossing: A Memoir* (University of Chicago Press, 2000).

McFalls, Joseph A., Jr., "Population: A Lively Introduction," *Population Bulletin*, 62(1) (2007), 1–31.

McFalls, Joseph A., Jr., Bernard Gallagher, and Brian Jones, "The Social Tunnel Versus the Python: A New Way to Understand the Impact of Baby Booms and Baby Busts on a Society," *Teaching Sociology*, 14 (1986), 129–132.

McGehee, Mary A., "Mortality," in Jacob S. Siegel and David A. Swanson (eds.), *The Methods and Materials of Demography*, 2nd edn. (San Diego, CA: Elsevier Academic, 2004), pp. 265–300.

McIntosh, C. Alison and Jason L. Finkle, "The Cairo Conference on Population and Development: A New Paradigm," *Population and Development Review*, 21 (1995), 223–260.

McKeown, Thomas, *The Modern Rise of Population* (New York: Academic Press, 1976).

McLaren, Angus, *History of Contraception: From Antiquity to the Present Day* (New York: Wiley, 1992).

McNicoll, Geoffrey, "Population," in Paul Demeny and Geoffrey McNicoll (eds.), *Encyclopedia of Population* (New York: Macmillan Reference, 2003), vol. 2, pp. 730–732.

Meadows, Donella H., Dennis L. Meadows, Jorgen Randers, and William W. Behrens, III, *The Limits to Growth: A Report for the Club of Rome's Project on the Predicament of Mankind*, 2nd edn. (New York: Universe, 1974).

Meadows, Donella, Jorgen Randers, and Dennis L. Meadows, *Limits to Growth: The Thirty-Year Update* (White River Junction, VT: Chelsea Green, 2004).

Mehlan, K. H., "Legal Abortions in Romania," *Journal of Sex Research*, 1 (1965), 31–38.

Meltzer, David J., *First Peoples in a New World: Colonizing Ice Age America* (Berkeley, CA: University of California Press, 2009).

Menzies, Gavin, *1421: The Year China Discovered the World* (New York: William Morrow, 2003).

Merton, Robert K., *Social Theory and Social Structure* (New York: Simon & Schuster, 1968).

Micklin, Michael and Dudley L. Poston, Jr., "Prologue: The Demographer's Ken: 50 Years of Growth and Change," in Dudley L. Poston, Jr. and Michael Micklin (eds.), *Handbook of Population* (New York: Springer, 2005), pp. 1–15.

Mill, John Stuart, *Principles of Political Economy with Some Applications to Social Philosophy*, 2 vols., eds. V. W. Bladen and J. M. Robson (University of Toronto Press, [1848] 1965).

Miller, G. Tyler, *Living in the Environment: Principles, Connections, and Solutions*, 13th edn. (Belmont, CA: Brooks/Cole Thomson Leaning, 2004).

Miller, Kerby A., *Emigrants and Exiles: Ireland and the Irish Exodus to North America* (New York: Oxford University Press, 1985).

Minino, Arialdi M., "Death in the United States, 2011," *NCHS Data Brief*, 115 (March 2013).

Minino, Arialdi M., Jiaquan Xu, Kenneth D. Kochanek, and Betzaida Tejada-Vera, "Death in the United States, 2007," *NCHS Data Brief*, 26 (December 2009).

Money, John, *Gay, Straight, and In-Between: The Sexology of Erotic Orientation* (New York: Oxford University Press, 1988).

Money, John and Anke Ehrhardt, *Man and Woman, Boy and Girl* (Baltimore, MD: Johns Hopkins University Press, 1972).

Monte, Lindsay M. and Renee R. Ellis, "Fertility of Women in the United States: June 2012," *Current Population Reports*, P20-575 (Washington, DC: US Bureau of the Census, 2014).

Morgan, S. Philip, "Late Nineteenth- and Early Twentieth-Century Childlessness," *American Journal of Sociology*, 97 (1991), 779–807.

"Is Low Fertility a Twenty-First-Century Demographic Crisis?" *Demography*, 40 (2003), 589–603.

Morgan, S. Philip and R. Chen, "Predicting Childlessness for Recent Cohorts of American Women," *International Journal of Forecasting*, 8 (1992), 477–493.

Morgan, S. Philip and Kellie J. Hagewen, "Fertility," in Dudley L. Poston, Jr. and Michael Micklin (eds.), *Handbook of Population* (New York: Kluwer Academic/Plenum, 2005), pp. 229–249.

Morris, Jan, *Conundrum: From James to Jan, an Extraordinary Personal Narrative of Transsexualism* (New York: Harcourt Brace Jovanovich, 1974).

Morrison, Peter, *Forecasting Population of Small Areas: An Overview* (Santa Monica, CA: Rand Corp., 1977).

Mosher, William D., Anjani Chandra, and Jo Jones, "Sexual Behavior and Selected Health Measures: Men and Women 15–44 Years of Age, United States, 2002," *Advance Data from Vital and Health Statistics*, 362 (2005), 1–56.

Mosher, William D., Gladys M. Martinez, Anjani Chandra, Joyce C. Abma, and Stephanie J. Willson, "Use of Contraception and Use of Family Planning Services in the United States: 1982–2002," *Advance Data from Vital and Health Statistics*, 350 (2004), 1–46.

Mumford, Lewis, *The Culture of Cities* (New York: Harcourt Brace, [1938] 1970).

Münz, Rainer, "Immigration Trends in Major Destination Countries," in Paul Demeny and Geoffrey McNicoll (eds.), *Encyclopedia of Population* (New York: Macmillan Reference, 2003), vol. 2, pp. 519–523.

Murdock, George P., *Social Structure* (New York: Macmillan, 1949).

Murray, S. O., *Homosexualities* (University of Chicago Press, 2000).

Myers, Dowell, *Immigrants and Boomers: Forging a Social Contract for the Future of America* (New York: Russell Sage Foundation, 2008).

Myers, Robert J., "Errors and Bias in the Reporting of Ages in Census Data," *Transactions of the Actuarial Society of America*, 41(2) (1940), 411–415.

"The Validity and Significance of Male Net Reproduction Rates," *Journal of the American Statistical Association*, 36 (1941), 275–282.

Nam, Charles B., "The Progress of Demography as a Scientific Discipline," *Demography*, 16 (1979), 485–492.

"Another Look at Mortality Crossovers," *Social Biology*, 42 (1995), 133–142.

Nam, Charles B., William J. Serow, and David F. Sly (eds.), *International Handbook on Internal Migration* (New York: Greenwood, 1990).

Nam, Charles B., Norman L. Weatherby, and Kathleen A. Ockay, "Causes of Death which Contribute to the Mortality Crossover Effect," *Social Biology*, 25 (1978), 306–314.

Nanda, Kavita, "Contraceptive Patch and Vaginal Contraceptive Ring," in Robert A. Hatcher, James Trussell, Anita L. Nelson, Willard Cates, Jr., Deborah Kowal, and Michael S. Policar (eds.), *Contraceptive Technology*, 20th rev. edn. (New York: Ardent Media, 2011), pp. 343–369.

National Center for Health Statistics (NCHS), "Deaths, Preliminary Data for 2000," *National Vital Statistics Reports*, 49(12) (2001).

"Life Expectancy at Birth, by Race and Sex, Selected Years 1929–98," *National Vital Statistics Reports*, 50(6) (2002).

"About the National Survey of Family Growth," National Center for Health Statistics, Hyattsville, MD, 2015.

National Park Service, "Fact Sheet," available at: www.nps.gov/npnh/learn/news/fact-sheet-elis.htm, 2015, last accessed June 13, 2015.

National Population and Talent Division, *A Sustainable Population for a Dynamic Singapore: Population White Paper* (Singapore: National Population and Talent Division, 2013).

Nelson, Anita L. and Carrie Cwiak, "Combined Oral Contraceptives (COCs)," in Robert A. Hatcher, James Trussell, Anita L. Nelson, Willard Cates, Jr., Deborah Kowal, and Michael S. Policar (eds.), *Contraceptive Technology*, 20th rev. edn. (New York: Ardent Media, 2011), pp. 249–341.

Neugarten, Bernice L. and Gunhild O. Hagestad, "Age and the Life Course," in Robert H. Binstock and Ethel Shanas (eds.), *Handbook of Aging and the Social Sciences* (New York: Van Nostrand Reinhold, 1976), pp. 35–55.

Nicholson, W. J., "Case Study I, Asbestos – The TLV Approach," *Annals of the New York Academy of Science, Occupational Carcinogenesis*, 271 (1976), 152–159.

Nolan, Peter, "Petty Commodity Production in a Socialist Economy: Chinese Rural Development Post-Mao," in Jan Breman and Sudipto Mundle (eds.), *Rural Transformation in Asia* (Delhi: Oxford University Press, 1991), pp. 218–255.

Noonan, John T., Jr., *Contraception: A History of Its Treatment by the Catholic Theologians and Canonists* (Cambridge, MA: Harvard University Press, 1966).

Norris, Tina, Paula A. Vines, and Elizabeth M. Hoeffel, "The American Indian and Alaska Native Population, 2010," *2010 Census Briefs*, C2010BR-10 (Washington, DC: US Bureau of the Census, 2012).

Notestein, Frank W., "Population – The Long View," in Theodore W. Schultz (ed.), *Food for the World* (University of Chicago Press, 1945), pp. 36–57.

Obregon, Misael, "Extending the Latino Paradox: Comparative Findings of STIs among Birth Giving Mexican Origin, Black and White Women," PhD dissertation, Texas A&M University, College Station, 2015.

O'Connell, Martin and Sarah Feliz, "Same-sex Couple Household Statistics from the 2010 Census," Working Paper No. 2011-26, US Census Bureau, Social, Economic and Housing Statistics Division, Washington, DC, 2011.

Oeppen, Jim and James W. Vaupel, "Broken Limits to Life Expectancy," *Science*, 296 (2002), 1029–1031.

O'Grada, Cormac, *Black '47 and Beyond: The Great Irish Famine in History, Economy, and Memory* (Princeton University Press, 1999).

  "Markets and Famines: Evidence from Nineteenth-Century Finland," *Economic Development and Cultural Change*, 49 (2001), 575–590.

  "Famine, Concepts and Causes of," in Paul Demeny and Geoffrey McNicoll (eds.), *Encyclopedia of Population* (New York: Macmillan Reference, 2003a), vol. 1, pp. 382–385.

  "Famine in Ireland," in Paul Demeny and Geoffrey McNicoll (eds.), *Encyclopedia of Population* (New York: Macmillan Reference, 2003b), vol. 1, pp. 390–392.

Oi, Jean C., *Rural China Takes Off: Institutional Foundations of Economic Reform* (Berkeley, CA: University of California Press, 1999).

Olshansky, S. Jay and Brian Ault, "The Fourth Stage of Epidemiologic Transition: The Age of Delayed Degenerative Diseases," *Milbank Quarterly*, 64 (1986), 355–391.

Olshansky, S. Jay and Bruce A. Carnes, *The Quest for Immortality* (New York: W. W. Norton, 2001).

Olshansky, S. Jay, Douglas J. Passaro, Ronald C. Hershow, Jennifer Layden, Bruce A. Carnes, Jacob Brady, Leonard Hayflick, Robert N. Butler, David B. Allison, and David S. Ludwig, "A Potential Decline in Life Expectancy in the United States in the 21st Century," *New England Journal of Medicine*, 352 (2005), 1138–1145.

Omran, Abdel R., "The Epidemiologic Transition: A Theory of the Epidemiology of Population Change," *Milbank Quarterly*, 49 (1971), 509–553.

Oppenheimer, Andres, "Immigration: Will China Be the New Mexico?" *Miami Herald*, May 9, 2015.

Orzack, Steven Hecht, J. William Stubblefield, Viatcheslav R. Akmaev, Pere Colls, Santiago Munné, Thomas Scholl, David Steinsaltz, and James E. Zuckerman, "The Human Sex Ratio from Conception to Birth," PNAS E2102-E2111 (March 30, 2015).

Osborn, Frederick, *This Crowded World* (New York: Public Affairs Committee, 1960).

Ostby, Lars, "Population Registers," in Paul Demeny and Geoffrey McNicoll (eds.), *Encyclopedia of Population* (New York: Macmillan Reference, 2003), vol. 2, pp. 763–765.

Paddock, William and Paul Paddock, *Famine, 1975* (Boston, MA: Little, Brown, 1967).

Paget, W. John and Ian M. Timaeus, "A Relational Gompertz Model of Male Fertility: Development and Assessment," *Population Studies*, 48 (1994), 333–340.

Palloni, Alberto and Elizabeth Arias, "Paradox Lost: Explaining the Hispanic Adult Mortality Advantage," *Demography*, 41 (2004), 385–415.

Palloni, Alberto and Jeffrey D. Morenoff, "Interpreting the Paradoxical in the 'Hispanic Paradox': Demographic and Epidemiological Approaches," in M. Weinstein, A. Hermalin, and M. Stoto (eds.), *Population Health and Aging* (New York: New York Academy of Sciences, 2001), pp. 140–174.

Palmore, James A. and Robert W. Gardner, *Measuring Mortality, Fertility and Natural Increase*, 5th edn. (Honolulu: East-West Center, 1994).

Papademetriou, Demetrios G., "International Labor Migration," in Paul Demeny and Geoffrey McNicoll (eds.), *Encyclopedia of Population* (New York: Macmillan Reference, 2003), vol. 2, pp. 570–574.

Parish, W. L., E. O. Laumann, M. S. Cohen, S. M. Pan, H. Y. Zheng, I. Hoffman, T. F. Wang, and K. H. Ng, "Population-Based Study of Chlamydial Infection in China: A Hidden Epidemic," *Journal of the American Medical Association*, 289 (2003), 1265–1273.

Parr, Nick and Ross Guest, "The Contribution of Increases in Family Benefits to Australia's Early 21st Century Fertility Increase: An Empirical Analysis," *Demographic Research*, 25 (2011), 215–244.

Passel, Jeffrey S., "Provisional Evaluation of the 1970 Census Count of American Indians," *Demography*, 13 (1976), 397–409.

"The Growing American Indian Population, 1960–1990: Beyond Demography," in Gary D. Sandefur, Ronald R. Rindfuss, and Barney Cohen (eds.), *Changing Numbers, Changing Needs: American Indian Demography and Public Health* (Washington, DC: National Academy Press, 1996), pp. 79–102.

"The Size and Characteristics of the Unauthorized Migrant Population in the U.S.: Estimates Based on the March 2005 Current Population Survey," Research Report, March 7 (Washington, DC: Pew Hispanic Center, 2006).

Passel, Jeffrey S. and Patricia A. Berman, "Quality of 1980 Census Data for American Indians," *Social Biology*, 33 (1986), 163–182.

Passel, Jeffrey S. and D'Vera Cohn, *Unauthorized Immigrant Totals Rise in 7 States, Fall in 14* (Washington, DC: Pew Research Center's Hispanic Trends Project, November 2014).

Passel, Jeffrey S., Jennifer Van Hook, and Frank D. Bean, "Estimates of Legal and Unauthorized Foreign Born Population for the United States and Selected States, Based on Census 2000" (Washington, DC: Urban Institute, 2004).

Passel, Jeffrey S., Wendy Wang, and Paul Taylor, *Marrying Out: One in Seven New US Marriages is Interracial or Interethnic* (Washington, DC: Pew Research Center's Social & Demographic Trends Project, June 15, 2010).

Patrick, Erin, "Demography of Refugees," in Paul Demeny and Geoffrey McNicoll (eds.), *Encyclopedia of Population* (New York: Macmillan Reference, 2003), vol. 2, pp. 825–830.

Paul, Maureen and Tara Stein, "Abortion," in Robert A. Hatcher, James Trussell, Anita L. Nelson, Willard Cates, Jr., Deborah Kowal, and Michael S. Policar (eds.), *Contraceptive Technology*, 20th rev. edn. (New York: Ardent Media, 2011), pp. 695–736.

Pebley, Anne R., "Infant and Child Mortality," in Paul Demeny and Geoffrey McNicoll (eds.), *Encyclopedia of Population* (New York: Macmillan Reference, 2003), vol. 2, pp. 533–536.

Pedraza, Sylvia and Ruben G. Rumbaut, *Origins and Destinies: Immigration, Race and Ethnicity in America* (Belmont, CA: Wadsworth, 1996).

Peel, John and Malcolm Potts, *Textbook of Contraceptive Practice* (New York: Cambridge University Press, 1969).

Peng, Xizhe, "Demographic Consequences of the Great Leap Forward in China's Provinces," *Population and Development Review*, 13 (1987), 639–670.

Perloff, H. S., E. S. Dunn Jr., E. E. Lampard, and R. F. Muth, *Regions, Resources, and Economic Growth* (Baltimore, MD: Johns Hopkins University Press, 1960).

Petersen, William, *Population*, 3rd edn. (New York: Macmillan, 1975).

Malthus (Cambridge, MA: Harvard University Press, 1979).

Pinkerton, James, "Anti-immigrant Mood Here Rising, Survey Says," *Houston Chronicle*, April 23, 2008.

Piore, Michael J., *Birds of Passage: Migrant Labor in Industrial Societies* (Cambridge University Press, 1979).

Pison, Gilles, "Fewer Births, but a Boy at All Costs: Selective Female Abortion in Asia," *Population and Societies*, 404 (September 2004).

"The Population of France in 2005," *Population and Societies*, 421 (March 2006).

"World Population, 7 Billion Today, How Many Tomorrow?" *Population and Societies*, 482 (October 2011).

Pison, Gilles and Sabine Belloc, "The World Population, and What About Me? An Exhibition at the Cité des Sciences et de l'Industrie in Paris," *Population and Societies*, 412 (2005), 1–4.

Plane, David A., "Population Distribution: Geographic Areas," in Jacob S. Siegel and David A. Swanson (eds.), *The Methods and Materials of Demography*, 2nd edn. (San Diego, CA: Elsevier Academic, 2004), ch. 5.

Plankey Videla, Nancy, "Maquiladoras," in William A. Darity (ed.), *International Encyclopedia of the Social Sciences*, 2nd edn. (Detroit, MI: Macmillan Reference, 2008), vol. 4, pp. 591–594.

Pollard, A. H., Farhat Yusuf, and G. N. Pollard, *Demographic Techniques*, 2nd edn. (Sydney: Pergamon, 1981).

Demographic Techniques, 3rd edn. (Sydney: Pergamon, 1990).

Popoff, Carole and Dean H. Judson, "Some Methods of Estimation for Statistically Underdeveloped Areas," in Jacob S. Siegel and David A. Swanson (eds.), *The Methods and Materials of Demography*, 2nd edn. (San Diego, CA: Elsevier Academic, 2004), pp. 603–641.

Population Reference Bureau (PRB), "World Population Highlights," *Population Bulletin*, 62(3) (2007).

Family Planning Worldwide, 2013 Data Sheet (Washington, DC: Population Reference Bureau, 2013).

2014 World Population Data Sheet (Washington, DC: Population Reference Bureau, 2014).

2015 World Population Data Sheet (Washington, DC: Population Reference Bureau, 2015).

Porter, Katherine Anne, *Pale Horse, Pale Rider* (New York: Harcourt Brace, 1939).

Portes, Alejandro and Ruben G. Rumbaut, *Immigrant America: A Portrait* (Berkeley, CA: University of California Press, 1990).

Portes, Alejandro and John Walton, *Labor, Class, and the International System* (New York: Academic Press, 1981).

Postel, Sandra, *Water and Sustainability: Dimensions of the Global Challenge* (Amherst, MA: World Watch Institute, 1992).

Poston, Dudley L., Jr., "Income and Childlessness in the United States: Is the Relationship always Inverse?" *Social Biology*, 21 (1974), 296–307.

"Social and Economic Development and the Fertility Transition in Mainland China and Taiwan," *Population and Development Review*, 26 (Supp.) (2000), 40–60.

"South Korea's Demographic Destiny: Marriage Market and Elderly Support Implications for the 21st Century," in *International Conference on the Longevity and Social, Medical Environment of the Elderly* (Taegu, South Korea: Institute of Gerontology, Yeungnam University, 2002), pp. 69–83.

"Age and Sex," in Dudley L. Poston, Jr. and Michael Micklin (eds.), *Handbook of Population* (New York: Kluwer Academic/Plenum, 2005), pp. 19–58.

"John Graunt," in Bryan Turner (ed.), *The Cambridge Dictionary of Sociology* (Cambridge University Press, 2006a), p. 254.

"Malthus," in Bryan Turner (ed.), *The Cambridge Dictionary of Sociology* (Cambridge University Press, 2006b), pp. 347–348.

"Human Ecology," in James D. Wright (ed.), *International Encyclopedia of the Social and Behavioral Sciences*, 2nd edn. (Oxford: Elsevier, 2015), vol. 11, pp. 283–288.

Poston, Dudley L., Jr. and Amanda K. Baumle, "Patterns of Asexuality in the United States," *Demographic Research*, 23 (2010), 509–530.

Poston, Dudley L., Jr., Amanda K. Baumle, and Michael Micklin, "Epilogue: Needed Research in Demography," in Dudley L. Poston, Jr. and Michael Micklin (eds.), *Handbook of Population* (New York: Kluwer Academic/Plenum, 2005), pp. 853–881.

Poston, Dudley L., Jr. and Yu-Ting Chang, "Patterns of Gay Male and Lesbian Partnering in the Metropolitan Areas of the United States in 2010," paper presented at the XXVII International Population Conference, International Union for the Scientific Study of Population, Busan, South Korea, August 26–31, 2013.

"The Conceptualization and Measurement of the Homosexual, Heterosexual and Bisexual Populations in the United States," in M. Nazrul Hoque and Lloyd B. Potter (eds.), *Emerging Techniques in Applied Demography* (New York: Springer, 2015), pp. 359–378.

Poston, Dudley L., Jr., Iris H. J. Chu, Jaime M. Ginn, Godfrey Jin-Kai Li, Catherine Hong Vo, Carol S. Walther, Ping Wang, Juan J. Wu, and Ming M. Yuan, "The Quality of the Age and Sex Data of the Republic of Korea and Its Provinces, 1970 and 1995," *Journal of Gerontology*, 4 (2000), 85–126.

Poston, Dudley L., Jr., Eugenia Conde, and Bethany DeSalvo, "China's Unbalanced Sex Ratio at Birth: Millions of Excess Bachelors and Societal Implications," *Vulnerable Children and Youth Studies*, 6 (2011), 314–320.

Poston, Dudley L., Jr. and Cristina Elizabeth Cruz, "Voluntary, Involuntary and Temporary Childlessness in the United States," paper presented at the XXVII International Population Conference, International Union for the Scientific Study of Population, Busan, South Korea, August 26–31, 2013.

Poston, Dudley L., Jr., Mary Ann Davis, and Chris Lewinski, "Fertility," in Bryan Turner (ed.), *The Cambridge Dictionary of Sociology* (Cambridge University Press, 2006), pp. 403–405.

Poston, Dudley L., Jr., Bethany S. DeSalvo, and Heather Terrell Kincannon, "Sex and Sex Structure," in Zeng Yi (ed.), *Demography. Encyclopedia of Life Support Systems (EOLSS)* (Oxford: UNESCO, Eolss Publishers, 2009), see at: www.eolss.net.

Poston, Dudley L., Jr., Bethany S. DeSalvo, and Leslie D. Meyer, "Malthusian Theory of Population Growth," in Dennis L. Peck and Clifton D. Bryant (eds.), *Encyclopedia of Death and the Human Experience* (Thousand Oaks, CA: Sage, 2009), pp. 684–687.

Poston, Dudley L., Jr. and Charles Chengrong Duan, "Nonagricultural Unemployment in Beijing: A Multilevel Analysis," *Research in Community Sociology*, 10 (2000), 287–301.

Poston, Dudley L., Jr. and W. Parker Frisbie, "Human Ecology, Sociology, and Demography," in Michael Micklin and Dudley L. Poston, Jr. (eds.), *Continuities in Sociological Human Ecology* (New York: Plenum, 1998), pp. 27–50.

"Ecological Demography," in Dudley L. Poston, Jr. and Michael Micklin (eds.), *Handbook of Population* (New York: Springer, 2005), pp. 601–623.

Poston, Dudley L., Jr. and Karen S. Glover, "Too Many Males: Marriage Market Implications of Gender Imbalances in China," *Genus*, 61 (2005), 119–140.

Poston, Dudley L., Jr. and Baochang Gu, "Socioeconomic Development, Family Planning and Fertility in the People's Republic of China: A Subregional Analysis," *Demography*, 24 (1987), 531–551.

Poston, Dudley L., Jr., Baochang Gu, Peihang Liu, and Terra McDaniel, "Son Preference and the Sex Ratio at Birth in China," *Social Biology*, 44 (1997), 55–76.

Poston, Dudley L., Jr., Kenneth M. Johnson, and Layton Field, "Natural Decrease in the Countries and Counties of Europe in the Context of the Second Demographic Transition," paper presented at the XXVI Congress of the European Society for Rural Sociology, Aberdeen, Scotland, August 18–21, 2015.

Poston, Dudley L., Jr. and Kathryn B. Kramer, "Voluntary and Involuntary Childlessness in the United States, 1955–1973," *Social Biology*, 30 (1983), 290–306.

Poston, Dudley L., Jr. and Hua Luo, "Chinese Student and Labor Migration to the United States: Trends and Policies since the 1980s," *Asian and Pacific Migration Journal*, 16(3) (2007), 323–355.

Poston, Dudley L., Jr., Hua Luo, and Li Zhang, "Migration," in Bryan Turner (ed.), *The Cambridge Dictionary of Sociology* (Cambridge University Press, 2006), pp. 384–386.

Poston, Dudley L., Jr. and Michael Xinxiang Mao, "Interprovincial Migration in China, 1985–1990," *Research in Rural Sociology and Development*, 7 (1998), 227–250.

Poston, Dudley L., Jr., Michael X. Mao, and Mei-Yu Yu, "The Global Distribution of the Overseas Chinese Around 1990," *Population and Development Review*, 20 (1994), 631–645.

Poston, Dudley L., Jr. and Peter A. Morrison, "China: Bachelor Bomb," *International Herald Tribune*, September 14, 2005.

"Chinese Workers Could Replace Mexican Immigrants," *Houston Chronicle*, August 13, 2011.

Poston, Dudley L., Jr. and Richard G. Rogers, "Toward a Reformulation of the Neonatal Mortality Rate," *Social Biology*, 32 (1985), 1–12.

Poston, Dudley L., Jr. and Heather K. M. Terrell, "Fertility," in Bryan Turner (ed.), *The Cambridge Dictionary of Sociology* (Cambridge University Press, 2006), pp. 201–203.

Poston, Dudley L., Jr., Carol S. Walther, Iris H. J. Chu, Jaime M. Ginn, Godfrey J. Li, Catherine H. Vo, Ping Wang, Juan J. Wu, and Ming M. Yuan, "The Age and Sex Composition of the Republic of Korea and its Provinces, 1970 and 1995," *Genus*, 59 (2003), 113–139.

Poston, Dudley L., Jr. and David Yaukey (eds.), *The Population of Modern China* (New York: Plenum, 1992).

Poston, Dudley L., Jr. and Li Zhang, "Ecological Analyses of Permanent and Temporary Migration Streams in China in the 1990s," *Population Research and Policy Review*, 27 (2008), 689–712.

Poston, Dudley L., Jr., Li Zhang, and Heather K. M. Terrell, "Fertility," in William A. Darity (ed.), *International Encyclopedia of the Social Sciences*, 2nd edn. (Detroit, MI: Macmillan Reference, 2008), pp. 126–130.

Potts, David Malcolm, "Birth Control, History of," in Paul Demeny and Geoffrey McNicoll (eds.), *Encyclopedia of Population* (New York: Macmillan Reference, 2003), vol. 2, pp. 93–98.

Potts, David Malcolm and Martha Campbell, "History of Contraception," *Gynecology and Obstetrics*, 6, ch. 8, 2002.

Potts, David Malcolm, Peter Diggory, and John Peel, *Abortion* (New York: Cambridge University Press, 1977).

Presser, Harriet B., "Demography, Feminism, and the Science–Policy Nexus," *Population and Development Review*, 23 (1997), 295–331.

Preston, Samuel H., "The Social Sciences and the Population Problem," *Sociological Forum*, 2 (1987), 619–644.

Preston, Samuel H. and Michael R. Haines, *Fatal Years: Child Mortality in Late Nineteenth-Century America* (Princeton University Press, 1991).

Preston, Samuel H., Patrick Heuveline, and Michel Guillot, *Demography: Measuring and Modeling Population Processes* (Malden, MA: Blackwell, 2001).

Prewitt, Kenneth, *What is Your Race? The Census and Our Flawed Efforts to Classify Americans* (Princeton University Press, 2013).

Purcell, L. Edward, *Immigration: Social Issues in American History* (Phoenix, AZ: Oryx Press, 1995).

Ramachandran, K. V., "An Index to Measure Digit Preference Error in Age Data," World Population Conference, 1965, Belgrade, 1967, III, pp. 202–203.

Ramchandran, Deepa and Ushma D. Upadhyay, "Implants: The Next Generation," *Population Reports*, Series K, No. 7 (Baltimore, MD: INFO Project, Johns Hopkins Bloomberg School of Public Health, 2007).

Rand Corporation, *Low Fertility and Population Ageing: Causes, Consequences, and Policy Options* (Santa Monica, CA: Rand, 1995).

Ravenstein, E. G., "The Laws of Migration," *Journal of the Royal Statistical Society*, 48 (1885), 167–277.

Raymond, Elizabeth G., "Contraceptive Implants," in Robert A. Hatcher, James Trussell, Anita L. Nelson, Willard Cates, Jr., Deborah Kowal, and Michael S. Policar (eds.), *Contraceptive Technology*, 20th rev. edn. (New York: Ardent Media, 2011a), pp. 193–207.

"Progestin-Only Pills," in Robert A. Hatcher, James Trussell, Anita L. Nelson, Willard Cates, Jr., Deborah Kowal, and Michael S. Policar (eds.), *Contraceptive Technology*, 20th rev. edn. (New York: Ardent Media, 2011b), pp. 237–247.

Rees, William, "Sustainable Development and the Ecosphere," in Arthur Fabel and Donald St. John (eds.), *Teilhard in the 21st Century* (Maryknoll, NY: Maryknoll Publications, 2004), pp. 1–12.

Reichert, Josh and Douglas S. Massey, "History and Trends in US Bound Migration from a Mexican Town," *International Migration Review*, 14 (1980), 475–491.

Renzetti, Claire M. and Daniel J. Curran, *Women, Men, and Society*, 4th edn. (Boston: Allyn & Bacon, 1999).

Women, Men, and Society, 5th edn. (Boston: Allyn & Bacon, 2003).

Riddle, John M., *Eve's Herbs: A History of Contraception and Abortion in the West* (Cambridge, MA: Harvard University Press, 1999).

Riley, Nancy E., "Research on Gender in Demography: Limitations and Constraints," *Population Research and Policy Review*, 17 (1998), 521–538.

"Demography of Gender," in Dudley L. Poston, Jr. and Michael Micklin (eds.), *Handbook of Population* (New York: Springer, 2005), pp. 109–142.

Riley, Nancy E. and James McCarthy, *Demography in the Age of the Postmodern* (Cambridge University Press, 2003).

Rindfuss, Ronald R., S. Philip Morgan, and Gray Swicegood, *First Births in America: Changes in the Timing of Parenthood* (Berkeley, CA: University of California Press, 1988).

Riosmena, Fernando, Bethany G. Everett, Richard G. Rogers, and Jeff A. Dennis, "Negative Acculturation and Nothing More? Cumulative Disadvantage and Mortality during the Immigrant Adaptation Process among Latinos in the United States," *International Migration Review*, 49 (2015), 443–478.

Ritchey, P. Neal, "Explanations of Migration," *Annual Review of Sociology*, 2 (1976), 363–404.

Roberts, Kenneth D., "China's 'Tidal Wave' of Migrant Labor: What Can We Learn from Mexican Undocumented Migration to the United States?" *International Migration Review*, 31 (1997), 249–293.

Roberts, Sam, "New Figure for 2010 Census: $1.6 Billion Under Budget," *New York Times*, August 10, 2010.

Robine, Jean-Marie, "Epidemiological Transition," in Paul Demeny and Geoffrey McNicoll (eds.), *Encyclopedia of Population* (New York: Macmillan Reference, 2003), vol. 1, pp. 307–310.

Rock, John, *The Time Has Come: A Catholic Doctor's Proposals to End the Battle over Birth Control* (New York: Alfred A. Knopf, 1963).

Rodriguez, Alex., "'Parental Glory' Counts in Russia," *Houston Chronicle*, January 29, 2009.

Rogers, Andrei, *Introduction to Multiregional Mathematical Demography* (London: Wiley, 1975).

Rogers, Richard G. and Robert Hackenberg, "Extending Epidemiologic Transition Theory: A New Stage," *Social Biology*, 34 (1987), 234–243.

Rogers, Richard G., Robert A. Hummer, and Patrick M. Krueger, "Adult Mortality," in Dudley L. Poston, Jr. and Michael Micklin (eds.), *Handbook of Population* (New York: Kluwer Academic/Plenum, 2005), pp. 283–309.

Rogers, Richard G., Robert A. Hummer, and Charles B. Nam, *Living and Dying in the USA* (San Diego, CA: Academic Press, 2000).

Rogers, Richard G., Robert A. Hummer, Charles B. Nam, and Kimberley Peters, "Demographic, Socioeconomic, and Behavioral Factors Affecting Ethnic Mortality by Cause," *Social Forces*, 74 (1996), 1419–1438.

Romero, Fabian, "The Residential Segregation of Latino Immigrants in the US: Exposure to Crime and the Effects of Place of Destination," PhD dissertation, Texas A&M University, College Station, 2014.

Roncari, Danielle and Melody Y. Hou, "Female and Male Sterilization," in Robert A. Hatcher, James Trussell, Anita L. Nelson, Willard Cates, Jr., Deborah Kowal, and Michael S. Policar (eds.), *Contraceptive Technology*, 20th rev. edn. (New York: Ardent Media, 2011), pp. 435–482.

Rosenberg, H. M., J. D. Maurer, P. D. Sorrie, N. J. Johnson, M. F. MacDonald, D. L. Hoyert, J. F. Spitler, and C. Scott, "Quality of Death Rates by Race and Hispanic Origin: A Summary of Current Research, 1999," *Vital Health Statistics*, 2(128) (1999), 1–13.

Rosenwaike, Ira, *Mortality of Hispanic Populations* (Westport, CT: Greenwood, 1991).

Rosenwaike, Ira and Samuel H. Preston, "Age Overstatement and Puerto Rican Longevity," *Human Biology*, 56 (1983), 503–525.

Rostron, Brian L., John L. Boies, and Elizabeth Arias, "Education Reporting and Classification on Death Certificates in the United States," *Vital and Health Statistics*, 2(151)(2010), 1–14.

Rowland, Donald T., *Demographic Methods and Concepts* (New York: Oxford University Press, 2003).

Rubenstein, Edwin S., "The Twin Crises," *The Social Contract*, 19 (2008/9), 3–83.

Rudacille, Deborah, *The Riddle of Gender: Science, Activism, and Transgender Rights* (New York: Pantheon, 2005).

Russell, Chris and Dudley L. Poston, Jr., "Overpopulation," in William A. Darity (ed.), *International Encyclopedia of the Social Sciences*, 2nd edn. (Detroit, MI: Macmillan Reference, 2008), vol. 6, pp. 95–96.

Ryder, Norman B., "Fertility," in Philip M. Hauser and Otis Dudley Duncan (eds.), *The Study of Population* (University of Chicago Press, 1959, pp. 400–436.

"Notes on the Concept of a Population," *American Journal of Sociology*, 69 (1964), 447–463.

Ryder, Robert E. J., "Natural Family Planning: Effective Birth Control Supported by the Catholic Church," *British Medical Journal*, 307 (1993), 723–726.

Sabagh, Georges, "The Fertility of French Canadian Women during the 17th Century," *American Journal of Sociology*, 47 (1942), 680–689.

Saenz, Rogelio,"Latinos in the United States 2010," *Population Reference Bureau Bulletin Update* (December) (Washington, DC: Population Reference Bureau, 2010).

Saenz, Rogelio and E. Colberg, "Sustenance Organization and Net Migration in Small Texas Nonmetropolitan Communities, 1960–1980," *Rural Sociology*, 53 (1988), 334–345.

Saenz, Rogelio and M. Cristina Morales, "Demography of Race and Ethnicity," in Dudley L. Poston, Jr. and Michael Micklin (eds.), *Handbook of Population* (New York: Kluwer Academic/Plenum, 2005), pp. 169–208.

Sampson, Robert J. and John H. Laub, "Crime and Deviance over the Life Course: The Salience of Adult Social Bonds," *American Sociological Review*, 55 (1990), 609–627.

Sanderson, W. C., "Quantitative Aspects of Marriage, Fertility and Family Limitation in Nineteenth Century America: Another Application of the Coale Specification," *Demography*, 16 (1979), 339–358.

Sane, K. and O. H. Pescovitz, "The Clitoral Index: A Determination of Clitoral Size in Normal Girls and in Girls with Abnormal Sexual Development," *Journal of Pediatrics*, 120 (1992), 264–266.

Sassen, Saskia, *The Mobility of Labour and Capital: A Study in International Investment and Labour Flow* (Cambridge University Press, 1988).

Sautter, Jessica M., Patricia A. Thomas, Matthew E. Dupre, and Linda K. George, "Socioeconomic Status and the Black-White Mortality Crossover," *American Journal of Public Health*, 102 (2012), 1566–1571.

Scharping, Thomas, *Birth Control in China 1949–2000: Population Policy and Demographic Development* (London: Routledge Curzon, 2003).

Scheidel, Walter, "Ancient World, Demography of," in Paul Demeny and Geoffrey McNicoll (eds.), *Encyclopedia of Population* (New York: Macmillan Reference, 2003), vol. 1, pp. 44–48.

Schmeckebier, Laurence F., *Congressional Apportionment* (Washington, DC: The Brookings Institution, 1941).

Schnore, Leo F., "Social Morphology and Human Ecology," *American Journal of Sociology*, 63 (1958), 620–634.

Schoen, Robert, *Modeling Multigroup Populations* (New York: Plenum, 1988).

Schumacher, E. F., *Small is Beautiful: A Study of Economics as if People Mattered* (New York: Harper Colophon, 1975).

Schwartz, Jill and Henry L. Gabelnick, "Contraceptive Research and Development," in Robert A. Hatcher, James Trussell, Anita L. Nelson, Willard Cates, Jr., Deborah Kowal, and Michael S. Policar (eds.), *Contraceptive Technology*, 20th rev. edn. (New York: Ardent Media, 2011), pp. 513–532.

Scribner, Richard S., "Paradox as Paradigm: The Health Outcomes of Mexican Americans," *American Journal of Public Health*, 86 (1996), 303–304.

Scribner, Richard S. and James H. Dwyer, "Acculturation and Low Birthweight Among Latinos in the Hispanic HANES," *American Journal of Public Health*, 79 (1989), 1263–1267.

Segal, Sheldon J., "Modern Methods of Contraception," in Paul Demeny and Geoffrey McNicoll (eds.), *Encyclopedia of Population* (New York: Macmillan Reference, 2003), vol. 1, pp. 170–174.

Segal, Sheldon J. and Olivia S. Nordberg, "Fertility Regulation Technology: Status and Prospects," *Population Bulletin*, 31 (1977), 1–25.

Sharpe, F. R. and Alfred J. Lotka, "A Problem in Age Distribution," *Philosophical Magazine*, 21 (1911), 435–438.

Sheehy, Daniel, *Fighting Immigration Anarchy: American Patriots Battle to Save the Nation* (Bloomington, IN: Rooftop Publishing, 2006).

Shepard, Marguerite K., "Nonsurgical Methods of Contraception," in Rochelle N. Shain and Carl J. Pauerstein (eds.), *Fertility Control: Biological and Behavioral Aspects* (New York: Harper & Row, 1980), ch. 6, pp. 71–84.

Sheth, S. S., "Missing Female Births in India," *Lancet*, 367(9506) (2006), 185–186.

Shilts, Randy, *And the Band Played On: Politics, People and the AIDS Epidemic* (New York: St. Martin's Press, 1987).

Shkolnikov, Vladimir M., "Mortality Reversals," in Paul Demeny and Geoffrey McNicoll (eds.), *Encyclopedia of Population* (New York: Macmillan Reference, 2003), vol. 2, pp. 676–679.

Shkolnikov, Vladimir M., D. A. Jdanov, E. M. Andreev, and James W. Vaupel, "Steep Increases in Best-practice Cohort Life Expectancy," *Population and Development Review*, 37 (2011), 419–434.

Shrestha, Laura B., "Life Expectancy in the United States," *CRS Report for Congress*, RL 32792 (Washington, DC: Congressional Research Service, 2006).

Shryock, Henry S., *Population Mobility within the United States* (Chicago, IL: Community and Family Study Center, 1964).

Shryock, Henry S., Jacob S. Siegel, and Associates, *The Methods and Materials of Demography*, condensed edition by Edward G. Stockwell (New York: Academic Press, 1976).

Shultz, Jackson Wright, *Trans/Portraits: Voices from the Transgender Communities* (Hanover, NH: Dartmouth College Press, 2015).

Siegel, Jacob S. and David A. Swanson (eds.), *The Methods and Materials of Demography*, 2nd edn. (San Diego, CA: Elsevier Academic, 2004).

Simon, Julian L., *The Ultimate Resource* (Princeton University Press, 1981).
  Population and Development in Poor Countries: Selected Essays (Princeton University Press, 1992).

Simpson, J. A. and E. S. C. Weiner (eds.), *Oxford English Dictionary*, 2nd edn (Oxford University Press, 2000).

Sivin, Irving, Harold Nash, and Sandra Waldman, *Jadelle Levonorgestrel Rod Implants: A Summary of Scientific Data and Lessons Learned from Orogrammatic Experience* (New York: Population Council, 2002).

Skeldon, Ronald, "Migration and Poverty: Some Issues in the Context of Asia," in Irena Omelaniuk (ed.), *World Migration, 2005: Costs and Benefits on International Migration* (Geneva: International Organization for Migration, 2005), ch. 13, pp. 253–268.

Smith, David P., *Formal Demography* (New York: Plenum, 1992).

Snipp, C. Matthew, *American Indians: The First of This Land* (New York: Russell Sage Foundation, 1989).

Solinger, Dorothy J., *Contesting Citizenship in Urban China: Peasant Migrants, the State, and the Logic of the Market* (Berkeley, CA: University of California Press, 1999).

Song, Jian, Chi-Hsien Tuan, and Jingyuan Yu, *Population Control in China: Theory and Applications* (New York: Praeger, 1985).

Song, Jian and Jingyuan Yu, *Population System Control* (Berlin: Springer, 1988).

Sonnega, Amanda, "The Future of Human Life Expectancy: Have We Reached the Ceiling or is the Sky the Limit?" *Research Highlights in the Demography and Economics of Aging*, 8 (2006), 1–4.

South, Scott J. and Katherine Trent, "Sex Ratios and Women's Roles: A Cross-National Analysis," *American Journal of Sociology*, 93 (1988), 1096–1115.

Spengler, Oswald, *The Decline of the West* (New York: Oxford University Press, [1918] 1991).

Spitz, I. M., C. W. Bardin, L. Benton, and A. Robbins, "Early Pregnancy Termination with Mifepristone and Misoprostol in the United States," *New England Journal of Medicine*, 338(18) (1998), 1241–1247.

Stark, Oded, "Migration Decision Making: A Review Article," *Journal of Development Economics*, 14 (1984), 251–259.
  The Migration of Labour (Oxford: Blackwell, 1991).

StataCorp, *Stata: Release 14, Statistical Software* (College Station, TX: Stata Corporation, 2015).

State of Wyoming Economic Analysis Division, "Resident Population of the United States," available at: http://eadiv.state.wy.us/demog_data/usdec_1790_10.htm, last accessed June 1, 2015).

Sternlieb, George and James W. Hughes, *Current Population Trends in the United States* (New Brunswick, NJ: Center for Urban Policy Research, 1978).

Stockwell, Edward G., Jerry W. Wicks, and Donald J. Adamchak, "Research Needed on Socioeconomic Differentials in US Mortality," *Public Health Reports*, 93 (1978), 666–672.

Stone, L. O., *The Frequency of Geographic Mobility in the Population of Canada* (Ottawa: Statistics Canada, 1978).

Stover, John, "Revising the Proximate Determinants Framework of Fertility: What Have We Learned in the Past 20 Years? *Studies in Family Planning*, 29 (1998), 255–267.

Stycos, J. Mayone, *Family and Fertility in Puerto Rico: A Study of the Lower Income Group* (New York: Columbia University Press, 1955).

Swanson, David A. and G. Edward Stephan, "A Demography Time Line," in Jacob S. Siegel and David A. Swanson (eds.), *The Methods and Materials of Demography*, 2nd edn. (San Diego, CA: Elsevier Academic, 2004), pp. 779–786.

Szreter, Simon, "The Right of Registration: Development, Identity Registration, and Social Security: A Historical Perspective," *World Development*, 35 (2007), 67–86.

Taeuber, Conrad and Irene B. Taeuber, *The Changing Population of the United States* (New York: John Wiley, 1958).

Taeuber, Cynthia M., *American Community Survey Data for Community Planning* (Victoria, BC: Trafford, 2006).

Taeuber, Irene B., "Demographic Research in the Pacific Area," in Philip M. Hauser and O. Dudley Duncan (eds.), *The Study of Population* (University of Chicago Press, 1959), pp. 259–285.

Taeuber, Irene B. and Conrad Taeuber, *People of the United States in the 20th Century* (Washington, DC: US Government Printing Office, 1971).

Tancredo, Tom, *In Mortal Danger: The Battle for America's Border and Security* (Medford, OR: WND Books, 2006).

Tavris, Carol and Carole Wade, *The Longest War: Sex Differences in Perspective*, 2nd edn. (New York: Harcourt Brace Jovanovich, 1984).

Teilhard de Chardin, Pierre, *The Phenomenon of Man* (New York: Harper & Row, 1959).
The Future of Man (New York: Harper & Row, 1969a).
The God of Evolution (Orlando, FL: Harcourt, 1969b).

Teitelbaum, Michael S., "Fertility Effects of the Abolition of Legal Abortion in Romania," *Population Studies*, 26 (1972), 405–417.
"Political Demography," in Dudley L. Poston, Jr. and Michael Micklin (eds.), *Handbook of Population* (New York: Kluwer Academic/Plenum, 2005), pp. 719–730.

Tentler, Leslie Woodcock, "Bitter Pill," *Commonweal*, 135(20) (2008), 22–24.

Thomas, Dorothy Swaine, *Social and Economic Aspects of Swedish Population Movement, 1750–1933* (New York: Macmillan, 1941).

Thompson, Kenneth, *August Comte: The Foundation of Sociology* (New York: Halsted Press, 1975).

Thompson, Warren S., "Population," *American Journal of Sociology*, 34 (1929), 959–975.

Thompson, Warren S. and David Lewis, *Population Problems* (New York: McGraw Hill, 1965).

Thompson, Warren S. and Pascal K. Whelpton, *Population Trends in the United States* (New York: McGraw Hill, 1933).

Thornton, Arland and Tom E. Fricke, "Social Change and the Family: Comparative Perspectives from the West, China and South Asia," in J. Mayone Stycos (ed.), *Demography as an Interdiscipline* (New Brunswick, NJ: Transaction, 1989), pp. 128–161.

Thornton, Russell, *American Holocaust and Survival* (Norman, OK: University of Oklahoma Press, 1990).

Tienda, Marta, "Demography and the Social Contract," *Demography*, 39 (2002), 587–616.

Tietze, Christopher, "History of Contraceptive Methods," *Journal of Sex Research*, 1 (1965), 69–85.

Tobler, Waldo, "Migration: Ravenstein, Thornthwaite, and Beyond," *Urban Geography*, 16 (1995), 327–343.

Trussell, James, "Contraceptive Failure in the United States," *Contraception*, 70 (2004), 89–96.

"Contraceptive Efficacy," in Robert A. Hatcher, James Trussell, Anita L. Nelson, Willard Cates, Jr., Deborah Kowal, and Michael S. Policar (eds.), *Contraceptive Technology*, 20th rev. edn. (New York: Ardent Media, 2011), pp. 779–863.

Trussell, James and Katherine A. Guthrie, "Choosing a Contraceptive: Efficacy, Safety, and Personal Considerations," in Robert A. Hatcher, James Trussell, Anita L. Nelson, Willard Cates, Jr., Deborah Kowal, and Michael S. Policar (eds.), *Contraceptive Technology*, 20th rev. edn. (New York: Ardent Media, 2011), pp. 45–74.

Trussell, James and Eleanor Bimla Schwarz, "Emergency Contraception," in Robert A. Hatcher, James Trussell, Anita L. Nelson, Willard Cates, Jr., Deborah Kowal, and Michael S. Policar (eds.), *Contraceptive Technology*, 20th rev. edn. (New York: Ardent Media, 2011), pp. 113–145.

Tucker, Catherine and Jennifer Van Hook, "Surplus Chinese Men: Demographic Determinants of the Sex Ratio at Marriageable Ages in China," *Population and Development Review*, 39 (2013), 209–229.

Tucker, Joseph D., Gail E. Henderson, T. F. Wang, Y. Y. Huang, William Parish, S. M. Pan, X. S. Chen, and M. S. Cohen, "Surplus Men, Sex Work, and the Spread of HIV in China," *AIDS*, 19 (2005), 539–547.

Tucker, Joseph D., Dudley L. Poston, Jr., Qiang Ren, Baochang Gu, Xiaoying Zheng, Stephanie Wang, and Chris Russell (eds.), *Gender Policy and HIV in China: Catalyzing Policy Change* (New York: Springer, 2009).

Turner, Frederick Jackson, *The Frontier in American History* (New York: Henry Holt, [1893] 1920).

Turra, Casio M. and Irma T. Elo, "The Impact of Salmon Bias on the Hispanic Mortality Advantage," *Population Research and Policy Review*, 27 (2008), 515–530.

United Nations, *Principles and Recommendations for National Population Censuses* (New York: United Nations, 1958).

The Determinants and Consequences of Population Change (New York: United Nations, 1973), vol. 1.

Patterns of Urban and Rural Population Growth (New York: United Nations, 1980).

1988 Demographic Yearbook (New York: United Nations, 1990).

"Principles and Recommendations for Population and Housing Censuses, Revision 1," *Statistical Papers*, Series M, No. 67/Rev. 1 (New York: United Nations, 1998).

Replacement Migration: Is it a Solution to Declining and Ageing Populations? (New York: United Nations, 2001).

World Population Prospects: The 2004 Revision and World Urbanization Prospects: The 2003 Revision (New York: United Nations, 2005).

World Urbanization Prospects: The 2005 Revision (New York: United Nations, 2006).

World Population Prospects: The 2006 Revision: Highlights (New York: United Nations, 2007).

Adolescent Fertility since the International Conference on Population and Development (ICPD) in Cairo (New York: United Nations, 2013a).

International Migration Report 2013 (New York: United Nations, 2013b).

International Migration Wall Chart 2013 (New York: United Nations, 2013c).

World Population Prospects: The 2012 Revision. Highlights and Advance Tables (New York: United Nations, 2013d).

World Fertility Patterns Wall Chart, 2013 (New York: United Nations, 2014a).

Urban and Rural Areas Wall Chart, 2014 (New York: United Nations, 2014b).

World Urbanization Prospects, Highlights. 2014 Revision (New York: United Nations, 2014c).

United Nations Department of Economic and Social Affairs (UNDESF), "Trends in Contraceptive Methods Used Worldwide," *Population Facts 2013/9* (New York: UNDESA, December 2013).

United Nations Fund for Population Activities (UNFPA), *Framework of Actions to the Follow-up to the Programme of Action of the International Conference on Population and Development, Beyond 2014* (New York: UNFPA, 2014).

United Nations High Commissioner for Refugees (UNHCR) *Mid-Year Trends 2014* (Geneva: UNHCR, 2015).

United Nations International Children's Emergency Fund (UNICEF), *Birth Registration Right from the Start* (Florence: UNICEF, 2002).

Levels and Trends in Child Mortality (New York: UNICEF, 2013).

Every Child's Birth Right: Inequities and Trends in Birth Registration (New York: UNICEF, 2014).

United Nations Joint Program on HIV/AIDS (UNAIDS), Fact Sheet, 2014, available at: www.unaids.org/sites/default/files/media_asset/20140716_FactSheet_en.pdf, last accessed May 26, 2015.

United Nations Office of the High Commissioner for Human Rights (UNOHCHR), *Fact Sheet: LGBT Rights, Frequently Asked Questions* (New York: UNOHCHR, 2013).

United Nations Statistics Division (UNSD), "2010 World Population and Housing Census Programme (2005–2014)," *Newsletter*, 14 (March, 2013).

US Bureau of the Census, *Historical Statistics of the United States* (Washington, DC: US Government Printing Office, 1975).

Statistical Abstract of the United States: 1994, 114th edn. (Washington, DC: US Government Printing Office, 1994).

Statistical Abstract of the US: 2003 (Washington, DC: US Government Printing Office, 2004).

American Community Survey, Design and Methodology, Technical Paper 67 (Washington, DC: US Government Printing Office, 2006).

Census Atlas of the United States, Series CENSR-29 (Washington, DC: US Government Printing Office, 2007).

Annual Estimates of the Population by Sex and Five-Year Age Groups for the US: April 1, 2007 to July 1, 2007 , NC-EST2007–01 (Washington, DC: US Government Printing Office, 2008).

"Census Bureau Releases Estimates of Same-Sex Married Couples," News Release, Bureau of the Census, Washington, DC, September 27, 2011.

"Methodology, Assumptions and Inputs for the 2014 National Projections" (Washington, DC: US Government Printing Office, 2014a).

Through the Decades, History: Index of Questions (Washington, DC: US Government Printing Office, 2014b).

"1790 Overview," 2015a, available at: www.census.gov/history/www/through_the_decades/overview/1790.html, last accessed June 1, 2015.

"World Population Clock," 2015b, available at:. www.census.gov/popclock, last accessed October 24, 2015.

"Calculating Migration Expectancy Using ACS Data," *Migration/Geographic Mobility*, Main Page (April 1) (Washington, DC: US Bureau of the Census Bureau, 2015c).

US Department of Commerce, *United States Life Tables, 1890, 1901, 1910, and 1901–1910* (Washington, DC: US Government Printing Office, 1921).

US Department of Homeland Security, *Yearbook of Immigration Statistics, 2013* (Washington, DC: US Department of Homeland Security, 2014).

van de Kaa, Dirk J., "Europe's Second Demographic Transition," *Population Bulletin*, 42 (1987).

van de Walle, Etienne and John Knodel, "Teaching Population Dynamics with a Simulation Exercise," *Demography*, 7 (1970), 433–448.

van Imhoff, Evert, "Cohort Analysis," in Paul Demeny and Geoffrey McNicoll (eds.), *Encyclopedia of Population* (New York: Macmillan Reference, 2003), vol. 2, pp. 155–157.

Veevers, J .E., "Voluntarily Childless Wives: An Exploratory Study," *Sociology and Social Research*, 57 (1973), 356–366.

Velkoff, Victoria A. and Valerie A. Lawson, "Gender and Aging Caregiving," *International Brief*, IB/98–3 (December) (Washington, DC: US Bureau of the Census, 1998).

Ventura, Stephanie J., Brady E. Hamilton, and T. J. Mathews, "National and State Patterns of Teen Births in the United States, 1940–2013," *National Vital Statistics Reports*, 63 (August 20, 2014).

Waite, Linda J., "Marriage and Family," in Dudley L. Poston, Jr. and Michael Micklin (eds.), *Handbook of Population* (New York: Kluwer Academic/Plenum, 2005), pp. 87–108.

Wallace, Ruth and Alison Wolf, *Contemporary Sociological Theory* (Upper Saddle River, NJ: Prentice Hall, 2005).

Waltzer, Michael, "The Distribution of Membership," in Peter G. Brown and Henry Shue (eds.), *Boundaries: National Autonomy and its Limits* (Totowa, NJ: Rowman & Littlefield, 1981), pp. 221–235.

Wang, Feng, Yong Cai, and Baochang Gu, "Population, Policy, and Politics: How Will History Judge China's One-Child Policy?" *Population and Development Review*, 38 (Supp.) (2013), 115–129.

Wang, Wendy and Kim Parker, "Record Share of Americans Have Never Married, As Values, Economics and Gender Patterns Change," Pew Research Center's Social & Demographic Trends Project, Washington, DC, September 2014.

Warner, Lee and Markus J. Steiner, "Male Condoms," in Robert A. Hatcher, James Trussell, Anita L. Nelson, Willard Cates, Jr., Deborah Kowal, and Michael S. Policar (eds.), *Contraceptive Technology*, 20th rev. edn. (New York: Ardent Media, 2011), pp. 371–389.

Warren, Robert and Donald Kerwin, "Beyond DAPA and DACA: Revisiting Legislative Reform in Light of Long-term Trends in Unauthorized Immigration to the United States," *Journal on Migration and Human Security*, 3 (2015), 80–108.

Warren, Robert and Jeffrey S. Passel, "A Count of the Uncountable: Estimates of the Undocumented Aliens in the United States 1980 Census," *Demography*, 24 (1987), 375–393.

Waters, Mary C., "The Social Construction of Race and Ethnicity: Some Examples from Demography," in Nancy A. Denton and Stewart E. Tolnay (eds.), *American Diversity: A Demographic Challenge for the Twentieth-first Century* (Albany, NY: State University of New York Press, 2002), pp. 25–49.

Wattenberg, Ben J., *Fewer: How the New Demography of Depopulation Will Shape Our Future* (Chicago, IL: Ivan R. Dee, 2004).

Weller, Robert H. and Leon F. Bouvier, *Population: Demography and Policy* (New York: St. Martin's, 1981).

Westoff, Charles F., Robert G. Potter, and Phillip C. Sagi, *The Third Child: A Study in the Prediction of Fertility* (Princeton University Press, 1963).

Westoff, Charles F., Robert G. Potter, Philip C. Sagi, and Elliot G. Mishler, *Family Growth in Metropolitan America* (Princeton University Press, 1961).

Whelpton, Pascal K., Arthur A. Campbell, and John E. Patterson, *Fertility and Family Planning in the United States* (Princeton University Press, 1966).

White, Michael J., Frank D. Bean, and Thomas J. Espenshade, "The US 1986 Immigration Reform and Control Act and Undocumented Migration to the United States," *Population Research and Policy Review*, 9 (1990), 93–116.

White, Theodore, *America in Search of Itself: The Making of the President: 1956–1980* (New York: Harper & Row, 1982).

Whitney, Craig R., "Jeanne Calment, World's Elder, Dies at 122," *New York Times*, August 5, 1997, available at: www.nytimes.com/1997/08/05/world/jeanne-calment-world-s-elder-dies-at-122.html.

Whitney, R. B., "Quinacrine Sterilization (QS) in a Private Practice in Daytona Beach, Florida: A Preliminary Report," *International Journal of Gynecology and Obstetrics*, 83(Supp.2)(2003), S117–S120.

Wilkinson, David O., *Deadly Quarrels: Lewis F. Richardson and the Statistical Study of War* (Berkeley, CA: University of California Press, 1980).

Williams, David R., and Chiquita Collins, "US Socioeconomic and Racial Differences in Health: Patterns and Explanations," *Annual Review of Sociology*, 21 (1995), 349–386.

Wilmoth, Janet., "Population Size," in Jacob S. Siegel and David A. Swanson (eds.), *The Methods and Materials of Demography*, 2nd edn. (San Diego, CA: Elsevier Academic, 2004), pp. 65–80.

Winch, Donald, "Malthus, Thomas Robert," in Paul Demeny and Geoffrey McNicoll (eds.), *Encyclopedia of Population* (New York: Macmillan Reference, 2003), vol. 2, pp. 619–621.

Wing, Steven, Kenneth G. Manton, Eric Stallard, Curtis G. Hames, and H. A. Tryoler, "The Black/White Mortality Crossover: Investigation in a Community-Based Study," *Journal of Gerontology*, 40 (1985), 78–84.

Wolfenden, Hugh H., *Population Statistics and Their Compilation* (University of Chicago Press, 1954).

Wooldridge, Frosty, *Immigration's Unarmed Invasion: Deadly Consequences* (Bloomington, IN: Authorhouse, 2004).

World Bank, *China 2020: Sharing Rising Incomes: Disparities in China* (Washington, DC: World Bank, 1997).

World Health Organization (WHO), *International Classification of Diseases*, 10th revision (Geneva: World Health Organization, 1992).

    Maternal Mortality in 2000 (Geneva: World Health Organization, 2004).

    Neonatal and Perinatal Mortality: Country, Regional and Global Estimates (Geneva: World Health Organization, 2006).

    "The Top Ten Causes of Death," *Fact Sheet* No. 310 (Geneva: World Health Organization, 2011).

    "HIV-AIDS," *Fact Sheet* No. 360 (Geneva: World Health Organization, 2014).

    Global Health Observatory (Geneva: World Health Organization, 2015a).

    Trends in Maternal Mortality, 1990 to 2015 (Geneva: World Health Organization, 2015b).

Wortman, Judith, "The Diaphragm and Other Intravaginal Barriers: A Review," *Population Reports*, Series H, No. 7 (Baltimore, MD: INFO Project, Johns Hopkins School of Public Health, 1976).

Woytinsky, Wladimir S. and Emma S. Woytinsky, *World Population and Production* (New York: Twentieth Century Fund, 1953).

Wrigley, E. A., *Population and History* (New York: McGraw-Hill, 1969).

Wu, Cangping and Lin Wang, "Contribution of Population Control in Creating Opportunities for China Arising from Fertility Decline Should not be Neglected," paper presented at the International Symposium on the 2000 Population Census of China, Beijing, 2004.

Yang, Jisheng, *Tombstone: The Great Chinese Famine, 1958–1962* (New York: Farrar, Straus & Giroux, 2012).

Yang, Xiushi, "Urban Temporary Out-migration under Economic Reforms: Who Moves and for What Reasons?" *Population Research and Policy Review*, 13 (1994), 83–100.

  "Labor Force Characteristics and Labor Force Migration in China," in *Changes in China's Labor Market: Implications for the Future* (Washington, DC: US Department of Labor, 1996), pp. 13–44.

Yinger, J. Milton, "Towards a Theory of Assimilation and Disassimilation," *Ethnic and Racial Studies*, 4 (1981), 261.

Young, Paul, *L. A. Exposed: Strange Myths and Curious Legends in the City of Angels* (New York: St. Martin's Griffin, 2002).

Yusuf, Farhat, Jo M. Martins, and David A. Swanson, *Methods of Demographic Analysis* (New York: Springer, 2014).

Zaba, Basia, "AIDS," in Paul Demeny and Geoffrey McNicoll (eds.), *Encyclopedia of Population* (New York: Macmillan Reference, 2003), vol. 1, pp. 37–43.

Zakaria, Fareed, *The Post-American World* (New York: W. W. Norton, 2008).

Zangwill, Israel, *The Melting Pot* (New York: Macmillan, 1909).

Zeng, Yi, Ping Tu, Baochang Gu, Y. Xu, B. Li, and Y. Li, "Causes and Implications of the Recent Increase in the Reported Sex Ratio at Birth in China," *Population and Development Review*, 19 (1993), 283–302.

Zhang, Li, *Male Fertility Patterns and Determinants* (New York: Springer, 2013).

Zhang, Li, Dudley L. Poston, Jr., and Chiung-Fang Chang, "Male and Female Fertility in Taiwan," in Dudley L. Poston, Jr., Wen Shan Yang, and D. Nicole Farris (eds.), *The Family and Social Change in Chinese Societies* (New York: Springer, 2014), pp. 151–161.

Zhou, Min, *Chinatown: The Socioeconomic Potential of an Urban Enclave* (Philadelphia, PA: Temple University Press, 1992).

Zinn, Howard, *A People's History of the United States* (New York: HarperCollins, 2003).

Zuehlke, Eric, "The Lucky Few Reveal the Lifelong Impact of Generation" (Washington, DC: Population Reference Bureau, 2008).

Name Index

Entries in bold typeface indicate figures or tables.

Subject Index

Entries in bold typeface indicate tables or figures.